CRITICAL ACCLAIM ACROSS AMERICA FOR
THE NEW CENTURY FAMILY MONEY BOOK

"COVERS EVERYTHING! . . . CLEAR, JARGON-FREE . . . One feature that sets this volume apart is Mr. Pond's self-scoring questionnaires, checklists, tables, charts and guides that helps the novice planner make judgments about where his or her personal finances stand. . . . A handy reference . . . a useful investment dictionary."—*The Atlanta Journal*

"A GREAT QUANTITY OF INFORMATION, BUT ALL OF IT WELL ORDERED AND BASED ON COMMON SENSE. . . . This financial consultant and author manages to keep interest piqued while explaining such concepts as annuities, high-yield municipal funds, and SEPs."—*Booklist*

"POND GOES BEYOND THE BASICS. He provides excellent, readable sections explaining economic events and exactly what they mean to your wallet. . . . Individual chapters are short and briskly written so readers can zero in on particular subjects, such as budgeting, children, insurance, taxes, investing or estate planning."—*Rochester Democrat & Chronicle* (New York)

"POND OFFERS A LOT. . . . He provides guides on how to save money, invest, plan for retirement, and he fills in the latest in tax laws."
—*Charleston Post & Courier* (South Carolina)

"A COMPREHENSIVE GUIDE TO A LIFETIME OF FINANCIAL SECURITY. This book helps you analyze your individual needs, assets, goals, and problem areas, then advises you on the course to take."
—*Oneonta Star* (New York)

Please turn the page for more extraordinary acclaim . . .

Also by Jonathan D. Pond

1001 Ways to Cut Your Expenses

Safe Money in Tough Times

Pond's Personalized Financial Planning Guide for Teachers and Employees of Educational Institutions

Pond's Personalized Financial Planning Guide for Salespeople

Pond's Personalized Financial Planning Guide for Self-Employed Professionals and Small Business Owners

Pond's Personalized Financial Planning Guide for Doctors, Dentists, and Health-Care Professionals

QUANTITY SALES

Most Dell books are available at special quantity discounts when purchased in bulk by corporations, organizations, or groups. Special imprints, messages, and excerpts can be produced to meet your needs. For more information, write to: Dell Publishing, 1540 Broadway, New York, NY 10036. Attention: Special Markets.

INDIVIDUAL SALES

Are there any Dell books you want but cannot find in your local stores? If so, you can order them directly from us. You can get any Dell book currently in print. For a complete up-to-date listing of our books and information on how to order, write to: Dell Readers Service, Box DR, 1540 Broadway, New York, NY 10036.

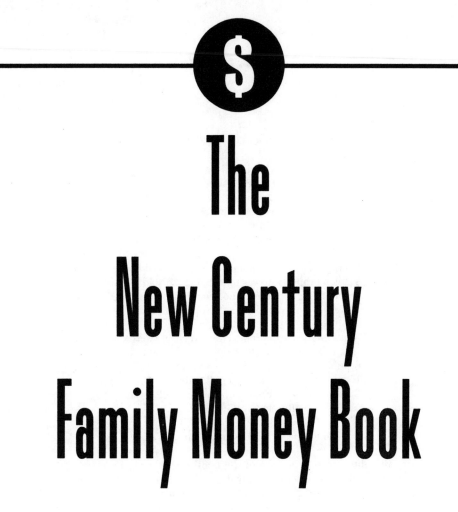

The
New Century
Family Money Book

Jonathan D. Pond

A Dell Trade Paperback

A DELL TRADE PAPERBACK

Published by
Dell Publishing
a division of
Bantam Doubleday Dell Publishing Group, Inc.
1540 Broadway
New York, New York 10036

This book was designed and produced by Michael Wolff & Company, Inc., New York. It has been wholly designed and produced by means of desktop-publishing technology. The text is set in the typefaces BellGothicRoman, New Baskerville, Toronto Belvedere, BureauGrotOneThree, BureauGrotOneFive, and BureauGrotOneSeven.

ISBN: 0-440-50693-X

Reprinted by arrangement with Delacorte Press

Printed in the United States of America

Published simultaneously in Canada

March 1995

10 9 8 7 6 5 4 3 2 1

RRH

For my family

Lois, Elizabeth, and Laura

Acknowledgments

This book has benefited greatly from the assistance of several capable and enthusiastic people. They share my belief that a book that provides unbiased and understandable guidance will enable you to manage your personal finances effectively so that you can achieve financial security. I gratefully acknowledge their dedication and sacrifice. Jim Lowell was instrumental throughout the development of this book. Don Carleton made important contributions during the writing and editing stages. Viveca Gardiner and Natalie Liu also provided very capable assistance.

The insights of Jeanne Cavelos and Leslie Schnur, my editors at Dell, were very helpful. The advice and encouragement of Peter Ginsberg, my agent, is much appreciated. The design and production of the book were skillfully overseen by Michael Wolff.

I would also like to acknowledge the contributions of the many people I have spoken with across the country over the past several years. Your questions, concerns, and observations have been indispensable in shaping this book. Many thanks as well to the numerous financial services professionals for their helpful comments and suggestions.

Anyone who says that writing a book is easy has never written one. The author suffers, the staff suffers, the editor suffers, but most of all the author's family suffers. I will always appreciate the encouragement and forebearance of my wife and daughters during the countless hours spent away from home working on this book and the countless hours spent at home worrying about it.

Contents

Part III—Your Career

Chapter

Part IV—A Greater Financial Perspective

Chapter

Part V—Insurance

Chapter

Part VI—Managing Your Credit

Chapter

Part VII—Investing

Chapter

Part VIII—Income Tax Planning

Chapter

Part IX—Retirement Planning

Chapter

Part X—Estate Planning

Chapter

Part XI—You Can Achieve Financial Security

Chapter

Introduction

Planning for a secure financial future is truly important for everyone. After all, we work hard for our money, and we want to be able to afford to retire comfortably without worrying about running out of money. During our working years, we want to build up a secure foundation so that we can both cope with whatever financial demands are thrust upon us and take advantage of any financial opportunities that may come our way. Achieving financial security is no easy task, but you will soon learn that you can do it. You will no longer be perplexed by the mystery and complexity of personal financial planning. You'll be able to take control of your financial future, confident of your ability to make the right decisions rather than having someone else make those decisions for you.

This book will help you do a better job with your money. You may not have paid a lot of attention to financial planning up to now, or you may think your finances are in reasonably good shape. Either way, this book contains a wealth of information that will help you manage your "wealth," no matter how modest it might now be. Even if you're starting from scratch or if debts have you in a financial hole, you'll find hundreds of ways to improve your financial well-being so that you will at last be able to enjoy the good feeling that comes from having financial peace of mind.

While money is the focal point, successful personal financial planning requires attention to a variety of areas, including:

- **SETTING** financial objectives and planning ahead to meet them

- **ORGANIZING** your personal records

- **MANAGING** your debt effectively and bringing your spending under control

- **SAVING** regularly and investing those savings wisely

- **ACCUMULATING** an investment portfolio that meets your lifetime needs

- **MINIMIZING** your income taxes

- **PLANNING** to retire when you want to, how you want to, and without fear of running out of money during your retirement years

- **PREPARING** and keeping up-to-date appropriate estate-planning documents

All these topics and many more will be covered here. This is not a get-rich-quick book. It is a get-rich-*sensibly* book. There is a lot of common sense in these pages, since common sense is the key to successful personal financial planning.

Don't be surprised if you find the financial-planning process rather overwhelming at first. There is a lot to do, even if your finances are already in pretty good order. The worksheets and checklists will help you identify areas that need attention. You won't be able to do everything, and those matters that need attention cannot be addressed all at once. But if you begin to do one or a few things, you will find that you *can* improve your personal financial status.

It isn't such a burden—in fact, it will be enjoyable to watch your investments grow, to finally get your debts and spending under control, to know that you are adequately insured, and to realize that you will be able to enjoy a long and financially fruitful retirement. You'll be able to enter the new century in full control of your financial future, confident of your ability to achieve lifetime financial security.

How to Use This Book

This book will help you and your family meet all of life's financial challenges. Each of the 87 chapters provides essential information and advice about a particular personal financial matter. You may use this book in a variety of ways:

1. First, it is a helpful guide to the world of personal finance. By perusing its pages, you will uncover a wealth of ideas that you can use in your own personal financial planning. Within most chapters you will find highlighted "Smart Money Moves" and "Money Savers"—timely suggestions to help you make better use of your money.

2. You may also use this book to review your current financial situation and to uncover areas that need attention. The "Personal Financial-Planning Questionnaire" in Chapter 2 is designed to highlight your financial strengths and problems—and to direct you to chapters that will help you address areas that need attention. Also, most chapters conclude with a checklist that summarizes important matters to consider.

3. The third use of this book is as an easy reference to answer the many financial questions that arise so often. Perhaps the biggest obstacle people encounter in their planning is gaining access to timely and objective information. You will want to refer to this book many times throughout the year for unbiased, down-to-earth answers and suggestions.

4. Finally, most chapters contain a variety of worksheets and checklists that you can use to evaluate your financial situation and determine what action you need to take. After all, successful personal financial planning is really based on exploiting our financial strengths and taking action to correct any weaknesses. It cannot be done overnight. But, if you begin gradually to make some changes, you will soon find that you are well on your way to achieving financial security.

The
New Century
Family Money Book

Part I

Getting Started

Achieving Financial Security

T he one thing we all share in common is our desire to achieve financial security. For most people, financial security means financial independence—the ability to meet all foreseeable financial needs out of their own resources. In other words, financial security means being able to afford to retire, whether one wants to retire or not. Everyone wants to be financially independent by the time they retire, but many fall short. Along the way, during our working years, we all want the financial security of being able to cope with whatever financial demands might be placed on us—buying a home, educating the children, and surviving disability, unemployment, or the death of a breadwinner.

You don't have to be lucky to achieve financial security. But you do have to work at it—and the earlier you begin, the easier financial security will be to achieve. As the next section shows, achieving financial security entails many different tasks. All of them are important, and each merits your attention.

The Keys to Achieving Financial Security

F FORMULATING OBJECTIVES. You can't get there from here unless you establish some important personal financial-planning objectives (see Chapter 3).

I INSURING THAT YOU HAVE ADEQUATE INSURANCE. Always maintain continuous and comprehensive insurance coverage (see Chapter 37).

N NEVER GIVING UP CONTROL OVER YOUR MONEY. Don't let other people tell you what to do with *your* money. You are your own best financial planner (see Chapters 36 and 50).

A ALLOCATING YOUR INVESTMENTS APPROPRIATELY. Deciding how to apportion your investments among stocks, interest-earning securities, and real estate is crucial to your investment success (see Chapter 52).

N CREATING A NEST EGG. There's nothing like money in the bank to give you financial peace of mind. Kick the spending habit, and get hooked on saving regularly (see Chapter 5).

C COPING WITH MAJOR LIFE EVENTS. Life deals each of us a variety of cards—some are good, and some are not. Preparing for the unexpected helps minimize financial disruptions (see Chapter 9).

I **INVESTING WISELY.** Learning about how to invest and putting your knowledge to work is one of the most important ingredients to your achieving financial security (see Chapter 52).

A **ASSURING THAT YOU MINIMIZE INCOME TAXES.** Income taxes take a large chunk out of your income, and there is no reason to pay any more than the minimum that the law obligates you to pay (see Chapter 63).

L **LEARNING TO LIVE BENEATH YOUR MEANS.** The only way to accumulate the investments necessary to achieve financial security is to spend less than you earn, and the only way to spend less than you earn is to live beneath your means (see Chapter 7).

S **SETTING YOUR RECORDS STRAIGHT.** Organize your records and prepare personal financial statements to get a better handle on your finances (see Chapters 4, 5, and 6).

E **PLANNING YOUR ESTATE.** You'll not only be doing your heirs a big favor by preparing the necessary estate-planning documents, you will benefit during your own lifetime (see Chapter 80).

C **MEETING COLLEGE EDUCATION COSTS.** The best way to meet college education costs is to undertake a realistic savings plan when the kids are young, then become familiar with the financial aid process as they near college age (see Chapters 21 and 22).

U **USING CREDIT WISELY.** Credit can be useful to achieving financial security, or it can destroy your financial security. It all depends on how you use it (see Chapter 47).

R **PARTICIPATING IN RETIREMENT PLANS.** Maximize your participation in tax-advantaged retirement plans to help assure a comfortable retirement (see Chapters 71 to 75).

I **INVESTING IN YOUR CAREER.** Devote the time necessary to improve your skills and advance in your career. Your career is your most important income-producing investment (see Chapter 27).

T **TAKING THE TIME TO ATTEND TO YOUR FINANCES.** The time you spend to work on your personal finances is always time well spent (see Chapter 84).

Y **YOU'RE RESPONSIBLE FOR ACHIEVING FINANCIAL SECURITY.** It's up to you to take the actions necessary to achieve financial independence. You *can* do it (see Chapter 87).

2

Finding Out Where You Stand

Your Personal
Financial-Planning Primer

S uccessful personal financial planning requires attention to three distinct yet interrelated areas: getting organized, accumulating and protecting your investments, and planning for later life. Within each of these areas, there are several important matters that require your attention, all of which will be discussed in detail in this guide. We all have areas needing attention in our personal finances, and this chapter will help you identify them.

Never Underestimate
the Value of Common Sense

L ooking at the table of contents of this book, you may think that the seemingly vast number of items covered would require that you work full time just on your personal finances. But as you will see in the chapters that follow, personal financial planning isn't really that complicated (although a lot of financial institutions and financial planners would like you to believe otherwise). All it takes is some discipline, a little time, and the willingness either to be your own financial planner or to make sure your financial-planning adviser(s) are acting in your best interests.

If successful financial planning can be boiled down to two words, they are common sense. If you think back on the dumb things you have done with your money in the past—and no one is immune to doing dumb things with their money—you will no doubt find that your money calamities were caused by lapses of common sense on your part. There's a wealth of common sense in this book!

This brings me to a rather thorny issue: Getting rich quickly. I don't believe in it. I don't advocate it. All I can do is recommend that, if you're looking for no-risk ways to get rich quickly, read no further. This isn't the book for you. If, on the other hand, you're looking for ways to get rich *sensibly* and/or to be able to achieve lifetime financial security by the time you retire, you'll benefit from the abundant advice in these pages.

Learn How to
Communicate about Matters of Finance

I n an age when business, economics, and household budgets dominate the news as well as everyday conversation, it's amazing how little most of us truly know about basic financial planning. While there's no excuse for this, there are a few good reasons for it. The primary reason is that we are neither taught nor told about the birds and the bees of finance. In the movie *It's a Wonderful Life,* Jimmy Stewart puts one "Momma dollar" and one "Poppa dollar" into a bank vault in order to raise more cash. Anyone who has a savings account but not a mutual fund account is doing the same, hopeless kind of "money-making." You need to open lines of money communication:

- **TALK** with your parents to learn about their financial errors and successes.

- **TALK** with your children to educate them about what worked and failed for you.

- **USE** your public library's financial-planning and investment section.

- **DON'T MAKE** talking about money taboo.

Finally, although talking about money with those who've experienced its guileful ways is strongly recommended, be sure nevertheless to take all that you hear with a grain of salt. Research and analyze financial-planning options as they pertain to your particular situation—which is precisely what this guide aims to help you do.

PERSONAL FINANCIAL-PLANNING QUESTIONNAIRE

This questionnaire will help you identify strengths and weaknesses in your own financial situation. After completing the questionnaire, refer back to your answers. Generally, but not always, a "no" response indicates a possible weakness, so you should refer to the appropriate pages that discuss the areas needing attention. Several "yes" responses also merit your attention. So whatever your response, if you need more information, refer to the pages indicated at the end of each question.

- Have you established some realistic short-term and long-term financial goals, such as purchasing a home and funding children's education? (See page 17.)   [ ] **YES**   [ ] **NO**

- Have you developed a personal record-keeping system that is simple enough to use yet comprehensive enough to be useful? (See page 25.)   [ ] **YES**   [ ] **NO**

»

• Do you have a safe-deposit box for storage of valuable papers and possessions? (See page 23.)   [ ] YES   [ ] NO

• Do you have a comprehensive and up-to-date inventory of your household furnishings and possessions? (See page 30.)   [ ] YES   [ ] NO

• Do you periodically prepare a personal balance sheet (i.e., a listing of your assets and liabilities)? (See page 32.)   [ ] YES   [ ] NO

• Do you periodically prepare a household budget that lists expected income and expenses? (See page 37.)   [ ] YES   [ ] NO

• Do you have enough savings to ensure that you are not financially strapped periodically because of unexpected expenses or large annual bills (e.g., insurance, property taxes, vacation expenses, IRA contributions)?
(See page 44.)   [ ] YES   [ ] NO

Insurance

• Do you have enough life insurance coverage to prevent your dependents from suffering financial hardship in the event of your death? (See page 291.)   [ ] N/A   [ ] YES   [ ] NO

• If you are married, does your spouse have sufficient life insurance coverage to prevent you and your dependents from suffering financial hardship in the event of your spouse's death? (See page 291.)   [ ] N/A   [ ] YES   [ ] NO

• Do you and all members of your household (if applicable) have comprehensive and continuous health insurance coverage?
(See page 311.)   [ ] YES   [ ] NO

• Do you and the working members of your household have adequate long-term disability insurance coverage (typically equivalent to at least 60 percent of your current salary)? Adequate cov-

»

erage includes both sickness and accident. (See page 345.) [ ] N/A [ ] YES [ ] NO

• Do you have adequate homeowner's or renter's insurance coverage? (See page 351.) [ ] YES [ ] NO

• Do you have additional insurance protection for jewelry, silverware, safe-deposit box contents, and other valuables? (See page 357.) [ ] N/A [ ] YES [ ] NO

• Do you have a personal liability (umbrella) insurance policy? (See page 371.) [ ] YES [ ] NO

• If your occupation warrants it, do you have professional liability insurance? (See page 372.) [ ] N/A [ ] YES [ ] NO

Borrowing and Credit

• Have you established your credit through borrowing for worthwhile purposes? (See page 384.) [ ] YES [ ] NO

• Are you aware of your personal credit rating as reported by the credit bureaus? (See page 401.) [ ] YES [ ] NO

• Have you secured, or are you now considering securing, a home equity loan (i.e., a loan secured by the equity in your home)? (See page 92.) [ ] N/A [ ] YES [ ] NO

• If you have children or grandchildren, will sufficient money be available to pay for their college, graduate school, or private school education? (See page 159.) [ ] N/A [ ] YES [ ] NO

• In order to meet a financial "emergency," do you have savings or investments equal to at least six months' salary? (See page 247.) [ ] YES [ ] NO

• Do you save through payroll withholdings or some other regular savings program? (See page 635.) [ ] YES [ ] NO

• With respect to your savings and investments, is more than one-half of the total invested

»

in the stock market? (See page 451.)   [ ] **YES**   [ ] **NO**

• Do you or would you like to actively choose your investments (as opposed to having someone else choose them)? (See page 439.)   [ ] **YES**   [ ] **NO**

• Do you periodically review your overall savings and investment portfolio? (See page 439.)   [ ] **YES**   [ ] **NO**

• Do you avoid making risky investments (e.g., stock options, commodity futures, speculative stocks, junk bonds)? (See page 455.)   [ ] **YES**   [ ] **NO**

• If applicable, do you participate in your employer's stock-purchase plan? (See page 468.)   [ ] **N/A**   [ ] **YES**   [ ] **NO**

• If you have stock market investments, do you avoid ever having a substantial amount of your total portfolio tied up in the stock of one or a few companies? (See page 439.)   [ ] **N/A**   [ ] **YES**   [ ] **NO**

• If you own stock directly or through mutual funds, do you participate in their dividend reinvestment plans? (See page 468.)   [ ] **N/A**   [ ] **YES**   [ ] **NO**

Real Estate

• Do you own a house or condominium? (See page 89.)   [ ] **YES**   [ ] **NO**

• If you don't own either one, do you plan to buy a home or condominium in the future? (See page 75.)   [ ] **N/A**   [ ] **YES**   [ ] **NO**

• Are you considering any future major home improvements? (See page 99.)   [ ] **YES**   [ ] **NO**

• Do you own a second home? (See page 98.)   [ ] **YES**   [ ] **NO**

• If you don't own a second home, are you considering purchasing a second home? (See page 99.)   [ ] **N/A**   [ ] **YES**   [ ] **NO**

• Have you purchased or are you considering purchasing a vacation time share? (See page 535.)   [ ] **YES**   [ ] **NO**

»

- Do you own directly (not as a limited partner) any investment real estate (e.g., apartments or undeveloped land)? (See page 533.) [ ] YES   [ ] NO

- Are you considering investing in income-producing real estate in the future? (See page 543.) [ ] YES   [ ] NO

Income Tax Planning

- Do you prepare your own income tax return? (See page 570.) [ ] YES   [ ] NO

- Do you consider yourself knowledgeable about tax-saving techniques and the latest changes in the tax laws? (See page 567.) [ ] YES   [ ] NO

- In your opinion, is your personal record-keeping system adequate to be useful in preparing your tax returns? (See page 580.) [ ] YES   [ ] NO

- Do you keep a notebook handy to record miscellaneous tax-deductible expenses? (See page 581.) [ ] YES   [ ] NO

- Are you familiar with the potential benefits of tax-advantaged investments? (See page 568.) [ ] YES   [ ] NO

- Are you self-employed either full time or part time (e.g., moonlighting)? (See page 235.) [ ] YES   [ ] NO

Retirement Planning

- Do you make payments to an individual retirement account each year? (See page 659.) [ ] YES   [ ] NO

- If you are self-employed, do you have a Keogh plan or SEP (simplified employee pension) plan? (See page 651.) [ ] N/A   [ ] YES   [ ] NO

- Are you currently enrolled in a company pension plan? (See page 627.) [ ] YES   [ ] NO

- Do you participate in your employer's salary-reduction (401 [k]) plans? (See page 635.) [ ] N/A   [ ] YES   [ ] NO

»

• Are you contemplating early retirement (prior to age sixty-five)? (See page 679.) [ ] **YES** [ ] **NO**

• Have you invested in tax-deferred annuities or are you considering doing so?(See page 671.) [ ] **YES** [ ] **NO**

• Have you estimated how much income you will have upon retirement? If not, skip the next question. (See page 601.) [ ] **N/A** [ ] **YES** [ ] **NO**

• If you have estimated your retirement income, do you think it's sufficient to provide you with a comfortable retirement? (See page 602.) [ ] **N/A** [ ] **YES** [ ] **NO**

If you are over age fifty but not yet retired, please answer the following questions. If you are under fifty, move to the estate planning questions below.

• Have you considered alternative places to live when you retire? (See page 595.) [ ] **YES** [ ] **NO**

• Have you thought about what you will be doing during your retirement (e.g., hobbies, travel, part-time work)? (See page 598.) [ ] **YES** [ ] **NO**

• Have you discussed your expected pension benefits with a company representative? (See page 627.) [ ] **N/A** [ ] **YES** [ ] **NO**

• Will you have the option of taking a lump-sum pension payment instead of an annuity at retirement? (See page 631.) [ ] **N/A** [ ] **YES** [ ] **NO**

• Have you checked with the Social Security Administration recently to see if it has an accurate record of your earnings? (See page 613.) [ ] **N/A** [ ] **YES** [ ] **NO**

• Have you recently estimated what your Social Security retirement benefits will be? (See page 613.) [ ] **N/A** [ ] **YES** [ ] **NO**

Estate Planning

• Do you have a will? (See page 720.) [ ] **YES** [ ] **NO**

»

• Is your will up-to-date? (See page 723.)	[ ] **N/A**	[ ] **YES**	[ ] **NO**
• Do you have a letter of instructions (i.e., a readily available document that provides your survivors with pertinent information about your insurance policies, investments, funeral wishes, etc.)? (See page 727.)		[ ] **YES**	[ ] **NO**
• If you are married, does your spouse have both an up-to-date will and a letter of instructions? (See page 723.)	[ ] **N/A**	[ ] **YES**	[ ] **NO**
• Have you discussed the contents and whereabouts of your will and letter of instructions with your immediate family? (See page 721.)	[ ] **N/A**	[ ] **YES**	[ ] **NO**
• If applicable, have you appointed a guardian for your dependent children? (See page 728.)	[ ] **N/A**	[ ] **YES**	[ ] **NO**
• Do you have a durable power of attorney or living trust for yourself (in the event that you become disabled or mentally incapacitated)? (See page 724.)		[ ] **YES**	[ ] **NO**
• Do you have a living will? (See page 726.)		[ ] **YES**	[ ] **NO**
• Have you evaluated the most advantageous way to designate the owner(s) of your investments and real estate (i.e., individual ownership or some type of joint ownership)? (See page 730.)		[ ] **YES**	[ ] **NO**
• Do you have real estate and/or other business interests in more than one state? (See page 711.)		[ ] **YES**	[ ] **NO**

On your mark, get set, go. Once you have completed the questionnaire, review your responses and begin referring to appropriate parts of the book for guidance on areas where you need improvement or where you simply would like additional helpful information. If you're like most of us, there's a lot of room for improvement. Don't feel overwhelmed, or you'll probably end up doing nothing. Instead, pick out a couple of relatively easy matters to attend to. Once you get a couple of them under your belt, you can begin to tackle the more challenging areas. Try it—you'll like it.

You should retake the above "test" periodically, because your answers will probably

»

change as your personal financial circumstances change. Retaking the test will also help you gauge your progress.

Finally, this questionnaire is by no means all-inclusive. You'll find a lot of information throughout this book that will help you meet the financial challenges that lie ahead—throughout your life.

3

Planning to Achieve Your Financial Objectives

Most people are so busy with the day-to-day demands on their personal and financial lives that they neglect to sit back periodically and reflect on what they want to accomplish with all their hard work. One thing you should do—if you haven't already—is establish some financial-planning objectives. What do you want to accomplish in your financial life? If you don't have at least some idea of what you want to accomplish, you'll have difficulty taking the necessary actions to achieve your financial dreams. This chapter will help you:

- **ESTABLISH** goals and objectives that are important to you

- **MAP OUT** strategies to accomplish your goals and objectives

- **ESTABLISH** the priorities to achieve the most important and urgent objectives first.

Your Most Important Financial Goal

Everyone's primary financial planning goal is financial security. Financial security means living the rest of your life without having to work or, if you're retired, not having to worry about running short of money in the face of constantly rising living costs. Most people don't achieve financial security until about the time they retire, and there's nothing wrong with this. What *is* unfortunate, however, is the number of people who never achieve financial security—not by age sixty-five, not by seventy-five, never.

Achieving financial security requires a lot of planning and some sacrifice because the only way you're going to be successful in reaching your most important goal of financial security is to save regularly. In other words, you must learn sooner, rather than later, to *live beneath your means*—even after you're retired.

17

Identifying Important Objectives

Goals are broad, relatively open-ended forecasts of what you want to achieve. As mentioned above, financial security is your most important financial-planning goal. *Objectives* are more specific ends that you want to achieve within a definite period of time. You probably have a variety of financial-planning objectives, although you may not yet have taken the time to think about them in much detail. Among the more common objectives are:

- **SAVING** more regularly

- **IMPROVING** personal record-keeping

- **REDUCING** debt

- **ASSURING** complete insurance coverage

- **INCREASING** income through a part-time job

- **BUYING** a home

- **MAKING** a major purchase

- **REDUCING** income taxes

- **MEETING** children's college-education costs

- **RETIRING** early

- **PROVIDING** support for elderly parents

- **MAKING** sure your estate is properly planned.

You should be pretty specific about the objectives you have and how you plan to go about achieving them. Be sure to write them down and discuss them with your spouse from time to time. Also remember that objectives may change for a number of reasons, including age, changes in income, and changing marital or parental status. For example, the arrival of children often dramatically alters a couple's financial-planning objectives. A worksheet is provided at the end of this chapter to help you identify your important financial-planning objectives.

Devising Strategies

Strategies are detailed plans that help you achieve your financial objectives. Identifying objectives is the easy part. Devising strategies to achieve them, and sticking to those strategies, is more challenging. For example, many people want to retire early, but far fewer are able to come up with a plan that will allow them to retire early—and comfortably. Even people who devise a realistic strategy often end up not sticking with it. This guide will help you devise workable strategies to meet your financial objectives.

Prioritizing Your Priorities

Some objectives are more important than others. Therefore, assigning priorities to your financial objectives is essential. Of course, your overall goal of achieving financial security by the time you want to retire is your first priority. But what's next? Many people would rank securing adequate insurance coverage pretty far down on the list of priorities, yet it is so essential to financial security that it should be a very high priority. Insufficient insurance may jeopardize years of past—or future—savings.

You should also set timetables for achieving your objectives. But be realistic—don't become obsessive. Rather, concentrate on achieving reasonable and sensible financial objectives. Also, take into consideration nonfinancial as well as financial concerns. For example, don't leave out your life-style wants and needs. While these shouldn't be extravagant, they also shouldn't be ignored.

FINANCIAL-PLANNING OBJECTIVES WORKSHEET

OBJECTIVES	VERY IMPORTANT	SOMEWHAT IMPORTANT	NOT IMPORTANT
Instructions: Indicate below those financial-planning objectives that are important to you. Then refer to the chapters that will help you achieve your objectives.			
• IMPROVING MY PERSONAL RECORD-KEEPING (CHAPTER 4)	[ ]	[ ]	[ ]
• SAVING MORE REGULARLY (CHAPTER 7)	[ ]	[ ]	[ ]
• BUYING A HOME (CHAPTER 12)	[ ]	[ ]	[ ]
• MEETING COLLEGE EDUCATION COSTS (CHAPTER 21)	[ ]	[ ]	[ ]
• ENSURING COMPLETE INSURANCE COVERAGE (PART V)	[ ]	[ ]	[ ]
• REDUCING DEBT (CHAPTER 50)	[ ]	[ ]	[ ]
• REDUCING INCOME TAXES (PART VIII)	[ ]	[ ]	[ ]
• IMPROVING MY INVESTING (PART VII)	[ ]	[ ]	[ ]
• ASSURING A COMFORTABLE RETIREMENT (PART IX)	[ ]	[ ]	[ ]
• MAKING SURE MY ESTATE IS PROPERLY PLANNED (PART X)	[ ]	[ ]	[ ]
• OTHER IMPORTANT OBJECTIVES			
•			
•			
•			

Setting Your Records Straight

S uppose your doctor tells you that you need to have major surgery within the next week and that the operation will be followed by a lengthy period of recuperation. Will your personal records be organized well enough to allow your spouse or a friend to take charge of your financial affairs on short notice? For many people, the answer is no. As modern life grows more and more complicated, we correspondingly accumulate greater numbers of personal financial documents. Yet too many of us never get around to putting our records in order. That is a *big* mistake. And the problems don't simply involve the possibility that you may be out of commission for a while. Poor record-keeping ends up complicating your financial life and may well cost you money—for example, in lost tax deductions.

This chapter will show how to go about setting up and maintaining your own straightforward and easy-to-use record-keeping system.

The Value of Good Record-Keeping

G ood record-keeping is valuable for at least two reasons. First, by making your financial documents easily accessible, you will save time. Admittedly, setting up a record-keeping system will take a while, especially if your records are extremely jumbled. Once your system is "up and running," however, you will no longer have to spend two hours hunting for a canceled check to prove a disputed bill. Nor will you have to rifle through innumerable drawers in order to find a medical receipt.

Second, the process of organizing your records and documents is an excellent way to reacquaint yourself with some of the more neglected areas of your lifetime personal financial planning. In organizing your legal documents, for instance, you might find that neither you nor your spouse ever updated your powers of attorney— even though you each assumed that the other had. Organizing your records will allow you to find out where you stand—which is essential to planning for the future.

A good record-keeping system is an indispensable component of sound personal financial management. If you have not developed sound record-keeping habits because you are not aware of how simple an effective record-keeping system can be, then read on! The

Smart Money Move

Save money and time by organizing and maintaining a simple personal record-keeping system.

advantages of having a good record-keeping system are clear:

- **GOOD RECORD-KEEPING** saves time in retrieving important information, such as insurance policies, brokerage advices, tax information, and other financial documents.

- **YOU WILL BE** better able to recognize problems that require attention.

- **A WELL-ORGANIZED** filing system eases the stress of family emergencies, particularly incapacity or an unexpected death.

Tax Record-Keeping

Record-keeping serves a dual function in tax planning. It eases the process of preparing tax returns, whether you do your own or have a tax professional prepare them, and it assures the availability of support information should the IRS audit your returns. An informal accounting system—which may consist only of a checkbook—should be maintained if you have a large number of deductible items. Recording all your expenses in your checkbook or elsewhere allows you to record more deductions and to avoid an end-of-the-year marathon tax-return-preparation session.

A filing system for receipts and pertinent papers is also helpful. Finally, a notebook or appointment calendar that records miscellaneous deductible items (such as charitable contributions and unreimbursed business expenses) helps you keep track of deductions that might otherwise escape your memory.

The IRS does not require specific types of records, but it does require that taxpayers keep "adequate, contemporaneous records" of their deductible expenses. For example, a taxpayer must keep adequate records to support the portion of automobile usage deducted for business purposes. Receipts and logbooks of automobile usage, calendars of appointments and activities, accounts of home computer use for business purposes, and other pertinent records should be maintained carefully and kept up to date in order to minimize conflicts with the IRS.

How Long Must Tax Records Be Kept?

You must keep records that support an item of income or a deduction on a return until the statute of limitations on the return runs out—usually three years from the filing or due date. Some records must be kept for longer periods of time. For example, in many transactions involving real estate, including your home, improvements made to property can change the basis of that property for purposes of computing capital gain or loss for income tax purposes. Therefore, you should keep receipts of home improvements you make to your house or rental property for as long as you own the property. For a further discussion of tax-preparation issues, consult Chapter 66.

Components of a Record-Keeping System

A good record-keeping system is one that is (a) complete enough to be effective and (b) simple enough that you will use it regularly. In general, the more complicated a system is, the less likely it is to be used regularly. The majority of commercially sold record-keeping systems are either too complex or too generalized for most people's needs. If you are a genuine computer enthusiast, buy a software program that allows you to put your personal records on-line. Be forewarned, however, that the vast majority of home record-keeping software sits at home collecting dust.

Every good record-keeping "system" has three main components:

- A SAFE-DEPOSIT BOX

- AN ACTIVE FILE KEPT AT HOME

- AN INACTIVE FILE KEPT AT HOME OR IN STORAGE

In addition, you may want to keep some documents at your attorney's office, with copies kept in the home active file. Both spouses, as well as at least one other adult family member, should know where these files are located, their basic contents, and the logistics of the family accounting system.

Home active and inactive files do not need to be particularly fancy. You really don't need a fireproof safe—desk drawers, a filing cabinet, or simple cardboard boxes work just as well. Reserving a separate manila folder for each category of documents or papers should suffice. The easier the setup is to use, the more likely it is that you will sustain an interest in and profit from record-keeping. The personal record-keeping organizer at the end of this chapter will assist you in organizing all your files.

Safe-Deposit Box

Your safe-deposit box should contain such personal papers as birth certificates and Social Security records, ownership papers like bond certificates and deeds, contract papers like insurance policies, and estate-planning papers like wills.

Keep two considerations in mind when renting a safe-deposit box. First, appoint a deputy who has the power to open the box if you are incapacitated or otherwise unable to open it yourself. Second, keep a duplicate copy of your estate-planning documents outside the box, in case it is sealed upon your death (see page 723).

It is sometimes necessary for each spouse to have a separate safe-deposit box because, depending on the state in which a couple resides, a jointly owned box might be sealed following the death of one spouse, just when the other needs to retrieve documents or valuables. The home active file should contain an inventory of all safe-deposit-box contents, updated whenever necessary. In fact, it is often wise to keep photocopies at home of important documents stored in the safe-deposit box—at least those for which there are no other records. The "Safe-Deposit Box Inventory Worksheet" at the end of this chapter will help you summarize the contents of your safe-deposit box.

If you store valuables in your safe-deposit box—jewelry, for example—obtain a floater on your homeowner's or renter's insurance policy to insure the contents of the safe-deposit box against loss. Most people don't realize that if their safe-deposit box is robbed or its contents damaged, items contained in the box are usually not insured by the bank (see page 356).

Home Active File

The main purpose of the home active file is to keep track of personal papers and important contractual obligations, and to help in preparing your current year's tax returns. The active file should also include tax working papers for the last three years, since the IRS can freely audit a return for that period. (In fact, three years is a useful time frame for holding most other papers as well.) The home active file should contain a range of documents, from bank statements and recently canceled checks to loan statements and payment books to income records. In short, all papers pertaining to current matters should be kept in the active file.

The accessibility of your active file is important if it is going to be useful. Otherwise, you'll end up postponing filing items. You should try to file bills, warranties, bank statements, and other records as they come in, or collect them all together in one location and sort them periodically for filing.

Because the active file needs to be easily accessible, it should be located in a convenient and pleasant location like a den. If the file is squirreled away in a dank basement or a stifling attic, you will be less likely to use it. If you use a desk with several drawers or a file cabinet, you could reserve each drawer or section of a drawer for a specific class of documents; one for estate-planning documents, for example, one for insurance records, one for current bills, and one for investment-related materials such as prospectuses and brokers' statements.

Home Inactive File

The main purpose of the home inactive file is to prove past tax returns. It should contain important papers—formerly in the home active file—that are over three years old. In certain instances, the IRS can examine tax returns going back more than three years, although after six years most people can safely discard their records.

A few other items should also be kept in your inactive file. Invoices and canceled checks pertaining to any home improvements should be kept until the home is sold. Brokerage advices (receipts of buy-and-sell transactions) should also be kept to substantiate capital gains and losses. You may also want to keep important personal papers that are not currently needed in the inactive file, such as family health records and proof that major debts and other contracts have been discharged. Some people keep canceled checks indefinitely, because they can be used to substantiate expenses long after other records have been discarded.

You may also want to keep old tax returns as a matter of curiosity—to show your great-grandchildren that it was once possible to live on less than $100,000 per year. At the present rate of inflation they'll probably be earning $100,000 per *month*!

PERSONAL RECORD-KEEPING ORGANIZER

This organizer serves two purposes. First, you can indicate next to each item where that particular item is now located. Second, you can organize your personal records by consolidating your documents into the three "files" noted below.

I. ITEMS FOR STORAGE IN SAFE-DEPOSIT BOX

Personal Papers

1. FAMILY BIRTH CERTIFICATES ....
2. FAMILY DEATH CERTIFICATES ....
3. MARRIAGE CERTIFICATE ....
4. CITIZENSHIP PAPERS ....
5. ADOPTION PAPERS ....
6. VETERAN'S PAPERS ....
7. SOCIAL SECURITY VERIFICATION ....

Ownership Papers

1. BONDS, STOCK, AND MUTUAL FUND CERTIFICATES ....
2. DEEDS ....
3. AUTOMOBILE TITLES ....
4. HOUSEHOLD INVENTORIES ....
5. HOME-OWNERSHIP RECORDS (E.G., BLUEPRINTS, DEEDS, SURVEYS, CAPITAL ADDITION RECORDS, YEARLY RECORDS) ....
6. COPIES OF TRUST DOCUMENTS ....

Obligation/Contract Papers

1. CONTRACTS ....
2. COPIES OF INSURANCE POLICIES ....
3. IOUs ....
4. RETIREMENT AND PENSION-PLAN DOCUMENTS ....

»

25

PERSONAL RECORD-KEEPING ORGANIZER < CONT'D >

Estate-Planning Documents

1. WILLS ....
2. LIVING WILLS ....
3. TRUSTS ....
4. LETTERS OF INSTRUCTION ....
5. GUARDIANSHIP ARRANGEMENTS ....

II. ITEMS FOR STORAGE IN HOME ACTIVE FILE

Current Income/Expense Documents

1. UNPAID BILLS ....
2. CURRENT BANK STATEMENTS ....
3. CURRENT BROKER'S STATEMENTS ....
4. CURRENT CANCELED CHECKS AND MONEY-ORDER RECEIPTS ....
5. CREDIT CARD INFORMATION ....

Contractual Documents

1. LOAN STATEMENTS AND PAYMENT BOOKS ....
2. APPLIANCE MANUALS AND WARRANTIES (INCLUDING DATE AND PLACE OF PURCHASE) ....
3. INSURANCE POLICIES
   - HOME ....
   - LIFE ....
   - AUTOMOBILE ....
   - PERSONAL LIABILITY ....
   - HEALTH AND MEDICAL ....
   - OTHER: ....
4. RECEIPTS FOR EXPENSIVE ITEMS NOT YET PAID FOR ....

Personal

1. EMPLOYMENT RECORDS ....
2. HEALTH AND BENEFITS INFORMATION ....
3. FAMILY HEALTH RECORDS

»

4.	COPIES OF WILLS	....
5.	COPIES OF LETTERS OF INSTRUCTION	....
6.	EDUCATION INFORMATION	....
7.	CEMETERY RECORDS	....
8.	IMPORTANT TELEPHONE NUMBERS	....
9.	INVENTORY OF AND SPARE KEY TO SAFE−DEPOSIT BOX	....
10.	RECEIPTS FOR ITEMS UNDER WARRANTY	....
11.	RECEIPTS FOR EXPENSIVE ITEMS	....

Tax

1.	TAX RECEIPTS	....
2.	PAID−BILL RECEIPTS (WITH DEDUCTIBLE RECEIPTS FILED SEPARATELY, TO FACILITATE TAX PREPARATION)	....
3.	BROKERAGE TRANSACTION ADVICES	....
4.	INCOME TAX WORKING PAPERS	....
5.	CREDIT STATEMENTS	....
6.	INCOME AND EXPENSE RECORDS FOR RENTAL PROPERTIES	....
7.	MEDICAL, DENTAL, AND DRUG EXPENSES	....
8.	RECORDS OF BUSINESS EXPENSES	....

III. ITEMS FOR STORAGE IN HOME INACTIVE FILE

1.	PRIOR TAX RETURNS	....
2.	HOME IMPROVEMENT RECORDS	....
3.	BROKERAGE ADVICES (PRIOR TO THREE MOST RECENT YEARS)	....
4.	FAMILY HEALTH RECORDS (PRIOR TO THREE MOST RECENT YEARS)	....
5.	PROOF THAT MAJOR DEBTS OR OTHER MAJOR CONTRACTS HAVE BEEN MET	....
6.	CANCELED CHECKS (PRIOR TO THREE MOST RECENT YEARS)	....

SAFE-DEPOSIT BOX INVENTORY WORKSHEET

LOCATION OF SAFE–DEPOSIT BOX ....

LOCATION OF BOX KEYS ....

NAME(S) OF BOX RENTER(S) ....

Personal Papers

FAMILY BIRTH CERTIFICATES ....

FAMILY DEATH CERTIFICATES ....

MARRIAGE CERTIFICATE ....

CITIZENSHIP PAPERS ....

ADOPTION PAPERS ....

VETERAN'S PAPERS ....

SOCIAL SECURITY VERIFICATION ....

OTHER: ....

Ownership Papers

BOND CERTIFICATES ....

STOCK CERTIFICATES ....

U.S. SAVINGS BONDS ....

OTHER INVESTMENT CERTIFICATES OR EVIDENCE OF OWNERSHIP ....

AUTOMOBILE TITLES ....

OTHER: ....

Valuables and Miscellaneous Papers

....

....

....

....

Measuring Your
Financial Progress

inancial statements are a necessary part of planning your personal financial future, just as they are for a business. In fact, your personal financial life is very similar to that of a business. Like a business, you have assets, liabilities, income, and expenses. Read on to learn how to prepare the two basic types of personal financial statements:

- **STATEMENT OF PERSONAL ASSETS AND LIABILITIES.** This statement, also called a personal balance sheet, summarizes your assets, liabilities, and net worth.

- **PERSONAL BUDGET.** Your personal budget lists your income sources and summarizes how you spend your income. (Chapter 6 explains how to prepare a personal budget.)

You don't need to be an accountant to prepare your own personal financial statements, although you do need to pull some records together.

Preparing a Statement
of Personal Assets and Liabilities

A Statement of Personal Assets and Liabilities is an excellent way to gauge your progress toward achieving financial security. It is a snapshot of what you own and what you owe. The principle behind preparing this statement is simplicity itself: You tally up your assets, then add up your liabilities. By subtracting liabilities from assets, you'll end up with your net worth. (If, on the other hand, your liabilities exceed your assets, you will have a "deficit" in net worth. This is a common affliction of recent college graduates as well as people who have suffered financial problems. But, as long as you realize you are in the financial plight of a nega-

Smart Money Move

Measure your financial progress by periodically preparing a statement of personal assets and liabilities.

tive net worth, you can begin to take action to move your net worth to the plus side.)

Adding Up Your Assets

Adding up all that you own can be the fun part of calculating your net worth. Although it can be a rude awakening, you may be pleasantly surprised at how much you have actually accumulated. Don't get carried away with the clink of gold coins, however, for a personal financial statement is only as useful as it is accurate. In "accountant-speak," personal assets must be listed at estimated "current value," the price at which a given asset could theoretically be sold.

In other words, the "current value" of your house, for example, is *not* the price at which you would be willing to let it go if you had to leave town within twenty-four hours. Nor, on the other hand, is it what a buyer would pay for your house if he or she absolutely *had* to find a home on your block within the same time span.

In short, the key to accurately estimating current value is to be objective. Most people overestimate the value of their home and other real estate. The more you rely on outside, objective sources like market prices and professional appraisers when valuing your assets, the more likely you are to develop accurate estimates. The following section is designed to help you place an accurate value on the main classes of your assets.

Checking and Savings Accounts and Cash-Equivalent Investments

Adding up the value of your cash and cash-equivalent investments (e.g., money-market funds) is by far the easiest part of your job. Sit down with your most recent statements—if necessary, you can get updated balances by calling your bank—and add them up.

Individually Owned Stocks, Bonds, and Options

Marketable securities are also easy enough to value. The fastest way to determine the value of your stock, bond, and option holdings is to check the prices in the financial pages of the newspaper. If you can't find the prices there, check with your broker or the bank that holds your securities.

Mutual Funds

The companies that operate your mutual funds all maintain investor-relations departments; the customer service representatives there can quickly provide you with up-to-date quotations of the value of your fund holdings. Current prices of most mutual funds are also listed in the financial pages of the newspaper.

Family Business

If you own part or all of a small business, you probably already know how difficult it is to estimate its value. The best way to determine the value of your small business is to obtain a professional appraisal, but this is expensive. If you don't want to go to the expense, make a conservative estimate.

Real Estate

Real estate, including your home, is another area where subjective factors can cloud your ability to make an accurate estimate of a property's worth. As anyone who has bought or sold a property will attest, there is always a difference between what the seller thinks a property is worth and what the buyer is willing to pay. In a soft real estate market, this is doubly true. Many property owners are unable or unwilling to come to grips with the fact that the price of their real estate holdings has sunk drastically.

One way to obtain an objective analysis of your property's value is to have a couple of real estate brokers appraise it for you. While brokers are by no means infallible, once you have some estimates in hand, you should be able to assign a reasonable value to the property.

Life Insurance Policies

To estimate the current value of a cash value life insurance policy, subtract from the policy's cash value the amount of any loans you have taken out against it. A term policy, of course, has no cash value unless the policyholder dies.

Collectibles (Antiques, Art, and Family Heirlooms)

While Aunt Hepzibah's settee may be of great sentimental value to you, don't count it as an asset unless you have had it professionally appraised. Nostalgia or sentimental attachment to family heirlooms or antiques can inflate their value in the owner's eyes. Only a gimlet-eyed professional can be trusted to come up with anything like an accurate appraisal of these items. (For further discussion of appraisers and appraisals, see page 357.)

Personal Property

Used cars, furniture, clothing, and other personal property aren't worth very much, so don't put much of a value on it.

Adding Up Your Liabilities

ow it's time to take a strong dose of reality—you have to add up all your debts. While this may be a painful exercise, it is a good deal easier than adding up your assets: valuing your obligations is usually a very straightforward process.

Unpaid Monthly Bills

First, tally up all your unpaid bills, including utility bills, all insurance premiums currently due, medical bills, and any other items which you have not yet paid.

Mortgages and Home Equity Loans

Next, tote up the unpaid principal on any mortgage(s) and home equity loan(s). Call the lender to obtain the current balance.

Consumer Loans

All consumer loans—including auto, student, credit card, and charge account loans—should be valued at their current unpaid balances.

Other Liabilities

You may have other liabilities that need to be listed on your statement of personal assets and liabilities. These may include money owed on investments, such as margin loans, and unpaid taxes.

The following worksheet provides a straightforward, convenient way for you to organize your estimates of personal assets and liabilities. It is followed by a more detailed worksheet, the "Statement of Personal Assets and Liabilities." You may, of course, choose whatever format you like, as long as it presents your financial information clearly.

QUICK STATEMENT OF PERSONAL ASSETS AND LIABILITIES

PERSONAL ASSETS		PERSONAL LIABILITIES	
CASH	$..............................	CREDIT CARD AND CHARGE ACCOUNTS DUE	$..............................
INVESTMENTS (E.G., STOCKS, BONDS, MUTUAL FUNDS, CDs)	....	AUTOMOBILE LOANS	....
REAL ESTATE (EXCEPT PERSONAL RESIDENCE)	....	MORTGAGES (INCLUDING HOME EQUITY LOANS)	....
PERSONAL RESIDENCE	....	OTHER BANK LOANS	....
INVESTMENT IN FAMILY BUSINESSES	....	OTHER LIABILITIES	....
VESTED INTERESTS IN RETIREMENT PLANS	....		
OTHER ASSETS	....		
TOTAL PERSONAL ASSETS	$..............................	TOTAL PERSONAL LIABILITIES	$..............................
		TOTAL NET WORTH (ASSETS LESS LIABILITIES)	$..............................

STATEMENT OF PERSONAL ASSETS AND LIABILITIES

This worksheet can be used to summarize your assets and liabilities in detail. Three columns are included so that you can periodically monitor your progress. This worksheet should be prepared at least once per year, and many people prepare it more frequently.

Date (month/day/year)	____ , 19	____ , 19	____ , 19

Assets

1.	CASH IN CHECKING AND BROKERAGE ACCOUNTS	$...............	$...............	$...............
2.	MONEY-MARKET FUNDS AND ACCOUNTS	....	....	
3.	FIXED-INCOME INVESTMENTS			
	• SAVINGS ACCOUNTS	....	....	....
	• CDs	....	....	....
	• GOVERNMENT SECURITIES AND FUNDS	....	....	....
	• MORTGAGE-BACKED SECURITIES AND FUNDS	....	....	....
	• CORPORATE BONDS AND BOND FUNDS	....	....	....
	• MUNICIPAL BONDS AND BOND FUNDS	....	....	....
	• OTHER FIXED-INCOME INVESTMENTS	....	....	....
4.	STOCK INVESTMENTS			
	• COMMON STOCK IN PUBLICLY TRADED COMPANIES	....	....	....
	• STOCK MUTUAL FUNDS	....	....	....
	• OTHER STOCK INVESTMENTS	....	....	....
5.	REAL ESTATE INVESTMENTS			
	• UNDEVELOPED LAND	....	....	....
	• DIRECTLY OWNED, INCOME-PRODUCING REAL ESTATE	....	....	....
	• REAL ESTATE LIMITED PARTNERSHIPS	....	....	....
6.	OWNERSHIP INTEREST IN PRIVATE BUSINESS	....	....	....
7.	CASH VALUE OF LIFE INSURANCE POLICIES	....	....	....
8.	RETIREMENT-ORIENTED ASSETS			
	• INDIVIDUAL RETIREMENT ACCOUNTS (IRAs)	....	....	....

»

STATEMENT OF PERSONAL ASSETS AND LIABILITIES < CONT'D >

- TAX-SHELTERED ANNUITY PLANS SCHOOL/COLLEGE ....
- KEOGH OR SIMPLIFIED EMPLOYEE PENSION PLANS ....
- VESTED INTEREST IN SCHOOL/COLLEGE PENSION PLANS ....
- EMPLOYEE THRIFT AND STOCK-PURCHASE PLANS ....
- OTHER RETIREMENT-ORIENTED ASSETS ....

9. PERSONAL ASSETS
   - PERSONAL RESIDENCE(S) ....
   - AUTOMOBILE(S) ....
   - JEWELRY ....
   - PERSONAL PROPERTY ....

10. OTHER ASSETS
    - ....
    - ....
    - ....
    - ....

11. TOTAL ASSETS $............... $............... $...............

Liabilities

1. CREDIT CARDS AND CHARGE ACCOUNTS $............... $............... $...............
2. INCOME TAXES PAYABLE ....
3. MISCELLANEOUS ACCOUNTS PAYABLE ....
4. BANK LOANS ....
5. POLICY LOANS ON LIFE INSURANCE POLICIES ....
6. AUTOMOBILE LOANS ....
7. STUDENT LOANS ....
8. MORTGAGES ON PERSONAL RESIDENCE ....
9. MORTGAGES ON INVESTMENT REAL ESTATE ....
10. BROKER'S MARGIN LOANS ....
11. LIMITED PARTNERSHIP DEBT ....

»

12. OTHER LIABILITIES ....

• ....

• ....

• ....

13. TOTAL LIABILITIES $ .... $ .... $ ....

14. NET WORTH (TOTAL ASSETS LESS TOTAL LIABILITIES) $ .... $ .... $ ....

Note: Assets should be listed at their current market values. Be realistic in valuing those assets that require an estimate of market value, such as your home and personal property.

Preparing a Personal Budget

Budgeting, for individuals and families, is one of the most important steps to personal financial security. The purposes of budgeting are:

- **TO DEFINE** possible problems in spending patterns
- **TO IDENTIFY** opportunities to overcome these problems
- **TO HELP YOU** plan realistically to balance your spending with your income.

A Budget Can Help You Reach Your Financial Goals

Most people think of budgeting as a punitive task rather than as a positive financial-planning step. Nearly all of us have areas (read: arrears) in our personal finances where we routinely overspend, or at least don't use our resources as prudently as we might. A budget can help you spot patterns of overspending so that you won't be doomed to repeat them.

Knowing the amount of income you can reasonably expect to earn—and how that income will be spent—can go a long way in preventing unforeseen financial problems. How? By knowing what your expenses are, you'll be less tempted to overspend. (That's the theory, anyway.) A sensible, practicable budget can instill a much-needed degree of discipline into your financial affairs. It can also help you devise a plan to reduce debt and increase savings. Even veteran savers, those self-disciplined people we love to hate, regularly prepare budgets.

A BUDGETER'S CHECKLIST

The following checklist will guide you through several steps necessary to develop a useful and user-friendly budget.

ESTABLISH REASONABLE FINANCIAL GOALS AND OBJECTIVES

If you don't know where you want to go financially, it will be more difficult for you to set up a useful budget. After all, you couldn't plan a vacation without a destination. (For information on setting some realistic financial objectives, see Chapter 3.)

SUMMARIZE YOUR PRESENT FINANCIAL SITUATION

If you haven't yet prepared a statement of personal assets and liabilities, you should do so. (Chapter 5 explains how to prepare these statements.) Once you understand your financial progress-to-date (or lack of progress), you can begin to prepare an appropriate budget.

SELECT—OR DESIGN—A BUDGET FORM THAT SUITS YOUR NEEDS

Budgets come in a bewildering variety of formats and styles. You will find a sample budget form—the "Personal Budget Planner"—at the end of this chapter. It will help you gain an understanding of how budgets are organized. You can use it as it is, or modify it to better suit your needs. If you are looking for a more comprehensive (and complicated) system, several "budget systems" are available in bookstores or in computer software. In my opinion, however, the simpler the better.

FORECAST YOUR INCOME

The "Personal Budget Planner" worksheet on page 40 will help you identify the various sources of income you have. Be sure to be realistic in estimating your income—particularly items that might be uncertain, like annual bonuses. It is better to err on the low side when projecting income.

SUMMARIZE YOUR PAST EXPENSES

Before you can estimate your future expenses, you should summarize your past expenses on one of the columns of your worksheet. Don't simply guess what your past expenses were. The more precise you can be, the better your budget will work. Summarize and categorize your canceled checks.

One way to get a handle on how you spend your pocket cash is to periodically account for it by carrying a notebook to record each item paid for in cash. You'll probably be amazed at how much your cash expenses mount up to. Incidentally, those day-to-day cash expenses are often among the easiest to cut back on.

ESTIMATE FUTURE EXPENSES

Now that you have forecast your income and estimated your past expenses, you should estimate your future expenses over whatever period you are budgeting—a month, a quarter, or a year. Your objective is to budget your expenses so that, at a minimum, they don't exceed your income. You should strive, of course, to spend less than you earn. (You've heard me say that before, and you'll hear me say that again.)

Irregular expenses—in other words, those that are paid less frequently than monthly—present a special problem. They include insurance payments, vacations, and IRA contributions. They should be summarized separately, and money should be set aside to avoid periodic crises in cash flow caused by large bills. Each month, you should put one-twelfth of the estimated total annual amount of these infrequent bills into a separate savings account. There the money should stay, only to be withdrawn when these bills come due. You should mark the due dates for large payments on your calendar, so you will see them coming well in advance. (You'll find an "Irregular Expenses" worksheet on page 39.)

■ COMPARE YOUR ACTUAL WITH YOUR ESTIMATED EXPENDITURES

At the end of the period you budgeted, you should compare the amount of income you actually earned and the expenses you actually paid against your budget. Once you have a few budgets under your belt, you will become very proficient at identifying areas where you can further reduce your expenses. Before you know it, you will be well on your way to putting your financial house in good order.

A successful budget should carefully balance the various needs of all family members. If everyone in your family can't agree on the way the budget is structured, it probably won't work. One way to keep everyone happy is to establish a personal allowance for each family member. Whatever form your own "budget reconciliation act" takes, however, remember to leave a comfortable margin for unexpected expenses. A budget that cuts too close to the bone will be too difficult to follow faithfully. And it could be completely thrown off by a single unanticipated expense.

Personal budgeting isn't fun, but it is necessary. The fun part comes when you can confidently predict where the money will come from and where it will go. The real fun is knowing that a good portion of the "where your money goes" part of the budget equation is going into an investment account.

IRREGULAR EXPENSES WORKSHEET

This worksheet can assist you in planning to meet large, irregular bills. You should set aside funds during the year sufficient to meet these bills when they become due. One method is to total the irregular expenses and divide the total by 12 to yield the amount that should be saved each month, preferably in a separate interest-earning account earmarked to pay these expenses. In filling out this worksheet, include the expected annual amounts for any expenses that are billed less frequently than monthly.

		ESTIMATED ANNUAL AMOUNT
1.	PROPERTY TAXES	$ ....
2.	HOMEOWNER'S/RENTER'S INSURANCE	....
3.	LIFE INSURANCE	....
4.	OTHER INSURANCE	....
5.	HOME IMPROVEMENTS/MAINTENANCE	....
6.	FURNITURE	....
7.	SEASONAL FUEL/ELECTRICITY	....

»

IRREGULAR EXPENSES WORKSHEET < CONT'D >

8. VACATION ....

9. HOLIDAYS/GIFTS ....

10. TUITION/SCHOOL EXPENSES ....

11. CLUB MEMBERSHIP DUES ....

12. CHARITABLE CONTRIBUTIONS ....

13. ESTIMATED TAXES ....

14. RETIREMENT PLAN CONTRIBUTIONS ....

15. OTHER: ....

....

....

....

TOTAL $ ....

PERSONAL BUDGET PLANNER

Individuals and families should prepare budgets just as corporations do. This Personal Budget Planner can be used to record your past cash receipts and cash disbursements and/or to budget future receipts and disbursements. You may want to use the first column to record your past receipts and disbursements; the second column to list your budget over the next month, quarter, or year; and the third column to compare your actual future receipts and disbursements against your budget in the second column. If you budget over a period of less than one year, be sure to take into consideration those expenses that you may pay less frequently than monthly, such as insurance, vacations, and tuition. You should be setting aside an amount each month that will eventually cover those large bills.

Indicate at the top of each column whether the amounts in that column are actual or estimated past figures or budgeted future figures. Also indicate the time period in each column—for example, "July 1993" or "Year 1994."

INDICATE IF ACTUAL OR BUDGET ....

INDICATE THE TIME PERIOD ....

»

Cash Receipts

1.	GROSS SALARY	$...............	$...............	$...............
2.	INTEREST	....	....	....
3.	DIVIDENDS	....	....	....
4.	BONUSES	....	....	....
5.	ALIMONY/CHILD SUPPORT RECEIVED	....	....	....
6.	DISTRIBUTIONS FROM PARTNERSHIPS	....	....	....
7.	INCOME FROM OUTSIDE BUSINESSES	....	....	....
8.	TRUST DISTRIBUTIONS	....	....	....
9.	PENSION	....	....	....
10.	SOCIAL SECURITY	....	....	....
11.	GIFTS	....	....	....
12.	PROCEEDS FROM SALE OF INVESTMENTS	....	....	....
13.	OTHER			
	●	....	....	....
	●	....	....	....
	●	....	....	....
14.	TOTAL CASH RECEIPTS	$...............	$...............	$...............

Cash Disbursements

1.	HOUSING (RENT/MORTGAGE)	$...............	$...............	$...............
2.	FOOD	....	....	....
3.	HOUSEHOLD MAINTENANCE	....	....	....
4.	UTILITIES AND TELEPHONE	....	....	....
5.	CLOTHING	....	....	....
6.	PERSONAL CARE	....	....	....
7.	MEDICAL AND DENTAL CARE	....	....	....
8.	AUTOMOBILE/TRANSPORTATION	....	....	....
9.	CHILD CARE EXPENSES	....	....	....
10.	ENTERTAINMENT	....	....	....
11.	VACATION(S)	....	....	....
12.	GIFTS	....	....	....

»

PERSONAL BUDGET PLANNER < CONT'D >

13.	CONTRIBUTIONS	....	....	....
14.	INSURANCE	....	....	....
15.	MISCELLANEOUS OUT-OF-POCKET EXPENSES	....	....	....
16.	FURNITURE	....	....	....
17.	HOME IMPROVEMENTS	....	....	....
18.	REAL-ESTATE TAXES	....	....	....
19.	LOAN PAYMENTS	....	....	....
20.	CREDIT CARD PAYMENTS	....	....	....
21.	ALIMONY/CHILD SUPPORT PAYMENTS	....	....	....
22.	TUITION/EDUCATIONAL EXPENSES	....	....	....
23.	BUSINESS AND PROFESSIONAL EXPENSES	....	....	....
24.	SAVINGS/INVESTMENTS	....	....	....
25.	INCOME TAXES AND SOCIAL SECURITY TAXES	....	....	....
26.	OTHER			
	•	....	....	....
	•	....	....	....
	•	$	$	$ ....
27.	TOTAL CASH DISBURSEMENTS	$	$	$ ....
	EXCESS (SHORTFALL) OF CASH RECEIPTS OVER CASH DISBURSEMENTS	$	$	$ ....

Learning to Live Beneath Your Means

Living beneath your means is the only route to take to enjoy a secure and comfortable standard of living throughout your working and retirement years. Living beneath your means isn't a suggestion. It's an imperative. Spend less than you earn! Of course, most of us have heard this before—from our parents. But who listened? Not too many people. All you have to do is look at where your spending habits have landed you. If you're like most people, you've simply ended up repeating your parents' financial mistakes rather than heeding their experience-based advice.

The single most important key to achieving financial security: live beneath your means.

Cutting back on expenses, increasing your savings, adding to your investments—these are things many of us are not accustomed to doing. We're too accustomed to getting what we want, when we want it, to concern ourselves with such fundamentals as actually *owning* what we've got. The problem is that without steadily increasing your savings and investments, you're literally living on borrowed time. If you don't own the home you live in, the car you drive, the furniture you sit on, or even the shirt on your back (let alone the washer and dryer you use to clean it), is it any wonder that, when a minor financial problem hits, it packs a heavyweight punch that can knock your finances for a loop? No, it isn't.

The fact is that America as a culture—a culture of conspicuous consumption—isn't the land of the free. It's the land of the indebted. It's time to stop shackling yourself with ridiculous spending habits, develop sound saving habits, and learn to invest regularly and wisely so that you can share in a piece of the American dream rather than the debtor's nightmares.

Frugality Is In

Is plastic out? Well, let's just say that the devil-may-care attitude about charging has (thankfully) lost a lot of its wattage. In fact, those who are still living on credit cards are now looked at for what they are—dim bulbs!

Spend Less and Enjoy Life More!

- **YOU'LL** no longer have to worry about living from paycheck to paycheck, wondering and worrying about how you're going to be able to meet next month's bills.

- **YOU'LL** no longer have to worry about losing the shirt off your back if you are laid off from work or suffer a pay cut.

- **YOU'LL** no longer feel compelled to keep up with the Joneses. (You'll be miles ahead of them when you retire.)

- **YOU'LL** no longer have to worry if you'll be able to afford your children's tuition, your own retirement, or even your own funeral.

How to Live Beneath Your Means

To succeed, you have to continually look for ways, both small and large, to cut your expenses. You may think that you have no fat to trim and can't possibly make your budget any leaner. You are wrong. Innumerable ways exist for you to pare small amounts off both your recurring and your annual expenses. While some of the savings may individually seem marginal, in total they will be significant. Unfortunately, people who don't get into the habit of living beneath their means—saving regularly—will never achieve financial security.

Remember, saving doesn't mean having to live like a miser. As your savings rise and your net worth increases, even savers can indulge in luxuries. But the ultimate goal is financial security—being able to maintain a comfortable standard of living after retirement. Imagine being able to maintain the same standard of living throughout your retirement as you did during your working years! It is in your grasp.

Putting Your Savings to Work

Smart Money Move

Financial security is not so much dependent on how much you earn as it is on how much you save.

A substantial portion of this book covers investing—extolling its virtues (for the most part), defining its jargon, and presenting and analyzing investment strategies. Investing is the focal point of the whole personal financial-planning process. Most of us have only a vague notion about the stock market's relationship to other people's money. Despite the stories you read about Wall Street—junk bond czars landing in jail, small investors landing in the poorhouse or on Easy Street—the world of finance has much to offer the average American. Yet most of America is missing the boat when it comes to investment. Prudent investment will enable you to take the money you've worked so hard to save and put it to work for you.

Be Self-Sufficient

When it comes to taking control of our financial lives, many of us have lost the pioneering spirit. But you cannot rely on others to provide sufficient resources to achieve financial security for you. You must do most of it on your own. Here's the secret to financial success revealed:

- **THE ONLY WAY** to get money to invest is to save regularly.

- **THE ONLY WAY** to save regularly is to spend less than you earn.

- **THE ONLY WAY** to spend less than you earn is to live beneath your means.

- **IF YOU DON'T** get into the habit of living beneath your means, you'll never save enough money to invest, and so you'll never achieve financial security.

Develop a Cost-Cutting Plan

Cutting expenses is never as difficult as one thinks. Like dieting, it's the thought of having to cut back that keeps us hungering for more—even when we aren't hungry. In most of the chapters of this book you'll find "Money Savers" specifically designed to help you cut costs (not corners) in every financial aspect of your life. These practical, sensible, straightforward tips can help save you money right off the bat so that you can make it around life's financial bases and still make it safely home to financial security.

Example

Mark and Celeste Burns, like many other couples in their thirties, haven't been able to save very much. But they're now sufficiently concerned about their future financial security that instead of saying the same old line, "There's no way we can afford to save," they've taken a hard look at where they're spending their money. They have come up with the following money-saving ideas:

	WEEKLY SAVINGS
CARRY LUNCH TO WORK RATHER THAN GO TO A RESTAURANT OR DELI	$14
SHARE A RIDE RATHER THAN DRIVE TO WORK ALONE	$27
REDUCE LOTTERY TICKET PURCHASES FROM $15 TO $2 PER WEEK	$13
REDUCE RESTAURANT DINING FROM THREE TO TWO TIMES PER WEEK	$18
ESTIMATED WEEKLY SAVINGS	$72

If they can stick to their plan, the Burnses can begin saving without a great deal of suffering. While $72 per week in savings may not sound like a lot, it sure adds up over the years. The following shows how much $72 per week in savings will accumulate at 8 percent interest:

1 YEAR $3,900

3 YEARS...$12,700

5 YEARS $23,000

10 YEARS $57,000

20 YEARS...$185,000

30 YEARS $468,000

Not bad, considering the small amount of sacrifice Mark and Celeste will have to "endure."

CHECKLIST FOR LIVING BENEATH YOUR MEANS

☐

Take a moment to look objectively at your spending habits. Are they reasonable in relation to your income and future financial needs?

☐

List below four areas where you can cut back on your expenses.

ESTIMATED WEEKLY SAVINGS

1. .... $ ....

2. ....

3. ....

4. ....

☐

If you are not yet saving enough to achieve financial security by the time you want to retire, begin now to implement a plan to live beneath your means.

Ways to Increase Your Income

Sometimes, a little extra money can make the difference between desperation and financial peace of mind. But that money won't come in the mail, grow on trees, drop from the sky, or be pulled from a hat. When it comes to making more money, there's no hocus-pocus remedy, just hard work. Many industrious people have found ways to increase their income in order to meet living expenses or increase their savings. But it takes a lot of elbow grease, stick-to-itiveness, and perhaps the most valuable thing of all—time.

The following ways to increase your income are tips of the iceberg—they're just a smattering of the numerous "Smart Money Moves," "Money Savers," and saving and investment strategies to be found throughout this book. But for starters, these items will help you weather a temporarily weakened financial situation—or, even better, help you increase your savings and investing plans.

Some of the tips will deliver small, immediate amounts of money—a quick fix to a bigger problem that you need to address—namely, your financial planning and security. Others will get you thinking about ways to change your overall financial situation so that you can make progress toward achieving the financial security you want—and deserve.

Ten Ways to Increase Your Income

1. Moonlight

Moonlighting is perhaps the best way for many people to augment their income. You may be able to take a part-time job evenings or on weekends. You may have a skill such as painting or word processing that you can turn into a lucrative part-time business.

If you look around, you will find ample moonlighting opportunities, and as long as they don't jeopardize your full-time work, you can supplement your job income nicely. Incidentally, if you do moonlight, you may be able to take advantage of certain tax breaks for self-employed people, including the opportunity to set up your own tax-advantaged retirement plan. (See Chapter 74.)

2. Work Part Time

Many people who are not currently in the workforce—like homemakers, retired people, students, and the temporarily unemployed—are finding that there's an abundance of part-time jobs available to augment their income. Many companies are effectively utilizing part-time employees and, in order to attract them, offer flexible working arrangements and working hours.

3. Take In a Boarder or Roommate

You could add hundreds of dollars to your monthly income by taking in a boarder or, if you're a renter, a roommate. Admittedly, this isn't everyone's cup of tea, but tough financial times may call for a temporary change of life-style. If you have adult children living with you who are employed, they should be paying you room and board. It's a great way to teach your children about the hardships of meeting monthly bills.

4. Take Out a Second Mortgage, or Refinance Your First Mortgage for a Higher Amount

This strategy should not be taken lightly, since it could jeopardize your home or, in the case of refinancing, potentially *increase* the overall cost of your mortgage. Unless your situation is desperate, it is unwise to use home equity financing to meet current living expenses or to make nonessential purchases. Two often worthwhile reasons to hock your home: to make needed home improvements and to help pay college tuition bills.

5. Buy and Sell at Yard Sales

A yard sale is a great way to get rid of items you no longer need and raise some money. Even ritzy neighborhoods have yard sales! If you no longer need some major possessions like pieces of furniture, place an ad in the local paper.

Also, some people make big money buying "junk" at yard sales and selling them as "antiques" to dealers or at flea markets. These people have an eye for value and a knack for identifying collectibles in people's front yards. You can make thousands of dollars a year by doing this. I know a woman who bought an original Rembrandt etching for ten dollars at a yard sale. It was worth $25,000!

6. Adjust Your Withholding

Are you sure too much money isn't being withheld from your paycheck for taxes? If you got a refund last year, if you are going to have higher deductible expenses this year, or if your income may drop this year, you may be able to increase the number of your withholding exemptions in order to decrease the taxes withheld. It's not that difficult to figure out, and it's worth it if you can increase your take-home pay.

7. Move to a State with Lower Taxes

Many people are beginning to realize that some states have much higher tax burdens than others. If you are young, or if you otherwise have some flexibility as to where you live, consider moving to a state where there is both opportunity and lower taxes.

8. Shift Investments into Higher-Yield Interest-Earning Securities

If your investments are concentrated in stocks, or if you have cash that's sitting in your checking account, you can increase your current income by moving your money into higher-yield interest-earning securities, like bonds and certificates of deposit (CDs). But be careful of investments that promise unusually high interest, since high interest means high risk.

9. Shop Around for the Best Yields on Interest-Earning Investments

Next time your CD comes due, don't simply roll it over without comparing the new interest rate with rates offered by other banks and financial institutions. You may be surprised to find that by transferring your money to another institution, you can increase your interest income. Your CD world is no longer limited to your home town. Brokerage firms, including the discounters, now have "CD shopping services" that scour the nation to find the highest CD rates. As long as your CD is in a federally insured institution, it doesn't matter whether it's on deposit in a bank down the street or two thousand miles away.

10. Buy Municipal Bonds

You can probably increase your interest income by selling taxable bonds and buying municipal bonds. After factoring in federal and state taxes, lower-yielding municipal bonds provide you with more income than taxable securities like CDs and government bonds.

Emergency Measures
Use These Only If You're In a Pinch

Reduce Your Contributions to Your Company 401(k) Plan or Other Savings Plans

This action should only be considered a temporary solution to increase your take-home pay to meet a short-term financial problem. Hopefully, you will be able to restore these important retirement-plan contributions as soon as your financial situation stabilizes.

Sell Investments

You can increase your income by selling some investments, but this should be viewed as only a temporary expedient, since you should normally be adding to your investments, not reducing them. But one of the comforting aspects of having money in the bank is that you can gain access to it in the event of a personal financial emergency. Selling investments can extend to cashing in IRAs or other retirement plans, but only as a last resort. Not only will you incur stiff penalties, but you'll jeopardize your retirement security.

MOONLIGHTING AND PART-TIME JOB IDEAS

Here are some creative ways to earn extra part-time income. Most of these skills are in great demand, and if you are already skilled or can develop skill in them, they are a great way to increase your income.

- GARDENING/YARD WORK

- HOUSE CLEANING

- PAINTING/WALLPAPERING

- HOUSE-SITTING

- BABY-SITTING

- PET-SITTING

- DOG-WALKING

- TEACHING EXERCISE CLASSES

- LEADING AEROBICS CLASSES

- TUTORING

- TYPING AND WORD PROCESSING

- TECHNICAL WRITING

- WORKING PART TIME AT DEPARTMENT STORES DURING HOLIDAYS

- PREPARING INCOME TAX RETURNS

- DOING BOOKKEEPING OR ERRANDS FOR BUSY FAMILIES

- ALTERING CLOTHING

- ORGANIZING AND CATERING PARTIES

9

Expecting the Unexpected

O ver the course of your lifetime, you will undoubtedly experience several "life events" that will make it necessary for you to reevaluate your personal financial status and plans. Some of these life events are pleasant, but most of them are unpleasant. The birth of a child, the death of a loved one, a new job, unemployment, an inheritance—these are but a few of the financial events that life may have in store for you. These events will usually require you to make some adjustments in your planning. Some—divorce, for example—may require major changes.

Certain major life events are unavoidable, while others are becoming more frequent— the "sandwich generation," for example. Many baby boomers are now reluctantly finding themselves in the sandwich generation. They have both dependent children and aging, dependent parents. For them, the financial and emotional problems of meeting the needs of elderly parents at the same time that they must raise and educate their children—not to mention provide for their own retirement—can create enormous financial strain.

Knowing what you can expect and, to the extent possible, preparing for it, can help lessen the effects of these changes in your financial circumstances. The box lists life events that most commonly lead to at least some modifications in people's financial planning. Note that many of these circumstances are quite common. In fact, you could lead a very typical life and experience eight to ten such events.

Smart Money Move

Many life events require a change in your financial planning. Anticipate them, and you won't get caught unprepared.

LIFE EVENTS THAT USUALLY REQUIRE A MODIFICATION IN FINANCIAL PLANS

Family
MARRIAGE

BIRTH OR ADOPTION OF CHILDREN

FAMILY MEMBER WITH SPECIAL FINANCIAL NEEDS

AGING PARENTS

DEATH OF A SPOUSE OR OTHER CLOSE FAMILY MEMBER

RECEIPT OF AN INHERITANCE

COHABITATION

SEPARATION OR DIVORCE

»

Occupation

BEGINNING A CAREER

CHANGING JOBS OR CAREERS

STARTING ONE'S OWN BUSINESS

DECLINE IN INCOME

UNEMPLOYMENT

Health

DISABILITY

OLD AGE

CHRONIC ILLNESS

TERMINAL ILLNESS

Coping with the Changes in Your Life

The nature and extent of the changes required by each of the above life events vary. For some, you may need professional assistance—a financial planner, lawyer, or CPA. But don't expect these professionals to handle all the necessary changes. An attorney who assists in the legal matters associated with separation and divorce will not necessarily deal with changes that need to be made in insurance policies and loan arrangements. While it is difficult to generalize about such a multiplicity of situations, the following financial-planning areas are often affected by your various life events:

- **BUDGETING AND RECORD-KEEPING.** Review and revise your personal budgets. Prepare projections, including possible changes in your tax situation, based on your changed status.

- **INSURANCE.** Review your beneficiary designations, adequacy of coverage, type of coverage.

- **CREDIT.** Establish or reestablish your credit standing. Revise your loan documentation.

- **FAMILY ASSETS.** Review your holdings. Change ownership designations. Evaluate the sufficiency of your diversification.

- **ESTATE PLANNING.** Review and revise your estate planning documentation. Utilize more advanced estate-planning techniques. Clarify or change your bequests to heirs or other will provisions.

The explanations and guidance appearing throughout this book will help you cope financially with these life events whenever they occur. The sooner you anticipate and deal with them, the better.

MAJOR LIFE EVENTS CHECKLIST

☐

To the extent possible, prepare for "major life events" before they occur to help reduce the financial problems and uncertainties.

☐

Seek the assistance of lawyers, CPAs, or other professionals to help you cope with major changes such as divorce or death of a spouse.

☐

When a major life event occurs, don't delay making the necessary changes in your finances, including:

- BUDGETING AND RECORD-KEEPING

- INSURANCE

- CREDIT

- OWNERSHIP AND INVESTMENT OF FAMILY ASSETS

- ESTATE PLANNING

Wise Banking

Remember when you opened up your first passbook savings account? A momentous occasion, but it was simple enough that a child *could* do it. Contrast that with today's consumer-banking environment. Even an adult can easily feel like a child who's lost his mother in a large and intimidating shopping mall. Consumer-banking, like everything else in our financial lives, has become increasingly complex.

It's no longer advisable to simply open up a checking and savings account at your friendly local bank. That local bank might charge you an astronomical sum for the pleasure of doing business with a teller who knows you by name. Nor is it more advisable to open up your accounts in a "big" bank, where there are usually no discounts for their streamlined retail services.

To make matters worse, interest earned on all types of bank accounts is low. From money-market accounts to CDs to regular savings and Super-NOW accounts, the rates are unreliable and almost always underperform other investment possibilities.

All this makes banking wisely much more difficult—and all the more imperative. To make matters more complicated, there are many different types of banks: commercial banks, correspondent banks, country banks, independent banks, industrial banks, insured banks, investment banks, member banks, mutual savings banks, private banks, savings banks, state banks, and trust companies that operate like banks—and of course, bankrupt banks. In addition to banks, you can also "bank" at credit unions and savings and loans (S&Ls) and despite the problems S&Ls have had of late, credit unions and S&Ls are often better places to do business.

Shopping for a Bank That Suits Your Needs

Shopping for low-cost banking services is one of the few remaining instances where shopping can *save* you money! The work required is as simple as picking up your phone and calling various banks in your area to find out what fees they charge for the accounts you need. Another good resource for discovering the best credit card and CD rates is *Money* magazine. *Money* also provides a monthly listing of top-performing money-market accounts.

Increasingly, banks big and small have been offering service-related incentives to lure new customers into their fold—and to keep old customers content. The most common incentive? Usually a limited-time (six months to one year) waiver of service-related fees for new checking and savings accounts. If you think that's small potatoes, think again. Average annual service fees for basic checking accounts run in the area of $100. And God forbid you should bounce a check or need to reorder a packet of them! That'll cost you between $10 and $35. Need a printout of your past two months' activity? Fifteen dollars to $30. Using your ATM card at a bank that is not part of your bank's network? A one- or two-dollar charge (per transaction) will likely be assessed. In fact, it's not unreasonable to expect to pay $150 to $200 in annual service fees to your friendly banker. No wonder they're always smiling.

How to Select a Bank That's Right for You

U sing convenience as the sole criterion for selecting what bank you'll use for your basic finances—checking and savings accounts—is not a good idea. Just ask any of the many depositors who lost big-time in the late 1980s and early 1990s, when hundreds of S&Ls were shut down across the country. Many haven't received a penny since their banks went under, and many will never receive more than a few pennies on the dollar—if and when their situation is rectified. The reason? There was no federal insurance, and/or the state or private insurance was inadequate to cover all the depositors' accounts.

Which brings me to one of the most important (banking) questions you'll ever ask: are your deposits federally insured? Make certain that they are insured by either the Federal Deposit Insurance Corporation (FDIC) or the Savings Association Insurance Fund (SAIF). The National Credit Union Association (NCUA) insures the majority of credit unions. As long as your deposits are federally insured and they don't exceed the maximum amount covered by the insurance, you are protected.

In general, such insurance will guarantee your deposits up to $100,000 per account. (You can increase your money's coverage by opening up three separate accounts—one under your name, another under your spouse's name, and another under your spouse's and your name. The end result will be that your accounts will be insured up to $300,000.) But why be fancy when you want to be safe? Contrary to what you might think, there are many good, respectable banks that are more than willing to service your banking needs. In other words, heed the financial commandment "thou shalt not put all thy eggs in one basket!"

Make sure that you select a bank based on the services you need, not on services it provides. Also, make sure you get what you need, not what they want you to have. What do you need from a bank? This question probably has as many answers as there are people—especially nowadays, when banks are capable of being brokerages, realtors, and even insurers. But for most people a bank is for two things: taking money out (checking account) and putting money in

Money Saver

Order your checks directly from Checks In The Mail, Inc. (telephone 800-733-4443) and save up to 50 percent of the cost.

(savings account). There are a range of checking and savings accounts that you probably already know about. There are also certificates of deposit and money-market deposit accounts (not to be confused with money-market mutual funds). People also go to the bank to take out more money than they have in their own accounts—by taking out a loan. From consumer loans, mortgage loans, and home improvement loans, to college tuition loans, banks are busy with our business.

Opening an Account

To open a bank account you'll need four items: money, your Social Security number, an address, and probably some form of identification—a driver's license should be fine. Whether it's a checking or savings account that you're opening, the procedure is straightforward. In fact, the procedure for opening an account (putting money into the bank) is, not surprisingly, the only really easy thing left in banking these days. For example, if you're opening up a checking account, you'll be faced with at least three different types of checking accounts, several checkbook options, and hundreds of check styles to choose from. (If you choose anything but the plain old blue or green check, you'll be paying more for something that only you and a machine will ever see.) And if you order the checks from your bank, you'll be paying top dollar. There are several services that offer discounted check-ordering, with savings to you of up to 50 percent when compared with what the bank charges. Then there is the cross-selling of everything from ATM cards to the bank's credit card and loan options. Many people are so exhausted after opening up a simple account that they forget to go home and set up a record-keeping file for their new account.

Smart Money Move

Order "top-stub" instead of regular checkbooks. It may cost a couple of dollars more, but you'll be able to balance your checkbook with greater facility—and avoid the steep fees for bouncing a check.

Failure to keep meticulous records can often lead to interminable delays when a clerical error occurs—and they will occur—costing you money (in terms of time and lost interest). It is easy to open an account—but have you ever tried to sort out a clerical problem with one? Many consumers don't realize, until it's too late, that they foot the bill when their friendly banker researches a problem that they discovered in their own account.

Take note: If you have several accounts at one bank and their total balance is under $100,000, consider combining them into one or two accounts. Make one of them your bill-paying account, and the other an interest-earning savings account. You'll simplify your record-keeping and receive lower service fees.

Types of Checking Accounts

I sn't it un-American not to have a checking account? But just because everyone has one doesn't mean that everyone has taken the time to ensure that their account is competitive with those of their neighbors. I've always found it peculiar that, when it comes to spending money to keep up with the Joneses we go for broke, but when it comes to saving money, we keep it a family secret. *Psssst!* Is the type of checking account you have in your best interest? Or your bank's?

If you have a choice between opening a checking account that offers free checking but requires a minimum balance, and opening a checking account with no minimum balance where you pay for each check, you'll almost always be better off with the first. Why? Even though you lose interest on the money that must be kept in your checking account to satisfy the minimum balance requirements, the amount of interest income you "lose" is far less than the expense of maintaining a checking account that charges a monthly fee.

There are three basic kinds of checking accounts available to you: regular, NOW, and Super-NOW. The majority of us have at least a regular checking account—no interest is earned on the money we deposit, and a "small" monthly fee ranging from four to fifteen dollars per month is charged. Why do we put up with this? The answer is that we don't have enough money to keep the minimum balance required in the NOW and Super-NOW accounts—usually $500 to $2,500. The benefit we pass up is that in a NOW account, service fees are waived by maintaining a small minimum balance, and in a Super-NOW, not only are service fees waived, but (modest) interest is earned. Ironically, many consumers keep a small savings account at the same bank where they have their checking account. The result—they're hit with two service fees and diminished interest-earning potential.

Types of Savings Accounts

T hough there are many variations on the theme, the basics remain unchanged. You put money into an account, and you receive, in return, a low rate of interest on the amount in your account. Liquidity is the biggest selling point of savings accounts. Growth of your capital is not. The average savings account rate is under 5 percent—sometimes *way* under.

Passbook and Statement Savings Accounts

The basic savings account has two transaction options. In a passbook account, all deposits and withdrawals are recorded in your passbook, while in a statement savings account, the bank records your transactions and sends along a monthly or quarterly printout for your review. Before banks were computerized, passbook accounts were the standard savings account—now statement savings accounts are the norm.

One advantage of this basic type of account is liquidity—your money is always readily available to you, twenty-four hours hours a day if you have an automatic teller machine (ATM) card. Another is safety (as long as your deposits are insured in full). The disadvantage is low interest.

Money-Market Accounts

Money-market accounts are essentially a higher-yield savings account with limited check-writing privileges. These federally insured accounts should not be confused with money-market mutual funds (see page 514). Usually, money-market account holders are permitted to write up to three checks per month free; additional checks written incur a steep fee. A money-market account is a great temporary parking place for cash en route to other investments; it is a poor place to invest money for the long term.

Optional Services

Overdraft Protection—A Service Worth Considering

The last thing you want to do is bounce a check. It is both embarrassing and costly. The average service fee charged for a check that is returned for insufficient funds is fifteen dollars. Overdraft protection solves the problem—but it can lead to another problem: overdraft abuse. Many people, as the result of their negative financial situation or simply bad money-management habits, use their current overdraft protection as a line of credit. In fact, many banks do little to discourage this type of activity because it's good news for them at 18 percent annual interest.

ATM CARDS: CONVENIENCE AT WHAT COST?

Advising readers against having an ATM card is probably completely quixotic, but you should at least realize the drawbacks of having a bank card. An ATM card increases your use of your account—on the withdrawal side of the equation—and with increased use comes increased service fees. The more you use your card, the more you become accustomed to using it, which means the more comfortable you become with a bad financial habit.

A final caution: Along with the increased use of ATMs nationwide has come an often unreported—or at least underreported—statistic, ATM-related crime. In fact, according to the FBI, ATM-related crime has skyrocketed. So while ATM cards are a necessity for most of us, be prudent in their use—both for your financial and physical well-being.   »

Follow these safety precautions for ATM use:

- Avoid using an ATM card when you're alone at night.

- Avoid using your ATM card if there is only one other person in the "chamber."

- Avoid ATM booths that are tucked in out-of-the-way places away from public view. ATM booths located at the back of a bank or on an unlit street should be avoided.

- Always be aware of who is around you when you enter and leave an ATM booth. All a thief has to do is hold you up when you leave, or worse, trap you inside and demand your card, password, and all your other valuables.

Club Accounts—A Service Worth Avoiding

Only someone who wears a loincloth and has lived in a deep, dark cave for the past few thousand years would consider club accounts a valuable option. Perhaps they're named for the feeling you get when the fact that you earned less interest than your son did on his passbook saving's account hits you! Thunk.

Cultivating a Good Banking Relationship

One of the best things you can do, especially if you plan to live in the same area for the next several years, is to develop a good relationship with a credit union, bank, or savings and loan. The reason? You will be more likely to get the service you desire, as well as some financial help and advice that you may need when it comes to making important financial decisions like buying your first home or improving your existing one.

Credit Unions—An Overlooked Alternative to Commercial Banks

A credit union is a banking cooperative that is operated for the benefit of its members, who are basically the company's stockholders. Because credit unions are nonprofit corporations, when a surplus is generated, it is paid out to account holders in the form of either a small dividend or rebate of loan interest at the end of the fiscal year. Not only are most credit unions federally insured (only around 10 percent still carry private coverage), they frequently offer better service at a lower cost than do commercial banks. Credit unions usually have low overhead, which translates into lower costs for banking products, including loans and mortgages, and higher payout for savings accounts and CDs.

While credit unions may seem like old-fashioned places to bank—given the technological sophistication of today's services industry—they can actually be as convenient and up-to date as typical commercial banks. Some credit unions even offer stock-brokerage services.

There is one catch, however. Most credit unions are sponsored by an employer or an association and are not open to the general public. Only about 50 percent of Americans have the option of using a credit union. But if you can belong to a credit union, you should definitely use it.

When evaluating a credit union, find out how your checking account interest is calculated. Some credit unions will calculate your interest based on your lowest monthly balance. An account that pays interest on this schedule could really be a bad deal. Suppose you had $1,000 in your account for three weeks, then withdrew $750 of this money at the end of the fourth week. You would earn interest only on the $250, not the full $1,000, since $250 was your lowest monthly balance.

How Safe Is Your Bank?

Many people today are concerned about the safety of their banks, savings and loan institutions, and credit unions. Hardly a day goes by without the announcement of some bad news on the banking front. Numerous deposit institutions have been liquidated or merged with stronger ones in the last few years. In the early 1990s, many financial institutions filed for bankruptcy or were on the verge of bankruptcy. In a few instances, depositors actually lost money.

For the most part, however, customers need not fear for the safety of their deposits as long as the banks are federally insured. As you read earlier, the vast majority of commercial banks, mutual savings banks, savings and loans, and credit unions are covered by some form of federal or federally backed deposit insurance.

How Can You Gauge Your Bank's Health?

As long as your deposits are federally insured, you don't need to lose sleep over the financial health of your bank. If you want to find out about your bank's financial condition, however, contact the rating service Veribanc (see box).

What Happens If Your Bank Fails?

If a bank fails, the regulators step in to liquidate assets, and insured depositors can expect to be paid shortly after the closing. In some instances there have been delays, but the insured depositors got their money back.

If you have deposits at an institution that is not federally insured, you should be concerned. While these banks may have private or state insurance funds, history has shown that such insurance funds cannot always make good on depositors' claims. It is best to stick with federally insured institutions. In the future, Congress may look at placing further limitations on federal deposit insurance. It may enact laws at any time that reduce or restrict, but don't eliminate, federal deposit insurance. If such legislation is enacted, find out how it will affect your bank, savings and loan, or credit union deposits.

QUESTIONS ABOUT A BANK'S RATING?

When it comes to examining the health of local banks, fewer accessible information sources are available to the banking consumer than to the investing consumer. One source that does rate the health of banks is Veribanc. If you have questions about the financial stability of your bank, you can call and, for $10, receive an immediate rating, $5 for each additional immediate rating—up to $45 for a full research report (most likely unnecessary!). Through Veribanc you can access enough information to scrutinize and check up on any bank—something that is probably a very good idea for those who are new to an area. The contact information is:

Veribanc, Inc.
P.O. Box 461
Wakefield, MA 01880
(800) 442-2675

ASSET MANAGEMENT ACCOUNTS

One type of checking account where you can hold your cash is outside of the banking industry entirely—the asset management account (AMA). AMAs, like money-market mutual funds, are available through many of the major brokerage houses. Some of the companies offering AMAs require a $1,000 initial deposit; others have set their initial deposit requirements as high as $20,000. (A variation of the AMA, the declaration cash account, has no minimum initial deposit requirement.) Unlike money-market accounts or money-market mutual funds, AMAs offer unlimited checking privileges.

Asset management account holders can also obtain debit cards that look and work just like credit cards—with one crucial difference. Purchases charged to the card are deducted directly from your AMA. The debit card offers the convenience of a credit card without the temptation of easy credit. With a debit card, you can't spend more than you have in your account.

AMAs are protected by the Security Investors Protection Corporation (SIPC), which while it is a private—rather than a federal—insurance program, is strictly regulated by the SEC. An SIPC-protected AMA is about as safe as any money-market mutual fund.

Why AMAs pay better interest than checking accounts
An AMA is no more of an investment than is a checking account. It is a way station »

between your paycheck and your creditors' accounts. Nonetheless, AMAs generally pay higher interest than do checking accounts. Since your money will spend some time in the account between the time it is deposited and the time the checks clear, you might as well get the highest return that is safely available.

The interest your AMA account pays falls into two categories—variable interest paid on your account balance, and the interest that results from the daily account compounding. The sum total of AMA interest almost always outpaces even the best Super-NOW accounts.

Opening an AMA

Opening an AMA is as simple as opening a money-market mutual fund account. You order a prospectus and application and return the application with your deposit. From this a yearly fee ranging from $25 to $125 will be deducted, although some accounts can be opened free of charge.

FOR MORE INFORMATION

On Evaluating Your Bank

Office of Consumer Affairs
Federal Deposit Insurance Corporation
(FDIC)
550 17th Street, N.W.
Washington DC 20429
(800) 424-5488

On Evaluating Your Credit Union

"Federal Credit Union Handbook" Cost: $3.50
National Credit Union Administration
1776 G Street, N.W.
Washington DC 20456
(202) 682-9600

"Why Save and Invest at Your Credit Union?"
Credit Union National Association
P.O. Box 431
Madison WI 53701
(608) 231-4000

BANKING CHECKLIST

Use only those bank products and services that you need; avoid unneeded and expensive "extras."

■□■

Make sure all of your deposits in a bank, credit union, or savings and loan are federally insured.

■□■

If you can join a credit union, do so.

■□■

Look for ways to lower your banking costs by, for example, combining checking accounts or using no-fee checking.

■□■

Consider opening an asset management account for convenience and to earn attractive interest rates on your checking account deposits.

Part II

Your
Home and Family

Renting

Whether you are a first-time renter or a seasoned renter, the following information will help you make the most of your rent dollars. Housing costs are usually the largest single living cost, so it behooves you to become a smart apartment-seeker and tenant.

Your First Apartment

You may luck into the apartment you want right off the bat, but chances are you won't. The general rule should be: The more time you give yourself to search for the right apartment for the right price, the more likely you are to find it.

Price Is Always the Object

Don't take on more rent than you can afford. Figure out what you can afford, and stick with it. If you're paying more than *28 percent to 30 percent* of your net income on rent—including utilities—you're paying too much! Just because an apartment is a temporary living space doesn't mean you should be less focused on more lasting financial goals. The quickest way to becoming a permanent renter is to take on more apartment than you can reasonably afford.

The affordability of your apartment will affect your savings plan for the future. If you are unable to save at least 10 percent of your net income, after taking care of all the necessary line items—rent, utilities, phone, food, and transportation—then you are either paying too much in rent, or you are squandering too much on ephemeral fun.

How to Locate

If you are new to a city or state, your best bet is to talk to a few realtors about neighborhood qualities, such as convenience to supermarkets, transportation, and entertainment. If you know that you will be moving to a new location, try to stay with a relative or friend for a period of two weeks to one month—offering to pay for your share of the food, utilities, and phone bills. That way you can have a base from which to launch your apartment search, as well as an in-

Smart Money Move

Don't become rent poor by paying more than 30% of your net income on rent.

home guide to where you might best situate yourself. Also, visit local realtors, read the local papers, and talk to your new colleagues at work. If you are familiar with the city or suburb in which you would like to reside, then chances are you will know what newspapers to go to for good rental listings.

A realtor may not be a renter's best friend, but he or she can be very helpful and may have just the apartment you've been looking for. Realtors can also offer advice—what prices you can expect to pay for the apartment you want, where the best deals are, what areas to avoid—on the rental market. You might even set up some appointments to view apartments with a realtor—you're under no obligation to rent any of them—so that you can get a better feel for what's out there.

Things to Look For

Advertised apartments must be seen to be believed. There's no other way to look for an apartment. But looks can be deceiving, too. Most people think that because they can read, they can understand the meaning of what is written. Likewise, most apartment-hunters think that because they have eyes, they can see what is right and wrong with a place.

Don't be deceived. When you cross the threshold into a prospective apartment, there are so many concerns vying for your attention that making objective observations and decisions is difficult. What you should do is create a notebook that contains a checklist of the pros and cons of each apartment you've seen. You might even go as far as to sketch out a rough outline of the rooms, the number of windows, and comments on the views (for example, the bedroom has no windows, and the living room's big plate-glass window looks out onto a golf driving range).

Renter's Guide to a Great Apartment

Be in Control

- ALWAYS view an apartment twice—at least once in bright daylight. Artificial lighting can hide material damage to walls and floors, and it can easily create artificial feelings about a place. You also want to be sure that you're not renting a dark, gloomy place.

- ALWAYS view a prospective apartment at night. Viewing an apartment by day won't give you a sense of how noisy your new neighbors may be.

- THE TOP FLOOR tends to be the safest floor, and the one with a view. (Of course, you might want to keep in mind that fire truck ladders reach only to the sixth floor.)

Know Your Limits

- **WHAT** can you afford to pay?

- **WHAT** terms (lease or tenant-at-will—see page 70)?

- **WHAT** utilities are you responsible for—and does the landlord have documented utility bills to substantiate the quoted figures?

- **IS** there another tenant that you can talk to about the apartment building and the landlord?

- **ARE** there laundry facilities in the building? If not, where is the nearest coin-op located?

Damage Control

- **CHECK** all appliances in the kitchen: stove, sink, dishwasher, refrigerator, and disposal. Let each item run until you are satisfied that it functions.

- **CHECK** all bathroom facilities: toilet, sink, and shower. Does the hot water work? Does the hot water change temperature when you run the sink or flush the toilet? If it does, you can be sure that when someone flushes the toilet in the apartment above or below yours, you will have a cold or scalding burst of water in your shower.

- **ASK** other tenants in the building if there have been any problems with bugs or rodents. If there have been, what was done about it, what is the situation now, and what are the procedures should the problem arise again?

- **HAVE** there been any break-ins into the apartment itself, or into the apartment building?

- **IF** there is no off-street parking, ask a few tenants what it's like to park on the street. Is it congested? Is your car radio safe? *(Note:* If you're living in a city, a car is probably an unnecessary expense and should be avoided if at all possible.)

Warning Signs

- **THE LANDLORD** is overly pushy in asking you to sign a lease.

- **THE LANDLORD'S** name is not disclosed to you.

- **THE BUILDING** looks run-down on the outside, inside, or both. (When it comes to heating and plumbing, there's no such thing as cosmetic surgery.)

Your Rental Agreement

One of the first things to know about renting an apartment is that you can often negotiate the price of the rent to your advantage. Don't hesitate to try to do so. Another important thing to know is that depending on the landlord, you might be required to fill out a lengthy application for the apartment you desire. Moreover, if you don't have a good credit history—delinquent student or credit card loans, for example—you might be turned down. So if your credit record is less than stellar, be prepared to do some explaining.

References

A reference is someone who can vouch for your reliability and responsibility, ideally as a tenant. But if you're a first-time renter, an employer or relative who lives in the area might do the trick. Most landlords will ask for references. So be sure to have at least two—three is better—readily available.

Deposits

Many landlords require first and/or last month's rent as a deposit. In addition, most landlords require a security deposit (usually equal to one month's rent.) Be sure they put that deposit in an interest-earning savings account (which may be required by law), and that you receive the interest!

Lease versus Tenant-at-Will

A lease locks you into a legally binding contract for a set period of time. A tenant-at-will is an open-door agreement between you and your landlord—you are free to terminate the agreement, but so is the landlord. If you are planning on living in the apartment for at least one year, then a lease will have the advantage of securing the apartment for you. (The last thing you want to do is to have to hunt for a new apartment on relatively short notice because the landlord wants to "rent" the unit to his ne'er-do-well son.)

If you are new to an area and are uncertain that the location of the apartment is ideal for your needs, or if you think you may tire of living in a basement studio before a year runs its course, then a tenant-at-will is probably your best bet. If you are thinking about a tenant-at-will arrangement, one thing you should be sure to do is to always keep enough money handy that if you have to move suddenly, you will have the resources to do so.

Money Saver

Negotiate for a lower rent. You have nothing to lose and a lot to gain.

Warning: Never sign a lease that's for longer than twelve months—unless you feel that the rent is likely to go sky high, and that you want to remain where you are for more than twelve months. The reason is that there are always deals to be made on better apartments. Your friends might decide to move to a new state, leaving their spacious, convenient, and low-rent apartment to you. Also, if you're just starting out or are new to an area, you probably don't want to tie yourself to a place for more than a year.

Tenants' Rights

You have certain rights as a tenant or prospective tenant. It is illegal to be turned down from renting an apartment because of your race, religion, or marital status. You have the right to receive the services (like fixing a broken window or leaky faucet) that are your landlord's responsibility. If you think your rights have been violated, contact your local housing authority to locate the specific department that handles such complaints.

Renter's Insurance

One of the most overlooked issues in renting an apartment is one of the most important ones. If you do not get renter's insurance—most policies cost under $200—you could wind up losing all the valuables in your apartment. The landlord does not insure the contents of your apartment! (See Chapter 43 for details on renter's insurance.)

Rent Control

Some cities and towns have rent-controlled apartments that can be spectacular opportunities for a would-be renter. The difficulty is getting them! The competition for them is fierce. One thing to consider, however, is that rent-controlled apartments aren't often located in the most desirable neighborhoods.

Renting a House

If the bulk living arrangements of the typical apartment don't suit your fancy, consider renting a house with some reliable friends—or maybe even with a sibling. *Caveat* renter: The heating and other utilities in a house can be much more costly than in an apartment.

Sharing the Rent

Sharing rent with friends is how many people start out. This enables you to live in a higher-quality apartment with a rent you can afford. But do prepare a written agreement between yourselves that spells out who pays for what. One of the disadvantages of roommates is that the time may come when your friends can't abide by the rental agreement. They might have to relocate to a new job, or worse—they might be laid off. This could suddenly leave you stuck with having to pay for the whole apartment yourself.

Warning: Sharing a lease can be hazardous to friendships. So can sharing the rent with strangers—either by moving into a shared house together, or renting rooms out. The positive side is that you will meet new people and live with lower rent in a nicer place than you could afford on your own. The down side is that you will have to live with these new people day in and day out. They might become annoying or, worse, unreliable. Use your best judgment, and be sure that every detail of the living and rental arrangement is spelled out—that means written down!

Renting on Your Own

Living in a crowded house—your parents' house or the one you rent with your friends—may quickly become more of a bother than a pleasure. The option of moving out and renting on your own presents new financial challenges and responsibilities. Don't be rent poor, in any event.

Renting with a Significant Other

Renting with your significant other, while more feasible, is an option that requires a great deal of maturity—financial and otherwise—on both sides. Who will pay what amount of each household bill needs to be clearly determined at the outset. The question of savings can be particularly tricky. (See Chapter 17 for helpful information about domestic partners and money matters.)

Prematurely Terminating Your Lease

This is a very difficult but nonetheless possible thing to do. First, talk to your landlord and give him or her the detailed reasons as to why you need to prematurely terminate your lease. Wanting to move to a new apartment isn't a very strong reason. But if the reason is serious financial difficulty—you may have been laid off—your landlord might agree. You might have to offer to find a suitable new tenant for the apartment. In this case you will need to talk with your landlord about the cost of advertising and showing the apartment, as well as what the cost and terms of the agreement should be. It might cost you $200 or more to advertise the apartment, but it may save you money and anxiety in the long run.

When to Begin Planning for the Home You Can Afford

Should you be a renter or a homeowner? It all depends. There are many advantages to home ownership, but it certainly isn't for everyone. Renting allows you much more flexibility and is particularly advantageous if you aren't sure if you'll remain in the same locale for at least four or five years. The major problem with being a renter is that your housing costs will continue to escalate, and rent increases often outpace inflation.

If your life is settled, on the other hand, and you can afford it, home ownership has a number of advantages. One is that you can get your housing costs under control. There are the income tax advantages as well as the ability to live in better, more spacious quarters and the sense of belonging to a community. Perhaps the biggest advantage of home ownership is that you can pay off your mortgage by the time you retire, so that you won't have to worry about ever-increasing housing costs during your retirement years, when most retirees' incomes are relatively fixed.

Rent-to-Own

According to the National Association of Realtors, renting with an option to buy, commonly known as rent-to-own, is becoming more and more popular today. Sometimes renting-to-own makes more sense than outright ownership. For instance, you might want to experience living in the area for a year before deciding that it is the best place for you to establish your home. Another consideration is the living space itself. Whether it's a condo or a house, you may be able to negotiate so that you can rent-to-own the property. The benefit is that if you don't like it for any reason, you can move on at the end of the lease term, and if you do like it, the payments you have been making for rent can, depending upon the contractual agreement, constitute a down payment or a principal reduction on the sale price.

Another advantage of rent-to-own is that if the real estate market rises or falls dramatically, you will be relatively unaffected by it. In other words, if market values drop considerably, you may be able to renegotiate your previously agreed upon purchase price or find a better property for a lower price. If, on the other hand, real estate prices rise rapidly, you will be able to hold your homeowner to the originally agreed-upon purchase price.

Warning: You will need to hire a real estate attorney to review the rent-to-own contract in order to ensure that it contains all the provisions asked for and agreed upon. Don't try to go this alone.

RENTING CHECKLIST

Take time to find the right apartment at the right price.

Always check a prospective apartment thoroughly to make sure it meets your needs and is free of defects.

Smart Money Move

Evaluate whether you are better off with a lease or renting as a tenant-at-will. On balance, a lease will provide you with more security.

If you're interested in becoming a homeowner, find desirable housing that you can live in on a rent-to-own basis.

If you have roommates, avoid future conflicts by preparing a signed agreement that outlines duties and responsibilities.

Consider buying a home as an alternative to renting in order to get your housing costs under control (see Chapter 12).

Buying a Home

Buying a home is no simple task. In fact, most first-time home-buyers end up getting at least mildly "taken" for two reasons. First, they get so emotionally attached to the home they want to buy that any serious efforts at negotiation fall by the wayside. Second, first-time home-buyers are simply uninformed about the many nuances of the real estate market. I can't help you if your emotions get the better of you, but the following information will help new and experienced home-buyers alike to be better informed purchasers.

There are advantages and disadvantages to home ownership, but on balance, most people benefit in many ways from long-term home ownership.

It's no secret that the new century family has less home-purchasing power than did the generation preceding it. Many home-buyers have to settle for a house that isn't quite as nice as the one in which they grew up. But remember, the most important thing is to get into your own home or condominium. You'll always have the opportunity to trade up in the future.

Many people find looking for a new home to be a disagreeable task. Going door to door, open house to open house, even realtor to realtor, can be exhausting. It is also an emotionally trying time. You're having to face up to the financial reality of what you can and cannot afford.

Are You Financially Prepared to Look for a House?

The Down Payment

One of the major barriers to buying a house is the down payment. This may be as low as 5 percent of the house value, but more commonly it approaches 10 or 20 percent. Thus, a $100,000 house may require an initial expenditure of as much as $20,000, plus closing costs. Closing costs may be as high as several thousand dollars, including loan origination fees (also known as "points") of typically 1 to 3 percent of the mortgage amount.

Figure Out the "Amount" of House You Can Afford

The amount of down payment and closing costs you will have to accumulate depends upon how much house you can afford. The first thing to do is to get an idea of how large a mortgage you can carry. Some rules of thumb:

- YOUR monthly mortgage payment should not exceed more than one and a half week's worth of your take-home pay.

- YOUR monthly mortgage payment should not exceed 28 percent of your net monthly income or 32 percent of your gross monthly income.

- YOUR total monthly debt obligations, including the mortgage, should not exceed 35 percent of your gross monthly income.

As you can see, a variety of loan-affordability measures are commonly used by lenders, but this will give you a way to estimate the amount of monthly mortgage payment you can afford.

Estimating Your Mortgage Payments

The following table provides a quick way to estimate the amount of your monthly mortgage payment. For example, if you're thinking of qualifying for a $120,000 thirty-year mortgage at 9 percent, multiply 120 times the applicable amount—$8.05 per $1,000 borrowed—to determine that your monthly principal and interest payment will be approximately $966.

PAYMENT PER $1,000 OF LOAN

INTEREST RATE (PERCENT)	15 YEARS	30 YEARS
7.00	$8.99	$6.66
7.25	9.13	6.83
7.50	9.28	7.00
7.75	9.42	7.17
8.00	9.56	7.34
8.25	9.71	7.52
8.50	9.85	7.69
8.75	10.00	7.87
9.00	10.15	8.05
9.25	10.30	8.23

The reality of how much or how little house they can afford knocks many first-time buyers for a loop. You may have to pull back from the search and rent for another year or two in order to save up enough for your first house.

Take note: Many banks' lending guidelines are based on those of the Federal National Mortgage Association (FNMA). These stipulate that your total monthly debt obligation on the house—principal, interest, taxes, utilities (including heat, hot water, and water), as well as a fraction set aside for current and future maintenance expenditures—should not exceed 28 percent of your gross monthly income.

Outstanding Debts

Banks look at your whole financial picture, past and present. If you have outstanding debts—credit cards, car loans, student loans—the bank will add the amount you owe monthly for these to make sure that, together with your monthly debt obligation on the house, your total monthly debt obligations will not exceed about 35 percent of your gross monthly income.

Before you apply for a mortgage, pay off as much of your consumer debt as possible. Your consumer debt includes everything from your Visa card to your gas credit cards, from your car payments to your student loans. The less debt you owe, the easier it will be for you to qualify for a mortgage.

Money in the Bank

Most banks will require that, in addition to the required application costs, down payment, and sundry closing costs, you have at least two months' worth of mortgage payments in a savings account.

Let the Banker Work for You

One way to determine the amount of mortgage you may qualify for is to simply contact a bank or mortgage company in your area and let them know that you are in the beginning stages of buying your first home. Ask if they would set up an informational meeting to discuss the process of applying for a mortgage, and ask them to discuss the various types of mortgages offered, and what they estimate the amount of mortgage available to you might be. The mortgage business is very competitive. Lenders are eager to lend to good customers.

Know What Is Available

As you estimate the amount of house you can afford and determine the location that suits your personal needs and your finances, you will also need to familiarize yourself with the different types of homes, condominiums, or cooperatives that are available in your price range.

Smart Money Move

Before beginning your home search, find out how much home you can afford to buy by speaking with a lender.

Check Your Credit Rating

A clean credit record for at least two to three years is an important part of getting the mortgage you want. See Chapter 49 for guidance on obtaining, reading, and correcting errors on your credit bureau report.

Warning: Don't count on last-minute ways to accumulate a down payment. It used to be as simple as calling your rich uncle—and begging him to lend you the necessary funds—but no more. In most cases, you'll still need to convince your lending officer that you're capable of good personal money management.

Where to Begin Your Search

One of the easiest ways to begin your search is to read the real estate section of the Sunday newspaper. Chances are it will contain an article or two about a particular neighborhood, as well as extensive sale listings town by town. If you haven't yet decided on one or two communities, you can surmise, at a glance, what towns you can and can't afford, and you can then visit these communities.

Location, Location, Location

Many people think that location is all-important, but affordability is just as important. A location's advantages—in terms of its conveniences, safety, public schools, transportation, shopping areas, and cultural centers—need to be weighed against the costs of a home in a prime location. Keep in mind that one of the benefits of buying—as opposed to renting—a home is that you're building equity in it. And location often can play a key role in the appreciation of the value of your home. One strategy many experienced homeowners use is to buy a less desirable home (smaller, less well situated, a fixer-upper) in the best part of town.

Network

Contact any acquaintances you have who are currently residing in—or who have recently moved from—the area in which you're interested. Ask them to recommend a real estate agency or two, and follow up on their recommendations by making requests for informational interviews with a few local realtors.

Smart Money Move

Never buy the best home in the neighborhood.

Another source of information, if you're moving to unknown territory, is your college alumni association. It can provide you with names of alumni living in the area to which you're moving. Call them up, introduce yourself, and ask if they wouldn't mind answering a few questions about where they live. This may sound too bold and personal, but most people are happy to introduce an outsider to their neighborhood. Anytime you give people the opportunity to demonstrate their knowledge, they'll be happy to do so.

Realtors

If you have never dealt with a realtor before, don't be overly impressed by a firm handshake and winsome smile. The first and most important thing to remember about realtors is that they represent the seller, not you (the buyer). Nevertheless, good realtors know what the fair market prices for the homes they are selling are. The difficulty is getting them to own up to it. Like all salespeople, realtors have their own best interests at heart, and if they can get you to pay a few thousand dollars more than the next guy, so much the better for them. As long as you understand a realtor's position in a sale, you will probably benefit from using one.

Buyer's Brokers

Some real estate agents have switched camps and work exclusively for buyers. Known as buyer's brokers, these real estate professionals negotiate the purchase price on the buyer's behalf. Buyer's brokers are listed in the Yellow Pages.

A buyer's broker may also be able to help you determine the areas where affordable housing exists. They charge either an hourly rate or a percentage of the selling price of the home that you purchase.

What's Out There

The decision to buy a particular home depends on several variables, the most common of which are:

- **LOCATION.** Is the home convenient to work, shopping, school, and recreation? Is the general neighborhood declining or improving? How heavy are the property taxes? Are there any crime or pollution problems? How good are the local schools, community facilities, and services?

- **TYPE OF HOME.** The traditional single-family house is facing stiff competition from newer types of housing, such as condominiums and multifamily units. Even traditional housing shows a tremendous amount of variety, especially between older dwellings and new ones. Typically, newer houses are more expensive and have more conveniences, but they may also have structural problems or inferior construction compared with older ones. Old houses, however, may be less energy efficient and may require considerable ongoing maintenance.

Types of Homes

Single-Family Homes

The old-fashioned single-family house is still the most popular choice for first-time home-buyers—perhaps because they are fed up with the clatter of apartment buildings and have a natural desire for their own private space. Purchasing a single-family home is a smart move. In a declining housing market, single-family home prices are more stable than prices of other types of residential real estate.

Multifamily Homes

Buying a two- or three-family home is a method used by many people who can't afford the costs of a single-family home but who nevertheless want to own a home. The rental income is used to offset a part of the mortgage payment. The problems with this option begin with the additional costs of such a purchase and include problems associated with being a landlord. Nevertheless, for those who don't mind being a property manager as well as a homeowner, multifamily housing is a great way to keep housing costs to a minimum while at the same time owning an excellent investment.

Condominiums

Condominiums represent an affordable way to have your own living space. You are also relieved of the chores of maintaining the outside and common areas of the condominium development. For many people, this added convenience is a big plus.

On the other hand, you are also a joint owner of the common space in the building in which your condominium is located—including stairways, light fixtures, parking lots, and recreational facilities. And condominium associations generally do not win awards for promoting good neighborliness. Another possible disadvantage is that condominiums and cooperatives (described next) have not appreciated as much as single-family homes in many areas of the country, particularly in areas where condominiums have been overbuilt.

Smart Money Move

Start yourself on the way to a rental real estate empire by purchasing a multifamily house as your first home.

Cooperatives

Not to be confused with a condominium, a cooperative is a corporation that sells shares of itself to willing buyers. Instead of buying space—as you do with a condominium—you are buying a share whose dollar value is roughly represented by the square footage of the space in which you want to live. Another difference is in financing. Many banks take a dim view of cooperatives, so they may be more difficult to finance.

Other Important Considerations

There are other factors that must weigh in your decision about what type of house you want. Two of the most important are:

- **SIZE.** Determining the optimal size of the house you want requires a projection of your future needs. Is your family likely to grow, or is it likely to shrink as your children leave the nest? Also, the size and the layout of the house may influence its resale value.

- **LENGTH OF STAY.** If you anticipate staying only four or five years in a neighborhood, you may have different priorities from someone who is anticipating a permanent stay. If you anticipate moving, the house you purchase should be easy to resell, and the size and location should fit the demands of the market more than your specifications.

Mortgages

Types of Mortgages

There are almost as many types of mortgages as there are types of homes. Familiarize yourself with the most common types, so that you can select the one most appropriate for your needs.

The two main types are fixed-rate and adjustable-rate mortgages. A fixed-rate mortgage is a loan whose rate of interest does not change during the life of the mortgage. As a result, your loan payment will be a constant amount. By contrast, an adjustable-rate mortgage is a loan whose interest rate fluctuates throughout the life of the loan.

Thirty-year fixed-rate

The old-fashioned thirty-year fixed-rate mortgage is still a desirable commodity, particularly if you can lock in a reasonable interest rate (perhaps 9 percent or less). While an adjustable-rate mortgage may offer a lower interest rate at first, the security of knowing that your monthly payments will never change is important to the many home-buyers who opt for fixed-rate mortgages.

Fifteen-year fixed-rate

Your monthly payments will be higher with this than if you take out a thirty-year fixed-rate mortgage, but the total interest you pay out over the life of the loan will be substantially lower. A fifteen-year

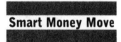

Smart Money Move

Save tens of thousands of dollars taking out a fifteen-year mortgage or by making extra payments against your thirty-year mortgage.

81

fixed-rate mortgage is a good idea if you can afford the higher payments. Want to turn your thirty-year mortgage into a fifteen-year mortgage at no cost? It's easy. Just make sufficient additional principal payments each month on your thirty-year mortgage so that it is paid off over the shorter period of time. You can also cut your mortgage-repayment period down by taking out a biweekly mortgage.

Two-step mortgage

A two-step mortgage is a variation of the thirty-year fixed-rate mortgage. There is one fixed rate for the first phase of the loan—typically five to seven years—with a one-time adjustment for the remaining life of the loan. If you are planning on moving before the first phase expires, consider this option.

Adjustable-rate mortgage

If you're thinking of staying in your home for only a few years—and this is a tricky thing to think about—an adjustable-rate mortgage is probably a good idea for you. Adjustable rate mortgages (ARMs) are commonly available, and are most beneficial when interest rates are low and are expected to stay low.

With an ARM, the interest rate and, hence, the monthly payment changes based on a financial index. Rather than locking in a fixed mortgage payment, ARM payments can and will change. The frequency of the interest rate change is spelled out when you take out the mortgage, but they typically vary from six months to three years. The initial interest rate is typically lower than those of fixed-rate mortgages. While this makes them attractive, payments can increase, sometimes sharply, if the index on which the adjustable rate is based increases. (If the initial ARM rate is super-low, you can rest assured that it will rise when the loan rate is first adjusted.) Many adjustable-rate mortgages have rate or payment caps, which means that your monthly payments won't go through the roof all of a sudden. However, you'll need to keep a weather eye on changes in the financial index, otherwise you may be caught unaware by a substantial increase in your monthly payments from one year to the next.

Smart Money Move

Cut your mortgage costs from day one by shopping for the best interest rates and loan terms.

Coming to Terms with Points

One of the most perplexing tasks the home-buyer will encounter is comparing mortgage terms. The impact of points on total carrying costs contributes to this confusion. Each point equals one percent of the loan amount. When comparing mortgages, one general rule of thumb is to equate each point with about 0.25 percent on the interest rate. For example, an 8.5 percent loan with two points is roughly equivalent to an 8.75 percent loan with one point. The significance of points diminishes as the period of time you own the home increases.

Difficulty Obtaining Mortgages

In some areas housing prices may have risen so much that people find themselves shut out of the housing market altogether. In other areas, depressed real estate markets may tend to make lenders wary. Today, the large number of foreclosures and the frequent practice of reselling mortgages on the secondary market are causing lenders to follow strict guidelines in assessing a prospective borrower's mortgage creditworthiness. The end result is that it is all the more important for you to carefully evaluate your creditworthiness prior to beginning your search in earnest.

Getting the Mortgage You Want

You have a much better chance of arranging for a favorable mortgage if you have maintained a good working relationship with a bank, and if you have a clean credit history. You should get to know a personal banker, and keep that person informed of your financial status. Even if you are not currently interested in purchasing a specific house, you should test for your mortgage-borrowing capacity. The banker should be able to gauge whether you are capable of assuming a substantial mortgage and may even be able to bend a few rules for you if you are a good customer. Nevertheless, you should check with as many other local lending institutions as possible.

Lending institutions vary both in the interest rates they charge and in mortgage terms and closing costs. If possible, the mortgage you arrange should be assumable—meaning that the next owner can assume the existing mortgage at the time of sale. Your agreement should not include a mortgage prepayment penalty, so that you will be able to repay the mortgage early, either with a lump sum or with periodic additional payments. Creditworthy borrowers should not hesitate to try to negotiate concessions on the loan terms.

Mortgage Shopping

In addition to scrutinizing lenders' fees for services rendered, you should compare lenders' mortgage rates. There are usually surprising differences among them. It is easy to get your hands on this information: Most local papers list the local lenders' rates in their financial sections. The next step is to ask your realtor or buyer's broker to run a computerized shopping service that can take your search for a suitable mortgage well beyond your local area. You don't have to take a mortgage from a bank in your area, and you may be able to get a better deal from an out-of-town lender.

The Purchase and Sale Agreement

A purchase and sale agreement (P&S) is the contract between a buyer and a seller that specifies the terms and price of the sale. Of course, the negotiation between buyer and seller occurs before the purchase and sale agreement is prepared. Negotiations are the time to hold your emotions in check. You obviously want the home, but until you have purchased it, it is just a house.

If this is the first time you have purchased a home, be sure to enlist the assistance of family members or friends who have purchased houses in the past. Otherwise, you can rest assured that you'll pay too much.

Prior to signing the P&S and forking over the deposit, you should probably ask an attorney to review it. You will want to include some contingencies in the agreement, typically including obtaining the financing (which will require the lender to appraise the property), a satisfactory home inspection, and a clear title. These are discussed below.

Appraisals

Appraised values are what bankers, realtors, buyers and sellers use as their standard to determine acceptable and unacceptable bids. If you are a potential buyer but are uncertain whether the asking price on the home that interests you is reasonable, spend some money and get an independent appraisal of the property. To find a qualified appraiser, check the Yellow Pages.

Don't confuse appraisals with another valuation that you have probably heard of—assessed value. The assessed value of a home is the valuation that the town or city places on the property to determine its property taxes. Assessed values are almost always lower than appraised values, except in areas where real estate values have declined dramatically and suddenly.

There is also a valuation known as fair market value. This valuation is based on recent sales prices of similar homes selling in the same vicinity.

Inspection

You need to hire a professional home inspector to give the home you want to buy a thorough physical exam. These are some of the items on which your inspector should report back to you.

The Foundation

A solid foundation is an absolute necessity. Be sure your inspector knows his or her masonry. Ask when the foundation was made, and whether and to what extent repairs have been required. Also, is the basement above or below the water table? This question sounds silly, but do you want to spend the rest of your days listening to the rhythm of a sump pump?

The Roof

The cost of roof repairs can run from a minor patch—$1,000—to a reroofing—$10,000 to $20,000. Make sure your inspector knows his or her way around a roof. You can't determine the quality of a roof from the ground or from a ladder. The inspector needs to get up on it, and get into the attic to track watermarks, damp rot, and more.

Windows

Do you know how expensive a replacement window can be? What if you need to replace all the windows in your house? They may not be insulated, for example, or they may be over fifteen years old—the age when glass becomes brittle.

Plumbing

The inspector you hire should be qualified to examine the plumbing. If he or she isn't, then hire a plumber to check all the pipes and water works. When were they installed? What repairs have been made? Are the pipe joints soldered with lead? It is expensive to replace or repair pipes, and you should know the extent and cost of the damage before you commit to a purchase. The same goes for the electrical work, and the heating and air-conditioning system.

Environmental Concerns

You can be held financially liable for lead paint and other hazardous or toxic materials on property you purchase. In some states there are no disclosure laws that require the seller of a property to tell the buyer whether there are hazardous or toxic materials on the premises. As the new owner of such a property, you could be held responsible for any hazardous-materials problems that crop up after the purchase. Fortunately, most states do have disclosure laws to protect prospective home-buyers from unscrupulous sellers. But be careful—don't discover a problem only when it's too late.

Title Search

Title Examination

When you have a signed purchase and sale agreement, you or the lender can then conduct a title examination of the property. A title search is a routine investigation undertaken to prove that the seller indeed has the right to transfer title of the property to you. Usually, a professional abstractor examines the transfer-of-property records for the house, often tracing the chain of ownership back sixty years or more. If no irregularities in previous titles appear, the sale can be concluded.

Title Insurance

In many areas, the lender requires buyers to purchase title insurance. This protects the lender against any defects that might appear in the transfer records, such as illegal transference or liens that supersede the transfer. Title insurance can be purchased from a number of insurance companies or through most attorneys. Usually, the buyer pays for it, although this item is sometimes negotiable.

Closing the Home Purchase

T he settlement is the legal closing of the property transaction. The buyer, the seller, the attorneys for both, the real estate broker, and a representative of the lender usually attend the settlement. Here all legal documents (abstract of title and deed to property drawn up by the attorneys) are signed, and all fees are paid, including the broker's commission.

As the buyer, you should be sure to bring along a stack of checks, because you'll be writing out checks to people you've never seen before and will probably never see again. The following is a list of the typical fees, categorized according to who usually pays them (although most of them are negotiable):

SELLER'S RESPONSIBILITY	BUYER'S RESPONSIBILITY	NEGOTIABLE
• BROKER'S COMMISSION	• SURVEY	• APPRAISAL FEE
• SELLER'S ATTORNEY FEES	• BUYER'S ATTORNEY FEES	• LOAN ORIGINATION FEE (COMMONLY KNOWN AS POINTS, WHICH ARE TAX-DEDUCTIBLE IF PAID BY THE PURCHASER)
• SELLER'S PERCENTAGE OF PROPERTY TAXES, INSURANCE, AND UTILITIES	• OWNER'S TITLE INSURANCE POLICY	
	• TITLE EXAMINATION FEE	
• INCOME TAX FROM PROFIT ON SALE	• FINANCING FEES	
• STATE TRANSFER FEES	• RECORDING FEES	

Closing Costs Add Up

Here's a list of just some of the fees you're likely to encounter when buying a home.

- **MORTGAGE-APPLICATION FEE** Depending on the lender, this can run from nothing to several hundred dollars.

- **ORIGINATION FEE.** This is the fee that a mortgage department or company charges to process your loan.

- **MORTGAGE-INSURANCE FEE.** If you don't have a 20 percent down payment but you're still a candidate for a mortgage, you may be required to insure that the difference between your down payment and the 20 percent figure can be paid.

- **APPRAISAL FEE.** You pay a professional to assess the market value of your desired home for the bank. This starts at $150, with no ceiling.

- **HOME INSPECTION FEE.** This fee—around $150—is what you pay a professional to inspect the house for defects.

- **CREDIT REPORT FEE.** You pay the bank to run a credit check that tells them how creditworthy you are. They start at $30.

- **BANK ATTORNEY FEES.** You pay the cost of the bank's legal work.

- **POINTS.** These are paid at closing to the lender: one percent to three percent of the loan amount. (Two points on a $125,000 mortgage, for example, would be $2,500.)

FOR FURTHER INFORMATION

The following publications are available from the Consumer Information Center:

Consumer Handbook on Adjustable-Rate Mortgages, Publication 423Y, Price: $0.50

A Consumer's Guide to Mortgage Lock-Ins, Publication 424Y, Price: $0.50

A Consumer's Guide to Mortgage Refinancing, Publication 425Y, Price: $0.50

The Mortgage Money Guide, Publication 122Y, Price: $1.00

Wise Home Buying, Publication 123Y, Price: $1.00

To receive copies, write to:
Consumer Information Center
Attention: R. Woods
Pueblo CO 81002

The Federal National Mortgage Association distributes the leaflet "How to Buy a Foreclosed Home," which is free, as well as a list of foreclosed properties owned by the FNMA. Fannie Mae also publishes "Introducing a New Adjustable Rate Mortgage (ARM) for Today's Homebuyer." Write to:
Fannie Mae
Public Affairs
3900 Wisconsin Avenue NW
Washington, DC 20016
(202) 752-6527

HOME-BUYERS' CHECKLIST

☐

First things first. Work hard to accumulate the down payment necessary to buy a home. While you are saving up for your down payment, be sure to pay off your old debts.

☐

Once you are close to accumulating the necessary down payment, find out how large a mortgage you can qualify for.

☐

Don't rush into making a home purchase. The more time you spend studying neighborhoods and visiting individual properties, the better. Plan to spend a year on your home search.

☐

Take out the kind of mortgage that best suits your circumstances.

☐

Comparison shop for your mortgage, to take advantage of competition among lenders.

Home Ownership

Homes are like children—they're expensive to acquire and even more expensive to maintain. What's more, the expenses of a home—like the expenses of children—never go away. This chapter is intended for Harry and Harriet Homeowner. It covers home economics (including refinancing your mortgage and using your home for credit), home improvements (including cost-efficient home repairs and getting a home improvement loan that won't leave your finances unimproved), and home remedies (which are sensible and financially sound ways to cut the costs of running your home). Using these cost-efficient ways, you can make your home your castle—without paying a king's ransom.

HOMEOWNER'S EMERGENCY MANUAL

Always be prepared for the worst when it comes to owning a home. If you wait long enough, the worst will happen. Here are some defensive measures you can take now in anticipation of homeowner emergencies.

- Create a household emergency fund. Set aside sufficient easily accessible money to pay for the next home emergency—a new hot water heater, burst pipes, and the like.

- Save receipts from major purchases. Chances are you're going to need them. Set up a file where you can keep these important receipts. The best place is away from your home—in your office, perhaps, so that if disaster strikes, you'll be able to show the insurance company what you owned and how much you paid for it.

- Put all warranties and owner's manuals in one location. That way you can find them when you need them.

- Inventory your household possessions. A detailed, handwritten inventory of your possessions, with photographs of them attached, is the best way to get a fair settlement from your insurance company, should disaster strike. (See page 357 for details on how and what to inventory.)

Your Mortgage

With home ownership come the trials and tribulations of a sizable mortgage. Figuring out how you're going to pay your monthly due is your first order of business, but figuring out how to reduce its total cost should be your second.

Refinancing Your Mortgage

At some point, you may wish to refinance your mortgage, either to take advantage of lower interest rates or to raise additional cash. (You should be cautioned, however, that if the refinanced mortgage amount exceeds the prior mortgage, the interest on the new mortgage may not be fully deductible.) Refinancing occurs most frequently when current interest rates have fallen below the rate on your original mortgage.

Is Refinancing Worth It?

The costs involved must be considered. Whether refinancing is worthwhile depends on the costs and the time it takes to recoup them. One rule of thumb states that refinancing makes sense if you can reduce your current interest rate by 2 percent or more, although it may be worthwhile for a difference of only 1.5 percent. This is most appropriate in situations where closing costs and points (that is, loan-origination fees, or the up-front interest often charged on mortgages) are low.

In addition to closing costs and points, there may be prepayment penalties of up to six months' interest. Several states either prohibit or limit prepayment penalties. Also, some banks waive this penalty for their own customers. You can estimate the amount of closing costs by requesting an estimate of closing costs from your lender. You should generally aim to recoup refinancing costs in five years or less.

Money Saver

Check to see if you will benefit from mortgage refinancing if you can obtain a rate at least 1.5 percent less than your current mortgage rate.

The worksheet in the box on page 91 is designed to help you make a quick approximation of the number of months it will take for you to break even, should you decide to refinance. There are four key ingredients: your existing mortgage payment, the refinanced mortgage payment, taxes, and closing costs. Points, application fees, inspections, attorneys fees, and a credit report can add several thousand dollars into the "bargain." Make certain that you know all the closing costs that a possible refinancing will incur before you sign on any dotted line.

MORTGAGE REFINANCING WORKSHEET

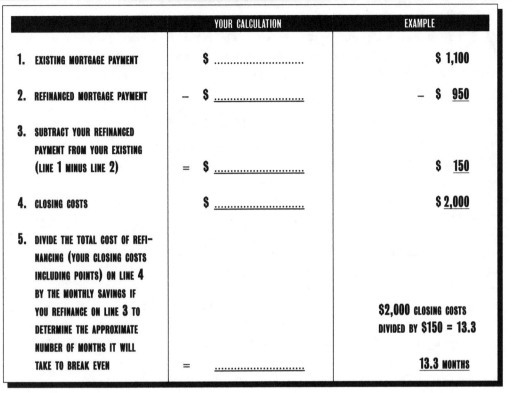

	YOUR CALCULATION	EXAMPLE
1. EXISTING MORTGAGE PAYMENT	$	$ 1,100
2. REFINANCED MORTGAGE PAYMENT	− $	− $ 950
3. SUBTRACT YOUR REFINANCED PAYMENT FROM YOUR EXISTING (LINE 1 MINUS LINE 2)	= $	$ 150
4. CLOSING COSTS	$	$ 2,000
5. DIVIDE THE TOTAL COST OF REFINANCING (YOUR CLOSING COSTS INCLUDING POINTS) ON LINE 4 BY THE MONTHLY SAVINGS IF YOU REFINANCE ON LINE 3 TO DETERMINE THE APPROXIMATE NUMBER OF MONTHS IT WILL TAKE TO BREAK EVEN	=	$2,000 CLOSING COSTS DIVIDED BY $150 = 13.3 13.3 MONTHS

Refinancing's Tax Impact

Although refinancing may often save you thousands of dollars, it does have an impact on your income taxes. Lower interest payments mean a smaller tax deduction, since interest payments on mortgages are tax deductible. Moreover, owners who pay points when they refinance their homes cannot take an immediate tax deduction for them. Instead, the points must be deducted over the life of the loan.

An immediate deduction is still allowed on points when the new loan is more than the value of the old mortgage and when the extra funds are used to remodel the home. In addition, home mortgage interest that can be deducted on a refinancing is limited to the value of the mortgage being refinanced plus $100,000, unless the proceeds are used for home improvements.

Appeal Your Property Tax Assessment

Another way to reduce the overall cost of home ownership is to have your home tax-reassessed for property tax purposes. The fact is that many people who appeal their property tax assessments end up with a lower bill! It's more often the result of bad fortune than good luck—property values having dropped in many locales.

Home Equity Lines of Credit

Financial institutions offer a wide range of financing plans specifically designed for people who have accumulated substantial equity in their homes or who have seen the market value of their homes appreciate but have not realized any of the gain. A home equity loan is usually more appropriate for a younger homeowner who has the time and ability to generate the funds necessary to pay off the loan. Other programs, such as a reverse annuity mortgage (RAM), can provide retirees with a monthly check, resulting from the partial conversion of their home's equity. The reason for the loan, the amount of loan you need, the terms of the loan, your ability to repay the loan in a timely manner, as well as your age are all important factors.

Substantial risks are involved in using your home for credit. The worst case is when you take on too much debt and lose your home to foreclosure. Nevertheless, if you are a homeowner who is facing major expenses—you need to finance a new roof, or your daughter has just been accepted by an expensive private college—consider taking out a second mortgage, or a home equity loan (HEL), using your home as collateral.

Choosing a Plan

In choosing a plan to finance a large expenditure, consider which option best meets your long- and short-term needs. If you take out a second mortgage, you have to choose between a fixed-rate mortgage and a variable-rate mortgage. The fixed-rate mortgage is more expensive but is more predictable than a variable-rate mortgage.

The main drawback of a second mortgage is the burden of additional debt and often higher interest rates. If you are still paying a first mortgage, you may have difficulty with a second mortgage added. Nevertheless, the second mortgage might be a flexible method for financing large expenditures.

Home Equity-Secured Credit

Home equity-secured credit is essentially a credit account, secured by a second mortgage. It operates like a checking account. Generally, the line of credit is 70 percent to 80 percent of the appraised value of the house, less what is owed on it. For example, a house worth $200,000, with $80,000 still unpaid on the mortgage, might qualify for a $70,000 line of credit (75 percent of $200,000 less $80,000). Usually, the amount of credit allowed depends on your income. The length of the loan may range from five to twelve years or longer at some institutions. It is wise to shop among local lenders, because interest rates and fees can vary substantially.

For Major Expenditures Only

A home equity line of credit is a convenient, flexible way to borrow that can preserve the deductibility of interest under the current tax laws. Once your line of credit is in place, you are not required to fill out a loan application again. But because such credit draws on the equity built up in your home (that is, the difference between the value of your home and what you owe on it), it should be used only for major expenditures and worthwhile purposes, such as home improvements, children's education expenses, major purchases (like an automobile), and, if you are committed to cleaning up your debt act, debt consolidation.

Rates Fluctuate

Home equity-secured credit usually offers a lower interest rate than other lines of credit because it is secured by the equity in your home. Most home equity lines of credit have variable interest rates, which are usually based on the prime rate or a government Treasury bill rate index. This allows you to secure the best rate available at a given time. These rates will fluctuate over time, however, sometimes raising monthly payments. Make sure you can afford this flexibility.

Evaluate

When evaluating and selecting a home equity loan, review the following considerations:

- IS a home equity loan most suitable for your needs?

- WHAT is the initial rate of interest? Is it fixed or variable? How often can the rate change? Is there a maximum cap on interest rates?

- ARE there application fees? Annual fees? Closing fees?

- WHAT is the minimum monthly payment? How much of it will go toward paying off principal?

- DO minimum monthly payments go up with variable interest rates? How much?

- ARE there conditions under which monthly payments can be reduced?

- CAN the bank demand refinancing of outstanding credit? Can any of the credit terms be changed without your approval?

Smart Money Move

Don't take out a home equity loan unless: (1) you're one of those rare people who never borrows for the wrong reasons and (2) you need to borrow for a good purpose. Otherwise, HELs can be hell on your personal finances.

- **IS** there an option to convert the line of credit into an installment loan with a specified term? If so, at what interest rate, and over what period of time?

- **IF** your income or the amount of available equity increases, can your line of credit be increased?

Exercise Caution

Home equity loans can represent an excellent source of available credit. They are flexible, and the interest on them may continue to be tax deductible. But proper financing remains essential. It's all too easy to jeopardize your home as a result of abusing this relatively easy and heavily marketed form of credit. In essence, the proper management of home equity loans is no different from proper debt management of a mortgage. The loan principal should be paid off over a time period consistent with the use of loan proceeds.

Short-Term Satisfaction

Home equity loan borrowers, like businesses, typically borrow for short-term purposes (like vacations, home maintenance and repairs, and payment of estimated income taxes), inter-mediate-term purposes (like automobiles), or longer-term purposes (like making major home improvements and paying off college tuition bills). Short-term loans should be paid off within a year, intermediate loans should be paid off over a few years at most, and longer-term loans should be paid off over a maximum of ten to fifteen years.

If you lack the self-discipline to manage your borrowing properly, particularly when you have such easy access to a large credit line, don't tempt yourself. A typical case of misuse is borrowing for a car through a home equity credit line and not making any payments against your principal. A few years later, you purchase another car by simply adding to your existing indebtedness. At this rate, you could eventually face serious credit problems. Financial institutions are already beginning to note a disturbing increase in the rate of home equity loan foreclosures!

Some lenders offer interest-only payments. This may be appropriate when special circumstances make it difficult or undesirable to pay down the principal. Generally, however, it is preferable to pay down at least some principal each month. In general, making only the minimum monthly payments on your home equity loan can be an early warning of potential credit problems.

Beware of Balloon Loans

With some plans, interest-only payments lead to a balloon payment at the end of the loan term. This arrangement may be appropriate for you if you can predict that you can pay off your loan at a future time (for example, if you are planning to sell the home). For others, it may be entirely inappropriate. In general, if you can repay your home equity borrowing over an appropriate period of time, it can be a very effective tool for credit management, despite the potential pitfalls.

Risks

Because the deductibility of consumer interest has been eliminated, home equity loans have become an attractive alternative for obtaining credit. Nevertheless, there are potential problems. If you fall behind on your payments, your home is at risk. Moreover, the variable interest rates on most home equity loans mean that if interest rates rise, payments will rise, too—perhaps dramatically. This is especially true of lines of credit with no cap on or maximum increase in the interest rate. In addition, although most home equity loans no longer charge points, many require fees. Finally, rules regarding home equity loan interest deductibility are complicated. The result: Home equity financing should not be seen as an easy and painless way to generate cash. The decision to convert home equity should be made only after a meticulous review of your options. An imprudent plan could be devastating.

Even people who manage their home equity credit lines reasonably well may find that, rather than entering their retirement years with little or no mortgage indebtedness (a very desirable financial planning objective), they are saddled with substantial mortgage payments well into their retirement years. Therefore, evaluate the long-term as well as the short-term implications of adding to your home indebtedness.

Using Your Home for Your Retirement

R etirees often face the problem of being cash poor, having limited income to cope with medical expenses, an increased cost of living, and other financial problems. Some specific home equity conversion plans allow retirees to supplement their incomes by converting some of their home's equity into needed cash. But while these programs may seem attractive, they tend to offer a lot less than meets the eye.

Reverse Mortgage

With a conventional mortgage, you repay the lender over a specified time period, at the end of which you own the home. With a reverse mortgage plan, the lender—typically a bank—issues you a loan based on a percentage (usually from 20 percent to 60 percent) of your home equity. You receive either a lump sum or periodic (monthly or quarterly) payments from the lender, based on an annual calculation. In most cases, the retirement of the debt entails the selling of the home.

Less than meets the eye

The size of the cash flow to you resulting from a reverse mortgage is determined by your property's value, the interest rates, and your age. The property value and your equity determine the size of the loan. Your age is a determinant of the loan term (that is, the time over which the cash flow is spread), and the interest rate affects the actual size of the flow. Therefore, a combination of a high interest rate and a long expected remaining life may not yield a cash flow great enough for you to consider taking out the reverse mortgage.

When to go forward

The reverse mortgage is ideally suited for a retiree who expects to move soon but needs money in the interim, or for a retiree who does not expect to outlive the mortgage. Current income from a reverse mortgage is maximized when interest rates are low and especially when the loan term is short. This short loan term, which makes the mortgage most attractive for people wishing to increase their income, is also the greatest danger of the reverse mortgage. If the loan comes due and you have insufficient funds to repay, the bank may foreclose, leaving you with no other housing options.

Warning: Outliving your mortgage may force you to sell your home and move! A reverse mortgage must include the possibility of outliving the loan at the same time that it provides you with enough income to make the mortgage worthwhile.

Reverse Annuity Mortgage (RAM)

The reverse annuity mortgage is similar to the reverse mortgage, but with a RAM you're guaranteed a home and income for life. Consequently, the income stream is almost always smaller than that from a reverse mortgage. For this reason you should consider the RAM as an income supplement, not an income generator.

How to get a RAM

To obtain a RAM, you first take out a mortgage. With the proceeds, you purchase an annuity from an insurance company. The insurance company subtracts the interest due on the mortgage, sends it to the lending institution, and sends the net amount back to you. When you die, the home is sold and the mortgage principal is repaid, and any remaining proceeds go to your estate.

> **Smart Money Move**
>
> Reverse mortgages and reverse annuity mortgages may be of limited assistance in providing extra income to retirees who need it.

The amount of the annuity payment depends on interest rates, the property's value, and your age and marital status. Because the insurance company is taking on a mortality risk and wants to ensure a profit for itself, the annuity payment is going to be smaller than a straight reverse mortgage payment over a fixed term. For example, a $50,000 liquidation at a 13 percent interest rate for seventeen years would yield a monthly annuity payment of $67.64.

Tax ramifications

The tax effects of a RAM can be disadvantageous. The rules for determining the amount of the monthly annuity that must be declared as taxable income are prescribed by the Internal Revenue Service, so of course they're very complicated. Suffice it to say, however, that if interest rates are high, the amount of taxable income that you must declare may actually be larger than the income you actually receive. In other words, you may wind up paying taxes on money you never received. Just as with a reverse mortgage, the interest rate plays a key role in determining the feasibility of a RAM.

Private Annuity

With a private annuity, you sell your home to a private party (often your children) and in turn receive an annuity for life. You also execute a separate agreement that guarantees you a lifetime tenancy in your home. The private annuity has both estate-planning and tax ramifications that must be weighed. A private annuity removes the asset from your estate. Assuming you will spend the income from the annuity, the transfer has the effect of lowering the total value of your estate.

There is an emotional advantage to keeping the home in the family. But a private annuity may be difficult to arrange. The children may be reluctant to assume ownership of the home, they may not be able to agree with their siblings as to the arrangement, or they may not have the resources to do so. Investigate the possibility of a private annuity, however, because it combines the advantage of the RAM—the guarantee of continued living in one's present house—with an increased cash flow.

Dealing with Your Mortgage Delinquency

A t some point in the life of the mortgage, you may encounter difficulty making timely payments because of disability, unemployment, death in the family, emergency home repairs, or just plain lousy planning. You should immediately notify your lenders of your problem, and you must be prepared to talk about the crisis in detail and discuss the following matters:

- **THE REASON FOR THE DELINQUENCY.** You should be prepared to supply details about the situation that created the financial crisis.

- **YOUR CURRENTLY AVAILABLE RESOURCES.** You should list all your sources of income, including wages, disability benefits, welfare, veteran's benefits, child support, Social Security, savings accounts, and your spouse's or children's income.

- **A PLAN FOR PAYMENT.** You should provide a schedule for meeting and maintaining your current mortgage payments, laying out all available options.

The lenders may choose to do one of several things. They may temporarily reduce or suspend regular monthly mortgage payments, or they may extend the payments over a longer period of time. They may recast the mortgage, increasing the amount of unpaid principal by the amount you are currently behind. If you know that you will not be able to resume payment within a reasonable period of time, a lender may suggest that you sell your home or sign over your property to the lender. Obviously, these are last-resort options, but they help you avoid foreclosure and a bad credit record.

If you are encountering financial difficulties, you should not hire individuals who say they will speak to the lender on your behalf. These are often professional con men who prey on the difficulties of others. The fee they charge is better applied toward mortgage payments. Finally, you should not borrow more money to meet your mortgage payments. Doing this only adds more misery to an already complicated situation.

Second Homes

Second homes, often referred to and used as vacation homes, are a popular form of real estate ownership because they can serve as both an investment vehicle and a home away from home. However, the tax benefits of second homes are generally very limited compared with owning property that is used solely for rental. In essence, if you often use the home for personal purposes, its tax deductibility is severely restricted. Still, if you rent your second home for fifteen days or fewer a year, the rental income need not be reported to the IRS.

Many people use their second homes for both rental and personal stays. In this event, the IRS allows the investors (owners) to deduct that proportion of expenses corresponding to the number of days that the house was used as an income-producing investment. Before maintenance and depreciation deductions can be taken, real estate taxes and mortgage interest allocable to rental use must be subtracted from rental income. More than likely, taking all the deductions will create a taxable loss that you cannot take on your income tax return if the property is used for more than 14 days or 10% of the total period, whichever is greater.

Example

Say a second home was used for a total of ninety days during the previous year. The owner stayed there for fifteen days and rented it for seventy-five days, earning a total of $3,000 in rental income. Maintenance for the year cost $1,900. The IRS will allow the investor to deduct 75/90 of the maintenance, or about $1,600, as a business expense.

Depreciation deductions are calculated in the same manner. However, property taxes and mortgage interest cost $4,500, and 75/90 of this amount is $3,750. Since rental income was only $3,000, no other deductions for maintenace and depreciation can be taken. (In such a case it might pay to stay at a nearby hotel and limit personal use of the home so that you can enjoy the maximum tax benefits, rather than spend those few extra days at the home and lose significant tax benefits.)

Smart Money Move

Don't buy a vacation home as an investment.

Be realistic

Unless you want to own the second home exclusively for your enjoyment, the most important economic aspect of the second home as an investment is its rental producing potential. Rents can provide solid returns but may also entail hidden costs. For example, extra maintenance expenses and marketing/brokerage fees affect the rental rate of return. Moreover, in most areas of the country (for example, Florida, southern California, and New England) the period of prime rentability is limited to a few months of the year. And, to make matters more difficult, the competition to rent during those months is either very keen or very slow (depending on such unforeseeable events as a bad economy or bad weather), the end result being low rent and/or slow rental periods. If you are thinking of investing in a second home you need to recognize how difficult it often is to get a lot of rent off the property. A realistic assessment of rent revenue, free of the attestations of the seller or the seller's broker, is essential.

Second homes aren't immune to falling home prices
Second homes in vacation areas are particularly susceptible to weakening real estate prices. In fact, soft regional real estate prices are often devastating to vacation home prices. While soft markets may present a buying opportunity, don't count on a dramatic appreciation in the home's value after you have bought it.

Home Improvements

This section has more ideas than a carpenter's toolbox has tools. Still, it only scratches the surface of the many home-improvement projects that you can do yourself. Granted you won't save time—but you will save money.

Try to Do It Yourself
Unless the task is too dangerous, try your hand at minor home repairs, renovations, cleaning, even plumbing. You don't have to be a carpenter to make home repairs, any more than you have to be an economist to figure out that doing some repairs yourself will save you money.

Keep good records of your home improvements
Hold on to every home improvement record in order to prove the adjusted cost of your home when capital gains taxes are assessed.

Be prepared to make emergency repairs
Household emergencies are certain to happen. You need to be able to keep a bad situation from getting worse. A power failure, a clogged drain, a leaky roof—don't think they can't happen to you. In order to prepare yourself for such problems, purchase and familiarize yourself with a homeowner's do-it-yourself book. Such books are a great resource of preventive maintenance tips, too.

Fix a broken appliance

Find out what's wrong with it. You may be surprised to find that repairing it rather than replacing it makes the most financial sense: "Use it up, wear it out, make it do, or do without."

Remodel yourself

Try making your own small improvements to your living quarters. If you call someone in, you're going to see a lot of your hard-earned money going out the door. Read that do-it-yourself book, and get some advice from the local hardware or home supply store.

Don't own the most expensive home in the neighborhood

Making improvements to your home so that it becomes the showplace of your neighborhood isn't a bright idea. When you go to sell it you will likely find your pricey abode has appreciated much less—in comparison with the money you've invested in it—than the more modest homes in the neighborhood.

Insulate your home

One of the more expensive aspects to owning a home is heating or cooling it. Insulating your attic is an easy and efficient way to reduce the costs of both.

Windows of opportunity

If you do not have storm windows or insulated (double-pane) windows, you are losing a lot of heat—and money—out of them. Replacement windows are difficult to install. A professional carpenter will be required. But be sure the quality of his or her work, as well as the quality of the windows to be installed, are first-rate.

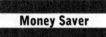
Money Saver

Resist the temptation of calling in a tradesman every time you need something done around the house. You'll be richer for it.

Weather-strip your doors

If you feel a chill from a draft, think of the chill you'll feel when you get your next heating bill. The simple use of weather-stripping to seal the trim around your doors will save you from such drafts—and high bills.

Install a dead bolt

Peace of mind and protection of valuables is the key ingredient to installing antitheft dead bolt locks on all your ground floor doors.

Paint yourself

Whether inside or out, painting your home is a great way to save a lot of money and feel that you're accomplished.

Touch up rather than repaint

Touching up the eyesore spots in a room is a quick and inexpensive way to bring a living area back to life.

Check the foundation of your house annually

This isn't as difficult as it sounds. Check for cracks, bulges, or excessive moisture on your basement walls.

Trim what is overgrown

Trees and shrubs engulfing your home can damage siding, break windows, clog gutters, and provide a squirrel an easy way to get into your attic. Cut back on such vegetation.

Clean the gutters

If you don't clean out your gutters annually, they won't drain properly. If that happens, expensive repairs could be in your future.

Clean your sewer pipes

Routing your pipes annually will save you from the unpleasant experience of sewage backing up in your house.

Clean house

If you want to decrease your household's expenses, clean it yourself. While you're at it, don't throw out your vacuum cleaner bag. Empty it. You can get two or three uses out of a single vacuum cleaner bag.

Home remedies

Use ammonia, water, and dishwasher soap or liquid detergent to remove stains (one part of each). Use baking soda instead of toothpaste. Use baking soda mixed with vinegar to clean your drain pipes. Make your own cleaning fluids rather than buying them—vinegar and lemon juice are great countertop cleaners.

Use grocery bags as trash can liners

Paper or plastic, they make great environment- friendly trash-can liners.

Recycle

Recycling is a financially smart thing to do. You don't need to waste a fortune on items that you throw away—plastic trash bags—any more than you need to stock your shelves with a hundred and one cleaning solvents. Why not be more friendly to the environment and your wallet?

Professional Projects

There are times when the expertise of a trained professional will be required. But just because expertise is required, doesn't mean expense is.

- **GET** several bids on home repair or improvement projects.

- **ASK** for competitive quotes.

- **REQUEST**, receive, and follow up on references of recent work.

- **NEGOTIATE** a further price reduction with your chosen contractor.

- **STICK** to your original plans—avoid the temptation to make expensive changes.

Don't make foolish home renovations

A good home renovation is one that will add value to the home when you resell it. A bad one won't. How can you tell the outcome of your investment ahead of time? Consider added living space, modernizing bathrooms and kitchens—these are smart moves. On the other hand, building a swimming pool—a major expense—won't add much, if any, value to your house.

Don't take out a home improvement loan

You can take out a home improvement loan, but it will cost you. Home improvement loans are similar to a collateralized consumer loan, in which a small amount is loaned for specific home improvements, rather than a sum issued against your home's equity for purposes of your own design. Unlike an equity line of credit, the interest paid on a home improvement loan is not deductible.

Warning: Home improvement scams are on the rise. If you don't know the contractor or home improvement company, and they can't furnish you with references, then show them the door.

Selling Your Home

Buy a house, raise your kids in it, and stay in it at least until you retire. It's the most economical and sensible thing to do. That's because trading up is only going to raise your housing costs. Is extra closet space really worth the additional cost? Why not just thin out your wardrobe? (Give the old clothes to the charity of your choice for a tax deduction.) Still, there may come a time when you want or need to sell your home. If so, heed this advice.

Sell your old home before you buy your new one

When you decide to sell your house and move, sell before you buy, even if it means temporarily renting before locating a new home. If you buy the new home before you sell the old one, your savings can easily be eroded, if not erased, while trying to carry your original mortgage plus a new one.

Investigate employer's assistance

When a change in housing is mandated by a job transfer, your employer may provide assistance, such as paying or helping to pay the monthly mortgage dues until the house is sold, or even buying your old house if you are having difficulty selling it.

Selling Your Home Yourself

Selling your home yourself may save you some up-front costs, such as the realtor's five to eight percent commission fee. But, the decision to sell your house yourself should not be taken lightly. There are many important steps you need to take to ensure that the outcome is profitable, if not pleasurable.

- **GET AN APPRAISAL.** You will need to hire an appraiser to estimate the value of your home. The appraiser will also tell you what similar houses are selling for in your area.

- **CLEAN UP YOUR ACT.** Make your house as appealing to a buyer's eye as possible. Starting outside, be sure that the yard is clean of debris, and that the house is clean and ship-shape. (This means no dangling gutters or unhinged shutters.) Paint your mailbox a cheery color. Keep the inside of your home spic-and-span. Consider moving some furniture out of crowded or cramped rooms (placing it into temporary storage) in order to create the appearance of greater living space. Keep fresh flowers in various rooms—they tend to liven up both the room and the buyer. Wash the windows, touch up any dents and scrapes on walls, floors, and trim. Perhaps most important, make your bathroom(s) immaculate.

- **PREPARE A FACT SHEET.** You might prepare a fact sheet that details the costs of heating, utilities, and taxes. Also provide floor plans. This way the buyer will have several important questions answered in advance. It also gives them a way to remember your home.

- **HIRE AN ATTORNEY.** You should learn all about the fair housing rules—what you should and should not say—unless you want to get slapped with a lawsuit. You should also hire a real estate attorney to draft the purchase and sale agreement.

Using a Real Estate Broker

Employing the services of a real estate broker won't get you out of doing most of the above. Rather, it will provide you with a broker's expertise and access to market listings and potential buyers, which could move your home more quickly. In addition, brokers are well informed about the local real estate market and may be able to help you plan your next purchase.

The contract

If you decide to use a real estate broker, a listing contract that sets out the terms of employment must be drawn up. You can choose from several types of contracts, including:

- **OPEN LISTING.** This is a simple oral or written agreement in which you agree to pay the broker a stated commission if the broker successfully completes a sale of the home on terms acceptable to you. You or any other broker may also complete the sale if you so desire. Brokers and sellers generally do not favor such a contract because it essentially asks the broker to commit time and energy to a project that will not necessarily produce a commission. Therefore, a broker contracted under an open listing contract usually has little incentive to market the home properly.

- **NET LISTING.** Here the seller provides the broker with a floor price below which the property cannot be sold. The broker adds his or her fee to this amount. Homeowners often prefer this type of contract because it guarantees them a base price for their home. However, most brokers dislike this type of listing contract as well.

- **EXCLUSIVE LISTING.** This is the most common form of contract. One broker holds the exclusive rights to the property for a specified period of time, usually three to six months. If the broker secures sale of the house during this period, he or she is guaranteed a commission. "Exclusive right to sell" is a similar contract, but it assures the broker of a commission even if the owner sells the property.

- **MULTILISTING.** This arrangement allows several brokers to try to sell the same property at the same time. The broker obtaining the listing and the broker arranging the sale share the commission. This type of listing, used in some parts of the country, is advantageous to the seller, for it assures him or her of a wide effort to find a buyer.

Specify the sale price

Regardless of the type of listing employed, the contract with the real estate broker should specify the sale price of the property, the terms of sale, and any personal property included in the transaction. The listing should also specify the brokerage fee, usually 5 percent to 8 percent of the selling price of the property. Sometimes the brokerage fee may be negotiable, particularly for high-priced properties.

Determine who negotiates with the buyer

Once a buyer has been found, the real estate broker usually negotiates a sales contract between the parties. The contract should include price, financing arrangements, type of deed, insurance requirements, title insurance, title examination, tax-payment agreements, settlement dates, possession date, a legal description of the property, and a list of any personal property included in the sale. You probably should have your attorney review the purchase and sale agreement.

Seller Financing

Seller financing should be a last resort. If the banks don't think your would-be buyers are creditworthy, they probably aren't. The last thing you need or should want to do is to get involved with a bad debtor. This can make your life miserable and expensive. The court costs for getting him or her out of your property, should they default on your financing, can exceed $10,000 in costs and loss of payments.

Nevertheless, if this is what you have set your mind on doing, the following steps should be taken:

- **HIRE** a lawyer to draft all the contracts relating to the financing. Make sure that all contingencies are written down, from when the first payment is due to what should happen if the buyers default on two or more payments.

- **GET** a thorough credit check on the buyer(s).

- **RUN** a property check on the buyer(s) to see if they have owned property before. If they have, where did they get the financing, and why are they coming to you this time? Contact their first lender, and ask for details about their payment history. If your would-be buyer(s) were renters, get the name and address of each landlord, and call them for their remarks.

- **ASK** for a substantial down payment if you're going to be the only lender. Nothing under 20 percent should be acceptable to you. Why? If you don't ask for and receive a substantial down payment, your buyer(s) might walk away from the property, since they've got little invested in it.

- **ALWAYS** insure your loan, making certain that the property is insured by the buyer(s) against fire, flood, and other potential disasters. Make sure they pay the insurance through you, with their mortgage payment, so that you can be sure the insurance payments are up-to-date.

The Tax Consequences of Selling Your Home

Be tax wise

The tax basis for a piece of real estate is your original investment, plus the cost of any improvements, less any depreciation claimed previously if you used part or all of the house for business or rental purposes.

If you have been using your home for business purposes—and taking advantage of the office-at-home deduction—but want to benefit from the $125,000 capital gains exclusion for people over fifty-five, only the portion of the house used as your principal residence will qualify for the exclusion. You can avoid the apportionment rules, however, if you claimed the deduction over no more than two years during the five-year period preceding the sale.

Capital gains

Capital gains may be deferred under the following circumstances:

1. IF the proceeds of a capital gain are reinvested in a second home within two years of the date of sale, or if another home was purchased within two years before the sale, no tax is paid. If the new home costs less than the original residence sold for, some taxation will occur. If a personal residence is sold for a loss, a capital loss cannot be taken.

2. TAXPAYERS over the age of fifty-five who are selling their principal residence may exclude the first $125,000 of capital gain, if they have owned and occupied the home as their principal residence for at least three out of the five years ending on the date of sale, from their income. If you are near fifty-five and contemplating the sale of your home at a substantial capital gain, waiting until you qualify for the $125,000 exclusion may make sense. It's up to you, but you should consider the ramifications of moving now or delaying your move until you qualify for the over-fifty-five tax break.

    The exclusion is a great opportunity for retirees to shore up their retirement funds. Moreover, by combining both the over-fifty-five exclusion and the capital-gains deferral provisions of the tax laws, you can take advantage of the $125,000 exclusion, and you can postpone paying taxes on any remaining capital gains by investing in a new home whose cost is greater than the sale price of the old house minus the $125,000 exclusion.

    You can rent your home and still qualify for the $125,000 exclusion. You must occupy the house for at least three out of the five years preceding its sale date.

Smart Money Move

Careful planning can postpone or avoid the capital-gains tax when you sell your home.

You could, however, rent the house for two of those years—including the two years between the time you move out and the date when the sale takes place.

3.   **PAYMENT** of capital-gains tax can be deferred through the installment method. Under this method, the seller receives the purchase price of the property over a period of two years or longer; the initial payment in the year of the sale cannot be more than 30 percent of the total purchase price. If additional payments are received over two or more years, the taxpayer can pay the income tax on the gain in the year he or she receives payment rather than in the year he or she sells.

Downward mobility

When all is said and done, downward mobility may be a good move, particularly for empty nesters and retirees. You not only reduce the utility and heating costs, as well as property taxes, but you also reduce the size of the space you have to keep up. Moreover, you can invest the difference between the sale price of your old home and the lower cost of your new one so as to increase your investment portfolio or retirement nest egg.

FOR FURTHER INFORMATION

For more information on home ownership, contact:

The American Homeowners Foundation
1724 South Quincy Street, Arlington, VA 22204
(703) 979-4663

Home-improvement contracts are available for $5.95.

HOME OWNERSHIP CHECKLIST

■□■

If interest rates have dropped at least 1.5 percent below the rate on your existing mortgage, check to see if you will benefit from refinancing.

■□■

While home equity credit lines are flexible and offer tax advantages, don't misuse them.

■□■

If you are a retired homeowner in need of extra income, consider reverse mortgages and reverse annuity mortgages, although the income potential of these programs is limited.

■□■

Vacation homes should be viewed more as a source of personal enjoyment than as an investment, since in most locales they offer limited rental potential. Prices may be particularly adversely affected by downturns in the real estate market.

■□■

Don't automatically go to the phone book for home improvements or repairs. You can do many of them yourself.

■□■

If you are trading up or relocating, always sell your current residence before buying the new one.

Automobiles

Before I discuss automobiles, it is only fair that I provide you with some background information. I hate cars. Most people spend far more money to own and maintain their cars than they can comfortably afford. It used to be that people spent the equivalent of about two months' salary on a car, and if they didn't pay cash for it, they financed it over eighteen months at most. Now people spend a fortune for a car, finance it over an eternity, and then turn around and buy another car within a few years. No wonder so many people can't afford to save for the important things in life, such as a home, a college education for their kids, and a comfortable retirement. I'm proud to drive around in an old clunker.

A few years ago a neighbor put the following note on my windshield: "Your car violates this neighborhood's standards of good taste." I took that as a compliment, because I knew that if I had fallen into the trap of always wanting a late-model car, I couldn't have afforded to live in that neighborhood.

In this chapter I'll show you how to get the most for the many dollars you have to spend on your "wheels." Car ownership is one area where a lot of people can benefit financially from shopping wisely and developing more sensible ownership habits. First, a few tips.

Follow your "spending" limit

If truth and advertising were one and the same, then this would be the bottom line in car advertising: "More of *our* car for more of *your* money." In fact, when it comes to purchasing a new or "preowned" car, we almost always exceed a reasonable spending limit—and pay the price for it.

Don't drive yourself to the poorhouse by buying expensive cars, financing them to the hilt, and then trading them every few years.

Plan sensibly from the word (Yu)go

We often set a precedent for our behavior when we bought our first car. That expenditure served as our introduction to substantial debt, loan qualification, and installment payments, and insurance arrangements and costs. In fact, for most of us, our first car was a four-wheeled symbol of our passage into adulthood, also known as consumerism—passage that we took without much thought of the financial toll the purchase would take on our budget three to four years down the road.

Learn from past mistakes

When it comes to purchasing our second and third car, do we demonstrate any signs of having grown up? No. In fact, many of us repeat the same old pattern of buying more car than our budget can afford.

A Buyer's Ed Course on the Rules of the Road

When it comes to providing driver's ed for our children, we spare no expense. But when it comes to educating ourselves about buying a car, we rarely spend more than the price of a newspaper to find out where the "best" deals in town are. What a mistake! Familiarize yourself with the basic car-buying rules of the road before you even think of test driving your gasoline dream.

Rule 1: Know What You Can Afford to Want

The hardest part of buying a car isn't deciding what color you want. It's coming to terms with the car you can afford, as opposed to the car you've been dreaming about. If you don't calculate a precise price that you can afford, you will only be making the decision process more difficult and increasing the likelihood of your car payments colliding with your budget.

Rule 2: Estimate What You Can Afford to Buy

Estimate the total monthly cost of car ownership before you leave your house. Don't forget to calculate the cost to you in terms of up-front sales tax, yearly taxes assessed by your town or state, registration, insurance payments, and a maintenance account. In the best of all worlds, this last is a savings account in which you deposit a monthly sum for future automobile repairs.

Rule 3: Insurance Is Costly

Call your insurance agent to get a rough estimate of your intended car's insurance cost. Find out which models are cheaper to insure. (See Chapter 44 for tips on getting the best coverage for the best price.)

Rule 4: Know Your Limits

Don't set foot in a car dealership before you have completed the above calculations and done your other homework. Always give yourself several weeks to study the various sources of information on purchase prices, preferred makes, financing options, dealer incentives, and the like before you go to the dealer. *Consumer Reports*, *Money* magazine, and *Road and Track* are but a few of the national magazines that review the minutiae of automobile performance and price.

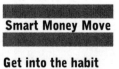

Smart Money Move

Get into the habit of buying used cars.

Rule 5: New or Used—You Decide

Once you've determined the amount you can afford to spend, you can take the next step: deciding whether to buy a new or used car. The used or "preowned" option is well worth considering. Many used cars are only a year or two old and in good shape. If purchased from a reputable dealer, these may even include warranties. In fact, buying a good used car is the only way you can truly get more car for less money.

Where and how to get used car quotes, estimates, and a bargain that won't leave you and your bank account stranded in a dead-end deal isn't as tough as you think. You can dig up the "Blue Book" value—the suggested retail price of the make and model you're considering—at your library or in a good bookstore or magazine stand. The annual *Consumer Reports Buying Guide* also provides useful information on prices and desirable used car models.

Another consideration is the number of previous owners. Most states require that the title to a car must list its previous owners. If the car has had more than two owners in as many years, you might consider looking for another one. In the end, the recommendation is the same: Arm yourself with pertinent information before you set foot on a dealer's lot.

Rule 6: Shop for the Best Price Around

You are your own best resource when it comes to getting the car you can afford for the bargain price you want. Simply pick up the phone and call the many dealerships within your area—most will give you quotes over the phone. (Be leery of those that won't.)

Rule 7: Get a Second Opinion

Once you have determined what a reasonable price would be and the dealer you may take your business to, always get a second and third opinion from other dealers. You can save *thousands* of dollars by shopping around from reputable dealer to reputable dealer. Have them put their cost quote in writing, then show it to the dealership down the block or in the next town and ask them to beat it. Chances are they will. Don't be afraid to play one dealer off another. Remember, car salespeople will, at the slightest opportunity, take every advantage they can of you, so turnabout is fair play. If anyone hassles you, simply walk out of the dealership—but expect someone to come chasing after you trying to get you to do business with them.

Rule 8: If You Can't Haggle, Hire Someone Who Can

For a nominal fee, you can hire a service to shop for the best deal on the model and make you want. To find the number of an auto broker near you, contact a branch of the American Automobile Association.

Smart Money Move

Do unto a car salesperson as he will do unto you.

Rule 9: When to Shop

There's a right and a wrong time to shop. The wrong time is when there are no discounts, rebates, or incentives to be found. The right time is almost always toward the end of the model year. The reason is that manufacturers and dealers alike need to clear the lot of the old-year models in order to make room for the new, more expensive ones that your spendthrifty neighbors will be eager to buy. Buying your car late in its model year (or early in the new model year—there are always "leftovers") will nearly always net you a bargain.

Financing

F inancing the total purchase price of your car—or part of it—is the shortcut to ownership that most of us take. But, unless you shop for the lowest rate, it can be a very costly "shortcut." Of course, paying cash for your car is the least expensive and best way to go. Remember to put on your financial thinking cap: If you have set aside $10,000 for a car and have over $8,000 worth of credit card debt, your best option is to pay off your high-interest credit card debt, put the remaining money toward a down payment on the car, and take out a loan with the lowest possible financing rate available—which will be way less than your credit card interest rate!

The second best way to pay is to increase the size of your down payment. That way you will borrow less and so pay less nondeductible interest. If paying for the car up front and outright—or for a good chunk of it—is not within your means, you are in the majority. You will have to arrange for financing. Translated into car buyer terms, this means that you will have to shop for the best terms. A word to the wise: The auto dealer is probably not the best place to get a car loan.

Today there seem to be as many different financing options as there are different models of cars.

Smart Money Move

Get into the habit of paying cash for cars. If you can't afford it, start saving now so you can pay cash for your next car.

Car loans

The most common financing option is, of course, a car loan. Car loans come in many different forms—your bank, credit union, and auto dealership are likely to have at least half a dozen different types with differing terms and interest rates.

New car loan rates should always be lower than used car loan rates. (If not, then look elsewhere for a more reasonable deal.) But just because new car loan rates are lower doesn't mean you should buy a new car. It will cost you a lot less to buy a $4,000 car at 12 percent interest than a $15,000 new car at 9 percent interest.

New car loans usually require a smaller down payment and offer you many repayment periods, from twelve to sixty months. The longer the loan, the less your monthly payment—but the more you will be paying in interest. And unless you use your car for business, the interest on the loan is not tax deductible.

Often, credit unions beat the best bank rates. If you can take advantage of such a deal, why go to a bank?

Home equity lines of credit

The tax benefit of paying for your car with a home equity line of credit is something to consider. As you know, there is no deduction for interest paid on any consumer loan, and that's what a car loan is. But by using a home equity loan—the interest of which *is* generally deductible—you can pay for your car in a cost-effective manner. But be sure to repay the loan as you would a regular car loan! Don't dig yourself into a financial hole by taking ten or fifteen years to pay off a car purchased with a home equity loan long after the vehicle has been replaced.

Discounts, rebates, incentives

They're out there, but you have to track them down. (They don't call it bargain-hunting for nothing!) Wrestling the pertinent information about discounts, rebates, and factory-to-dealer incentives out of your salesperson might qualify you for a World Wrestling Federation title, but it's worth it. Thousands of dollars can be at stake—although $500 to $1,500 is the norm.

- **ASK** what, if any, discounts there are on the car you want to buy. Discounts can be from the manufacturer or the dealer, and these may be either specific or spontaneous. A discount may be an amount subtracted from the gross or net cost of the car, or it may be discounted from a range of options that you might be inclined to buy. Another kind of discount is purchasing the floor model.

- **REBATES** come directly from the manufacturer to you. They are the car seller's equivalent of coupons. You buy the product, send in your sales slip, and receive several hundred dollars or more back.

- **FACTORY-TO-DEALER** incentives usually increase toward the end of the year because the manufacturer wants to help the dealer clear space on his or her lot for the new model year. But be wary of incentives. Many are used to lower the discount that the dealer would otherwise have given you from the list price.

Trade-in allowance

This is the amount of money the dealer "gives" you for your old car. This amount is subtracted from the purchase price of your new car. As a general rule, if your old car is in relatively good condition, you'll get *less* money by trading it in than you would by selling it yourself. On the other hand, if your car is a wreck, some dealers will give you more than you could ever hope to sell it for as an incentive for you to buy your new car from them.

Warning: Negotiate a deal on the car you want *before* you mention that you have a possible trade-in. The reason is that you may get the same amount off prior to introducing the trade-in as you would have if you mentioned the trade-in up front. This way, you may be able to reduce the dealer's "lowest offer" substantially.

Packaged options and service warranties

Why let someone tell you what you want and then charge you for it? That's what packaged options amount to. You don't need an eight-speaker stereo when four speakers drive you wild. You don't need a moon roof unless you're Count Dracula. And you certainly don't need to pay for those two items simply to get the free fog lights that make the package a "deal." The same goes for those ridiculous service warranties. You'd be far better off opening up a savings account and putting a small monthly amount into it for pending car repairs. Remember, it's better to have a roof over your head at night than a sun roof in your car by day.

Leasing

L easing is an increasingly popular way to acquire a new car—especially a more expensive, sporty or luxury car. Many manufacturers offer leasing as an alternative option to purchasing, and for good reason. The cars are too bloody expensive to pay for by other means. Leasing allows Mr. Jones to "buy" the BMW his better half never wanted, although, of course, he never really "owns" it.

Types of Leases

There are numerous types of leases, and rest assured that each is complex, more troublesome and less financially advantageous than ownership. Leasing lets you take the financial rap for the fact that a car's value declines more in its first two years than it does for the remainder of its life. When your lease is up, the dealer is left with a prime preowned car to sell.

Smart Money Move

Don't lease a car. It is more expensive than financing a car yourself, and leasing causes you to trade cars too often.

Closed-End Lease

If you think you might want to purchase the vehicle at the end of the leasing period, make sure you take a "closed-end" lease, which gives you the option to buy the vehicle at a stated and specific purchase price. That way, when your lease expires, you can compare the option purchase price with current used car prices of the same make and model and see where you can get the best deal.

Advantages and Disadvantages

Leases can reduce the hassle of acquiring and maintaining a car (some come with service plans), and you don't have to worry about selling it at the end of the lease. On the other hand, it's safe to say that leasing is almost always more expensive than owning. In my opinion, it also encourages people to trade in their cars too soon. Often you must make a substantial "deposit," sometimes as much as 25 percent of the cost of the car, in order to start a lease plan. There are often penalty fees, too, if you need to leave the lease early. Another hidden cost of leasing lies in the "excessive wear and tear" clause, which states that you will be charged extra for damage to the vehicle. Make sure that those "damages" are specified in writing. Otherwise a coffee stain on the backseat might end up costing you.

Maintaining Your Car (and Its Value)

Whether you buy a new or used car—and I recommend the latter—take good care of it. As with your own health, preventive maintenance is the least costly route to take. Read your ownership manual's section on oil changes, tune-ups, tire rotation, radiator cleaning, and so on. You don't have to be a certified auto mechanic to appreciate the value of keeping your car fine-tuned regularly and on schedule. In the end, it will pay off in terms of reduced wear and tear on the vehicle itself. (This means the resale value will be the highest possible for your model.) And it will make for a more pleasurable and less expensive ownership experience.

Take note: Join the American Automobile Association. In the event of a road trip or a breakdown, it's a service worth having.

When to Sell

Most car owners trade in their iron and plastic master far too soon. Unless you've got tons of money, trading a car every three or four years is truly a waste. Don't tell me that car repairs on an older car make it more expensive to run than a new car. Unless your old clunker has a truly catastrophic problem in the motor or the transmission, no amount of repairs will come close to the cost in terms of depreciation and financing of a new car. So think twice before getting rid of your middle-aged car. How would you like it if your spouse got rid of you when you became middle-aged?

Ten Money Savers That Will Save You Thousands of Dollars in Car Ownership Costs

1. Keep Your Car Longer

There's no reason why you can't keep a car for seven to ten years or even longer. People who trade their cars in every three, four, or five years are simply throwing money away. Sure, a late-model car feels good, and you probably think people are impressed by it. But is it worth the cost?

2. Buy a Used Car Rather Than an Expensive New Car

The quickest way to lose $2,000 is to drive a new car off a dealer's lot. So many people are obsessed with frequently trading in their cars that many excellent used cars go begging. If you get into the habit of buying used cars, you'll save literally tens of thousands of dollars over your lifetime.

3. Do Your Homework

The only way to assure a good deal from a car salesman is to march into the showroom heavily armed with facts and figures. You should know exactly what the dealer has paid for the particular car you want to buy. You can obtain information on dealer cost by referring to the "Blue Book," available at bookstores and in many libraries. Or you could pay for a service that will provide you with this price information. Two such services are listed at the end of this chapter. Let's face it: It's you against the dealer, and if you don't have the right information, you're at a big disadvantage.

4. Finance over Three Years or Less

Some people never manage to get out from under their car loan. Ideally, you should pay cash. If you can't afford to finance a car over two or three years, you can't afford that car.

5. Avoid Cars That Are More Costly to Insure

Insurance companies are not dummies. They maintain extensive records on the claims they have to pay out by car model. Don't waste money buying a car that, for whatever reason— perhaps it has twenty-five cylinders and three hundred valves and can exceed the speed of sound—incurs higher premiums than more ordinary vehicles.

6. Don't Get Frivolous Options

A "loaded" car means two things. First, it is loaded with all the available options. Second, it is going to be loaded with problems as each option starts to fall apart. When you next buy a car, evaluate your "need" for each option. Some of them, such as a sun roof, cost a lot of money and serve no apparent purpose. Not only does a loaded car cost several thousand dollars more up front, you will end up paying dearly to keep these options functioning in the future.

7. Don't Buy the Dealer's "Extras"

Such extras are commonly called "packs." They're as close to worthless as anything you could ever buy. They include items such as undercoat, overcoat, racing stripes, and of course, the infamous fabric protector. If the dealer asks if you would like to add one of these packages to your gleaming new car, just laugh. If you don't, have your head examined. If the dealer informs you that they already have been added to the car, thank them kindly and then say you're not going to pay "extra" for them.

8. Sell Your Old Car Yourself

Chances are that you can sell your old car for quite a bit more money than a dealer would give you for it as a trade-in on a new car. Sure it takes a little effort, but the time is well spent if you can make a little extra money to put toward your next chariot. (If you keep your car as long as I do, only the junk dealer will buy it.)

9. Perform Routine Car Maintenance Yourself

Have you noticed the labor charges for car maintenance and repairs lately? While not quite equal to neurosurgeons' fees, they're getting there. You can perform more routine maintenance tasks on your car than you think.

10. Find a Good Mechanic

Auto dealers don't have a monopoly on good mechanics. As a matter of fact, some of them don't have any good mechanics. Like locating any other competent professional, word of mouth is often your best resource.

FOR FURTHER INFORMATION

Consumer Reports For a back issue of their annual auto buyer's guide (April issue), send $5 to Consumer Reports, P.O. Box 2015, Yonkers NY 10703. *Consumer Reports Auto Price Service* For a printout of dealer cost on base price and options of any car, send $11 to Consumer Reports Auto Price Service,	P.O. Box 8005, Novi, MI 48376, or call (303) 745-1700. *Car/Puter* This national car pricing and referral service has a 900 number. For $2 per minute, it can give you instant dealer base prices on most automobiles. The live operator can answer most of your questions, too. The number is 900-226-CARS.

AUTOMOBILES CHECKLIST

☐ Buy a sensible car that won't drive you to the poorhouse.

☐ If you can't pay cash for a car, finance the car over no more than three years, preferably two years.

☐ Do not trade cars too frequently. Most cars will last at least seven to ten years.

☐ Become an informed car shopper and car loan shopper.

Your Good Health

Do you know how expensive poor health can be? Are you willing to take the financial risk of finding out? Then again, do you know the expense that some people go to to shed a few pounds? Fortunately, there is a happy, healthy median that doesn't require you to be a financial heavyweight. Control your health care expenses. Practice preventive medicine for both your physical and financial well-being. Exercise and eat the right foods. Take maximum advantage of health-care-expense tax deductions, and follow the money-saving tips at the end of this chapter so that you can protect both your health and your pocketbook.

Don't overlook the many financial benefits of staying healthy.

Preventive Medicine: The Craze

Some Americans look with suspicion at the current fitness and nutrition "crazes." But few of them will be guilt-free if they aren't already exercising and eating well. The problem is pronounced among baby boomers. Back in the 1960s and 1970s—formative years for many of today's citizens-in-need-of-exercise—they grew up on smoking, drinking too much, and eating more and more red meat. Granted, youth, health, and athletic prowess have been over worshiped in the United States, but it is only comparatively recently that average Americans have started to make physical fitness part of their daily lives.

Insurance companies now recognize the fact that good health should be rewarded. Increasingly, Americans who don't smoke, aren't obese, and otherwise take good care of themselves pay lower health and life insurance premiums, not to mention fewer doctors' bills.

Take good physical care of yourself. Not only will you enjoy life more and live longer, you'll spend less money on junk food and health care.

Exercise: A Sine Qua Non of a Fit Life

As in your financial life, set realistic objectives for exercise. If you take up jogging, you won't be able to run a marathon in a month. You want exercise to be enjoyable so that you will continue with a regular exercise regimen.

Walking

Walking is a great way to begin, since it doesn't require any specialized equipment except a good pair of walking shoes or sneakers. (It is also a great way to reacquaint yourself with the neighborhood you live in.) In fact, walking is the fitness rage these days. There are numerous walking clubs—for all levels. (Don't forget that speedwalking is an Olympic sport.) There's even a national magazine, *Walking*, devoted to tales from the trails.

Swimming

One of the best things you can do for yourself physically and financially is to swim. Most local high schools (it doesn't have to be your alma mater) and many communities have pools and a range of adult swim times to fit your schedule and your budget.

Biking

Better for the joints than high-impact exercises like jogging, biking is an appropriate and popular form of exercise for many, although biking in some cities could be hazardous to your health. The costs may initially be high, but once you've purchased your bike, there's little more expense in pursuing your new-found sport.

Exercise Machines

Stairmasters, exercise bikes, Nautilus, NordicTrack, rowing machines, and more have become very popular. Despite the youth-oriented image of these devices, there is no reason why any average Jane or Joe can't take advantage of them—except the exorbitant price tag that accompanies many of them. Don't rush out and buy an expensive exercise machine that is too big for your living space or too narrow in function to perform all your exercise needs. Instead, consider buying a low-cost temporary membership to a health club so that you can experiment with various exercise machines before buying one. Don't extend your health club membership, however (see below).

For Those with Money and Calories to Burn

Health Clubs and Gyms

Often expensive, and seldom—in spite of the hype—paid for in part or in full by your health insurance company or employer, health clubs and gyms are a common way to exercise your wallet—and gums—more than your biceps. Mirroring the images of "club members" working their way around a "circuit," spending a certain amount of time working out on each of a succession of different weightlifting machines, thereby exercising their whole bodies, will cost more time and money than you or I can afford to spend.

Fat Farms

These are expensive. The one thing that's certain about a spa or clinic is that your wallet will come out of it a lot lighter than it went in.

Five Ways to Shape Up without Straining Your Wallet

- **RENT** a low- to high-impact workout video from your local video store.

- **CONTACT** the high school nearest you to find out about adult exercise classes offered during postschool and postwork hours.

- **CREATE** a home gym by buying an exercise machine. Unless you overdo it with exotic equipment, the price will be less than the cost of a health club.

- **AVOID** exercise gimmicks and paraphernalia.

- **SCHEDULE** a time to exercise with one or more partners and/or friends. Not only does this greatly increase motivation, it makes it harder to ditch your workouts.

The IRS Diet

I f your out-of-pocket medical expenses exceed 7.5 percent of your adjusted gross income (AGI) for the tax year, you can qualify for a medical expense deduction. Let's say you have medical expenses of $10,000 and an AGI of $100,000. All medical expenses above $7,500 ($100,000 x .075)—in this case, $2,500—can be deducted from your taxable income. Include your share of your insurance premiums as a medical expense.

Keep good records of all your unreimbursed medical expenses in order to take maximum advantage of this tax break.

The health-care travel deduction is often overlooked. If you have to travel any distance to go to a doctor or hospital, you can deduct your travel expenses as medical expenses (subject to the 7.5 percent of AGI threshold). If you use your car, either deduct the actual cost of gas and oil or take a simpler approach by using the standard mileage rate.

Ten Ways to Cut Your Health-Care Costs

1. Stay well

Preventive medicine is the most effective and inexpensive medicine. Learn how to stay healthy. Do it. Then spend some of the money you save on yourself.

2. Always maintain good health insurance coverage

The quickest way to lose what money you've accumulated to date, as well as a large chunk of your future income, is to suffer an uninsured illness. Do whatever is necessary to maintain adequate health insurance coverage for you and every family member. If you are sixty-five or older, Medicare gap insurance is a must. Also, make sure your adult children have health insurance coverage through their place of employment. Or, if they are between jobs, make sure they've purchased a temporary health insurance policy.

3. Get regular physical checkups

Get a periodic physical, and follow your doctor's advice. Chances are you could use some health care advice from your doctor, and if there is a problem, it's far better (and cheaper) to find out sooner rather than later.

4. Don't wait until it's too late

If you don't feel all-well, don't postpone seeing your doctor. The worse the health problem gets before you see a doctor, the more expensive it is going to be, no matter how comprehensive your health coverage.

5. Use medical and dental schools for low-cost, professional services

If you live near a university medical or dental school, consider taking advantage of the health and dental services it offers. The price is reduced, and the student who is examining or treating you is fully supervised.

6. Use public health nurses

If you or a loved one requires some home care, contact your local health department or the Visiting Nurse Association (VNA) to find out what services it offers and how you can qualify to receive them.

7. Lose weight

Consult your doctor, buy a recommended diet book, and really try to lose weight on your own before going to an expensive weight-loss clinic.

8. Quit smoking

Smoking is hazardous to your financial health. The habit can easily cost over $1,000 per year, not to mention what it does to your health and life insurance premiums and dental bills.

9. Review alternative health plans offered by your employer

If you are fortunate enough to have an employer that offers a choice of health-care plans, don't assume that the one you have is the best. Review the alternatives. Some plans may cost you less while meeting the health-care needs of you and your family.

10. Brush and floss regularly

Brushing and flossing can save you a lot of physical and financial pain. Remember the tacky sign that stares you in the face as you sit in your dental chair? "You don't have to brush and floss all of your teeth—just the ones you want to keep."

Marriage

This chapter looks at love through a financial lens. Certainly this isn't the most romantic way to perceive it, but it is still important. Why? Because money concerns can bring out the worst in a relationship. Yet they don't have to. In fact, if you periodically discuss your financial concerns and goals with your spouse, you will avoid countless marital money squabbles.

Premarital Agreements

Nothing, it seems, can throw cold water on a romance better than a premarital agreement (also known as an antenuptial or prenuptial agreement). Whether it makes sense for you to draw one up depends on your circumstances. Even if it does, you have to be concerned about how your betrothed will react when you bring up the subject. Such an agreement should be prepared with the advice and assistance of your lawyer. Actually, two lawyers—one for each partner—are often appropriate when one party brings a substantially greater number of assets into the marriage than the other or when both parties have substantial assets.

Premarital agreements define each partner's separate properties that are brought into the marriage and describe your financial intentions after you're wed. Premarital agreements are particularly popular among previously married partners who want to avoid a repeat of a financially chaotic marital breakup.

Premarital agreements may contain a limitation or waiver of alimony should you ever divorce, or a provision under which one spouse gives up all rights or limits his or her rights to the other's estate. It may even discuss more personal matters, such as the division of housework or how much time will be spent with in-laws!

Advisability

Premarital agreements are advisable if one partner is much wealthier than the other and is concerned with the protection of assets should the marriage dissolve. If a divorce occurs later, the agreement usually stipulates a transfer, or the promise of a transfer, of a stipulated amount of property from the wealthier spouse to the other. The transfer may be outright, or in a trust in exchange for a release of all claims the other may have for support or against the transferor's estate. Also, if you or your partner already have children from a previous marriage, a prenuptial agreement can protect the children's financial stake in the parents' estate.

Legal Precedent

Legal precedent favors adherence to premarital agreements as long as both parties to the contract are open and honest about their assets and liabilities and both have access to legal advice. Most states will allow spouses to give up or limit their interest in their partner's estate under certain conditions, but fewer allow contracts that limit or forbid alimony. The concern is that these latter contracts may encourage divorce and therefore violate public policy. Nevertheless, some states have concluded that a properly advised adult should be free to agree to make do without alimony.

Postmarital Agreements

Postmarital agreements can be used by already-married couples to settle beforehand, under more amicable circumstances, what will happen to their property in the event of a divorce. They can be used for business as well as personal reasons to clarify which spouse has rights to certain property (for example, an interest in a family business or summer home).

Postmarital agreements are also used to update or renegotiate an outdated premarital agreement. Because postmarital agreements can face legal barriers, expert legal assistance is necessary, and each party should be represented by independent counsel.

The Wedding

I t's no wonder parents cry at weddings. Most of them realize too late that, in under six hours, they have spent a fortune on the biggest single cash expenditure of their post-house-purchasing lives. And then there's the bride and groom, suddenly wed and confronted with all the complexities of a financial as well as a spiritual union.

Simplifying your wedding plans can save thousands and thousands of dollars, which in turn can be put to much better use.

Invest Some of What You Receive

If you receive monetary gifts on your wedding day, don't spend them. Invest them, instead, in one or more good mutual funds. Start your marriage off on the right financial foot.

Smart Money Move

Be kind to your parents. Either elope or have a modest-cost wedding.

Review and Revise All Essential Financial Documents

Everything from health, property, casualty, and life insurance to checking, savings, investment, and retirement accounts will need to be revised. If children from a previous marriage are involved, tuition planning that was in the works will need to be revised and recalculated—or begun. Devise a budget, based on your increased or decreased income, that spells out what percentage of whose paycheck goes to the paying of which bills.

Your personal circumstances may have changed for the better, but be sure your financial circumstances don't suffer as a result of marriage. Be certain that you and your spouse devise a budget for household expenses and a financial plan for the stages in your newly linked lives: purchasing a home, having children, paying for their education, and building your retirement nest egg. Set aside one day each year to review your financial progress and plans for the future. Couples not only need to agree on what financial goals they want to accomplish in the long run; they must also decide how to go about reaching these goals. The best way to avoid money squabbles is to sit down annually to review your progress and discuss plans for the upcoming year. When you and your spouse have your "summits" you will also need to decide where to spend—and where to cut back—in the context of your overall savings program.

Revise Your Record-Keeping

You will need to sit down together and create a record-keeping system that you both can live with. Record-keeping is often neglected until a major, stressful event like tax time rolls around. Then there's a scramble for all the important documents, and arguments tend to ensue. If you each want your own checking account, that's fine. You don't have to carry togetherness to a ridiculous extreme.

Insurance Matters

You will need to discuss your various insurance needs. Most important, you may need to consider purchasing life insurance for the first time. Also, you will need to review your health insurance policies in order to ensure that your coverage is inclusive but not excessive or redundant.

Take Stock of Investments

A thorough review of your respective investments needs to be made. (If neither of you has any investments to speak of, you've got to start sometime. Now is a good time.)

Combine your investment accounts so that you pay only one account-maintenance fee. Banks and brokerage firms are beginning to nickel and dime us to death. If you and your spouse maintain separate investment and savings accounts, each of which assesses a fee, consider combining at least some of them to save these annoying and costly charges.

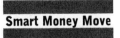

Smart Money Move

Set aside one day each year to review your financial progress and plans for the future.

Tax Filing Status

You will need to change your filing status from single to married, filing jointly. It's a good idea to determine whether filing jointly or separately results in the lower tax when tax time rolls around. One way to estimate whether your new tax status is going to save or increase your taxes is to resurrect your previous year's returns and rerun the numbers, assuming you're filing jointly.

Retirement Planning

Retirement planning may be the last thing on your and your spouse's minds, but it should take priority over many if not most other financial considerations. Review your retirement plans, if any, to see how far along the retirement-planning road you are. No matter how young you are, start to set aside money for retirement through participation in company-sponsored plans, like 401(k) plans, and/or do it yourself with annual IRA contributions.

Draft or Revise Your Wills

If you don't have a will or other important estate-planning documents, now is the time to draft them. If you or your new spouse has a will, now is the time to revise it. (See Chapter 80 for details.)

Always Work to Keep Your Marriage Intact

Divorce is one of the worst things you can do to your financial health. It usually takes a tremendous financial as well as emotional toll. Work hard to keep your marriage afloat. It can be both emotionally and financially rewarding.

PREMARITAL CHECKLIST

☐ Have a mutual talk/disclosure about money. What you earn, what you owe, and what assets you own need to be common knowledge so that you can plan for your joint future.

☐ Figure out your net worth. Don't just talk about money matters—figure out exactly where you stand. This will only make it easier to discuss such matters as buying a house, raising children, and investing for retirement.

☐ Cover the topic of insurance thoroughly. Make certain that both of you are adequately insured for health, life, and the ownership of property.

☐ Discuss savings and investing accounts. How active has each of you been in creating a financial future? How active should and will you be able to be? Remember that by consolidating your accounts, you will save service fees and so have more money to invest.

☐ List the credit cards each of you has, what debts you have run up, and how you plan to pay down the debt. Also, consider eliminating all but one credit card each. The same holds true for department store charge cards. Talk about what charge accounts you have and which of them you truly need.

☐ Try to agree on a budget, and then try to live on it.

☐ Consider the mutual benefits of a premarital contract.

☐ Recognize that arguing about money is inevitable but doesn't have to be a regular occurrence.

NEWLYWEDS' CHECKLIST

☐ You probably need to change the beneficiary designations on the following:

- **LIFE INSURANCE**
- **PENSION PLANS**
- **INDIVIDUAL RETIREMENT ACCOUNTS**
- **LIVING TRUSTS**
- **ANNUITIES**

☐ Prepare or revise your wills, and revise other estate-planning documents.

☐ If applicable, notify Social Security of your new name.

☐ Consolidate savings, investment, and credit card accounts.

■□■

Establish joint checking, savings, and investment accounts.

■□■

Establish a joint financial file and filing system.

Cohabitation

"**D**omestic partners" are persons of the opposite or same sex sharing living quarters. There is an acronym that refers to opposite-sex cohabitants—POSSLQs, which means "persons of the opposite sex sharing living quarters." But with the exception of common law rights, there's little else that officially defines the increasingly common practice of cohabitation—whether with someone of the opposite or the same sex.

This chapter will discuss a variety of financial matters that may be important to all domestic partners.

Daily Money Matters

Deciding to "move in together" is a bigger deal—personally, and perhaps even more important, financially—than most people think. It is not a simple matter of having twice the income. In fact, perhaps as a result of the need for larger living space, some domestic partners find that they have less disposable income than they had when they were living apart.

Budgeting Is Essential

All married couples argue over money. All cohabitants do too. The easiest way to avoid cash-spats is to establish a clear-cut budget that accounts for income and expenses. It is always a good idea to base the amount of expenses—from food to rent—for which each partner is responsible on his or her ability to pay. For example, if one partner earns more income than the other, then that partner should consider covering more than half of the expenses.

Joint Property and Accounts

Saving and investing are difficult enough propositions for people who are single or married. It is an even more complicated and difficult proposition if you are cohabiting. Why? In the event that you separate, the division of your jointly held property will fall to your good graces and sense of ethical duty and responsibility—not always the most reliable foundation on which to rest a division of property. Certain state laws may intervene if you have the time and money to take your former partner to court (in the event that he or she will not negotiate fairly or at all). It is probably best to play it safe and keep your accounts separate.

A joint savings account may be all right. Many cohabitants open joint checking and savings accounts for shared items like food costs, rent, utilities, and insurance. Not only does a joint account save you service fees, it introduces you to the subject of mutual financial responsibility.

Financial Commitments

side from all the other important considerations that go into home buying and other major financial commitments, domestic partners have to convince lenders that they are legitimately and mutually committed borrowers.

Home Ownership

Property ownership is a big step up from renting an apartment together. And even though buying a home together may represent a sign of good faith, it rarely represents a sign of financial smarts. Why? The worst-case scenario in a rented apartment is that you are left having to pay the remainder of the lease by yourself, should your relationship sour. But a home, complete with a monstrous mortgage, is obviously a different matter and a much bigger commitment. The problem is not the length of the mortgage, but the length of the commitment. If you want to take the property out of joint ownership and your partner refuses, it could be very difficult for you to do so—even if you contributed 90 percent of the purchase and mortgage payments. If you and your partner are going to buy a home, seek the advice of a lawyer who can help you avoid the many pitfalls.

Insurance

You are better off making certain that each of you is adequately covered by separate policies. Why? Your partner may decide to leave and not keep up her or his payments to your plan. Of course, if you want to go ahead and co-insure, you might turn to your company plan and see if there is a domestic partner option. Nowadays, some companies are extending insurance protection and other benefits to domestic partners. This trend will continue.

Every financial move you make should be put in writing. From buying or selling a car, to investing, to making larger purchases like a home, you and your partner need to be deliberate and diligent about writing down the transaction costs and agreements. It's unromantic, yes, but it's prudent.

Your Will

Leaving property to your domestic partner may not be to the liking of your relatives. You must make a written will that states specifically who gets what, and why. Otherwise, no matter how long you have been with your partner, he or she might end up losing all that you bequeathed to an aggressive relative who has enough money to invest in a good probate attorney. Be sure that your will and other estate-planning documents are bullet-proof if they favor your partner.

Cohabitation Agreements

U nder the current family court system, unmarried couples do not have the same rights as married couples to share property or to receive alimony or maintenance payments. Unofficial relationships are governed under contract laws. An unmarried couple that will be residing together over a long period of time should draw up a written agreement that specifies each partner's rights and obligations. Such a statement will provide some protection and could be important for settling disputes over issues of entitlement to property gained before or during the relationship, should the couple separate. A written agreement can also create a feasible alternative to what could potentially erupt into a financially and emotionally taxing legal battle. This agreement should be prepared by an attorney. Ideally, each partner should have his or her own attorney review the agreement to make sure that it is fair to both parties.

COHABITATION AGREEMENT CHECKLIST

Written agreements for unmarried couples who are living together should stipulate the terms that will direct the division of their assets if the relationship is terminated. Some specific suggestions concerning issues that may arise in developing such a document include:

☐ Record each partner's assets and determine whether either partner has rights to the property or income of the other partner. Assets should be listed along with their approximate values and the dates they were acquired. Such a provision will protect each partner from unforeseen claims that the other partner may place on his or her assets.

☐ Delineate the responsibility for the debts incurred during the relationship. Both partners are generally responsible only for debts that have been cosigned and loans for acquiring assets or producing income that are commingled.

Smart Money Move

Consider a cohabitation agreement to clarify important matters and protect the rights of both you and your partner.

☐ Determine what respective contributions to the relationship justify the agreement. Each person's contribution to the household, which can be in the form of money or services, should be assessed for purposes of specifying the respective contributions of both.

☐ Establish how either partner will take title to assets acquired while the couple is living together. Couples can choose to own property individually, as joint tenants with the right of survivorship, as tenants in common, or as a combination of these. A partner can pass his or her share of property owned as a tenant in common to anyone in his or her will. But joint tenancy property that is automatically passed to a survivor could be interpreted as a gift and be subject to federal gift tax.

◼️

Decide whether the relationship is a common law marriage. If a couple resides in a state in which common law marriages are recognized, the couple should state in their agreement whether their relationship is one.

◼️

Determine the disposition of the home you both reside in. Decide the circumstances and the terms under which either partner can continue to live in the home. If the house will eventually be sold, determine how the proceeds will be divided.

◼️

Arrange for the personal and financial care of any children.

◼️

Specify the circumstances that would terminate the agreement. Typically, agreements are invalidated by the death of one of the partners, marriage, or a written agreement that ends the partnership.

◼️

Decide whether a mediator should be used to help solve disputes and forestall going to court.

Advice for Single People

Increasing numbers of Americans are staying single, and staying single longer. From 1970 to 1990, one-person households increased from 11 million to almost 25 million. But as the number of singles grows, it becomes increasingly difficult to make broad generalizations about them as a group. Singles can, however, be roughly separated into three main groups: singles without children, unmarried individuals with children, and unmarried couples living together. (See Chapter 17 for advice for cohabitants.) Your personal financial needs and strategies will often differ somewhat depending upon which of the three categories you are in.

You Do Have Different Needs

You may find that financial-planning publications and financial-planning service providers have not directed sufficient attention to singles' unique needs. The main difference between the financial-planning needs of the single person compared with the married person begins with estate planning and extends to other areas as well, including insurance, saving and investing, and retirement planning.

The Single Most Important Goal

The most important financial goal of everyone, single or married, is financial security. But many single people have more difficulty achieving financial security since, compared with their dual-earner, married counterparts, a higher proportion of their income will probably have to be spent on living expenses (although I know many singles who are excellent savers and could teach the yuppies a lot about frugality). This means that saving is comparatively more difficult for singles.

Myths about Singles

The difficulty of saving isn't helped by the fact that many singles harbor longstanding notions about their personal finances that are at best out-of-date and that at worst will result in mistakes that will be financially penalizing for many years. Some of these notions (which you need to discard) are:

- SINGLE PEOPLE should not buy (or can't afford to buy) homes.

- SINGLE PEOPLE should invest very conservatively because they have less money available to make up for losses on risky investments (like stocks).

- **SINGLE PEOPLE** with no dependents don't need life insurance.

- **ESTATE PLANNING** is either unnecessary for singles or requires nothing beyond a simple will.

While your needs are different in several respects from your married counterparts', they are identical in most others, in spite of preconceived notions to the contrary.

The Importance of Planning

Planning is particularly important. Many singles may not have paid adequate attention to it in the past, or they may simply think that planning is not necessary for them. Make specific plans, both short and long term, about what you want to accomplish—financially and personally.

Record-Keeping

Organize your personal records so that, in the event of disability, a designated individual (a relative or friend) can readily assume important record-keeping chores, including bill-paying, banking, and income tax preparation. Ideally, someone should be designated to perform these tasks should the need arise. The designee should be shown where the records are located and how they are organized. Also, instructions should be prepared to show what needs to be done in the event someone else has to take over.

Insurance

Smart Money Move

Make arrangements for a relative or friend to take over your personal record-keeping chores in the event of your disability.

The need for comprehensive insurance is as crucial for singles as it is for couples. There are, however, some differences that may need to be addressed when reviewing your insurance policies. For example, many singles who have no dependents see no need for any life insurance at all (and some are quite correct). But your parents or siblings may become financially dependent at some future time. Life insurance, should you die before them, would be particularly helpful to them. Also, life insurance proceeds may be useful in providing a bequest for a particular charity of your choosing.

If you are a single parent, you need life insurance to provide for your child(ren) should you die before they leave the nest. Even if you have established a guardianship for them—and you should do this (see page 728)—you also need to provide for their financial security with adequate life insurance.

Another area of insurance that may merit particular attention is disability coverage. Singles do not have the luxury of falling back on a spouse's income in the event of an under- or uninsured disability. Therefore, maintaining sufficient disability insurance is particularly crucial.

Investing

While the investment strategies of singles generally do not differ from those of couples in similar financial circumstances, the need to accumulate a financial cushion against financial adversity is more crucial because there is no second breadwinner to take up the slack. Accumulating sufficient capital to meet life's adversities, as well as funding a comfortable retirement, may therefore be a greater challenge for you. (See Part VII for investing.)

If you have been investing too conservatively, remember that investing for growth is every bit as important for you as it is for families bringing home two paychecks. (See Chapter 54 for asset allocation suggestions.)

Estate Planning

Make no mistake about it—estate-planning rules and strategies favor married couples. For this reason, single people and unmarried persons living together often have more difficulty planning their estates. (For more on cohabitation, see Chapter 17.) Selection of fiduciaries and designation of beneficiaries may be particularly perplexing if you have no partner or immediate relatives whom you want to inherit your estate. Nevertheless, estate planning is essential, unless you want to bequeath all that you've worked for to the state. Make sure that you also prepare and keep up-to-date other important estate-planning documents (see Chapter 81).

One idea is to make your alma mater or other favored charity a beneficiary, particularly if your parents, siblings, nieces, and nephews are all in reasonable financial shape.

If you are charitably inclined and you choose not to leave all or most of your estate to heirs, you may choose from among a variety of giving strategies that benefit both the charity and you—during your lifetime (see page 743).

Dating Tips

You may not always be single. But when you look at the high cost of courtship, you might be better off financially by staying home alone. If you do become love-struck, here are some tips to help you avoid spending your way to the poorhouse.

Don't try to buy affection

It's a surefire way to lose both money and the object of your desire. Yet the temptation to spend as wildly as your heart beats overcomes many rational financial instincts. Try to stem your money's flow if you or someone you know is struck by Cupid's arrow.

Go dutch

The convention that one party—usually the man—must shoulder the entire cost of a dinner, movie, or other entertainment has been jettisoned. It's fair to share, and the sooner you establish cost-splitting as a ground rule in a relationship, the better off you'll be—especially if you are the one who normally picks up the tab.

Date on the cheap

Take advantage of the many free opportunities for amusement that make a good excuse for a date. The list is endless—biking, hiking, a visit to the park, free concerts, and so on.

Don't go overboard on gift-giving to your sweetie

Ain't love grand—and ain't it expensive! Even though passion may be clouding your judgment, you must try to avoid spending more than you can afford on gifts for your significant other. You'll be glad to have saved some money if you ever decide to move in together. You can't sit or sleep on a sapphire ring or a gold watch.

Recognize that long-distance courtships are costly

Before you get involved with a melancholy Ukrainian beauty, consider the costs that long-distance relationships invariably incur. Your phone bill will skyrocket, and you will find yourself earning many more Frequent Flyer miles than you had ever dreamed possible. And if the relationship blossoms, one of you is going to have to move a long, long way.

Don't fall for someone who has a lot of debt

This happens a lot more often than you might realize—victims of it are too embarrassed to admit that they've been had. Say you fall for someone who is having debt problems. In a rush of love, you lend them money to set them on an even financial keel. Suddenly, the relationship sours. Kiss your money good-bye. (Many charlatans go from relationship to relationship in this manner.) Take my advice—avoid falling for anyone who can't manage their personal finances.

Fall for someone who's rich, or at least affluent

There is nothing inherently romantic about falling in love with a poor person. It's just as easy to love a rich one. If you are looking for ways to ensure a secure financial future, "marrying well" is certainly a sensible way to reach that goal.

Shop carefully for an engagement or wedding ring

It's awfully easy to get taken when you are buying an engagement ring. Most of us don't buy diamond rings often enough to be informed bargainers. So educate yourself enough about diamonds that you can at least be an educated consumer. Visit only established dealers. Finally, don't spend more than you can comfortably afford.

The Arrival of Children

I f marriage hasn't inspired you to take control of your finances, if buying your first home hasn't prompted you to start balancing your checkbook, then news that the stork is flying in your direction is likely to make you start planning for the future as you never have before. Even the most profligate, spendthrift characters have been known to get personal financial religion when faced with the prospect of having to provide for their posterity.

If you think a house is expensive, it's chickenfeed compared with the cost of raising a child. By the time your little bundle of joy has graduated from college and left the nest, he or she will have cost you somewhere around the equivalent of two houses. And don't expect to get off the financial hook when junior starts working—just ask your friends who have adult children. You can pretty much expect to be doling out money for the rest of your life.

But first things first. In this chapter, we'll review the various financial matters relating to the birth or adoption of children, then some financial matters to take into consideration once the little one arrives on the scene. My objective here is to make sure that you don't lose sleep worrying about the inevitable changes in your financial status. You'll lose enough sleep when the little one arrives.

Preparing for the New Arrival

W hen you get the news that your family is going to expand, your first impulse may well be to spend a lot of money decorating and furnishing the baby-to-be's room and buying clothes for the little tyke. Don't make the mistake of getting too carried away at this juncture, however. As far as baby clothes and toys are concerned, the judicious use of hand-me-downs makes a lot more sense than does splurging on glitzy new items that will be quickly outgrown. Furthermore, seven or eight years down the line, Sally will probably tell you that she hates having "baby" wallpaper in her room. So if you find yourself struck with an uncontrollable urge to spend $500 on a six-foot-tall stuffed rabbit for your heir, why not start a college-tuition fund instead by investing the money in a stock mutual fund?

Financial Details

Before the arrival of a child, you should attend to several important financial details. First, review your health insurance to get a handle on how much of the childbirth costs you will be expected to pay. Also, see whether your disability income insurance or other employer-provided benefits are available to you or your spouse while on maternity leave.

Once you have estimated your out-of-pocket childbirth costs and maternity leave benefits, you will know how much money you need to set aside for the blessed (and expensive) event. If your current resources fall short, it is better to start saving now than to have the money run out just after the baby arrives.

Housing

If you don't have a spare bedroom to convert into the baby's room, you're probably contemplating a move either before the baby arrives or in the near future. You may be able to cope with having the baby sleep in your bedroom or the living room for a while. You will quickly realize, however, that such a makeshift arrangement is fairly unsatisfactory.

While you are out looking for new digs, you and your spouse will have to consider a variety of factors that may have heretofore been of little interest to you, such as the availability of day care and the quality of the local school system. Whether you are looking at apartments or a home, you should keep the following points in mind as you evaluate properties.

- **DOES** the property have an enclosed or enclosable yard or play area where your child can play safely?

- **IS** the home or apartment located on a quiet street or a busy thoroughfare?

- **IS** the property conveniently located? As a new parent, you'll be surprised at how much more frequently you will use grocery and convenience stores. Also, sooner than you think, you will have to be concerned about easy access to day care, the local public library, and schools.

- **WILL** your child be able to find companions nearby? If a given neighborhood is populated by retired World War II veterans, it's unlikely that your tyke is going to find many playmates there.

Smart Money Move

Financial planning for a new child should begin before the little one is born.

Birthing Alternatives

Back when you were born, there was only one option for "civilized" families as to where a birth would occur—in the hospital. During the baby-boom years, our technology-obsessed nation wanted to do everything in the most modern, up-to-date manner. The idea of home birth seemed repugnant and old-fashioned to most American parents-to-be. Today, due to a variety of factors, including the influence of the feminist movement and revelations of sloppy practices in some big-city hospital delivery rooms, attitudes have shifted considerably. The emphasis is now on choice—expectant mothers can choose to give birth in a variety of different settings, based upon her and her family's wishes. There are four main alternatives.

The Hospital Delivery Room

This was the traditional—and is now the most expensive—place to give birth. The average cost for a hospital delivery is over $3,000. One reason that giving birth in a hospital is more expensive than elsewhere is that hospitals require lengthier postnatal stays. If there is any possibility that a pregnancy will have complications, you have little choice but to use the obstetrics ward. But if medical complications aren't anticipated, you may want to consider the other alternatives.

The Hospital Birthing Room

While the cost of giving birth in a so-called birthing room is comparable to that of a standard delivery room, many mothers prefer the more comfortable, familiar atmosphere that these rooms try to create. The past fifteen to twenty years have witnessed a steady movement away from the antiseptic births of the 1950s and 1960s. Hospital birthing rooms are an attempt to reconcile the safety of a delivery-room birth with the more "mother-friendly" atmosphere of the at-home birth. During the birth itself, either an obstetrician or a nurse-midwife is present. Furthermore, family members can be present during the birth in a pleasant, homelike atmosphere.

The Birthing Center

Over half the states have now licensed birthing centers. These centers essentially duplicate the hospital birthing rooms described above, with one salient difference: They are not attached to hospitals. Birthing centers are staffed by certified nurse-midwives; consulting physicians are on twenty-four-hour call. These centers encourage one-day stays, and the cost for a delivery is less expensive—about $2,000. But you should check with your doctor first. If complications are likely to arise, you don't want to risk being any distance from a hospital.

The Home

Seventy-five years ago, the average four-poster saw a lot more of life's key moments—conceptions, births, and deaths—than does today's average waterbed. Yet giving birth the way our ancestors did is coming back into vogue. Many women are loath to bring their children into the world in the chilly, antiseptic atmosphere of a hospital delivery room. Instead, they are rediscovering the world of home birthing and midwives.

While the very word *midwife* would have caused most 1950s American mothers to wrinkle their noses, the profession has since climbed out of near-extinction to a high degree of respectability. Modern nurse-midwives are state-licensed, just like RNs, and you can find their names in the Yellow Pages. (You would do well, however, to make sure that the one you choose has sterling references.) Home births usually cost between $800 and $2,000. Remember, however, that unless your doctor is fairly certain that the birth will be uncomplicated, home birthing is not a wise choice.

Adoption

Many American couples turn toward adoption as a means of starting or expanding a family. There are a bewildering variety of agencies through which one can adopt a child, but they can be divided into two broad categories, public and private. No matter which route you take, however, you won't be able to escape paying legal fees: typically, adoption papers cost about $1,000 to prepare.

Public Adoption Agencies

Many states and localities maintain their own adoption agencies, and procedures vary widely from state to state. Many have substantial waiting lists—some couples have had to wait years to receive a child. The chief advantage to adopting through a public agency is that it is usually free (although you will still need to pay the above-mentioned attorney's fees). You should contact your state's social-service agency for information about agencies and procedures in your state. State social-service agencies can also provide you with a list of licensed private adoption agencies in your area.

Private Adoption Agencies and Organizations

Not surprisingly, private agencies can be more flexible and less bureaucratic in their procedures. If you are willing to pay a good sum of money, you can get results much more quickly through the private sector. By the same token, some licensed private agencies have engaged in questionable practices, including collecting large sums of money up front and then failing to provide babies to eager prospective parents.

It is important that you thoroughly research an agency's background before you sign any checks. One organization that can be of help is the National Committee for Adoption (1930 17th Street, N.W., Washington DC 20009). This group publishes *The Adoption Fact Book*, which is a good guide to reputable, established private adoption agencies.

If prospects look dim for finding a suitable American girl or boy, you could consider adopting a foreign child. West European children, however, are as difficult to obtain as U.S. ones; children from impoverished Third World countries are easier to obtain. Adopting a foreign child can be expensive, however, costing between $4,000 and $8,000. The International Committee for Children (911 Cyprus Drive, Boulder CO 80303) publishes a list of well-established agencies called *The Report on Foreign Adoption*.

When considering the adoption of a foreign child, it is very important that you check an agency's references, as the field seems to attract more than its share of shady operators. The federal government also publishes a booklet that may be of interest, "The Immigration of

Adopted and Prospective Adoptive Children." (You can obtain it for $1.75 from the Superintendent of Documents, U.S. Government Printing Office, Washington DC 20402-9325.)

Independent Adoption

There is one additional means by which you can adopt a child, but it is the most difficult and risky. You could try to adopt a child directly, without the assistance of a middleman. Usually this is done "a priori"—in other words, you find a pregnant woman who wants to give up her child, and you agree to pay her medical expenses for a future interest in her off-spring. The chief benefit of independent adoption is that it allows you to take the baby straight home from the delivery room. Doing it yourself also enables you to circumvent the sometimes-onerous qualifications that agencies require of adoptive parents.

But the process is fraught with danger. The birth mother could at any time change her mind, especially after she has actually given birth to the child, leaving the adoptive parents holding the bag. Furthermore, some states take a very dim view of the practice, and it is actually illegal in a few states. Finding a suitable expectant mother is a difficult, word-of-mouth business. You have to talk to a lot of people, including doctors and clergymen, as you go about your search. The National Adoption Center (1218 Chestnut Street, Philadelphia PA 19107; tel.: [215] 925-0200) can provide you with additional information on independent adoption.

After the Blessed Event

Social Security

The baby is far more concerned about eating than retirement, but the sooner you obtain a Social Security card for your scion, the better. The IRS now requires that each child who reaches age one in a given tax year have a Social Security number. For example, if your child is born in September 1993, you will have to list the child—along with his or her Social Security number—on your 1994 income tax return. Why? Because the child will reach age one in 1994. If you neglect to list each child and his or her Social Security number, you could incur a $50 penalty. To avoid penalties, the child's Social Security number must also be provided to banks, brokers, and other payers of interest and dividends.

To obtain a Social Security number for your new family member, contact your local Social Security administration office and request Form SS-5. If you apply for a Social Security number but your child is not yet assigned one by the filing due date, write "applied for" on the tax return.

Insurance

Your insurance needs have changed. The following areas of your coverage are all going to need to be reviewed and probably modified to meet your changed circumstances:

Health insurance

You need to update your policy so that it covers your child. Furthermore, it is more important than ever that your and your spouse's *own* health be well insured. If your employer offers a choice of health insurance policies, this may be a good time to reconsider the alternatives that are available, since your family will become a more frequent user of health-care services.

Life insurance

Most new parents find that their life insurance needs have changed dramatically. The birth notice in the newspapers is likely to unleash legions of insurance salespeople who are anxious to tell you how much your life insurance needs have changed. Don't let them tell you how much you need. Rather, take a look at Chapter 38 for assistance in assessing how much insurance you may need—and to find economical ways to obtain it. Incidentally, it wouldn't hurt to bolster your life insurance coverage before the baby arrives. You'll be busy enough afterward without having to undertake the time-consuming task of adjusting your life insurance coverage.

Smart Money Moves

Review all your life insurance to make sure it is adequate in light of your new financial responsibilities.

Ask your attorney if your will needs to be revised when the baby is born. If you haven't yet prepared a will, do so now.

Other insurance areas

With your new parental responsibilities, you should also review the other areas of insurance coverage to ensure that you now have coverage and that you have enough of it. The plain fact is that you can no longer afford to take chances by skipping or shortchanging certain areas of insurance. You need sufficient disability income insurance to replace 60 to 70 percent of your income, and, if applicable, your spouse's income. You need a renter's insurance policy because you can no longer afford the risk of going without. You need umbrella liability insurance, because you don't want to risk what you've saved and, perhaps, future earnings, to a lawsuit.

Estate Planning

As a new parent, it is more important than ever that you have an up-to-date will, durable power of attorney, and living will. If you haven't already prepared these documents, have them drawn up now. If these documents already exist, they will likely need to be changed in light of your new family circumstances.

If you still doubt the need to prepare estate-planning documents, let me scare you into taking action. If neither of you has a will and you both die in an accident, the courts—not you—will appoint a guardian for your child or children. If one of you dies without a will, most state laws will divide your estate evenly between the surviving parent and the child or children. Had you prepared a will, you could have insured that your spouse received full control of your estate.

Child Care

For the majority of parents these days, child care is a financial necessity, and an expensive necessity, at that. Be sure to take a look at the various day-care alternatives available to you well before your child arrives on the scene. First, ask your employer whether any company-provided programs or financial assistance will be at your disposal. Second, given the available options, consider how you can best satisfy your child-care needs at a reasonable cost. Be forewarned that child-care in any form is an expensive proposition, although the tax code is structured to provide some relief to overburdened parents.

You can take advantage of the child-care income tax credit. Or if your company provides a flexible-benefits plan, you may be able to pay child-care bills out of your pretax income. Whether the flexible-benefits plan or the income tax credit results in greater savings depends upon your particular tax situation, but usually the flexible-benefits plan provides the greater. Note also that not only day care, but nursery and kindergarten tuition costs are also eligible for the child-care credit.

Ten Ways to Cut Your Child-rearing Costs

P arents must resign themselves to the fact their bundles of joy are also bundles of expenses. There are, however, ways to keep these expenses under control, including four magic words that can be deployed at strategic junctures—"We can't afford it." Read on and learn.

1. Invite grandparents to visit often

Why? Because grandparents always bring presents, and they baby-sit for free.

2. Don't send your kid to private school—move to a town with a good public school system

Despite all the current lamentation about the state of American public education, many affluent suburban school districts still provide fine educations at bargain rates. Even high property taxes will look reasonable when compared with the cost of private school tuition. So if you are unhappy with your town's public schools, consider moving to a town with a superior public system before making the substantial financial commitment that a private school education entails.

3. Get hand-me-down toys from relatives and friends

If you put out the word that you are in the market for used toys, you'll end up with a roomful of toys from family and friends. Why? For some reason, when our kids have outgrown their toys, we usually put them away rather than get rid of them. So the toys sit in the attic, awaiting a good home. What better place for them than the home of a child of a friend or relative?

4. Form a baby-sitting cooperative

Baby-sitters are a scarce and expensive commodity. It's getting to the point where parents find that the biggest cost for a night on the town is the baby-sitter. That's why a lot of parents are forming baby-sitting cooperatives, where they trade taking the chores of baby-sitting one another's broods. After all, it's already chaotic enough with your own kids around the house; taking care of a few more is sometimes no big deal.

5. If you think you are going to have more than one child, buy quality clothing for the first one

Here's one place where spending a little more is a good idea. By buying well-built, durable clothing for child number one, you can rest assured that children numbers two and three will have good baby clothes, while your bank account will be preserved. There's no point in buying a whole new set of clothes for each new addition to the family.

6. Remove expensive furniture and knickknacks when children are around

Put young children in a room with any pretensions to style, and within five seconds they will take the most expensive knickknack in hand and launch it into orbit. Give children a crayon and a coloring book, and they'll be hard at work in short order—coloring the mahogany cocktail table or the reproduction William Morris wallpaper. Be forewarned.

7. Avoid buying expensive dress clothing for young children

Your kid may look spectacular in a Laura Ashley dress or a Brooks Brothers blazer, but these things will be worn only a few times before they are outgrown. If you want to lavish that kind of money on your offspring, buy a more practical garment, and purchase a U.S. savings bond with the difference.

8. Buy "preowned" toys

If you think about it, quality toys can't be used up. Most children tire of a particular bauble long before the bauble is ready to be retired. So keep your eyes peeled for places like yard sales and used toy emporiums. Both are good sources of inexpensive, barely used toys.

9. Save shirt cardboards and corrugated boxes for kiddie-craft projects

Shirt cardboards and corrugated boxes are marvelous raw materials for kiddie projects. Large boxes can be made into stockades, express passenger trains, or men-of-war; shirt cardboards can be used as painter's canvases or to make anything from masks to suits of armor.

10. Make your youngster's Halloween costume instead of buying it

These days a Halloween costume can cost as much as a new set of clothes, but it will probably be used only once. You can save a lot of money by making your child's costume yourself. It's a wonderful parent-child co-production, and with a little luck and skill, you may design something that far surpasses any store-bought costume anyway!

BIRTH OR ADOPTION CHECKLIST

☐ Obtain and file a copy of your child's birth certificate for safekeeping.

☐ Ask your attorney to review your child's adoption papers. They should be appropriately filed for safekeeping.

☐ Revise your budgets to reflect changes in your living expenses.

☐ Take account of the effect that having a child will have on your long-term planning and forecasting.

☐ Determine whether your life insurance coverage is adequate to protect your expanded family.

☐ Amend your health insurance coverage to account for your new child.

☐ Review your disability insurance coverage to account for your new parental status.

☐ Inform your umbrella liability carrier that you now have a child.

☐ Obtain a Social Security number for your child.

☐ Ask your employer to revise your income withholding tax to reflect the additional exemptions—and possibly increased credits—for which you may qualify.

■□

Revise both your own and your spouse's wills to reflect your changed family circumstances.

■□

If your new child has an interest in the estate of your parents (or your spouse's parents), see to it that their wills are revised.

■□

Appoint (and inform of your appointment) personal and, perhaps, property guardians for your new child.

Teaching Children About Money

I t is essential to prepare your children for the financial responsibilities of adulthood. This chapter shows how parents can help their children become financially literate adults, by helping them learn about investing, budgeting, and becoming a good money manager.

Allowances

A llowances are a good springboard for teaching sound money habits. Many parents, however, have trouble determining what a fair allowance is. Your child's allowance should be large enough to cover fixed expenses and still leave something to save or spend as your child chooses. The following are guidelines for establishing allowances for children of different age groups.

Preschoolers

Even preschoolers can begin to understand the value of money, so this may be an appropriate time to begin an allowance. Fifty cents to a dollar a week should be sufficient to start a small child planning his or her finances with your encouragement. A preschooler's allowance should be expected to cover only luxury items, such as candy and toys.

Remember that giving too much is just as bad as not giving enough. Especially at this young age, it is easy for children to confuse money with love or attention. Divorced parents who pay their kids hefty allowances to compensate for their absence are only hurting them.

Grade Schoolers

Grade schoolers can begin to assume responsibilities for their own club dues, hobby materials, sports equipment, and friends' presents. Some parents expect their child's allowance to cover necessary expenses such as food and clothing, while others prefer to continue to pay these separately so that the child will not be tempted to spend money earmarked for necessities on frivolous items. In setting the allowance, you should take into account what your child's friends and classmates receive, but remember that there will always be a

Smart Money Move

Use allowances to teach children the value of money and the importance of managing it well.

friend who gets that extra quarter you refuse your child. It's an age-old bargaining technique.

Your child should learn early on where your money comes from and the effort that goes into earning it. Children can often be taught simple lessons of earning and spending by being paid extra for special household tasks or for outside work, such as baby-sitting and mowing lawns. Payments for exceptional chores should be kept separate from your child's regular allowance and regular chores and should not be carried to the point where he expects payment for any help he gives. Otherwise, you might find a mutiny on your hands.

High Schoolers

As children reach high school age, their expenses increase, and so therefore should their responsibilities and allowances. It is entirely reasonable to ask a high schooler who asks for an allowance "raise" to submit a budget of his or her expenses, showing actual expenditures on social activities, cosmetics, jewelry, clothing, cassettes and compact discs, food, and school activities. Teenagers need to be encouraged to budget. A tight budget will also force them to comparison shop and cut expenses. Longer-term planning and budgeting should also be encouraged. While it may be appropriate to pay younger children a weekly allowance, high schoolers can be expected to budget a month at a time.

You should encourage your child to open his or her own savings account in order to learn about the mechanics as well as the importance of saving. Many banks offer teenagers special accounts with low fees.

Coping with Inherited Wealth

Several trillion dollars will be inherited in the United States over the next twenty years. Some parents and children will be receiving very large inheritances. (Alas, I will not be one of them.) A number of problems accompany large inheritances, and you may have to address them for either yourself or your children. There are many ways to resolve these monetary problems with your children, especially if you yourself are the beneficiary of affluence, and for inheritors themselves to face the specific problems and responsibilities their wealth brings them.

Children of wealth often suffer from low self-esteem. Many are uncertain whether they could achieve anything significant or be liked and respected by others if they were not affluent. This can also result in a continuing and irrational fear of losing their wealth, which may prevent them from taking the initiative and the risks required for personal and vocational achievement.

Even more than in normal cases, it is essential to familiarize children of affluence with the value of money. After all, with so much around, it might seem to them as if it grows on trees, which is hardly how you want your child to become accustomed to the presence of money. Children should be expected to earn their allowances through the accomplishment of specific chores. Paid summer jobs, always a good idea, can help your children to believe that they can support themselves.

Being active participants in the decisions that affect their lives also alleviates some of the problems that can accompany being passive inheritors. Choosing a school is a particularly good example. Your child should feel that his point of view and feelings are at least heard and respected. Do not pressure your child to attend your alma matter or some school that you could not attend.

Because many young inheritors are spared their share of life's challenges, they are often slow in their personal development. The comfort and security that money provides can avoid, diminish, or delay the crises and challenges that are necessary for emotional and intellectual development. For many people, however, being able to provide this level of security and comfort for their kids is one of the main goals for which they worked. Teach your child to endure the pain and frustration of delays and disappointments, and to resist the temptation to quit when things are not going their way, rather than shield them from all of life's stresses.

A large inheritance can make it difficult to sustain an interest and commitment to anything, including most jobs and relationships that require continuing effort or the endurance of ambiguity, setbacks, and frustration. Lack of motivation is related to lack of discipline. Many inheritors have trouble finding and putting energy into meaningful pursuits long enough to obtain satisfying outcomes. Self-discipline requires concentration and the ability to postpone gratification in the interest of higher, ultimately more satisfying rewards.

Developing a Sense of Purpose

The best solution to the lack of motivation, discipline, and interest that often accompanies inherited wealth is to never allow money to substitute for these things in the first place. You may want to discuss the obligations and ethical issues that accompany affluence with your children, so they realize that their fortunes carry certain responsibilities to society. Wealth should become a reason to accomplish, not a replacement for it. Young inheritors who are troubled at not having to "earn their living" may find an answer in "earning the right to live." This can mean careers or avocations in the arts, academia, or public service. It may mean devoting as much time and effort as money to charities or investing in noncharitable, "socially responsible" companies. Whatever their interest, your children should be advised to fight the tendency to give up when the level of their frustration and discouragement becomes unpleasant; a sense of success and competence can only occur once an inheritor's obstacles are confronted and overcome.

Power presents a particular peril for inheritors, since they have

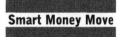

Smart Money Move

If your children are likely to be the beneficiaries of a large inheritance, be aware of ways to help them cope adequately with it.

not earned it and may not feel entitled to it. They may handle power in extremes: by avoiding it, by denying its reality, or by exercising it arbitrarily and self-servingly as overcompensation for their sense of inadequacy. Most inheritors suffer from guilt. They find it hard to accept unearned good fortune and have trouble finding ways to prove themselves worthy of it.

The solutions to the problems of dealing with guilt and power are the same: your children need to attain a constructive attitude toward their financial good fortune. This starts with you yourself being comfortable with your wealth, free of pride or shame about it. One experience that seems to distinguish those who function well with inherited wealth from those who do not is that their parents have dealt with them straightforwardly about the money itself.

Wealthy people can be afflicted with feelings of alienation and suspicion. They sometimes find it difficult to understand the lives and experiences of those in more ordinary circumstances, and they are equally convinced (with some reason) that those others cannot understand theirs. Adding to this alienation is the suspicion that many of those they encounter want something from them and are ready to manipulate them for their own purposes.

You can help this by suggesting work situations where your children are not identified as being wealthy, and where they have opportunities to succeed on their own merits. Generally it is preferable for a child to seek work outside the family business, if there is one. The young affluent must also risk making favorable assumptions about friends and associates and making true commitments to these relationships. This will expose them, like anyone else, to the possibility of being hurt, but it is the only way to full and rewarding relationships.

Don't Spoil the Child

One of the hardest but most important things you must do for your children is to learn to avoid both negligence and intrusion. Some rich parents lead active lives and purchase child care, thus neglecting to give their children the personal attention they need and deserve. Other parents may be too intrusive in their children's lives. Their legitimate concern that their wealth be preserved and used properly too often results in excessive interference. This dichotomy between negligent and intrusive parenting is reflected in the provisions they set for inheritance. Most people find it wise to wait until children show some responsibility and understanding of their positions and obligations, as well as some signs of being able to support themselves, before entrusting them with their fortunes. Whenever you make the decision to withhold money from your children, however, make it clear why you are doing so, what you expect in return, and what your children can expect from you. It is not fair to bring the child up with one set of expectations, then suddenly and inexplicably deny them their inherited wealth.

Although substantial inheritance should depend on some demonstration of your heir's ability and inclination to handle money responsibly, avoid the temptation to use the promise of an inheritance as a means of coercing children to behave a certain way. Children should not be encouraged to dissemble or deny their true nature, and your distribution of wealth among your children should be fair to all. It might help to arrange trusts or wills that make a portion of your children's inheritances available to them at a relatively young age, with the understanding that the forthcoming portions will depend on their demonstration of responsibility.

Some Common Kids' Money Questions and Their Answers

"Jimmy down the street gets a dollar allowance. Why do I only get eighty-five cents?"

Don't fall for this: it's an age-old bargaining technique that you have probably used yourself. If it seems as if everyone your child knows is getting spoiled, look into it. Chances are she's exaggerating. If she's not, she gets a firsthand lesson on the injustices of wealth distribution.

"If I don't get those hundred-dollar sneakers, I'll die!"

Tell him how much you can pitch in for his shoes budget, and let him cover the difference. But remember, your contribution had better be fair. Unless you're really strapped for cash, don't force your child to undergo the humiliation of showing up in school with a pair of neon red bargain sneakers from a warehouse past the city limits. This sort of thing can be intensely damaging to a child's psyche. Figure out how much a pair of decent sneakers really costs. Also, remember that your kid is constantly subjected to advertising that has been specially designed to sucker him. Watch TV with him and teach him about advertising tricks: he'll probably be fascinated by the corruption of the industry. Go to stores with him so he can see for himself the difference between the giant slime-monsters in their ooze kingdom on TV and the cheap plastic dolls that drip goo out of their mouths in the box.

"Why won't you pay for my New Kids on the Block tickets? You just don't understand: of course they're worth thirty-five bucks!"

This sort of thing is pretty complicated: there are some things that your child will view with something akin to a religious awe and will therefore have trouble relating to your concerns about its price. Imagine if your long-dead idol (Napoleon or Elvis or whoever) were coming to town for a series of lectures or performances. You would probably be willing to dish out big bucks to see the great man or woman in the flesh. As harsh as it may seem, putting your foot down is often the best solution, providing you explain why. If she's getting an allowance, you can encourage her to plan ahead and save up for these things. Reward her discipline by matching her savings, or at least chipping in a little. If your child is old enough, try some hands-on treatment: Make her do the bills one month, and let her see how much is left.

In the long run, she will learn not from your long speeches about when you were a child, but from how you behave now. If you trade in your car for the new model with the talking sun roof, then trade that in two years later because the manufacturer has finally introduced one with a distinguished burgundy paint job, your child is unlikely to learn good spending habits. On the other hand, she needs to realize that you have a little more leverage than she when it comes to family finances. "When you're supporting yourself, you can buy as many central remote-control systems as you like" will suffice, even if you did just buy one for your own study. Or a simple line my mother always used whenever I announced that I wanted anything: she would simply reply wistfully, "I want a big coffee ice cream soda." After about ten or twelve years, I got the point.

"Why are you so cheap when Grampa always brings me lots of toys?"

Again, your kid is smarter than he's letting on. It doesn't take much to realize that there's a difference between relatives you only see occasionally and the immediate family. Point this out in a friendly manner, making it clear that you know that he understands. His act may require an expression of dumbfounded bewilderment, but he will still love you.

"Fine, don't give me any allowance. I'm still not making my bed."

You are raising a mercenary. Your child needs to be aware of her responsibilities around the house that have nothing to do with money. This can be difficult: if she knows that she'll get her allowance whether or not she does her chores, she might be doubly inspired to go to the arcade and forget the trash. You'll have to work out some other kind of disciplinary system—perhaps suspending her TV privileges for the week. A good middle ground is to have additional, optional chores that are linked to payment: baby-sitting, mowing the lawn, cleaning the garage.

"There's no way I'm saving my allowance for college!"

Hear, hear! Unless you have an angel in your fold, no kid in his right mind is going to look far enough ahead to save money for serious later expenses. You can nurture those tendencies, however, by getting him started on smaller projects with clearer, sooner rewards. Like those New Kids on the Block tickets. By the time he's seventeen or eighteen, you'll be surprised how mature he's become about saving.

TEACHING FINANCIAL SAVVY FOR PENNIES A DAY

You can use their weekly allowance to teach young children—even preschoolers—how to manage their money wisely. The following suggestions are provided by Neale S. Godfrey, author of *The Kid's Money Book* (Checkerboard Press, 1991), a book I recommend highly.

A young child should be encouraged to divide his or her allowance into three parts:

- **THE FIRST PART** can be spent immediately on whatever the child wants.

- **THE SECOND PART** should be saved so that the child can purchase a more expensive item when he or she has accumulated enough money. For example, rather than buy the eight-crayon box now, the child might be encouraged to set aside this part of the allowance to buy a sixty-four-crayon box later.

- **THE THIRD PART** should be considered long-term savings. You should set up a savings account or investment account so that your child can learn the importance of saving regularly for the future. The youngster can also begin to see that money set aside can grow in value as interest or dividends are added to the account.

The allowance can be used for older, grade-school children to impart other important money lessons. Encourage your older child to divide the allowance into five parts. In addition to the three parts described above, you can teach your child the importance of charity and taxes. The fourth part of the allowance could be set aside for charitable purposes, with the child having a say as to which charity will receive his or her contributions. The fifth part introduces income taxes. (Most of us were not introduced to income taxes until we got our first paycheck, and it was indeed a rude introduction.) Even though the child's allowance will not be subject to federal or state income taxes, there is no reason why a "family tax" could not be withheld from the allowance. The tax receipts should be set aside and accumulated so that they can be used to pay for part of a major family outing—a vacation, perhaps. The lesson here is that everyone has to pay taxes, and these taxes are used to benefit society as a whole—just as the "family tax" benefits the family as a whole.

21

Planning Early to Meet the High Costs of Higher Education

ollege costs have been increasing at a much higher rate than inflation, and that's not likely to change. Unfortunately, the costs of college look so staggering that many parents are discouraged from taking the first step toward meeting these costs. In this chapter, you will first learn the brutal truth about expected future college costs and, to make matters worse, how little financial aid you're likely to qualify for. Then, on a more upbeat note, I will describe a variety of good and not-so-good college-fund investment alternatives, including a reasonable strategy for investing college-earmarked money based upon the age of your young scholar-to-be.

Chapter 22 will help bring you up to speed on the college financial aid process. It should be of interest to parents of all college-bound children, particularly those whose children are within a few years of enrolling.

How Much Will College Cost?

ost experts, including the universities themselves, estimate that the tuition costs will increase at an annual rate of six to seven percent—well above the expected rate of inflation. If inflation heats up again, college costs will escalate even more.

The following table projects current average four-year education costs, assuming a six percent annual increase in costs. These figures do *not* include the students' out-of-pocket costs for such necessities as books and supplies, transportation, and entertainment. These "extras" could easily add many thousands of dollars to the four-year college tab.

How, you and millions of other parents ask, will you ever be able to afford to send your children to college? Unfortunately, many parents give up at the outset, simply believing that it's impossible. Others begin a savings program designed to accumulate 100 per-

Smart Money Move

Don't let the high cost of college discourage you from saving to meet those costs. The important thing is to start saving for college now, even if you can only put aside small amounts.

AVERAGE FOUR-YEAR EDUCATION COSTS

YEAR ENTERING	PUBLIC SCHOOL	PRIVATE SCHOOL	SELECTIVE PRIVATE SCHOOL
1993	$ 27,422	$ 69,780	$ 98,528
1994	29,067	73,967	104,440
1995	30,811	78,405	110,706
1996	32,660	83,110	117,348
1997	34,620	88,096	124,389
1998	36,697	93,382	131,853
1999	38,899	98,985	139,764
2000	41,232	104,923	148,150
2001	43,706	111,219	157,039
2002	46,329	117,893	166,461
2003	49,109	124,966	176,449
2004	52,055	132,464	187,036
2005	55,178	140,412	198,258
2006	58,489	148,837	210,153
2007	61,998	157,767	222,762
2008	65,718	167,233	236,127
2009	69,661	177,267	250,295
2010	73,841	187,903	265,313
2011	78,271	199,177	281,232
2012	82,967	211,127	298,106

cent of the child's college costs, only to abandon the savings program in a few months because they can't afford it. So part of the process of planning early to meet the high costs of higher education is to devise a realistic program that will help you over the college-cost hurdle. The key, initially, is to *do something*.

Sources of Money for College

There are a variety of sources of funds for college.

Parents' Income

A good-size portion of your income while your child is in college will probably go toward helping meet college expenses. While you may have little money to spend now, chances are that you'll have more discretionary income later on when your child is in college.

Student Jobs

There is no reason not to expect your child to work during the academic year, and/or during vacations to help meet college expenses.

Gifts and Inheritances

Grandparents may be a source of help in meeting college expenses if they can comfortably afford it. Many elderly people have a strong desire to see that money passed on after their death be used to help educate the grandchildren or great-grandchildren.

Loans

Student and personal loans are a common way to bridge the gap between money needed for college and money available for college.

Financial Aid

Financial aid is available only to the neediest families. This means that you can probably expect to qualify for little or no financial aid, even though it will be a struggle to get your child through college. (To get an idea of what financial aid you might qualify for, if any, see the table on page 170–71).

Savings and Investments

Unless you are very poor or are wealthy enough to pay for college out of your current income, you will have to use personal savings to fund your children's education. Otherwise, you will end up accumulating astronomical debts. Read on to learn of the various investment alternatives for college-earmarked money.

Save What You Can

Don't set your sights too high when planning to save for college. Always remember that:

- **ANY AMOUNT OF SAVINGS IS BETTER THAN NONE.** Set a reasonable target savings level, then try to stick to it. Perhaps your goal should be to save 30 percent or half of expected college costs. That's certainly a lot better than doing nothing. Don't fall into the trap of setting up an overly ambitious savings program. It will probably be easier for you to save money a few years from now, when your income is up and your living expenses are under control. But by all means begin a modest savings program now.

● **KEEP IT SIMPLE.** Most savings or investment accounts will help the money grow over the years, but some investments are better than others, as shown in the next section. Don't fall for the elaborate college-savings strategies that are so heavily promoted in advertisements and by commissioned salespeople. You'll be better off keeping it simple.

College Investment Alternatives

I don't know how many times I've heard it said that *saving* for your children's college costs is critical. But in most cases, such advice goes only halfway. In fact, those savings need to be *invested* appropriately in order to keep up with the ever-rising costs of college. Simply putting the money into a savings or money market account is really doing a disservice to your hard-earned money. What follows is a summary of some good and not-so-good places to invest college funds.

Everyday Investments

Investing for college, particularly when your child is young and you have a relatively long time during which to invest, is not unlike investing for any other worthwhile purpose. My three favorites are the following:

Smart Money Move

Invest your college savings in stock mutual funds, bonds, and U.S. savings bonds. Avoid investments that are too conservative or too risky.

Stock Mutual Funds

You may think that putting college funds in stocks is too risky, but if you're ten years or more from writing out those tuition checks, stock mutual funds are a good place for a good portion of your college investments. Rather than buy individual stocks and lose sleep over them, the stock mutual fund is the route to take (see Chapter 59).

Bonds

Buying bonds whose maturity is tied to the years when you will be paying tuition may provide you with attractive returns. By timing the maturities to coincide with the years your child will be in college, you eliminate the potential loss of principal that can happen if you sell a bond before maturity, after interest rates have risen.

What kinds of bonds should you buy? They run the gamut from ultrasafe U.S. Treasury bonds to municipal bonds to corporate bonds. Part of the decision will hinge upon your federal and state tax situation and whether the bonds are in your name or your child's name. Incidentally, you'll hear a lot of talk about investing in zero-coupon Treasury bonds (see page 474) for college-savings funds. They aren't a bad investment, and you can time the maturity to coincide with college, just as you can with straight bonds.

The problem is that zero-coupon Treasury bonds require the payment of taxes on the imputed interest. So you will end up paying taxes on money you haven't received. If this is okay with you, they are a nice, worry-free investment. Alternatively, you may be able to find some zero-coupon municipal bonds whose imputed interest is not taxable because it is a tax-free investment in the first place (see Chapter 57).

Series EE Bonds

Don't turn up your nose at old-fashioned U.S. savings bonds. While the returns aren't spectacular, the tax-deferred buildup feature and state tax exemption make Series EE bonds an excellent and safe place to put some of the money that's headed for college. An added benefit for bonds bought any time after 1989—so long as they're not carried in your child's name—is that if you redeem the saving bonds to cover college fees and tuition and you meet an income test (which rises each year with inflation), the interest on these bonds is tax-free. But be careful—the interest on these bonds when you cash them in is added to your income in order to determine whether your income level qualifies for tax exemption (see page 482).

In summary, you can't go wrong with a combination of stock mutual funds, U.S. savings bonds, and, when you have enough money to buy individual issues, bonds. Now, on to a few unique investments designed specifically for college savers.

Special College-Savings Investment Plans

These much-ballyhooed investments offer, in my opinion, less than meets the eye, although they may be useful for some college savers.

Prepaid tuition plans

A variety of states, colleges, groups of colleges, and banks offer prepaid tuition plans. Basically, you invest a certain amount of money, and the sum you invest is guaranteed to meet the future tuition costs. My advice: You could probably do better with the above-mentioned old-fashioned investments. Also, the state and college plans usually limit your child's choice of colleges to those in the state or to the specific college that offers the plan. Perhaps I'm an idealist, but I'd rather let my child choose the college he or she wants to attend.

Bank-prepaid tuition plans, originated by the College Savings Bank in Princeton, New Jersey, provide a variable CD rate pegged to somewhat less than the annual rate of increase in college costs. Of course, the interest on the CD is taxable, and you can probably do just as well, if not better, with a Series EE savings bond whose interest rate varies with inflation and offers more tax advantages than the bank CD.

Baccalaureate or "college saver" bonds

These are municipal bonds, pure and simple, that are sold by some states as a college-savings vehicle. While the states may offer a variety of inducements to invest in them, the main advantage is tax-exempt interest. So before investing in a baccalaureate bond, compare it with other investment alternatives described here. These munis may or may not play a role in your college-savings arsenal. You can probably do better elsewhere.

Investments to avoid

Although you may be told differently, there are several investments that don't make as much sense for college-savings plans. Don't get me wrong, these are certainly better than nothing. But you can probably do better. Cash value life insurance, whether the policy insures you, your spouse, or worse, your child, won't deliver the kinds of returns you need to build up a sizable college nest egg, despite what the insurance company projections might tell you. Similarly, tax-deferred annuities are more a retirement-savings vehicle than a college-savings vehicle. Unless you're a pro, investment real estate doesn't provide enough investment security to make a good college-savings vehicle. And limited partnerships—forget them!

Savings and Investment Strategies

While there are many good investments that you can make, your investment strategy will be influenced by the age of the college-bound child. The reason for this is that the nearer the child is to entering college, the less risk you can afford to take with funds earmarked for college costs. There aren't many times in our lives when we should invest for the short term, but one of those times is when a child nears college age. Timing is an important element to any investment plan. The best time to invest for a child's future education is probably before he or she is born. More realistically, however, the best time is as soon as you can.

Smart Money Move

Adjust your college savings investment strategy as your child nears college age.

Preteens

If your child is under thirteen, you should be investing for the long term. Therefore, stock mutual funds should play an important role in your college savings plan. Why? Stocks have proven, time and again, to provide better returns than bonds or short-term interest-earning investments like money-market accounts if held long enough. How much of a younger child's college fund should be in stocks? Probably about half, with the other half in various kinds of bonds, including U.S. savings bonds, whose maturity will be timed to coincide with the college years.

Teenagers

As if having a teenager weren't difficult enough already, you're also going to need to spend some time worrying about his or her college funds. The trick here is to gradually shift your money out of stocks into more conservative interest-earning securities. With college just a few years off, it's time to become a short-term investor. You can't afford the risk of having too much money invested in stocks.

Be careful if you have been investing regularly in U.S. savings bonds—you have to hold them at least five years in order to pick up the full interest rate. Also be careful not to invest overly conservatively on behalf of your soon-to-be collegian. Rather than money-market accounts and savings accounts, consider short-term bonds or CDs to pick up a bit more yield.

Who Should Be the Owner of the College Fund?

Should you keep the college savings fund in your name or your child's name? Far too many parents transfer a lot of money to their children. But this can backfire in more ways than one. The financial-aid gods require that most of the investments owned by the student be used to meet college expenses (roughly 35 percent per year), whereas, had the money been in the parents' name, a much lower percentage of these same investments would be required to fund the college education. *Many* parents have made this mistake (often at the suggestion of their financial advisers). Also, if you put pencil to paper, you'll find that investing in your child's name really doesn't save a lot in income taxes.

Once children reach the age of eighteen they can't legally be stopped from using the money any way they want. Imagine this scenario: In lieu of going to college, your daughter joins a cult and falls in love with the chief guru. His highness urges your daughter to "release" herself from all worldly goods (so that he can buy another Rolls-Royce, of course). This has happened!

Smart Money Move

Don't put a substantial amount of college money in your child's name. This strategy has limited tax benefits and could end up backfiring.

FOR FURTHER INFORMATION

U.S. Savings Bonds: Now Tax-Free for Education
Publication 449-Y
Cost: $0.50

Consumer Information Center
Attention: R. Woods
Pueblo CO 81009

HIGHER EDUCATION COST CHECKLIST

■ □ ■

Set reasonable college-savings goals so that you can begin a college-savings program as soon as possible.

■ □ ■

Invest college-earmarked funds for a younger child in stock mutual funds, bonds, and U.S. savings bonds. These should do better than alternative investments such as prepaid tuition plans, baccalaureate bonds, and cash value life insurance.

■ □ ■

Change your college savings investment strategy for a teenage child to account for a shorter investment period.

■ □ ■

Don't put college money in your child's name until you understand the risks of doing so.

Getting the Most Out of College Financial Aid

eeting the cost of a college education is a struggle for all but the most affluent families. You and your college-bound children need to learn about the many ways to finance a college education and become acquainted with the financial aid process.

The Financial Aid System: Determining the Need

The amount of financial aid a student receives is determined by what is called the financial need of the family. Need is calculated through a process known as *needs analysis*. Through a complicated formula, assets are evaluated and reasonable family contribution is determined. This amount is subtracted from the total cost. The college usually appoints one of two agencies, either the College Scholarship Service (CSS) or the American College Testing program (ACT), to conduct this analysis. The table on page 170 shows, according to family assets and pretax income, approximately how much a family will be expected to pay toward a child's college education.

FAF

Along with its application materials, the college sends the family a computerized form called a financial aid form (FAF). This form must be filled out immediately and returned to the above agencies so that they can perform their needs analysis.

Needs Analysis

After the agency completes the needs analysis, it sends the information to the selected colleges. Information is also sent to the government-based Pell grant to determine eligibility. The analysis assigns an "aid index" to the student and notifies the student if he or she may be eligible for a grant. Once the college receives the information, it conducts its own needs analysis. Finally, when the student receives notification of acceptance by the college, he or she should receive notice of the amount and type of aid being awarded.

State Aid

State aid corporations may also require information from the CSS or the ACT. Most states have an agency that assists in giving student aid. The student should find out the name and address of the state agency (a guidance counselor will be of help here) and what family financial information the state needs. State student aid, at its best, covers only a small amount of total college costs.

Initiating the Needs Analysis Process

When your child begins applying to schools, he or she should receive financial aid forms along with the application materials. Deadlines for these forms are *very, very* important to meet and should be noted as soon as they are received. Failure to file on time will always result in a delay of processing and decreases the chances of receiving aid.

Application questions are based on income tax returns, so you should make every attempt to complete your taxes as early as possible. Estimates can still be made if tax returns are not complete, but it is important to be as accurate as possible. Any errors will have to be corrected later and will delay the process and jeopardize the student's chances for aid.

Fortunately, financial aid materials are generally accompanied by explicit directions, so there should be no problem understanding what information is needed—and no excuse for missing deadlines.

The Bad News

The bad news is that the calculated "need" only accounts for about 70 percent of the actual need. You'll still probably need thousands—yes, thousands—of dollars each year to land your child a diploma. Additional funds are almost always necessary even if your son or daughter has selected a public college. Why? The average cost of a four-year public college is nearing $30,000, and a selective private college can cost you nearly $100,000 for the same four-year period. Even with maximum financial aid, you could still have to shell out $3,000 (public college) to $9,000 (private college) *per year* to cover the many expenses that financial aid doesn't. Count on thousands of additional dollars being spent, per year, on travel expenses, room, board, textbooks, and other sundry and related items.

Smart Money Move

File your financial aid forms accurately and on time.

Safety Net

Fortunately, there's a safety net of sorts: Colleges often find a way to help your child supplement his or her aid package with work-study and other programs. And, of course, loans are available to bridge the gap between needs and resources.

What You Can Expect to Pay

Just how much you should expect to pay for your child's college costs will depend on the cost of their college—tuition, room and board—as well as their particular financial aid package. You can estimate how much you will be asked to contribute toward college expenses by using the following expected parental contribution table and worksheet.

Government Aid

What You See Isn't Always What You Get

There are numerous sources of federal, state, private, and personal loans that you can combine to fund your child's college tuition—but you may only qualify for some of them. The following sections detail leading loan options. The facts and figures for Government AID are based on loans taken out on or after 7/1/93. You can easily bring yourself up-to-date on current changes in available financial aid by contacting the financial aid office at the college or university.

Federal Pell Grants

These are outright "gifts" from the federal government of up to $2,400. You apply simply by checking the appropriate box on the family financial statement or the financial aid form. Between four and six weeks after the information is sent in, your child receives a student aid report, assigning him or her an aid index that determines whether he or she is eligible. An index lower than 1700 usually qualifies the child for a grant. The form comes in three parts, and whether or not your child is eligible, all three parts must be sent to the school that he or she will be attending.

Federal Stafford Loans (Guaranteed Student Loans)

Commonly known as GSLs but now officially known as subsidized Federal Stafford loans, these are the most common and equitable way to help finance a college education today. Your child may take out a Stafford loan at an interest rate of eight percent. The rate for the first loan taken out will remain the same for all subsequent loans. Your child may take out up to $2,625 in the first year, $3,500 for the second year of his or her undergraduate study, and up to $5,500 per year for the remaining two to three years that it takes to graduate. The total loan limit for an undergraduate is $23,000. Graduate students may borrow up to $8,500 per year of graduate study, amounting to not more than $65,500, including the undergraduate loans. Yearly loans cannot exceed tuition amounts.

The loan rate for *subsidized* Federal Stafford loans, for loans received on or after 7/1/93, is a variable rate based on the 91-day Treasury bill as of July 1 of each year, plus 3.1 percent. The rate is capped at nine percent.

The government subsidizes the loan until six months after graduation. At this point, the

APPROXIMATE EXPECTED PARENTAL CONTRIBUTION FOR THE ACADEMIC YEAR 1993-94

A Worksheet for Parents to Estimate How Much They Will Be Asked to Contribute Toward College Expenses

The following chart shows the approximate yearly amounts the standard financial need analysis system expected parents to pay for college in 1991-1992.

1. PARENTS' TOTAL 1990 INCOME BEFORE TAXES

A. Adjusted gross income (equivalent to tax return entry)

———— A

B. Add nontaxable income (Social Security benefits, child support, welfare, etc.)

———— B

Total Income:

A + B = ———— (1)

2. PARENTS' TOTAL ASSETS

C. Home residence and other real estate equity (estimated value less unpaid balance on mortgage)

———— C

D. Total of cash, savings, checking accounts, stocks, bonds, mutual funds, etc.

———— D

Total Assets:

C + D = ———— (2)

3. FAMILY SIZE (include student, parents, other dependent children, and other dependents)

———— (3)

4. EXPECTED PARENTAL CONTRIBUTION
Find the figures on the chart that correspond to your figure on lines 1, 2, and 3 to determine your approximate expected parental contribution for one child in college in 1991-92, and place the results here.

———— (4)

ASSETS / FAMILY SIZE	INCOME BEFORE TAXES							
	$ 5,000	10,000	15,000	20,000	25,000	30,000	35,000	40,000
$ 10,000								
3	$ 0	0	0	600	1,400	2,100	3,000	4,200
4	0	0	0	0	800	1,500	2,300	3,300
5	0	0	0	0	200	1,000	1,700	2,500
6	0	0	0	0	0	300	1,100	1,800
$ 20,000								
3	$ 0	0	0	600	1,400	2,100	3,000	4,200
4	0	0	0	0	800	1,500	2,300	3,300
5	0	0	0	0	200	1,000	1,700	2,500
6	0	0	0	0	0	300	1,100	1,800
$ 30,000								
3	$ 0	0	0	600	1,400	2,100	3,000	4,200
4	0	0	0	0	800	1,500	2,300	3,300
5	0	0	0	0	200	1,000	1,700	2,500
6	0	0	0	0	0	300	1,100	1,800
$ 40,000								
3	$ 0	0	0	700	1,400	2,200	3,200	4,300
4	0	0	0	100	800	1,600	2,400	3,400
5	0	0	0	0	300	1,000	1,800	2,600
6	0	0	0	0	0	400	1,200	1,900
$ 50,000								
3	$ 0	0	200	900	1,700	2,500	3,500	4,700
4	0	0	0	300	1,100	1,900	2,700	3,800
5	0	0	0	0	500	1,300	2,100	3,000
6	0	0	0	0	0	700	1,400	2,200
$ 60,000								
3	$ 0	0	500	1,200	2,000	2,900	3,900	5,300
4	0	0	0	600	1,400	2,100	3,100	4,100
5	0	0	0	0	800	1,600	2,400	3,300
6	0	0	0	0	200	900	1,700	2,500
$ 80,000								
3	$ 0	100	1,000	1,700	2,600	3,600	4,800	6,400
4	0	0	400	1,100	1,900	2,800	3,800	5,200
5	0	0	0	600	1,300	2,100	3,000	4,100
6	0	0	0	0	700	1,500	2,200	3,200
$100,000								
3	$ 0	600	1,500	2,300	3,200	4,400	5,900	7,600
4	0	0	900	1,700	2,500	3,500	4,700	6,300
5	0	0	300	1,100	1,900	2,700	3,800	5,000
6	0	0	0	500	1,200	2,000	2,900	4,000
$120,000								
3	$ 200	1,200	2,000	2,900	4,000	5,400	7,100	8,700
4	0	500	1,400	2,200	3,100	4,200	5,800	7,400
5	0	0	800	1,600	2,400	3,400	4,600	6,200
6	0	0	100	1,000	1,800	2,600	3,600	4,800
$140,000								
3	$ 800	1,700	2,600	3,700	4,900	6,600	8,200	9,800
4	100	1,000	2,000	2,800	3,900	5,300	6,900	8,500
5	0	400	1,300	2,200	3,100	4,200	5,700	7,300
6	0	0	600	1,500	2,300	3,300	4,400	6,000

»

INCOME BEFORE TAXES								ASSETS	FAMILY SIZE
$ 45,000	50,000	55,000	60,000	70,000	80,000	90,000	100,000		
								$ 10,000	
$ 5,600	7,200	8,500	10,000	12,900	15,800	18,800	21,700		3
4,400	6,000	7,400	8,800	11,800	14,700	17,600	20,600		4
3,600	4,700	6,300	7,800	10,700	13,600	16,600	19,500		5
2,700	3,700	5,000	6,500	9,500	12,400	15,300	18,300		6
								$ 20,000	
$ 5,600	7,200	8,500	10,000	12,900	15,800	18,800	21,700		3
4,400	6,000	7,400	8,800	11,800	14,700	17,600	20,600		4
3,600	4,700	6,300	7,800	10,700	13,600	16,600	19,500		5
2,700	3,700	5,000	6,500	9,500	12,400	15,300	18,300		6
								$ 30,000	
$ 5,600	7,200	8,500	10,000	13,900	15,800	18,800	21,700		3
4,400	6,000	7,400	8,800	11,800	14,700	17,600	20,600		4
3,600	4,700	6,300	7,800	10,700	13,600	16,600	19,500		5
2,700	3,700	5,000	6,500	9,500	12,400	15,300	18,300		6
								$ 40,000	
$ 5,800	7,400	8,700	10,200	13,100	16,000	19,000	21,900		3
4,500	6,200	7,600	9,000	11,900	14,900	17,800	20,800		4
3,700	4,900	6,500	7,900	10,900	13,800	16,800	19,700		5
2,800	3,900	5,200	6,700	9,700	12,600	15,500	18,500		6
								$ 50,000	
$ 6,400	7,900	9,300	10,700	13,700	16,600	19,500	22,500		3
5,000	6,700	8,100	9,600	12,500	15,500	18,400	21,300		4
4,100	5,500	7,100	8,500	11,400	14,400	17,300	20,300		5
3,100	4,200	5,800	7,300	10,200	13,200	16,100	19,000		6
								$ 60,000	
$ 7,000	8,500	9,800	11,300	14,200	17,200	20,100	23,000		3
5,700	7,300	8,700	10,100	13,000	16,000	19,000	21,900		4
4,500	6,100	7,600	9,100	12,000	14,900	17,900	20,800		5
3,500	4,700	6,400	7,900	10,800	13,700	16,700	19,600		6
								$ 80,000	
$ 8,100	9,600	11,000	12,400	15,300	18,300	21,200	24,200		3
6,800	8,400	9,800	11,300	14,200	17,100	20,100	23,000		4
5,600	7,200	8,700	10,200	13,100	16,100	19,000	22,000		5
4,300	5,900	7,500	9,000	11,900	14,900	17,800	20,700		6
								$100,000	
$ 9,200	10,800	12,100	13,500	16,500	19,400	22,400	25,300		3
7,900	9,600	10,900	12,400	15,300	18,300	21,200	24,200		4
6,700	8,300	9,900	11,300	14,300	17,200	20,100	23,100		5
5,400	7,000	8,600	10,100	13,000	16,000	18,900	21,900		6
								$120,000	
$ 10,300	11,900	13,200	14,700	17,600	20,500	23,500	26,400		3
9,000	10,700	12,000	13,500	16,500	19,400	22,300	25,300		4
7,800	9,500	11,000	12,500	15,400	18,300	21,300	24,200		5
6,500	8,100	9,700	11,200	14,200	17,100	20,100	23,000		6
								$140,000	
$ 11,500	13,000	14,300	15,800	18,700	21,700	24,600	27,500		3
10,200	11,800	13,200	14,600	17,600	20,500	23,500	26,400		4
9,000	10,600	12,100	13,600	16,500	19,500	22,400	25,300		5
7,600	9,200	10,900	13,400	15,300	18,200	21,300	24,100		6

Source: Peterson's College Money Handbook 1992

5. ADJUSTED EXPECTED PARENTAL CONTRIBUTION

If there were two or more family members in college attending half-time or more in 1991-92, divide the contribution in (4) by the number in college, and place the result here.

——— (5)

Note: The expected parental contribution that you determined with the help of this chart is intended to give you a rough idea of how need analysis works. While the figure should be useful as you make financial plans for college, you should realize that your family's financial situation is likely to be more complicated than the simple model used here. For example, the table is based on the assumptions that there are two parents (of whom only one works), state and local taxes average 8 percent of income, standard deductions apply, and there are no unusual expenses. Factors such as high medical expenses, two working parents, private secondary-school tuition payments, business ownership, and special family circumstances may all affect the eventual calculation of the expected parental contribution by the financial aid office at the colleges you apply to. Also, consistent with the recent change to the federal student aid law, the value of the home or farm has been removed from the calculation. It is possible that some colleges will continue to collect this information and use it to raise the expected parental contribution. A more detailed analysis is available as part of Peterson's Financial Aid Service.

student must start paying it back monthly and is allowed ten years to repay. It is up to you and your child to find a lender that offers a Stafford loan and that is approved by the government. The school or the state loan guarantee agency can supply a list of lenders close by. You can also call the United Student Aid Fund Agency's toll-free number: 800-428-9250.

Take note: The check received will be somewhat less than the amount actually borrowed—there is a five percent origination fee. In addition, the guarantee agency in the state may charge an insurance premium.

There is also an *unsubsidized* Federal Stafford loan which has, for the most part, the same terms and conditions as the subsidized Federal Stafford loans. This loan is open to all students who do not qualify for the subsidized Stafford, or who only qualify for a partial subsidized Stafford. There are exceptions: The borrower must begin making interest payments from the time he or she receives the loan. Unsubsidized Federal Stafford borrowers will also have to pay a combined 6.5 percent origination fee/insurance premium—compared to the five percent origination fee or a subsidized Stafford.

Federal PLUS Loans

Federal Parent Loans for Undergraduate Students (PLUS) enable graduate students and the parents of undergraduates to borrow up to the annual cost of education minus any financial aid the student receives. The parents may receive this money in addition to the amount their child receives through a Stafford loan. Graduate students may borrow it in addition to their $65,500 maximum outstanding Stafford debt.

All PLUS loans carry an interest rate of 3.10 percent over the rate for one-year Treasury bills, with a 10 percent cap. There's a catch: Parents must start paying back the loan within sixty days. Graduate and independent undergraduate students can defer the principal until they leave school, but *interest* payments start within sixty days. Application is made in the same manner as for the Stafford loan, but *no* needs test is required, although parents may have to undergo a credit check.

Campus-Based Federal Aid

Federal aid is available not only directly from the government but through the college of your son or daughter's choice. The government gives the college a specific amount of money to distribute to the college-designated recipients. This money is in the form of grants, loans, and subsidized jobs. A qualified student can participate in more than one program at a time for the purpose of meeting need that has not already been met.

Federal SEOG Grants

Supplemental Education Opportunity Grants (SEOG) are for undergraduates only and range up to several thousand dollars. The difference between Pell grants and SEOGs is that the government guarantees that a school will get enough money for all its Pell grant awards, whereas it gets only a fixed amount for SEOGs. Thus, SEOGs are awarded on a first-come, first-served basis—another reason why it is important to send in your application materials on time. The school will notify your child if he or she is going to receive a SEOG and will either pay the student directly or credit his or her account. *Note:* Part-time students may also be eligible for this grant and should check with the school.

Federal Perkins or NDSL Loans

National Direct Student Loans (NDSLs), or Federal Perkins loans as they are now called, are special education-assistance loans offered at below bank loan interest rates. An undergraduate may borrow a yearly sum with a cumulative maximum for the first four years. Graduate students can receive additional money on top of money they borrowed as undergraduates. Payments begin six months after graduation or after the student drops below half-time status, and the loan must be paid back within ten years. Students may defer payments by joining the Peace Corps, enlisting in the military, or teaching in an inner-city public school. The college's financial aid office is in charge of the program for that school.

Federal College Work Study

In college work study (CWS) programs your child finds a job with an approved employer, such as a nonprofit organization or a professor, either on or off campus. The government subsidizes a certain percentage of the payback, usually about two-thirds. By taking a CWS job, your son or daughter can become an attractive candidate for employment and thereby have an edge in getting a future job while, at the same time, helping share the cost of their current education. Wage rates vary but are at least the federal minimum, although the student is given a wage ceiling and may not earn more than that.

Military Aid

That's right. The Army, Navy, Air Force, and Marine Reserve Officers Training Corps want *you*—your child, actually. The military offers scholarships that pay all tuition, fees, and books and that provide a tax-free stipend per month to be used at the participating school. The student in turn incurs a long service obligation—six years, four of them on active duty. The school must have a base on campus in order to offer this scholarship, and the student must report to an ROTC class weekly while enrolled in school. To learn more about how ROTC can help put your child through college, contact your local Army, Navy, Air Force or Marines recruiting center. The recruiting center, which is listed in your local white pages, can put you in touch with the nearest ROTC office.

The National Guard also offers substantial tuition help after a two-year enlistment. Veterans' benefits may also be applied toward a college education if the student is a veteran or is the spouse or child of a deceased or disabled veteran.

College Aid

College aid is direct aid from the college of your choice. Each school has its own way of packaging aid and provides its students with information on the available options. Installment plans, loans, merit scholarships, athletic scholarships, and discounts for more than one family member attending the university are all possible forms of aid. Many of the most competitive schools, including the Ivy League colleges, offer financial aid strictly on the basis of need. You may find that some of the more expensive colleges are better sources of financial aid. Many colleges offer scholarships on a nonneed basis, such as for academic, athletic, or other talent. But schools that give scholarships to attract better students may not continue the scholarships after the freshman year. Always know the conditions and length of your award.

Tuition Payment Options

Many schools offer a variety of methods of payment in order to make the expense as painless as possible. Explore the available options. Many plans are unique to particular schools, and information is available for the asking.

Tuition prepayment

One option that is becoming available at more and more universities is called the tuition prepayment option. When the student enters, the entire four years are paid all at once at the price of the freshman year. The idea is to hedge against future increases in tuition, which has been increasing at a higher rate than inflation and is expected to continue to do so. The savings from such a plan can be in the thousands of dollars, but it is useful only to families that have sufficient capital to make the prepayment. For parents who don't have a pile of cash, some schools have a loan plan to spread out the cost at a nominal interest rate.

Another common type of payment option is the monthly payment plan, which allows the semester bill to be paid in monthly installments rather than all at once. This may be convenient for families that are paying a lot of the tuition bill out of their paychecks.

Private Aid

Scholarships that come from sources other than the school or the government are sometimes based on merit and are sometimes available through affiliation, such as your employer, the Rotary Club, or other community organization or church. Finding out about such aid takes initiative, but the rewards can be worth it. A good place to start looking is a school guidance counselor's office or your local library. And since the process may be overwhelming for your child, it is a good way to share with him or her the hard work involved in making his or her dreams come true.

Organizing Your Approach to Financing College Costs

More often than not, parents delay planning for their child's education and are left with little time to organize the financing. Sometimes, however, even after maintaining a responsible and far-sighted savings program, parents still find that the cost of college far exceeds the amount saved. Both situations necessitate a methodical examination of financing alternatives, including the following steps.

- **ASSESS** all family resources available for funding college costs. These resources may include equity that has accumulated in the family home, gifts from grandparents, and inheritances.

- **EXHAUSTIVELY REVIEW** all sources of possible scholarships. A multitude of scholarship opportunities exist. Scholarships for academic, athletic, and leadership achievement are very common. Parents and students should also consider any military, company, union, trade, civic, religious, or ethnic affiliations they have that could lead to sources of funds.

- **INVESTIGATE** available loan and grant opportunities. Not all loans are created equal. Students displaying appropriate financial need may qualify for other federally sponsored low-interest loans aside from Stafford loans (formerly GSLs). Programs such as the Pell grant, college work study, and Perkins loan (formerly NDSL) provide funds for the neediest candidates in the form of outright grants or very-low-interest loans. In addition, many states offer their own educational-assistance programs. Finally, institutions themselves offer loans on favorable terms, although resources are usually limited. Candidates should apply for such loans as early as possible in order to be considered while funds last.

  The PLUS program can provide another source of funds. These loans are incurred by the parents of a student. While their interest rates are relatively low compared with those of commercial loans, they usually run about 4 percent above those of Stafford loans. Also, repayment of the loan begins two months after it has been granted. Therefore, parents should assume a PLUS loan only if they do not qualify for a Stafford loan.

Reducing College Costs

The Family Contribution

Since a student's need, and therefore eligibility for aid, is directly determined by the family's expected ability to pay (family contribution), you should investigate ways in which institutions' estimates of this figure can be reduced.

- **AVOID** overstating the value of family assets. When completing the section of a financial aid application concerning the family's assets, don't overestimate, particularly when it comes to the value of your home.

- **DON'T TRANSFER** assets to your college-bound children. If there is any possibility that you might qualify for financial aid, you should generally not transfer any assets to your children. Such a transfer might result in lower taxes, since the parents are usually in a higher tax bracket. But the transfer could backfire because colleges and universities require a much higher percentage of assets in the student's name to be used to meet college expenses than they do assets in the parent's name.

- **IF POSSIBLE,** have your child declare him- or herself financially independent. If your college-bound child can declare him- or herself financially independent, he or she should do so. Why? The federal government, state governments, and educational institutions can't consider the parents' income and assets if a student is independent. The income and assets of the student are normally more limited if he is independent, and this usually results in a larger aid package. But tests to establish independence vary from state to state and from institution to institution, and federal criteria for establishing independence may be more or less strict than those of the student's state and college.

The Aid Package

Students should attempt to obtain packages that consist of few loans and many grants and work-study awards. Since much student aid is distributed on a first-come, first-served basis, students must be prompt in applying to college and financial aid programs. Don't be afraid to appeal the college's financial aid "offer." They may up the ante. Obtaining outside sources of funding through scholarships is also an ideal way to reduce a student's loan obligation.

Smart Money Move

Appeal the college's financial aid offer, particularly if it's your child's first choice college. They may be able to provide additional aid.

Miscellaneous Costs

Neither you nor your child should ever sacrifice quality of education for a few dollars' savings that can be repaid in the future once a fine education is in hand. But frugal living while in school is one way that a student may significantly reduce the amount of money, and therefore the amount of aid, needed. A few ways to minimize expenditures are:

Books

Although it's easier to go to the campus bookstore and buy new books and textbooks, shopping for used books from fellow students, from on-campus stores, or from off-campus bookstores can result in substantial savings.

Room and board

Many colleges provide a choice between on- or off-campus housing. Although it's often more convenient to live on campus, a student may find room and board cheaper off campus. Investigate whether living on or off campus is more economical.

Insurance

Often your medical insurance policies will cover your child through college until graduation. Therefore, don't pay for a college-sponsored program *if*, in fact, your child is already insured.

FOR FURTHER INFORMATION

The Student Guide: Five Federal Financial Aid Programs, Publication 522Y (Free)
This guide describes all federal sources of financial aid in great detail and lists sources for information on state aid for every state.
Consumer Information Center
Dept. 522Y
Pueblo, CO 81009
(719) 948-3334

Applying for Financial Aid (free)
American College Testing Program
P.O. Box 168
Iowa City, IA 52243
(319) 337-1040

The College Cost Book, Item #004329 ($15.00 plus $2.95 shipping and handling.) This reference book is available in most libraries and high school guidance counselors' offices.
College Board Publications

Box 886
New York, NY 10110-0886
(800) 323-7155

Don't Miss Out
($6.00 plus shipping and handling)
This financial aid book is available in most libraries and high school guidance counselors' offices.

The A's and B's of Academic Scholarships
($6.00 plus shipping and handling)

Earn and Learn
($4.00 plus shipping and handling)
This publication lists co-operative jobs offered by federal agencies.
Octomeron Associates
P.O. Box 2748
Alexandria, VA 22301
(703) 836-5480

Paying Less for College ($22.95)
This handbook gives financial informa-

»

---

tion on 1,700 colleges in the nation, including the average percentage of need met at each school.

Peterson's
Attention: Book Order Department
P.O. Box 2123
Princeton, NJ 08543
(800) 338-3282

A Selected List of Fellowship Opportunities and Aids To Advanced Education, NSF 88-119 (free)

Publication Office
National Science Foundation
1800 G Street, N.W.
Room 527
Washington, DC 20550
(202) 357-7861

The following nonprofit agencies administer a variety of student loan programs:

Student Loan Marketing Association
(Sallie Mae)
1050 Thomas Jefferson Street, N.W.

Washington, DC 20007
(800) 831-5626

New England Education Loan
Marketing Corporation (Nellie Mae)
50 Braintree Hill Park, Suite 300
Braintree, MA 02184
(800) 634-9308

The following private organizations can provide information on scholarships and grants:

National Scholarship Research Service
2280 Airport Boulevard
Santa Rosa, CA 95403
(707) 546-6781
(707) 545-5777
(24 Hour Message Center)

National College Services
600 South Frederick Avenue, 2nd floor
Gaithersburg, MD 20877
(301) 258-0717

Inventory of College Funding Sources

Grants, scholarships, and fellowships

Pell grant

Supplemental Education Opportunity grant

State financial assistance

☐ School financial assistance

☐ School scholarship/fellowship/private aid programs

☐ Military benefits or officer training program

☐ Social Security benefits

Education loans

☐ Perkins loan (formerly called National Direct Student Loan)

☐ Stafford loan (formerly Guaranteed Student Loan)

☐ Parent Loans for Undergraduate Students (PLUS loans)

☐ School loan programs

☐ State loan programs

☐ Private education loan programs

Personal loans

☐ Home equity loan

☐ Other secured financing

Unsecured loans

Personal resources

Income of parents

Income of student—school job

Income of student—summer job

Parents' savings/investments

Student's savings/investments

Gifts from relatives

College Students

I f you're like most college students, you don't think once about *saving* money while in school. And guess what—you're always strapped for cash. Of course, if you're like me when I was in your shoes, I had ready reasons to explain my constant need for more money. But today's students are faced with extremely high tuition bills and a steadily decreasing supply of financial aid. The result is that most or all of any job income is spent on tuition, room, board, books, and of course the occasional libation.

Yet the fact that you are cash-strapped shouldn't be confused with the notion that you're not involved in some very fancy financing. In fact, a combination of parents' money, grants, scholarships, fellowships, financial aid, and your own personal contributions (from work study, summer jobs, or off-campus work) creates the complex financial package needed to foot the overall expense of your higher education. Unfortunately, the twain seldom meet— and any leftover income is almost always viewed as spendable rather than savable.

Ways to Make and Save Money

Summer Jobs
Even if you don't work while in school, most college students work in the summer months: as lifeguards, camp counselors, landscape workers, carpenter's assistants, and retail salespersons—be it ice cream, clothing, or videos. I hope your parents insist that most of your summer earnings go toward the upcoming year's tuition. Save the remainder? Rarely. Invest it? Not a chance!

Become an Employee of the College
Would you like to reduce your tuition costs dramatically? If you work at a college or university, chances are your tuition will be reduced or, in some instances, waived. It's a good way to get a college eduction on the cheap.

Live in a Dorm
Unless you plan to share an apartment with a horde of other people, your most economical housing bet may well be a dormitory (it depends on the school). The desire to live off campus often clouds students' judgment. What initially appears to be cheaper than living in a dorm may end up costing a lot more.

Buy Used Textbooks

Textbooks are unbelievably expensive. Pretty soon, textbooks are going to cost more than tuition. But you can reduce the cost of owning textbooks. If the particular text or texts you need haven't been newly revised, there is no reason you can't buy used editions. Before you buy the texts from the school bookstore, where the used textbooks may have been given a stiff markup, try to buy them from a fellow student. If you eliminate the middleman—in this case, the school bookstore—you will come out ahead. Don't forget to sell them when you're finished with the course.

Part-Time Work

College towns usually offer a host of part-time employment opportunities, and you may be able to work in a college work-study program. If working won't interfere with your studies, a part-time job is a good way to take some of the financial heat off you and your parents. You might even make some contacts that will help you find a real job after you graduate.

Cost-Sharing

To avoid financial misunderstandings, you and your roommate(s) should agree on how to divvy up expenses like phone service at the beginning of the school year. Just as good fences supposedly make good neighbors, a fair cost-sharing arrangement should make for a more harmonious relationship with your roommates. You won't have to be so worried about getting "stuck" by your roommate(s).

Make Sure Your Personal Possessions Are Insured

Chances are that the valuables you have at school are covered under your parents' home-owner's or renter's insurance policy. Double-check that they are. If these items aren't covered, go to an insurance agent in your college's town and inquire about student policies. These policies are usually inexpensive, and it's probably worthwhile for you to purchase the coverage. Another thing to consider: If you have some particularly valuable items such as expensive jewelry, a stereo, or a computer, verify that the policy does indeed cover your high-ticket items.

Do You Really Need a Car at School?

Taking a car to school is a big expense. As difficult as it may be, try to envision getting by without a car. Sometimes having a car on campus is a necessity, but in many instances, students can get along quite well without one.

Carpool Home on Vacations or Weekends

If you are driving home on a vacation or weekend, take a bunch of your comrades with you and ask them to kick in some gas money. If you're heading home without a car, hitch a ride with another student. It will be cheaper than other modes of transportation.

Finally, Get Good Grades

Good grades can accomplish a lot. First, they will keep your parents off your back. Second, you may qualify for some merit-based scholarship or grant. Third, many automobile insurance companies offer a "good student discount" if you maintain a B average or better. Finally, good grades may help you land a job in a competitive job market.

THE HOW-TO-MAKE-ENDS-MEET CHECKLIST

This Financial Planning 101 checklist is designed to help you develop good spending habits and to balance your spending with your income. Knowing the amount of income that you can reasonably expect and what expenses you will have can go a long way to preventing complete financial chaos in the event of an unforeseen financial problem. This checklist will help you develop a financially feasible life-style.

PREPARE A REALISTIC BUDGET

You will find a student budget worksheet at the end of this chapter. It should help you gain an understanding of how budgets are generally set up. Use it as is, or adapt it to your own needs—whatever works best for you.

LEARN HOW TO MAKE A LUMP SUM LAST

Many college students earn the majority of their yearly pocket money during the summer months. Your allowance probably comes in lump sums, too. Budgeting is imperative for college students, since what you earn in the summer has to last you for nine months.

BE REALISTIC AND WISE ABOUT YOUR MONTHLY CASH FLOW

If you have a work-study job, or are working part time off campus, or if you are fortunate enough to have an allowance, you may be able to generate not only spending money but some saving and investing money, too. See if you can work out a budget that leaves you with something extra to save on a monthly basis.

If you really want to impress your parents and classmates, open up a mutual fund account. Some mutual funds have no minimum investment requirement, and investing in a stock mutual fund is a great way to introduce yourself to real-world finance. (See Chapter 59 for details on how to invest in mutual funds.)

MARK YOUR DUE DATES FOR LARGE PAYMENTS ON YOUR CALENDAR

That way you will see them coming well in advance. You will know when your semesters begin, for example, and you will know when substantial book costs will be due. Don't be caught short.

COMPARE YOUR ACTUAL WITH YOUR ESTIMATED EXPENDITURES

Periodically review and revise your budget. Simply compare your budget with what you actually earned and spent. In this way you will gradually develop two important habits: realistic budgeting and financial responsibility.

YOUR COLLEGE EXPENSE WORKSHEET

EXPENSE	FIRST SEMESTER BUDGET	FIRST SEMESTER ACTUAL	SECOND SEMESTER BUDGET	SECOND SEMESTER ACTUAL
TUITION	$	$..........	$..........	$..........
FEES	....	....	....	....
ROOM	....	....	....	....
MEALS	....	....	....	....
BOOKS	....	....	....	....
EQUIPMENT AND SUPPLIES	....	....	....	....
LAB FEES	....	....	....	....
TRAVEL TO AND FROM SCHOOL	....	....	....	....
ALL OTHER TRAVEL	....	....	....	....
RECREATION/ENTERTAINMENT	....	....	....	....
CLOTHING	....	....	....	....
LAUNDRY	....	....	....	....
FRATERNITY/SORORITY DUES	....	....	....	....
GROOMING (HAIRCUTS, ETC.)	....	....	....	....
HEALTH EXPENDITURES	....	....	....	....
PROPERTY AND AUTOMOBILE INSURANCE	....	....	....	....
SNACKS	....	....	....	....
CHURCH AND CHARITABLE CONTRIBUTIONS	....	....	....	....
MAJOR EXPENDITURES (E.G. CAR, BIKE, STEREO, GUITAR)	....	....	....	....
MISCELLANEOUS COSTS	....	....	....	....
TOTAL	$	$..........	$..........	$..........

Surviving a Divorce

Divorce is never pleasant, but if you have the right information, the split can at least be as amicable and fair as possible under difficult circumstances. While it's hard to separate the financial and emotional elements of divorce, the more both parties are able to view the financial settlement with cool heads, the better and fairer the final divorce agreement will be.

Current Attitudes toward Divorce

Attitudes toward divorce—and expectations of settlements—are important factors to consider. Currently, most divorces are negotiated without regard to "fault" or marital conduct. Property settlements are made on the grounds of fairness and need, without reference to moral judgments. The result is that the rationale behind property settlements is changing, which, in turn, means that the types of settlements negotiated are also changing.

Alimony

The original purpose of alimony was to enforce the husband's obligation to continue to support his wife, for whom employment opportunities were practically nonexistent. (Authorities have differed as to whether alimony was also intended to compensate the wife for her contribution to the marriage.) The awarding of alimony is within the discretion of the court at a divorce trial, and it is generally awarded only in situations where the divorced spouse cannot support him- or herself or where there are not presently sufficient marital assets to support both spouses.

Divorced spouses who are disabled or caring for dependents are often awarded some form of alimony, but this more and more often takes the form of temporary or rehabilitative support while the spouse acquires job skills. The court expects most divorced spouses who are of working age to find their way to gainful employment.

Distribution of Assets

Alimony is being increasingly replaced by distribution of marital assets. The most common form is called equitable distribution, although a few states use community property to determine division. Equitable distribution does not mean equal distribution. The determination of claim to ownership is made by a number of criteria.

Basically, community property attempts to divide all marital property between the divorcing spouses, whereas equitable distribution weighs each partner's contributions to the marriage, including nonfinancial considerations, to determine a fair claim.

Many divorce settlements achieve some balance between maintenance and asset division. A spouse who receives a large property settlement, even when he or she is over fifty and has never worked outside the house, can expect to have his or her alimony substantially decreased or eliminated from the settlement. In effect, property is traded for income.

Divorce Alternatives

I f you are going to divorce, you need to consider the cost of the divorce process itself. Some people do not realize the range of legal fees and related expenses, including such costly minutiae as fees to property appraisers and accountants that may be incurred during divorce proceedings. Depending on the location and size of the firm, legal fees generally range from $75 to $350 an hour. Such fees add up. In New York, for instance, the costs for one affluent party of a contested divorce can easily run to $100,000 or more! Indeed, if separating couples realized the true cost of a contested divorce, they might be more willing to sit down and attempt some sort of negotiated settlement on their own.

Before a final agreement is signed, each party should hire a lawyer who specializes in matrimonial law to review the proposed settlement. Moreover, if your attorney has little tax expertise, you are probably well advised to hire a separate lawyer or accountant to review the divorce's tax ramifications.

If, after considering the daunting costs, you and your spouse can agree to negotiate a less costly solution—both financially and emotionally—so much the better.

Although lawyers should be hired to review the final agreement, alternative professional help is available to mediate an agreeable settlement at a fraction of the legal eagles' cost.

Mediation

The most common alternative is a professional divorce mediator. While mediation is not recommended for hostile couples, it can help nonadversarial couples come to realistic and reasonable terms. Often, it helps both sides to understand and accept the finality of the divorce more easily than they might accept an extensively litigated decision imposed on them by the court. Mediation generally costs $70 to $100 an hour, and uncomplicated divorces can usually be resolved in less than twelve hours.

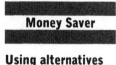

Money Saver

Using alternatives to an adversarial divorce can be a big money-saver.

Do-It-Yourself Divorce

Another alternative to litigation is doing it yourselves. Amenable couples with no dependent children can, in many states, negotiate their own settlement and file for divorce themselves. Remember, if you choose this route, consult with a lawyer before filing the final agreement so that nothing egregious will be overlooked.

Dividing Your Assets

While new divorce legislation strives to split property both fairly and finally, the final settlement that you reach with your spouse can vary depending on the state in which you live. As already mentioned, there are two main types of divorce codes that govern property division.

Community Property States

In these states, the court will try to divide marital assets in half. Unlike equitable distribution states, which weigh various factors in order to reach an equitable but not necessarily equal division of property, community property states occasionally still weigh marital conduct or fault in settling divorces.

Marital Property States

Marital property is defined as all assets acquired since the marriage that were not acquired as a gift from a third party, through an inheritance, or from personal injury. It doesn't matter which spouse originally purchased a certain property if the property is owned jointly.

Equitable Distribution States

Equitable distribution states view marriage as an economic and emotional partnership. They base their division on the couple's proportionate contributions to the partnership. Contribution to the marriage is weighed as consideration and may include in addition to financial contributions those made as a homemaker or parent in support of the other spouse's career potential.

Some of the criteria used by equitable distribution states to guide division are the length of the marriage; the age, health, and position in life of the parties; the occupations of the parties; the amount and sources of income; vocational skills; employability; the estate, liabilities and needs of each party; the opportunity of each to acquire further capital assets and income; the contribution of each party in acquiring and preserving marital property and assisting in its appreciation or dissipation; loss of inheritance or pension rights; and the possibility of property distribution in lieu of support.

Division of Property

Some property divisions cause specific problems, and some properties are not divisible. If an indivisible property, such as a car, goes to one spouse, the other is generally compensated elsewhere. Sometimes the property, such as a family home, will be sold, and the couple will divide the proceeds. Family businesses also present specific problems.

Update Insurance Coverage

The status of your insurance policies and future coverage will need to be addressed in your final divorce settlement. Notify your insurer of your change in marital status. Where appropriate, you should also transfer title and ownership of property, especially on vehicles and real estate.

Life Insurance

Without further spousal maintenance, you may wish to change the beneficiary designation on your existing insurance policies. In cases where life insurance replaces alimony for the recipient spouse after the payor's death, the recipient spouse should insist on a clause in the agreement giving her or him authority to obtain information periodically from the insurance company.

Health and Medical Insurance

Divorcing couples need to assure that they are adequately and continuously covered by health and medical insurance. The obligation to provide health insurance coverage is often included in the separation agreement. If one ex-spouse is fully insured under Social Security, the other is entitled to Medicare at age sixty-five as long as the ex-spouse is also age sixty-five or over (even if he or she is still working) or is dead. An ex-spouse is entitled to full Social Security disability benefits if the other spouse is eligible.

Borrowing and Credit

Credit may be a new and critical issue as a result of your changed marital status. You may have to establish credit on the basis of your changed financial position, but in most instances your rating cannot legally be affected by your marital status. If, however, your credit was based in any way on your ex-spouse's income, you may not have the borrowing capacity you once enjoyed. A divorcée applying for credit individually can cite as proof of creditworthiness the credit history of accounts carried in the name of the ex-spouse, if both spouses used them. On the other hand, a divorced person may also have to give reasons why a bad joint credit history does not reflect on personal ability or willingness to pay.

Smart Money Move

Revise insurance coverage and beneficiary designations upon the divorce.

Credit Rights

If you receive alimony, you need not reveal that fact to a creditor unless you wish to use it to demonstrate your creditworthiness. If you do include alimony as part of your income on your credit application, however, the lender is entitled to examine whether your ex-spouse can be depended upon to make regular payments. The creditor might conclude that your ex-spouse is a poor credit risk, in which case alimony could be legally discounted as income, which could be detrimental to your application. Unless the lenders can prove that your ex-spouse is a poor risk, however, they cannot automatically discount alimony.

Notify the Credit Bureau

You should notify the credit bureau of both your and your ex-spouse's new addresses and specify that those accounts should henceforth be reported separately. Otherwise transactions may be reported on the wrong spouse's account, and the records can get tangled, especially if one of the two remarries. Occasionally, one or both spouses will have credit problems during the separation period preceding the final divorce period, especially if the marital assets are frozen to negotiate the settlement. In this situation, the credit bureau and lenders should be informed of the circumstances. Lenders may be more lenient in restoring the credit ratings of the parties to a divorce once the situation stabilizes.

Tax Consequences

The emphasis in most contemporary divorces on property division, income division, or alimony still exists, especially in cases where there are insufficient assets to support both households. For some couples there are significant tax advantages to using ongoing support in structuring a settlement. For others, a lump sum settlement is more advantageous. While the tax implications of your divorce may be the farthest thing from your mind as you undergo the stressful divorce experience, it is important that you understand the various alternatives available to you and your spouse.

Adjusting to Your Changed Financial Status

Divorce almost always results in at least a temporary decrease in the standard of living for both spouses. The income and assets that once supported one household must now support two. The earlier you plan for this situation, the better you will be able to cope. You should prepare budgets and revise your financial objectives to account for your changed financial status. Careful advance planning will also help make the divorce settlement as fair as possible. The budgeting information and worksheets in Chapters 5 and 6 will help you plan financially during and after your divorce.

Changes in Estate Planning

Divorcing spouses should each ask an attorney to review and revise basic estate-planning documents to account for the new marital status. Most states will not allow couples who are in the process of divorcing but are still legally married to completely disinherit the spouse. During the period of separation preceding a divorce, you may wish to reduce your spouse's bequest to the minimum amount required by law. When the divorce is finalized, you will probably need to redraft the will as well as other estate-planning documents to change beneficiaries and trustees, at least. Pay careful attention to guardianship arrangements for children (see page 728).

A number of estate and gift tax opportunities and pitfalls may arise as a result of a divorce. Certain trusts can protect a former spouse who is financially inexperienced and can protect the children's inheritance in the event that the former spouse remarries and subsequently divorces. As in all estate-planning matters, expert legal and tax counsel is essential.

Be Reasonable, Be Fair

A reasonable financial settlement takes projected income and assets into account. The division should provide for necessary and foreseeable expenditures, including the costs of medical care. For older couples undergoing divorce, the allocation of pension and retirement-plan benefits, which are considered marital property, is obviously a most important issue. If the value of these retirement vehicles is not divided on an equal basis, you should make sure that you are otherwise compensated in your divorce settlement. Above all, if you are going through a divorce, be reasonable, be fair.

DIVORCE CHECKLIST

If you are going to divorce, learn about trends in the way divorce settlements are structured.

Try to avoid an adversarial divorce proceeding. Consider alternatives such as mediation.

Many changes in your financial planning will be necessary after the divorce, including:

- ADJUSTING INSURANCE COVERAGE

- ESTABLISHING CREDIT

- ADJUSTING TO A CHANGED FINANCIAL STATUS

- CHANGES IN ESTATE PLANNING DOCUMENTS.

Elderly Housing Concerns

This chapter is intended to help seniors deal with the housing concerns and problems they will face in their advanced years. People who are planning for their retirement, and who are trying to determine what sort of retirement life-style makes sense, should consult Chapter 68.

Housing Options for the Older Retiree

Retirees with fixed incomes who can no longer afford to maintain their homes or pay high rent in private housing, or whose health does not allow them to live alone comfortably, are increasingly turning to alternative housing arrangements. Your local office on aging can assist you to locate specific housing facilities in your chosen community.

Housing possibilities are now more extensive than ever before, ranging from homesharing—which enables older people to stay in their own homes—to nursing home care. This chapter contains descriptions of some of the housing options currently available to older people in many communities as well as a discussion of options for retirees looking for a new place to live.

Retirement Homesite Developments

Over the last decade, thousands of people have been lured by newspaper and magazine advertisements to invest in retirement homesites across the Sun Belt. Developers may put on a hard and elaborate sales pitch, including paying for prospective buyers' airfare and accommodations so they can visit the site. Persons paying reasonable amounts to honest developers may be able to find a lovely site where they can enjoy their golden years. But overbuilding and high promotion costs virtually ensure these lots will not prove lucrative investments. Worse, many real estate development operations are forced to delay building through hard times or tight credit, and occasionally, promised developments never materialize.

- **DO NOT** be pressured into buying property you cannot afford, and do not count on projected appreciation in your calculations.

- **ASK** the local Better Business Bureau about the property's developer and promoter. Also, ask for material to compare the asking price with similar projects.

- **CAREFULLY** review the required "property report" for details on the project and costs.

- **RESEARCH** the area. Find out how far the site is from transportation, hospitals, refuse removal services, shopping, and recreation. Never buy without visiting the development.

- **HAVE** a lawyer review any documents you plan to sign.

- **NEVER** be pressured into signing up for any property, no matter how good the deal sounds or how nice the salesperson is.

Retirement Communities

Retirement communities are a sensible choice for older but healthy and independent retirees who desire social interaction with people their age. Typically, older individuals rent or purchase an apartment and have access to recreational and other facilities and easy access to health-care facilities. Many retirement communities have been thriving for years and therefore do not have the same risks associated with retirement homesite developments.

Motor Homes

For many retirees who have extensive travel plans, motor homes represent the ultimate in freedom and convenience. You decide when you're leaving, you set your own pace, and you always get to sleep in your own bed. You never miss the boat, and you never have to wait for the plane. Your home can even follow the seasons.

Today's motor homes are more comfortable than ever before, but they are also more expensive. Still, even if you don't plan to spend more than a few months in it each year, your motor home can qualify as a second home, and your interest payments are deductible—as long as it has cooking, sleeping, and bathroom facilities and your first mortgage doesn't exceed certain limits.

You can also rent your motor home when you aren't using it. The rental income will help offset your loan payments, and it may make a portion of the nonmortgage expenses you incur from it (such as insurance, maintenance, and repairs) deductible to the extent of the rent you receive. (The rental income is taxable. For more tax details see page 98) Many dealers who sell motor homes have programs to arrange to rent such homes to others when the owners aren't using them.

If you are going to use a motor home only occasionally, consider renting one rather than buying one.

Houseboats

A boat can qualify as a second home if it has a head, galley, and berth. Just as with a motor home, you may be able to charter it out when you aren't using it. If you can afford it and will use it, houseboats are great. But, oh, the expense!

Housing Options for People Who Need or Anticipate Needing Extra Care

As many older Americans have discovered, healthy habits and good medical care have broken the link between advanced age and poor health. With the aging of the nation, more and more alternatives are being developed for the relatively well elderly—that increasingly large group who need a modest amount of help with the chores of daily living but can still manage pretty well by themselves. The housing alternatives vary in the kinds of life-style they promote and in the amount of medical and custodial care they offer. The spectrum of housing options available to the relatively infirm elderly is also broadening.

Homesharing

Homesharing is a means by which an older person who owns a home shares expenses and household tasks with a younger person who needs affordable housing. The younger person might agree to do cleaning or yard work in exchange for inexpensive or free room and board at the elderly person's home. There are local community groups or government agencies in most areas that match homeowners with potential homesharers. Check the references of any potential homesharer, and prepare a written agreement spelling out the details of the arrangement.

If you are considering homesharing, you should think carefully about your needs and desires. For example, if you need someone to prepare meals for you, you should be prepared to ask the potential homesharer questions such as the following:

- ARE you on a special diet that may differ from what I generally eat?

- WHO will determine the menu?

- WHO will shop for food?

- HOW many meals a day will you provide?

- DO you expect to eat meals with me?

- HOW will food costs be allocated?

Smart Money Move

Senior citizens who need or anticipate needing extra care should explore the wide range of housing options available to them.

An alternative to homesharing that retirees have is to share someone else's home. In many communities there are organizations to match up interested homeowners with interested retirees. Some will match two retirees who wish to rent together and will even find them an apartment. Zoning regulations that prohibit multifamily dwellings or the rental of part of a house often make exceptions for people over sixty-five or people living as one "family" instead of in separate apartments within the same house.

Some potential drawbacks of homesharing arrangements include the effects of the extra income on Social Security benefits and the adjustments of living with a stranger.

Home Care

Home care is for people who wish to remain in their own home but for whom the unskilled companionship and guardianship of a homesharer will not be adequate. When you remain in familiar surroundings, you usually feel more at ease, more in control, and more comfortable. Furthermore, staying there is much cheaper than moving into a nursing home or other institution. Home care is particularly appropriate for persons with Alzheimer's or other debilitating diseases and for people who are recovering from recent hospitalization and who still require nursing care or help with life's daily activities.

Different levels of home care service are available, ranging from custodial care (for people who need some assistance with daily tasks but don't need medical supervision) to skilled nursing care. Many programs are also available for persons who need some help but don't need someone to move in. Meals on Wheels, for example, delivers hot meals or provides transportation to a meal site. State community care programs for the elderly provide homemaking services and meals and run errands for homebound persons.

Accessory Apartments

Accessory apartment arrangements are similar to homesharing, but each dwelling space has a separate kitchen. In some locales, such housing is known as mother-daughter homes because often the older person is renting or staying in an apartment within a son's or daughter's home. The apartment gives parents more independence and privacy than they would have if they were sharing their children's household.

Like homesharing, this arrangement can be reversed for elderly people who own their homes and want to take in tenants to give them a sense of security as well as to boost their income.

In a new twist on accessory apartments known as Elder Cottage Housing Opportunity (ECHO), temporary, self-contained units are installed in the side or back yard of an adult child's home to accommodate the elderly parent(s). The units are removed when they no longer are needed. The units can also be privately purchased and installed at a cost of $14,000 to $20,000. They are generally portable and reusable, but many people find the purchase price and installation costs prohibitive. Also, they can raise property taxes, and the additional utility costs may exceed those of an apartment. On the other hand, ECHO units offer their residents a degree of independence they would not have in a shared-home arrangement, yet with the same closeness and safety of family.

Congregate Housing

Congregate housing is a group living situation for older people who are basically in good health but whose functional abilities are somewhat limited. The basic services provided include one to three meals per day in a central dining area, light housekeeping, laundry services, and organized recreational activities. Residents share common areas such as the living room, bathroom, kitchen, and dining room. The services of a social worker and/or homemaker, meal delivery, transportation, and recreational programs may also be available.

Congregate housing, varying in size and physical design, is sometimes sponsored by nonprofit organizations that offer the housing at a low rate. If you are considering a move to congregate housing, you should:

- **TOUR** the facility, talk with residents, and, if possible, participate in a meal and some other activity.

- **EXAMINE** the lease or contract carefully, checking to see if there is a penalty for terminating the lease. If you are hospitalized, is your room reserved for your return?

- **FIND OUT** what the monthly fees are and what additional charges for extra services exist.

- **ASK** about regulations. For example, some facilities place restrictions on visitors or pets.

Many congregate housing facilities are being built in or near the urban areas of the North and Midwest. Residents who don't wish to relocate to the "retirement belt" of the Southeast and West can move in without losing touch with their families, friends, clergy, and community.

Senior Housing

Senior housing, subsidized by a branch of local, state, or federal government, often offers rents based on the older person's income. To be eligible, you must meet established income requirements. Senior housing usually consists of a one-bedroom apartment with a living room, bathroom, and kitchen and is accessible to persons with disabilities. There are often waiting lists for admittance to senior housing.

Continuing Care Communities

Designed to meet the changing needs of their residents, continuing care communities offer a variety of housing alternatives in one location: town houses for independent, active older adults; apartment buildings with meals, homemaker, and laundry services; and in many communities a nursing home. Because this is a relatively new concept, you should check:

- **THE FINANCIAL STATUS** of the owners and developers

- **THE CURRENT LEVEL** of occupancy

- **WHETHER** the continuing care community has sufficient resources to remain solvent

- **WHETHER** the down payment is refundable if you move out

- **WHETHER** any of the down payment is refundable to your estate upon your death

- **WHAT SERVICES** are included in the monthly fee

- **HOW MUCH** the monthly fee has increased over the community's history

- **WHETHER** the facility is located near public transportation and is accessible to family, friends, and shopping.

As with any housing alternative, you should always visit the community and talk with residents, and have a lawyer review any documents. Unfortunately, several such communities have failed, leaving their residents in a lurch.

Many elderly people who are faced with or concerned about declining health and increasing medical costs enter continuing care communities to protect themselves against these risks, because no additional costs will be incurred even if their health care expenses increase. Life-care contracts offer the elderly person the advantages of independent living, long-term security, and affordable nursing home care.

Different continuing care communities make different arrangements for payment, but they typically require a large entry fee ($100,000 to $250,000), for which mortgages are not available, and a monthly charge of $1,000 to $2,000, depending on the size of the unit and other variables. The monthly charge includes some meals and services. Ask about extra fees for extra services. The entry fee is normally refundable when the resident leaves or is payable to his or her estate, but no interest is paid. Some facilities offer units on a rental basis with no entry fee.

Adult Day Care

Adult day care is often appropriate for elderly persons who are still mobile and have their faculties but who may not be entirely self-sufficient. Adult day care is available at a lower cost than residential care, and retirement communities often offer this care daily or several times a week at a much lower cost than nursing home or home nursing care.

Transportation, games and puzzles, exercises, physical therapy, field trips, performances, classes, snacks, and hot midday meals are the staples offered by adult care centers, in addition to having registered and licensed practical nurses on hand to monitor residents' health.

When choosing an adult care center, ask what is included in the daily rate. Program supplies, transportation, and excursions may cost extra, and individualized services for the severely handicapped, physical therapy, and psychiatric care will add substantially to the total cost that is not covered by Medicare or most private medical insurance. Some insurers are beginning to offer policies that cover adult day care, and financial aid may be available to lower-income individuals.

Points to consider in choosing a center include: the center's conformity to state regulations, the sufficiency of available medical staff and services, quality of the meals and the center's capacity to accommodate special dietary regimens, client-to-staff ratio, and safety and cleanliness of the facilities. Geriatric social workers and consultants can assist you in evaluating your suitability for this level of care and in identifying an appropriate center.

Nursing Homes

E ntering a nursing home is an event of intense personal and financial concern for many elderly persons and their families. Often the decision to enter a home follows a period of serious illness or loss of a loved one, leaving little time for planning. The high cost of nursing home care can rapidly deplete the resources of residents. Nursing homes should be chosen on the basis of location, recommendations, financial arrangements, facilities, a thorough inspection and tour, and your specific needs and preferences.

Nursing home care is expensive, and private health insurance for such care is available but inadequate. Such coverage is itself quite costly and often does not cover the full range of nursing home expenses. Medicare generally pays only for skilled nursing care, generally after a hospital stay, in a skilled nursing facility. Patients who need less extensive care must pay for it themselves or qualify for Medicaid reimbursement. Some prospective nursing home residents try to qualify for Medicaid by transferring their assets to a spouse or children or into an irrevocable trust, but there are risks and limitations associated with such transfers (see page 340).

Choosing a Nursing Home

The decision to enter a nursing home or to place a spouse or parent in a nursing home is a particularly difficult one to make. Once this decision is made, however, an appropriate nursing home must be selected. Few homes will offer everything you want for your loved one. Since any home visited will, of course, present its best features to you, it is important to know what to look for and what to ask. (The comments in this section also apply to selecting a continuing care community or other alternative housing.)

All nursing homes are required to have a current license from the state or a letter of approval from a licensing agency. For nursing homes operating under Medicaid, the administrator should also have a current state license or waiver. Ask for a copy of the nursing home's license, its certification for participation in government programs, and reports of any recent violations.

The general atmosphere of the home and staff should be pleasant and cheerful. Most nursing homes are trying to provide the best service they can within the limits of the income they receive, the staff they can afford to pay, and the cooperation they receive from the patients and their families. Listen to what patients, other visitors, and volunteers have to say about the home and see if the patients look well cared for and generally content. Consider how the staff acts toward the patients. Do they show them genuine interest and affection? Some nursing homes do not allow patients to wear their own clothes or decorate their rooms. Others have written statements of patients' rights that they enforce. Make sure there is a place for private visits with family and friends. Visiting hours should be convenient for both patients and visitors.

Some of the things to look for in a nursing home are fairly obvious. Is it clean and orderly? Is it reasonably free of unpleasant odors? Is it well lighted? Other things can be easily overlooked. Are toilet and bathing facilities easy for handicapped patients to use? Are the rooms well ventilated and kept at a comfortable temperature? Are wheelchair ramps provided where necessary? Certain areas should be posted with no smoking signs, and staff, patients, and visitors should observe those signs.

Safety Is Particularly Important

Toilet and bathing facilities should have grab bars, and hallways should have handrails on both sides. Bathtubs and showers must have nonslip surfaces. One good indication of how seriously the home takes its patients' safety is how strictly it adheres to standard building safety ordinances. Exit doors should be kept unobstructed and unlocked from the inside, and they should be marked clearly with illuminated signs. Portable fire extinguishers should be accessible, and the sprinkler system and emergency lighting should be automatic. Check to see if an emergency evacuation plan is posted prominently.

Unfortunately, the quality of medical, dental, and even nursing care in nursing homes varies broadly. An acceptable home will have a physician available for medical emergencies at all times, either on staff or on call. At least one registered nurse or licensed practical nurse should be on duty day and night. A registered nurse should serve as director of nursing services, and nurse call buttons are ideally located at each patient's bed and in toilet facilities. The home should have an arrangement with an outside dental service to provide patients with necessary dental care. Many homes have arrangements with nearby hospitals for quick transfer of patients. Nursing homes are required to give Medicaid recipients annual checkups. Find out whether regular checkups are also given to patients paying privately.

Pharmaceutical services should be supervised by a qualified pharmacist in a room set aside for storing and preparing drugs. Full-time programs of physical therapy, occupational therapy, and speech therapy should be available to patients who need those services.

Check Behind the Scenes

Try to check behind the scenes as much as possible. See how clean the kitchen is, if food is refrigerated properly, and whether waste is disposed of appropriately. At least three meals should be served every day at normal hours (with no more than fourteen hours between the evening meal and breakfast the next morning), with plenty of time for leisurely eating. Nutritious between-meal and bedtime snacks should be available. The home will usually allow you to sample a meal—make sure it matches the one on the posted menu. It should look and taste appetizing, and it should be served at the proper temperature. The dining room should be attractive and comfortable. Make sure the patients are given enough food and that special meals are prepared for patients on therapeutic diets. You may wish to ask how patients who need help eating are assisted.

Insist on visiting patients' rooms, and make sure they are shared according to the residents' preferences and compatibilities. Every room should open onto a hallway, and every room should have a window to the outside. Each patient should have a reading light, a comfortable chair, and a closet and drawers for personal belongings. Bathing and toilet facilities should have adequate privacy and be located conveniently, and each bed should have a curtain or screen to provide privacy whenever necessary. Does each patient have a locked drawer or safe box?

Daily Activities

Once you have established that the nursing home is clean and well kept and treats its patients decently, try to determine what the residents do all day. Is there an activities coordinator on the staff who organizes a varied program of recreational, cultural, and intellectual activities? Suitable space, tools, and supplies should be provided for such activities. Activities should also be offered for patients who are relatively inactive or confined to their rooms. Activities should be scheduled each day and some evenings.

Besides the scheduled activities, there should be a lounge where patients can chat, read, play games, watch television, or just relax away from their rooms. Is there an outdoor area where patients can get fresh air and sunshine? How easy is patient access to drinking water and telephones? Also find out what extra services are offered. If any particular service is important, find out how convenient it will be and how much it will cost. For example, will the resident have access to a barber or beautician, a manicurist, a masseur or masseuse, or a podiatrist? Are social services available to aid patients and their families? Do patients have an opportunity to attend religious services and talk with clergy both inside and outside the home?

Financial and Related Matters

Compare the estimated monthly costs (including extra charges) with those of other homes. Make sure that the financial terms are clear and in writing and that the contract specifies that the home will provide a refund for unused days paid for in advance. The rate at which you sign on should be guaranteed for a reasonable period of time. Is the home certified to participate in the Medicare and Medicaid programs? Will the patient be able to remain if he or she is forced to fall back on Medicaid?

Your Ongoing Relations with the Home

When you have chosen a home and your family member is ready to be admitted, label all belongings and leave a complete list with the home administrator. On each visit, check to see that nothing is missing, and if it is, report it immediately. Discuss any problems with the supervisor. If they are not handled properly, file a complaint with the ombudsman council or regulatory authority. These volunteers have the right to visit the home at any time, investigate complaints, and require corrective action and even closure.

The checklist will assist you in choosing the right nursing home for your loved one.

FOR FURTHER INFORMATION

"Consumer's Directory of Continuing Care Retirement Communities"
American Association of Homes for the Aging
AHA Publications
901 E Street
Suite 500
Washington DC 20004-2037
(202) 783-2242

"Consumer Information on Continuing Care"
American Association of Retired Persons
Research Information Center
601 E Street, N.W., A2-402
Washington DC 20049
(202) 434-6240

National Council of Senior Citizens
1331 F Street, N.W.
Washington DC 20004
(202) 347-8800

"How to Choose a Home Care Agency"
National Association for Home Care
519 C Street, N.E.

Washington DC 20002-5809
(202) 547-7424

"Directory of Accredited Home Care Aide Services" and "All About Home Care"
Foundation for Hospice and Home Care
519 C Street, N.E.
Washington DC 20002-5809
(202) 547-6586

National Alliance of Senior Citizens (a senior citizens' lobbying group; write for information on becoming a member)
1700 18th Street, N.W.
Suite 401
Washington, DC 20009
(202) 986-0117

National Council on the Aging (write for a complete list of publications)
Attention: Publications
409 3rd Street, S.W.
Suite 200
(202) 479-1200

»

Aging magazine ($6.50/year)

Request an order form from

The Superintendent of Documents
Government Printing Office
Washington, DC 20402-9371
(202) 783-3238

ELDERLY HOUSING CHECKLIST

☐

Examine the wide variety of housing options available to the active older retiree and to the retiree who needs extra care.

☐

Exercise extreme caution prior to making a commitment to a particular care facility, particularly if it requires a major financial investment.

☐

Evaluate thoroughly a nursing home prior to placing a loved one in it, since the quality of nursing home care varies.

26

Death of a Family Member

This chapter provides surviving family members with the information necessary to make sound financial judgments and decisions in situations involving the death of a family member. In the midst of an extremely trying situation, you must be prepared to examine every aspect of your financial situation.

You will need to come to financial terms with your changed circumstances. Although substantial changes will not be required in each area, changes—some substantial and some incidental—will inevitably be required.

There are also a variety of things to attend to before focusing in on the numerous details regarding the settlement of the deceased's estate.

Immediate Decisions

Following the death of your spouse or other family member, you must identify the resources available to meet your financial needs until the estate is settled. These expenses must account for everything from the fifteen dollars you still owe the paper boy to the mortgage, insurance, and taxes due on your property. Furthermore, you must make important financial decisions in the months after your spouse's death.

Money in the Bank

You need readily available cash, not only to support you during this period but to enable you to pay debts and funeral expenses, administration expenses, federal and state death taxes, and cash bequests. You or the executor of the estate (who may well be you) need to determine what liquid assets (in other words, readily accessible assets) are available to you, and what outside resources are available. (Your parents or children may be able to help you meet costs that you can't cover yourself.)

Even when the assets are considerable, they may not be liquid (for example, they could be tied up in real estate), or they may be inaccessible during the administration of the estate.

Fortunately, even if your (and the estate's) immediate cash needs have not been provided for by prudent advance estate planning, there are a number of ways the executor may be able to obtain sufficient funds:

- JOINT CHECKING or savings accounts and other assets that don't have to go through probate may help you cover immediate needs.

- **IF** the executor—the person designated to settle the estate—receives the required authority to do so, he or she can distribute assets in lieu of cash bequests in some cases. Distributions of this kind will reduce the cash needs of the estate.

- **IF** the decedent's will creates a trust, the executor may elect to place any liquid assets in the trust and sell more marketable assets.

- **THE ESTATE** can raise cash by borrowing from a beneficiary of the estate, or from the beneficiary of a trust established by the estate.

- **THE ESTATE TAX** on a family business interest may be deferred for up to fourteen years, with the estate making annual interest-only payments for the first four years and paying the balance in ten annual installments of principal and interest. In order to qualify, the value of the business must exceed 35 percent of the value of the decedent's estate.

Decision Making

Haste makes waste. Although your changed circumstances will cry out for some immediate revisions, some important decisions can be delayed.

When in Doubt, Procrastinate

It's important to realize that your judgment—your ability to make the right decisions—during this emotionally trying time may be impaired. Therefore, you should be extremely conservative. In fact, putting all death benefits or insurance proceeds in money-market accounts, CDs, Treasury bills, or other short-term investments that are safe (federally insured) and accessible makes good sense. In six months or a year, you will be better able to consider important investment decisions.

Look Out for Scam Artists

Families who have lost a loved one are prime targets for charlatans and frauds. You may be subject to fraudulent demands for repayment of loans your late spouse never took out, or you may receive false notices of overdue premiums on life insurance policies, or receive merchandise C.O.D. that the decedent never actually ordered. My recommendation: Unless you knew about the debt or purchase in advance, do not pay it. Turn any unusual bills over to the estate executor or to your lawyer or other professional adviser. On the other hand, you should try to pay legitimate bills without undue delay to avoid hurting your credit rating now and in the future.

Family Financial Matters

dult children and close friends are often important sources of assistance in dealing with financial-planning matters during this difficult time.

Required Documents

You will need as many as *ten* copies of the death certificate for insurance claims, Social Security benefits, and will probate. Many parties need to be notified of your loved one's death, including the Social Security Administration, the insurance companies, the current or former employer, and, if the decedent was an honorably discharged veteran, the Veterans Administration. (See the "Action Checklist" at the end of this chapter.)

Insurance

You'll need to determine the deceased's death benefits and advise the beneficiaries on the distribution of their proceeds. You should also review possible changes in your overall family insurance coverage. (These matters are discussed in detail below.)

Notify the Deceased's Life Insurance Agent

You should notify the life insurance agent or company and file the necessary claims. Besides employee benefits and life insurance, you may also be eligible for Social Security or Veterans Administration benefits and should contact the appropriate offices.

Death Benefits

It's important to determine any death benefits that are due. If applicable, Social Security orphan's benefits should also be investigated. You should also notify the employee benefits office if the decedent was employed at the time of death. You may be eligible to receive a last paycheck, payment for accrued vacation and sick leave, company life insurance, a pension benefit, deferred compensation, profit sharing, and/or accident insurance.

Insurance Proceeds

If you are the beneficiary of a life insurance policy, you may have several options of how to receive the money. These options should be very carefully evaluated. Don't rely solely on the insurance agent's recommendation. If necessary, pay for an independent opinion. You can always leave the insurance proceeds with the insurance company, earning interest until a final decision is made.

Budgets

Reevaluating your financial position in light of your changed circumstances is easier said than done. Nevertheless, you need to organize many important financial records, and at the same time, you should prepare a budget that reflects your changed circumstances. A revised budget may affect many other decisions, such as whether it's necessary to remain in or reenter the work force.

Expenses

Expense projections should take into account any increased expenditures, such as child care or household help. You may require additional travel expenses to visit children and other relatives and friends. If your loved one's final illness was protracted, increased expenditures may be necessary for purchases and activities that were suspended during the illness.

Three Ways to Receive Insurance Proceeds

There are three main ways you can elect to receive the proceeds of a life insurance policy with lesser variations within each method.

Lump-Sum Settlements

Lump-sum payments—getting the whole amount at once—are usually appropriate for small policies and/or for those beneficiaries who are capable of investing wisely or who can rely on competent investment advisers. Lump-sum payouts occur automatically when insurance proceeds are payable into a trust.

Fixed Payments

You can opt to have the insurance company distribute the proceeds and interest thereon over a fixed period of time, usually in installment payments of a fixed amount paid at stated intervals until the money is used up. You should make certain that you can change your mind and withdraw the entire sum at a later date. If you have not received the entire payment and have not exercised the power to withdraw a lump sum by the time of your own death, the unpaid balance will be payable at your election to your estate or to some other beneficiary.

Alternatively, the insurance company can pay you fixed payments of interest only, with the principal of the policy payable to either your estate or to a designated beneficiary.

Annuities

With an annuity, the insurance company agrees to pay a certain sum for life, usually monthly, the amount depending on the size of the insurance policy and your age. Annuities assure that you will never outlive the monthly payment.

This option may be particularly useful where your resources and/or investment expertise is limited, where you have spendthrift tendencies, or where there is danger of your incurring uninsured health care costs (see page 677).

If you want to purchase an annuity, the settlement-option plan offered by the life insurance company that issued the policy may not be the best deal. Other insurance companies may offer you a higher monthly income. If you want to purchase an annuity from a company other than the one that paid the death claim, you should have the two companies transfer the funds directly to avoid adverse tax consequences. (See Chapter 76 for a detailed discussion of annuities.)

Important Financial Matters

Revise Your Coverage

Insurance coverage will need to be reviewed after the death of a spouse. If your spouse handled your insurance, you may be unfamiliar with policy features, etc. In this case, you will need to educate yourself on your insurance needs. Besides revising and changing the beneficiary designations on existing policies, you have to assess your own insurance needs as a result of the changed circumstances. If you were formerly covered as a spouse under a health insurance plan, continuing coverage will have to be acquired. Appropriate coverage in your name for auto, homeowner's or renter's, and umbrella liability insurance is also necessary. Depending on individual circumstances, you may need to acquire or increase the limits on your disability and life insurance coverage.

Review the Debt Situation

Your changed circumstances will necessitate a review of your debt situation. The loss of the decedent's income may tempt you to borrow more than you should. Don't. If you are concerned about your ability to pay off existing debts, don't delay in preparing realistic budgets. It's better to face these matters now (see Chapter 47).

Cancel Credit Cards

You will need to cancel the decedent's credit cards or convert the accounts to your own name. Outstanding loans should be reviewed, since some may be covered with the lender by credit life insurance that will pay off the debt in full.

Individual credit accounts that were granted solely on the basis of your income cannot legally be closed without evidence that you will not be able to pay. (*Note:* Skipping two monthly bills may be considered such evidence.) If, on the other hand, the credit accounts were based even partially on your late spouse's income, the lender can require a new application, which it may refuse if your present financial situation does not meet its requirements.

Account for Tuition

Projections of any remaining children's education costs should be reviewed. Changed family financial circumstances may mean that the child qualifies for financial aid, for more financial aid, or even for an emergency loan from his or her school. Orphan's benefits may also be available.

Investments

A thorough review of your savings and investments should be conducted in light of the new family circumstances. You should assess how the money is invested as well as your ability to manage the investments. Other matters may also need to be addressed, including revising ownership designations on investment accounts and real estate and deciding what to do with a family business.

Revise Your Investment Strategies

Professional investment management may be appropriate where it was not prior to your spouse's death, especially if you are unfamiliar with investment management and/or if you are quite elderly. Regardless, your changed circumstances often warrant a change in investment strategy and plans. For example, you may have a greater need for stable income from your investments, in which case a more conservative strategy might be appropriate.

Savings Bonds Owned by the Decedent

The interest income on U.S. Series E and EE bonds (or Series H or HH bonds acquired by the decedent in exchange for E or EE bonds) is usually reported upon the bonds' redemption unless election has been made to report such income on an annual basis. If the deceased did not report the interest annually, the income tax liability on the interest that accumulated during the deceased's lifetime passes to the beneficiary. It may be advantageous, however, to report all of the accrued income on Series E or EE bonds on the decedent's final income tax return, particularly if death occurred early in the final taxable year before the deceased received much in the way of taxable income. Even if the election results in the imposition of federal income taxes, the tax liability is deductible on the estate tax return.

Worthless Assets

If there are any loans owed to the decedent or investments that are worthless as of the date of death, it should be determined whether worthlessness occurred during the year of death or in a prior tax year. If worthlessness occurred during prior tax years, a claim for tax refund may be possible.

The Family Business

If the decedent owned a family business, some important decisions will have to be made. The owner's stock in the business is often the principal asset in his or her estate, and when its value depends on the owner's presence, the business may be difficult to sell. Even when it can be sold, it may have lost value.

The hardest decision may be whether to continue, try to sell, or close the business. Closing the business should usually be avoided if possible, since it almost invariably means severe loss in value. You may wish to keep the business in the family, or you may wish to sell it to an outsider. The sooner you decide, the better.

Possible Spouse's Benefits

I f you are a widow or widower who is not yet retired, you should revise your retirement income and expense projections. You may be eligible to receive retirement benefits as a surviving spouse in addition to whatever benefits you may have earned on your own. These are some of the sources you should check for possible spouse's benefits.

Social Security

If your spouse was a worker or retiree covered by Social Security, you and your dependents may be entitled to various benefits. If you are an ex-spouse of a decedent, you also may be eligible for benefits (see Chapter 70).

Veterans Administration

If the decedent was a veteran whose discharge was honorable, you may be eligible for a funeral allowance and/or a pension.

Pension plan

To qualify for your spouse's pension, generally, the two of you must have been married for a full year before your spouse retired and also for a full year before your spouse died. In many plans, if he or she died before the official early retirement age, you are ineligible to receive benefits.

IRA or spousal IRA

If the IRA owner dies before his or her entire interest has been distributed, the balance is distributable to the named beneficiary.

Qualified employee benefit plan

Qualified plans may provide annuity or lump-sum death benefits to you in place of or in addition to retirement benefits.

Other employee benefits

The employer may be contractually obliged to pay death benefits to a designated recipient. The employer may pay benefits in the nature of extra compensation for services performed or may choose to make a pure gift. Voluntary payments of death benefits flowing from affection or charity are viewed as a gift and not subject to income tax. Voluntary payments made in anticipation of some economic benefit to the employer or in recognition of past employee services are taxable.

Death and Taxes

You may be unfamiliar with taxes and tax filing—or you may be familiar enough with tax matters to want little or nothing to do with them! Unfortunately, understanding tax matters as they relate to decedents and their survivors is essential. This section details tax matters as they relate to you, to the deceased, and to the estate. Why all three? Because all have to file tax returns. If preparing any of these tax returns is likely to cause you fits, hire a tax professional.

Tax Status of a New Widow or Widower

You are allowed to do the following:

- **FILE** a joint return for the year in which the death occurred.

- **CLAIM** a personal exemption for the late spouse in that year.

- **FILE** a joint return as a surviving spouse for two years after the death of your spouse, as long as all of the following conditions are met:

  1. **YOU** were entitled to file a joint return the year before your spouse died, whether or not you elected to do so.

  2. **YOUR** children qualify as your dependents, and your home is their principal residence.

  3. **YOU** provide over half the cost of maintaining your household.

  4. **YOU** have not remarried. If you have, your may file a joint return with your new spouse.

If you are the executor of the estate, you may choose to waive the executor's commission, especially if you will otherwise receive an equivalent amount as a bequest or legacy. This would be advantageous because the inheritance is not taxable, but the executor's commission qualifies as regular income. It may also be preferable to waive the commission if the marital deduction exempts the estate from estate tax, so that an estate tax deduction for the commission is not needed.

Tax Status of the Decedent

The taxable year of the decedent is his or her normal tax year regardless of when death occurs. Medical expenses incurred before death and paid within one year after death may be claimed as medical deductions on the decedent's final return or on the estate's tax return. To prevent a double deduction, the executor must file a waiver of right to claim the estate tax deduction if it is to be claimed on the decedent's return. Of course, the tax consequences of each option should be weighed before the waiver is made. Choose the option that requires the lesser payment of tax.

Income taxes owed

All income earned up to the time of death must be reported on the decedent's income tax return. Income earned by a decedent but not included in his or her final income tax return because it was not received before death is known as "income in respect of a decedent" and is generally reported on the estate's income tax return.

Administrative expenses, taxes, interest, business expenses, and other items that have accrued at the date of the decedent's death can be claimed as income tax deductions.

Tax status of the estate

If death taxes are due and the will does not specify which assets shall bear the burden (or if there is no will), state and federal laws specify what is required. All taxes must be paid before a beneficiary can receive any property. In states that impose an inheritance tax, the amount of this tax comes directly from the property to be received. Any estate taxes must be apportioned among all property, subject to such tax. When property is left to someone who would be entitled to a deduction because of this bequest, the property shall be exempt from having to share in paying the tax. Property left to the surviving spouse, for example, which qualifies for the marital deduction, does not pay federal estate taxes.

The alternative valuation date

An alternative valuation date may be used to value the estate at a date other than the date of death, in order to reduce estate taxes. The alternative valuation date is generally six months after the death. Once the election is made, it cannot be changed. Alternative valuation is available only where both the total value of the gross estate and the amount of the estate tax liability are reduced as a result of the election.

Stepped-up basis

Whether the alternative valuation is elected or not, the valuation of the property for estate tax purposes also establishes the basis in the property for the recipient. The "basis" is the amount used to compute gain or loss from the subsequent sale of the property by the person who inherits it—usually, the fair market value of the property at the time of death. (The recipient's basis is "stepped up" from the cost the decedent originally paid to the fair market value at the date of death or alternative valuation date.)

Administering the Decedent's Estate

S urviving spouses or children are often the ones designated as estate executors. If you take on this burden—and it is a burden, unless you also happen to be an estate-planning attorney—you should be aware of the increased demands that it will place on your time, emotions, and problem-solving abilities.

Carrying Out the Decedent's Wishes

The decedent may have left some instructions that were not in the will. Instructions outside the will may take various forms, from letters of instruction to spoken promises or other informal declarations of intent. Such outside instructions can be very useful. For example, decedents may will their personal property to one beneficiary, then write a letter suggesting how the property might be disposed of or explaining why that beneficiary was not left other assets.

Instructions outside the will may also present some special difficulties for you, especially if you disagree with the decedent's wishes and disagreements aren't uncommon. It is very difficult to separate the legal from the moral obligations involved, and it is sometimes difficult for heirs to differentiate between nonbinding suggestions, guidance, and legally enforceable commands.

If the decedent's estate planning was thoughtful and timely, the will provisions, the specific property beneficiary designations, and the joint property laws usually result in an equitable and agreeable property division and estate transfer.

Revising the Will's Provisions

In the rare cases when circumstances have changed since the will was executed or where you take issue with any of its provisions, you may be able to effect a change. Some common ways of revising a will's provisions are as follows.

Disclaim part or all of an inheritance

A disclaimer is primarily used by surviving spouses who do not need the bequest and who would bequeath it at their own eventual death to a certain beneficiary anyway. (Inheritors who might need the property should not disclaim it, even if they assume the recipient of the disclaimer will support them.) The advantage of disclaiming is that it may allow the transfer to be made without incurring gift tax liability. Disclaimers by surviving spouses are valid even if the will directs that the property disclaimed passes to a trust in which they have an interest. Disclaiming, also known as "renouncing," gives up all future interest in the property disclaimed.

Elect against provisions of the will

If you feel that you have not been adequately provided for by the will, you may be able to elect against it. *Contrary to what many people think*, in most states, spouses cannot be disinherited. In fact, if your late spouse's will does not provide you with the minimum spousal bequest as established by law, you are entitled to that amount before the distribution of the remaining estate. The amount will vary, but it is based on a minimum percentage of the decedent's individual estate, regardless of what other property you inherit. If you were not disowned entirely, depending on state law, the right of election may give you the necessary sum in addition to what you were bequeathed in order to reach the minimum amount, or it may supersede any provisions in the will for you.

Contest part or all of the will

Interested parties (those who have something to gain or lose) who believe that a part or all of the will is not valid may be able to contest the will or protest probate. Usually, only interested parties adversely affected by a codicil or subsequent will are entitled to object to probate of a will. The one who objects bears the burden of proving his or her contentions. Mechanical defects (such as not signing the will in the presence of two witnesses), or substantive defects (such as drafting the will under undue influence or when misinformed by fraud), are common grounds for protesting probate.

The Survivor's Estate

T he transfer of the estate occasioned by the death of your spouse or other family member often has a considerable effect on your own estate planning. For example, you may find your estate greatly enlarged and/or greatly complicated.

Review Your Own Estate-Planning Documents

At the least, the deceased will have to be replaced in any capacity in which he or she appears in your estate-planning documents. Documents to be reviewed—and usually revised—include your own will, durable powers of attorney, living will, and letter of instructions. Trust documents will also have to be reviewed. Legal assistance in all of these matters is, of course, necessary.

The death of a spouse usually has far-reaching financial consequences as well. Your income may be substantially reduced by the death of an income-earning spouse, or your assets may be reduced. Conversely, the estate may be substantially increased by death benefits, insurance proceeds, or bequests. Any of these situations will affect your financial planning.

The possibility of remarriage merits considering how such a remarriage might affect the eventual transfer of the estate to heirs. Prenuptial contracts may be appropriate (see page 125).

What You Will Need to Do Following the Death of a Family Member

Professional help

- **CONTACT** the decedent's attorney. He or she should know where all the important, pertinent documents of the deceased's estate are to be found.

- **CONTACT** the decedent's accountant, financial planner, investment counselor, or other money manager. There may be some financial details that the deceased's attorney may not be aware of.

- **CONTACT** your own attorney. If you don't have a good probate attorney, chances are you will need one. The difficulty is finding an attorney with whom you can be comfortable sharing the most intimate details of your emotionally charged situation. Ask your friends for references, and always make an appointment with two or more attorneys. The first consultation should be free of charge—if it isn't, something's amiss. Discuss services rendered and fees charged, and compare and contrast them with those of the other attorneys you visit.

- **IF** you and your immediate family members are not familiar with finance, then consider hiring an accountant or financial planner to review all the ramifications of the deceased's estate.

Personal affairs

- **YOU** will need at least ten copies of the death certificate. The reason you will need so many is that, every time you make a claim for a benefit, you will have to present a copy of the certificate.

- **LOCATE** the *original* will and insurance policy. If they can't be found immediately—a good place to start is with a known safe-deposit box—contact the deceased's attorney, bank, insurance agent, or anyone else who might know the whereabouts of these important items.

- **OBTAIN** duplicate wills and other pertinent information from the deceased's safe-deposit box in a manner consistent with the law.

- **LOCATE** the deceased's Social Security number. You will need this more than once!

- **THE LETTER** of instructions, if one exists, should be located and read thoroughly so as to ensure that the specific desires of the deceased regarding, among other things, his or her funeral are carried out. (If the letter of instructions is thorough, it will also provide useful information concerning the location of documents pertinent to the probate process as well as a wealth of other important matters.)

- **YOU** should probably obtain five copies of your marriage certificate or license, for reasons relating to making claims.

- **IF** the deceased had children, then several copies of their birth certificates should be obtained. You won't be able to establish claims for certain Social Security benefits without them. Again, if you can't find the documents, contact the state and/or county where the children were born and request that certified copies be sent to you pronto.

- **YOU** will need copies of your spouse's certificate of honorable discharge in order to claim any veteran's benefits. If there isn't a readily available copy, write to the Department of Defense's National Personnel Record Center, 9700 Page Boulevard, St. Louis MO 63132. The inquiry should be addressed to the branch of the armed services in which the decedent served. The whole process can be speeded by contacting the Record Center by phone at: (314) 538-4261 (Army), (314) 538-4141 (Navy, Marines and Coast Guard), or (314) 538-4243 (Air Force).

- **CONTACT** the deceased's employer for details about pension plans and other retirement-plan (stock options, 401[k] plans) benefits. Get copies of pertinent documents.

- **DETERMINE** titles and ownership of all properties (such as home, automobile, boat), and all stocks, bonds, and other investments.

- **ASCERTAIN** whether the deceased's credit accounts, mortgage payments, bank, and utility bills have been kept up-to-date.

- **NOTIFY** the deceased's creditors.

ACTION CHECKLIST

DO THE FOLLOWING:	DONE

1. Locate important papers

Death certificate	☐
Insurance policies	☐
Marriage license	☐
Birth certificates	☐

»

ACTION CHECKLIST < CONT'D >	DONE
Naturalization papers	☐
The will	☐
Veteran's discharge papers	☐
Social Security benefits	☐
Most recent tax returns	☐

2. Contact an attorney ☐

3. File for probate of will ☐

4. Apply for benefits ☐

Life insurance proceeds	☐
Retirement plan benefits	☐
Veterans' benefits	☐
Other employee benefits	☐
Social Security benefits	☐

5. Change titles and ownership

House	☐
Insurance policies	☐
Automobiles	☐
Your will	☐
Credit cards	☐
Bank accounts	☐
Stocks, bonds, other investments	☐
Safe-deposit boxes	☐

6. Complete notifications of death ☐

7. Review finances ☐

8. File and pay applicable taxes ☐

FOR FURTHER INFORMATION

"On Being Alone" (free)
Publication # D150
American Association of Retired Persons
Fulfillment Department
601 E Street, N.W.
Washington DC 20049
(202) 434-2277

Part III

Your Career

Starting Out in the Work World

G raduation. The "real world." Scrambling for jobs. (Hopefully) moving out of your parents' house. Starting out! No one ever said it was going to be easy, but no one ever said how difficult it would be to meet basic living expenses—paying for rent, food, clothing, and entertainment, let alone buying and maintaining a car and last, but not least, saving some of your hard-earned dollars. This chapter isn't going to make real-life financial difficulties go away. Instead, it will help you know what lies ahead so that you can begin to develop sound financial habits that will achieve your life's dreams.

Graduating Magna cum Loans

I f you graduated with a loan coupon book about as thick as a phone book, welcome to the real world. Graduating with debt is becoming commonplace. Whether it's debt in the form of school loans (a reasonable debt) or credit card debt (a ridiculous debt), you're now faced with having to pay it off.

The last thing on many students' minds is their financial future. And the thought of a career seems secondary, not second nature. Most of them approach the job market the way they approached their course of studies—with a random interest and the sense that work might be fun. Let me break the ice by saying that work is seldom *fun*, but that it can be very interesting and downright compelling if you take the time to select a job that relates to your own interests and skills.

You'll have to be patient, however. The president of the company isn't going to move aside just because you've breezed in with an idea or two about how things could change for the better. Instead, you'll need to develop many new skills and exercise many old ones: typing may be key among them at first. But what's to worry? You've landed a job. Everything is hunky-dory, right? Wrong. You've got expenses!

Credit Card Insanity

If you fell prey to one of the millions of credit card solicitations that flood college campuses, chances are you've also fallen victim to your own bad spending habits. The sad thing is that, even before college graduates can begin to develop good saving and investing habits, they have to correct bad spending habits. To many recent graduates, credit card balances of a few thousand dollars are as normal as charging dinner three nights a week. After all, when you're just starting out, who has the time to cook? (Besides, brown-bagging it to work looks so depressingly unprofessional.)

Unfortunately, living on borrowed money is like living on borrowed time—you exceed sensible limits that will affect your future in ways you can't even begin to imagine. Fortunately, many recent grads are waking up to this fact. They're the ones who, instead of buying a new Ford Mustang convertible, are buying a secondhand Toyota. They're the ones who are contemplating career changes even before they've become dissatisfied with their first real job. And they can afford to contemplate such changes, because they've got a reasonable amount of debt that won't force them to stay put at a job whose only value is that it keeps the creditors at bay.

There are a lot of things you can and should do to protect yourself from financial problems that will affect your future well-being. Of course, some problems are probably beyond your control, like a layoff. But you can expect increased living expenses—moving out in the real world and moving up into it don't have to lead you to the poorhouse. In fact, you can learn to avoid many potential financial problems by learning some sensible, realistic planning techniques and, perhaps, learning about sacrifice. The strategies that follow will help you take control of your financial future from the word go, so that you can avoid the avoidable and manage the unavoidable.

Build up your savings

One of the most important things you can do when starting out is to build a cushion of savings to fall back on. In spite of what may look like limitless prospects for your future, it wasn't that long ago that many like-minded people had their hopes dashed. (In the early 1990s, the ranks of the unemployed were swelling by more than fifteen thousand *per week*.)

Smart Money Move

The single best thing that you can do to assure a secure financial future is to begin saving regularly as soon as you begin your career.

Nothing can beat money in the bank (or in an investment account) to help you shoulder these burdens should they arise. Another benefit of setting aside emergency funds is that you'll worry a lot less about what's going to happen to you and your new apartment. It is crucial that you begin to set aside some money—five or ten dollars per week is better than nothing. The easiest way to save is to never see the money. Most credit unions and banks will be more than happy to take your money out of your paycheck or checking account and put it into a savings account. If you can get into the habit of saving ten percent of your gross income throughout your career, you'll retire on Easy Street.

Get your debts under control

Millions of people are choking on consumer debt—don't let yourself become one of them. You may already know that you're sitting on a house of cards: The slightest disruption in your personal financial situation, and you may be headed for big trouble. Whatever your debt situation, take the necessary steps to get your debts under control.

First and foremost, don't add to your indebtedness. If necessary, take the scissors to your credit cards. Second, keep up-to-date on all your obligations. And third, work to reduce your credit debts if they aren't excessive. Even if it means putting your spending on a crash diet, keep up-to-date on your college loan payments.

Maintain your good credit

Whether you have a lot of debt, a little debt, or no debt, you need to build a good credit rating so that you can access credit when you need it (to buy your first secondhand car and your first home, for example). Dipping into your newly started savings is, if necessary, preferable to incurring more credit card debt.

There is an additional advantage to good credit that you may not yet have experienced: convenience. If you manage your credit properly, it allows you more flexibility to manage your day-to-day finances, and you won't have to waste time worrying about unpaid bills.

REPAYING STUDENT LOANS

As the cost of higher education rises in the United States, so do the debts accumulated by you-know-who—the graduates of universities and professional schools. Many new graduates are confronted with aggregate student loans that resemble the balance of a mortgage more closely than a student loan.

But hey! Uncle Sam cares. In fact, there's a federal program that now can assist you in handling your education debts by enabling you to consolidate your federal student loans. The program is especially helpful if your outstanding loans exceed $10,000. If you take advantage of the program, you can start writing only one monthly repayment check. More important, consolidation allows you to extend the repayment period from ten years to as many as twenty-five, which can mean as much as a 40 percent drop in monthly payments. Still, you should know that in some cases, the interest rate will be higher on the consolidated loan, which leads to an increase in the total cost of the borrowing.

To be eligible, you must have at least $5,000 in debt under any of four federal loan programs: Stafford loans, Health Professional Student loans, Perkins loans, and Supplemental Loans for Students. Separately, these loan programs offer widely varying interest rates. If you consolidate your loans, the interest rate is generally calculated as the weighted average of the various loans rounded to the nearest whole percent. (Married couples can consolidate loans jointly; minimum consolidation amount is $7,500.)

You also have several repayment options from which to choose, unless consolidation is offered by the state guaranty agency holding your loan or by a bank or other lender. In that case you must consolidate with that institution. But, if you have your choice, I'd rec-

»

ommend looking for lenders who offer graduated repayments that start out lower during the first years out of school rather than fixed monthly payments over the entire repayment period. Presumably, your income and thus your ability to pay will rise after your first years in the job market. In any case, if you consolidate you'll pay no penalty for early repayment—just as with original loans.

Some students may have legitimate reasons for extending their college loan repayment schedule, including the inability to comfortably afford monthly payments on current income or the need to lower the monthly payments in order to qualify for a mortgage. Nevertheless, extending these schedules can considerably increase the total cost of borrowing, particularly since college loan interest is considered consumer interest and is therefore not deductible. Moreover, think about the burden of making monthly college loan repayments over a period of time that may be roughly equivalent to a mortgage loan. Yikes!

Prepare a budget and review it regularly

This may sound like something only married people with children need to do. It isn't. Ideally, you should be creating your first budget even before you get your first paycheck. You'll also need to review and revise it to reflect the many actual and/or expected changes in your income or expenses. If you think something particularly troublesome might happen, like difficulty staying employed, prepare a budget that reflects that condition, so you can figure out what you'll need to do to make ends meet.

Control your spending

If there is one key to starting out on the right financial foot, it is learning to live *beneath* your means. Until you get into the habit of spending less than you earn, you will never be able to save. If you can't save, you will never be able to acquire the very things that you should be working for—whether it's your first home or your graduate school tuition. Many recent grads say that it's impossible for them to save, that they spend their money only on absolute necessities and there is still never anything left. Of course, you know as well as I do that they really haven't looked very hard at how and where they spend their money. There are always ways to cut back spending, and most of them are painless.

Smart Money Move

Don't jeopardize your financial future by taking a chance going without needed insurance coverage.

Maintain your insurance coverage

Unfortunately, many people just starting out think little or nothing at all about being insured. It seems to be a relatively needless thing—after all, you're young and healthy. For example, you may think a renter's or health insurance policy is a waste of money. Let me assure you that both represent money well spent.

The problem with leaving even a single gap in your insurance coverage—no matter how youthful you are—is that it exposes you to a possible uninsured loss, which could end up jeopardizing not only the few assets that you currently own but also some of your *future* earnings.

Make your own investment decisions

Investments? Absolutely. You're never too young to start investing your money. And while the opinions and advice of others may be helpful, you should be making your own investment decisions. That way, you'll understand what you're investing in and keep current on market conditions. A subscription to *Money* magazine or *Kiplinger's Personal Finance* can go a long way toward curing your lack of knowledge about investing. No matter what, avoid investing in extremes—liking stocks one week, loving bonds the next week, hating them both the next month. Instead, consider mutual funds, whose advantages—too numerous to list here—are detailed in Chapter 59.

Once you get into the saving and investing habit, open up an IRA. You don't have to put the full $2,000 per year into your IRA if you can't yet afford it. The important thing is to get into the habit of making tax-advantaged retirement investments as soon as possible. You have forty or more years to let these investments grow, so it doesn't take much investing at your age to amass prodigious retirement resources.

Try to anticipate contingencies

Don't deceive yourself. You need to review your current financial situation periodically, so that you can anticipate any problems before they occur. The younger you start, the more benefit this sound personal financial management technique will have. These problems could include the loss of your job, salary freezes or reductions, credit problems, or difficulty meeting your budget. Uncertain times call for careful evaluation and planning. Starting out in your career is definitely an uncertain time, no matter how confident you are in your ability to succeed.

Smart Money Move

Get help if adversity strikes

Finally, don't be too proud to ask for help when you truly need it. Being reluctant to get the help that is available to assist you simply doesn't make sense. Making tough choices—you may have to move back home, for example—is certainly preferable to letting your situation deteriorate to the point where it harms your future prospects for fame and fortune!

Contributing to an IRA at this stage in your life will put you well on the road to financial security.

STARTING OUT IN THE WORK WORLD CHECKLIST

Develop a plan to repay your student and other loans over a reasonable period of time.

Get into the saving habit, even though you may have to start small.

Always maintain adequate and continuous insurance coverage, particularly health insurance and disability insurance.

Start planning for retirement now. Annual contributions to an IRA are a good start.

Starting a Business

T he appeal of being their own boss has led many people down the entrepreneurial path. While owning your own business offers the opportunity for both job satisfaction and wealth, the majority of small-business startups end in failure. The reasons that new small businesses go belly-up are manifold; some are beyond the control of even the most talented businessperson. Many common mistakes, however, can be avoided with a little planning and foresight. If you ever contemplate launching your own business, this chapter will provide you with just the necessary dose of reality to change you from a dreamer into a hard-headed man or woman of business.

Deciding What Sort of Business to Establish

I f you have given much thought to starting up a business, you probably already know what kind of business you want to launch. Before you move full-speed ahead, however, a little self-scrutiny is in order. You should be confident that you are *really* up to the task that lies ahead. It is important, for instance, that the venture you envision calls on skills you've already developed. Jumping "cold turkey" into a line of business in which you have no experience is only a recipe for disaster. The last thing you want to do is to have to learn the business as you go along. Although a few extraordinarily lucky entrepreneurs have done just that, many more have failed miserably when striking out in untried directions. As a matter of fact, your business could well begin as a hobby or as a sideline to your regular, nine-to-five job. Many successful small business people started their businesses as part-time endeavors.

Drawing Up a Battle Plan

S tarting with a thorough and well-written business plan is essential to launching your business successfully. The very act of writing down your ideas in a structured, coherent form will force you to think through and refine them. Without a solid—and well-researched—business plan, your hopes and dreams of entrepreneurial success have little chance of realization. Whatever format you choose for your plan, it should address in clear, concise language the following questions:

- **WHAT** product or service will I offer?

- **WHO** constitutes my market?

- **HOW** will I organize the business?

- **WHAT** is the long-term economic outlook for my chosen field of endeavor?

- **HOW** much startup capital do I need?

- **HOW** much emergency capital can I put aside to cover periods when things are slow?

- **WHAT** will my annual business expenses be for each of the next five years?

- **WHAT** will my annual business income be for each of the next five years?

- **HOW** will I market my service or product?

Of course, just because you've drawn up a well-organized plan doesn't mean you have to adhere to it slavishly. Indeed, as your business starts to grow, you may well find that your original assumptions were partially or entirely inaccurate. Don't be afraid to rethink your plan if real-world business conditions warrant it.

If at all possible, begin your new venture on a "moonlighting" basis. Having the security of a steady paycheck will do much to steady your nerves, not to mention your bank account, in the hard days when your business is a struggling enterprise. But once things begin to get going, you will eventually come to a crossroads: Choose either the business or the job. At that point, it will have become quite clear that continuing with a full-time job is simply impossible. Be prepared to cut back on your life-style during the first few years of your business's operation. Most likely, all of your disposable income—not to mention a good deal of your other income—will be used up capitalizing your venture.

Smart Money Move

Start a business that you already understand by virtue of your work or hobby experience.

Striking Out on Your Own Without Striking Out Financially

For every story of the fabulously wealthy entrepreneur who started a business with $500, there are scores of untold stories of unsuccessful entrepreneurs who risked their life savings, went deeply into debt, and then lost everything. Job security has been the biggest victim of the recent recession, so it's not surprising that more people are thinking about starting their own businesses. Starting any business is risky, but there are ways to manage the financial risk so that you don't jeopardize your financial future.

First, if at all possible, don't quit your day job until the business is established and it is clear that you can draw enough salary to support yourself. If this is not possible, you should have two years' worth of living expenses already in the bank.

Second, figure out how to start your business on a shoestring. High overhead at the outset can kill a business before it has had a chance to succeed. Can you work out of your home or a shared office space? If you must have a store, negotiate a short-term lease on favorable terms, and buy used furniture and equipment. In short, do whatever you can to keep your overhead to a minimum.

Third, don't risk all your personal savings and investments on your new venture. There is nothing as discouraging as seeing a lifetime's worth of savings evaporate, only to be left deeply in debt and have to rejoin the work world. Obviously, you are going to have to risk some of your personal wealth when starting a business, but if you have to bet the ranch, the odds are that you'll lose it.

Finally, try to arrange financing that does not require your personal guarantee. This may mean getting someone to provide financing in exchange for stock in the new company, but it is better to own 50 percent of a successful and adequately capitalized business than to own 100 percent of a failing business.

In spite of all these caveats, starting a business is filled with excitement and promise. The satisfaction of launching a successful venture cannot be matched. But if you want to strike out on your own, make sure your personal finances don't strike out in the process.

The Importance of Good Sales Skills

N o matter how good your service or product may be, if you can't effectively thrust it into the public eye, your business may as well not even exist. If you don't have good sales skills, you need to develop some quickly. The technical and managerial skills you bring to your business will all go for naught should you be unable to promote and sell your product and yourself.

Some people are uncomfortable selling. Others, who have never sold before, adapt quite readily. If you don't have a sales background, you need to take a close and objective look at how comfortable you will be in a sales capacity. It is quite likely that you will spend a substantial portion of time selling your product or service, at least for the first two years your business is in operation.

Smart Money Move

Sales skills are crucial to succeeding in a new business. You must either have them already or develop them quickly.

Hot Prospects for the 1990s and the New Century

Even though the overall economy is currently languishing, certain areas remain robust. While no one can predict the future with certainty, it is unlikely that the 1990s will be a repeat of the economic boom of the 1980s. More likely, the end of this decade and the beginning of the new century will likely be characterized by inconsistency—high rates of growth in some sectors, stagnation or shrinkage in others.

Selecting the right kind of business to enter is always important, but it may be even more important when economic prospects are less than terrific. The key to finding the right business to start is to first identify the area or areas where you are experienced, then match your expertise to the kinds of businesses that have attractive growth prospects. What areas are likely to experience above-average growth? Here are some:

- HEALTH CARE

- PRODUCTS AND SERVICES FOR THE ELDERLY

- ENERGY EFFICIENCY

- ENVIRONMENTAL PROTECTION

- PRODUCTS AND SERVICES THAT MAKE HOME LIFE EASIER

- COMPUTER AND SOFTWARE PRODUCTS AND SERVICES

- PRODUCTS AND SERVICES THAT ARE APPEALING TO FOREIGN MARKETS

Insurance—Look Before You Leap

If you are planning to set up your own business, your mind is probably chock-full of cost estimates, five-year plans, and sales projections. But one item that may not be first on your list of items to include in your cost-benefit equations is how much you will have to pay for insurance once you are no longer under your employer's umbrella. This could be a big mistake, for once you are out on your own, insurance premiums will take a big bite out of your income.

How much could it cost? The numbers vary greatly based on geographical location, age, and other factors. In the most expensive metropolitan areas, coverage for a family of four—where the breadwinner earns $75,000 at his old job—assuring continuity in health, disability and life insurance, could cost as much as $10,000 annually. Premiums can be reduced by taking actions like opting for higher deductibles.

Nonetheless, the fact remains that insurance could become a major expense once you set up your own shop, so make sure you include its cost in your expense calculations. It pays to look before you leap.

Paring Down Your Operating Costs

E very penny that you can cut from your new business's operating budget is one more penny of profit (or one less penny of loss). The following twenty tips will help you stretch to the limit each dollar you spend to keep your business running.

1. When you start your business, select the form of business organization that will be cheapest in the long run

The decision to form a corporation or proprietorship is not an easy one. You may benefit from the advice of an attorney or accountant when you set up a business. One major consideration is to select the form of business organization that will be the least expensive in the long run. If you cannot afford to obtain professional advice, go to the library or bookstore and find one of the many available books on starting your own business. The cheapest way to organize is a sole proprietorship.

2. Work out of your home

One of the biggest mistakes budding entrepreneurs can make when their businesses are new is to saddle themselves with too much overhead. If at all possible, start your business out of your home rather than renting an office, with all the costs associated with rental space. Of course, some businesses, such as retailing or food service, cannot effectively be run out of a home. But all too often new entrepreneurs delude themselves into thinking that they must have fancy digs. They end up regretting the decision later.

3. Find low-cost rental space

If and when you need an office, warehouse, or retail space, search around for the lowest-cost location that will still meet your needs. Rents can vary dramatically in a single locale and even on a single block. Avoid the temptation to rent in a higher-cost building. While it may not seem significant now, a high rent can really drag down a growing business. Look at it this way: Your customers will probably appreciate the fact that your quarters are modest rather than located in domains of mahogany and marble.

4. Obtain free media publicity

The media are always starved for good stories. If you can put together a good story about your business that will appeal to a particular newspaper, magazine, or radio show, you have a good chance of gaining free publicity. Moreover, positive comments about your business in a column, article, or radio or television program are usually much more convincing than the usual advertisements.

5. Buy your business cards, stationery, and forms on the cheap

Chances are you don't need to spend a lot of money on designing a fancy logo and on purchasing expensive business cards, stationery, and forms. You can get perfectly satisfactory printed items at much lower cost by using a mail-order stationery company or a local print shop. Remember, too-fancy stationery may send the wrong signal in the 1990s. Your customers want to know that you are as concerned about controlling expenses as they are. Engraved stationery printed on thick bond paper could send the wrong signal.

6. Establish an in-house advertising agency

This is one of the oldest tricks in the book. Advertising agencies receive a 15 percent discount from publications and broadcasters. But you don't need an advertising agency to take advantage of the discount. All you need to do is establish your own "in-house." How do you go about it? The absolute most you'll typically need is some stationery and a separate checking account with the agency's name on it. But you probably won't even need that.

7. Contact the SBA (Small Business Administration) and SCORE (Service Corps of Retired Executives) for free advice

Both the SBA and SCORE are excellent sources for free consultations. Why pay a consultant wearing a thousand-dollar suit when you can probably get free advice?

8. Purchase advertising space in regional editions

You can advertise in big-name publications for a lot less than you think by purchasing space in regional editions. This is a good idea especially if your customers are located in a particular region, or if you simply want to advertise in a big publication so you can brag about it (not a bad idea in and of itself).

9. Buy office supplies at discounters

Don't pay full price for office supplies. It's easy to get handsome discounts at one of the many office-supply discount houses. None are located in your area? Contact a mail-order discounter.

10. Consider employing your spouse and/or children

If you own a business, there may be a variety of advantages in putting your spouse and/or children on the payroll. But be sure they really work, lest you cross the IRS. Still, it's in your financial best interest to keep your money flowing into the family coffers.

11. Use bulk-rate postage when sending out large mailings

Many small business owners make the mistake of sending out large mailings using first-class postage. If they used bulk-rate mail, they would save a bundle.

12. Buy used office furniture

Used, low-cost office furniture is in abundant supply. There's no reason for a small business to adorn its offices with fancy new furniture when attractive preowned furniture is available.

13. If you use your car for business travel, you can deduct unreimbursed expenses relating to the use of your vehicle

Does your business take you out on the road frequently? If you use your personal car for these trips but are not reimbursed for the costs of operating your chariot, you may be entitled to deduct these expenses on your income tax return. Calculate your deduction by using either a standard mileage rate or by keeping a log of the actual costs of operating your automobile during business trips.

14. Use independent contractors if you can legally

If you can use independent contractors, you can avoid paying the high costs associated with full-time employees, including Social Security and fringe benefits. But be careful: The IRS is clamping down on business owners who abuse the rules pertaining to independent contractors.

15. Be firm in your accounts receivable collection efforts

Don't let your customers take advantage of your good nature—it ends up being the "nice guy" who gets paid last. So if some of your customers are stringing you out, be firm in your collection efforts. Don't worry about alienating the customer. Your business will never survive if your customers are unwilling to pay you within a reasonable period of time.

16. Don't pay your accounts payable too soon

Although vendors will love you if you pay your bills early, it only ends up costing you money. Set a file for your accounts payable so that you pay them no sooner than on time.

17. Don't entertain customers lavishly

In the frugal 1990s, three-martini lunches are as passé as $100-a-head dinners. If you end up entertaining customers lavishly, you not only end up spending a lot of precious money, you risk sending your customers the wrong message. It's okay to entertain them, but be sure to project a "lean and mean" image when you do.

18. Bargain hard if you want to buy an existing business

If you are going into business for yourself, you have two choices. One is to start the business yourself; the other is to buy an existing business. If you choose the second route, be sure not to overpay. Most sellers have an inflated view of the value of their businesses—just as we all do when we go to sell our homes. You can probably settle for considerably less than the asking price. Just as with any major purchase, don't hesitate to walk away from an intransigent seller. Also, it wouldn't hurt to hire a professional appraiser to give you an objective assessment of the business's value.

19. Encourage free word-of-mouth advertising

Whatever business you're in, word-of-mouth advertising is the best and cheapest. Do what you can to stimulate positive word-of-mouth advertising, first by satisfying your customers, and second by asking them to spread the good word about your business. You'll be pleasantly surprised at how effective this can be.

20. Cut your losses if your business is not working out

If you start your own business, the odds are regrettably high against your succeeding. There may well come a time when you have to realistically evaluate whether you should continue your business. If you do find yourself facing this difficult decision, you may want to seek the counsel of an accountant or other financial professional. What you don't want to do is throw good money after bad. Far too many entrepreneurs, by nature an optimistic lot, have risked their homes, their savings, and almost everything else to support doomed businesses. It is far preferable to cut your losses or, at a minimum, sharply cut back your business aspirations.

STARTING A BUSINESS CHECKLIST

☐ Start a business in which you can exploit your experience and skills. Don't start a business that you don't understand.

☐ Look for a business that will thrive in the 1990s and the next century.

☐ Prepare a thorough business plan—it is essential to business success.

☐ Avoid risking all your personal savings or going into a lot of debt to start a business.

☐ Cut your expenses to a minimum. High overhead can kill a new business.

Small Business Owners and Self-Employed Professionals

I f you are a self-employed professional or run your own business, you share many common financial goals and concerns with other occupations. You belong, however, to a group that faces a number of financial-planning concerns and opportunities that are quite different from those of the wage-earning world. Your employment status can and should influence the course of your personal financial planning. This chapter will show you where you must concentrate your efforts to assure a comfortable and secure financial future.

The Financial-Planning Quandaries of Self-Employment

I ndependent businesspeople are often so engrossed by their work that they lack the time, energy, and sometimes the knowledge to manage their personal finances effectively. This is hardly surprising: When every ounce of energy is devoted to your profession, the sometimes mundane details of personal finance all too easily fall by the wayside. For a variety of reasons, if you are your own boss, you must—even more than your wage-earning counterparts—focus on planning your financial future. The following sections address areas of particular concern to the small business owner.

The Big Picture

Frugality is a virtue much needed by the self-employed: Independent businesspeople must exercise particular care in their personal spending and borrowing. You should always be prepared for the onset of a business slump—an event that may require dipping into your personal resources to meet business expenses. Ideally, to be truly prepared to face whatever adversity comes your way, you should be able to sustain your business for at least a year on significantly lower revenue.

The entrepreneur who always keeps an eye trained on the horizon is best able to survive the inevitable business downturns. You must be prepared to pay both your personal living expenses and business overhead during this period.

The biggest mistake a small business owner can make is to assume that his or her business, in and of itself, will be able to be sold for enough money to be able to provide lifelong financial security. Few small businesses create enough value to do so. Therefore, most self-employed people must accumulate investments outside the business—just like any wage-earner—and at the same level. At least 10 percent of income should be set aside, outside the business, although more is even better.

Investments Outside Your Business

Small business owners often have a substantial portion, if not most, of their wealth tied up in their businesses. The risk of "having all your eggs in one basket" is a serious one. One of the most important things you can do to assure your long-term financial security is to build up a diversified investment portfolio outside your business.

Ideally, this portfolio should be hedged with investments that will perform reasonably well when economic conditions do not favor your business. For example, if you're in a business that is susceptible to downturns in the general business cycle, concentrate your stock investments in stocks that thrive even when business is down, like food and pharmaceutical companies. (See Chapter 52 to learn about how to invest effectively.)

Insurance Coverage

While securing the right kind of insurance coverage is important to people of every occupation, many independent businesspeople have particular needs and problems that must be addressed in order to assure comprehensive coverage. For one thing, self-employed people often cannot afford to provide comprehensive insurance coverage for themselves and for their employees through their businesses. It is simply too costly. If this describes your situation, you need to obtain adequate health, disability, and life insurance coverage outside the business.

As a business owner, you must also be concerned about how your business will run in the event of your disability or death. An owner's disability or death can seriously jeopardize the health of a small business. You should speak with the agent who handles your business insurance coverage about special policies that cover these eventualities.

The need for personal and professional liability insurance is greater if you are an independent businessperson. Successful self-employed professionals and small business owners are often high-profile members of their communities, and they need correspondingly higher limits of liability insurance than might otherwise be necessary. Sadly, whether it is true or not, business owners are viewed as having deep pockets: they make attractive lawsuit targets.

Taxes

I t is important to understand the effects of taxes on both your business and your personal financial situation. Fortunately, the tax laws look favorably upon the self-employed. As you probably realize, the tax code allows you to take a number of deductions for business-related expenses, and you should take full advantage of these deductions.

Deductible expenses for professionals include the cost of supplies, the expense of operating and maintaining an automobile used in the business, dues paid to professional organizations, rent for office space, the cost of fuel, light, water, and telephone used in the office, the cost of hiring assistants, and the cost of books, instruments, and equipment when such items have a short useful life. The cost of items with a long useful life, like office furniture and equipment and professional books, are not deducted in the year purchased; rather, they are depreciated over several years.

Expenses incurred in attending business conventions and the cost of subscriptions to professional journals or information services bought in connection with the performance of your business or professional duties are normally deductible as a business expense. You can also deduct any contributions you make to a qualified pension plan. You may be allowed a deduction for business entertainment, as long as there is a direct relationship between the expense and the development or expansion of your business.

If you have an office at home, you may qualify for beneficial tax treatment. You must be able to prove, however, that you use your office home exclusively or on a regular basis as either (1) a place to meet with clients or customers in the normal course of business or (2) your principal place of business.

Smart Money Move

Insure your business to assure that it will continue to operate in the event of lawsuit or your disability or death.

All in the Family

Many independent businesspeople are discovering the tax advantages of hiring family members in their businesses. For instance, if your spouse helps with keeping the books or any other duty for the benefit of the company, he or she should be put on the payroll. The compensation paid must be "reasonable" for the IRS to accept the deduction. In essence, this means you should pay the prevailing rate that other employers pay for the same type of work. In addition to the pay, your employed family members may enjoy a variety of other benefits, including participation in the company retirement plan, qualification for an IRA, and insurance coverage.

Finally, remember that a loss incurred in your proprietorship, partnership, or Subchapter S corporation is deductible from your other income. Conversely, any net taxable income from your business, unless it is a Subchapter C Corporation, is added to your other income on your personal tax return.

Retirement

Smart Money Moves

Take maximum advantage of tax-deductible and tax-deferrable pension plans available to the self-employed.

Provide for the orderly succession or disposition of your business in your estate planning.

Consider the many advantages of hiring family members.

Self-employed professionals and small business owners must take the initiative to establish and maintain their own retirement plans. While many independent businesspeople simply assume that the eventual sale of their business will fund their retirement, most small businesses and professional practices cannot be easily sold or liquidated. Selling a closely held or family-owned business is often a tricky and difficult proposition, and owners frequently think their businesses are worth a lot more than they eventually fetch. The sure way to provide for a secure retirement is to accumulate funds outside your business. This may be accomplished in one of two ways. Either save money the old-fashioned way, or let Uncle Sam subsidize your retirement by taking advantge of one of the tax-deductible, tax-deferred retirement plans available to the self-employed (see Chapter 74).

Estate Planning

Estate planning for self-employed professionals and small-business owners is usually more complex than it is for wage-earners. In some instances, it can be very complex. For small business owners, the overriding concern is how—and whether—to pass the business on to family members, either at the time of retirement or upon your death.

If family members are not going to take over your business, your estate plan must address the question of how to dispose of it, whether through the provision of a successor management or through the orderly sale or liquidation of the business. In any case, make sure that your estate plan provides sufficient liquidity to allow the continuation and/or orderly liquidation of your business. You must also have enough cash available to cover your survivors' immediate needs and estate tax bills.

Self-employed people often accumulate larger estates than wage-earners, and they can benefit from more advanced estate-planning techniques. These techniques not only maximize the amount that can be transferred to the next generation, they may provide certain protections and benefits during your lifetime (see Chapter 82).

Cutting Your Business Expenses

Even successful and seasoned independent businesspeople can benefit from learning new techniques to reduce the costs of running a business. The following tips will help you send less to your creditors and more to your bank account.

1. Pay business expenses in the current year rather than deferring payment until the next year

The more deductible expenses you can accumulate during a profitable tax year, the smaller your tax bill will be. To the extent possible under IRS regulations, pay as many business expenses during the current year as you possibly can.

2. Do your own accounting or have a low-cost service do it

So many small business owners are so intimidated by accounting that they think they must use an accountant. Chances are you can do your own accounting, because for a small business accounting really isn't that difficult. In fact, you can do most of your accounting right out of your checkbook. A number of companies offer inexpensive "one-write" checkbook systems that will allow you to make accounting entries at the same time you make a deposit or write out a check. Alternatively, a number of inexpensive software programs make accounting easy. Therefore, while you certainly should be preparing accounting statements to measure how your business is doing, try to do it yourself first rather than hiring someone to do it for you.

3. If you expect your business to be in a higher tax bracket next year, accelerate the billing and collection of receivables into the current tax year

The rules are simple. If rising income will push your company up into a higher tax bracket in the next tax year, accumulate as much profit as possible in the current year.

4. If you're selling your business or part of your business, consider timing the sale so as to minimize or postpone taxes

The sale of a business requires as much professional counsel as the acquisition of a business. Mistakes can have a very serious effect on the ultimate amount you realize from the sale of your business.

5. Negotiate interest rates on business loans

Next time you apply for a business loan, remember that you might be able to negotiate an interest rate that is lower than the rate first offered to you. Often there is some room for negotiation, so it doesn't hurt to try.

6. Structure business loans to maximize tax benefits

Be sure to understand the tax benefits or drawbacks of any loans you are contemplating for your business. Generally, this is particularly important for small business owners who are using a mixture of personal and business loans to finance their business. Proper advance planning (and the help of a tax accountant or tax lawyer, if a large sum of money is involved) can assure that you get the maximum tax benefit out of your business loans.

7. Barter your goods or services for advertising, if possible

You may be able to find an advertiser who needs or can make use of your business's goods or services, which can save you a great deal in advertising costs.

8. Send out bills regularly

Don't let your accounts receivable mount. It's easy to overlook or postpone billing when you're immersed in the day-to-day operations of your business, but collections are your lifeblood. Prepare bills on a regular schedule.

9. Become active in your community

Are most of your customers located in and around your city or town? If so, become active in your community. Potential customers who are aware of your civic activity are more likely to support your business. If you don't think so, check out the occupations of the people who are active in your town. Many of them will be small business owners.

10. Send nonurgent faxes after hours when phone rates are lower

If you are like most small business owners, you're working well into the night anyway. So send faxes in the evening or on weekends, when phone rates are lower.

CHECKLIST FOR THE SELF-EMPLOYED PROFESSIONAL AND SMALL BUSINESS OWNER

☐ Accumulate an investment portfolio outside the business in order to sustain the business in the event of a downturn, as well as to provide a nest egg independent of the business.

☐ Take advantage of the many tax breaks that are available to self-employed professionals and small business owners.

■

Accumulate retirement-oriented resources outside the business, since most small businesses and professional practices do not create enough value to provide, in and of themselves, sufficient resources to assure their owner's financial security.

■

Make provisions in both your lifetime financial planning and your estate planning to assure business continuity in the event of your disability or death.

30

Living with a Fluctuating Income

This chapter will help commissioned salespeople—and members of other occupations whose incomes fluctuate—do a better job managing their money. If you are an insurance agent, a stockbroker, a real estate agent, or a commissioned salesperson of any sort, you should be prepared to weather difficult periods when your income declines.

And you don't have to work on commission to be subject to a fluctuating income. Perhaps you are paid an annual bonus based on your performance and/or the performance of your company, or you may be able to earn overtime at your job. Of course, you can't bank on bonuses and overtime continuing indefinitely. They could evaporate almost overnight. Or you may own a business where your income level fluctuates depending on the business's success.

Granted, salespeople and others whose income fluctuate are often among the highest-paid employees in many industries. And yes, their higher incomes provide them with the opportunity to build up savings and to take advantage of many investment opportunities. On the other hand, the high-income aspect of the job seduces all too many salespeople into living beyond their means—they simply adjust their spending to equal their income in the good years. That's fine when times are fat, but financial travail can be only a paycheck away when the lean times come—and they always do.

If you're in sales, chances are that you're too busy hustling for business to devote the amount of time necessary to plan your finances effectively. Yet developing a good financial plan is critical. Otherwise, even a slight downturn in your business could drastically reduce your paycheck for an extended period of time. The following sections address financial planning issues that are especially important if your annual income is likely to fluctuate.

Spending and Saving

If you can't discipline yourself to live off your base salary, you should build up sufficient savings to allow you to live for a year on your base salary—without commissions, bonuses, or overtime. You may have to cut back on your life-style in order to divert enough income into your savings fund, but having a good cushion could be crucial. If you can't start saving now because you have to make payments on the vacation home, the motorboat, or the third

Smart Money Move

Set aside sufficient savings to be able to live on your base salary alone.

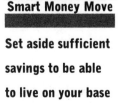

car, now is the time, perhaps, to cut back a bit on these luxuries. Once you have built up your reserve, you may be able to indulge yourself once again, but meanwhile, pare down your consumption enough to begin accumulating an emergency investment fund.

With a solid investment reserve, you will be able to weather an economic downturn without facing a drastic alteration in your life-style, and you will be able to keep current on your debts even though your income is down. By the way, don't consider your retirement savings as part of your investment reserve. Your retirement funds should be kept intact until you retire.

Insurance Coverage

I f your total compensation has a large commission- or bonus-based component, your employer may be basing your disability and life insurance benefits on your base salary alone. If so, should you become disabled or die, your company-provided benefits will probably be inadequate to support you or your survivors. To avoid this eventuality, you should obtain enough supplementary insurance to bridge the gap between your company-provided benefits and what you and/or your family would need to support a reasonable life-style. (Consult Chapters 38 and 42 for in-depth discussions of how to obtain the supplementary insurance coverage you need.)

Tax Planning

Smart Money Move

If your disability and life insurance benefits are based on your base salary, bring your coverage up to an adequate level by purchasing coverage individually.

M any people with fluctuating incomes—salespeople, in particular—are able to take advantage of a number of tax deductions that are not available to members of many other occupations. What's the reason for this? Many salespeople incur certain expenses in conjunction with their work, particularly with respect to activities in selling and promoting, that may be tax-deductible. Unreimbursed employee business expenses, including car expenses and travel, can be claimed as "miscellaneous itemized deductions." Since miscellaneous itemized deductions must exceed a two percent floor of your adjusted gross income (AGI) before the deductions are allowed, it is quite possible that none of your unreimbursed expenses will be of help in reducing your taxable income. But add them up anyway to see if they are high enough to shave a bit off your tax bill.

Note: If you are claiming business expenses as an employee, you are required to file Form 2106, "Employee Business Expenses," with your tax return. Self-employed salespersons will generally record all business expenses on Schedule C of Form 1040.

Record-Keeping for Business Expenses

Good record-keeping is essential if you are to maximize your business-related deductions and substantiate them later. Salespeople are usually pretty good about keeping records of business contacts and meetings. These good record-keeping habits should also extend to tax matters. Perhaps the best way to do this is to keep a diary with you at all times in which you can note day-to-day business-related expenses, as well as travel itineraries and notations of business meetings.

Retirement Planning

People whose incomes are subject to fluctuation have two retirement-planning concerns, which, while not unique to them, are nevertheless more commonly encountered among them. First, if you work for a company that provides few or no pension benefits, or if the pension benefits are based upon your base salary (exclusive of commissions and bonuses), then you'll have to accumulate retirement resources outside any company-sponsored retirement plan. Unfortunately, the spending temptations that accompany a higher income leave many salespeople short when retirement time rolls around.

The second matter that affects people who work on commission perhaps more than members of other occupations is job-hopping. If you find yourself moving from one company to another in pursuit of a better deal, you may pay a price in terms of your ultimate pension benefits. Frequent job-hoppers accrue few if any vested pension benefits because they never work long enough for one company. Even periodic job-hoppers who work for companies with pension plans usually end up with far fewer pension benefits than do their more sedentary colleagues. While there may be many valid reasons for changing jobs, remember that there is a "price" to be paid with respect to your retirement. The answer, of course, is to save and invest enough money to offset the lower company pension benefits that you will receive. Ignore this advice at your own peril.

LIVING WITH A FLUCTUATING INCOME CHECKLIST

Smart Money Move

People who change jobs with any frequency should offset the loss of retirement benefits with a greater level of savings.

☐ Avoid the temptation of adjusting your spending to equal your income in a good year, then having to cut back when the bad years follow.

☐ Be sure that you have adequate insurance coverage, particularly if your employer bases your disability and life insurance on your base salary.

If you are a commissioned salesperson who cannot participate in your company pension plan to the full extent of your income, increase your participation in personal retirement savings plans.

Unemployment

Losing your job is traumatic under any circumstances. If you've recently joined the ranks of the unemployed, you need to attend to two important but difficult matters. First, you must strive to overcome the personal anxiety you are almost certainly experiencing. Second, you need to assess your financial situation so that you can cope with the loss of income. Above all, don't panic. You *can* and *will* overcome this temporary setback. If you're still in the workforce but fear that you may lose your job, don't delay preparing for that eventuality (see page 250).

Overcoming Anxiety

Before you can get your feet back on the ground, you must overcome the inevitable psychological and emotional stress. Most people go through three stages of anxiety:

1. **IMMEDIATE PANIC.** Your first reaction to losing your job may be to hide this fact from your family and friends. Some people even go to the extreme of leaving home every day as if they were going to their job. Avoid this temptation. Your family and friends will provide enormous support, and the more support you have, the easier it will be for you to get back on your feet and find another (probably better) job.

2. **GUILT AND LACK OF SELF-WORTH.** After your initial panic has subsided, you may begin to blame yourself for your plight. You may feel that you have let yourself and your family down and be convinced that job prospects are going to be pretty poor. Obviously, these feelings are not going to help your situation, but you need to recognize that you are likely to go through this stage.

3. **ANGER AT THE WORLD.** Finally, you will begin to feel angry about your situation. It is not until you get through this last stage that you will be in the frame of mind to present yourself to a prospective employer convincingly. This stage typically leads to renewed self-confidence and determination.

Most important, you must be willing to ask for help. Other people can offer you emotional support and can be a source of information about new employment opportunities. The sooner you face up to your situation, the sooner you will be able to evaluate your financial

status, and the sooner you will be able to begin the search. Let the world know you're looking for a new job.

Coping with the Loss of Income

In spite of the emotional trauma, you must evaluate your current financial situation
realistically so that you can adjust to your temporarily changed financial circumstances. This is particularly important if you lose your job during a tight job market,
when you may spend more time unemployed than you would during more prosperous
times. You need to address the following matters.

Understand Severance Benefits

Be sure you understand your employer's severance benefits, such as salary continuation,
payment for accrued vacation, and insurance benefits. If you are about to be laid off or have
just been laid off, it may be possible for you to negotiate additional severance benefits from
your employer. Experts suggest that this be done within a day or two of the layoff, when the
employer is most apt to respond to your appeal.

Assure Continuation of Health and Life Insurance Coverage

It is advantageous to continue to carry your employer-provided health and life insurance
coverage as well as all other insurance coverage. Most employers are required by a federal
law known as COBRA to allow you to continue your company health insurance plan for up
to eighteen months without a medical checkup as long as you pay the premiums (see page
314). While the premiums may be steep, you should not go one minute without health
insurance coverage. Alternatively, you might be able to save some money by purchasing a
temporary insurance policy, which usually covers periods from three months to one year.
Acquiring a new policy, even a temporary one, may require a medical checkup and/or pre-
clude preexisting conditions. Be sure that the temporary health insurance coverage does
not leave any gaps that could cost you dearly when you can least afford it. (Should you need
to purchase a temporary health insurance policy, see Chapter 39.)

Smart Money Move

Never allow impor-
tant insurance cov-
erage to lapse while
you're unemployed.

If your employer does not continue your life insurance coverage,
you may be able to convert your employer's group policy to an individual policy. Otherwise, you may be able to purchase low-cost life
insurance coverage to replace your company-provided policy by
shopping around for the best rates (see pages 299 and 375).
Unfortunately, you will not be able to continue or obtain disability
insurance coverage while you're unemployed.

Apply for Unemployment Compensation Benefits

If you've been let go, you are entitled to collect unemployment compensation benefits. Strange as it may seem, some people—perhaps out of a sense of pride or embarrassment—don't want to collect these benefits even though they are eligible. But realize that your employers have been paying into the unemployment benefits fund ever since you entered the workforce.

Take Stock of Your Ready Resources

Your primary financial concern is how you're going to meet your financial obligations during your period of unemployment, so you should begin by taking stock of your available resources. Your available resources consist of your cash reserves as well as any investments that can be sold and converted into cash in a short period of time. The worksheet will help you summarize your ready resources. Once you know how much (or how little) you have available, you can begin to prepare a budget that will sustain you during your period of unemployment.

READY RESOURCES WORKSHEET

LUMP SUM SEVERANCE BENEFITS	$ ....
CASH IN BANK ACCOUNTS	....
SAVINGS, MONEY-MARKET ACCOUNTS	....
CDS AND OTHER INTEREST-EARNING INVESTMENTS	....
STOCK INVESTMENTS	....
MUTUAL FUNDS	....
OTHER AVAILABLE RESOURCES	....
TOTAL READY RESOURCES	$ ....

Reduce Your Spending

Unless you are one of the few who are blessed with a lot of money, you are probably going to have to reduce your spending at least for a while. Before you can do this, you should summarize your past spending patterns so that you can identify ways to cut expenses. If you are unclear as to where your wage income has been going, you should take a look at Chapter 6 to get a handle on setting up a budget.

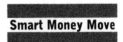

Smart Money Move

Prepare a realistic budget of income and expenses, then devise a plan to cover any shortfall.

Prepare a Budget

Once you have figured out what income and resources you have and how you have been spending your money, you are ready to prepare an unemployment budget. Ideally, this should ensure that you will be able to meet your important bills over the next six months. The budget worksheet provided in Chapter 6 may be used for this purpose.

First, determine what your income sources will be, including severance and unemployment benefits, income from your spouse's job, and investment income—unless you will have to liquidate those investments to meet living expenses. Next, summarize your expected expenses, starting with the expenses that must be paid (rent/mortgage and groceries, for example) and ending with those expenses that can be forgone (restaurant dining and vacations, for example).

After you have summarized your projected expenses, you can compare them with your expected income and decide how you are going to close the gap between income (probably too little) and expenses (probably too much). The key to dealing with the financial strain of unemployment is to reduce expenses as much as possible. If your unemployment income is insufficient to meet your reduced expense level, you will have to use your ready resources to help meet expenses.

Your Job Search

Whether your financial situation is pretty good or pretty dismal, you need to approach the job search with the same enthusiasm and dedication with which you would approach any new and challenging task. Sure, you'll be discouraged by any rejections, but you *will* succeed sooner rather than later, as long as you sustain your effort.

While you are unemployed, consider doing volunteer work. It will keep you busy during time not spent looking for work. Also, it can account for the period of unemployment on your résumé, and employers may be impressed by your resourcefulness during a time when far too many unemployed people sit at home feeling sorry for themselves.

If You Think You May Lose Your Job

Assess the Situation

Perhaps the first thing to do if you are worried about losing your job is to assess, as realistically as possible, the probability that the ax might fall. Rumors of massive layoffs can circulate around large companies for years without any occurring. Many more people fret about being laid off than actually join the ranks of the unemployed. It can be difficult to predict how, where, and when company layoffs may occur. You can still try, however, to make an objective assessment of the likelihood that you are going to lose your job and when it might occur. Has the company gone through previous layoffs? How essential is your department, and how is it doing during the recession?

If you fear that you may lose your job because of poor business conditions, company restructuring, or other circumstances, you should start planning now. Even if you don't lose your job, you won't be any worse off from making these preparations. Preparing in advance for the loss of a job can reduce the disruptions to your career and personal finances that are almost inevitable should you be handed a pink slip.

Examine Job Opportunities

Should you look for another job? If your assessment leads you to believe that you may be one of the victims, there is no reason to delay taking action. Begin your job search now—but do it discreetly!

Arm Yourself with Information

Another advantage of being realistic about your job prospects is that you can prepare for the fateful day not only from a financial standpoint (discussed below), but from the standpoint of dealing with your employer. Even though most layoff victims anticipate that they are going to lose their jobs, they are often so shocked when it happens that they are not in a position to negotiate a better severance arrangement.

Your employer is much more likely to accommodate your needs if you express them immediately at the time of severance. Experts suggest you will be able to do this much better if you are prepared for the layoff. Remember, the company is as uncomfortable about letting people go as the employees are about being let go. Even if you are not in a position to improve your severance arrangement, by being mentally prepared you will be well on your way to landing on your feet and finding another job.

Reviewing Your Financial Status

You can take several financial actions prior to your expected unemployment that can help reduce your fiscal duress. Incidentally, many of these suggestions are a good idea under any circumstances, not just under threat of imminent unemployment.

Prepare a Survival Budget

You should prepare a budget that assumes that you will be unemployed for a period of six months. First, estimate your income during unemployment, including unemployment compensation benefits and severance payments. Look carefully at your past expenses and classify them according to expenses that must be paid (such as the mortgage or rent), necessities that could be reduced somewhat in the event of dire financial straits, and discretionary expenses like clothing, vacations, and meals at restaurants. (Chapter 6 provides guidance on preparing personal budgets.) If your expected income during unemployment is going to be insufficient to meet your

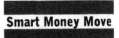

Smart Money Move

If you think a layoff is imminent, plan to negotiate a better severance deal.

expenses—and it probably will—you can plan how you will close the gap. It will probably involve a combination of reducing your living expenses and finding other sources of income.

Reduce Current Spending in Order to Increase Savings

The two best things that you can do to prepare for financial adversity go hand in hand: reduce your current level of spending, and increase your savings. Setting aside some savings now may come in very handy in helping you meet your living expenses later if you become unemployed. A financial cushion is the best way to soften the trauma of unemployment. It is bad enough that you may have to go through the job-hunting process. But it would be doubly unfortunate to have to worry about making ends meet.

Manage Your Debt

If you have outstanding debts, such as auto and credit card loans, you may be wondering whether you should reduce them in anticipation of unemployment rather than increase your savings level. In general, if you are concerned about losing your job, you should be careful not to fall behind in debt payments, but you're better off putting extra money in savings rather than further reducing your debt. Why? If you do lose your job, you may have to dip into savings to meet your living expenses. If you had used the money to reduce your debts, this potential financial cushion would not be available to you. Paying down high-interest debt is a good idea under more normal economic circumstances. Your financial uncertainty, however, requires that you establish a generous emergency fund rather than reducing your indebtedness any more than necessary.

Adjust Your Tax Withholding

If you are quite certain that you are going to be laid off, you might want to arrange to have less income tax withheld from your paycheck (by increasing the number of exemptions) so that your take-home pay is increased. This will provide extra income for you to use when you are unemployed. Since your income will almost certainly drop when you are laid off, the taxes owed will probably balance out by the end of the year, even though you decreased your tax withholdings while you were still employed.

Defer Large Expenditures

Now is *not* the time to make any large purchases like a new car or home improvements. These commitments should be deferred at least until you are confident that your job is not in jeopardy.

Plan for Continuity of Insurance Coverage

One of the worst things people can do during a period of financial adversity is to let their insurance coverage lapse. Stories abound of people who thought they couldn't afford to continue their health insurance coverage, only to find their finances wiped out by an uninsured illness. Be sure to include a provision in your budget for paying insurance premiums.

Also, decide ahead of time how you are going to replace your employer-provided health and life insurance when it expires. Your company is probably required to allow you to continue your group health coverage for a period of 18 months after termination as long as you pay the premiums—look into it.

Review Your Investments

If you are expecting to lose your job, you should review your investments for two reasons. First, you need to assess how much of your invested funds can be readily converted into cash to meet living expenses if the need to do so arises. Second, you want to consider selling some "low-yield" investments like stocks that pay little or no dividends. Reinvest the proceeds from selling these investments into interest-earning securities; these securities will provide you with higher current income to help meet expenses while your salary is temporarily eliminated. You have to weigh the tax effects of any investment transactions, however. For example, it may not make sense to sell very-low-tax-basis stock investments in order to buy interest-earning investments, since the capital gains taxes you will have to pay on the sale will reduce the resources available for reinvestment in interest-earning securities.

MAKING ENDS MEET WHILE UNEMPLOYED

- **KEEP UP** with your mortgage payments since your house is probably your largest investment.

- **YOU MAY BE ABLE** to borrow from your company salary reduction plan (401[k]) or pension plan. But tapping into these important retirement plans should not be taken lightly.

- **CONSIDER** tapping other retirement accounts like IRAs and deferred annuities if you must, though you'll incur a penalty.

- **CONSIDER** part-time work to augment your income.

- **RESIST** the temptation that many laid-off people have of starting their own business.

- **IF** it appears likely that you are going to have trouble meeting your obligations to creditors, be sure to contact them and work out a more comfortable payment schedule. (See Chapter 50 for more information on keeping creditors at bay.)

UNEMPLOYMENT CHECKLIST

Above all, don't panic. You will survive this setback, just as you have survived the other setbacks we all experience during our lifetimes.

Accept the fact that you are going to experience a lot of stress, particularly right after you lose your job. Seek and welcome the support of your family and friends.

Take advantage of unemployment compensation benefits to which you are entitled.

Continue or replace all important employer-provided insurance coverage.

Summarize the ready resources you have available to meet living expenses during the period of unemployment.

Budget carefully for the future by analyzing past spending patterns, determining ways you can cut back on expenses, and figuring out where you are going to obtain sufficient resources.

Begin your job search quickly and enthusiastically.

Keep yourself occupied. Consider doing volunteer work.

Part IV

A Greater Financial Perspective

32

Understanding the Economy

T here are almost as many economic theories as there are economists. It's no wonder that getting a commonsense definition of economics (that is, one that you can use) proves difficult. But the bottom line is that economics deals with the basic consumer law of supply and demand. Not surprisingly, the themes of scarcity and production are central to most economic theories. The greater the demand, the greater the incentive to increase production (supply) to satisfy it. If the resources needed for production aren't scarce, demand reduces the cost of the product or service to the point where more consumers can afford it. But if the resources needed are scarce and the demand is strong, then prices will rise.

We are bombarded with economic information, but most people don't understand what is being said. Terms like *GNP*, *leading economic indicators*, and *prime rate* are used as if their meaning were common knowledge. But what do these terms and the numbers that accompany them mean? And what is their relevance to your own financial life? This chapter will help you understand the economy, show you how to tell where it may be heading, and explain what you might do to take advantage of economic trends rather than having them take advantage of you.

How Economic Developments Affect You

E veryone knows the value of a healthy, growing economy, but not many understand exactly why. A growing economy sets a chain of events in motion that generally benefit almost everyone in the economy, although there are often pockets that stay depressed. Conversely, in a recession, the economic pain is also distributed unevenly: While some areas of the country may suffer only a cessation of long-lasting growth, others may fall into a severe recession.

In Theory, Nearly Everyone Benefits from a Robust Economy

In the ideal model of the growing economy, jobs are created. As jobs are created, unemployment goes down. As unemployment goes down, wages rise—employers have to compete for workers by offering higher salaries. As wages rise, workers have more income to buy more goods and services. This prompts the creation of still more jobs.

Economic growth can have a bad side effect—*inflation*, although inflation can also occur in a stagnating economy. In an economy experiencing rapid growth—like several South

American countries—the heating up of the cycle of buying and spending can lead to very high inflation indeed. Monetary policy, set by the Federal Reserve, attempts, among other things, to keep inflation in check while stimulating growth.

Terms You Should Know

The U.S. economy is watched by legions of economic analysts and other pundits—at universities, think tanks, corporations, and in the government. These analysts look at a variety of so-called *economic indicators* to assess how the economy is faring and where it is headed. Since these figures are constantly in the news, understanding what they mean and how they affect you is important.

- **CAPACITY UTILIZATION.** This indicator tracks the operating activity of leading manufacturers. If the manufacturers are operating at more than 85 percent capacity, it's viewed as positive.

- **CONSUMER PRICE INDEX (CPI).** The CPI (also known as COLI, the cost-of-living index) tracks the changes in costs for consumer goods and services, from catsup to your utility bill.

- **GROSS NATIONAL PRODUCT (GNP).** The GNP is the total value of all finished goods produced and services rendered over a set period of time (usually six months to one year). This indicator relates the expansion or contraction of the economy as a whole.

- **INDEX OF LEADING ECONOMIC INDICATORS.** There are twelve economic indicators (detailed below) that reflect upward and downward trends in the overall economy. You'll hear this term ad nauseam from business reporters.

- **NEW CAR SALES.** Cars are big-ticket items, requiring large cash transactions or long-term repayment plans. The number of car sales reflects the number of people who think they can afford to spend large sums of money, which in turn reflects optimism or pessimism about the economy.

- **RETAIL SALES.** The retail sales indicator also indicates confidence in the economy. The more you buy, the more optimistic about the economy, your job prospects, and your continuing purchasing power you seem to be.

- **DEPARTMENT STORE SALES.** Every time you buy a T-shirt at J.C.

Definition

Inflation: The increase in a nation's overall price level. Generally, it's caused by either (1) an increase in demand, or (2) a reduction in supply without a change in demand.

Penney, you contribute to this indicator of, among other things, consumers' willingness to buy nonessential items.

- **UNEMPLOYMENT.** The higher the unemployment, the worse off the economy is. This indicator is followed weekly and is always worth noting.

- **FEDERAL FUNDS RATE.** The "Fed funds rate" is the interest rate that banks charge one another. This rate affects the rates of interest on bank loans to consumers and businesses.

- **PRIME RATE.** The prime lending rate is the interest rate reserved for a bank's best customers. It is usually the bank's lowest available rate. The lower the rate, the greater the motivation to borrow, therefore the greater the motivation to spend.

- **BROKER LOAN RATE.** This is the interest rate charged to brokers who are borrowing from banks. If interest rates are low, borrowing tends to increase. The result is an increase in investing that may or may not send an optimistic message to the market.

- **HOUSING STARTS.** This refers to new home construction across the nation. The number of housing starts indicates the level of consumer optimism and willingness to spend.

- **WAGE SETTLEMENTS.** The results of major wage contracts can indicate the magnitude in the rise in the cost of goods and services. Agreements with lower annual salary increases usually mean lower inflation.

- **PAYROLL EMPLOYMENT.** This figure—the number of employees on company payrolls— is issued on the first Friday of each month in most major newspapers. Not only does it reflect the employment situation, it best predicts future consumer spending patterns, which depend heavily on employment.

- **THE DOLLAR INDEX.** This index shows the value of the dollar against a group of foreign currencies.

- **INVENTORY-TO-SALES RATIO.** This is a crude but useful measure of the extent to which the demand for goods is satisfied. It therefore indicates sales patterns that affect corporate profits. It consists of the dollar value of business inventory nationwide divided by sales and is issued monthly. When the economy is flagging, this ratio may be as high as 1.5 to 1, because inventories build up and sales slow. A 1.3-to-1 ratio is considered balanced, because businesspeople like to keep a little extra inventory on hand.

- **THE STANDARD AND POOR'S (S&P) STOCK INDEX.** The stock market predicts general economic

259

recoveries as no other indicator can, but as the old joke goes, it also predicted nine of the last five recessions. The S&P 500-Stock Index is quoted daily in most newspapers. It's considered a better predictor of the economy's future prospects than the Dow Jones Industrial Average because the S&P index is based on many more stocks than is the Dow.

- **MONEY SUPPLY.** This refers to the amount of the nation's money that is available to spend.

The Index of Leading Indicators

Information from the U.S. Department of Commerce is also important to figuring out what is going on in the economy. Among the data published regularly is the composite index of leading indicators. This index has twelve components, which are appraised monthly. The data for each component are collected monthly and are then combined to form one index. These measures, when taken together, show how the general business climate will move in the future.

Changes during a single month may not be significant. Changes over short periods may reflect the influence of random events. Examples of such events are unusual or extreme weather patterns, or a prolonged strike by members of a large labor union, such as the teamsters, the U.A.W., or the mine workers. But when the composite index shows continued gain month by month, this is an indication that business will improve—and vice versa.

The twelve components of the composite index of leading economic indicators are as shown in the box.

TWELVE LEADING ECONOMIC INDICATORS

1. AVERAGE WORK WEEK OF PRODUCTION WORKERS

2. LAYOFF RATE IN MANUFACTURING

3. VALUE OF MANUFACTURERS' NEW ORDERS FOR CONSUMER GOODS AND MATERIALS

4. INDEX OF NET BUSINESS FORMATION

5. STANDARD & POOR'S INDEX OF 500 COMMON-STOCK PRICES

6. CONTRACTS AND ORDERS FOR PLANT AND EQUIPMENT

7. INDEX OF NEW PRIVATE HOUSING UNITS AUTHORIZED BY LOCAL BUILDING PERMITS

8. VENDOR PERFORMANCE—PERCENTAGE OF COMPANIES REPORTING SLOWER DELIVERIES

9. NET CHANGE IN INVENTORIES ON HAND OR ON ORDER

10. CHANGE IN PRICES OF KEY RAW MATERIALS

11. CHANGE IN TOTAL LIQUID ASSETS—THE LIQUID WEALTH HELD BY PRIVATE INVESTORS

12. MONEY SUPPLY

Consumer Confidence

One of the greatest problems of capitalist economies is their susceptibility to consumers' fears and insecurities. When consumers, investors, and businesspeople feel pessimistic, the wheels of the economy can slow dramatically, even if the economy is actually in reasonable shape. In an age where the media transmit ideas at lightning speed, gloominess can be extremely infectious. The key to surviving in bad economic times is to break free of this "crowd mentality," take stock of where you stand, and act accordingly. Opportunities often abound when most people are pessimistic.

The Fed, the Money Supply, and the Prime Rate

In most advanced industrial countries, the monetary system is run by a semi-independent national bank. In theory, at least, this central bank is above the political fray; it sets monetary policy on a rational and dispassionate basis. In the United States, a system of banks—rather than one single bank—acts as our national bank, and it is called the Federal Reserve System. Congress created the Fed in 1913, granting it the power "to coin money and regulate the value thereof," and it has been running our monetary system ever since.

A board of governors, whose members are appointed by the President, presides over the Fed. The Fed chairman wields a great deal of power in deciding how monetary policy should be set; indeed, whomever is the chairman personifies the system as a whole. The Fed chairman, while technically free to regulate this monetary system as he thinks best, must in actuality work closely with the Treasury Department. Since the Secretary of the Treasury is a political appointee and therefore subject to political pressures himself, the Fed is indirectly influenced by politics. Furthermore, Congress can summon the Fed chairman to testify about monetary policy and the state of the economy. Congress can thus make its displeasure about monetary policy quite clear, and if it wishes, really hold the chairman's feet to the fire.

How does the Fed set monetary policy? The Fed uses several tools, the most important of which is the discount rate. The discount rate is the rate the Fed charges for the money it loans federally-chartered banks. These banks use funds borrowed from the Fed to bolster their reserves, which in turn allows them to lend more money to their customers. If the Fed wants to restrict the amount of money going into the economy, it can raise the discount rate, discouraging borrowing by making loans more expensive. On the other hand, should the Fed want to increase the flow of cash into the economy, it can lower the discount rate, making borrowed money cheaper.

Because the Fed has such massive cash reserves, it is also free to buy or sell large blocks of U.S. government securities in order to reach its interest rate targets. These activities are called open-market operations, and they are another one of the Fed's important tools for setting monetary policy. If the Fed starts aggressively buying up government securities, it will be pumping great amounts of cash into the monetary system. Conversely, by selling securities, the Fed can soak up a large number of greenbacks, thus restricting the money supply.

Finally, the Fed can set reserve requirements, the amount of money U.S. banks are required to have on hand in liquid form. The lower a bank's reserve requirement, the more money it can lend out to businesses and individuals. By raising or lowering reserve requirements, the Fed can therefore regulate how much money finds its way into the economy.

Does the President Have Much Control Over the Economy?

Whenever the economy goes off track, the President's popularity slips in the public opinion polls. As the country's leader, the President is a natural target for people's frustration with poor economic conditions; he is similarly the first to benefit politically when the economy is booming. But does the President deserve the share of blame and credit that he gets for the course the economy takes?

The President does have direct control over several important levers to the nation's economic machinery. In general, however, government action is slow and ponderous. It is not like a little car that can be jump-started but is more like a supertanker, whose direction and speed take considerable time and effort to change. Many people think the federal budget can strongly influence the economy and it can. But there is a great deal of lag time between the time the President presents an idea and its effect is actually felt. By the time the proposal that the President submits to Congress has made its way through the House Ways and Means Committee, been reconciled with other competing budgets, and been signed by the President, as much as ten months have elapsed. Then and only then will whatever economic policy actions are included in the act take effect. The upshot of all this is that the effects of federal government actions can be so slow that the economy will have either improved or worsened on its own accord long before the impact of the new budget or other presidential actions, for that matter, are felt.

Coping with Inflation

C oping with inflation entails understanding what inflation is in the first place. Generally, *inflation* is an increase in the costs of goods and services throughout the economy. (The higher inflation is, the less purchasing power a dollar has over time.) Compared with the second half of the 1970s and the early 1980s, when (if you don't remember) inflation was at times in the high teens and low twenties, inflation has been much more bearable of late. In the late 1980s and early 1990s, it was under 4 percent.

But don't be fooled by a 3 percent to 4 percent annual inflation rate. It may represent a breather after the high inflation experienced in the 1970s and early 1980s, but 4 percent is still a number to reckon with. Not only can the rate increase rather swiftly, it can be a wolf in sheep's clothing. Ten years' worth of 4 percent annual inflation means your cost of living will increase by almost 50 percent! So you need to account for inflation's toll even if—thank heavens—it's not as bad as it has been. Furthermore, while the long-term outlook continues to be for moderate inflation, the economists could be wrong—it wouldn't be the first time. The following table shows how much prices will rise at various inflation rates.

HOW TO CALCULATE THE EFFECT OF INFLATION

This table shows how much the price of something that costs one dollar today will rise in the future at different rates of inflation. For example, at 5 percent annual inflation, something that costs one dollar today will cost $2.65 twenty years from now.

YEARS FROM NOW	ANNUAL INFLATION RATE					
	3%	4%	5%	6%	7%	8%
5	$1.16	$1.22	$1.28	$1.34	$1.40	$1.47
10	1.34	1.48	1.63	1.79	1.97	2.16
15	1.56	1.80	2.08	2.40	2.76	3.17
20	1.81	2.19	2.65	3.21	3.87	4.66
25	2.09	2.67	3.39	4.29	5.43	6.85
30	2.43	3.24	4.32	5.74	7.61	10.06

Unlike our most recent recession, which has really put a damper on both inflation and interest rates, recession and inflation can combine to produce a double-whammy called *stagflation.* We've had two bouts with stagflation since 1970: during the 1973-1974 recession, and again in 1981. During both of these recessions, business was down, stock prices declined, and prices of consumer goods soared. Stagflation is indeed the worst of all possible worlds.

The inflation fighter's checklist will help you cope with the vicissitudes of inflation, whether it stays at a bearable rate or starts to creep up to the heights we experienced in the 1970s.

INFLATION FIGHTER'S CHECKLIST

If a period of higher inflation is likely, you should account for those costs in your budgeting, and make the necessary changes in your spending to reflect increased costs. While wages typically rise with inflation, there is always a lag between rising costs and rising income, which is going to have to be made up somewhere.

If prices rise, so must your savings. You will need to set aside more money to meet the higher costs of whatever you will use your savings for, including coping with family financial emergencies and accumulating enough resources to be able to retire comfortably.

Review your insurance coverage limits in the light of higher inflation, particularly your homeowner's or renter's insurance policy. While some insurance companies automatically increase the limits of coverage each year to bring the protection into line with current costs, many do not. Even those who do adjust for inflation, may not increase the limits sufficiently to account for higher inflation. This applies both to your home and to your personal possessions. The cost if insuring valuables in particular may increase significantly during a period of high inflation. Your life insurance coverage may also need to be revised. That $100,000 life insurance policy you took out ten years ago may have been adequate at the time, but inflation may now render it inadequate.

If you find that consumer goods costs are increasing rapidly (as they did in the early 1980s), consider buying household necessities in bulk. But don't go overboard and spend money you may need for other purposes.

■□

Don't accept the advice that borrowing is a good thing to do during a period of high inflation because you can repay these loans with "cheaper dollars." Many families have been ruined financially by taking that advice during inflationary periods. The reason? They borrowed for silly reasons and didn't have any "cheaper dollars" around to repay their loans.

■□

You may want to switch to a fixed-rate mortgage if you now have an adjustable-rate mortgage and you expect that inflation will heat up and continue indefinitely. Check the provisions of your adjustable-rate mortgage to see how high the interest rate can go. While you may not be able to lock in a very attractive rate on a fixed-rate mortgage now, it may be better than having to suffer from an even higher rate on your adjustable mortgage.

■□

Retirees should put at least a portion of their personal retirement funds in investments that offer a hedge against inflation. Retirees also should save some of their income well into their old age, so that they will be able to increase their income in their later years to meet inflation-fueled increases in living expenses. Inflation is a tremendous problem for any retiree whose income is wholly or partially fixed. Social Security benefits generally rise with the cost of living, but most pensions and annuities do not.

■□

So-called "hard assets," such as home and investment real estate, tend to do well in times of rapid inflation, although this is not always the case. Long-term fixed-income investments, namely bonds, do rather poorly during an inflationary period as inflation pushes up interest rates, so the value of older bonds with lower coupons sinks, sometimes dramatically. A safe harbor during periods of high inflation is short-term cash-equivalent investments whose interest rates tend to rise as inflation rises. Once interest rates get quite high, you can lock in the attractive yields by buying longer-term bonds. It's hard to know when inflation is at its peak, so you probably should hedge your bets by "laddering" the maturities on your fixed-income investments (see page 485).

■□

Since real estate generally has been a good inflation hedge, your home becomes an even more attractive investment during a period of high inflation. You could well profit from worthwhile home improvements. You may also want to invest in additional real estate (as described in Chapter 60). Nevertheless, real estate, like any other worthwhile investment, is not immune from declining values.

■□■

In periods of high inflation, money invested in stocks and other property is not as likely to lose its purchasing power as is money that is simply set aside in fixed-income securities that have a fixed-dollar value. Of course, stocks do not provide a guaranteed hedge against inflation. There is simply no close connection between inflationary (or deflationary) conditions and the movement of stock prices. *Note:* Many experts advise against purchasing utility stocks during a period of threatened or actual inflation, because utilities have a great deal of trouble performing well in an environment where their debt costs are rising due to higher interest rates. Due to strict regulation, utilities have difficulty passing higher costs on to customers.

■□■

Don't fall for the hard-sell tactics that may be leveled at you by salespeople intent on protecting your home and hearth against the ravages of inflation. They want to sell you "guaranteed" inflation hedges such as rare coins, gemstones, gold bullion, and the like. The only guarantee in these offers is that you are going to be taken if you take them up on their offer.

Surviving a Recession

T he decade of the 1990s opened with the U.S. economy mired in recession. Recession will come again, for it is an integral part of the business cycle. (The business cycle is an economic cycle consisting of prosperity, decline, then prosperity. The cycle usually, but not always, covers a period of two to eight years.) Even if the economy is completely healthy at the time you read this, if the new century is going to be anything like the old one, periodic recessions will be a fixture of the economic landscape.

What Is a Recession?

A recession is generally a period of decline in the country's total output of goods and services, corporate income, employment levels, and foreign trade. Many sectors of the economy contract during a recession. A recession reduces employment and demand for goods, so that wages and corporate profits decline, thus reducing the government's tax revenue.

Four leading economic indicators historically have been reliable in signaling an impending economic downturn:

1. DECLINING STOCK PRICES

2. DECLINING CONSUMER CONFIDENCE

3. DECLINING OR FLAT FACTORY ORDERS

4. RISING UNEMPLOYMENT CLAIMS

The United States is a huge, sprawling and heterogeneous country. Not surprisingly, how much you are affected by a particular recession depends to some extent on where you live. During the early stages of a recession, some locales may already be in deep trouble, while others are only at the brink. As a recession progresses, some areas may be recovering while others are just slipping into recession. Some parts of the country may even make it through relatively unscathed. For instance, the agricultural sector went through very hard times in the mid-1980s but felt little impact from the recession of the early 1990s.

How a Recession
Affects Your Investment Portfolio

During a recession, many investment experts urge investors to restrict themselves to the highest-quality securities. A major stock-price retreat can, however, provide opportunities for venturesome stock investors who want to invest for the long term. But you must be prepared for the possibility that stock prices may go down before they go up: contrarian investing is not for the weak of heart. During a recession, you should concentrate your stock investments in so-called "defensive" industries (see page 558).

Quality is of particular importance for interest-earning investments during a weak economy. Bonds or notes of marginal companies, of companies in troubled industries, and of weak municipalities should be avoided. Interest rates generally decline in a recessionary economy. Individuals who have invested heavily in short-term, interest-earning securities like money-market funds and Treasury bills therefore often see their interest income decline. The interest paid on these investments fluctuates with overall interest rates, so when interest rates fall, so does interest income.

Investors in bonds fare much better when recessions hit. Why? Bonds pay a fixed interest rate, a fact that benefits investors in two ways when interest rates decline. First, interest income is protected because interest paid on bonds does not change when overall interest rates fall. Second, should you wish to sell some of your bonds, you will be happy to find that the value of your bonds has increased because of the decline in interest rates (see page 472).

Real estate, the third major investment category, is very difficult to evaluate, in part due to wide variations in real estate prospects in various regions of the country. Bargains can be had, but they are a lot more difficult to find than many investors think. And many a "bargain" real estate investment has turned into a dog after all.

How to Recover from a Recession—and Better
Prepare for the Next One

Recessions do end, thank heavens. Millions of people find their finances in a shambles as a result of a recession. And once the economy starts to turn around, you should begin to plan for better times ahead. Whatever your circumstances, you can begin to rebuild so that you will be able to look forward to a more secure financial future. The following checklist is for recession victims. It will help you take action to get back on your feet.

- REVIEW your debt situation. You may have been preoccupied with your indebtedness during the recession, and now that matters have settled down, you probably would like to forget about them. That's not possible, of course, but at least your finances may have stabilized sufficiently to begin making progress on getting your loan balances reduced. This should be a high-priority item as you emerge from the recession. By all means, don't let postrecession euphoria motivate you to add to your loan balances if they already were causing you problems.

- **IMPROVE** your credit standing. Because so many families are hurt by a recession, many will emerge with bad credit ratings. If this applies to you, you should make an extra effort to assure that you reestablish your good credit standing as soon as possible—not so you can borrow yourself into trouble again, but to restore your ability to borrow in the event you need to in the future for worthwhile purposes or to meet financial emergencies.

- **RESTORE** your savings. If you, like many people, have had to dip into your emergency fund to make ends meet during an economic downturn, restore it to a comfortable level. If you didn't have any savings in the first place, you may have seen how important it was as you struggled through the recession. Since your financial situation should be improving somewhat, you can now focus on building up your savings.

- **EVALUATE** postponed expenses. The financial strain of the recession may have caused you to postpone some necessary household expenses. If your financial situation has improved, review these items to see if it would be prudent to incur these expenses now. For example, if you postponed making needed car repairs, home repairs, or appliance replacements, you may decide that now is the time to make the repairs or purchase the appliances.

- **BE REALISTIC.** Getting back on your feet won't happen overnight. This is one of the frustrating things about personal finance. We can get into financial trouble in a matter of weeks or months, but it takes a lot longer to recover. Don't let financial recovery get you down. If you can make progress each day, whether it involves forgoing an expense that can be forgone, looking for ways to improve your job performance or earn outside income, or putting a few dollars in a savings account, you are on the road to financial recovery. And that progress, however small it might seem, will snowball.

- **DON'T REVERT** to your old habits. If you were victimized by the recession because you lacked a sufficient financial cushion, take action now so that you won't revert back to your old habits. Sadly, many people in this country are consigned to a lifetime of living hand-to-mouth. I am not talking about the impoverished. I am talking about middle-income and even high-income individuals and families. You know what your past financial experience has been. Do you really want to go back to your old ways, or do you want to make some progress so that you don't have to live in constant fear of creditors, or illness, or whatever other conditions might befall you? Do you really want to have to work the rest of your life? Believe me, it doesn't take that much effort to change your life-style so that you can turn the corner. You know that you should change, and there is no better time than now to begin to manage your finances more sensibly.

Caveat Emptor—Avoiding Ripoffs

"**B**uyer Beware." How many times have you heard it said? Yet surprisingly, countless numbers of people continue to neglect its basic truth. In fact, so many people fall victim to fraudulent schemes that P. T. Barnum's estimation of consumer savvy—"there's a sucker born every minute"—needs to be updated. According to the Council of Better Business Bureaus, which admits that it can't even begin to quantify the *actual* number, a lot more than one person a minute is swindled.

This chapter will wake you up to consumer ripoffs, investment scams, and other types of fraud. It should help you know what to look out for and what sources you should trust for guidance concerning businesses and individuals who are interested in giving you that slick-sounding but "once-in-a-lifetime deal." Of course, the burden of insuring yourself against becoming a victim of one investment scheme or another is up to you. Even the best-funded consumer protection agencies can't look out for everyone. Still, there are many sources at your beck and call. You'll find a list of selected consumer protection and rights agencies at the end of this chapter.

Famous Last Words

"**N**ew and improved" is the credo of a product's progress. Yet how many times have you actually purchased a product because of such a claim? Since most of us have been active consumers for many decades, we aren't convinced that a dazzling new package and a glitter of rhetoric translates into substantial improvements in an old product. Nevertheless, when it comes to investments that cost more than a bread box—a new roof for our home, a land investment in a sunny clime, or the chance to get in on the bottom floor of a new stock of a company we've never heard of—we prove time and again that we're gullible. Granted, there isn't always an easy warning signal like the catchphrase "new and improved." However, there are some commonly used catchphrases listed in the following box:

FINANCIAL SCHEMERS' PREFERRED VOCABULARY

- "Unconditional lifetime money-back guarantee"

- "Big savings"

- "Will last forever"

- "It's now or never"

- "If at any time you're not completely satisfied"

- "You can't lose"

- "Trust me"

Words to live by include:

- **KNOW THE PRODUCT**

- **KNOW THE SALESPERSON**

- **KNOW THE COMPANY**

- **KNOW WHEN TO SAY "NO!"**

A Skunk Is a Skunk

If someone comes knocking at your door or starts talking a mile a minute to you on your phone or is sending you glitzy mailgrams that tell you that you are a "definite, absolute, guaranteed winner if only you ...," politely shut the door, hang up the phone, and/or make a contribution to your recycling bin.

Believe me, bunk is bunk, no matter how pretty the wrapping or flowery the words. In fact, the prettier the wrapping and the more flowery the words, the greater the likelihood that you're being duped. So if it sounds too good to be true, it probably is. If it sounds too simple to be believed, it is probably very complex. If you think you are being misled, you probably are. And if you feel you're being pressured, you most likely are being pressured. Words alone won't suffice. The scam artist knows how to tell a tall tale and make it sound convincing.

Themes that could land you the leading role in your own financial tragedy include:

- **ANYTHING** that requires up-front cash quickly. The only person who stands to get rich quick this way is the person who is pitching the scheme to you.

- **ANYTHING** that requires you to pay for the secrets of someone else's success. We all like secrets, but how secret can it be if it is broadcast every morning on your local TV station? The true secret to such success lies in the ability to sell the products that the expensive TV ad is pushing on the gullible.

- **ANYTHING** that promises to make you or your house the envy of your neighbors. Does a fake brick facade really enhance the look of your home more than a decent paint job? The price, usually with the temptation to finance the project, often leaves you twice as much in debt for your newly adorned, fake brick "showplace."

- **ANYTHING** that costs you money in order to save you money. An "inspector" comes to your home unannounced and performs a free furnace inspection. He recommends that you buy a new gas furnace, pointing out that a new furnace will save you hundreds of dollars over the next several years. If this happens, simply ask him what if anything is wrong with the old one. Chances are, the cost of the new furnace will not save you enough money over the next many years to make up the difference of your "inefficient" old one. Often, a brand-new furnace will lead you to the poorhouse faster than the perfectly competent one you now have. The same goes for water-filtration systems.

- **ANYONE** who tells you that rather than working for your money, you should let your money work for you. Making your money grow is the hardest, but the most rewarding work you'll ever do.

- **ANYONE** who doesn't tell you in plain English what it is you're putting your money into. If you can't understand what you're being told to buy, don't buy it.

- **ANYONE** who doesn't have the time, inclination, or willingness to let you get a second opinion about the proposed investment idea. What's the rush? A good investment should always be long-lived.

Same Old Story

From tragedy to philosophy: Forewarned is forearmed. It was the Greek philosopher Socrates who affirmed that a knowledgeable person is distinguished by knowing what he or she doesn't know. In financial matters, this should be your philosophical maxim: Know what you don't know. The reason—it will help you avoid whimsical or impulsive spending or investing. (Never buy on impulse, especially from a complete stranger. The likelihood of disaster, no matter how safe it seems, is guaranteed to be titanic.)

Same Old Song and Dance

Some of the most common scams seem as simple as a stone, but they prove to be complex webs of deception whenever they're turned over and examined. In the end, the only way to be 100 percent positive that you will never be the victim of a scam that leaves you short of cash and pride is to never buy or invest in anything at all. However, since abstinence is not a practicable consumer proposal, it is best to familiarize yourself with the scam artist's temptations. Here are some classics:

Bait and switch

The most common consumer scam is known as the "bait and switch." Stated simply, it's when someone puts an expensive lamp in their store window with a tag that says, "Lamp Sale! 75% Off!" You rush in to buy the lamp, but lo and behold—there are no more of that model left. But it just so happens that many just as handsome lamps are available. Of course, *they're* not on sale. The principle is that, once you've been hooked, you'll be an easier sell—and it works time and again.

Pyramid power

Perhaps the most ingenious scam going is called a "pyramid scheme." Pyramid schemes are something of which many consumers have firsthand knowledge. While there are numerous categories of pyramid schemes, the original racket is still around. A letter arrives promising untold riches that will materialize if only you would participate and pass it on. Lo and behold, participation is so simple, you only have to remove the name at the top of a list of, say, six people, send the person whose name you removed a sum of money that may range from $1 to $100, then put your name at the bottom of the list. You then send the revised letter to the same number of people on the list; six new unsuspecting lambs. When your name hits the top of the list, you supposedly will have it made in the shade. Here's how: Say a list of six names comes to you. You remove the name at the top, insert your own, and send it along to 6 new people. At the end of the day, a day that never comes, you will receive your original amount multiplied to the sixth level—or 279,936 people participating. By the time the letter reaches the tenth level, 362,797,056 people would have to be participating. Sound too good to be true? It is. Pyramid schemes always fall apart, leaving you and the majority of the beguiled participants with less money and potentially fewer friends.

The Ponzi scheme

This one's named in honor of Charles Ponzi, a 1920s scoundrel. Although he didn't pioneer the scheme, he certainly popularized its use.

In a Ponzi scheme, an unfortunate investor is asked to give the scam artist a sum of money today that, the scamster promises, will be returned with substantial interest in only thirty days. In thirty days the scamster delivers on his or her word and returns your money, with substantial "interest" applied, to your eagerly outstretched hand. The victim is then asked if he or she would like to do the same transaction for another thirty days, and, of course, he or she consents. Often, the victim will "loan" even more money the second time around.

But how the money grew so quickly is never disclosed. The reason: It grew as a result of the scam artist's ability to recruit a second tier of gullible investors whose money was used to pay off the first tier. By the time the second tier's money is due, the scamster will have a third tier (consisting of the repeat first tier and new recruits) signed on. But sooner or later the Ponzi artist will just close shop—lock, stock, and barrel—and walk off with three or more tiers of willing investors' cash. It's one of the oldest but most successful investment schemes going.

Paradise lost

"Private getaway with water views" (swampland), or "your own Ponderosa in the heart of the old West" (treacherous mountain land with no plumbing and no access nine months of the year due to avalanches)—that's what you're likely to be buying if you don't research a purchase of undeveloped land very carefully. Less than greener pastures, gussied up in promotional advertising campaigns that look too professional not to be believed, convert many a sane person into a money-spending dolt.

If the land is inexpensive, there's probably a good reason for it. Usually zoning laws prohibit building on it, or it lacks something as basic as running water. But who hasn't heard of Florida real estate that ended up being nothing but an acre of some uninhabitable alligator swamp? Aren't we all the wiser?

Most of us are "wise" enough not to let on that we have been so swindled. The fact is that those who are swindled seldom tell the tale. Vanity and the dislike of being seen as someone who has been taken to the cleaners are the reason. But if you have been victimized, why not tell your friends? At the very least you'll get some sympathy, and you could be doing them a world of good. The scam artist's greatest ally is the silence of his or her victims. If you think you are being swindled in a land "deal," contact the Interstate Land Sales Registration Division in Washington, D.C. (telephone: 202-708-0502).

The vinyl home

We all are concerned about maintaining the value of our property. That translates into a concern for maintenance, which in turn plays nicely into the hands of a home improvement scamster. Home improvement dreams often lead to sleepless nights and financial nightmares. You probably don't need expensive vinyl siding—even if a salesperson insists you do. *You* should be the one to decide what home improvements *you* need. The home improvement business is filled with charlatans, so be sure to check and double-check the references of anyone *you* hire to improve or repair your home.

The boiler room

Boiler room operators will try to sell you virtually anything. Often it is an investment or a product that plays on people's fears and greed. It is simply unbelievable how many people get taken over the telephone. If you are ever tempted to send in your money or give out your credit card number over the telephone, do the following. First, request information in writing. Of course, they'll tell you that you must act now, but be firm. Chances are the information will never arrive, but if it does, you can examine it without the sales pitch. Show the information to a relative or friend so that you can get a "second opinion." You get a second opinion before having surgery—you should also get a second opinion before somebody removes a good portion of your savings account.

Prime Targets

While everyone who has any money at all is a target for a scam artist, some people are more attractive than others. The older you are, the greater the likelihood that someone out there is going to test your financial mettle. Retirees, especially widows, are a preferred target, as are people who have just inherited money or won it in the lottery. The simple reason is that they tend to have the most amount of readily available cash—usually placed in easy-to-access savings accounts. Because they are unfamiliar with managing money, they often demonstrate more willingness to listen to anyone's advice—a scamster's dream.

Double-Check

One way to ensure a margin of safety is to double-check any commitment of money for any reason with a trusted friend, accountant, or lawyer—even your parents or children—before you plunk down a large chunk of cash. (I consider a large chunk to be anything over $500.) In the end, most of us will be or already have been taken advantage of by one scheme or another. For the most part, it will have been a relatively harmless reminder that, when it comes to financial decisions, we should always let prudence be our guide.

Consumer Protection

Smart Money Move

Always double-check with someone else any major expense or investment that you have even the slightest doubt about.

Before spending your money on a product or service, make sure that you will get what you pay for. If you have any doubts, take the time to check with all the appropriate consumer protection agencies to find out whether a company is on the level. Of course it's time consuming, but it's also the only way for you to avoid being taken.

CONSUMER PROTECTION AGENCIES

Consumer Federation of America
1424 16th Street, N.W., Suite 604
Washington DC 20036
(202) 387-6121

Consumer Education and Protective Association
6048 Ogontz Avenue
Philadelphia PA 19141
(215) 424-1441

Consumers' Research
800 Maryland Avenue, N.E.
Washington DC 20002
(202) 546-1713

Consumers Union of the United States
101 Truman Avenue
Yonkers NY 10703
(914) 378-2000

Your state will also have an office that handles consumer questions or complaints. Finally, your local Better Business Bureau may be able to answer your questions.

FOR FURTHER READING
"Investment Swindles: How They Work and How to Avoid Them" (free)
National Futures Association
200 West Madison Street
Chicago, IL 60606
(312) 781-1300

CHECKLIST: WAYS TO AVOID BEING RIPPED OFF

■ Don't fall for home improvement scams. Home improvement scams are on the rise. All homeowners are vulnerable, particularly the elderly. Always take your sweet time deciding whether to go ahead with a home improvement. Always check out the person who wants to do the work. One clear warning sign: The home improver comes to you rather than you going to them. If you have elderly parents, encourage them to check with you before committing themselves to any kind of home repair or home improvement, no matter how small.

■ If it sounds too good to be true, it is. Don't buy anything that guarantees to make you money without having to work for it, to lose weight without dieting, or to grow hair where no hair grows.

■ Don't invest in anything you don't understand. If the person who's trying to sell you an investment can't explain it to your satisfaction in one sentence, don't buy it. Even if you make your own investment decisions, never invest in anything you have difficulty under-standing.

☐

Be wary of anything "free." Jonathan's Law: Everything that's free ends up costing you money.

☐

Don't buy a "get rich quick in real estate" course. You've seen them on late-night televi-sion, promising endless riches by following their real estate investment techniques. Aren't they generous in sharing their knowledge for a mere $200? If you want to make money this way, write one of these courses and go on television instead.

☐

Always be wary of charlatans who prey on senior citizens. Sadly, seniors are often victim-ized by unscrupulous individuals who sell them things they don't need at vastly inflated prices. Always be on the lookout for these scalawags, and if you ever have the slightest doubt, don't buy anything until you have checked them out.

☐

Check with your children, parents, or close friends before making any major financial commitment. Whenever you are contemplating making a financial decision—a change in housing, a home improvement—be sure to check out your plans with your children or close friends. It's always useful to get a second (or third) opinion on important financial matters.

Selecting the Right Professionals to Help You Achieve Financial Security

Many people already know a lot more about personal finance than they give themselves credit for. Consider your own situation. If you are like most Americans, you manage your personal finances, control your spending, insure against the unforeseen, borrow judiciously, minimize your taxes, and (hopefully) invest your resources carefully. You may not always know the answers and you may sometimes even feel financially illiterate, but in fact you probably already have the basic skills. They just need honing.

In fact, each aspect of your personal financial life is simply too important to ignore or to pass on to someone else. It doesn't matter how professional an accountant, broker, or financial planner may be, and how little you may think you know. The first—and most important—thing to remember is that you should never give up control of your own money! Information on managing your personal finances, in addition to this guide, is available in daily newspapers, magazines, radio, and television. Believe it or not, most of the information that you receive from these sources is trustworthy (so long as you don't feel compelled to act on every recommendation).

You may think you don't have the time to attend to all your money matters, let alone read about matters of finance. As you will see from this book, good personal financial planning doesn't require a lot of time. Rather, it requires discipline, patience, and an interest in achieving financial security. Most of the important areas—insurance, retirement planning, and estate planning—need be addressed only once or twice a year. You could be well rewarded for paying closer attention to the most dynamic area, investments, but, on the other hand, if you spend too much time studying the investment markets and reviewing your investments, you probably will be prone to making the wrong decisions, because when it comes to investing, often the best thing to do is nothing.

Selecting and Managing Your Advisers

Many people fail to select appropriate financial advisers or neglect to work with them effectively. You probably need to take a more active role in making sure your advisers or the advisers you are thinking of hiring are providing you the best possible advice and service. The three most common family advisers are:

Insurance Agents

It is usually, but not always, better to select an independent insurance agent who has the capability and willingness to shop among several insurance companies for the best possible coverage rather than an agent who represents a single company. Insurance agents also have a conflict of interest in that certain insurance products pay them much higher commissions than other products.

In the worst instances, mediocre agents may not even suggest essential coverage to you (such as umbrella liability insurance) because it provides them with such a low commission. The better agents will review your coverage with you at least annually and will be willing to shop for appropriate policies. Moreover, effective agents will go to bat for you when necessary. If you are having difficulty securing disability insurance because of a health problem, for example, a good agent will work hard to find you the necessary insurance at the best possible price. To assure a good relationship, you must keep your agent informed of changes in your circumstances and, if necessary, insist on a periodic review of your coverage.

Attorneys

You may not yet have a family attorney. But you'll need one at least to prepare necessary estate planning documents like wills and powers of attorney. You should use an attorney who is approximately your age or younger, since you will probably use the same attorney over the years, and you don't want to be burdened by having to find a new lawyer when your current one retires. On the other hand, you may outgrow your attorney's expertise if your estate grows to a level that would benefit from more sophisticated estate-planning techniques. These techniques usually require the expertise of an attorney who devotes all of his or her time to estate planning matters. Whatever attorney you select, he or she should be responsive to your needs and should conduct his or her work in a timely manner.

Smart Money Move

The best source for finding good professionals: word-of-mouth recommendation.

Stockbrokers

It is certainly no secret that stockbrokers have an inherent conflict of interest in advising you on your investments. You are usually better off keeping the investments you buy for a long time, while a broker is under pressure to generate transactions (and hence commissions). In addition, a broker is often given incentives to promote products that his or her firm wants to be promoted. Nevertheless, there are many excellent stockbrokers who can deal with these conflicts and still act in your best interest. Often, these brokers are those who have established themselves in the business (as opposed to a new broker who is usually under an inordinate amount of pressure to sell his employer's products). On the other hand, if you make your own investment decisions, why do you need a "full service" stockbroker at all? Use a discount broker (see page 445).

A final note on full-service stockbrokers. Don't do business with a stockbroker who cold-calls you and is unwilling to meet face-to-face with you. As a matter of fact, don't even invest on the advice of someone you've never met.

Finding the right advisers is well worth the effort. There is no ideal way to locate these professionals, but word-of-mouth recommendation can be an important first step. Finally, if you are unhappy with one of your advisers, it may be because you have not taken an active role in the relationship. First, try to resolve the problem with your adviser. If the problem persists, do not hesitate to make a change. It's amazing how many people dislike or distrust their advisers yet continue to do business with them.

Who Needs a Financial Planner?

You may be wondering why I haven't mentioned financial planners as part of your team of financial advisers. I am a firm believer that you are your *own* best financial planner. While financial planning sounds like a service everyone could use, many people do not benefit significantly from the services of a financial planner. First, many people think, unrealistically, that a planner can turn their finances around. But financial planners aren't miracle workers. Second, many financial planners are simply not capable of dealing with the multiplicity of matters that affect a person's financial well-being, including insurance, investments, credit management, pensions, and estate planning. That's because a lot of people who call themselves financial planners are primarily salespeople. They may understand a lot about investments or insurance, but they don't know a lot about other important financial planning areas.

Some people—typically those who have a major matter that needs evaluation, like setting up an education fund or planning for retirement, or those who have a lot of money and too little time available to manage it—may well benefit from an evaluation of their financial situation. If you feel you need a financial planner (perhaps for a particular problem rather than for a comprehensive review), you obviously have many to choose from, since all sorts of people call themselves financial planners. In fact, anyone can call himself or herself a financial planner.

Smart Money Move

Be your own financial planner.

How Planners Earn Their Pay

Financial planners are compensated for their efforts on your behalf through fees, commissions, or a combination of the two. A *fee-only planner* is paid on an hourly or retainer basis. If one of these planners spends ten hours devising a portfolio strategy for you, you are billed for ten hours' work at a fixed hourly fee. Whether you buy a single bond or a million dollars' worth of bonds makes no difference to this type of planner, for he or she has no monetary stake in the investments you purchase. In fact, a fee-only planner may well steer you to lower-cost ways to buy investment and insurance products. But is it worth the fee? Perhaps— and perhaps not.

A *commissioned planner*, on the other hand, doesn't get paid on the basis of the time he or she spends working on your behalf. A commissioned planner's income is generated purely by what—and how much—he or she sells you. The more transactions you make, and the more products you purchase, the more money the planner takes in. Do these obvious conflicts of interest mean that you should avoid commissioned financial planners? Not necessarily. Many excellent and well-qualified financial planners earn commissions. But if you take this route, beyond the obvious matter of finding one of the good ones, you must *always* be aware of the inherent conflict of interest.

Some planners combine these two means of compensation, earning their keep through both fees and commissions. Fees are earned by providing a review of your overall financial situation together with recommendations. If you accept their recommendations, then the planner will earn commissions on the investment and insurance products that you purchase.

Certification

The fact that a planner is a certified member of a financial planning organization does not necessarily prove that he or she is going to be competent. After all, the same could be said about licensed lawyers and CPAs. One planner, as a joke, actually got his schnauzer certified (the organization has since tightened up its requirements). Nonetheless, accreditation is a starting point, and at the least it shows that the planner has taken the initiative to learn about the diverse field of financial planning. Most accredited planners are stockbrokers and insurance agents who have taken the accreditation courses. There are three main "degrees" financial planners can earn:

Accredited Personal Financial Specialist (APFS)

This degree is conferred by the American Institute of Certified Public Accountants (AICPA) and this designation can be held only by CPAs. The vast majority of APFSs operate on a fee-only basis.

Certified Financial Planner (CFP)

The CFP is granted to individuals who have completed a study program and passed an examination, and who have fulfilled an experience requirement. The degree is given by the Denver-based College for Financial Planning.

Chartered Financial Consultant (ChFC)

This degree is awarded by the Bryn Mawr, Pennsylvania-based American Society of Chartered Life Underwriters and Chartered Financial Consultants to individuals who complete a ten-section course of study and who have passed two exams.

Some planners boast of being "registered investment advisers." This merely means that the planner is registered with the Securities and Exchange Commission. But the law requires *everyone* giving investment advice to register with the SEC, and the only skills it requires are being able to complete an application form and sending in $150 with the completed application.

Finding a Good Planner

What constitutes the right kind of planner for you depends on your needs. If you want to be assured of getting objective advice, use a fee-only planner—but be prepared to pay for the service. If you don't want to pay what can amount to a large fee, consider a commission-only planner—but be sure to select one that would put your interests first, not the opportunity to earn a fat commission. Look around, they're out there.

Whomever you choose, be sure he or she is truly qualified to be a financial planner. As I said before, anyone can call himself or herself a financial planner, but a precious few are truly qualified to provide good analysis and advice in all areas of financial planning. Accreditation is certainly a plus, but it doesn't guarantee competency. If your situation is particularly complicated—for example, if you have unusual tax problems or estate-planning needs—the best route is probably a CPA or lawyer who is actively involved in financial planning.

The way to find a good financial planner is no different from the way to find a qualified lawyer, insurance agent, or tax preparer: word-of-mouth. Ask your acquaintances, co-workers, or your banker for referrals. I would avoid using the Yellow Pages. It's a pig in a poke. A lot of financial planners run seminars to drum up business, but don't be swayed by a slick, prepackaged presentation. Finally, I go back to my first comment: Do you really need a financial planner at all?

FOR FURTHER INFORMATION

To obtain background information on individual brokers and financial services firms, contact: **North American Securities**	**Administrators Association (NASAA)** **555 New Jersey Avenue, N.W., Suite 750** **Washington, DC 20001** **(202) 737-0900**

»

The following organizations can provide information on pursuing arbitration claims:

American Arbitration Association
Director, Commercial Department
140 West 51st Street
New York, NY 10020
(212) 484-4000

National Association of Securities
Dealers
Director of Arbitration
33 Whitehall Street
New York, NY 10004
(212) 480-4881

New York Stock Exchange
Arbitration Department
20 Broad Street, 5th Floor
New York, NY 10005
(212) 656-2772

Complaints against commodities brokers should be directed to:

National Futures Association
Arbitration Administrator
200 West Madison Street, Suite 1600
Chicago, IL 60606
(800) 621-3570
(800) 572-9400 (IL)

If you are weighing the possibility of hiring a financial planner, the following publications and organizations may be useful:

Tips on Financial Planners ($1 plus a self-addressed, stamped envelope)

Council of Better Business Bureaus,
Inc.
4200 Wilson Boulevard, Suite 800

Arlington, VA 22203
(703) 247-9310

How to Select a Financial Planner (free)

Institute of Certified Financial
Planners
Consumer Division
7600 East Eastman Avenue, Suite 301
Denver, CO 80231
(800) 282-7526

Consumer Guide to Financial Independence ($1.00)

International Association for Financial
Planning
Customer Service
Two Concourse Parkway, Suite 800
Atlanta, GA 30328
(404) 395-1605

Fee-Only Planners (free)
Questions That Could Change Your Financial Future (free)

National Association of Personal
Financial Advisors
1130 Lake Cook Road, Suite 150
Buffalo Grove, IL 60089
(800) 366-2732

American Institute of CPAs
Personal Financial Planning Division
Harborside Financial Center
201 Plaza 3
Jersey City, NJ 07311-3881
(800) 862-4272

Part V

Insurance

37

Assuring Comprehensive Insurance at a Reasonable Cost

This part of the book will help you to cut through the obfuscation that characterizes the insurance industry. When it comes to buying insurance, knowledge most certainly is your most potent weapon and your trustiest ally. As an informed consumer, you will be able to separate the nuggets of fact in insurance sales pitches from the blanket of blarney. No longer will the salesperson be your only source of "objective" information.

Coverage Matters

Whatever kind of insurance you are investigating, there are several elements that you should always keep in mind:

Cover all gaps
You and your insurance agent must be sure that all foreseeable areas of risk are covered with insurance. The most common gaps in coverage are lack of an umbrella liability policy (also called personal liability insurance), inadequate long-term disability coverage (particularly if you are self-employed), and insufficient coverage on valuable personal possessions such as jewelry and silverware.

Obtain the correct policy coverage
Each of the policies that you need to purchase must be evaluated carefully so that you are assured of receiving the coverage that you need. As you will find in the following chapters, policies can vary significantly as to extent of coverage they offer. This does not necessarily mean you need to purchase the most comprehensive policy, but you need to assure that the coverage meets your needs. Policy limits are also an important consideration. For example, an otherwise excellent health policy might have a major medical cap that is too low.

Adjust coverage to meet your changing needs

Even though you may have adequate coverage now, your needs will undoubtedly change in the future. Therefore, you need to review the adequacy of your insurance coverage at least annually, and if there is an obvious change in your status—for example, the birth of a child or a job change—you need an immediate review.

Minimize the cost of insurance

Many segments of the insurance industry are intensely competitive, and premiums for similar policy coverage can vary dramatically. You may well be able to achieve significant savings with careful shopping and selection of policy features. Cheaper does not necessarily mean better, but studies have shown that many people pay far more for their insurance coverage than they need to.

IMPORTANT AREAS OF INSURANCE COVERAGE

TYPE OF INSURANCE	DESCRIPTION/FEATURES
LIFE INSURANCE (CHAPTER 38)	Replaces part or most of your wage income in the event of your death and covers nonrecurring expenses of your dependents during a readjustment period after death.
HEALTH INSURANCE (CHAPTER 39)	Protects you from both the smaller out-of-pocket costs of health care and large medical bills a major illness can bring.
DISABILITY INSURANCE (CHAPTER 42)	Replaces part or most of your wage income in the event of disability.
HOMEOWNER'S INSURANCE (CHAPTER 43)	Insures property—such as a home, other structures, personal property, and general contents of the dwelling—against theft or destruction.
RENTER'S INSURANCE (CHAPTER 43)	Protects the personal possessions of the tenant.
AUTOMOBILE INSURANCE (CHAPTER 44)	Protects automobile owners from the potentially large bills an accident could bring. Automobile insurance also protects the car owner from theft.

»

PERSONAL LIABILITY INSURANCE (CHAPTER 45)	Protects you from forfeiting personal assets or future earnings as a result of a personal liability suit; provides additional protection on top of homeowner's and automobile liability coverage.
PROFESSIONAL LIABILITY INSURANCE (CHAPTER 45)	Protects you from lawsuits arising out of job-related activities.

Five Ways to Control Your Insurance Costs

1. Raise the Deductibles on Your Insurance Policies

You can save hundreds of dollars by raising the deductibles on your automobile and homeowner's or renter's insurance policies.

2. Don't Underinsure

While it's great to look for ways to save on insurance, don't be penny wise and pound foolish. Many people are adequately insured in some areas but underinsured in others. This can be financially disastrous should you suffer an uninsured or underinsured loss.

3. Earn Discounts by Purchasing All Your Insurance Coverage from One Company

Many insurance companies offer discounts to customers who purchase all their policies, like automobile, homeowner's, and umbrella insurance, from that company.

4. Don't Buy Insurance Through the Mail Without Comparison Shopping

You may periodically receive direct-mail offers for insurance from credit card companies, associations, or famous TV personalities. While most of these offers are junk, some may be worth considering. How do you decide? Never buy a policy through the mail without thoroughly investigating the financial health of the company offering it. Just as important, compare the premiums and terms of the mail-order policy with those of a comparable policy offered by your insurance agent.

5. Buy Insurance Only from Highly Rated Companies

It used to be a minor concern, but those days are over. Be sure to buy insurance only from companies that have high ratings from agencies that measure insurers' financial health. This goes double for life insurance because you expect to stick with your life insurance company for life—literally.

As you review the following insurance chapters, use this checklist to summarize the adequacy of your insurance coverage.

INSURANCE COVERAGE CHECKLIST

TYPE OF INSURANCE	ADEQUATE	ADDITIONAL OR IMPROVED COVERAGE NECESSARY	NOT NEEDED
● LIFE	[ ]	[ ]	[ ]
● HEALTH	[ ]	[ ]	[ ]
● DISABILITY	[ ]	[ ]	[ ]
● HOMEOWNER'S/RENTER'S	[ ]	[ ]	[ ]
● AUTOMOBILE	[ ]	[ ]	[ ]
● PERSONAL LIABILITY (UMBRELLA)	[ ]	[ ]	[ ]
● PROFESSIONAL LIABILITY	[ ]	[ ]	[ ]
● COMMENTS			

....
....
....
....
....
....
....
....

Life Insurance

S houldn't life insurance be called death insurance? After all, you have to die in order to collect. At its best, life insurance can be both a safety net for your dependents and an investment. On the other hand, life insurance can be a major expense. If it is, I'll show you ways to get insurance costs under control. Moreover, if it's used as an investment, chances are it will be a pretty mediocre investment. No one with a spouse and children to support should go without life insurance. Your loved ones need this protection.

Confusion Abounds

Let's face it—the insurance industry in general thrives on obfuscation, and the life insurance industry in particular is tailor-made to confuse the consumer. Even the people who sell life insurance coverage don't always understand how their products work.

All life insurance policies can be divided into two broad categories—term and cash value. But there are numerous variations upon these two categories. For the first-time buyer of life insurance, the number and range of options can be daunting. Even seasoned insurance buyers may sometimes be tempted to buy the first policy the salesperson pitches simply to avoid the ordeal of hearing another spiel. Whether you are a first-time buyer or an "old hand," you must be aware of what the life insurance industry is trying to do *to* you—as well as *for* you—so you can find a policy that meets your needs.

You must first determine the amount of coverage you need, then the type of policy that is appropriate, and finally, the source from which to buy it. This chapter will help you master all three moves in the life insurance game. Don't rely solely on someone else to figure out how much life insurance you need, or to tell you where you should buy your insurance.

Deciding How Much Life Insurance You Need

B efore you start talking to insurance salespeople and reading policy booklets, you should first determine how much coverage you are going to need. The last thing you want to do is talk to an insurance broker when you have no idea how much coverage you need. The broker will try to shoehorn you into a predetermined needs category based on insurance company-designed formulas. Accuse me of being cynical if you want to, but if you bought the amount of life insurance that the fancy computer printout told you you needed, believe me, you wouldn't have to fear being underinsured. One agent prepared a life insurance needs analysis for me a few years ago. The resulting number—the amount of life insurance the computer said I needed—looked more like the federal deficit than a reasonable amount of life insurance.

Make Your Own Estimate

You need to come up with your own estimate, but even before that, you must first determine whether you need life insurance at all. If you have no dependents, you may not need it. But be careful. You may have dependents and not realize it. Obviously, a stay-at-home spouse and children who haven't yet left the nest qualify as dependents. But you also may have other dependents. Is it possible that your parents may at some time in the future need to rely on you for financial support? Even DINK couples (dual-income no kids) may need life insurance because they have managed to get their spending up to a level that the surviving spouse could not sustain in the event of the death of the other spouse. Finally, even though you have no dependents, you may want to use life insurance to provide a bequest to a long-term partner or favorite charity.

If you determine that you do need life insurance, the next step is to realistically estimate your minimum needs. Once you know the bare minimum of coverage you require, you will be prepared to determine which kind of insurance is right for you and then compare premiums so that you get the best value. If you have family members who are truly dependent on your income, a bare minimum life insurance coverage should be the equivalent of four or five years' worth of your current net income (in other words, after-tax salary). If you have young children, you should have six to seven times your salary in coverage. In theory, this will give your family some breathing space to get back on its financial feet. If, as is the case in the majority of families, you and your spouse both have jobs, you may not need as much life insurance as this bare minimum, but you will probably need at least the equivalent of a couple years' net income in life insurance coverage, and probably more if there are young children.

Once you have determined your bare-minimum life insurance needs, you can make a rational assessment of the amount of life insurance that you think is appropriate. This way, you (not your insurance agent) will be responsible for the level of coverage you ultimately buy. For example, you may be confident that your family will be fine with your bare-minimum amount of coverage. Others would like to increase their coverage to assure a sound financial

> **Smart Money Moves**
>
> Figure out the minimum amount of life insurance you need, then work up from there.
>
> More often than not, life insurance is "sold" rather than "bought." Don't wait until you are "sold" a policy. Rather, determine your life insurance needs, and go out and "buy" the best policy to meet your needs.

future for the family. For example, you may want to add insurance over the bare minimum to pay off the home mortgage, or use additional insurance to set up a college fund for the kids (or grandchildren).

It's not that difficult to estimate how much life insurance you should carry. The following example illustrates one of many ways to do so.

Case Study

Roderick Random is age fifty-five. Roderick and his forty-seven-year-old wife, Clarissa, have two children, a senior in college and a junior in high school. The Randoms have a combined annual income of $75,000. (Roderick earns $45,000, Clarissa earns $25,000, and their investment portfolio returns about $5,000 a year.) Should Roderick die tomorrow, his pension, in which he has only recently been vested, would be worth $5,000 a year.

At Roderick's death, annual income would be available from the following sources:

CLARISSA'S EARNINGS	$25,000
INVESTMENT PORTFOLIO	$5,000
SURVIVOR PENSION BENEFITS	$5,000
TOTAL	$35,000

Roderick estimates that in order to finish educating the children while maintaining his family's current standard of living, and to provide Clarissa with a fund that would provide for her retirement, the family would need about 80 percent of their current income level, or $60,000 of income ($75,000 x 80 percent).

Based on these assumptions, Clarissa would have an annual income "shortfall" of $25,000 ($60,000 - $35,000) should Roderick die. Assuming that the insurance proceeds could be withdrawn at a rate of 5 percent per year, Roderick would need life insurance in the amount of $500,000 to provide $25,000 in annual investment income. Actually, Roderick estimates that the investments could earn 8 percent interest, so Clarissa would actually earn $40,000 per year from the invested insurance proceeds. She would, however, have to reinvest $15,000 ($40,000 - $25,000) to insure that the amount that is to be withdrawn will increase each year to keep up with inflation. Roderick's $500,000 in insurance is a lot more than a bare minimum of four to five years' net income, but he prefers to provide the family with a higher level of financial security. Now that he has determined how much insurance he needs, Roderick can shop for the best policy or policies.

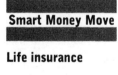

Smart Money Move

Life insurance needs vary. Typically, they decline as you age. Therefore, review your life insurance coverage every few years.

Changing Insurance Needs

Family insurance needs follow a cyclical pattern, so you may be best served by purchasing insurance that allows you to change the level of coverage. As your family grows, your insurance needs increase. The needs peak when the children are young, but they decline as the kids get nearer to leaving the nest. In the above example, Roderick's insurance needs will decline over the next several years—his pension benefits will increase and hopefully his investment portfolio as well. Roderick's children will graduate from college and leave home for good. Should Roderick die five years from now, his need for coverage would be reduced. Indeed, many people's life insurance needs decline significantly once the children are permanently out on their own (if they're *ever* permanently on their own). Retirees may not need any life insurance at all. In order to help you determine how much insurance you need, the worksheet at the end of this chapter can assist you.

As if all this weren't confusing enough, there is one more matter to worry about. If you think that your estate will be subject to estate taxes, life insurance may be used to help pay those taxes. And if your estate is likely to incur estate taxes, your life insurance policies should probably be placed in a so-called "life insurance trust." (This is covered in Chapter 82.)

The Varied Menu of Life Insurance Policies (It's Enough to Give You Indigestion)

O nce you have an idea of how much life insurance coverage you need, and before you start shopping, it is important to understand the kinds of life insurance products that are available. Life insurance comes in two basic flavors—term and cash value—plus a hybrid, universal life. The basic distinction between term and cash value insurance is that term insurance is pure life insurance, while cash value provides both insurance protection and a savings/investment feature. Beyond this basic distinction, how do they differ? And what about all those new variations on whole life and term insurance policies that have been recently introduced? The following will help you make sense out of all the confusion.

Smart Money Move

Make sure any term insurance you buy is "annually renewable."

Term Insurance

Term insurance is designed for one purpose only: protection for your dependents if you die. Only your heirs will benefit from the money you spend on term insurance premiums. On the other hand, term insurance is comparatively cheap, which makes it the coverage of choice for young heads-of-household. When you are just starting out in life and have young children, protection is crucial but funds are scarce. Young breadwinners usually don't have a lot of money to spend on life insurance premiums, so the low cost of term coverage makes it most attractive. You can buy term coverage that is quite flexible, allowing you to up- or downgrade coverage as your need for protection changes. For some individuals, term insurance could therefore provide good coverage during all of their working years.

One of the problems of term insurance, however, is that the older you get, the more expensive it becomes. On the other hand, for many people, the older they get, the lower the level of insurance protection they need. Term insurance may therefore not end up being as prohibitively expensive as people trying to sell you a cash value policy will claim.

Annual renewable term

If the term insurance you purchase has a fixed lifespan, when the policy expires you have to buy an entirely new policy. You will have to have a physical all over again and endure all the other hassles associated with buying an insurance policy—even if you are buying a policy identical to the old one. If health problems have arisen, you may not be able to get a new policy. The solution to this potentially serious dilemma: Buy an "annual renewable" term (ART) policy, which allows you to renew your insurance without having to prove your insurability all over again. Make sure any term insurance you buy is annually renewable for as long a period of time as you are likely to need the insurance protection.

You can *buy decreasing face value ART* policies, in which premiums stay level—or decrease slowly—while the value of death benefits decrease. More common is a *fixed face value ART* policy, where the premium goes up with each renewal while the value of the death benefit stays constant.

A *convertible term* policy, on the other hand, gives you the option of transforming your insurance from term to whole life with no questions asked. This feature may not, under ordinary circumstances, seem particularly thrilling. But should your health condition decline, owning a convertible insurance policy could be advantageous since you could convert the term policy before it expires, thereby providing you with insurance for the rest of your life.

Cash Value Insurance

The debate on the merits of cash value life (and its numerous offspring) versus term insurance is one that will continue as long as people buy and sell insurance. This section discusses the many varieties of cash value policies.

Whole life insurance

With whole life, you pay a fixed premium as long as you live, and the insurer pays a set death benefit. Since both the face value and the death benefit are fixed, the whole life policyholder overpays for coverage at first but pays comparatively lower premiums later on.

Whole life combines the protection offered by term insurance

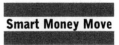

Smart Money Move

Don't impoverish yourself with too much cash value insurance.

with a savings aspect. A portion of each premium that the whole life policyholder pays goes directly to pay for the protection; the insurer invests the amount remaining on behalf of the policyholder. The policyholder's "investment portfolio" constitutes the policy's "cash value," which can be withdrawn in the form of loans, added to the death benefit, or used to reduce future premiums.

While whole life's forced savings aspect may make it attractive to some people, premiums are steep when compared to term insurance. Furthermore, with their fixed death benefits, whole life policies cannot be altered to reflect changes in the level of coverage a policyholder may need as his or her life progresses. Because of these drawbacks, whole life insurance is being surpassed in popularity by universal life insurance and other cash value products, which offer more attractive opportunities to build up cash values and greater policy flexibility.

Universal life insurance

Introduced in the late 1970s, this insurance product combines the protection of a conventional term insurance policy with the current yields available from short-term investments. Universal life policies separate the insurance component from the cash value. A charge is made for pure protection—the equivalent of term insurance, company fees, and profits—and the money that remains is the cash value of the policy, which earns interest according to a company contract or agreed-on financial index. Unlike the cash value of a traditional whole life policy, the cash value of a universal life policy grows at a variable rate.

Universal life's great virtue is the flexibility it offers the policyholder, who can buy additional insurance with the built-up cash value should the need arise. (A medical examination may be necessary.) Furthermore, you can vary premium payments within the limits established by the policy, a useful feature if your income is subject to periodic fluctuations. The cast-in-stone premiums of most whole life policies leave little room for maneuver should your income fall or be disrupted.

Universal life policies also offer greater flexibility to tap into cash value than do other types of insurance. Under most traditional whole life policies, you must either take out a loan or surrender the policy to have access to their built-up cash value. With universal life— and *some* whole life policies—you can make partial withdrawals from the policy's cash value through the receipt of dividends.

Universal life does have its drawbacks. As an investment product, the returns offered by universal life—like most insurance products—do not stack up against other saving and investment alternatives. Also, company fees and agent commissions are generally quite high, and they eat away at overall investment return.

Variable life insurance

This hybrid policy gives you a large measure of control over the buildup of cash value. As with whole life and universal life insurance, a portion of the premium buys pure protection, while the rest is invested by the carrier on the policyholder's behalf.

While whole life premiums are invested in low-yielding but safe securities, the variable life policyholder is presented with an array of investment choices. You can direct the company to invest premiums in one of several combinations of stock, bond, and/or money-market mutual funds. Variable life insurance is an attractive product if you like to take a hands-on approach to money management, and the returns you can achieve are an improvement over the generally dull performance of whole life portfolios.

There are two kinds of variable life policies. *Straight* variable life has a fixed annual premium. The more popular *universal* allows more flexibility insofar as the policyholder can vary the premiums that are paid as long as the basic minimum payments for death benefits are paid. So in addition to deciding how the money will be invested, you can choose how much to invest in a universal variable life policy.

But with the increased possibility of reward comes an increased risk, in the form of an uncertain cash value. The death benefit of a variable life policy is paid for by the pure insurance part of the policy and never falls below a certain "level or floor." But the amount of cash value is not guaranteed and could be severely reduced in the event that the company's portfolios perform badly. While the policyholder can choose the type of investment, insurance company money managers still choose the underlying securities.

Increasingly, though, variable life insurance policies are giving policyholders greater flexibility and choice in how premium proceeds are invested. The final drawback to variable life insurance is its expense. You can expect to pay a high sales commission and steep service fees, both of which will reduce the amount of money that actually ends up invested. For example, over fifteen to twenty years, policy fees would reduce a 12 percent investment return to 9 or 10 percent. Variable life insurance cash values, like all cash value insurance, do receive favorable tax treatment, however, in that cash value increases are not taxed until the money is withdrawn from the policy. In other words, policyholders get tax-deferred buildup of cash values.

Single-premium life insurance

If you have substantial cash reserves, single-premium life insurance may be an attractive option to build up some tax-deferred savings for retirement. By paying a single lump sum—which can be as low as $5,000—you can purchase death benefits and a cash value that grows free of current taxation. These policies may offer attractive interest rates but they usually impose stiff penalties for canceling the policy in the first few years after purchase. Policyholders do have access to cash value through loans. Given the way single-premium policies are structured, the emphasis is on investment, not insurance. Nevertheless, if you've got the money to spare and you want to buy an insurance product or accumulate cash-deferred retirement

Smart Money Move

A deferred annuity is a better bet than single-premium life insurance if you want to build tax-deferred retirement savings.

savings, I'd recommend a deferred annuity (see Chapter 76) over single-premium or variable life insurance.

Modified life insurance

This type of insurance is a variant of whole life, in which the premium is lower for the first five to ten years and then increases. Modified life is designed to entice younger people, even college students, to sign up for a whole life policy. I've met a lot of young people over the years who've started their careers "life insurance poor" because they had been sold modified life insurance policies with a whopping annual premium.

Limited payment life insurance

This product is another subspecies of whole life. Policyholders pay premiums for ten to twenty years; once payments cease, the interest paid on the cash value buildup pays for both the insurance and the increase in cash value. Premiums on this option may be even higher than ordinary whole life, which can make a bad deal even worse.

Smart Money Moves

Warning to college students: Life insurance agents working around the dorm can be hazardous to your financial health.

Don't waste your money on credit life insurance, travel insurance, or life insurance for children.

Useless Insurance

Credit life

Credit life insurance is a life insurance policy issued on the life of a borrower to cover the unpaid balance on a particular loan in the event of the borrower's death. Credit life insurance should be avoided unless you're about to die. Lenders often try to strong-arm borrowers into buying this coverage to cover a substantial loan like an auto or home loan. Fortunately, in most states lenders cannot require this insurance as a condition of the loan.

Credit life insurance is almost always outrageously expensive. It is completely unnecessary so long as you already have adequate life insurance—enough to pay off your loans while still providing for your dependents. If you want to take out life insurance to pay off a loan, purchase a less expensive term insurance policy and save a bundle of money. Years ago, the bank that gave me my mortgage tried to sell me a life insurance policy that would—in the event I died—pay off my mortgage. The first year cost: $750. I could have bought an equivalent term policy for $60!

Travel insurance

You no doubt have seen ads for accidental death insurance in airports. Policies are sometimes sold right out of vending machines at what appears to be a ridiculously low cost. The cost is ridiculously low because the chances of your survivors ever benefiting from one of these policies are also ridiculously low. *Don't buy travel insurance.* Some credit card companies now offer travel insurance at an extra cost. Believe me, they are making a bundle on this outrageously expensive insurance.

Life insurance for children

When the new bambino arrives, you may be bombarded by people who want to sell you life insurance for tots. Often, it's sold on the basis of providing a college fund through a buildup in cash value. You don't need it. Almost anything you put your money in instead of a child's life insurance policy will end up being a better investment. If you want to use life insurance to provide Junior with a college fund, insure yourself and/or your spouse.

Tip-offs to useless life insurance

Life insurance touted on television or the radio by some down-on-his-luck celebrity, and any life insurance offers you receive in the mail, are useless. No, no, no.

A Plan for Buying the Right Kind of Life Insurance at the Best Price

Once you have estimated the amount of life insurance that you need, and you understand the various types of life insurance that are available, it is time to become a wise insurance buyer. If you take control of the insurance purchase decision, you're bound to save money. If you use an insurance agent, understanding the alternatives that are available to you will help you get the right coverage at the right price. Even if you already have sufficient life insurance, the following tips may help you save money in the future, because most people over-pay for their life insurance coverage.

Term or Cash Value?

The debate over whether term or cash value life insurance is preferable will never be resolved. One thing is for sure, however: Term insurance is usually cheaper in the long run than cash value insurance, despite what the person who is desperately trying to sell you a cash value policy will say. If you're concerned about providing the most insurance coverage at the lowest cost now, buy term.

Nevertheless, many people have benefited, are benefiting, and will benefit from cash value insurance. People who are otherwise unable to discipline themselves to save regularly can benefit from cash value insurance's forced savings feature. Even disciplined savers

Smart Money Move

Don't buy travel insurance unless you are convinced your plane is going to crash. (If you are convinced, take the bus instead.)

can take advantage of the tax-deferral feature of cash value life insurance as part of a program for saving for retirement. In spite of the ever-present and annoying fees and commissions, the newer breed of cash value life insurance products can offer attractive tax-advantaged returns on the investment portion of the policy. The problem with trying to meet all or most of one's life insurance needs through cash value insurance is simply that it can become prohibitively expensive.

What's the upshot? Like most things in our financial lives, term versus cash value insurance should not be viewed as an either/or proposition. You may well be best served by a combination of term insurance to provide needed insurance protection for your dependents and cash value insurance to provide additional life insurance protection and, more important, to accumulate tax-deferred savings.

Sources of Life Insurance Coverage

You can do nothing but benefit from vigorous comparison shopping for the lowest price and best policy terms. Identical policies have carried price disparities as much as 1,500 percent. The following is a list of the many available sources of life insurance. As you can see, there are many ways to buy life insurance without an agent.

Employer-Provided Insurance

Your employer may already provide some insurance as part of your compensation package. If your employer pays the premiums, that's great. If you have to pay part or all of the premiums yourself, chances are that the coverage is still a very good deal. You may also have the option of purchasing additional life insurance beyond what the company provides. If so, investigate it, because it's very likely to be very attractively priced. Remember that if you leave your job, you may not have the option of continuing this life insurance. You or your family could be at risk if you have no additional coverage.

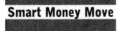

Smart Money Move

Cash value life insurance is expensive life insurance and is a mediocre investment.

Social Security Benefits

Don't forget to include in your life insurance projections possible Social Security benefits that are available to survivors who have been paying into Social Security and meet certain conditions. Benefits may be available to a surviving spouse, surviving children who are under age eighteen or are disabled, and dependent parents age sixty-two or older. (See Chapter 70 for information on Social Security benefits.)

Savings Bank Life Insurance

If you live or work in Connecticut, Massachusetts, or New York, consider yourself lucky, at least as far as life insurance is concerned.

Savings banks in those states provide low-cost term and cash value coverage. The amount of the insurance is limited, but it is well worth investigating.

Low-Load Life Insurance Companies

Some companies are now offering both term and cash value insurance directly to the public. These policies have lower fees because they don't incur a sales commission, so the premiums are often quite attractive. You have nothing to lose by contacting these companies and asking for some information and a quotation. The addresses and telephone numbers of several prominent low-load life insurance companies appear at the end of the chapter.

Purchase Through an Agent

Although this alternative is listed last, it doesn't necessarily mean that purchasing insurance from an agent is the least desirable way to obtain coverage. Many insurance agents will work hard to find attractively priced coverage for you, and their advice can be helpful at times.

Games agents play

As when finding any good professional, ask your friends or co-workers for a recommendation for an insurance agent. It's so common to be dissatisfied with one's insurance agent that once you find someone who really appreciates what their agent is doing, you've probably found a marvelous one.

When dealing with an agent, be wary of a few things. First, it is not uncommon for companies to offer agents two otherwise identical policies with different commission structures. You guessed it—the policy with the higher commission structure provides less attractive policy features than does the lower-commission policy. Don't be afraid to ask if you are thinking of making a purchase.

Second, be wary of agents who encourage you to cash in one cash value policy for another or a term policy. While there are situations where you may benefit—for example, the new cash value policy may offer a more attractive rate of return than a policy you recently purchased—you are generally better off sticking with the old policy. By staying put, you'll avoid having to pay another commission, not to mention the hassle of filling out reams of application forms. If you do cash in a cash value policy, you can avoid paying taxes on it by transferring the money into an annuity or another life insurance policy.

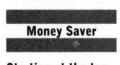

Money Saver

Starting at the top, use this section to find low-cost life insurance.

Finally, be very skeptical of the policy projections that are provided to you. Many are just pie-in-the-sky, as a lot of policyholders found out amidst the declining interest rates of the early 1990s. For example, policies that forecast that they would be paid up in eight to ten years are requiring premium payments of twenty years or more because low interest rates are slowing the cash value buildup.

(A paid-up policy is a policy that needs no further premium payments.) Therefore, the only life insurance cash value projections to believe are those based on the insurer's guaranteed minimum return.

How Can You Tell Whether You're Paying a Good Price?

I f you spend some time comparison shopping, you are likely to uncover dramatic differences in the cost of an otherwise identical insurance policy. This is why comparison shopping can pay off so handsomely. But even though you think you've found just the right policy at just the right price, you should consider having an independent third party give you an opinion. There are several consumer organizations that will provide an analysis of life insurance policies to help you find the best coverage at the lowest cost. Perhaps the best known and most respected is the National Insurance Consumer Organization (NICO). (You can write NICO at 121 North Payne Street, Alexandria VA 22314.)

If you're buying term insurance, this table (provided by James Hunt, author of *How to Save Money on Life Insurance*) will help you determine whether you're overpaying.

THE MOST YOU SHOULD PAY FOR TERM INSURANCE

NONSMOKERS	ANNUAL PREMIUM*		SMOKERS	ANNUAL PREMIUM*	
AGE	MALE	FEMALE	AGE	MALE	FEMALE
18–30	$ .76	$ .68	18–30	$ 1.05	$ 1.01
31	.76	.69	31	1.10	1.05
32	.77	.70	32	1.15	1.10
33	.78	.71	33	1.21	1.15
34	.79	.72	34	1.28	1.20
35	.80	.74	35	1.35	1.25
36	.84	.78	36	1.45	1.31
37	.88	.82	37	1.56	1.38
38	.92	.86	38	1.68	1.45
39	.97	.90	39	1.81	1.52
40	1.03	.95	40	1.95	1.60
41	1.09	1.00	41	2.12	1.73
42	1.17	1.05	42	2.30	1.89
43	1.25	1.10	43	2.50	2.05
44	1.34	1.15	44	2.72	2.22
45	1.45	1.20	45	2.95	2.40
46	1.59	1.29	46	3.22	2.59

»

Smart Money Move

Don't cash in a life insurance policy without careful consideration. Chances are it's not in your interest to do so.

NONSMOKERS			SMOKERS		
AGE	ANNUAL PREMIUM*		AGE	ANNUAL PREMIUM*	
	MALE	FEMALE		MALE	FEMALE
47	$ 1.74	$ 1.41	47	$ 3.52	$ 2.79
48	1.91	1.53	48	3.85	3.01
49	2.10	1.66	49	4.21	3.23
50	2.30	1.76	50	4.60	3.50
51	2.49	1.90	51	4.97	3.79
52	2.70	2.06	52	5.38	4.10
53	2.96	2.22	53	5.82	4.44
54	3.40	2.40	54	6.29	4.80
55	3.40	2.60	55	6.80	5.20
56	3.66	2.79	56	7.31	5.58
57	3.94	3.00	57	7.87	5.99
58	4.23	3.22	58	8.46	6.43
59	4.55	3.46	59	9.10	6.90
60	4.90	3.70	60	9.80	7.40
61	5.43	3.98	61	10.83	7.95
62	6.02	4.28	62	11.98	8.54
63	6.67	4.60	63	13.25	9.18
64	7.40	4.93	64	14.65	9.86
65	8.20	5.30	65	16.20	10.60

* Per $1,000 of coverage, per year.

Source: National Insurance Consumer Organization

Notes to the table:

• The table shows the premium rate per $1,000 of coverage. If you're buying a $100,000 policy, multiply the cost by 100 and add $60 (for the insurer's fixed policy expenses) to see the most that you should pay.

• Policies smaller than $100,000 cost a little more. Policies written for $500,000 and up cost a little less.

• Nonsmoker rates are preferred health risks.

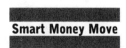

Smart Money Move

Find low-cost insurance by buying a life insurance analysis from an independent party.

Finally, you need to be concerned about the financial health of the company issuing your life insurance policy. Remember, if you're buying a cash value policy, you're going to be stuck with your insurer for life. Make sure that the company has a rating of A or better from A. M. Best. Not even a current high rating necessarily assures that the company will remain strong over the long run, but there's no sense in making a financial commitment to a company that is currently weak.

What if you have a life insurance policy with a company whose financial condition has deteriorated? This is a very difficult call. First, don't panic. Second, evaluate carefully the ramifications of cashing in the policy, which could result in some financial loss as well as an interruption in protection. Third, there has been a pattern of healthy insurance companies coming in and taking over policies held by ailing companies. However, if concern over the financial health of your insurer is causing you to have health problems—stress or lack of sleep—by all means get out of the policy.

FOR FURTHER INFORMATION

The following publications will help you better understand the vagaries of life insurance:
A Consumer's Guide to Life Insurance (Pub. #436Y, $0.50)
> **Consumer Information Center**
> **Attention: R. Woods**
> **Pueblo, CO 81009**

How to Save Money on Life Insurance ($13.95)
> **James H. Hunt**
> **National Insurance Consumer Organization**
> **121 North Payne St.**
> **Alexandria, VA 22314**

The following firms can provide you with premium quotes for a wide variety of life insurance policies. The information these companies furnish will help you find the best insurance for the lowest cost. You will easily recoup the money you spend on quote fees in reduced premiums.

> **Insurance Information, Inc.**
> **Cobblestone Court #2**
> **Route 134**
> **South Dennis, MA 02660**
> **(800) 472-5800**

Insurance Quote
3200 North Dobson Road
Building C
Chandler, AZ 85224
(800) 972-1104

Selectquote
140 Second Street
5th Floor
San Francisco, CA 94105
(800) 343-1985

You can also save money by buying your coverage directly from low-load life insurance companies like the ones listed below:

> **American Life of New York**
> **New York, NY**
> **(212) 399-5555**

> **USAA Life**
> **San Antonio, TX**
> **(800) 531-8000**

> **Ameritas Low-Load**
> **Houston, TX**
> **(800) 552-3553**

If you have lost your policy documenta-

»

tion, request a "policy search form" (make sure to include a stamped, self-addressed business-size envelope with your request) from:

American Council of Life Insurance
Attention: Policy Search Department
1001 Pennsylvania Avenue, N.W.
Washington, DC 20004
(800) 942-4242

LIFE INSURANCE NEEDS WORKSHEET

This worksheet can be used to estimate your life insurance needs. If you enter amounts for each category of need, the resulting estimate should be viewed as a *maximum* amount of insurance that will meet all foreseeable needs of your survivors. (*Note:* All amounts should be expressed in terms of current dollars.)

Expenses

1. Final expenses (one-time expenses incurred by your death)

   A. Final illness (medical costs will probably exceed health insurance deductibles and coinsurance, so assume you will have to fund at least those amounts) $ ....

   B. Burial/funeral costs   ....

   C. Probate costs (if unsure, assume 4 percent of assets passing through the probate process)   ....

   D. Federal estate taxes (for most estates over $600,000 willed to someone other than spouse)   ....

   E. State inheritance taxes (varies by state)   ....

   F. Legal fees, estate administration   ....

   G. Other   ....

   H. Total final expenses $ ....

2. Outstanding debt (to be paid off at your death)

   A. Credit card/consumer debt   ....

   B. Car   ....

   C. Mortgage (if it's to be paid off at your death; otherwise include payments in life income)   ....

   D. Other   ....

   E. Total outstanding debt $ ....

3. Readjustment expenses (to cover the transition period of immediate crisis)

»

LIFE INSURANCE NEEDS WORKSHEET < CONT'D >

  A.   Child care $ ....

  B.   Additional homemaking help   ....

  C.   Vocational counseling/educational training (for a non-working or underemployed spouse who expects to seek paid employment)   ....

  D.   Costs of continuing business and/or disposing of business in an orderly fashion (if business does not already provide sufficient life insurance coverage)   ....

  E.   Other   ....

  F.   Total readjustment expenses (add lines 4A - 4E) $ ....

4.   Dependency expenses (until all children are self-supporting)

  A.   Estimate your household's current annual expenditures   ....

  B.   To remove the deceased person's expenses, multiply this figure by:

        .70 for a surviving family of one

        .74 for a surviving family of two

        .78 for a surviving family of three

        .80 for a surviving family of four

        .82 for a surviving family of five

        $ .... (Line 4A) x .... (factor) = ...

  C.   Deduct spouse's estimated annual income from employment   (........)

  D.   Equals current annual expenses to be covered by currently owned assets and insurance   ....

  E.   To determine approximate total dependency expenses required, multiply by number of years until youngest child becomes self-supporting:

        $ .... (Line 4D) x .... (years) = ...

  F.   If support for dependent parent(s) is to be provided, multiply annual support by the number of years such support is expected to continue:

        $ .... x .... (years) = ...

  G.   Total dependency expenses (add Lines 4E and 4F) $ ....

5.   Education expenses

  A.   Annual private school tuition in current dollars (if desired)   ....

»

B. Multiply by number of years and children left to attend:

$ .... (Line 5A) x .... (years) = $ ....

C. Annual college costs in current dollars   ....

D. Multiply by number of years and children left to attend:

$ .... (Line 5C) x .... (years) = ...

E. Total education expenses (add Lines 5B and 5D) $ ....

6. Life income (for the surviving spouse after the children are all self-supporting)

    A. Annual amount desired (in current dollars)   ....

    B. Deduct spouse's estimated annual income from employment   ....

    C. Equals annual expenses to be covered by currently owned assets and insurance   ....

    D. Multiply by number of years between when the youngest child becomes self-supporting and the surviving spouse begins receiving Social Security benefits and other retirement income, if any:

$ .... (Line 6C) x .... (years) = $ ....

7. Retirement income for surviving spouse

    A. Annual amount desired in current dollars (less Social Security and any pension income)   ....

    B. Multiply by number of years of life expectancy after retirement begins:

$ .... (Line 7A) x .... (years) = $ ....

8. Total funds needed to cover expenses: (add Lines 1H, 2E, 3F, 4G, 5E, 6D, and 7B) $ ....

Assets currently available to support family

Proceeds from life insurance already owned $ ....

Cash and savings   ....

Equity in real estate (if survivors will sell)   ....

Securities   ....

IRA and Keogh and/or other pension plans   ....

Company savings plans   ....

Other sources   ....

9. Total available assets $ ....

»

LIFE INSURANCE NEEDS WORKSHEET < CONT'D >

Additional life insurance required

Subtract available assets (Line 9) from total funds needed to
cover expenses (Line 8). This shortfall represents the estimated
amount of additional life insurance that is needed if you desire $ ....

LIFE INSURANCE POLICY ALTERNATIVES

TYPE OF POLICY	DESCRIPTION OF FEATURES
TERM	*Term* insurance only provides death protection. A term policy does not build a cash value. If the insured discontinues insurance premiums payments, the coverage simply lapses after a specific grace period. This is the cheapest form of immediate insurance protection. There are many kinds of term insurance. Term insurance premiums increase with age for the same amount of coverage, although most people's life insurance requirements decrease with age. A *renewable term* policy covers the insured for a fixed period of years or until a specified age. With renewable term, the insured may usually renew the policy each year without a medical examination. *Decreasing term* provides constant premiums over time with a declining amount of death protection.
WHOLE LIFE	Also called *straight* or *ordinary life.* Requires level premium payments over the lifetime of the insured and provides cash value that increases slowly in the early years and more rapidly in the later years of the policy. The rate of increase in the cash value is predetermined. A number of variations are also available. Under a *limited payment life* policy, premium payments remain level up to a certain age and then cease. *Adjustable life* plans allow the insured to change both the premium payments and the face amount of the policy as needs and income vary.
UNIVERSAL LIFE	*Universal life* permits flexible premium payments. The cash value portion of the policy is deposited into an interest-bearing account that is usually tied to a predetermined index. Most universal policies allow the insured to increase the death protection, although another medical examination may be required. Universal life insurance policies have been designed to provide considerable flexibility to the amount of coverage and the amount of premium.

»

VARIABLE LIFE	The cash value portion of *variable life* is invested in one or more stock, bond, and money market funds of the policyholder's choosing. Therefore, the cash value will fluctuate based on the performance of these separate investment accounts.
SINGLE–PREMIUM WHOLE LIFE	*Single-premium* policies are paid up in one or very few installments. The emphasis in these policies is on investment, not insurance. Like other cash value policies, the cash values build up tax free.

LIFE INSURANCE CHECKLIST

Make your own estimate of how much life insurance you need. Don't rely entirely on others to tell you how much you need.

Periodically review your life insurance needs since they usually change over your lifetime and will likely decline as you get older.

Don't spend a lot of money on cash value life insurance because it is a very expensive way to obtain life insurance protection and a mediocre investment.

Shop around for low-cost term and cash value life insurance coverage. If you "buy" this insurance rather than having it "sold" to you, you'll save.

Before buying a life insurance policy, consider obtaining a low-cost analysis of it from an independent organization.

Don't waste your money on overpriced credit life insurance, travel insurance, or life insurance for children.

Health Insurance

For a great many Americans, the cost of health care heads their list of worries. It's not so much the illness that causes concern as its cost. Health-care costs have risen so dramatically that even individuals with generous company-provided health insurance plans are being asked to assume an ever-larger percentage of their medical bills.

The issue of rising health-care costs takes on particular urgency for the tens of millions of Americans who can't even take advantage of employer health insurance plans. These people are confronted with having to choose between obtaining their own health insurance policies—often at very high cost—or taking the terrible risk of going uninsured. For those who must take the latter course, every illness, every surgical procedure, every prescription drug drains precious financial resources. Whether you enjoy the security of an employer-sponsored plan, pay for your own insurance, or are not presently insured but hope to obtain coverage, this chapter will help you make the most of your situation. I strongly urge you to become a well-educated consumer, not only of health-care services but also of health-care insurance. It is crucial for your long-term financial security to obtain and maintain adequate health insurance coverage—at a reasonable cost. (If you are having trouble obtaining *any* coverage, consult Chapter 46.)

Make sure that you and all of your family members maintain continuous and comprehensive health insurance coverage.

The issue of national health insurance is one that won't go away—but it's also an issue that is not likely to be resolved soon. According to a recent national survey, Americans are fed up with their health-care system. Over 60 percent believe that the system needs fundamental change. While this dissatisfaction may become a stimulus for change, it's important to remember that currently there is no national health insurance policy in existence. In other words, if you're not funding your own health insurance or if your employer is not providing such coverage for you, then, like an estimated 31 million other Americans, you're uninsured.

The consequences of lacking adequate health insurance can be devastating. The average cost of a day in the hospital is approximately $400. The average stay for a heart attack is nine days, and for a hernia, it's three days. Add such basic costs to the costs of your physician's care, and you can see how easily you could bankrupt yourself by suffering an uninsured illness.

The bottom line is, don't go a day, an hour, or a minute without making certain that you and your loved ones are adequately covered by a solid health insurance policy. Some form of universally available health care may well become available, but don't believe for a moment that you can afford to wait for its arrival.

Basic Terms and Concepts

While many of the following insurance terms and concepts may sound familiar to you, review them anyway. You are sure to gain some knowledge that will help you in choosing and evaluating a medical insurance policy so that you set the coverage you need and avoid any unpleasant surprises when you file a claim.

Deductible

The deductible is the amount of money you must pay on a policy before your insurance coverage takes effect. If, for instance, your policy has a $100 deductible, you would pay the first $100 before the insurance policy kicks in. The deductible is often based on a per-person basis, so in this example, a family will have a total deductible of $100 per person, up to a specified maximum per family per year.

There is an inverse relationship between deductibles and premiums: the higher the deductible, the lower the premium. Policies that have no or low deductibles have correspondingly higher premiums. On the other hand, a policy with a high deductible—say, $1,000—will have a lower premium. If you have to buy insurance on your own, check into the possibility of taking a policy with a high deductible. It could lower your premiums significantly, but remember—you need to have the money available to pay the deductible.

Coinsurance

Another method insurance companies use to pass some of the costs of health care back to policyholders is coinsurance. A coinsured expense is one that is shared by the policyholder and the insurer. Unlike a deductible, which is a stated dollar amount, the insurer pays a fixed percentage share of a coinsured expense. A policy might, for example, pay 80 percent of daily hospital bills, with the policyholder paying (or coinsuring) the remaining 20 percent of the cost.

Stop-loss clause

Fortunately, most medical insurance plans include a "stop loss" clause. As its name suggests, this clause limits the amount of money you will have to spend on coinsurance, cost sharing, or deductibles during the benefit year. If your policy has a $1,000 "stop-loss" ceiling, once you've paid $1,000 in deductibles, cost sharing, or coinsurance, the company picks up all your remaining expenses for that year.

The Medical Information Bureau

It is important that you be honest in filling out your insurance application and claim forms. The reason for being honest is not only that virtue is its own reward. The Medical Information Bureau keeps track of your medical history, just as credit bureaus record your credit history. If an insurer discovers that you have lied or falsified information, you could have benefits denied or your policy revoked entirely.

Basic coverage

Basic medical coverage usually includes hospital room and board; hospital services such as diagnostic services, surgical care, anesthetics, drugs, medical equipment, and supplies; regular, health care service to a maximum limit, and sometimes outpatient care. Coverage of medical expenses is provided on an indemnity or service basis (see below).

Major medical

Major medical insurance picks up where basic coverage leaves off. The maximum benefits given by a major medical insurance plan may be as low as $10,000 or as high as $1,000,000, and sometimes they have no maximum. If your maximum major medical benefits are $250,000 or less, you should obtain an excess major medical policy (see page 318) to protect you against the possibility, however small, that a catastrophic accident or illness could run up medical bills exceeding your maximum coverage.

Indemnity benefit

An indemnity benefit pays a *fixed sum* toward the amount of each covered medical bill. For instance, an indemnity policy might pay you $275 per day toward daily hospital charges.

Service benefit

A service benefit pays a *percentage* of each covered medical bill. If you get very sick and your medical bills balloon, a service benefit will leave you in better shape financially than an indemnity benefit.

Employer-Sponsored Health Insurance

I f you work for a reasonably large corporation, you are, as far as health insurance is concerned, a member of the privileged class of America's workforce. Employees of large firms as a rule enjoy the best in employer-paid health insurance. Coverage in smaller firms can range from comprehensive to nonexistent, but usually falls short of big-company coverage. Generally, however, the smaller the company, the more difficulty it may have in coping with the rising costs of health insurance. The problems, however, cut across the board. These days, even well-insured employees of large companies are likely to receive company memos informing them of coverage changes designed to shift costs to the employee.

This trend will continue, so it is all the more important that you become an educated health insurance consumer.

Employer Cost Cutting

Employers are using a wide variety of cost-cutting tools. Increasingly common practices include adding or raising deductibles, requiring employees to coinsure hospital bills, and switching from traditional health insurance plans to health maintenance organizations (HMOs) and preferred provider organizations (PPOs). (Both HMOs and PPOs are discussed on page 315.) Some companies now require employees to discuss elective surgery with the insurance provider's medical representative. Mandatory second opinions are also becoming common. If you are employer-insured, it behooves you to pay attention to office memos and circulars about your insurance. You don't want to have any unpleasant surprises about changes to your coverage. Unfortunately, no matter how much you may dislike changes to your plan, you have little recourse but to make the best of the situation.

While you may be tempted to strike out on your own, it is very unlikely that you will benefit in the long run from opting out of your company's plan. Buying your own coverage will cost you a lot more money, or else the coverage you purchase will be much more limited than the employer-provided policy. Employer-sponsored group plans typically offer savings of 30 to 40 percent over equivalent individually purchased plans.

Understanding COBRA

Many people, especially those working in companies where layoffs have been occurring, are very concerned about losing their health insurance along with their job. Fortunately, federal law ensures continuing group health coverage for most former employees and their dependents. Passed in 1985, the Consolidated Omnibus Budget Reconciliation Act (COBRA) directs businesses with more than nineteen employees to give employees and their family members the option of continuing group health coverage for at least eighteen months after termination or resignation. The only exception—employees who have been fired for gross misconduct. Terminated employees who elect to take the continuing coverage must pay the entire premium plus an administrative surcharge (up to 2 percent of the premium). Nonetheless, even with this surcharge, the rate you pay is probably much lower than what you would pay for an individual policy.

Smart Money Move

Take the time to learn about your company's insurance plan(s), so that you can take full advantage of it.

The COBRA health-care provisions can be a godsend for many people who are "between jobs" or who resign from work to start their own business. It has one big potential pitfall—it only lasts for a fixed period of time. Since COBRA runs out, you will eventually need to secure your own coverage or find a job in a company with a health-care plan. Should you or any of your family members develop a serious health problem while covered under COBRA, you may, when COBRA expires, have a lot of difficulty obtaining good health insurance. One way to protect yourself against this eventuality is to purchase your own guaranteed renewable insurance coverage as soon as possible. Once this coverage is acquired, you can drop the "temporary" COBRA coverage.

Should you leave your job because of disability, you can receive up to twenty-nine months of continuing health insurance coverage under COBRA's provisions. Social Security and Medicare benefits for disabled people under age sixty-five don't begin until twenty-nine months after the onset of the disability, so COBRA plays an important role for these individuals. Disabled persons should be aware that employers do have the option of raising disabled employees' premiums by as much as 50 percent from the base price during the last eleven months of the twenty-nine-month period.

In addition, should you die while still employed, COBRA requires your company to continue covering at its own expense your dependents for the thirty-six months following your demise. The law also mandates that group coverage be continued for you and your dependents under some other circumstances, including divorce.

HMOs and PPOs

Health Maintenance Organizations (HMOs)

As the name implies, HMOs provide for all your health-care needs with an emphasis on the preventive end of medicine. An HMO gives an almost total health-care service: doctors' appointments (including routine physical exams), hospital stays, operations, and in some cases prescription drugs, eyeglasses, and podiatry. Like a conventional insurance company, an HMO typically charges a monthly premium. HMO members must go to a designated health center or centers for treatment and can usually see only physicians who are part of the HMO. If you've worked for a company that offers a choice of health-care plans, the chances are an HMO is one alternative. You may find that if you have no choice of plan, your employer has opted for an HMO. Finally, if you have to obtain your own health insurance coverage, an HMO is one alternative to consider.

The problem with HMOs is that they severely limit your choice. Once you've chosen a doctor, he or she determines what sort of treatment you'll get and whether you will see a specialist or go to a hospital. Traditionally, if you wanted to consult a physician outside the HMO, you would be expected to pay the entire bill yourself. Now, however, some HMOs cover a portion—sometimes as much as 75 to 80 percent—of outside doctors' bills.

While some HMOs are in effect large, self-contained clinics, other HMOs called individual practice associations (IPAs) contract with doctors who practice in their own clinics. Each type of HMO has its drawbacks and its benefits; if you like the idea of one-stop medical shopping, however, an HMO that operates its own clinic is a very convenient way to receive care.

As with any sort of medical plan, it makes sense to understand exactly what a prospective HMO will give you in return for your premium. The following checklist will help you evaluate an HMO.

HMO CHECKLIST

☐

Does the HMO pay for "extras" like
- unlimited hospital stays
- annual physical exams
- eye care contact lenses
- hearing aids
- foot care

☐

Does the HMO cover the expense of emergency care from a non-HMO provider, especially if you require care while you are outside of the HMO's region?

☐

Does the HMO allow you to select your own doctor?

☐

Does the HMO allow you to change doctors if you're not satisfied with the service or treatment?

☐

Does the HMO cover the cost of a second opinion from an HMO doctor? What about from a non-HMO doctor?

☐

Does the HMO have established procedures for redressing grievances or a hotline for customer questions and complaints?

Smart Money Move

If you cannot purchase health insurance through your employer, try to obtain group coverage before purchasing an individual policy.

Preferred Provider Organizations (PPOs)

Groups of physicians sometimes band together into preferred provider organizations (PPOs) in order to provide medical care at discount rates. PPO participants generally pay little or nothing to see member physicians and hospitals, but they pay more if they go outside the PPO for treatment. PPOs are becoming an increasingly important player in the health insurance marketplace. Insurance companies and employers have come to recognize the cost-benefits of working with PPOs. A number of cooperative arrangements between insurers and PPOs have been developed recently.

Membership in a PPO can also be obtained on an individual basis. Here, they offer an interesting alternative to an HMO for the individual seeking personal health insurance coverage. PPOs combine features of HMOs and orthodox medical insurance plans into a hybrid product that allows for more flexibility. It may be the ticket for you.

Individually Purchased Insurance and Insurance for the Self-Employed

When you are out on your own or if your company doesn't offer coverage, obtaining medical insurance can be difficult and frustrating—and expensive. If you are willing to shop around and put some time into your insurance hunt, however, you can probably find insurance that won't break the bank. (If you are healthy, that is. If you are already seriously ill, finding insurance is extremely tough. See Chapter 46.) There are several routes to finding a policy. You can affiliate yourself with a group so that you get coverage reasonably similar to the employer-sponsored variety, or you can get it strictly as an individual, whether from an insurance company, HMO, or PPO.

Group Coverage

One way to find coverage is to enroll in a professional or fraternal association or trade group. If you are self-employed, chances are that there is an organization established to promote the interests of your field of endeavor. Many organizations, particularly those that are based in your locale, offer their members group health insurance policies.

Be forewarned, however, that group insurance can have problems of its own. For one thing, group policies can be canceled at any time. Should the insurer decide to pull the rug out from under you, the company has no obligation to find another plan for ex-enrollees. Furthermore, since state insurance agencies don't regulate group insurance as closely as individually purchased insurance, yearly rate increases can be steep. Finally, these group policies often have low benefit limits. The upshot? Do consider group coverage if you can find it, but make sure it is comprehensive enough to meet your health-care needs.

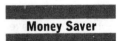

Money Saver

Reduce your health insurance premium costs by raising the deductible (but only if you can afford to pay the out-of-pocket costs).

Individual Coverage

Buying insurance individually is almost certain to be more expensive than buying it through a group plan, but finding a decent policy isn't impossible. An individual policy that is guaranteed renewable may also give you a greater degree of security than a group policy. The key to buying an individual policy is first that you, your spouse, and your dependents all be healthy enough to qualify for coverage. Next, you need to figure out how high (or low) a deductible you can afford. Get sick often? You'll probably want to pay a higher premium and obtain a lower deductible. Never been in a hospital? While you shouldn't delude yourself into thinking that you're medically invulnerable, you can probably opt for a higher deductible and a correspondingly lower monthly premium. If you can afford to coinsure the cost of certain items like hospital stays, you may also be able to shave your premium.

If you are fairly healthy, it makes sense to look at those exclusive policies that are laden with exclusions for preexisting conditions. You may have to have a physical to qualify, but the savings on a more selective health policy are well worth it. It may seem callous, but you can profit from the fact that a particular policy excludes everyone who has stubbed a toe or used cough syrup. The company will see you as an excellent risk, and your premiums will actually run lower than the national deficit. Just make sure that, should your health start to fall apart, the policy will meet your needs and continue to cover you.

On the other hand, if you have preexisting conditions, be prepared to forgo coverage on them for a period of time, often around a year. It's almost impossible to find a cost-effective policy that will cover an ailment that you have at the time of signing up. If the conditions are serious, you may have to join Blue Cross/Blue Shield or an HMO. While they have their drawbacks, most states require HMOs to have yearly enrollment periods during which they take all comers, although preexisting conditions can be excluded temporarily from the coverage. Finally, whatever type of policy you buy, make sure that it is guaranteed renewable, so that the insurance company can't pull the rug out from under you.

Supplemental Health Insurance

Smart Money Move

If your health insurance policy has a low benefits ceiling, purchase a low-cost excess major medical insurance policy.

Excess Major Medical

Whether you own a group or individual policy or belong to an HMO, and whether your employer pays part or all of your health insurance costs, if your medical plan has a benefits ceiling, consider getting supplementary coverage. Excess major medical insurance is designed to take effect when your ordinary benefits have been exhausted. While benefit ceilings can be as low as $100,000 and sometimes even less, hospital bills of $250,000 or more have been run up by more than one unfortunate patient. The price of excess major medical is quite reasonable and may be able to be obtained as part of an umbrella liability insurance plan. Don't risk a financial disaster by having too-low limits on your health care.

Avoid These Money Wasters

Most other types of supplemental policies, such as dread disease or hospital indemnity, are a waste of good money. These policies are almost always so narrowly defined that benefits kick in under only the rarest circumstances. Dread disease insurance is often marketed as a protection against cancer-treatment cost, but while cancer is a major cause of death, your individual chances of getting the disease are still relatively small. Furthermore, even should you "luck out" and develop cancer, the policy may cover only certain parts of the disease's overall cost. Side effects and conditions related to the cancer are often not covered by these policies.

Hospital indemnity insurance is similarly useless. You've seen these policies. They offer a daily benefit of $50 or $100 while you are hospitalized. If you have good health insurance, why do you need one of these meretricious policies? If you don't have health insurance, $100 a day won't even get you through breakfast in most hospitals. Most plans take effect after you've been hospitalized for a week or longer, even though the average hospital stay is under seven days. Premiums for hospital indemnity and dread disease insurance seem low, but the chances of receiving benefits are even lower, so they end up being a big waste of money.

Cutting Your Health-Care Costs

A s expensive as health care is today, only one thing is certain: Health-care costs will continue to escalate. Is there anything you can do to fight back? Yes. We'd all be financially healthier if everyone took a hard look at how they use the health-care system. The following suggestions will help you and your family become better consumers of medical services and products.

Recuperate at Home

In some cases you may be able to limit your hospital stays by recuperating at home with the assistance of professional home health caregivers. Even with the expense of hiring a professional nurse, recuperating at home is still a medical bargain compared with staying in the hospital, and it's better on the psyche.

Smart Money Move

Don't waste your money on extra insurance that covers only certain illnesses or has limited benefits.

Home recuperation typically involves visits by a nurse or other health-care professional, who provides therapy or other medical services and monitors your progress. Many health plans pay 100 percent of the cost of such care for a specified number of days each year. Some insurers waive their basic plan deductibles for policyholders who take advantage of the home health-care alternative. Naturally, only your doctor can authorize at-home recovery, but before you go into the operating room, consult with your physician to see whether it might be feasible.

If recuperation can't take place at home, moving to a skilled nursing facility is an appropriate alternative to a prolonged hospital stay. Skilled nursing facilities, which are often connected with hospitals, provide around-the-clock nursing care and effective rehabilitation for far less than the cost of traditional hospital care.

Self-Audit Your Hospital Bill

Hospital bills can be long, complicated, and dense. Nevertheless, make a point to read them over closely. Mistakes and billing errors *can* happen, and there's no point in overpaying. So if you are about to approve or pay a lump-sum bill, don't sign the bill and send it into the insurer or reach for your checkbook until you first receive an itemized account of the services rendered.

If you do find a charge you can't identify or are billed for a service you can't remember, ask the hospital's billing office to explain it. If it turns out you've been overcharged (as is often the case), insist that the hospital accounting office correct its error.

Ask for Generic Drugs

Most health insurance plans pay only part of the cost of the pharmaceuticals your doctor prescribes—about 80 percent is average. Thus, if a prescription costs $20, the policyholder usually pays about $4 out of his or her own pocket, with the insurance covering the remainder. While $4 here and $5 there may not seem like much, these expenses add up. Furthermore, how many medicines cost a mere $20 these days?

In many cases, the amount you pay for prescriptions can be cut by as much as half by using generic drugs. Generic drugs must pass the same Food and Drug Administration tests as their brand-name equivalents. You won't compromise quality one bit by taking your medicine in generic form. If you're in doubt, ask your doctor.

When the System Breaks Down: Contesting a Claim

You're insured with what seems to be a good company: the terms of the policy are acceptable, and the premium and deductible are bearable. Then you file a claim and the insurance company informs you that the claim has been denied. What can you do?

When a claim is turned down, the company will usually give a reason for the denial. The first thing you must do is obtain from your employer or agent a "true copy" of your policy. If you only received a certificate with a simplified description of your coverage at the time of your enrolling in a plan, without a "true copy" you won't be able to hold your own when arguing with your insurer. If you have a group policy, your benefits booklet serves as your "true copy" of the policy.

Check the fine print of your policy to see whether the reason that your claim has been denied indeed meets the policy's rules. There is a good chance that the company is right; perhaps your agent (or your company's insurance administrator) never correctly explained your policy's terms and limitations. If, however, after carefully reading (and rereading) your policy, you are still convinced that the company, and not you, is in error, your next step depends on whether your insurance is employer-provided.

If you have an employer-sponsored plan, you should first talk to the company's benefits administrator or the company officer who acts as a liaison between your company and the insurer. The Employee Retirement Income Security Act (ERISA) requires that your employer explain to you how to file an appeal. If the insurer denies your appeal and a significant amount of money is at stake, you can sue under ERISA for the amount of benefits under contention plus legal fees. This can be an expensive and painstaking process to which you hopefully won't have to resort.

If you have an individual policy, you should call your insurer and ask to speak with a claims representative. In some cases, you may be able to resolve the problem with the representative's assistance. If the company gives you no redress, you still have legal recourse under the "bad faith" provisions of the law.

HEALTH INSURANCE CHECKLIST

- Review your health insurance policy to make sure you fully understand the extent of its coverage and its limitations.

- Make sure all family members have adequate medical insurance, including children away at school, parents, and adult children.

- If you become unemployed, disabled, or divorced, take advantage of the provisions under COBRA to continue health-care coverage.

- If your employer does not offer health insurance coverage or if you are self-employed, investigate the purchase of insurance on your own, preferably through a group, but if necessary on an individual basis.

- If you have satisfactory health insurance coverage, there is no need for supplemental insurance like cancer or hospital indemnity insurance. An exception: Excess major medical insurance is helpful if your health insurance policy has a low benefits ceiling.

40

Medicare and Other Health Insurance for Seniors

Our health-care system for senior citizens is a mess. The fact that our elderly have to spend their golden years worrying about the specter of being wiped out financially to pay medical and nursing home bills is a disgrace. This chapter can do nothing to address the fundamental health-care financing problems of older Americans. What we can do, however, is to provide you with vital information on Medicare and other health insurance for seniors, so that at least you can make the most of the programs available to you. It's bad enough that our senior citizens have to pay so much out of their own pockets for basic health-care needs, but it's even worse when seniors have to pay their medical costs because they don't understand the fine points of the insurance rules and regulations.

For people age sixty-five and over, Medicare provides some measure of relief from high health-care costs. But Medicare all too often comes up short: The rate of increase in Medicare payments hasn't kept pace with the rise in health-care costs. As a result, the elderly must pay more and more of their health-care costs out of their own pockets. To achieve better health-care coverage, older people need to combine Medicare with private Medigap medical insurance plans. Also, many seniors are considering the purchase of long-term care policies. These provide some protection—not provided by Medicare and Medigap—against nursing home and home health-care costs.

Understanding Medicare

Whatever its deficiencies, the fact remains that Medicare is the core of most retired persons' medical coverage. The Medicare program provides health-care benefits to every American over age sixty-five who is eligible for Social Security, plus certain disabled persons.

Medicare consists of two parts. Part A pays for the costs of a hospital stay—it is provided at no cost to everyone who is automatically eligible for Social Security. Part B is an optional medical insurance plan designed to pay doctors' bills. Medicare Part B participants pay a monthly premium, which is automatically deducted from their monthly Social Security checks.

Enrolling in Medicare

You can sign up for Medicare Part A (hospitalization) coverage any time around or after your sixty-fifth birthday. Applications for Part B, however, must be submitted within special enrollment periods. Fortunately, the Part B enrollment rules don't present a problem for most people. If you retire early on Social Security or sign up for Social Security and Medicare right before you retire, your Part B coverage should be available when you need it. If you delay enrolling in Medicare Part B, you will likely pay a surcharge on your premiums. Furthermore, you may have to wait as long as a year or more for your Part B coverage to begin. The following Medicare enrollment policies should be familiar to every person nearing age sixty-five who wants to ensure full Part A and Part B coverage.

Enroll between the beginning of the ninth month of your sixty-fifth year and the end of the fourth month of your sixty-sixth year

The federal government gives you a seven-month window of opportunity to enroll in Medicare (generally at age sixty-five) called the "initial enrollment period." If you sign up during the first three months of this period, your Part B coverage will begin in the month you first become eligible for benefits. If you sign up during the last three months of this period, your coverage will begin up to three months later.

If you miss the initial enrollment period, you must enroll during the next "general enrollment period"

If you don't sign up for Part B during your initial enrollment period, you must wait until the next general enrollment period to apply. The general enrollment period runs from January 1 to March 31 of each year. If you sign up for Part B during this period, your coverage will begin the following July.

Late Part B enrollees will be penalized

The basic Part B premium is indexed to the overall cost of health-care as calculated by the federal government. Individuals who don't enroll within a year after first becoming eligible for Medicare benefits pay a 10 percent penalty for each year they delay signing up for Part B. Thus, a person who waits until age seventy to enroll may pay 50 percent (10 percent times five years) more for Part B coverage than someone who signs up at age sixty-five. Worst of all, the premium surcharge continues for life.

Smart Money Move

Don't delay signing up for Medicare Part B coverage. Sign up before your sixty-fifth birthday.

If you retire after age sixty-five, you may be exempt from the late enrollment penalty

If you continue to work after you've reached retirement age and are covered by an employee health plan, you may escape this penalty. While you continue to work, you can elect to keep the company health insurance and postpone enrolling in Medicare Part B. Essentially, you will postpone your initial enrollment period to the time when you finally do retire (or if your company plan coverage is based on your spouse's employment, at the time he or she retires). If you don't sign up within thirty days after you retire, you will have to sign up during the next general enrollment period. You would then be subject to the late-enrollment penalty.

Even if you plan to continue working past age sixty-five and will be covered by your company health plan until you retire, you might still want to enroll in Medicare Part A around your sixty-fifth birthday. After all, Part A coverage is free. And Medicare Part A may pay for some hospitalization costs that aren't covered under your company plan. You can then sign up for Part B—without a late-enrollment penalty—when you retire.

On the other hand, should you plan to retire at age sixty-five, be sure to contact your Social Security office a month or more before your sixty-fifth birthday to find out exactly how the Medicare enrollment rules affect you. If you want your Medicare coverage (or Social Security retirement benefits) to begin as soon as you turn sixty-five, file your application three months early to ensure that you don't have to wait for your benefits to begin.

What Medicare Covers

Like any private insurance plan, Medicare covers some procedures, medicines, and doctors' bills and doesn't cover others. It is important to know the ins and outs of the system to avoid unpleasant surprises.

What Medicare Part A covers

Under Part A, you pay a one-time deductible for the first 90 days of in-patient hospital care; Medicare pays the remainder of your covered costs. For days 61 through 90, Medicare pays all covered services except for a daily coinsurance charge. For hospitalizations longer than 90 days, you can draw upon a lifetime reserve of 60 days of coverage. When reserve days are used, you pay a coinsurance charge. These reserve days are not renewable.

Benefit periods begin the first day you receive Medicare-covered service in a hospital, and they end when you have been out of a hospital or skilled nursing facility for 60 consecutive days. If you enter a hospital again after 60 days, a new benefit period begins. These are the common medical expenses covered under Medicare Part A:

- **MEDICALLY NECESSARY INPATIENT CARE IN A HOSPITAL ROOM.** Unless a private room is necessary, however, be prepared to share a room if you plan to have your hospital stay covered by Medicare.

- **HOSPICE CARE**

- **ALL SERVICES CUSTOMARILY FURNISHED BY HOSPITALS AND SKILLED NURSING FACILITIES.** Private nursing, private rooms (unless medically necessary), or convenience items such as a telephone or television are not covered by Medicare.

- **ALL BUT THE FIRST THREE PINTS OF BLOOD RECEIVED DURING A CALENDAR YEAR.** You cannot, however, be charged for blood if it is replaced by a blood plan or through a donation on your behalf, or if you have met the Part B deductible for the year.

- **SKILLED NURSING FACILITY (SNF) CARE.** Medicare Part A pays for 100 days of care in a skilled nursing facility during the calendar year. For the first 20 days, Medicare pays 100 percent of the approved cost. For the next 80 days, the patient must pay a coinsurance charge.

   To qualify for Medicare coverage in an SNF, an individual must have been in a hospital for at least three consecutive days, not counting the day of discharge. Generally, admission to an SNF must be within 30 days of the discharge. A physician must certify that nursing home care is necessary and will treat the same condition that originally brought the patient into the hospital. Finally, the SNF must be Medicare-certified.

- **HOME HEALTH CARE.** Part A pays the cost of medically necessary home health care for homebound beneficiaries. Covered services include:
  - **OCCASIONAL** visits by a skilled nurse
  - **PHYSICAL**, occupational, and speech therapy and medical social services provided by Medicare-certified professionals
  - **80 PERCENT** of the cost of physician-approved durable medical equipment.

   Not covered are such services as full-time nursing care, drugs, home-delivered meals, homemaker services, and assistance in meeting personal or housekeeping needs.

What Medicare Part B covers

Medicare Part B pays 80 percent of the "reasonable cost" of all covered physicians' services, while the enrollee pays the remaining 20 percent as coinsurance. In addition, Part B participants pay an annual deductible fee. Covered expenses under Medicare Part B include the following:

- **PHYSICIANS'** and surgeons' services, regardless of where they are provided.

- **HOME HEALTH-CARE VISITS** for persons who are not covered under Medicare Part A. People who are ineligible for Medicare can have medically necessary covered home health visits paid for under Part B. There are no deductibles, but the enrollee must pay 20 percent of the cost of durable medical equipment supplied under the home health benefit.

- **PHYSICAL THERAPY** and speech pathology services obtained either as an outpatient or at home.

- **OUTPATIENT PRESCRIPTION DRUGS** furnished to hospice patients.

- **DRUGS** administered by physicians and immunosuppressants provided during the first year after an organ transplant.

- **MEDICAL SERVICES** and supplies such as outpatient hospital services, X-rays, laboratory tests, certain ambulance services, and the purchase/rental of durable medical equipment such as wheelchairs.

- **SECOND OPINIONS.** If you ever face the prospect of major surgery, you should always get a second opinion before going ahead with it. The designers of Medicare recognize this fact and will cover the cost of obtaining an informed second opinion. You can get the names of Medicare-certified physicians in your area by calling the Health Care Financing Administration's Medicare Telephone Hotline: (800) 638-6833.

A vexing problem that Part B participants often encounter is the discrepancy between the Medicare-defined "reasonable cost" of medical supplies and services and what you actually pay for these items. Suppose you are charged $1,000 for a standard procedure whose "reasonable cost" Medicare has already set at $750. You will have to pay $400 of the bill yourself. (Medicare will calculate its 80 percent share on the reasonable cost—$750—leaving you to pay 20 percent of $750, or $150, plus *all* of the remaining $250.)

One way to close the gap between the Medicare-approved cost and your out-of-pocket expense is to find a doctor who accepts assignment. In that case, the doctor will agree to accept Medicare's reasonable amount as full payment for the medical procedure involved and agrees not to bill you for anything above that amount. You can obtain "The Medicare Participating Physician/Supplier Directory" through your local Social Security Office. All the physicians listed in this booklet accept assignment. In those cases where you can't find an appropriate physician who accepts assignment, federal and state guidelines limit how much you can be charged.

What Medicare Does Not Cover

Just as with most private health insurance policies, there are a number of items that Medicare does not cover under either Part A or Part B. They include:

- **PRIVATE DUTY NURSING**

- **ROUTINE PHYSICAL EXAMS**

- **SKILLED NURSING HOME CARE BEYOND 100 DAYS PER BENEFIT PERIOD**

- **CUSTODIAL NURSING HOME CARE**

- **INTERMEDIATE NURSING HOME CARE**

- **MOST OUTPATIENT PRESCRIPTION DRUGS**

- **DENTAL CARE AND DENTURES**

- **ROUTINE IMMUNIZATION**

- **COSMETIC SURGERY**

- **ROUTINE FOOT CARE**

- **OPTICAL EXAMINATIONS FOR EYEGLASS FITTINGS**

- **AURAL EXAMINATIONS FOR HEARING AIDS**

- **MEDICAL CARE** received outside the United States, except under very limited circumstances in Mexico and Canada (If you are 65 or over and are traveling abroad, you should obtain a short-term health insurance policy prior to the trip. Several companies offer this coverage, and your travel agent can probably assist you.)

Disputing Your Medicare Bill

If you feel that you have been overcharged, call the local Medicare office to ask for a full explanation of the bill. If you find the explanation unsatisfactory, you can obtain and file a "Request for Review of Medicare Part B Claim." This automatically entitles you to a more detailed examination by the Medicare Review and Adjustment Unit, which will report in six to eight weeks as to whether it upholds the original decision or agrees with your viewpoint.

If the unit turns you down and the amount in dispute is over $100, you can request a hearing before an administrative law judge in your Medicare region. Plaintiffs usually represent themselves at these hearings—generally, there is no need to hire a lawyer unless the sum in question is large. Disputed sums over $1,000 can be appealed to federal court.

Obtain a comprehensive Medigap policy.

Smart Money Move

If you're 65 or over and are going to travel overseas, buy a short-term health insurance policy to cover you during your sojourn.

Filling the Gaps in Medicare with Medigap Insurance

While Medicare provides an important health-care "safety net" for retired Americans, this net has several large holes through which you might someday fall. Purchasing a supplemental Medicare Gap or "Medigap" insurance policy can provide you with valuable additional coverage for health-care expenses. As its name implies, Medigap insurance is designed to limit the out-of-pocket health-care costs associated with Medicare, including deductibles, portions of the 20 percent Plan B coinsurance charge, and other uninsured expenses.

Shopping for a Medigap Policy

Medigap insurance plans—like most insurance products—run the gamut from overpriced and misleading to cost-effective and ironclad. In response to the apparent plethora of Medigap policies on the market, Congress has mandated that Medigap insurance be sold as one of ten standard packages. This welcome simplification took effect in most states in 1992, although a few states have until 1993. The following chart will help you compare the ten types of Medigap insurance plans.

NAIC MODEL MEDICARE SUPPLEMENT COVERAGE PLANS

Medicare supplement insurance can be sold in only ten standard plans. This chart shows the benefits, in addition to the basic benefits, available in each plan. Every company must make available Plan A. Some plans may *not* be available in your state.

Basic Benefits: Included in all plans.
- Hospitalization: Part A coinsurance plus coverage for 365 additional days after Medicare benefits end.
- Medical Expenses: Part B coinsurance (20 percent of Medicare-approved expenses).
- Blood: First three pints of blood each year.

A	B	C	D	E	F	G	H	I	J
Basic Benefits	Basic Benefits	Basic Benefits	Basic Benefits	Basic Benefits	Basic Benefits	Basic Benefits	Basic Benefits	Basic Benefits	Basic Benefits
		Skilled nursing coinsurance	Skilled nursing coinsurance		Skilled nursing coinsurance		Skilled nursing coinsurance	Skilled nursing coinsurance	
	Part A deductible	Part A deductible	Part A deductible	Part A deductible	Part A deductible	Part A deductible	Part A deductible	Part A deductible	Part A deductible
		Part B deductible			Part B deductible				Part B deductible
					Part B excess (100%)	Part B excess (100%)		Part B excess (100%)	Part B excess (100%)
		Foreign travel emergency	Foreign travel emergency	Foreign travel emergency	Foreign travel emergency	Foreign travel emergency	Foreign travel emergency	Foreign travel emergency	Foreign travel emergency
			At-home recovery			At-home recovery		At-home recovery	At-home recovery
							Basic drugs ($1,250 limit)	Basic drugs ($1,250 limit)	Basic drugs ($3,000 limit)
				Preventive care					Preventive care
					Excess doctor charges 100%	Excess doctor charges 80%		Excess doctor charges 100%	Excess doctor charges 100%

Source: National Association of Insurance Commissioners (NAIC)

The best Medigap policy is your employer-sponsored insurance plan, so if you have the option of continuing it after retirement—even if you must pay the premiums yourself—you should probably do so. Unfortunately, most employer-provided postretirement health-care benefits are becoming a thing of the past. So if you are unable to continue with your company-sponsored plan after you retire or your employer's plan is unsatisfactory to begin with, you will have to shop around for a good Medigap policy. Keep the following in mind when evaluating a particular policy.

Check on the quality and reputation of an insurer before buying a policy

Unfortunately, despite their conservative reputation, events of recent years have proven that insurance companies are not always the financially strong organizations that they appear to be. To get a clear idea of a company's financial stability, refer to the current edition of A. M. Best's insurance reports, or have your insurance agent provide you with a Best's report on the company. This reference work—available in most library reference rooms—evaluates the financial strength of insurers. You should avoid buying a policy from any company that does not receive at least an A rating. The company should also have a reasonably high loss ratio (that is, the amount the company pays out in benefits for every dollar of premium). Federal law requires a minimum payout of 60 percent.

Review policy descriptions carefully

Take the time to read those acres of gray print and obfuscation that insurers like to use. Compare the restrictions, benefits, and costs of a few policies to see which one comes out ahead. When reading a policy description you should note the following:

- HOW MUCH per day is paid for room and board in a hospital

- HOW MUCH is paid for medicines and other expenses

- THE SIZE of the deductible

- WHETHER the policy covers other family members

- THE MAXIMUM amount paid for each illness or injury

- WHETHER limits apply to future illness and injury.

Smart Money Move

Be wary of questionable Medigap insurance policy sales practices.

Be forewarned that most Medigap policies don't pay for the extra cost of a private hospital room, routine immunization, medical expenses while traveling abroad, psychiatric care, eyeglasses, hearing aids, and dental work. If, despite your best attempts at consumer savvy, you buy a policy and then realize you've made a mistake, the law provides you with an escape hatch. Buyers of Medigap policies are guaranteed a thirty-day "free look" period during which they may cancel the policy without cost.

Be skeptical of policies that are aggressively promoted

Most, although not all, of the policies advertised via direct mail and radio and TV are shoddy and overpriced products. The established insurers rely on name recognition and legions of loyal, longtime insurance salespeople and brokers to sell their policies.

Buy only one policy

Amazingly, more than seven million elderly individuals own more than one Medigap policy, even though the law proscribes overpayment for medical care. In other words, if one policy is adequate to cover your expenses, all the others are worthless. If you need multiple Medigap policies because none of them is comprehensive enough, you should probably find a new insurer so that you can consolidate your coverage.

Be accurate and truthful when filling out your application

An incorrect or incomplete medical history will give the insurance company grounds for rejecting your application, or worse, for denying payment of your claim. List preexisting conditions such as physical ailments for which you have received medical advice or treatment prior to applying for your Medigap policy. Some companies will not pay a claim if they can prove you knew, or should have known, about an illness at the time you signed up

One final note: Don't let the insurance agent fill out the form on your behalf. The agent may be so eager to sell you the policy that he or she glosses over areas where your medical record might cause problems with the insurer.

Never buy "dread disease" insurance

Any policy that insures you against a specific disease—whether it be cancer, leprosy, or elephantiasis—should be avoided like the plague. These policies may have low premiums, but the chance you'll ever collect is even lower. Being insured to the hilt for cancer won't yield a penny when you have a heart attack.

Check the policy's renewal terms

A policy that is "renewable at the option of the company" is a policy that can be canceled at the whim of an insurance executive. Your policy will be more likely dropped at the order of an eagle-eyed actuary, who will cancel your coverage the moment you become too great a risk or liability to the company—precisely when you need the insurance most. Buy a policy that is guaranteed renewable for life.

Check out the length of the waiting period

Most policies don't become effective for weeks.

Finally, if you have a complaint about a Medigap policy or the way it is being marketed, call Health Care Financing Administration's Medicare Telephone Hotline: (800) 638-6833.

The Role of HMOs for Seniors

For some retirees, the total care offered by health maintenance organizations (HMOs) offers an attractive alternative to combined Medigap and Medicare Part B insurance. Premiums may be competitive with those charged for Medicare Part B, but HMO members give up some choice and flexibility. HMOs are more thoroughly discussed in Chapter 39. The following questions, however, may be useful to older individuals who are thinking about joining an HMO:

- **DOES** the HMO cover the same services and treatments as Medicare?

- **DO** the HMO's doctors, therapists, and nurses make house calls for home-bound patients?

- **DOES** the HMO make arrangements for assistance from visiting nurses?

- **DOES** the HMO enroll individuals at any time? If not, what are the enrollment periods? (HMOs with Medicare contracts must offer an annual thirty-day enrollment period.)

- **DOES** the HMO allow individuals to leave the plan at any time? Changing from an HMO to Medicare can sometimes be a slow and time-consuming process.

You're probably better off saving the money that you would be spending on long-term care insurance.

Long-Term Care Insurance

The statistics are startling: 40 percent of all Americans age sixty-five or older will spend at least some portion of their lives in a nursing home although most stay in a nursing home only temporarily. Half of all couples exhaust their entire life's savings within a year of one spouse's being admitted to a long-term care facility. The average annual cost of a nursing home stay is $25,000—a figure that can reach $50,000 or more in some metropolitan areas.

Furthermore, costs are increasing well ahead of inflation. Annual increases of 10 to 15 percent are not unusual. Moreover, for every person who is in a nursing home, there are several other elderly who are being cared for by family members, often at great financial cost.

Yet Medicare—even when coupled with private Medigap coverage—generally pays only for posthospitalization stays in "skilled nursing facilities." Custodial and intermediate care, the kind of care that most people in nursing homes receive, is not covered by either Medicare of Medigap.

Faced with these alarming statistics, many seniors are considering a relatively new and increasingly popular type of coverage known as long-term care (LTC) insurance, also called nursing home insurance. Unfortunately, this insurance has been vastly oversold, and it often falls far short of meeting the expectations of the people who buy the policies. Recently, however, policy features and benefits have shown some marked improvements. LTC insurance can be a partial solution to the nursing home and home health-care cost dilemma.

Long-term care insurance is usually offered as a separate policy, but it is sometimes available as a life insurance policy rider. Under certain circumstances—like being confined to a nursing home or requiring home health care—these riders permit the policyholder to take the death benefit in the form of a monthly annuity. If you elect to take this coverage as part of a cash value life insurance contract, you may even be able to leave intact the bulk of the policy's death benefit.

The Mechanics of Long-Term Care Policies

Who can be covered

Long-term care insurance is issued to those as young as forty and as old as eighty-four. Level premiums are based on the current age of the insured; discounts are available for married couples. Most policies are guaranteed renewable and include a waiver of premium during the benefit period.

How benefits work

Generally, a long-term care policy covers four basic types of care: skilled, intermediate, custodial, and home. The first three types of care are usually provided in a hospitallike institution, with different floors or wings dedicated to different types of care. At-home care requires the services of a paid nurse or attendant: depending on the individual's condition, the caregiver might be on duty anywhere from around the clock to only a few hours each day.

Long-term care policies provide daily benefits ranging from $50 to $100 or higher for the first three types of care; benefits for home care are often about half that for nursing home care. The maximum benefit period is usually five years. In place of the deductible required by most standard medical policies, most LTC policies impose an "elimination period"—a time period after admission to a long-term care facility during which no benefits are paid. Elimination periods vary from policy to policy, and some companies offer policies with no elimination period at all. While a longer elimination period does lower the premium, remember that the average nursing home stay is only sixty days, so it doesn't make much sense to purchase a policy with an elimination period that is longer than the average nursing home stay.

Policyholders can typically lower their premiums by 15 percent by waiving the inflation-adjustment and hospice coverage. But the inflation-adjustment provision can be crucial given the escalating costs of nursing homes. Policyholders desiring lifetime coverage, as opposed to a five-year cap, must pay a premium that is around 20 percent higher than that for ordinary coverage. When the policy covers home health-care, benefits amount to about half of the institutional payment. For a policyholder to qualify for the home health-care benefit, a physician must periodically certify the fact that the individual suffers from disabilities that make an independent life-style unfeasible. Some long-term care policies now cover adult day care as well.

Choosing an appropriate policy

In evaluating a long-term care insurance policy, take the following important matters into account:

- **DOES** the policy cover illnesses like Alzheimer's and Parkinson's disease?

- **ARE** preexisting conditions covered?

- **IS** prior hospitalization required for nursing home admission at any level of care?

- **DOES** the policy provide inflation protection that automatically increases benefits with each passing year?

- **IS** the coverage renewable for life? It should be as long as you pay your premiums.

- **DOES** the premium remain the same throughout the life of the policy?

- **IS** your premium waived after you have been receiving benefits for at most ninety consecutive days?

Smart Money Moves

If you're going to purchase a long-term care policy, be sure the policy includes an inflation adjustment provision.

Learn all you can about long-term care insurance before purchasing a policy.

Should you purchase a long-term care policy?

Being insured against a nursing home confinement may help you sleep better at night, but you pay a heavy price for this reassurance. Moreover, if and when you eventually receive policy benefits, you may be surprised to learn just how little LTC policies provide. While the insurance industry has made great strides in improving these policies over the years (in response to competition), there are still a lot of problems associated with LTC insurance. A report by the General Accounting Office (the congressional watchdog agency) noted many deficiencies in long-term care insurance. Questionable sales practices were widespread, and the policy language was such that many policyholders had no idea how limited these policies were.

Perhaps a better alternative to long-term care insurance is to invest the money you would pay in LTC premiums. Chances are that you could accumulate a significant amount of money by the time you enter a nursing home—if you ever enter a nursing home. If you're worried about you and your spouse becoming impoverished as a result of a nursing home confinement, consider investing in an annuity, which will at least assure you of a lifetime income source. Finally, it is not inconceivable that the trend toward universally available health care will eventually include some sort of government-provided nursing home coverage that doesn't first require families to impoverish themselves before they receive the benefits.

If you are considering the purchase of a long-term care policy, the most important thing to do is to become an expert on this coverage. Find out what LTC policies can—and cannot—do for you. Examine critically the various features that LTC policies contain. Review many LTC policies before making a purchase. Don't fall for the first sales pitch you read or hear. Let's face it: You are probably going to spend far more on this coverage than you will spend on your automobile over the same period of time. This insurance could be one of your biggest expenses. It requires considerable effort to ensure that you make the most of your hard-earned dollars.

FOR FURTHER INFORMATION

The following publications will help you gain a further understanding of the health insurance issues facing seniors:

Consumer's Guide to Long Term Care Insurance (free)

Consumer's Guide to Medicare Supplement Insurance (free)

Health Insurance Association of America
P.O. Box 41455
Washington, DC 20018
(202) 223-7780

Medigap: Medicare Supplement Insurance (publication #D14042, free)

American Association of Retired Persons (AARP)
Fulfillment Department
601 E Street, N.W.
Washington, DC 20049
(202) 434-2277

Guide to Health Insurance for People with Medicare (publication #518Y, free)

Medicare and Prepayment Plans
(publication 509x, free)
Consumer Information Center
Attention: S. James
Pueblo, CO 81009
(719) 948-3334

The following organizations can also pro-

»

FOR FURTHER INFORMATION < CONT'D >

vide information on Medigap insurance:

Health Care Financing Administration (HFCA)
6325 Security Boulevard
Baltimore, MD 21207-5187
(410) 966-3000

National Insurance Consumer Organization
121 North Payne Street
Alexandria, VA 22314
(703) 549-8050

INSURANCE FOR SENIORS CHECKLIST

■ ☐

Sign up for Medicare Part A and Part B during the initial enrollment period to avoid a surcharge.

■ ☐

Obtain and maintain a single, comprehensive Medigap policy. Or, enroll in an HMO as an alternative to Medicare and Medigap insurance.

■ ☐

If you travel overseas after age sixty-five, purchase a short-term health-care policy to cover your trip.

■ ☐

Don't let your justifiable concern over the possibility of a nursing home confinement push you into buying expensive long-term care insurance. If you do want to consider this coverage, research it thoroughly before making a purchase.

Medicaid

I nstituted during the Depression to provide medical care for the poor, Medicaid is jointly administered by federal and state governments. Essentially by default, Medicaid is now the one government program that underwrites the cost of long-term custodial care for America's elderly.

The current system leaves much to be desired. Indeed, when it comes to long-term nursing home care, you are well advised to be either quite wealthy or utterly destitute. The very well-off can easily afford nursing home expenses, while the poor automatically qualify for Medicaid. For all too many of us in the middle, however, paying for long-term nursing home care is a problem that causes a great deal of apprehension.

Spending Down (Almost) to the Poorhouse

Exhausting Your Resources

Generally, average middle-income people pay for their care in two phases. During the first, they pay nursing home bills with their personal savings, insurance coverage, and other assets until those are largely exhausted. During the second phase, the individuals—having qualified as indigent under the laws of their state—have Medicaid pay both their nursing home bills *and* Medicare Part B premiums.

Before an application for Medicaid benefits will be approved by a state, the applicant must have spent down the bulk of his or her personal assets and have little or no source of income. Given this scenario, many married couples worry that one spouse's catastrophic illness will wipe out the savings of both, leaving the healthy spouse bankrupt. The spousal impoverishment provisions of the Medicaid law somewhat ameliorate this otherwise cheerless situation.

Noncountable and Countable Assets

The spend-down rules are the rules that stipulate the amount by which you or your spouse must reduce your assets in order to qualify for Medicaid. Not all assets are "countable" for the purposes of the indigency requirement. While they vary in their particulars from state to state, noncountable assets generally include:

- PRINCIPAL RESIDENCE

- CAR (PRIMARY VEHICLE)

- PREPAID FUNERAL

- BURIAL ACCOUNT

- PERSONAL JEWELRY AND HOUSEHOLD EFFECTS

- TERM LIFE INSURANCE

Everything that is not classified as noncountable is by definition countable, including:

- CASH (GENERALLY OVER $2,000)

- CASH-EQUIVALENT INVESTMENTS like money-market accounts, savings accounts, and treasury bills

- SECURITIES OF ALL TYPES

- REAL ESTATE BESIDES PRINCIPAL RESIDENCE

- AUTOMOBILES BESIDES PRIMARY VEHICLE

How the Spend-Down Rules Work

On the surface, it appears that every asset on the countable list must be exhausted before an individual can qualify for Medicaid. But as was mentioned earlier, in the case of married couples, the law limits the healthy spouse's liability. At the same time, the federal spousal impoverishment rules also keep the states from being too generous.

Smart Money Move

If you expect to someday qualify for Medicaid, consult with an attorney who specializes in Medicaid to get up-to-date information on the regulations in your state.

When a married person is institutionalized

If you or your spouse is institutionalized, Medicaid will take stock of *all* your property, including both singly and jointly owned assets. Half of this property is shielded under the spousal impoverishment provisions of the law, and half—the share belonging to the Medicaid applicant—must be spent down. At least $12,000 of countable assets is guaranteed to be shielded on behalf of the healthy spouse. For instance, if a couple had $20,000 in countable assets, the spouse could keep $12,000, even though it is more than half of countable assets.

A limit to what you can shield

On the other hand, the healthy spouse may shield no more than

$60,000 from the spend-down requirements. So if a couple has $150,000 in countable assets, the healthy spouse can only keep $60,000, even though it is less than half of the total. (The amounts vary by state and are subject to periodic adjustment for inflation.)

The implementation of these rules varies from state to state, and there are many local variations. Be sure to consult a local attorney who is familiar with your state's Medicaid regulations if you have any doubts about what constitutes marital assets in your state or about how the Medicaid rules are applied there.

How the spend-down rules affect your home

Under federal rules, your principal residence is exempt from state spend-down requirements for at least the lifetime of you and your spouse. As the home is often the largest single piece of marital property, this exemption is very important.

Suppose that at the time of your spouse's entering a nursing home, you have $100,000 in a variety of jointly owned investments and a $50,000 mortgage balance on your home. The law would ordinarily require your spouse to spend down $50,000 of these jointly owned investments. (The other half would be protected under the spousal impoverishment provisions.) But your spouse could use that $50,000 to pay off the mortgage balance, thus greatly increasing your home equity while satisfying the law.

In general, then, you can use countable assets to purchase noncountable ones. Take note, however, that once both spouses have died, Medicaid could put a lien upon the home. (See the section on Medicaid trusts beginning on page 341 for an explanation of how to keep your home in the family after the death of you and your spouse.)

If you think you or your spouse may have to spend down to qualify for Medicaid, don't make the mistake of converting noncountable assets into countable assets. For example, if you have a lot of equity in your home and you either refinance it or take out a home equity line, the cash that is freed up from the equity in your home will be included as a countable asset for Medicaid rules.

How the spend-down rules affect income

Many older people rely on income from sources like pensions and annuities for financial support. The federal government has instituted rules that dictate how much income the states may take for Medicaid reimbursement purposes. When one spouse is institutionalized, states must allow the stay-at-home spouse to keep at least $815 (but no more than $1,500) of the Medicaid recipient's monthly income. Any income remaining must go toward nursing home bills. When income exceeds the amount of nursing home bills, patients pay the entire bill themselves.

Medicaid does allow the patient to use some income for non-medical personal expenses. Typically, a Medicaid recipient may

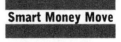

Smart Money Move

Careful planning can avoid costly mistakes when qualifying for Medicaid.

keep a small portion of his or her income for:

- **A PERSONAL NEEDS ALLOWANCE**

- **HOME MAINTENANCE** (single patients with a reasonable chance of returning home within three to six months of entering a nursing home)

- **MEDICAL INSURANCE PREMIUMS.**

Once again, the states have considerable latitude in determining how much to allow and under what circumstances. Some states do not allow some of these personal allowances at all.

Take note: Spouses of Medicaid recipients with independent incomes or salaries may enjoy them free of Medicaid requirements. If, however, this income is derived from investments, the underlying investments are subject to the spend-down requirements.

Asset Shifting

There is a third class of assets in addition to countable and noncountable ones: inaccessible assets. As the name implies, inaccessible assets cannot be tapped by Medicaid. Given the way federal and state Medicaid laws are structured, shifting assets into inaccessibility might appear to be a failsafe way to instantly turn you into a Medicaid-qualifying pauper. But it isn't as simple as it appears.

Transfers to Relatives

Asset shifting usually involves the establishment of a trust, although it can be done through simple gift giving. (Should you give assets to your children or other relatives, you'd better be sure that they can be trusted to preserve them in the event you need them later. Stories abound of well-meaning children who ended up squandering their parents' money while their parents were in a nursing home.) Unfortunately, while some lawyers may try to convince you that asset shifting is easy, rest assured that it is a precipitous action that you may quite justifiably feel nervous about undertaking. Nevertheless, our crazy health-care system certainly motivates many seniors to take these actions in order to preserve their assets.

Smart Money Move

Don't give any money to your children or other relatives that you may eventually need.

The thirty-month rule

This regulation restricts your ability to circumvent Medicaid's asset rules. It states that if you transfer assets in any way that makes them inaccessible to Medicaid, you are disqualified from receiving Medicaid for a thirty-month period. In addition, already-institutionalized patients who transfer countable assets are disqualified from joining the Medicaid program for thirty months.

Loopholes

There are several loopholes in the regulations that exempt from the restriction certain individuals who acted in good faith. For instance, someone in apparently good health at the time of the asset transfer who had no reason to think institutionalization was imminent will usually be exempt from the thirty-month rule. Individuals with a record of making transfers for estate planning or gift purposes would also be treated in a relatively lenient manner.

Implications for your home

The thirty-month rule also has implications for your home. Under the rule, a single individual who transfers his or her home to another party at below-market value will be disqualified for Medicaid for thirty months. If nursing home bills accumulate to the value of the transferred property before thirty months have elapsed, however, the patient becomes eligible for Medicaid.

Consider all the implications before you establish a Medicaid trust to shield your assets from the Medicaid spend-down rules. It may not make sense for you.

Medicaid Trusts

So-called Medicaid trusts, or trusts established to make a person's countable assets inaccessible to Medicaid, can work under some limited circumstances, but they shouldn't be taken lightly. For one thing, if a person's assets are placed in trust within thirty months of institutionalization, he or she will run afoul of the regulations (see above). In addition, only an irrevocable trust can effectively protect countable assets.

Case study

Jane and Joe Gradgrind are concerned about the possibility that future institutionalization will jeopardize their $200,000 in savings and investments. Their concern is that if either of them requires long-term care, their funds could be depleted. So they transfer their assets into an irrevocable trust that provides that all the income from these assets—but only the income—will be paid to the two of them for the rest of their lives, providing that if either enters a nursing home, the income will then all be paid to the healthy spouse for life. After the death of both, the trust will terminate and whatever is left will be paid out to their children. The trust allows the trustee to (a) distribute income but no principal to Mr. and Mrs. Gradgrind as long as they are alive, (b) make gifts of income to their children and grandchildren after their death, and (c) distribute the trust's principal to the children five years after the surviving spouse dies.

The assets in trust are now effectively beyond Medicaid's reach, although the income is not. If, however, the trustee had been given the right as trustee to distribute both the income and the principal on the Gradgrinds' behalf, Medicaid would have access to the principal. Why? In that case, as the trustee *could* make principal available to the beneficiaries,

Medicaid would therefore assume that the trustee *should* use that discretionary right to make funds available for nursing home care.

Keeping the family home in the family

A properly structured Medicaid trust is also a useful way to keep a home in the family after the death of both the husband and the wife. Even though a home is technically a noncountable asset, it may well be subject to a Medicaid lien once the surviving spouse dies, necessitating its sale. But you can place your house—unlike the countable assets discussed above—in a *revocable* trust. By placing the home in such a trust, it can be protected from a Medicaid lien, although some states are moving to restrict the rights of nursing home patients to put their homes in trusts.

If you are single but have relatives whom you want to inherit your home, you could also put it in trust. (Some states have adopted a federal rule forcing the sale of a single person's primary home six months after institutionalization if the patient cannot prove that he or she will be able to go home. An irrevocable "Medicaid" trust may protect against that eventuality.) You could also hold the home jointly with the person who will inherit the property. On your death, the home would pass directly to the beneficiary.

Disadvantages

If you think the Medicaid trust sounds too good to be true, you haven't considered its disadvantages. One problem is that putting assets into the trust triggers a 30 month waiting period for either spouse to qualify for Medicaid benefits. This problem could be addressed by including a provision in the trust that empowers the trustee to make payments of principal to the couple over the 30 month waiting period which could be used to provide financial resources if either spouse had to enter a nursing home within the first 30 months.

Perhaps the biggest drawback is that neither spouse would have access to the principal of their trust. While some provisions may enable access to trust principal in the event of a family emergency, don't count on it. I've found that many elderly people who look objectively at Medicaid trusts are very uncomfortable with the idea of parting with their assets forever.

You need the services of an experienced estate-planning attorney (probably not your family attorney) to set up an ironclad Medicaid trust. The bill could run to $2,000 or more.

As with all the other big financial decisions that we all have to make from time to time during our lives, don't jump at the prospect of setting up a Medicaid trust without doing a thorough evaluation of both the pros and the cons as well as some soul-searching. Remember, once you've done it, there's no turning back.

MEDICAID CHECKLIST

☐

If you may eventually need to spend down in order to qualify for Medicaid, familiarize yourself with the Medicaid rules or regulations in your state.

☐

Avoid mistakes that could jeopardize your financial status if and when you have to spend down—for example, taking equity out of your home shortly before entering a nursing home.

☐

Evaluate carefully and thoroughly the ramifications of asset-shifting strategies designed to shield assets from the spend-down rules.

Disability Insurance

C ontemplating the prospect of a serious physical or mental disability is about as pleasant as standing on a precipice and looking into the depths of an abyss. The idea that either our bodies or our minds might someday be so damaged as to render us unable to work productively—let alone lead a meaningful life—is not especially cheering. Yet disability could someday rob you of the wherewithal to earn a living. In fact, most people don't realize how common disability is. You are *seven* times more likely to become disabled before you retire than you are to die. In fact, one out of four people suffers a disability of six months or longer at some point before they retire.

You may think that Social Security and worker's compensation alone will provide you with an adequate safety net. Neither of these sources of protection, however, is likely to provide you with anywhere near the financial cushion you'll need should you become disabled. Indeed, the Social Security administration denies disability benefits to over half the individuals who apply. And worker's compensation pays only for job-related disabilities. Most accidents and illnesses are not job-related. While you may blanch at the idea of having to buy yet another insurance policy, you may find that the coverage you have is inadequate and that you need to buy additional disability insurance (insurance against loss of income due to partial or total disability) to protect yourself against a financially catastrophic event. In the following pages, you'll find out whether you'll need additional coverage, and if you do, you'll learn some cost-saving ways to purchase it.

Protecting Your Earning Potential

L ack of adequate disability insurance is one of the most common gaps people have in their insurance. Yet you could wipe out years of hard-earned savings if you suffer a disability that is under- or uninsured. And remember, the young and healthy need as much, if not more, disability insurance protection than do the middle-aged. That's because younger people usually have limited investments, and they have to rely almost entirely on their many productive money-making years to achieve financial security. If younger persons' earning power is compromised by a long-term disability, their potential to achieve financial security may be seriously impaired if they do not have disability insurance coverage.

Protect your earning potential by maintaining comprehensive disability insurance coverage sufficient to replace 60 to 70 percent of your job income.

Therefore, it is important to assure that you—and any other working family member—have the right kind and amount of disability insurance protection.

Determining How Much Disability Coverage You Need

I deally, all of your disability coverage taken together should provide you with benefits equal to 60 to 70 percent of your current gross salary. If your disability benefits are received tax-free (more on that in a moment) and your benefits fall around the 60 to 70 percent mark, your disability income will compare favorably with your current after-tax work income. Your policy or policies should guarantee benefits until you either recover or reach age sixty-five—when you will be eligible for Social Security retirement benefits.

Sources of Disability Insurance Coverage

Y ou can obtain disability insurance from a variety of sources. This bears repeating: While Social Security and worker's compensation are automatically provided to disabled workers, they come nowhere near to providing adequate protection against disability. There are three common sources of disability insurance.

1. Company-Provided Insurance

Your employer may—or may not—already provide you with some disability coverage (in addition to worker's compensation). Take a careful look at your company's policy. Make sure you know:

- **HOW** much does it pay?

- **HOW** long do you have to be disabled before benefits begin?

- **WHAT** other policy provisions determine how, where, and when you receive disability payments?

The reason you need to review your policy is that company-provided insurance may have low monthly benefits and a short benefit period. By itself, it may not offer adequate protection against disability. Note also that disability insurance may be included in your company health insurance plan or life insurance plan.

A word to the taxwise

You may be fortunate enough to have your employer pay for your disability insurance coverage. Even so, you may want to reimburse your employer for it. "Why in the world," you might ask, "should I pay for something my employer provides me at no cost?" The reason is that paying the premiums yourself could result in big savings if you become disabled. By paying your own disability insurance premiums, any disability benefits you receive will not be subject to federal income tax. On the other hand, if your company pays the premiums, you will have to pay income taxes on those benefits. A little extra expense now may result in big savings later, should you become disabled.

If, after you have reviewed your company insurance, you find that you really need additional disability coverage in order to be adequately protected, you have a couple of ways to acquire the coverage.

2. Group Insurance

You may be able to get the advantages of group disability coverage similar to what employers provide by acquiring insurance through a professional group or fraternal organization. For example, self-employed people may be able to obtain disability coverage for themselves through the local Chamber of Commerce, small business organizations, or trade associations. Even if you are not self-employed, it may be worth your time investigating group disability coverage offered by various organizations that you may already belong to or may be able to join.

3. Individual Insurance

You may find that you will need to purchase a disability policy on an individual rather than group basis. Individual disability policies are expensive. But the good news is that you can obtain much more comprehensive coverage—coverage that meets your exact needs—than you can with a group policy. Make sure any individually purchased disability insurance is coordinated with any company-sponsored insurance that you may have so that you don't risk paying for more coverage than you need.

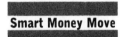

Smart Money Move

Consider reimbursing your employer for your own disability insurance premiums to save on taxes if you become disabled.

The Mechanics of Disability Insurance

Somewhere along the line, you've no doubt at least once or twice encountered an insurance salesperson who tried to sell you more homeowner's or life insurance coverage than you could ever possibly need. You don't have to worry about such a salesperson ever doing the same with a disability policy. Insurance companies will sell only limited amounts of coverage because they don't want to encourage goldbricks who might, if too well insured, have little incentive to go back to work after an injury.

How much coverage can and should you obtain? Insurance companies typically limit the *total* amount of disability insurance coverage to 60 percent to 70 percent of your job income. To a disability insurance underwriter, the best customer is someone who will scramble to get back in the workforce quickly should he or she suffer a disability.

The Basic Structure

As with any insurance, you (or your employer) pay a periodic premium for disability coverage. The two main types of insurance are *any occupation* coverage and *own occupation* coverage. Any occupation coverage will take effect only if your disability prevents you from working at even the simplest, most menial, or low-paying job. Own occupation coverage takes effect if your disability prevents you from working at your own occupation. For obvious reasons, you should be sure that your disability insurance provides *own occupation* coverage. Some insurance policies define disability as any condition leading to a loss of income. These policies are the most comprehensive, but they are also the most expensive.

Once you're insured, if you do have the misfortune to become disabled, your policy won't take effect until the *elimination period* has expired. The elimination period is the time that elapses between the onset of disability and the beginning of the benefit period. During the elimination period, which is analogous to health and automobile insurance deductibles, you must fend for yourself.

Smart Money Move

Be sure your disability insurance provides "own occupation" coverage.

Money Saver

Lower premiums by increasing the waiting period on your disability insurance.

As with health insurance deductibles, the more substantial the elimination period, the lower your premium will be. Most carriers give you the option of taking an elimination period ranging from thirty days to one year. Taking a long elimination period will only work, of course, if you have enough savings in reserve to replace your salary. If you can salt away the equivalent of one year's after-tax salary, there is no reason not to opt for a 365-day elimination period. The premium savings can be substantial if you can afford to support yourself in the intervening time. Your employer may provide short-term disability insurance, which may also allow you to opt for a relatively long elimination period.

Choosing riders intelligently

Like most insurance products, disability insurance can be "souped up" by purchasing riders that broaden your coverage. While riders are not cheap and some certainly will take you for a "ride," others are well worth considering. First things first, however. Be sure that any policy you purchase is *guaranteed renewable*. With these policies, the insurer must renew the policy at your request (as long as you continue to pay your premiums). No questions are asked, and no physical examinations are required.

The *COLA (cost-of-living adjustment) rider* is—at least on the face of it—a worthwhile adjustment. If you are saddled with a long-term disability, you would ordinarily be forced to watch the buying power of your fixed monthly benefit slowly erode. The COLA rider is designed to index your benefit to inflation, so that your benefit will stay constant in real dollars. Unfortunately, some insurers use simple, rather than compound, interest in calculating the COLA. This means that your benefit still won't keep pace with inflation, despite the sales pitch. Other COLAs have a cap that limits how much your benefit can grow. Despite these duds, a COLA that truly fulfills its promise is an investment worth considering—particularly if you're young and could really be hurt by inflation if you suffered a permanent disability.

Another rider designed to ameliorate the effects of inflation is the *automatic benefit increase rider,* which increases your benefit each year while you are healthy. If you buy a policy today and become disabled ten years from now, inflation will have significantly diminished the value of that benefit. It will cover much less of your salary loss, assuming your salary has kept pace with inflation. Once the insurance takes effect, however, the benefit is fixed at the level it reached at the time of your disability. Ideally, should the cost be acceptable, you ought to combine this rider with a COLA rider. You would then be sure that, no matter how many years have elapsed since you bought your policy, inflation won't have wiped out the value of the disability benefit. You would also know that your benefit would continue to grow once disability had set in.

Even with these two riders in place, you should also consider purchasing a *guarantee of physical insurability rider.* Why? Your salary may rise so much in your peak earning years that an old disability policy may have become inadequate. But if your health has deteriorated over these intervening years, you may be unable to renegotiate your policy. With the guarantee of physical insurability rider, the carrier will have to sell you a new policy, regardless of the condition of your health.

Riders that will take you for a ride

Two riders you should definitely avoid are the cash value and return-of-premium riders, both of which allow you to bet on staying healthy. In theory, the idea behind these riders seems sensible. The insurance company has made a great deal of money on your policy because you haven't drawn on any of its benefits—so why not try to get some of your money back? The problem is that these riders are much too expensive to be worth the limited savings that purchasing them will achieve.

Limitations that render policies worthless

Some disability insurance policies cover only disabilities that result

Smart Money Move

If you purchase your own disability insurance, a COLA rider is often worth the extra cost, particularly if you're young.

from rather specific causes, such as accidental injury. These policies are just as useless as dread disease health insurance, so avoid them. Make sure that you purchase a multiperil policy that will protect you from disabilities resulting from any cause.

FOR FURTHER INFORMATION

"Consumer's Guide to Disability Insurance" (free)

Health Insurance Association of America
P.O. Box 41455
Washington DC 20018
(202) 223-7780

DISABILITY INSURANCE CHECKLIST

☐

Obtain and maintain sufficient disability insurance coverage to replace 60 to 70 percent of your work income.

☐

Make sure you understand your disability insurance policy's features and limits, particularly your company disability policy.

☐

If you need to purchase disability insurance on your own, first check to see if you can obtain a group policy.

☐

If you need to purchase a disability policy individually, compare several policies and evaluate carefully the various features they offer.

Homeowner's and Renter's Insurance

ne of the most important purchases a homeowner makes is a purely defensive one—homeowner's insurance. Without it, you could lose more than your shirt—you could end up losing the roof over your head! And while most homeowners are aware of their need to insure, many remain unwittingly underinsured.

Don't play with fire. Always maintain adequate homeowner's/renter's insurance coverage.

For renters, it's a different story. The majority of renters, especially the younger set just starting out, are uninsured—perhaps because they view their situation as a temporary station on the road to home ownership, or perhaps it's out of ignorance. Whatever the reason, the results can be disastrous. This chapter examines the whys and wherefores of homeowner's and renter's insurance—how much is enough, how much is too much, and how to go about getting the coverage you need at the best possible price.

Levels of Coverage

There are three levels of private residence (home) insurance: HO-1, HO-2, and HO-3. The higher the number, the broader the coverage. Renter's coverage is HO-4, and condominium coverage is HO-6. HO-3 policies are the most popular choice for homeowners because of its broad-based coverage, and because the cost is only slightly more expensive than HO-2. The table summarizes the various levels of coverage.

COMPARISON OF RISKS COVERED UNDER VARIOUS HOMEOWNER'S INSURANCE PLANS

RISKS	BASIC HO-1	BROAD HO-2	SPECIAL HO-3	RENTER'S HO-4	UNIT OWNER'S HO-6	OLDER HOME HO-8
• FIRE OR LIGHTNING	A,B	A,B	A,B	B	B	
• WINDSTORM OR HAIL	A,B	A,B	A,B	B	B	A,B
• EXPLOSION	A,B	A,B	A,B	B	B	A,B
• RIOT OR CIVIL COMMOTION	A,B	A,B	A,B	B	B	A,B
• DAMAGE FROM AIRCRAFT	A,B	A,B	A,B	B	B	A,B
• DAMAGE FROM VEHICLES	A,B	A,B	A,B	B	B	A,B
• DAMAGE FROM SMOKE	A,B	A,B	A,B	B	B	A,B
• VANDALISM AND MALICIOUS MISCHIEF	A,B	A,B	A,B	B	B	A,B
• THEFT	A,B	A,B	A,B	B	B	A,B
• DAMAGE BY GLASS OR SAFETY GLAZING MATERIAL THAT IS PART OF A BUILDING	A,B	A,B	A,B	B	B	A,B
• VOLCANIC ERUPTION	A,B	A,B	A,B	B	B	A,B
• FALLING OBJECTS		A,B	A,B	B	B	
• WEIGHT OF ICE, SNOW, OR SLEET		A,B	A,B	B	B	
• ACCIDENTAL DISCHARGE OR OVERFLOW OF WATER OR STEAM FROM WITHIN A PLUMBING, HEATING, AIR-CONDITIONING, OR AUTOMATIC FIRE PROTECTIVE SPRINKLER SYSTEM, OR FROM WITHIN A HOUSEHOLD APPLIANCE		A,B	A,B	B	B	
• SUDDEN AND ACCIDENTAL TEARING APART, CRACKING, BURNING, OR BULGING OF A STEAM OR HOT-WATER HEATING SYSTEM, AN AIR-CONDITIONING OR AUTOMATIC FIRE PROTECTIVE SPRINKLER SYSTEM, OR AN APPLIANCE FOR HOT WATER		A,B	A,B	B	B	
• FREEZING OF A PLUMBING, HEATING, AIR-CONDITIONING, OR AUTOMATIC FIRE PROTECTIVE SPRINKLER SYSTEM, OR HOUSEHOLD APPLIANCE		A,B	A,B	B	B	
• SUDDEN AND ACCIDENTAL DAMAGE FROM ARTIFICIALLY GENERATED ELECTRICAL CURRENT		A,B	A,B	B	B	
• ALL PERILS EXCEPT FLOOD, EARTHQUAKE, WAR, NUCLEAR ACCIDENT, AND OTHERS SPECIFIED IN POLICY			A,B			

Notes:

A = Dwelling

B = Personal property

Source: Insurance Information Institute

Condo and Co-op Owners

Condominum and co-operation owners need to know the legal responsibilities that come with their form of ownership. Condo owners, for example, are liable if the condominium association is sued and is not able to cover the full settlement; in such an instance, each unit owner is assessed to cover the gap. Check the adequacy of the association's master policy to ensure there is a loss-assessment insurance endorsement. If none exists, the association should add it. Otherwise, one can be added to your own insurance policy for a minimal fee.

Mimimal Homeowner's Coverage

Before you begin to shop for the most suitable policy, you need to understand what you're shopping for. Consider the following items as minimums for basic homeowner's coverage:

- THE HOUSE itself

- OTHER STRUCTURES on the property, like a porch, garage, or outbuilding

- PERSONAL PROPERTY and the main contents of the main dwelling, usually up to 50 percent of the coverage of the main dwelling

- LIVING COSTS above the current expenditures incurred while repairing damages caused by an insured risk, usually up to 20 percent of the coverage on the main dwelling

- LOSSES of personal property while away from home, including the possessions of children residing at school, usually with a limit and under certain conditions

- PERSONAL LIABILITY up to a maximum for each occurrence, usually up to $25,000

- MEDICAL PAYMENT for injuries that occur on the premises, up to a maximum per occurrence, usually set at $500 per person

- DAMAGES to trees, shrubs, and plants up to 5 percent of the coverage on the main structure

- DAMAGE to property of others, usually up to $250.

Note to renters

With the exception of areas pertaining to the structure itself, most of the above items are also included in a standard renter's policy.

Buy replacement cost coverage on your home and its contents.

Replacement Cost Coverage

T
he replacement cost is the value of a lost or damaged item based on what it would cost to replace the item, regardless of age or condition. Homeowner's/renter's insurance should cover at least 80 percent of the replacement cost of the home, allowing for annual inflation. The basic insurance coverage usually specifies actual cash value or market value. (Actual cash value is the value of a lost or damaged item that takes into consideration its age and condition immediately prior to the loss or damage.) Using these estimates can lead to underinsurance. Repair costs rise faster than the market value of your home, and thus the rebuilding costs may be much higher than the market value.

Replacement cost coverage on your home is more expensive (usually 10 to 15 percent higher) than the basic coverage, but it's worth it. The reason is simple: It provides much more protection. Insurers, however, are not always willing to underwrite this insurance unless the house is covered to 100 percent of its replacement value as appraised by the company. Furthermore, such coverage on the main structure does not also cover the contents of the house at their replacement values; such coverage is normally available under a separate policy rider.

Replacement Cost Coverage for Household Contents

This is an extremely valuable option for both homeowners and renters. It avoids disputes with the insurer over the "actual cash value" of losses and provides for peace of mind knowing that no economic loss will be sustained in a claim settlement. If you have this added coverage, the insurance company will pay to replace your lost items with new ones, subject to some limits. Adding replacement cost coverage to personal property coverage will raise the premium for homeowners by about 10 percent, while renters and owners of co-ops or condominiums, who are insuring the contents alone, not the structure, may face increases of up to 30 percent.

Standard Policy Exclusions

Smart Money Move

Be sure to insure business-related property that is kept inside your home or apartment.

Household Contents

Household contents are normally insured to 50 percent of the coverage on the main structure, although you can increase this coverage to 70 percent for an additional premium. The real problem with homeowner's and renter's policy exclusions pertains to valuables. Silverware typically is limited to between $1,000 to $2,000, jewelry is limited to $500, and coins to $100. An endorsement allows you to raise the limit in any category by paying a higher premium—for example, $20 for a $1,000 increase in coverage on jewelry or $5 for an equal increase in coverage on silverware.

There are limits on endorsements. Separate "floaters" can increase the limits on valuables, and they are well worth considering if you have expensive valuables (see page 356).

Business-Related Property Inside the House

This is not normally covered. Personal computers and other equipment used to operate a home-based business must be insured separately. Basic home-office coverage is often available as a rider to the regular homeowner's policy for some, but not all, occupations. Such riders extend homeowner's liability to include business-related injuries and reimburse damage to business equipment. The liability limit and deductible on home-office riders are generally identical to those on the homeowner's policy, although they can be expanded. Office equipment coverage is typically limited to $10,000. Basic home-business policies are also available separately.

Host Liquor

There has been a recent spate of lawsuits against hosts whose guests are later involved in alcohol-related accidents. Such liability may not be covered unless you have added "host liquor" coverage or have a comprehensive policy. Be sure to check with your insurance agent or company about this coverage.

Earthquake

A standard homeowner's insurance policy does not cover either earthquakes or floods (although a fire caused by an earthquake is covered). These disasters may generally be covered by an addition to the homeowner's policy. Even though more than half of all earthquake policies have been sold in California, earthquakes can strike virtually anywhere. Costs of these policies vary according to the region's vulnerability to earthquakes and to the type of house to be insured. Whether you want to pay for this added coverage is a tough call. Certainly, if it will make you sleep better at night, it's worth the cost.

Flood

A flood is another frequently overlooked event that could cause catastrophic damage to your property. Flood insurance is available from the federal government for flood-prone areas, and some private companies offer coverage. There are limits to the total amount of coverage that is available for the home and its contents.

Purchase a floater policy on your valuables (unless you can afford to lose them).

Smart Money Move

Buy flood insurance if you are at risk.

Floater Policy

A floater policy provides extra coverage for specified valuable possessions. It does not relate to flood insurance. If you keep these valuables at home or use or wear them, they should probably be covered under a floater policy. This will require a professional appraisal unless they have just been purchased. A floater provides a specific amount of insurance for each object on an itemized basis, guaranteeing full replacement value and eliminating deductibles. The cost varies, but it usually averages about $5 per $1,000 of value for silverware, $15 per $1,000 value for jewelry, and $4 per $1,000 of value for furs. In high-risk urban areas, if theft insurance on valuables is available at all, it may cost considerably more. (Maybe you should move to Butte.)

All-Risk Coverage

Be sure that the floater policy provides "all-risk" coverage that will reimburse you no matter what the cause of the loss, including "mysterious loss" where you don't know how you lost something you lost. Some policies are written on a "named-peril" basis, which means the insurance company will provide reimbursement only when the type of loss is listed on the policy. If the loss is caused by an unnamed peril, your reimbursement would be zero. The all-risk coverage of a floater will also eliminate the need to prove theft, which is often difficult under the guidelines set by insurance companies.

All-risk coverage is provided on an item-by-item basis. As a result, companies usually require that applications for floaters be supported by sales slips or professional appraisals (more on this on page 357). If items in a collection are bought and sold frequently, or if there are many items to be insured but none are of exceptional value, the blanket coverage provided by an endorsement may therefore be more convenient than a floater. Some companies provide special blanket coverage policies for people who are lucky enough to have extensive collections of valuables.

Safe-Deposit Box Coverage

Smart Money Move

If you store valuables in a safe-deposit box, be sure to obtain safe-deposit insurance.

If jewelry or other valuables are stored in a safe-deposit box, insurance is probably a good idea. Many people do not realize that the contents of safe-deposit boxes are not insured by the bank, and insurance under a regular homeowner's policy is limited to $500 or less. If you store only stock and bond certificates in your name in your safe-deposit box, insurance is not necessary since they can be replaced if stolen or lost. But if you store valuables there, you need safe-deposit box insurance, which is simply a rider to your homeowner's or renter's insurance policy. A rider on your homeowner's policy can add safe-deposit box insurance for only about $6 per $1,000 of coverage.

By the way, whatever you keep in your safe-deposit box, be sure to maintain an up-to-date inventory of its contents, including the serial numbers on stock and bond certificates. Not only will this provide you with important information to replace lost items, it will also help you avoid making a wasted trip to the bank in search of an item that isn't there.

Take an inventory of your personal possessions and keep it up to date.

Personal Inventory

Taking a personal inventory is crucial to assuring that you get back what you deserve in the event you suffer a loss. Your insurance agent may be able to provide you with a worksheet to help you take a complete inventory. Record all identifying information, including serial numbers as well as a complete description of your personal possessions. Photographs of furniture, appliances, and the like will be a big help. Make no mistake about it—taking a household inventory is one of the most boring things you'll ever do! Save it for a rainy Saturday, but don't wait too long to do it. (Don't forget the garage.)

By the way, store your inventory and photographs somewhere away from your house—in your safe-deposit box or in your desk at the office. Also, remember to keep your inventory up to date by adding receipts for possessions subsequently acquired to your inventory file.

Companies offer videotaping services that can identify unique items more positively than a photograph. But since this service allows an outsider access to your personal property, you should check the reputation of the videotaping service with the local police and the Better Business Bureau before the videotaping session. *Note:* Only some practitioners in this field are bonded. A better alternative, perhaps, is to videotape your possessions yourself.

Appraisals

In order to qualify for a floater policy on valuables, you must submit recent appraisals or sales receipts of the items to the insurance company. There are two types of appraisers: generalists and specialists. Generalists usually appraise the contents of entire homes in one visit, using instruments and reference books. Specialists are usually extremely well informed in one area, such as jewelry, silverware, art, or the furniture of a single era. Most of us can get by with a specialist, and we can save a lot of money by taking our silver or jewelry to an appraiser rather than having him or her come to us. If you are blessed with a lot of valuables, read on.

Most homes can be appraised in an afternoon, and some appraisers charge a flat fee based on that much time. Others require that they be hired for a minimum period that may be anywhere from one hour to a whole day, which may or may not include travel

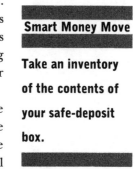

Smart Money Move

Take an inventory of the contents of your safe-deposit box.

and research time. Rates usually range from $100 or $300 an hour for both generalists and specialists.

One way to reduce the expense of an in-home appraisal is to prepare your home beforehand. Belongings should be clean and, along with any sales slips and receipts, easily accessible. Valuables like jewelry and silverware, which are usually stored in drawers or cupboards, should be spread out on a blanket in a convenient location.

Alert the appraiser that the appraisal is for insurance purposes. Tax appraisals are made at fair market value, which may be significantly lower than the replacement value used in insurance settlements. A good appraiser will report the condition, size, age, and value of an object. He or she will also include a disclaimer that lists the purpose of the appraisal and states that the fee was not contingent on the value of the objects.

Appraisers can sometimes evaluate the original worth of items that have already been lost, stolen, or destroyed. For this, you should provide all sales slips and photographs of the object as well as the remains if the item has been broken.

Appraisal fees paid at the time of insurance purchases are not tax deductible. In case of loss, they can be included as a miscellaneous itemized deduction when the casualty loss is computed because they constitute an expense incurred in determining tax liability. But miscellaneous itemized deductions are subject to a floor of two percent of your adjusted gross income.

When to Reappraise

Some objects fluctuate in value upward or downward with changes in the market or inflation. These should be reappraised every few years. Yes, this costs money, but it assures that you will maintain the right amount of insurance coverage.

Reducing Premium Costs

B argains aren't always your best bet. Unlike shopping for a car, shopping for an insurance bargain may not be a good idea. This doesn't mean that you should sign up with the first policy that comes along. There's work to be done to ensure that your insurer is a solid, reliable company that will provide you with the service you want at a price that is not out-of-line with its reputable competitors. Homeowner's insurance should be as comprehensive as necessary, although some cuts in premium costs are possible without seriously affecting your overall level of protection. For example, you can select a higher deductible, or take steps to increase home security, thereby reducing your premium somewhat. Also, you may find that you can get along without some of the "optional extras" that are attached onto your policy—at extra cost.

Smart Money Move

Eliminate nonessential homeowner's/renter's insurance options.

Shop Around for a Good Deal

Different companies' rates can vary according to the location, age, and condition of your house, as well as other factors. You may find that some insurance companies are less interested in your business than others, and that is reflected in much higher premiums. Hopefully, your insurance agent will shop around for the best deal, but you may want to do a little shopping yourself if you suspect you can get a lower premium. A few years ago I reduced a homeowner's policy premium by almost two-thirds just by making a few phone calls. But remember, the financial soundness of the insurer and its responsiveness to claims should not be sacrificed for lower costs.

Alarming Your Home

Increasing the security of your home has two advantages for the homeowner: It results in a safer home, and it reduces your insurance premium. Companies warn, however, that the reduction in premiums may not be as extensive as you might expect. Smoke detectors, for example, are not considered an adequate improvement by some companies, and expensive items such as an alarm system directly linked with the local police station may translate into a modest 5 to 10 percent premium reduction.

When to Review and Revise

No homeowner's or renter's policy should go beyond three years without updating. And these days, no insurance company should go without a financial health checkup for more than a year. Many people would benefit from an annual review of their property insurance coverage. As I've said before, make your agent earn his or her commission. Demand a periodic review of your policy.

Filing Claims

I f worse comes to worst, having a complete record of your personal possessions contained in your household inventory reduces some of the misery associated with having to detail all that you have lost. Expect the claims process to be disconcerting. The following list of steps should help to minimize the problems associated with filing claims and maximize reimbursement in the event of your personal property loss.

1. **CONTACT** your insurance agent, or the insurance company if you bought the insurance without an agent. This person will start the claims process and advance you cash for your immediate expenses in appropriate circumstances. (They're not being kindhearted—the advance is eventually deducted from your settlement.)

2. **IF** a police report has not been filed, find out from the agent or the insurer if a report is necessary to collect on a claim.

3.   **TOUR** your house or apartment and make a record of whatever is lost and of whatever is salvageable of what remains. Provide as much detail as possible on the articles destroyed, and make reasonable estimates of the value if there is no record. (Borrow a neighbor's videocamera if you have to.)

4.   **IF NECESSARY**, secure your house against vandals and children—this is sometimes required by law. A boardup service, which patches holes in walls and doors, can be found through the insurance agent or in the Yellow Pages under "glass." Most glaziers can refer you to a boardup service. Costs for securing the house may go into the thousands of dollars, but they are eventually reimbursed by the insurance company.

5.   **OBTAIN** the household inventory, insurance policy, and house deed from wherever they are stored. (It's at this point that you'll be thankful you didn't keep the inventory at home!) The lawyer and the insurance agent cannot process your loss claim without these papers.

6.   **SIGN NO PAPERS** until they have been examined by your lawyer. You should not make any statements or sign any papers, especially those proffered by a representative of the insurer, unless they have been approved by your lawyer or unless you have read through the agreement—including all the small print—and unless you know thoroughly and exactly the conditions and consequences of the agreement and have agreed to the settlement.

7.   **IN CASES OF EXTENSIVE LOSS**, you might consider contacting your lawyer, who will find and engage a public adjuster and advise you on any settlement. The public adjuster is the key to handling negotiations with the insurance company. Currently, over half the states require public adjusters to have a license; usually the adjuster is awarded 10 to 12 percent on small settlements and 3 to 7 percent on major claims. The adjuster is invaluable in reading and understanding your insurance policy, taking inventory of the remains of a disaster, and ensuring that any replacements meet the quality of the original. *Note:* Don't confuse public adjusters with insurance adjusters. The latter operate on behalf of their employers, the insurance companies.

HOMEOWNER'S AND RENTER'S INSURANCE CHECKLIST

Always maintain adequate homeowner's or renter's insurance coverage.

Review your coverage every few years at least, and change it when necessary.

■□■

Maintain replacement cost coverage on your home.

■□■

Maintain replacement cost coverage on your personal possessions.

■□■

If you have valuables, insure them separately with a floater or with an endorsement on your policy.

■□■

Take a personal inventory of your household possessions (and the contents of your safe-deposit box), and keep the inventories up to date.

■□■

Look for ways to reduce premium costs, including comparison shopping.

Automobile Insurance

A ll too often, the family car creates headaches—and runs up bills—that seem disproportionate to its utility. Yet the automobile is an indispensable part of most of our lives, and if you own a car, you have to insure it. This chapter will help you make the most of your automobile insurance dollars. If you both drive and shop carefully, you *can* keep your automobile insurance premiums down to a manageable level. In fact, you can save a lot of money on your auto insurance if you follow my recommendations.

What a Policy Should Cover

D riving an insufficiently insured vehicle could be financially disastrous. If you think about it, the amount of damage a ton of metal moving at forty or more miles an hour can do is positively frightening. One wrong twist of the steering wheel, and your vehicle could be transformed from an innocuous means of transportation into an agent of death and destruction. Fortunately, the majority of drivers never make that wrong turn, but it's a good idea to remember the fine line that separates a safe car from a dangerous one. And let's face it: Even the most prudent of us sometimes err while we're at the wheel.

Kinds of Automobile Insurance

G iven the dangers inherent in driving, a good automobile insurance policy protects more than the value of your vehicle. It protects your entire financial well-being, which could be jeopardized by a single underinsured accident. But buying automobile insurance is a complicated business, and the marketplace abounds with different policies and features. The following broad types of automobile insurance coverage provide protection from about every kind of calamity that could befall you and your car.

Bodily Injury and Property Liability Insurance

This insurance covers injury to pedestrians and occupants of other cars and damage done by you to the property of others. Automobile insurers routinely categorize bodily injury and property liability insurance with a numerical code. For example, in a policy coded 10/20/5 (or $10,000/$20,000/$5,000), the first number is the highest amount the insurer will pay for bodily injuries suffered by one person; the second, for all persons injured in one accident; and the third, for damage to property.

The amount of bodily-injury and property-liability insurance you need depends in part upon how much you've accumulated in the way of assets. Sadly, the more assets you have, the more attractive you are to plaintiffs' lawyers. It's the old "deep pockets" syndrome. If you are beginning to accumulate investments, you probably want at least $100,000 in coverage for each injured person, with a maximum of $300,000 per accident.

Many companies now offer a single-limit policy that covers total payments for both property damage and personal injury. Beyond the basic policy, most companies also offer an umbrella policy that covers personal liability, including liability associated with operating your automobile, that goes beyond coverage provided by the automobile policy (see Chapter 45).

Medical Payments Insurance

This insurance covers medical payments for the policyholder and his or her family members, as well as other passengers, as a result of any accident involving the insured's car, no matter who caused the accident. This is a relatively inexpensive, optional insurance, but it is probably not necessary if you have adequate health insurance.

Uninsured Motorist Coverage

Unfortunately, the drivers who most need ironclad insurance—the scofflaws whose speeding and reckless driving causes so many accidents—are the ones least likely to have it. For these drivers, the fact that state law imposes stiff penalties on uninsured drivers is of little consequence. Because of this little irony, you'd be well advised to include uninsured motorist coverage to protect yourself against the possibility of becoming entangled with an uninsured driver. This insurance covers the policyholder and any passengers riding in the car at the time of the accident. It also covers members of your family if any of you are hit by an uninsured motorist while walking or riding a bicycle. Reasonably priced coverage is commonly available.

Collision Insurance

Money Saver

Drop collision and comprehensive coverage if you have an old car.

Collision insurance covers damage to your vehicle no matter what or who caused the accident. Premium costs vary with the amount of the deductible, the type of car, and the type of coverage. If your car is more than a few years old, however, collision coverage makes little sense. Why? When a vehicle is damaged, the insurer will pay you either the cost of repair, or the actual cash value (ACV) of the vehicle, whichever is less. Older cars have low ACVs; the repair bill for anything more than minor damage to an aged vehicle will usually exceed the ACV. When this happens, the vehicle will be deemed "totaled." Chances are that the ACV of a totaled older vehicle won't be enough to cover its true replacement cost, especially if your departed car was well maintained. So unless you have a fairly new car, you should drop collision insurance altogether.

Comprehensive Coverage

This insurance takes effect where all of the previously mentioned policies leave off. Comprehensive coverage protects your vehicle against theft, damage from falling objects, vandalism, earthquakes, floods, collisions with animals, and a host of other risks. Unfortunately, should a meteorite flatten your 1981 Chevette, your comprehensive coverage will only entitle you to the vehicle's ACV, which would be about $3.99. Unless you are a genuine Chicken Little or you own the sort of luxury car that suffers relatively little from depreciation, comprehensive coverage may be superfluous. If you simply adore old clunkers, don't even waste your time thinking about buying comprehensive coverage.

Sizing You Up:
How Insurers Decide What to Charge You

T he more likely a driver is to send a claim to his or her insurer, the more likely the insurer is to charge a higher-than-average premium. Just as life insurance companies use complex formulas and equations to determine when you are likely to die, auto insurers must determine how likely it is that a particular driver will get into an accident or have his or her car stolen. Not surprisingly, city dwellers pay high premiums, for the chance of theft is far greater in New York or Boston than it is in Cedarburg, Wisconsin. In addition, insurers look very closely at the applicant's age and driving record—it's no secret that younger drivers are more accident-prone.

Another reason that geography so profoundly affects insurance rates is the fact that insurance regulations vary greatly from state to state. The absence or existence of a state "no-fault" law can affect your premium, as can a whole host of other legislative variables. While many states have adopted no-fault insurance plans, they vary in their features. In essence, no-fault insurance means that your own insurance company pays if you are in an accident whether you are at fault or not.

Finally, drivers who are convicted of motor vehicle offenses ranging from speeding to drunk driving also face higher-than-average premiums. While a speedster's surcharge may be an annoyance, the premium that a convicted drunk driver must pay can be absolutely prohibitive.

TEN WAYS TO REDUCE PREMIUMS

These pointers show you how to keep your premiums from ballooning out of control.

1. **DRIVE SAFELY.** Unsafe drivers are now universally penalized with increased premiums. If you steer clear of trouble, you may qualify for a reduced premium. You may also accumulate points toward "accident forgiveness," which will come in handy should you be unlucky enough to spoil your fine record with a fender-bender.

2. **BUY A CONSERVATIVE CAR.** If you purchase a hot pink Porsche with a speedometer that goes up to 300 mph, your insurer will assume you plan to test the "performance" of your performance vehicle. Since an accident that occurs at 250 mph is a lot more spectacular than one that happens at 30, your rates will be adjusted (upward) accordingly. A boring sedan, on the other hand, does not give an actuary nightmares, and he or she will be happy to reward you for being dull.

3. **MAKE YOUR CHILDREN TAKE DRIVER-TRAINING COURSES.** No matter what you do, having a young driver covered under your policy raises your premium sharply. If your child takes a driver-training course, however, the insurance company won't jack it quite as high as they might had little Jane learned how to drive from Dad.

4. **PUT ALL FAMILY VEHICLES ON ONE POLICY.** You can reduce your per-vehicle premium by about 15 percent when you insure several vehicles on the same policy.

5. **RAISE YOUR DEDUCTIBLE.** Just as with medical insurance, if you are willing to pay a higher deductible, you can usually qualify for a lower premium.

6. **TAKE A DEFENSIVE DRIVING COURSE.** Some states require automobile insurers to reward even seasoned drivers for taking defensive driving courses. If you live in one of these states, take the course: It will help you defend your pocketbook from high auto insurance premiums.

7. **BUY AN ANTITHEFT DEVICE.** In many states, insurers now penalize car owners who don't safeguard their cars with antitheft devices. Even though these gadgets can be expensive, the one-time cost is nothing compared to the interminable burden of paying an inflated premium each year.

8. **JOIN A CARPOOL.** An increasing number of insurance companies now recognize the all-around benefit of reducing the number of cars on the road. If you are willing to join a carpool, you will save money on transportation costs as well as insurance premium costs.

»

9.   DO YOUR OWN COMPARISON SHOPPING. Many people who put in a little effort comparison shopping (or whose agents are willing to do the same) can save quite a bit of money. Automobile insurance rates are competitive in most states, so you should check the rates offered by several companies.

10.   DON'T DUPLICATE THE MEDICAL COVERAGE PROVIDED BY YOUR HEALTH INSURANCE POLICY WHEN PURCHASING AUTO INSURANCE. If you have an adequate health insurance policy, you may not need to take the medical-payments or insured-motorist coverages in those states that do not require such coverage.

Car Rental Insurance

Generally, you don't need to purchase collision damage waiver insurance—often costing more than ten dollars a day—when you rent a car. Before you go out to rent a car, check your own automobile insurance policy. It probably covers you even when you are driving a rented car. You may even want to copy the section of your policy description that covers rental cars so that you can refer to it when you're in the rental agency. Having your policy in writing in front of you will bolster your resolve to resist the collision damage waiver "hard sell" that the rental agent may give you.

An exception to waiving collision-damage waiver: If you are renting a car outside the United States, you may be subject to so many hassles should you be involved in an accident that it is probably worthwhile accepting this coverage to ensure your peace of mind during foreign sojourns. Other kinds of insurance offered with your rental car contract—including personal accident insurance, personal effects insurance, and liability insurance supplement—are equally unnecessary. You probably already have this coverage in your other insurance policies.

The Claims Process

The auto insurance claims process is sometimes difficult and often frustrating. The key to success with it is patience, and if you are willing to wait the few weeks it takes to settle a claim, you will probably end up with more money. If your car is stolen—here in Massachusetts this seems to happen to each of us three or four times a year—the typical insurance company will wait for a few weeks for it to show up, albeit minus certain vital parts. Whatever your reason for filing a claim, the following list of steps will help you take appropriate actions.

1.   TELEPHONE the insurance agent or local company representative as soon as possible. Ask how to proceed and what forms and documents will be needed to support the claim.

2. **IF NECESSARY**, provide a "proof of loss" form as well as documents related to the claim (for example, medical and auto repair bills, a copy of the police report).

3. **IMMEDIATELY TURN OVER** to the insurance company copies of any legal papers received in connection with the loss.

4. **KEEP CAREFUL RECORDS** of expenses incurred as a result of an automobile accident or theft that may be reimbursed under your policy.

5. **CONTACT** the insurance agent or representative regularly to insure that the claim is being settled fairly and promptly.

To File or Not to File

What should you do if you have a small claim? Many people are reticent to file small claims because they are afraid that their insurance premiums will be raised as a result. Actually, many minor automobile insurance claims will not result in an increase in premium. You may also get into some trouble by not filing a claim. If the company discovers such "concealment," it is often grounds for policy termination. Also, by not giving notice of an accident, you may forfeit certain policy rights, such as legal defense, in the event you are sued later on.

AUTOMOBILE INSURANCE CHECKLIST

☐ Buy sufficient automobile insurance coverage in essential areas, but reduce or eliminate unnecessary coverage.

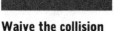

Money Saver

Waive the collision damage waiver when you rent a car if your auto insurance already covers it.

☐ Look for ways to reduce your automobile insurance premiums, particularly by comparison shopping.

☐ Don't buy unneeded rental car insurance.

Personal and Professional Liability Insurance

urs is a litigious age, and despite the pieties we hear about limiting lawsuits, Americans sue each other for almost every reason under the sun. Unfortunately, because U.S. citizens continue to sue one another in record numbers, extended personal liability insurance (often called umbrella liability insurance) is essential for most individuals and families. You probably assume your homeowner's or renter's policy and/or automobile policy give you an adequate level of protection against lawsuits. In fact, with awards increasingly topping the $1 million mark, even the $300,000 liability limit that a deluxe homeowner's policy offers could be sadly inadequate when facing a major personal injury lawsuit.

If you are a self-employed professional or small business owner, your personal liability insurance won't protect you from liability arising out of your professional or business activities. Indeed, your homeowner's policy probably doesn't even protect the equipment in your home office, if you maintain one. (See page 355 for information on insuring business equipment kept in your home.)

For most people, therefore, the best protection against the threat of lawsuit is to purchase an umbrella liability insurance policy. You could get sued because of your business activities, so you may also need professional liability insurance in addition to your umbrella policy. Remember, neither policy is a substitute for the other. This chapter explains both the danger that lawsuits could pose for your financial well-being and how umbrella liability and professional liability insurance work to protect you from that danger.

Understanding Tort Law

In order to understand the risks that a lawsuit could pose, it is important to have at least a basic knowledge of how the U.S. legal system treats civil suits. Personal and professional suits are almost always brought under the jurisdiction of what is called tort law. Quite simply, a tort is any wrongful act (other than breach of contract) that injures an individual or damages his or her property. If you commit a tort, even if your action was involuntary, you may be liable for damages. For better or worse, personal injury torts now include such items as "psychological trauma," and while many legitimately injured individuals do use the courts to win fair recompense, the current system of tort law does stack the deck against the accused.

Negligence

The tort for which you stand the greatest chance of being sued is negligence. To determine whether an accused is guilty of negligence, the court must determine whether the individual had a duty to act in a particular manner, and if so, whether he or she deviated from the standard of duty (that is, behaved negligently). Even if it is found that the person bringing the suit behaved negligently, you—the accused—may still be liable for damages on the basis of comparative negligence. In other words, the court might find that your negligence was greater than that of the plaintiff, and make an award accordingly. If this sounds scary, that's because it is. There are plenty of lawyers floating around who are more than happy to represent plaintiffs in their lawsuits against you and other average citizens. If you look at your Yellow Pages, the advertisements on local TV, and the ads in your newspaper, you'll realize that there are hordes of personal injury lawyers out there.

Joint and Several Liability

If you are in an accident for which several persons are deemed liable, you might be held responsible for the plaintiff's injuries under the rule of "joint and several liability"—even if you were only slightly at fault. Joint and several liability would come into play should your fellow defendants lack the means to pay the settlement. For instance, they might all declare bankruptcy. If you were the only person with the means to pay (perhaps you have a large retirement nest egg or college fund), even though your role in causing the plaintiff's injury might be a minor one, you could be asked to pay the entire award yourself. Another factor tipping the scales of justice in favor of the plaintiff is the "collateral source rule," which excludes from the courtroom discussion of other awards that the plaintiff may have received for his or her injury. Under this rule, a plaintiff could win a large personal-injury award even though disability insurance already covered all that person's medical expenses and income loss resulting from the accident. In some jurisdictions, the plaintiff could thus make a double recovery. Unfortunately, there are some people who make handsome livings out of suing others for all measure of supposed "negligences."

It Gets Worse

Two other points need to be raised to emphasize the importance of protecting yourself from a lawsuit. First, if you lack sufficient resources to pay the damages that are assessed, the courts may award the "injured" a portion of your future earnings to satisfy the judgment. Also, be mindful of the high cost of defending yourself from a lawsuit. Even if you "win," you could end up financially devastated just from paying legal fees. So the scales of justice are really stacked against the average person. While the plaintiff's lawyer works on a contingency fee basis, the attorneys defending you will demand to be paid up front for every hour (or fraction of an hour) that they work on your case.

Out, Out, Damned Plaintiff's Attorney!

N ow that you understand how calamitous being on the losing end of a lawsuit can be, you should consider how best to protect yourself and your family. There is no need to fear getting out of bed in the morning because a lawsuit may lurk behind every tree; indeed, unless you are accustomed to behaving recklessly, you probably don't even have to worry about modifying your life-style. Instead, simply invest in a good umbrella liability policy and, if necessary, a professional liability insurance policy.

Purchase an umbrella liability insurance policy to prevent the financial devastation of an uninsured lawsuit.

Personal Liability (Umbrella) Insurance

U mbrella insurance is designed to supplement the liability coverage included in your homeowner's or renter's and automobile insurance policies. Stand-alone policies may also be available. Fortunately, while—as we have seen—it is very important to have this coverage, an umbrella policy can be obtained at a reasonable cost. Typically, premiums range from $100 to $200 per year for $1 million to $2 million in protection. Naturally, the premium will vary depending on your personal circumstances—the size of your family, number of homes you own, and so on.

Don't be surprised if the company that issues your umbrella liability insurance (most often the company that handles your homeowner's and automobile policies) requires you to boost the liability limits on your homeowner's (or renter's) and automobile policies. Umbrella insurance is designed to take over when the underlying homeowner's and automobile policy liability limits have been exceeded. So in addition to the umbrella insurance premium, you may also have to pay somewhat increased homeowner's and auto insurance premiums to boost those policies' underlying liability coverage.

A good umbrella policy will protect yourself, family members living in your home, children attending school away from home, and even pets. In addition, the policy should cover legal defense costs, which are crucially important since even the successful defense of a lawsuit can be financially ruinous. Some policies even provide worldwide coverage, although coverage restricted to the United States and Canada is the norm.

Smart Money Move

Understand what your umbrella policy does and doesn't cover. Make sure it covers all family members, including pets.

Evaluate Policies Carefully

When evaluating a policy, keep an eye on the fine print. Policies won't cover intentional injury or damages unless they resulted from self-defense on the part of the policyholder. Nor do they cover damage to the policyholder's property, which is the proper province of homeowner's and automobile insurance. Liabilities willingly assumed are also not covered.

Volunteer Work

You may be concerned about potential liability in the murky area of volunteer work. You may find that volunteer work is excluded from both umbrella insurance policies and professional liability policies. This situation got so bad a few years ago that some lawyers were advising people to stop doing volunteer work because of the potential liability. But reason has prevailed in many states, where laws have been enacted that protect most—but not all—areas of volunteer work from lawsuit. Still, it is better to be safe than sorry. Ask the organization for which you do volunteer work and/or your attorney about any potential liability. In some instances, you—or preferably, the organization for which you are working—may need to obtain liability insurance protection.

If your professional or business activities warrant it, purchase a professional liability insurance policy.

Professional Liability and Malpractice Insurance

Professional liability insurance isn't something only doctors and lawyers need. This coverage—also called errors and omissions insurance—is used by a diverse array of professionals, including veterinarians, medical technicians, nurses, accountants, architects, insurance and real estate agents, and engineers. Find out about your exposure to professional liability by speaking to your employer or trade association. How much will premiums cost? Be prepared for a shock, particularly if you're a physician. But the shock of paying a stiff premium for professional liability insurance is nowhere near the shock of having to cope with a lawsuit arising out of your professional activities.

Determining what kind of insurance you need—and where to obtain it at reasonable cost—can be perplexing. But as in all areas of insurance, a little detective work on your part is time well spent. First, check with your insurance agent or an insurance agent who specializes in insuring small businesses. Also, check with your professional or trade association(s) about liability insurance. You may be able to purchase it through the association, which can refer you to companies that insure members of your profession. Another source of information might be professional colleagues or people who own businesses similar to yours.

If you are a self-employed professional or small business owner, you may well need liability insurance that covers both your office and your professional activities. Why both? Say you are a lawyer, a client comes in for a consultation, and he is somehow physically injured in your office. Your professional liability insurance won't protect you.

If you serve as a trustee or director, you should determine whether you are already covered by directors' and officers' liability insurance. This insurance—usually purchased by corporations and larger nonprofit organizations—protects directors and officers against suits for wrongful acts such as breach of duty, neglect, error, misstatement, or omission. If you are not protected, you should consider purchasing a professional liability insurance policy on your own—or resigning your post. Insurance is also available for individuals who have other fiduciary responsibilities such as guardianships or executorships.

Prepaid Legal Plans (Legal Insurance)

A variation on liability insurance is the prepaid legal plan. Like medical insurance, this coverage pays a portion of your lawyer's bills in return for a monthly premium. Many plans give you several free hours of general lawyerly consultation during each benefit year in addition to covering part of the expenses of defending yourself in court. At best, a well-chosen plan could save you several thousand dollars in lawyers' fees in the event of a lawsuit. (In addition, it provides legal assistance for other personal matters—assistance that you might forgo if you had to pay a lawyer directly for it.)

While the sum that a legal plan would contribute to the cost of defending a "typical" lawsuit would by no means cover all your expenses, the extra cash would give you a financial shot in the arm at a time when you are likely to most need it. On the other hand, the worst policies are so riddled with exclusions and limitations that they aren't at all useful. The upshot: Prepaid legal plans should not be considered a substitute for umbrella or, if necessary, professional liability insurance.

PERSONAL AND PROFESSIONAL LIABILITY INSURANCE CHECKLIST

☐ Protect yourself and your family from financially devastating lawsuits with personal (umbrella) liability insurance.

☐ Examine your umbrella policy to make sure that you understand the policy limits and that all family members are covered.

☐ If you do volunteer work, inquire as to your liability exposure, and if necessary, take action to protect yourself.

Smart Money Move

Don't consider a prepaid legal plan to be a substitute for a personal liability insurance policy.

Self-employed professionals or small business owners should examine the need for professional or business liability insurance.

46

Insurance for the Hard to Insure

I f you shop around for an insurance policy only to be repeatedly told that you are ineligible for coverage or a high risk, don't despair. True, you probably have your work cut out for you, but there are a variety of ways to obtain the coverage you need. Just because you are deemed a "substandard risk" doesn't mean you absolutely, positively can't get insurance.

Of course, your circumstances may require you to seek alternative ways to get the coverage. For example, you may need to find an insurance agent who specializes in substandard risks. (Good insurance agents are worth their weight in gold. They will go to bat for you in discussions with the insurance companies, and they often make the difference between being accepted and rejected.) There are even insurance companies, and very profitable ones at that, that concentrate on insuring the hard to insure.

Will it cost you more to get the coverage? Probably. But you'll probably be surprised by the fact that in most cases it won't cost that much more. And whatever extra it does cost, it is far cheaper than the expense of suffering an uninsured illness, disability, or property loss.

Life Insurance

A round three percent of life insurance policy applications are turned down on the basis of being substandard risks. Eight out of ten of the turndowns are due to physical factors such as heart condition, obesity, and high blood pressure. The other 20 percent involve occupational hazards, excessive traveling, foreign residence, or less common medical problems. One major source of coverage for such people is group insurance policies, which do not require individual assessment of insurability. (For information on sources of group life insurance, see Chapter 38.) In addition, some individual insurance may be available without a medical examination, but the limits are usually quite low.

Even in those cases when you do have to fill out medical questionnaires to obtain a life insurance policy, you'll be happy to know

Definition

Substandard risk: A condition (health, driving record, etc.) that prevents a person from meeting normal requirements of standard insurance policies.

Smart Money Move

A little persistence can go a long way if you are having trouble obtaining insurance coverage.

that insurance companies vary in their definitions of substandard risks. Often, one company's uninsurable applicant is another company's customer, so apply to several companies. Some companies even specialize in substandard risks. Furthermore, if the physical condition or occupational hazard that caused you to be designated a substandard risk no longer exists, you are entitled to new insurance at standard rates.

You should evaluate the advantages and disadvantages of the various categories of substandard life policy as you would any policy. Term life, for example, still costs less than whole life, and usually carries the same automatic renewability.

A relatively recent twist in whole life insurance provided to substandard risks is the graded-death-benefit policy, which does not require evidence of insurability. If death occurs during the first few years, however, the benefits are the total value of the premiums you paid in. The benefits gradually increase over time and ultimately equal the face value of the policy.

Some insurance agents have experience in or specialize in obtaining life (and disability) insurance for substandard risks. If you have difficulty in obtaining this coverage, ask some local insurance agents if they can refer you to a specialist.

Health Insurance

F inding an adequate and affordable health insurance policy is possible—even if you have preexisting conditions or have been turned down by other companies. It may take some shopping around to find the right policy, but then, you would need to shop around for a policy even if you weren't hard to insure. The Blue Cross/Blue Shield in your state may, for example, periodically offer an open enrollment period when every applicant must be accepted—no matter what their medical history—at standard rates. (Even AIDS patients must be admitted.) However, you will likely find that there are preexisting-illness clauses that may not cover you for a specific illness for a period of time not to exceed two years. Also, in some states, there are special insurance programs for people with chronic health problems. Check with your state insurance department.

Smart Money Move

If you are deemed a substandard life insurance risk, apply to several different life insurance companies.

Additionally, some plans will accept anyone regardless of their medical condition. While these policies often contain severe limitations in coverage, they are better than nothing and may be helpful temporarily until you find more suitable coverage.

Don't give up until you've got what you need. If you still find it impossible to locate an insurer—and you are well enough to work— you may be able to sign on to a large company's group policy. Many don't require any medical examination. The coverage will last for as long as you work, and in most cases, you will be allowed to keep the policy at the group rate for eighteen months after you terminate your employment. Other tips for locating a policy that's right for you:

- **HAVE** your spouse include you on his or her company insurance policy plan. Or have your spouse change jobs to a bigger company that provides such plans.

- **IF** you're a member of a professional group or union that offers an insurance plan, you may be able to participate in it. If you're not a member of such a group but you think you might qualify for their insurance plan, consider joining.

- **CALL** independent insurance agents and see what they can do for you. Chances are, the policy they may be able to provide will be an expensive one, but if it's a last resort, it's worth it.

- **CONSIDER** the junk-mail insurance policies, the "no questions asked" policies advertised on TV and on the back of matchbox covers, but only as a last resort—and only after checking the company's credentials with your state's insurance department.

Disability Insurance

Disability insurance is especially difficult to obtain if you have a dangerous job or hobby, a previous medical problem, are self-employed, or are a homemaker with no monetary compensation. People in these groups, if they can get disability insurance at all, face higher premiums—sometimes as much as three times higher than those for substandard-risk individuals but more often just somewhat higher. You can reduce these high costs by accepting a lower monthly benefit or a longer waiting period. If you have a medical problem, you should consider buying a policy that does not cover disabilities caused by the preexisting condition. If you are willing to purchase such a policy, the premium may well be comparable to that of a regular policy, but depending on your malady, it may not be worth the risk. Some insurance agents are experienced in acquiring disability insurance for persons with health problems, and they can provide valuable assistance in acquiring this essential coverage.

Smart Money Move

If your insurance agent can't find acceptable insurance coverage for you, find an agent who is experienced with hard-to-insure clients.

Beware of Nonmedical Policies

A policy offered without a medical examination should be closely examined. The definition of disability in this kind of policy may be much more stringent than it is in other policies. Or it may cover only accident-caused disability (which, as the insurance companies are well aware, is almost always independent of any existing health problems).

Women face special problems in securing disability insurance, because they are overrepresented in certain occupations, including part-time workers (more than 70 percent are female) and homemakers. Insurers are reticent to issue policies to individuals in these occupations. The justification for this practice is that these occupations do not have a stable salary against which to peg the disability benefits. Women and other workers facing this problem should not be discouraged from shopping for disability protection, however, because some companies do sell to special-risk groups. This is another instance where a good insurance agent can be indispensable.

Auto Insurance

I f you have a less-than-sterling driving record, you may find that auto insurance is expensive and difficult to obtain. However, "assigned-risk" pools do offer one means of getting coverage for you and your vehicle. The insurers in your state are required to take on poor risks in proportion to how much business the companies do there.

You can also purchase auto insurance on the "nonstandard market." The companies that offer this sort of coverage are not always the most scrupulous, however, so investigate the reputation and financial health of the prospective insurers before buying coverage from one of them. This coverage is not cheap, but it may be better than the rates that the well-known insurance companies would charge. Paying a stiff premium, while unpleasant, probably beats having to take the bus.

Honesty Is the Only Policy

Definition

Assigned Risk: A risk that insurers do not wish to insure but that, because of state law or regulation, must be insured through assignment to a specific insurance company.

D on't lie or omit important information on your insurance policy application in an attempt to secure coverage. It will only come back to haunt you (or, in the case of life insurance, your survivors). The insurance industry is very scrupulous in examining your policy application *after* you have made a claim against it.

CHECKLIST FOR THE HARD TO INSURE

☐ If you have been denied needed insurance coverage, don't give up. Programs are available to insure substandard risks.

☐ If your problem is life insurance, look for group coverage that does not require individual assessment of insurability, and/or obtain several quotations from insurance companies that will write substandard coverage.

■□■

If health insurance is your problem, get coverage that includes your preexisting condi-tion, even though it may cost more. If this is not possible, obtain a policy that temporarily excludes the preexisting condition so that you and your family have at least some protec-tion.

■□■

If your problem is disability insurance, ask your insurance agent to obtain quotations from several companies. If this coverage is unobtainable or prohibitively expensive, con-sider a policy that does not cover disabilities caused by the preexisting condition.

Part VI

Managing Your Credit

Obtaining and Maintaining Good Credit

 good credit rating takes time and effort to obtain, but it is easy to lose. Unless you were born with a silver spoon in your mouth (and a bag of gold ingots in both hands), you will need to borrow in order to meet your personal financial objectives. But borrowing is a double-edged sword. When used wisely, it can be very useful. On the other hand, when it is abused, it can lead to serious and long-lasting financial problems.

Credit Pro and Con

The Advantages of Credit

- **ACCESS** to credit allows you to make major purchases—a home and a car, for example—that you otherwise may not be able to afford or that would require you to deplete your savings.

- **CREDIT** provides security by allowing you to deal promptly with financial emergencies.

- **CREDIT** is convenient for shopping. Credit cards and charge accounts eliminate the need to carry large sums of cash and provide monthly itemized statements that allow you to monitor your spending.

The Disadvantages of Credit

- **CREDIT**, which has been and will continue to be too easily available, makes it easy to overspend. At best, too much debt will tie up a lot of your future income as you struggle to pay down your loans.

- **OVERBORROWING** can lead to many more problems than the inconvenience of paying off loans. It can lead to a negative credit rating or, worse, repossession, foreclosure, or personal bankruptcy. All these will jeopardize the use of future credit and may even impair your future employment opportunities, because many employers perform a credit check on prospective employees.

Unfortunately, many people overdosed on the easy credit of the 1980s, and many will spend most of the 1990s getting out from under their credit problems.

Establish and maintain your credit by borrowing for worthwhile purposes and paying off the loans on time.

Establishing and maintaining a good credit history is crucial. While nothing can beat money in the bank—or, better, in an investment account—to give you a sense of security, the ability to borrow on a moment's notice in case of an emergency ranks a close second.

Tax Savings on Interest Is No Longer Interesting

Interest paid on loans used to save people quite a bit on their taxes. But consumer indebtedness, which includes just about all kinds of debt except home mortgages and investment loans, hasn't been tax-deductible since 1990. Even debt that still is tax-deductible doesn't save much in taxes anymore since tax rates are much lower than they used to be. In short, any way you look at it, debt is less attractive than it used to be.

Judging by the ever-increasing level of credit card indebtedness, this hasn't deterred many people from borrowing more and more. In fact, a recent study indicated that American consumer debt as a percentage of disposable income is at its highest level since World War II. The conclusion: Millions of Americans are still using debt to support their comfortable life-styles.

Good Debt and Bad Debt

J ust as there's a difference between essential spending and frivolous spending, there are good reasons to borrow and bad reasons to borrow. If you list your current loans and what they were used to purchase, you will be able to see that distinction easily. In fact, at the very moment when you take out a loan (or charge something on your credit card that you know you can't pay off next month), you know whether you are incurring good debt or bad debt. If you've always been able to pay off your loans, you may begin to feel that borrowing is the easiest way to purchase something. That attitude has led more than a few people into financial trouble. Don't get lulled into a false sense of complacency when the credit card companies reward your "good behavior" with a higher credit limit or the home equity lenders line up at the door to give you a home equity loan. It's wonderful to have a $25,000 credit line—as long as you don't use it.

The best way to manage your personal debt is to borrow only for appropriate reasons and to pay off all loans within a reasonable period of time. Good debt finances something worthwhile that will benefit you well into the future. Bad debt usually finances something that you use up almost immediately or from which you never receive any real benefit (borrowing to consolidate loans, for example). Thus, a home mortgage is good debt, and credit card indebtedness is almost always bad debt. Borrowing to invest can be good or bad depending on how the investment fares, but it's seldom a great idea, because chances are your interest payments will exceed the return on your investment.

GOOD DEBT AND BAD DEBT

GOOD REASONS TO BORROW:

- TO BUY A HOME

- TO MAKE SENSIBLE IMPROVEMENTS THAT ADD VALUE TO YOUR HOME

- TO HELP MEET THE COSTS OF EDUCATING YOUR CHILDREN

- TO INVEST IN INCOME-PRODUCING REAL ESTATE, IF THE PROPERTY PRODUCES ENOUGH INCOME TO SUPPORT ITSELF

- TO MEET UNEXPECTED FAMILY FINANCIAL EMERGENCIES

NOT-SO-GOOD REASONS TO BORROW:

- TO BUY A CAR

- TO START A BUSINESS

BAD REASONS TO BORROW:

- EVERYTHING ELSE

Establishing Your Creditworthiness

I f you're trying to establish your creditworthiness by applying for a loan for the first time, you may be frustrated by rejections. Even people with good jobs and respectable backgrounds often are turned down if they haven't borrowed in the past. First-time borrowers will have a much tougher time in the 1990s because lenders have been so badly burned by the easy credit in the 1980s that they are much more stringent in granting credit.

It seems ironic that you have to incur debt in order to prove you can handle debt. But it's worth pursuing; a sound credit rating can be a godsend in an emergency. Those rejections don't go on your credit record, by the way, so keep trying and good luck.

HOW TO APPLY FOR A LOAN

Picture this: Someone walks in off the street and asks to see a bank officer. Upon meeting the officer, the person says, "I'm wondering what's the most money you can lend me

»

so that my payments will be two hundred dollars per month." This is what lenders have to put up with.

It doesn't take a lot of effort to put your best foot forward when you meet with a lender. If you go in well prepared, you will already stand way above the average person looking for a loan.

1. **GATHER YOUR RECORDS.** The lender will probably need to see information pertaining to your financial situation, including your most recent income tax return, W-2 forms, bank, brokerage, and mutual fund statements, and a list of credit card account numbers and balances. You may also want to request a copy of your credit bureau report (see Chapter 49). If there are any errors in the report, you can point them out when you meet with the lender and indicate that you are taking action to get the errors corrected. If there are legitimate problems noted on your credit report, you can also address those when you meet with the lender. Obviously, you will have to demonstrate that you have mended your ways.

2. **PREPARE WRITTEN DOCUMENTS.** Show the lender that you really have your financial act together by preparing and neatly organizing:

   - **A STATEMENT** of your personal assets and liabilities (see Chapter 5)

   - **A PERSONAL BUDGET** that shows how you will be able to repay the loan (see Chapter 6)

   - **A WRITTEN SUMMARY** that shows how much you want to borrow, the reason for the loan, and the period of time over which you expect to pay back the loan.

   IF you have one handy, you might also attach a copy of your résumé or prepare a brief summary of who you are, what your background is, and what you do.

Smart Money Move

Increase your chances of getting a loan by being well prepared for your meeting with the loan officer.

3. **MAKE AN APPOINTMENT.** Don't walk in off the street. Rather, make an appointment and show up with your neatly organized documentation. This won't assure that you'll get the loan, but you can be assured that the lender will be impressed with your preparation and thoroughness. After all, you're not just someone walking in off the street.

Qualifying for Credit

L enders often base their loan decisions on what is referred to as the "three Cs." These are:

- **CHARACTER.** Character denotes your personal qualities. It is revealed through factual records that indicate to the lender how you are likely to perform as a borrower.

- **CAPACITY.** Capacity is your financial ability to repay the loan. It is judged on the basis of the job you hold, the amount of money you earn, the length of time you have been at your present or previous job, and your future job prospects.

- **CAPITAL.** Capital includes all the assets that can serve as collateral for the loan. Your home, car, investments, bank accounts, jewelry, and other tangible property are examples of your capital assets.

Although these three items form the foundation of a credit-granting decision, the decision is far more involved. Here are some important areas that lenders look at to evaluate your creditworthiness:

- **EMPLOYMENT RECORD.** The lender will want to know how long you have worked with the same company and whether you frequently move or change jobs. (If you move frequently because you are advancing in your career, however, this will not be viewed negatively.)

- **PREVIOUS LOANS.** If you have previously paid back a loan on time (a student loan, perhaps), the bank is likely to anticipate that you will do the same again. If you have defaulted before, then you may have a hard time convincing lenders that you've mended your ways.

- **HOME OWNERSHIP.** It's generally a positive sign if you own your home (or have lived in the same apartment for several years). Otherwise, your condition might be judged unstable.

- **CHARGE ACCOUNTS.** A record of paying charge accounts regularly indicates a sense of responsibility to pay.

- **CHECKING AND SAVINGS ACCOUNTS.** Having a substantial amount in a bank account is a great help, especially if the account is at the bank where you're applying for the loan.

Smart Money Move

Don't be a stranger to your lender. Meet with your lender periodically to discuss your current financial status and your financial plans.

Maintaining Your Good Credit

M aintaining your good credit is a no-brainer. Make the required loan payments on time. The more debt you have, of course, the more difficult it is to keep up to date on your payments, particularly if temporary adversity strikes, like a job loss, an illness, or a huge repair bill on your car or home.

Ironically, the better you are at paying off your bills, the more temptation you will have to run up big loan balances, because credit card companies will increase your credit lines. Believe it or not, the banks will fall all over themselves trying to lend more money to you.

The best way to avoid this temptation is to adhere strictly to the following rule: You should borrow money only to acquire items that will benefit you for many years. Thus, it is perfectly all right to finance a home or major home improvement over many years. Similarly, college education costs will benefit you or your child for a long period of time and therefore could be financed over several years. Credit card loans are another matter. Nothing you purchase with a credit card justifies your paying it off over a period exceeding a few months.

Developing a personal relationship with your lending officer is a good way to preserve your credit. Individuals who periodically discuss their personal financial objectives and plans with their bankers put themselves in a good position to prove their worth as good credit risks.

Ask your lender if he or she would like you to send information on your financial status and plans periodically. (You should be preparing them anyway, so it's easy to make a copy to send to the lender.) Demonstrating that you are in control of your financial situation gives you a real advantage, both when you need a loan, and if and when you get into some temporary financial difficulty. Few of us escape financial difficulties at least once in our lives. Being well-known to your lender can be advantageous when financial adversity strikes (see Chapter 50).

CAR LOAN FOLLIES

Smart Money Move

Never finance a car over more than three years.

Car loans are a special case, since they involve borrowing to buy something that declines in value (as opposed to a home or home improvements, which over the long run should rise in value). Therefore, a car should be financed over no more than two to three years, although the average car-loan length now approaches five years. If you borrow over a period much longer than two years, you will start incurring repair bills while you're still making loan payments—hardly an appealing situation. If you can't afford to finance a car over three years or less, you can't really afford that car. Young people often spend more to

»

own and maintain a car than they do on housing. No wonder they can't seem to save up enough to make a down payment on a home!

If you find yourself constantly saddled with car loans, do some serious thinking about how much it is costing you to drive around in your steel (and plastic) master. I prefer old, unappealing cars. They're a lot cheaper in the long run, and I'd rather put my money to more productive use. Sure, people laugh at my old clunker. Am I bothered by that? Not for one second, because I know I'm not wasting my money on car loans that for many people never seem to get paid off. Why don't they get paid off? Because as soon as one car loan is paid off, they go out and finance another car. Worse, some people trade their cars even before their old car loan is paid off. Tell me, how much sense does that make?

CHECKLIST FOR OBTAINING AND MAINTAINING GOOD CREDIT

◼◻◼

Establish good credit by borrowing for worthwhile purposes and paying off all loan obligations on time. Good credit is an indispensable asset in the achievement of financial objectives.

◼◻◼

Gather and organize your documents before you apply for a loan so that you can show the lender that you take your personal finances seriously.

◼◻◼

Strive to reduce and eliminate all loans except those taken out to purchase or improve your home or to pay for education costs. Debt is "out" in the 1990s.

48

Types of Loans and Other Borrowing Arrangements

The rainbow should have as many colors! There are many available loan options just waiting for you. Familiarity with the most common types is therefore not only a good idea, it is in your best financial interest. The reason is straightforward: The more you know about what types of loan options are available to you, the more likely you will be to select the most appropriate and advantageous one.

Loan Basics

There are two basic types of consumer loans: secured and unsecured. (Automatic overdrafts and lines of credit should also be thought of as loans.) Both types share some basic characteristics. For example, both secured and unsecured loans may be repaid either in installments or in a single payment. Installments of twelve, twenty-four, or thirty-six equal monthly payments are the norm. Single-payment loans, also called term loans, are repaid in a lump sum at the end of the loan period, which can range from thirty days to several years.

Secured Loans

These loans are secured by some property or asset. The two common types are car loans and mortgage loans on real estate, both of which are paid in installments. If payments are not made on time, your lender can take back the secured property to satisfy the loan. Other possible collateral includes savings passbooks and various acceptable investment certificates. For example, Treasury bills are accepted by commercial banks as collateral; U.S. savings bonds are not. Stocks and bonds are commonly acceptable as collateral, but not at full value. For example, if you put up stock certificates with a current market value of $10,000, the bank will not lend you the full $10,000 against those certificates. Instead, they might lend seventy percent, or $7,000, against the $10,000 in stocks.

Unsecured Loans

No collateral is required for unsecured loans. Instead, you pledge your "full faith and credit" to repay. If payments are not made on time, the lender can initiate legal action against you, and your credit rating could be adversely affected.

Credit card loans are unsecured loans. Unsecured loans at banks, savings and loans, or credit unions are often referred to as "signature loans," since the money is lent on the basis of your signature on the loan agreement. The ability to borrow money from a bank on an unsecured basis is the best evidence of your creditworthiness.

Where to Get a Bank Loan

Whenever you apply for a loan, you want to accomplish two things. First, you want your loan application to be accepted, and second, you want the most advantageous (to you) loan terms.

Where to Apply

Apply first to the financial institutions where you already do business. Lenders prefer to lend money to people they already know. Start at the top of this list and work down.

- **YOUR CREDIT UNION.** Credit unions often have the most favorable loan rates.

- **A SAVINGS AND LOAN** where you do business. S&Ls may beat the banks when it comes to interest charged on loans.

- **A BANK** where you do business.

- **OTHER SAVINGS AND LOANS AND BANKS.** While they might not know you, they might be anxious to lend money on favorable terms.

- **FINANCE COMPANIES.** Consider a finance company only after all of the above sources haven't worked out. While finance companies can approve loans very quickly, the interest they charge is usually considerably higher.

Smart Money Move

Apply for a loan first at your credit union. Credit unions often have lower interest rates than the next two loan sources that you should consider, savings and loans and banks.

Pick the Right Terms

Make sure you get as favorable an interest rate as you can, although I wouldn't recommend taking your business somewhere else for a slightly cheaper loan if you have a long and satisfactory relationship with a particular credit union, S&L, or bank. Even though it may cost you a little more money, loyalty to your bank can pay off in the long run. Be sure to get the "annual percentage rate" on the loan.

That's the only way you will be able to compare loan rates. Also, if your borrowing position is quite strong, you may be able to negotiate a somewhat lower rate than that which is first offered to you. It certainly doesn't hurt to try. By the way, find out if they'll knock a bit off the interest rate if you agree to have your loan payments made directly out of your checking account. Some lenders will do this.

Finally, make sure that the term of the loan is reasonable. Balance your need to keep your monthly loan payments affordable against the higher interest charges (probably not tax-deductible) you would pay over the life of a longer loan. Generally, you want to keep the length of a loan as short as possible, except on investments that are likely to appreciate in value—namely, homes and home improvements. Be particularly wary of car loans—keep them as short as possible.

Nonbank Loan Sources

There are other sources of loans in addition to credit unions, S&Ls, and banks. They are often more convenient, but each has its risks.

Life Insurance Policy Loans

If you have a cash value insurance policy that has accumulated some cash value (many policies have little or no cash value in the first couple of years), you can borrow up to the full amount of the cash value at interest rates ranging from 5 percent to 13 percent depending on the type and age of the policy you carry. This is a good source of emergency cash. You can generally get the money quickly, with few questions asked. In fact, it is common practice for policies to be bought with the intention of borrowing against their cash value. But there's a limit to what you can borrow. Check your policy for specifics.

Be advised, however, that as long as a policy loan is outstanding, the insurance company may reduce the interest rate earned on the cash value well below its preloan rate. Check out the details with your agent or the insurer itself.

A policy loan may also affect death benefits and future premiums adversely. The death benefit is automatically decreased by the amount of the loan, but it rises as the loan is repaid. The slower growth of the cash value during the life of the loan may reduce the potential death benefits on variable life policies and raise later premiums on policies with level death benefits to compensate for the loss of expected cash accumulation. In spite of the various pitfalls,

Smart Money Move

Borrowing from yourself through a life insurance policy loan, pension plan loan, or margin loan may be an excellent and convenient way to meet your loan needs. But be aware of the potential pitfalls of borrowing in this manner.

the cash value of a life insurance policy is an excellent source of funds that are needed temporarily, unless the loan reduces your insurance protection below the amount needed to protect your dependents.

Keogh, 401(k), Pension Plan, and IRA Loans

You may be able to borrow from your Keogh, 401(k), or company pension plan, although various restrictions apply. You may have to demonstrate financial hardship, and even then there are restrictions as to the amount and loan duration. One advantage of these loans is that the interest you pay on the loan is paid into your own account—in other words, you're paying yourself interest. But, never borrow from one of these pension plans unless you fully expect to be able to repay the loan. If you cannot, not only will you incur tax penalties, but you will jeopardize important retirement-earmarked funds.

Qualified company retirement plan loans are subject to further restrictions. In general, the rules are intended to ensure that your plan assets are used for your retirement purposes and that loans are actually repaid. Loans from company pension funds must be made at market interest rates and are subject to ceilings on the amounts borrowed.

Technically, you cannot borrow from an IRA. However, it is possible to use this account to get cash on a temporary basis. No more than once a year, you can withdraw your IRA money for sixty days without penalty. You must be very careful, however. If the money is not returned within sixty days, you must pay income tax on all or most of the amount withdrawn plus, if you are under age fifty-nine and one-half, a 10 percent penalty.

Brokerage Accounts and Margin Loans

Most brokerage firms allow you to borrow an amount up to 50 percent of the market value of the stocks and 80 percent of the market value of the bonds in your accounts. These are called *margin loans.* Traditionally, margin loans have been used to buy stocks and bonds without paying the full price. Investors pledge the stock they have in the brokerage house as collateral for the loan. Interest rates on these loans fluctuate with market rates. A possible tax advantage: Interest paid on margin accounts to buy or carry other investments is deductible only up to the extent of net investment income for the year (that is, interest, dividends, and capital gains).

Generally, you must maintain a minimum balance in your account to qualify for a margin loan. Individuals with small portfolios should not borrow against them: if the value of the securities in a margin account falls, the investor could be forced either to pledge more securities or to pay back part of the loan. Margin investors have been wiped out in the past by rapidly declining stock prices—a sobering reminder of the need to use margin loans very judiciously, if at all.

Types of Credit Cards

What would a chapter on loans be without discussing the nemesis of living beneath your means—credit cards? In the real world—as opposed to the dreamworld of debt-free living—credit cards are a necessary way of life for most Americans.

THE BENEFITS OF CREDIT CARDS

Credit cards are a great convenience and, for those who properly manage their credit card obligations, an effective way to manage daily expenses without having to carry large amounts of cash. Those who make the most effective use of their credit cards understand what each type of card can and cannot do. Furthermore, they understand the nuances of credit card repayment terms.

The benefits of credit card **loans**: None.

By now, you know that credit cards come in a variety of forms and are issued by banks, oil companies, retail establishments, and travel and entertainment enterprises (like American Express, Carte Blanche, and Diners Club). But, there are important differences among these types of credit cards, and all of them must be further distinguished from another card that looks like a credit card but isn't: the debit card.

Bank Credit Cards

Known to us as Visa or MasterCard, these cards are issued by banks, brokerage firms, and other organizations throughout the United States and are honored by hundreds of thousands of establishments worldwide. Typical terms for these bank cards include the following:

- SMALL ANNUAL FEES (though a few banks still issue free cards)

- CREDIT LIMITS from $500 for first-time cardholders to $5,000 or more

- NO INTEREST on new charges that are paid within twenty to thirty days of receipt of the bill

- INTEREST RATES usually ranging from 14 percent to 22 percent depending on the state in which the card is issued

- SMALL MINIMUM MONTHLY PAYMENTS.

Although most cards offer twenty to thirty days' grace without incur-

Smart Money Move

Avoid the single most common cause of financial problems by paying off your entire credit balance each month.

ring interest charges, some have shorter grace periods, and others have none at all. Some cards also have transaction fees or other fees that are similar to check-writing fees and that are charged each time the card is used. The best way to use a credit card is to pay off the entire balance due each month. If you have credit card loans, devise a plan now to get rid of them. Credit card problems are the single greatest cause of personal bankruptcies. Don't succumb to credit card temptation.

What's in a name?

Not all Visa and MasterCard cards are the same. The difference in interest rates, how your monthly balance is computed, and annual fees can be substantial from one bank to another and from state to state. Comparative information on bank credit card interest rates is published in *Barron's* and may also be available in local newspapers.

Premium cards

Visa and MasterCard issue premium cards as rivals to the American Express Gold Card. Interest rates for premium cards are usually the same as those for regular cards, but annual fees may be more than twice the amount. In addition to higher credit limits, these premium cards often include no-fee traveler's checks, higher cash-advance and check-cashing limits, and free credit life insurance. Unless you are so lacking in self-esteem that you need to impress a department store clerk with your gold card, save your money and stick with a regular card like the rest of us mortals.

Whichever card you choose, it is important to read the applications carefully. Read the fine print: if the interest rate is not apparent, ask about it.

Cash advances

Most credit cards offer cash advances. Don't consider these advances to be free money. In fact, they represent incredibly expensive loans. In addition to interest that begins to accumulate as soon as the advance is made, loan fees are charged, often two percent of the loan amount. So don't use your cash advance "privilege" unless it's an emergency.

Smart Money Move

Obtain six to eight weeks of free credit by understanding your credit card company's billing cycle and procedures.

Beating the credit card companies at their own game

There are various factors that affect the billing of credit cards. Use them to your advantage. For example, if you know the billing cycle, use your cards on days that will give the longest use of the money without interest. Obtain six to eight weeks of free credit by buying just after the billing date and paying in full just before the due date.

If you expect to have to run card loan balances, one card may actually be cheaper than two because of the break point. For example, if the annual percentage rate (APR) is 18 percent on the first

$500 and 12 percent on amounts over that, it is better to run a $1,000 balance on one card than a $500 balance on two. (If your cards are issued by the same bank, ask the bank to combine the billing and charge the lower combined rate.)

Enhancements

Card-issuers are trying to lure customers by augmenting their cards with incentives known as enhancements. These may include cash advances, luxury suites, toll-free message services, check-cashing services, and card and travel insurance. Think twice before signing up for these enhancements. Some of them are of little value to begin with (like credit card insurance). Even if the issuer doesn't charge for these services directly, you will probably end up paying for them through larger annual fees and higher interest rates. No matter what, remember that prompt payment of credit card bills is in your best interest.

Debit cards

Many banks issue MasterCard, Visa, and/or their own debit cards. Debit cards look like regular credit cards, but instead of sending monthly bills, the bank transfers payments directly from your checking, savings, or asset management account as soon as it receives notice of the charge. Because the cards are directly linked to your bank accounts, you must monitor them as closely as you do your checkbook.

Debit cards offer some convenience in paying bills, forcing you to pay immediately and therefore not carry a balance on which you'd pay interest. Unless you need the forced discipline of paying your bills immediately, however, debit cards, on balance, don't have any additional virtues.

Travel and entertainment cards

American Express, Diners Club, and Carte Blanche are the major travel and entertainment cards. On balance, the American Express card offers the most advantages and is accepted at more establishments than all the other travel and entertainment cards combined. These cards are honored at some establishments that do not honor regular bank cards, such as some prestige clothing stores and restaurants. On the other hand, many establishments that honor bank cards do not honor the travel and entertainment cards.

Unique features

Usually, payment of travel and entertainment card bills must be made in full, within twenty to thirty days of receipt of the bill. There are limited exceptions to this policy, however. There is no interest if charges are paid on time, but credit privileges may be canceled if they are not. There is no preset spending limit, but eligibility requirements are much stricter than with other cards. Technically, these cards are charge cards, not credit cards; their main purpose is convenience, not credit. Since you have to pay your bill in its entirety each month, these are excellent cards to have if you have difficulty resisting the temptation to run up loan balances on your bank credit card.

If you are planning a trip, travel and entertainment cards offer some advantages over regular bank cards. An airline ticket and hotel and meal charges might quickly exhaust the credit line on a Visa or MasterCard, whereas travel and entertainment cards have no preset spending limits. Just as with premium bank credit cards, don't waste your money on travel and entertainment gold (or worse, "platinum" cards), unless you will really benefit from the extra features that these premium cards offer.

Be a Smart Loan Shopper

No matter what type of loan you are thinking of, when it comes to taking out a loan or selecting a credit card, be sure to shop around for the best available rates and terms. There are several sources for comparisons of consumer and mortgage loan interest rates. For example, local newspapers in many cities list consumer credit and mortgage interest rates comparing local banks and other credit sources. Believe it or not, lenders want your business, and the only way they can earn it is to offer better interest rates and terms than the competition. Therefore, you will benefit from shopping for the best interest rate and loan or credit card terms.

TEN GREAT WAYS TO CUT CREDIT COSTS

1. **PAY OFF** your entire credit card bill every month. Consumer credit incurs just about the steepest interest rates of any debt. Pay your bills every month and spare yourself the exorbitant finance charges, which are no longer tax-deductible.

2. **OPT FOR** low-or-no-cost credit cards. Several issuers offer credit cards at a low or no annual fee. In spite of what the ads say about "amenities," a credit card is a credit card. There is no justification to pay more than a minimum for the privilege of having one.

3. **IF** you're going to run up credit card loans, use a credit card that charges a low interest rate. When we talk about low interest rates for credit cards, low is relative. Most of the major card-issuers charge nearly 20 percent while other issuers, whose cards are just as good, charge much less. If you're going to run up a credit card loan, use a credit card that charges a lower interest rate. *Barron's* provides a list of lower-interest credit cards each week.

4. **DON'T PAY** extra for a gold card. You may be flattered to be offered a gold (or platinum) card on the basis of your credit standing. But you should ask yourself whether it's really worth it to pay the hefty annual fee. The words, "Thanks all the same, but I can get along quite well without your gold card," come to mind.

5. **SCRUTINIZE** your credit card bills. Mistakes can and do happen—be careful, as somehow they never work in your favor.

6. **SHOP AROUND** for the cheapest loans. Although you may read in the newspapers that no one wants to lend money anymore, the fact is that loan interest is by far a major source of income for banks, and banks compete vigorously with each other for the privilege of lending you money. So if you need a loan, shop around for the lowest rate and the best loan terms.

7. **BORROW** only for worthwhile purposes. Good debt, bad debt—never borrow for unnecessaries. You're only going to dig a deep hole for yourself, and it will take you years to climb out.

8. **PAY OFF** higher-interest-rate loans first. If you have several loans, pay off the ones with the highest interest first.

9. **MAKE** loan payments automatically from your checking account. Many lenders will reduce the interest rate a bit if you agree to have your loan payments automatically taken out of your checking account. Doing so also saves you time and a stamp.

10. **CONVERT** nondeductible personal debt into deductible home equity debt (see, Chapter 13). Home equity loans obviously can jeopardize your house if you get into financial trouble, but they're the borrowing source of choice. Under most circumstances, home equity loan interest is deductible, whereas most other loan interest is now considered nondeductible "personal" interest.

LIST OF DEBTS

CREDITOR	REASON FOR LOAN	MONTHLY PAYMENT	TOT. AMOUNT OWED
....	....	$	$ ....
....	....	....	....
....	....	....	....
....	....	....	....
....	....	....	....
....	....	....	....
	TOTAL MONTHLY PAYMENTS $	$	
	TOTAL AMOUNT OWED $		

$$\text{LOAN PAYMENTS AS A PERCENTAGE OF INCOME} = \frac{\text{TOTAL MONTHLY PAYMENTS}}{\text{NET MONTHLY INCOME}} = \frac{\$ ....}{\$ ....} = ... \%$$

Note: Total loan payments, except mortgage, should not exceed 20 to 25 percent of net income.

FOR FURTHER INFORMATION

The following publications can help you find a good, low-fee credit card:

Low Interest Rate/No Annual Fee List ($4.00)

How to Choose a Credit Card ($1.00)

Bankcard Holders of America
560 Herndon Parkway
Suite 120
Herndon, VA 22070
(703) 481-1110

BORROWING CHECKLIST

☐ Obtain the kinds of loans you need under the right terms by understanding the many available sources of loans. You may even be able to borrow from yourself.

☐ Shop for the best interest rates and loan terms, but give the financial institutions with which you do business the first crack at lending to you.

☐ Consider borrowing from a cash value life insurance policy, a pension plan, or a brokerage account, although there are potential pitfalls to each.

☐ Be judicious in your use of credit cards. Used correctly, they are a wonderful convenience, but if a credit card is abused, it could be a one-way ticket to financial disaster.

Credit Bureaus and Your Rights

Credit bureaus serve as clearinghouses for information about our consumer debts and bill-paying habits. Credit bureaus keep files on a borrower's address, occupation, employer, marital history, moving habits, and salary. In short, they profile your creditworthiness. As a result, credit bureaus play as significant a role in your loan application's acceptance as SAT scores played in your being accepted by the college of your choice.

Some public-record information is also included (like bankruptcies, lawsuits, judgments, and tax liens) that could affect a person's creditworthiness. The records that credit bureaus compile are just that—records and not ratings—and are subject to qualification.

Credit bureaus tell potential creditors (and sometimes potential employers) the details of an individual's credit history, thus saving creditors the time and trouble of checking credit references themselves.

Reviewing Your Credit History

You should request a copy of your credit report periodically to identify and correct possible errors before they result in the rejection of a credit application. Even if you're not applying for a loan, reviewing your file is a good idea—mistakes do occur. In fact, many credit reports are loaded with mistakes. Requesting your credit report is easy and inexpensive. In addition, the Fair Credit Reporting Act prohibits credit bureaus from charging a fee for review of a record within thirty days of being denied credit.

On the basis of the information provided by the credit bureau, lenders and credit card companies decide whether you are a safe credit risk. Lender requirements vary depending on how much credit is going to be extended. A department store may be satisfied if a person is in the habit of repaying charges within thirty to sixty days. Banks usually require a close-to-spotless record of loan installments paid on time. Most people have an occasional credit slip-up, like a late payment noted on their records, but lenders are very forgiving of these.

A credit report is not a rating (your potential creditors—not the credit bureaus—rate your credit applications), but it is a record of your credit history. However, not only will your credit history appear

Smart Money Move

Check your credit bureau report for errors by periodically requesting a copy of your report.

on the report, but the agency compiling the report will provide marginal comments on the status of various accounts, placing individuals in categories as a convenience to creditors. Comments usually indicate whether creditors perceive your history to be positive, negative, or neutral. Timely payments, of course, are perceived as positive; if you are behind in payments, the account may be neutral or negative, depending on the type of account, how far behind your payments are, and similar factors.

What Is in a Credit Report?

For each credit account, the report lists the creditor, type of account, terms, amount of the original debt or credit limit, and balance outstanding on the most recent report. A payment profile for the previous twelve months is made that indicates whether the individual fell behind on payments at any time during the previous year.

A credit report is not necessarily a complete credit history. For example, some card issuers do not supply credit bureaus with any information on cardholders' accounts, claiming that this would be a violation of the customers' right to privacy. Many gas credit cards report only delinquent accounts. Mortgage lenders seldom supply information to bureaus, because creditors assume that those obligations will be met even if you are behind on others.

Generally, credit grantors are interested only in more recent information, usually for the past twelve to twenty-four months. Many credit bureaus routinely delete older data from their files. However, bankruptcy can remain on a record for ten years, and debts written off by creditors as uncollectible can remain for seven years.

How to Obtain a Credit Report

Three companies dominate the credit reporting business: *TRW, Equifax,* and *Trans Union.* On the local level, there are hundreds of small credit-rating companies—you should be able to obtain their names from local merchants. To find out what your credit rating is with the "big three," write or phone each of them and request that they send you a credit report request form. (Their headquarters' addresses appear at the end of this chapter.) You may also contact them or local credit bureaus by checking the Yellow Pages under "Credit Reporting Agencies." When you receive the form, note that you will have to pay for your report—it usually costs anywhere from $2 to $15—and that you will be asked to provide your Social Security number and other personal information. If you have been denied credit within the last thirty days, the Fair Credit Reporting Act requires that the credit bureaus provide a report at no cost.

Reading Your Credit Report

Once you receive your credit report, you will probably have to spend some time puzzling over it before you piece together precisely what it means. Why? Credit reports are generally designed to be updated and read by computers, not by humans. They are often filled with a variety of abbreviations and codes that allow computers to scan reports easily. The figure shows a sample credit report and explanations:

SAMPLE CREDIT REPORT

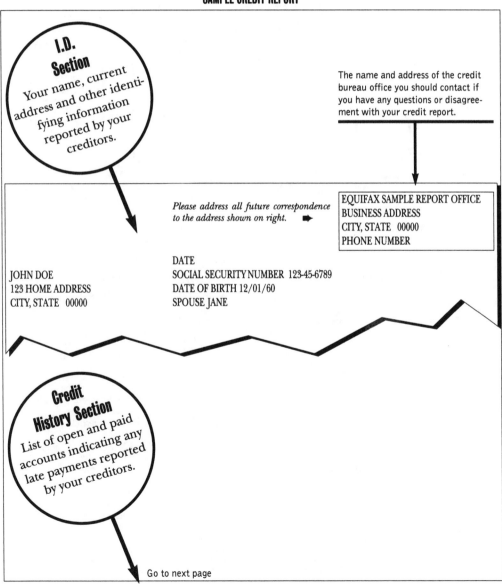

I.D. Section
Your name, current address and other identifying information reported by your creditors.

The name and address of the credit bureau office you should contact if you have any questions or disagreement with your credit report.

Please address all future correspondence to the address shown on right. ➡

EQUIFAX SAMPLE REPORT OFFICE
BUSINESS ADDRESS
CITY, STATE 00000
PHONE NUMBER

JOHN DOE
123 HOME ADDRESS
CITY, STATE 00000

DATE
SOCIAL SECURITY NUMBER 123-45-6789
DATE OF BIRTH 12/01/60
SPOUSE JANE

Credit History Section
List of open and paid accounts indicating any late payments reported by your creditors.

Go to next page

CREDIT HISTORY

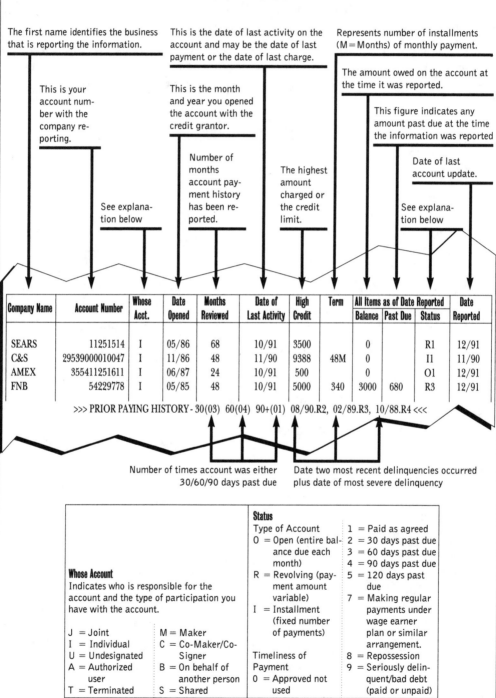

The first name identifies the business that is reporting the information.

This is the date of last activity on the account and may be the date of last payment or the date of last charge.

Represents number of installments (M=Months) of monthly payment.

This is your account number with the company reporting.

This is the month and year you opened the account with the credit grantor.

The amount owed on the account at the time it was reported.

This figure indicates any amount past due at the time the information was reported

Number of months account payment history has been reported.

The highest amount charged or the credit limit.

Date of last account update.

See explanation below

See explanation below

Company Name	Account Number	Whose Acct.	Date Opened	Months Reviewed	Date of Last Activity	High Credit	Term	All Items as of Date Reported			Date Reported
								Balance	Past Due	Status	
SEARS	11251514	I	05/86	68	10/91	3500		0		R1	12/91
C&S	29539000010047	I	11/86	48	11/90	9388	48M	0		I1	11/90
AMEX	355411251611	I	06/87	24	10/91	500		0		O1	12/91
FNB	54229778	I	05/85	48	10/91	5000	340	3000	680	R3	12/91

>>> PRIOR PAYING HISTORY - 30(03) 60(04) 90+(01) 08/90.R2, 02/89.R3, 10/88.R4 <<<

Number of times account was either 30/60/90 days past due

Date two most recent delinquencies occurred plus date of most severe delinquency

Whose Account

Indicates who is responsible for the account and the type of participation you have with the account.

J = Joint
I = Individual
U = Undesignated
A = Authorized user
T = Terminated

M = Maker
C = Co-Maker/Co-Signer
B = On behalf of another person
S = Shared

Status

Type of Account
O = Open (entire balance due each month)
R = Revolving (payment amount variable)
I = Installment (fixed number of payments)

Timeliness of Payment
0 = Approved not used

1 = Paid as agreed
2 = 30 days past due
3 = 60 days past due
4 = 90 days past due
5 = 120 days past due
7 = Making regular payments under wage earner plan or similar arrangement.
8 = Repossession
9 = Seriously delinquent/bad debt (paid or unpaid)

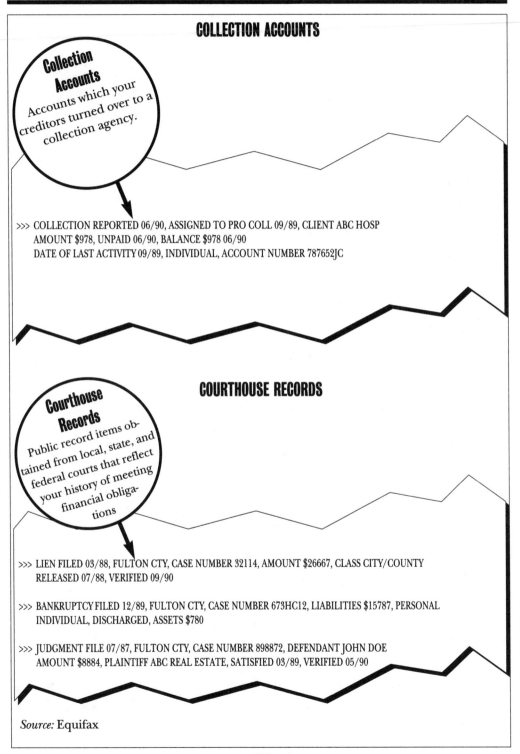

COLLECTION ACCOUNTS

Collection Accounts
Accounts which your creditors turned over to a collection agency.

>>> COLLECTION REPORTED 06/90, ASSIGNED TO PRO COLL 09/89, CLIENT ABC HOSP
    AMOUNT $978, UNPAID 06/90, BALANCE $978 06/90
    DATE OF LAST ACTIVITY 09/89, INDIVIDUAL, ACCOUNT NUMBER 787652JC

COURTHOUSE RECORDS

Courthouse Records
Public record items obtained from local, state, and federal courts that reflect your history of meeting financial obligations

>>> LIEN FILED 03/88, FULTON CTY, CASE NUMBER 32114, AMOUNT $26667, CLASS CITY/COUNTY
    RELEASED 07/88, VERIFIED 09/90

>>> BANKRUPTCY FILED 12/89, FULTON CTY, CASE NUMBER 673HC12, LIABILITIES $15787, PERSONAL
    INDIVIDUAL, DISCHARGED, ASSETS $780

>>> JUDGMENT FILE 07/87, FULTON CTY, CASE NUMBER 898872, DEFENDANT JOHN DOE
    AMOUNT $8884, PLAINTIFF ABC REAL ESTATE, SATISFIED 03/89, VERIFIED 05/90

Source: Equifax

ADDITIONAL INFORMATION

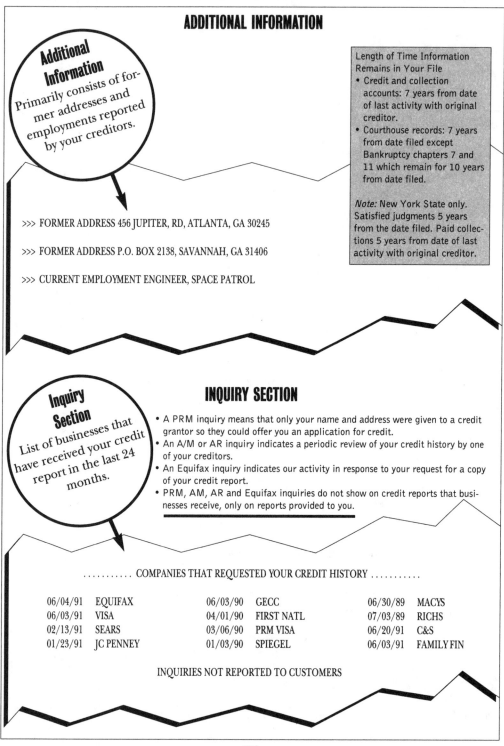

Additional Information
Primarily consists of former addresses and employments reported by your creditors.

Length of Time Information Remains in Your File
• Credit and collection accounts: 7 years from date of last activity with original creditor.
• Courthouse records: 7 years from date filed except Bankruptcy chapters 7 and 11 which remain for 10 years from date filed.

Note: New York State only. Satisfied judgments 5 years from the date filed. Paid collections 5 years from date of last activity with original creditor.

>>> FORMER ADDRESS 456 JUPITER, RD, ATLANTA, GA 30245

>>> FORMER ADDRESS P.O. BOX 2138, SAVANNAH, GA 31406

>>> CURRENT EMPLOYMENT ENGINEER, SPACE PATROL

INQUIRY SECTION

Inquiry Section
List of businesses that have received your credit report in the last 24 months.

• A PRM inquiry means that only your name and address were given to a credit grantor so they could offer you an application for credit.
• An A/M or AR inquiry indicates a periodic review of your credit history by one of your creditors.
• An Equifax inquiry indicates our activity in response to your request for a copy of your credit report.
• PRM, AM, AR and Equifax inquiries do not show on credit reports that businesses receive, only on reports provided to you.

. . . . COMPANIES THAT REQUESTED YOUR CREDIT HISTORY . . . .

06/04/91	EQUIFAX	06/03/90	GECC	06/30/89	MACYS
06/03/91	VISA	04/01/90	FIRST NATL	07/03/89	RICHS
02/13/91	SEARS	03/06/90	PRM VISA	06/20/91	C&S
01/23/91	JC PENNEY	01/03/90	SPIEGEL	06/03/91	FAMILY FIN

INQUIRIES NOT REPORTED TO CUSTOMERS

What to Do If Your Credit Report Contains Inaccurate Information

A great deal of media attention has been focused on the "big three" credit-rating agencies. These companies, it seems, have been running rather sloppy operations. Examples abound of sober citizens being summarily denied credit, only to later find that some erroneous information had found its way onto their credit reports. The offenders—embarrassed by the sudden deluge of publicity accorded a usually low-key industry—have since taken steps to improve the accuracy of their credit reports. Nonetheless, there is a reasonable chance that if you find what looks like a mistake on your credit report, you are right.

Fortunately there are several avenues of redress under the Fair Credit Reporting Act and various state regulations. The first step in getting an error in your report removed is simply to contact the credit agency. Photocopy your report, note the errors on it, and return it, along with an explanatory note. The law requires the agency to follow up on a consumer complaint. If the agency can't *prove* you wrong within an approximately twenty-five-day period, it must remove the disputed information from your report.

If the mistake is the fault of one of your creditors—perhaps it incorrectly reported your account activity—you may be in for a lot more hassle. It is likely that you'll have to go straight to the source, clear up the dispute, then have the store or business with whom you have the account notify the agency of its mistake. In cases where you have had a longstanding argument with a store over a bill, fixing your credit report may first require you to settle your dispute.

Your Bill of Rights

A ll of your dealings with credit agencies are governed by the provisions of the Fair Credit Reporting Act. These are your rights under the Act:

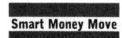

Smart Money Move

1. TO LEARN the name and address of the consumer reporting agency whose report impaired your application in connection with a credit or job application.

2. TO DISCOVER on request the nature and substance of all information, except medical, that a credit agency has on file about you.

3. TO KNOW the sources of such information, except investigative sources.

4. TO GET the names of all people who have received reports on

If your credit report contains inaccurate information, take action to have the errors corrected. It is your right under the law.

407

you within the previous six months, or within the previous year if the report was furnished for employment reasons.

5. **TO HAVE** all incomplete or incorrect information investigated, and if any information cannot be found or is found to be inaccurate, to have that information deleted from your file.

6. **TO HAVE** a credit bureau notify all agencies of the credit bureau's mistake, at no cost to you.

7. **TO HAVE** your side of any controversy included in a creditor's report, if difference with that creditor cannot be resolved.

8. **TO HAVE** no information sent out that is more than seven years old (ten years if you have been bankrupt), with two exceptions: There are no time limits if you are applying for an insurance policy over specified limits, or if you are applying for a job with a salary over specified limits.

FOR FURTHER INFORMATION

TRW Credit Data
P.O. Box 2350
Chatsworth, CA 91313-2350
(800) 392-1122

Equifax Credit Information Services
P.O. Box 740241
Atlanta, GA 30375-0241
(800) 685-1111

Trans Union Corporation
P.O. Box 7000
North Olmsted, OH 44070
(312) 408-1050

FOR FURTHER READING

Fair Credit Reporting (free)
Federal Trade Commission
Public Reference Branch
Room 130
6th and Pennsylvania, N.W.
Washington DC 20580

CREDIT BUREAU CHECKLIST

■□■

Periodically request a copy of your credit bureau report to check up on your credit history and to make sure there is no inaccurate information on the report.

■□■

Don't let errors remain on your credit report. Take the necessary steps to have erroneous information corrected.

■□■

Understand your rights under the Fair Credit Reporting Act. Don't jeopardize your creditworthiness over others' mistakes. Exercise your rights under the law.

50

Managing Financial Problems

No matter what your age, occupation, or income level, chances are that sooner or later you will run into financial problems. They may be of your own making—heaven knows, credit is too easy and too tempting. You may have been caught up in the "live beyond your means" hysteria that still afflicts many people. Or your problems may be caused by conditions beyond your control—a layoff, an illness or disability, or a parent or adult child who needs unexpected financial assistance. The purpose of this chapter is not to point blame (although I will not be able to resist the temptation to gently remind debt abusers to mend their ways). Rather, I will guide you through the process of getting out of your financial difficulties. Ideally, you will be able to get out on your own. Otherwise, you may need to seek assistance.

Are You Headed for Debt Problems?

Most people don't get into debt trouble overnight. It builds up gradually, and impending problems become obvious after a while:

- **AMOUNTS OWED** on various charge accounts rise steadily, so you are never out of debt to local stores.

- **BEFORE** you have finished paying last month's bills, this month's are stacking up. Payments are always late, and you are regularly receiving notes about delinquent accounts and perhaps some notices threatening legal action.

- **YOU ARE TAKING** cash advances on credit cards or using savings to pay basic monthly bills (for example, rent or utilities).

- **SO MANY** separate bills are received each month from so many sources that you borrow from a lending institution to have them consolidated into one loan. Yet credit buying continues, adding more and more new bills to this one big debt.

- **AN EVER-INCREASING PORTION** of your net income goes to pay debts.

- **YOU ARE SPENDING** more than 25 percent of your after-tax pay on installment debt (not including your mortgage).

411

- **YOU ARE USING** large credit lines (like a home equity loan) to pay for current living expenses or to make frivolous purchases.

- **YOU ARE MAKING** only the minimum required monthly repayments on credit cards or a home equity loan.

WATCH FOR THESE WARNING SIGNS

Prevent serious credit problems by recognizing the early warning signs. If you find *any* of the following happening to you, take action immediately to regain control of your debt.

- **YOU USE** savings or credit to meet normal household expenses.

- **YOUR CREDIT CARDS** are always at their limits.

- **YOU ALWAYS MAKE** the minimum payments, but your credit card balances are rising each month.

- **YOU START** falling behind on important monthly payments, like rent, the mortgage, or a car loan.

- **YOU USE** one form of credit to make payments on another.

- **YOU CAN'T NAME** all your creditors or cite the total amounts you owe them.

- **YOU ROUTINELY GO** to more expensive restaurants and stores because they accept credit cards and you are short of cash.

Getting Out of Your Debt Problems

There is no easy way out of debt problems, but you should first try to get out from under your hill of bills yourself before taking more drastic action—seeing a credit counselor or filing for personal bankruptcy. One way or another, you can and will emerge from your debt problem. It's not the end of the world. In fact, many who have trod the well-worn path of overindebtedness emerge with much-improved money habits and a bright financial future.

First Try to Solve the Problem Yourself

Here are six steps you can take to try to resolve your financial problems. There are no quick fixes, so you should expect to endure some psychological and financial pain. But working through these problems yourself is far more preferable than the alternatives that are discussed later.

1. Find out where you stand

Summarize *all* of your debts, including the total amount due, the amount overdue, and the minimum monthly payment requirements.

2. Prepare a bare-bones budget

You must prepare a budget that cuts your living expenses to the bone so that you can meet your monthly loan-payment obligations. As a matter of fact, after housing payments and food, debt payments should be the third most important item on your emergency budget. That means you'll have to live on whatever is left over after you have provided for housing, food, and debt payments. If, like most people in your predicament, credit cards caused the problem, take the scissors to all but one credit card. (You'll need one credit card as a form of identification. Ideally it should be a travel and entertainment card like American Express, since these cards require you to pay your entire bill each month.)

3. Prioritize

If you have many debts from different sources and you aren't sure that you'll be able to pay them all on time, work out a plan for paying the most important bills and for avoiding late charges. Figure out just how costly—in terms of interest, late charges, and the possible jeopardy to your credit rating—not paying the minimum amount due on each bill is. Then, prioritize. Missing an important bill might lead you to your car being repossessed or to the shutting off of your electricity. Beyond meeting minimum payments for all your bills, pay off the bills with the highest interest rates (like credit cards) first. Then pay any money you can spare toward other debts. For example, don't reduce your 11 percent car loan before reducing your 19 percent credit cards.

Smart Money Move

If you are experiencing debt problems, try to work out the problems yourself before seeking the services of a consumer credit counselor or taking the drastic step of filing for bankruptcy.

4. Speak with your creditors

If you are unable to make a loan payment on time, contact the lender (before they contact you) to explain your circumstances and work out a payment plan. They may agree to grant you a temporary reduction or delay in payments, or they may waive your late charges. Don't expect them to work miracles, but if you keep the lender informed of your circumstances, many will be more accommodating. Also, don't avoid calls or letters from creditors under any circumstances. Creditors would rather know that you are trying to work things out than fear that you are trying to evade your debt.

5. Don't be easily seduced by debt consolidation loans

The idea behind debt consolidation is that you take out one loan to cover all your debts. Paying only one loan in low monthly installments sounds like just what the debt doctor ordered—but this may well be the kind of thinking that got you into credit trouble in the first place. Lower monthly payments usually mean the loan is extended over a longer period of time. True, some people can consolidate their high-interest bills into a lower-interest loan (like a home equity loan), but generally if your financial situation is iffy, any debt consolidation loan you'll be able to get will charge high interest and may require you to pledge your hard-won assets, like your car, as security.

Moreover, consolidating loans often leads to incurring even more debt, because you can regain access to your credit cards. If you have no choice but to arrive at a lower monthly payment, discuss loan consolidation with a lending officer at your bank. With a good prior credit history, a banker may grant you an installment loan to consolidate your debts—*provided* that you would use the funds to pay off all existing loans and cancel all but one credit card.

6. Don't become a debt recidivist

If you're able to repair your credit yourself, the time will come (it may seem like an eternity) when you will return to a firmer financial footing. Many people, armed with generous credit card balances once again, lapse back into their old free-spending ways. It's the equivalent of successful dieters subsequently regaining all their lost weight. The other road that can be taken is the "saving road."

It's a lot easier to save when you know you'll get to keep the money, instead of feeling that it's all going toward paying off last year's binge. (If the cause of your debt problems was something beyond your control, you already know how important it is to save and will welcome the opportunity to resume saving.) It feels good to accumulate some savings, and if your finances catch the flu again, you'll be able to recover a lot faster. Remember, until you get into the habit of spending less than you earn—*living beneath your means*—you won't save a penny.

If you find that you are over your head in debt—beyond your ability to work out of it with your current income, *speak with your creditors again.* Contact each creditor and explain why you are overextended. They may be able to arrange an easier repayment plan. Many creditors will go along with a reasonable plan under which they will receive their money slowly, if you show that you are trying to pay your debts as opposed to avoiding them. Most creditors prefer doing this to repossessing the goods or taking you to court, which is expensive and time-consuming.

Next, Try Credit Counseling

If you have financial problems that you can't resolve on your own, the next step is to consult a credit counselor. Various institutions offer such counseling, including the following:

Many banks and credit unions

They often offer formal or informal debt counseling for their customers or members.

Family service agencies

Hundreds of these throughout the country can provide financial counseling or will make referrals to an appropriate professional.

Nonprofit consumer credit counseling organizations backed by local banks and merchants

These provide services to anyone, particularly to overextended families and individuals. If you are slightly overextended, the agency will usually help you develop a repayment plan for a nominal monthly fee. The agency may take monthly payments from you and distribute them to your creditors. The agency also talks to the creditors and often gets them to agree to a delayed or reduced payment. Because these groups are backed by local merchants, they will do everything possible to get you to repay debts.

By the way, make sure that you are dealing with a credit counselor who is affiliated with a *nonprofit* consumer credit counseling service. There are a variety of charlatans out there who hold themselves out as credit counselors but will do nothing more than wreak further havoc on your predicament.

One important thing to remember: If you use a consumer credit counseling organization, it will be reported to the credit bureaus and noted on your credit record. That fact should not deter you from using a credit counseling service, particularly if your only other alternative is filing for bankruptcy. While you may ultimately have to do so, give credit counseling a try first.

Personal Bankruptcy, the Last Resort

If you find that neither your own good efforts nor those of a credit counselor can salvage your situation, personal bankruptcy may be your only alternative. Some attorneys make it sound easy, but you should consider it only as a last resort. But if your situation is hopeless, bankruptcy will allow you to get a fresh start. (Personal bankruptcy is discussed further in the next chapter.)

The Psychological Side of Money Problems

Everyone experiences money problems sometime during their lives, and everyone argues with family members about money matters. But that's of little comfort if your family is going through financial problems now.

Communication Is the Key

Sadly, money is so important to our self-esteem in this country that money problems, even temporary money problems, can be devastat-

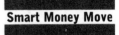

Smart Money Move

Don't make your money problems worse than they have to be by borrowing from family and friends—and creditors.

ing to us. For example, some people who have lost their jobs are afraid to tell anyone; they leave the house each morning as if they were going to work and return home in the evening. These same people probably aren't going to the unemployment office during their daily sojourns, because pride won't allow them to accept what they are entitled to and probably need.

When confronted with money problems, we tend to retreat at a time when we should be seeking help. We often spend too much time worrying about our problems and too little time working to address and resolve them. If there is one positive thing to say about financial problems, it is that they can be resolved. It will require a lot of work, it will probably require a lot of sacrifice, and it may well take a long time, but they can be resolved. One other thing is certain: They won't be resolved as easily as they might be if you don't share your problems with others, including family members.

It All Boils Down to Communication

Good communication is important to your financial health, not just with family members and close friends but with people who can help you with your financial problems. For example, in Chapter 13 we discussed what you should do if you fall behind or think you'll fall behind in your mortgage. The answer? *Communicate* with the lender. Similarly, this chapter maintains that anxious creditors should be coped with not by avoiding their calls and letters. You need to *communicate* with them openly and honestly. Creditors have a vested interest in helping you resolve your credit problems. They are usually well prepared to assist you, because you're not alone in your problems.

But, oh, does pride get in the way! It's not easy to get on the phone soon after you have been laid off to tell your friends and professional colleagues that you are in the market for a new job. How do you think they'll react? Is it really that embarrassing? If a friend or colleague called you to tell you the same thing, how would you react? When adversity strikes, don't let pride get in the way of good sense. Use the many resources available to you.

The Best of Times, The Worst of Times: You, Money Problems, and Your Family and Friends

Families Survive Financial Crises

You've probably heard your parents or grandparents talk about the Great Depression. Families survived then. If you're going through your own great depression, you'll survive now. Open communication with family members or close friends is important, just as it is with creditors—although you may feel that it is easier to talk with creditors about your problems than with family members. Generally, family members should share in any sacrifices that will be necessary to resolve the problem. Even if there is no immediate crisis but you want to prepare for that eventuality during a recession, involve other family members in the planning and actions that must be taken. A spirit of cooperation will go a long way toward minimizing the family stress that inevitably accompanies a financial crisis. If your money problems seem to be causing you and/or your family too much stress—and they may—by all means consult with a mental health professional.

When Your Financial Life Returns to Normal

If you want to start an argument with your spouse, money is the easiest excuse. You probably can find a money matter to complain about in less than ten seconds. So when your money problems are resolved and your outlook is rosy once again, you'll still argue with your spouse or other loved ones over money. It seems that the only married couples who have never had an argument over money are those who are on their way to their own wedding receptions.

But money disputes are not necessarily indicative of deeper problems. Actually, the vast majority of couples agree on important family financial matters such as buying a home, educating the kids, and preparing for a comfortable retirement. Your disagreements tend to be over smaller day-to-day financial matters. There are a couple of easy things you can do to minimize interspousal money tensions. First, set aside one day every year to sit down with your spouse or partner, review your financial status, and make some plans for next year. The date you select shouldn't be around tax-return preparation time, however. That's already stressful enough.

Second, write down some realistic financial goals that you both want to accomplish over the next few years. What this all boils down to, of course, is improved communication with your spouse. Lack of communication about family finances or about any aspect of marriage, for that matter, is a recipe for strife. But don't expect the arguments to go away entirely. Chances are you and your spouse will always have somewhat different approaches toward family money management. In fact, if you think about it, spenders tend to marry savers. While these couples may never eliminate marital money strife completely, they can, with a little communication, turn these warring extremes into a happy median.

FOR FURTHER INFORMATION

National Foundation for Consumer Credit **8611 2nd Avenue** **Suite 100** **Silver Spring MD 20910** **(800) 388-2227**	**Family Service America** **Public Inquiry Specialist** **11700 West Lake Park Drive** **Milwaukee WI 53224** **(800) 221-2681**

MANAGING FINANCIAL PROBLEMS CHECKLIST

☐

Try to nip developing financial problems in the bud by recognizing the warning signs of debt overload and taking action to curtail your borrowing, then pay down your debt.

☐

Follow the six-step program to try to resolve your financial problems yourself before seeking outside assistance.

☐

If you cannot resolve your credit problems on your own, try credit counseling before taking the drastic step of filing for personal bankruptcy.

Personal Bankruptcy

For centuries, unfortunately, the very word *bankruptcy* has carried heavy connotations of shame and failure; a thoroughly wicked person was, in the literary language of the nineteenth century, a "moral bankrupt." Nonetheless, when you are surrounded on all sides by creditors and your back is firmly pressed against the wall, bankruptcy can be a heaven-sent means of escape. It is a measure of last resort. It won't allow you to escape your problems in the long run. What filing for bankruptcy *can* do, however, is either relieve you of most or all of your debt obligations, or give you a measure of breathing room during which you can establish a payment plan and settle some or all of your obligations.

Bankruptcy law has come a long way since the days of debtors' prison. Modern bankruptcy law is flexible and humane. It recognizes that rescuing a hopelessly debt-burdened individual—not allowing him or her to fall to pieces—is the right thing to do. Nonetheless, declaring bankruptcy is an extreme step to take. For up to ten years, your credit record, for instance, will note that you have declared bankruptcy, no matter how much you subsequently improve your financial situation. For this reason alone, it is essential to consult with an attorney before taking the bankruptcy route.

Some attorneys, particularly those that advertise in the newspaper and on television, make bankruptcy sound easy. Rather than go to them, find an attorney that can give you a more objective assessment of what bankruptcy will do for and to you. Furthermore, a debtor who has declared bankruptcy may have to wait six years before doing so again, no matter how dire his or her financial situation. You should also realize that going bankrupt can be the cause of great emotional upheaval and family stress.

If you have recently filed for bankruptcy or expect that you will need to, you're not alone. In fact, between 1990 and 1992, almost one out of thirty families in the United States declared personal bankruptcy.

The Forms Bankruptcy Can Take

There are two chapters of federal law that apply to individual (as opposed to business) bankruptcy: Chapter 7 and Chapter 13; Chapter 11 bankruptcy, while generally associated with businesses, is available to individuals and may be preferable for those who have substantial assets and can afford the high expense of a Chapter 11 bankruptcy proceeding.

Chapter 7 Bankruptcy

Often called "straight bankruptcy," Chapter 7 is the most drastic and severe type of bankruptcy. Indeed, in some cases, debtors may have no choice over whether they file under Chapter 7—angry creditors may try to force them into involuntary bankruptcy. Otherwise, you file for Chapter 7 bankruptcy by completing a form and by paying a fee to the court. The court will then issue an injunction to stop harassment from creditors. Should Chapter 7 proceedings be initiated against you by your creditors, the court might require them to file a bond to indemnify you for court costs and liabilities incurred during the proceedings.

You will also have the right to file an answer to the creditors' petition. When and if bankruptcy proceedings actually commence, creditors are prohibited from attempting to collect on their debts: They can, however, require immediate payment from any cosigners. (Never, never, never cosign a loan unless it is for a close relative and you can afford to pay up when the creditor comes knocking.) Some creditors will schedule a meeting to question the debtor regarding possible omission of property from the required list of assets. Meanwhile, the court will appoint a trustee to supervise the liquidation of your assets. Once the proceeds from the asset liquidation have been used to settle creditors' claims, the court will grant you a discharge that voids any judgments previously made against you.

While severe, Chapter 7 bankruptcy does allow you to keep some property in so far as certain "exempted" property does not have to be liquidated in order to pay off debts. Debts linked to property, such as mortgages or automobile loans where the home or car is collateral, must be paid off or you will lose the property. The following is a list of exempted property:

Smart Money Move

Before filing for bankruptcy, seek the opinion of a credit counseling organization. Then seek the opinion of an objective attorney.

- UP TO **$7,500** in equity over and above mortgages and liens on your real estate

- **HOUSEHOLD GOODS**, clothes, appliances, books, and other personal items, up to $200 per item and up to a $4,000 total

- **$500 WORTH** of jewelry

- **$750 IN** professional implements, books, or tools

- **THE DEBTOR'S INTEREST** in other property, up to $400, plus up to half of any unused real property exemption

- UP TO **$4,000** in cash value life insurance

- **SUCH BENEFITS** as Social Security, unemployment compensation, public assistance, disability benefits, alimony, child support, and separate maintenance reasonably necessary, and payments of pension, profit sharing, annuity, or similar plans.

Certain other exclusions may also apply. These figures can be doubled for a husband and wife filing bankruptcy jointly. Finally, the following debts cannot be canceled under Chapter 7 bankruptcy:

- **CERTAIN TAXES** and customs, including unpaid withholding and Social Security taxes and the penalties associated with them

- **DEBTS INCURRED** because of fraud, embezzlement, or larceny

- **LIABILITY INCURRED** for willful and reckless acts committed against another person or against his or her property

- **STUDENT LOANS** less than five years old.

Chapter 13 Bankruptcy

Filing for bankruptcy under Chapter 13 will leave you with more of your property intact. Indeed, it can be argued that Chapter 13 isn't true bankruptcy at all—the full title of the law is Adjustments of Debts of an Individual with Regular Income. This form of bankruptcy is often called a "wage-earner" plan. If you file under Chapter 13, you are allowed to keep your property in exchange for assigning a portion of your income to repay your debts. Chapter 13 is generally used by individuals who have a regular income and debts manageable enough to make substantial repayment feasible. If you operate a business, you will be allowed to continue to do so under Chapter 13 bankruptcy.

As with Chapter 7, the creditors may no longer harass you once a petition is filed under Chapter 13. Also, your property is afforded the same minimum protection described in the preceding section. If some of your debts are cosigned, the cosigners are not immediately liable: the creditors must wait until it is clear that they will not be fully repaid under the court-approved plan. Only then can creditors collect the balance of the debt from cosigners. Ultimately, cosigners are responsible for any remaining debt they cosigned.

You are required to file a monthly budgeting plan with the court, indicating how much income will be left after living expenses are met. Your plan will be examined at a hearing, and the judge must either approve or modify your plan. The court will appoint a trustee to control your income; depending on your circumstances, you will have generally around three years to repay anywhere from 10 percent of your debts to the entire amount(s) owed. After the payments mandated by the court-approved plan have been paid in full, you will be granted a discharge of all debts.

Finally, you can change your bankruptcy status from Chapter 13 to Chapter 7 at any time. You can even agree to pay off all your debts in full, although the judge must decide whether taking that action is in your best interest, and you have a thirty-day escape clause to nullify the agreement.

Is Chapter 7 Preferable to Chapter 13?

Deciding which bankruptcy proceeding is better really depends on your individual circumstances in consultation with your attorney. Chapter 7 rids you of your obligations but rids you of most of your assets. Chapter 13, on the other hand, allows you to keep more property, but you must have an income in order to qualify and you still have to make payments on your debts. A Chapter 13 bankruptcy shows that you made more of an effort to make good on your obligations than a Chapter 7, but your credit record is still sullied for many years to come.

Emerging from Personal Bankruptcy

Some lenders may be willing to grant a loan to a family or individual who has recently declared bankruptcy, particularly if the bankruptcy was caused by factors beyond their control. But it is usually very difficult for an ex-bankrupt to obtain the kind of credit that previously supported his or her life-style. This may be just as well.

The type of bankruptcy you file may also affect your future credit. If you filed Chapter 7, creditors may be reassured by the fact that you are prohibited from filing again for six years. If you filed Chapter 13 and paid back a major portion of your debts, potential lenders may be willing to take a chance on you. However, you should recognize that many people are forced to reduce their standard of living for quite some time after declaring bankruptcy.

Whatever your situation, whatever the forces that compelled you to declare bankruptcy, the worst is over, and you will be able to emerge and begin anew. Rebuilding your credit will take time and perseverance. The best way to do so is gradually to rebuild your banking relationships, so you can demonstrate your creditworthiness. You may want to start by obtaining a credit card that is fully secured by a deposit you have on hand with the bank that issues the card. Once you have accumulated some savings, you should be able to borrow by fully securing the loan. That gives you a chance to first get the loan and then show the lender that you can pay off the loan on time. If you work hard to get your spending under control and build up your savings, you could probably begin to reestablish your creditworthiness within three to four years, sometimes earlier.

Smart Money Move

If you have filed for bankruptcy, devise a plan to restore your creditworthiness as soon as possible.

BANKRUPTCY CHECKLIST

Try to work something out to avoid filing for bankruptcy. Bankruptcy is a last resort, not an easy way out.

Consult with a credit counselor and an attorney before filing.

☐ Familiarize yourself with the two types of bankruptcy proceedings and decide in consultation with an attorney which would be more advantageous to you.

☐ Determine whether enough of your debts would be discharged by bankruptcy proceedings to make it worthwhile.

☐ Determine how you will use your property exemptions.

☐ Work with a credit counselor to devise a plan to pay debts that will not be discharged through the proceedings.

☐ Work hard to rebuild your creditworthiness when you emerge so that you won't repeat your credit problems.

Part VII

Investing

Investing Wisely

 ccumulating savings and investing those savings wisely is crucial to achieving financial security. As the figure below illustrates, investing is really the focal point of financial security. Unless you are fortunate enough to inherit or marry a lot of money, the only way you're going to achieve financial security is to:

1. **SPEND LESS THAN YOU EARN.**

2. **SAVE WHAT YOU DON'T SPEND.**

3. **INVEST THOSE SAVINGS APPROPRIATELY.**

Chapters 52–62 will help you become a good investor—one who doesn't follow the crowd (the crowd is always wrong). As you read on, you'll learn how to make your own investment decisions. Once you become educated, you will no longer have to rely on someone else to tell you what kind of investments you need. (That "someone else" may not have your best interests in mind.)

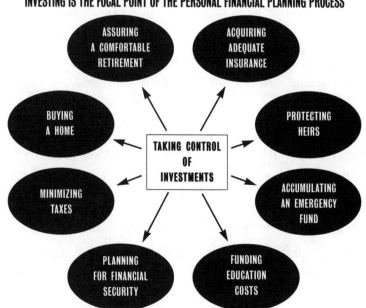

INVESTING IS THE FOCAL POINT OF THE PERSONAL FINANCIAL PLANNING PROCESS

Deciding on What You Want to Accomplish with Your Investments

As important as investing is, most people don't do a very good job of it. What's the secret to successful investing? First, you must decide what you want to accomplish with your investments. Ultimately, you will want to use the money to guarantee that your retirement years will be comfortable. Your investment income will supplement your Social Security benefits and, if you have one, your company pension plan. Your investment portfolio will provide steadily increasing income during your retirement years to keep up with inflation. In addition to providing retirement income, investments are often used along the way to retirement to meet such important needs as buying a home and educating the children. Investments can also help you weather life's setbacks, such as unemployment, divorce, and disability.

As corny as it sounds, if you don't have some clear idea of what you're going to do with the money, you're not going to be able to organize your investments to meet those targets. Chapter 3 provides some guidance on setting lifelong objectives. Once you have established some realistic objectives, you can then begin to map out a savings and investment plan that will help you achieve them.

The right kind of investments are undoubtedly the ones with which you are already pretty familiar. They are not new types of investments, nor are they the kinds of investments that you have to buy and sell all the time. In a word, they're "old-fashioned."

Finally, successful investors, whether they invest themselves or use investment advisers, won't let anyone persuade them to alter their objectives or their investments significantly. As you will see, the key prerequisite for success in investing is to *take control* of your investments.

Financial Security—Your Number One Goal

Everyone's foremost financial planning goal is financial security. Financial security means that your investments (combined with Social Security and pension benefits) will provide you and your spouse with an adequate income for the rest of your lives. In essence, then, financial security means you can afford to retire. Some people achieve financial security a lot sooner than others. Unfortunately, some people never achieve it.

Of course, the single most important ingredient in achieving financial security is accumulating enough money to be able to provide the income necessary to be "financially independent."

Why it's getting tougher and tougher to achieve financial security:

1.   OUR RETIREMENT ASPIRATIONS are ambitious. Many people want to retire early, and everyone wants to be able to maintain the same life-style when they're retired that they enjoyed during their working years.

2.   **WE ARE LIVING LONGER**—it is not unreasonable for some people to expect to spend one-third of their lives in retirement.

3.   **INFLATION** is a lot higher than it used to be.

4.   **COMPANY PENSION PLANS** are not as generous as they used to be.

What this all means is that most of us are or will be responsible for funding the lion's share of our retirement income or income needs. Social Security and pension plans alone are no where near enough.

While the emphasis in this and the following chapters is on investments, remember that financial security requires that all areas of financial planning—including insurance, tax planning, and estate planning—be attended to. You may eventually accumulate a large investment portfolio (I hope you do), but if you are not properly and completely insured, for example, you are not financially secure. (These important topics are discussed elsewhere in this book.)

Developing an Investment Plan

Once you have a clear idea of your overall financial objectives, you can begin to develop an investment plan designed to help you achieve those objectives. Your investment plan will require you to make the following decisions:

1. The amount of your current income to be set aside periodically for investment purposes

If you are not yet sure how much you will need to save and invest, various chapters in this book can help you estimate how much you will need to cover big expenses. These chapters include Chapter 13 for first-time homeowners, Chapter 21 on meeting educational costs, and Chapter 69, on projecting retirement income needs.

2. A reasonable target long-term rate of return on investments

Permit me to give you a target: You should strive to earn a rate of return on your investments that exceeds inflation by three percent after taxes. This is easier said than done, however. I would suggest for planning purposes that you assume a three to five percent long-term inflation rate. As the table on page 432 shows, you would have to earn a very high rate of return in order to beat inflation at all, let alone beat inflation by three percent. (One big reason why you should put as much money as possible into tax-deferred retirement accounts is that it's much easier to stay ahead of inflation that way, since income from these accounts is not taxed until you retire.)

3. The allocation of your investments among the three major investment categories

These are stocks, interest-earning securities, and real estate. By allocating your investments appropriately, you will be able to achieve an inflation-beating rate of return without subjecting your investments to undue risk.

These various categories of investment are discussed briefly in the next chapter and in more detail later on. The all-important matter of allocating your investments among the various investment categories is described in Chapter 54.

Saving Is Not Investing

Don't confuse saving with investing. Although you have to have savings in order to have investments, they are not one and the same. Short-term savings accounts, money-market accounts, and CDs may play a role in your investment program, but they should play only a minor role. You pay a big price for safety when you save. And that price is that your investments will not grow sufficiently to help you achieve your financial goals.

Be Patient—and Diversify

Successful investors are patient and disciplined. They take a long-term view of how to allocate their investments, and they rarely alter the proportions significantly. They don't overreact to market conditions by shifting their investments hither and yon, or seek the safety of no-risk savings accounts when market conditions are uncertain. They emphasize diversification of their investment assets—and they reap the benefits, as the following table illustrates.

This table illustrates the compound annual returns of various portfolios from 1970 through 1990. While the 100 percent stocks portfolio tied with the BB&K Index (a mixture of stocks, bonds, and real estate) for the best annual return, the more diversified portfolios also produced very attractive annual returns with considerably less risk than having all of your money in stocks. Investors who had all their money in Treasury bills over the same period would have had a compound return of only 7.7 percent.

THE BENEFITS OF DIVERSIFICATION

YEAR	100% STOCKS	100% BONDS	60% STOCKS/40% BONDS	STOCKS/BONDS/CASH (1/3 IN EACH)	BB&K INDEX
1970	4.0%	12.1%	7.5%	8.0%	4.7%
1971	14.3%	13.2%	14.1%	10.8%	13.7%
1972	19.0%	5.7%	13.5%	9.4%	15.1%
1973	-14.7%	-1.1%	-9.1%	-3.0%	-2.2%
1974	-26.5%	4.4%	-14.9%	-5.4%	-6.6% »

YEAR	100% STOCKS	100% BONDS	60% STOCKS/40% BONDS	STOCKS/BONDS/CASH (1/3 IN EACH)	BB&K INDEX
1975	37.2%	9.2%	25.7%	17.0%	19.6%
1976	23.8%	16.8%	21.2%	15.2%	11.5%
1977	-7.2%	-0.7%	-4.6%	-0.9%	6.1%
1978	6.6%	-1.2%	3.7%	4.4%	13.0%
1979	18.4%	-1.2%	10.8%	9.1%	11.5%
1980	32.4%	-4.0%	17.5%	13.2%	17.9%
1981	-4.9%	1.9%	-2.0%	4.1%	6.4%
1982	21.4%	40.4%	29.0%	24.0%	14.4%
1983	22.5%	0.7%	13.4%	10.5%	15.4%
1984	6.3%	15.4%	10.1%	10.8%	10.4%
1985	32.2%	31.0%	31.9%	23.4%	25.4%
1986	18.5%	24.4%	21.1%	16.6%	23.3%
1987	5.2%	-2.7%	3.6%	3.9%	8.6%
1988	16.8%	9.7%	14.0%	11.0%	13.2%
1989	31.5%	18.1%	26.2%	19.2%	14.3%
1990	-3.2%	6.2%	0.6%	3.6%	-1.4%
COMPOUND ANNUAL RETURN					
	11.2%	8.7%	10.5%	9.6%	11.2%
NUMBER OF YEARS WITH POSITIVE RETURNS					
	15	14	16	17	17

Stocks: S&P 500 Index
Bonds: Long-Term Treasury bonds
BB&K Index: 20% U.S. stocks, 20% bonds, 20% real estate, 20% foreign stocks, 20% cash
Note: Results assume annual rebalancing of portfolio allocations.
Sources: Bailard, Biehl & Kaiser and Ibbotson Associates, Inc.

In Addition to Death, Two of Life's Certainties

I t has always been said that the two things in life that are certain are death and taxes. However, there is now a third certainty: inflation.

Inflation

Inflation affects your investing in two ways. First, in projecting how much money you are going to need to reach your financial goals, you must factor in the impact of inflation on living cost. For example, assuming that inflation averages 4.5 percent per year, your living expenses will double every fifteen years. If you are fifty years of age, you might estimate that if you were to retire today, you would need $20,000 in personal investment income (in addition to Social Security and your pension). You would actually need a higher income when you reached retirement age in order to have the same "purchasing power" that $20,000 has today. In fact, if living costs do double every fifteen years, you will need twice as much money, or $40,000, in investment income commencing at age of sixty-five.

The second area of inflation that needs to be considered in your investment planning is the effect inflation has on your investments. Your investment program should assure—over the long run—that your investments provide you with a rate of return in excess of inflation.

Taxes

Most investors don't fully realize the impact of taxes. When CD rates reach nine or ten percent, many investors think they have died and gone to heaven. Yet after taxes have been taken out, they are actually staying just ahead of inflation. When CD rates are in the four or five percent rate range, investors may in fact be losing ground to inflation. Check out the following example.

Example

The following table shows the after-tax return on investment and inflation premiums on a $10,000 taxable CD investment for an investor with a combined state and federal tax rate of 33 percent.

ANNUAL RATE OF RETURN

	CD RATE 6%	CD RATE 9%
ANNUAL INTEREST INCOME ON $10,000 CD	$600	$900
LESS INCOME TAXES @ 33%	$200	$300
ANNUAL INTEREST AFTER TAXES	$400	$600
AFTER-TAX RETURN ON $10,000 CD INVESTMENT	4.0%	6.0%
INFLATION RATE (ASSUMED)	4.5%	4.5%
DIFFERENCE	-0.5%	+1.5%

The 6% CD loses ground to inflation while the 9% CD beats inflation by 1.5%.

Taxes are important. In fact, taxes can turn an apparently attractive investment into an inflation loser.

Two for the Money

Successful investors are disciplined savers and disciplined investors. Here are two wonderful ways to put yourself on the road to investment success.

Automatic Investing

How many times do you set out to save a certain amount of money each week or each month, only to give up after the first few times? Thanks to modern technology, you can save and invest automatically. All you need is a bank or credit union account or an investment account with a brokerage or mutual fund company. With your instructions, any of these financial institutions would be happy to withdraw some money from your paycheck or checking account and place it in an investment or savings account. Automatic investing is a great way to begin and, more important, to stick with a regular savings program. Be careful, automatic savings can become an addiction—but what a marvelous addiction!

Dollar-Cost Averaging

One of the best ways to add to your investments gradually is to use "dollar-cost averaging"— simply invest a fixed amount in a particular stock issue or mutual fund account on a regular basis. The trick is to stick with your schedule regardless of whether stock or bond prices go up or down.

Because you're investing a fixed amount at fixed intervals, your dollars buy fewer shares when stock or bond prices are high and more when they are low. As a result, the average purchase price is lower than the average market price over the same time frame. You can't beat that.

You can use dollar-cost averaging with individual stocks, but it often is easier with stock or bond mutual funds. While dollar-cost averaging won't dramatically improve the performance of your portfolio, it does add discipline to your investing and give you the benefits of saving regularly.

The table illustrates dollar-cost averaging.

	AMOUNT INVESTED	PRICE	NUMBER OF SHARES PURCHASED
1ST PERIOD	$4,000	$13 3/8	300
2ND PERIOD	4,000	8	500
3RD PERIOD	4,000	6 5/8	600
4TH PERIOD	4,000	8	500
5TH PERIOD	4,000	20	200
	$20,000		2,100

Total amount invested over 5 periods: $20,000...Number of shares purchased: 2,100...Average market price: $11.20...Average cost: $9.52

Many investors have benefited from dollar-cost averaging. To be successful, you must discipline yourself to invest at regular intervals. This discipline is put to its sternest test when the stock or bond prices are depressed, because more shares can be acquired when prices are low.

INVESTING WISELY CHECKLIST

☐

Set some "lifetime" investment objectives, since the best way to begin to accumulate the money you'll need is to decide what you want to do with it.

☐

Develop a realistic savings and investment plan that will help you achieve your objectives.

☐

Always factor in the effects of inflation and taxes in your investment planning.

☐

Use automatic investing and dollar-cost averaging to build financial security and retire rich.

The Basics of Investing

This chapter presents some basic information on investing. The later chapters provide more detailed and complex mechanics of investing, but the old saw that you need to learn how to walk before you learn how to run should be heeded by even experienced investors. Many of them, no doubt, could do with a refresher course on investing basics.

Investing Is a Way of Life

Stages. At twenty we still harbor doubts about our mortality. Potential success seems more worthy of our focus than the reality of our lives. As a result, investing tends to remain something our parents "do." At thirty, we tend to believe that thinking about retirement is what you do when you're retired. But the reality of home ownership, children, and the costs associated with each begin to turn us toward financial and investment planning. Passing forty, thoughts of retirement may begin to take root—only to be uprooted by the looming costs of children's tuition. At fifty, the issue of retirement blossoms into a major financial concern.

You're Never Too Young to Invest

In investing, as in life, we can't predict the future. Nevertheless, history serves as a good indicator of what may or may not happen. Historically, investors who have invested regularly over many years have been amply rewarded. The result: The sooner you start to invest, and the more investing becomes a rule and not an exception to your financial planning, the greater the chances of your success are.

You're Never Too Old to Invest

If your children have been put through school and the mortgage is mostly paid off, start concentrating on accumulating enough capital for a comfortable retirement. If, on the other hand, one or more children are still college-bound, you may well have to defer *some* of your retirement-oriented investing for a *few* more years.

The Earlier You Start, the Better

Ideally, you will have started a savings and investment regimen in your twenties or early thirties—and have stayed with it. The benefits are obvious, as the following table shows.

Unfortunately, most of us don't think about our as-yet unborn children's college tuitions, let alone funding our own retirement while we're still young.

YOU'RE NEVER TOO YOUNG TO START SAVING

IF YOU START SAVING $2,000 AT AGE	THE TOTAL AMOUNT YOU'VE SAVED IS	AT AGE 65, YOU'LL HAVE
19	$92,000	$837,000
27	$76,000	$441,000
37	$56,000	$191,000
47	$36,000	$75,000

Note: Assumes annual $2,000 savings until age 65 and an 8% annual growth rate.

Commonly Selected Investment Alternatives

Investing is a serious business. Many investments are appropriate for serious investors, while others are appropriate only for seriously impaired investors. The following table reflects my obviously biased opinion about various good, not-so-good, and downright awful investments.

MY BIASED ASSESSMENT OF INVESTMENTS

TYPE OF INVESTMENT	ASSESSMENT

Stock and Other "Ownership" Investments

COMMON STOCK...................................Has been, is, and will continue to be good long-term inflation hedge. Buy and hold.

PREFERRED STOCK ....Not very exciting unless you want the dividend income.

STOCK MUTUAL FUNDS...........................Good way to get diversification; cheap way to have your money managed.

OPTIONS ....For suckers or professional investors. You are probably not the latter and hopefully not the former.

COMMODITY FUTURES............................For the gullible.

STOCK–INDEX FUTURES ....Has a role in sophisticated portfolio-hedging strategies, which means they're not for you.

IPOS (INITIAL PUBLIC OFFERINGS)..................You don't pay a commission on a new issue, which » helps offset the loss you will probably experience after you buy one.

FOREIGN STOCKS...................................There is always a bull market somewhere in the world. Difficult to evaluate, so use international mutual funds.

PRECIOUS METALS.................................The only reason you should own a lot of gold is if you need to have a lot of teeth filled.

COLLECTIBLES ....Nice to sit on, walk on, or look at. Don't expect to retire on the profits.

Interest-Earning Investments

CERTIFICATES OF DEPOSIT.........................Generally lackluster returns after you finish giving Uncle Sam his piece of the interest. Chances are your local bank doesn't offer the best rates you can get, so shop around.

TREASURY SECURITIES.............................Yields fluctuate, and they usually become attractive once or twice per year. Safe, but how much safety do you need?

MORTGAGE-BACKED SECURITIES.....................Nice yields, but ever-present danger of getting back principal if interest rates drop.

MUNICIPAL BONDS ....Compare muni returns against after-tax returns on taxable securities. You may well find munis to be preferable.

CORPORATE BONDS ....Okay if you can get a much better yield than Treasuries. Otherwise, they don't justify the risk.

JUNK BONDS ....Reserved for people who like high income and deteriorating principal.

FOREIGN BONDS..................................Emerging investment area that is highly specialized; usually subjects you to currency risk. Buy through mutual funds only.

BOND MUTUAL FUNDS..............................Good way to let someone else worry about the direction of interest rates. Offers diversification and inexpensive management.

SAVINGS ACCOUNTS ....Better than nothing, but not much better.

U.S. SAVINGS BONDS ....Nice gift—much better than they used to be.

MONEY-MARKET FUNDS ....A temporary parking place only, please, since you »

---

can't beat inflation by very much on an after-tax basis. Money-market mutual funds almost always beat bank money-market accounts. Beware of "global" money-market funds.

Real Estate Investments

INCOME-PRODUCING REAL ESTATE ....The average person's best route to wealth, if you buy at the right price and can stomach being a landlord.

UNDEVELOPED LAND ....An expensive little lot is better than a lot of cheap lots. In other words, 50 square feet in Manhattan, New York, is a better investment than 50 square miles in Manhattan, Montana.

LIMITED PARTNERSHIPS ....Probably a good investment—next century. In the meantime, perhaps one deal in a hundred is worthwhile.

ANY "NEW" INVESTMENT, LIKE "LONG BOND
YIELD DECREASE WARRANTS" ....Excellent money-making opportunity, if you happen to be selling them to an unsuspecting public.

PRINCIPLES OF SUCCESSFUL INVESTING

- The only way you can invest is to save money. The only way you can save money is to spend less than you earn. The only way you can spend less than you earn is to live beneath your means.

- Invest so that your money will grow faster than inflation.

- Don't rely on your pension and Social Security benefits alone for a comfortable retirement income that will keep pace with inflation.

- Your financial well-being is your own responsibility. Don't rely too much on others to help you achieve it.

Managing Your Investments

Divide and Conquer

Successful investors spread their money around. Your money should be invested in various types of securities. For example, your interest-earning investments might consist of short-term investments (money-market accounts, certificates of deposit) and longer-term investments like municipal bonds, corporate bonds, and Treasury bonds—or bond mutual funds that invest in those types of securities.

Control Your Investments

Taking control of your investments means staying involved and keeping up to date on market issues and investment particulars. If you rely on someone to recommend investments, fine, but be sure that you understand each investment and decide whether it is appropriate for you. If you develop a sensible, disciplined, and consistent approach to investing, you can be your own best investment manager—or you can ask the most effective questions and receive the most important answers from your own investment manager.

Monitor Your Investments

In order to manage your money more effectively, you need to spend some time (not a lot of time) keeping up to date with market conditions in general and your own investments in particular. Whatever time you spend will be time well spent.

Don't Worry, Be Happy

For the beginning investor, the temptation to track investments can easily become an obsession. But don't subscribe to all sorts of investment newsletters. Rather, focus on the well-respected publications, including *Money* magazine and *Kiplinger's Personal Finance* magazine. They are good sources for novice investors to learn about the market. But the best source remains *The Wall Street Journal.* There you will find in-depth articles on investing and current information on the goings-on in the investment markets. Market analysis, economic reports, hot and cold stocks are scrutinized. Other sources of information are listed below.

Where to Find the Information You Need

When it comes to investing in stocks and bonds, information is an essential asset. However, many investors never use the information that is available to them. For example, if you are looking for basic financial information about a particular company that you think you might invest in, you can request that company's annual report.

Annual report

An annual report—usually free for the asking—is a company's summary statement about its past and most recent financial health. In an annual report you will find the company's financial statements, as well as a lot of commentary. Annual reports tend to be glossy marketing tools rather than substantial disclosures, but they're a good item to have on hand when making a decision about investing in the company.

Analyst's recommendations

Every stock brokerage firm has a bevy of analysts who produce numerous reports on particular companies, industries, and even the economy in general. Analysts' reports are available from your broker, or may be available from a brokerage house with whom you are considering opening up an account. Call and find out.

Standard & Poor's

S&P is a great source for stock and bond reports. The S&P *Stock Reports*, available at larger public and university libraries, provides substantial historical and current performances of thousands of stocks. S&P also publishes a monthly *Stock Guide* which tracks the performance of more than five thousand stocks.

Moody's investors services

Like S&P, Moody's is considered to be an invaluable source by professional and nonprofessional investors alike. Again, it lists substantial company data that you can use to determine the health of a particular investment prospect. Like the S&P stock manuals, Moody's should be available at larger public libraries.

The financial press

The Wall Street Journal, Barron's, and *Investor's Daily* are the three main financial newspapers. (*Barron's* is a weekly; the other two are dailies.)

Financial magazines

Financial magazines are increasing in number. Many are specifically investor-oriented, while some focus more on the overall economy, market and business. *Kiplinger's Personal Finance, Money, Worth, Financial World, Forbes, Business Week,* and *The Economist* are the tip of the iceberg.

Value Line investment survey

Value Line surveys 1,700 stocks and provides some of the best analysis in the business. You should be able to find Value Line at your public library.

On-line information

If you have a computer and are willing to pay for the service, you can link up to direct sources of stock information from a variety of databases.

How to Read the Financial Pages

T he stock, bond, and mutual fund listings in the financial pages contain abbreviations, symbols, and words that make them seem inscrutable to the novice investor. The following is a stock, bond, and mutual fund listing primer.

Stocks

- **52 WEEKS HI/LO:** the highest and lowest price per share of the stock during the previous fifty-two weeks

- **STOCK:** the name of the issuer

- **SYM:** the stock's trading symbol

- **DIV:** the latest annual dividend paid by the stock

- **YLD:** the stock's latest annual dividend, expressed as a percentage of the stock's price on that day

- **PE:** the price/earnings ratio—the price of a stock divided by the issuing company's past four quarters of earnings

- **HI/LO/CLOSE:** the stock's volatility, expressed in terms of a single share's price movement on that day. The close is what the price of the stock will open at on the next trading day

- **S OR X:** these symbols may appear in the left-hand column. An *s* indicates that the stock has split or the company issued a stock dividend within the last year. An *x* stands for "ex-dividend," meaning that new investors won't receive the next dividend.

Bonds

- **ISSUE:** the issuer's name

- **COUPON:** interest rate at which the bond was issued

- **MAT:** maturity date—the year in which the bond matures

- **PRICE:** the price at which the bond closed. For example, a price of 98 3/4 means it closed at 98 3/4 percent per $1,000 of par value, or $988.

- **CHG:** change reflects the amount at which the bond closed, as compared with its previous day's closing

- **BID YLD:** the bond's yield to maturity

- **CV:** the issue is a convertible bond—that is, it can be exchanged for a fixed number of shares of common stock from the issuer

Mutual Funds

- **NAV:** net asset value, or what a share of the fund is worth today

- **OFFER PRICE:** what you would pay per share were you to purchase shares in the fund that day

- **P:** the fund charges a 12b-1 fee

- **T:** the fund charges both a 12b-1 fee and a redemption fee

- **NL:** no load, meaning there are no up-front sales charges

- **R:** redemption charge. (Some are as high as six percent!)

- **X:** ex-dividend, meaning that new share buyers will not receive the fund's next dividend payout

- **NOTE** that a fund can have either a "p" or an "r" symbol listed next to it and still be called a no-load fund. However, a fund with a "t" cannot be so listed.

Common Mistakes Investors Make and How to Avoid Them

Definition

12b-1 fee: A fee charged by some funds to pay for distribution costs, such as advertising and broker compensation. This fee is taken out of the fund assets.

Even well-educated investors sometimes make mistakes. Here are cures for the common mistakes they make. The saying goes, "The way to win in investing is to avoid losing." But there is a lot more to achieving investment success than avoiding bad investments.

Investing Too Conservatively

Many first-time as well as experienced investors erroneously believe that they cannot afford to take any risk in their investing—especially as they near or enter retirement. The result—they restrict all or most of their investments to safe but low-yielding securities like money-market accounts and CDs. Investing too conservatively always risks losing purchasing power because investment returns simply do not keep up with the always-increasing cost of living.

Solution

If your investments don't include a generous portion of securities with capital-appreciation potential like stocks, gradually move some of your money into stocks. You need not restructure your portfolio overnight, but don't delay too long, either. You need to start investing for capital appreciation so that you can enjoy inflation-protected income for the rest of your life.

Chasing Yield

Yields on interest-earning investments can rise and decline dramatically. Many investors, particularly those who are retired on fixed incomes, have become so concerned about declining yields on their short-term investments that they end up, often unknowingly, taking on a lot more risk in order to gain more yield. Remember that the higher the yield, the higher the risk, in spite of what many investment salespeople like to tell you.

Solution

Don't blindly chase high-yielding investments. Instead, shop carefully for better yields that you can get now, taking into consideration the risk inherent in each investment that you're considering.

Making Inappropriate Investments

It's no surprise that unscrupulous salespeople love to sell shoddy investments to novice investors and gullible senior citizens. Despite being forewarned, many end up making investments that are far too risky or are defrauded outright.

Solution

Stick to investments that you understand. If you're considering a new investment, don't rush into it. Always ask someone you trust to review your contemplated investment. Also, research your intended investment to see how well it has performed in the past. While the past won't guarantee future success, it can serve as a sound indicator of the type of company or security you're investing in.

Overemphasizing Income Tax Savings

The gyrations many people go through in order to save taxes on their investments are astonishing. Many fail to realize that tax rates now are considerably lower than they were in the past and that, as a result, there is less of a need to focus on tax savings as an investment issue. (There's a lot of difference between a 45 percent to 50 percent federal income tax rate and 28 percent to 31 percent rate.) Nevertheless, many investors, in their zeal to avoid paying taxes on their investments, end up with less money.

Solution

Consider tax-free investments (see Chapter 57 for details). Always compare the after-tax equivalent of alternative taxable investments with tax-exempt investments. While municipal bonds and tax-deferred retirement plans can provide attractive investment opportunities, don't overlook the opportunity provided by taxable investments as well.

Holding On to Investments for Sentimental Reasons

Some people insist on holding on to investments for a variety of sentimental reasons—at great expense. Such attachments almost always lead to lousy investment performance.

Solution

Unless you can afford to do otherwise, view each of your investments with the cold detachment of a grizzled money manager. If a stock or bond no longer meets your investment objectives, sell it. If you simply have to keep some of it for sentimental purposes, sell the rest.

Maintaining Too Many Investment Accounts

Why is it that when people reach the age where they can finally devote some attention to managing their investments, they begin opening up numerous investment accounts? The only people who benefit from this are those who like to receive stacks of statements in the mail and those who enjoy the added complexity that multiple investment accounts provide at tax time.

Solution

If you are awash with accounts, start consolidating them so that you can ease your investment life a bit. Some of the big discount brokerage firms now offer accounts that allow you to combine no-load mutual funds with all the other kinds of investments traditionally offered by discount brokers into one account. Check them out.

Failing to Take Advantage of Mutual Funds

There's probably no better investment vehicle for individual investors. Mutual funds have really come into their own over the past decade, and they offer marvelous opportunities for those active and not-so-active investors (see Chapter 59).

Solution

If you haven't already, look into mutual funds. Go to the library to obtain some background information and/or contact the large mutual fund companies who will gladly send you detailed information on mutual fund investing. (For a list of no-load mutual fund companies, see page 528.)

Giving Up Control

Perhaps the biggest mistake that investors can make is giving up control over their investments to someone else. "I don't want to be bothered with my investments anymore. You manage my investments for me" is music to the ears of an unscrupulous investment adviser. It's a tried-and-true recipe for disaster.

Solution

Never, never, never lose control of your investments. If you reach a time when you feel that you're unable to manage them adequately, be absolutely certain that whomever you entrust them with is indeed totally trustworthy. What's more, ask a relative or close friend to help you monitor the activities of your investment manager.

TEN GREAT WAYS TO SAVE MONEY ON YOUR INVESTMENTS

One of the best things about living beneath your means is that you have money to invest. But, there are numerous ways to continue cutting your expenses in the investment arena. Why waste part of your hard-earned savings by paying more than you need to have your money invested or, worse, by making money-losing investment decisions? The key to investing successfully and parsimoniously is to take control of your own investments. There is no reason why you can't be an effective and efficient manager of your own investments, whether you have $1,000 or $100,000 to invest.

1. **DON'T INVEST IN ANYTHING YOU DON'T UNDERSTAND.** If the person who's trying to sell you an investment can't explain it to your satisfaction in one sentence, don't buy it. Even if you make your own investment decisions, never invest in anything that you have difficulty understanding.

2. **DON'T AUTOMATICALLY FOLLOW THE ADVICE OF THE EXPERTS.** They're often wrong, and they may tempt you to make big (and expensive) changes in your investments.

3. **BUY NO-LOAD OR LOW-LOAD MUTUAL FUNDS.** I can't understand why people want to pay someone four, five, even eight percent to recommend a mutual fund when, with very little effort, you could select an equivalent or better fund with little or no sales commission.

4. **USE DISCOUNT BROKERS.** If you want to make good investment decisions, make them yourself, and when you do so, use discount brokerage firms. (A list of discount brokers appears on page 467.) They'll save you a lot of money on commissions, and they won't call you at dinnertime to recommend that you buy "Nikkei put warrant" or some other get-poor-quickly investment.

»

5. **COMBINE YOUR INVESTMENT ACCOUNTS SO THAT YOU PAY ONLY ONE ACCOUNT MAINTENANCE FEE.** Many people have far too many investment accounts: a little bit here, a little bit there. While you might not realize it, each of those accounts is probably being hit with an annual maintenance fee.

6. **BUY STOCK THROUGH A DIVIDEND REINVESTMENT PROGRAM.** This is one of the best inventions since thumbs. DRPs, as they're affectionately called, allow you to buy additional shares of the stock you already own without paying a commission. It's a nice, low-cost way to build up a stock portfolio with a small amount of money, regularly invested.

7. **ASK YOUR BROKER FOR A BREAK ON COMMISSIONS.** If you do business with a stockbroker, ask for a reduction in the commissions that he or she charges. Many investors, particularly active ones, receive a reduction in commissions just for the asking. The brokerage business is very competitive, and you may be pleasantly surprised to find that even as a smaller investor you can get commission reductions.

8. **DON'T BUY A VACATION HOME AS AN INVESTMENT.** Vacation homes are a huge expense, and many people buy them with the expectation that they will generate a lot of rent. Don't believe what the people trying to sell you the home say. Its rent potential probably won't come anywhere near their estimates.

9. **DON'T BUY A "GET RICH QUICK IN REAL ESTATE" COURSE.** You've seen them on late-night television, promising you endless riches if you follow their real estate investment techniques. Aren't they generous to share their knowledge for a mere $200? If you want to make quick money in real estate, you should write one of these courses and go on television instead.

10. **BUY AND HOLD.** You have nothing to gain from frequently changing your investments. The only thing you end up doing is to pay a lot of commissions that slowly but steadily eat away at your investments. The only time your family benefits from your frequent trading is if your son or daughter is a stockbroker—and one who works for you. Select your investments carefully, and you should be able to hold on to them for a long time.

Creating an All-Weather Portfolio

Think of an all-weather portfolio as your very own Noah's ark. This chapter focuses on building, maintaining, and evaluating a portfolio of investments that will help you achieve your financial dreams. You don't have to have megabucks in order to have an investment portfolio. In fact, you can invest your money just as the billion-dollar pension funds do with as little as $1,000. I will take you step by step through this process. You'll be happy to know that it isn't very difficult once you understand what you want to accomplish in your financial life.

Many experts predict that the volatility in the stock, bond, and real estate markets that was so prevalent in the late 1980s and early 1990s will become the norm for the rest of the decade and beyond. Therefore, your all-weather portfolio must be well diversified. One crucial element of diversification is asset allocation—that is, the proportion of money you put into the various investment categories. In addition, you will have to learn to cope with continuing rather than sporadic market jitters.

It's crucial to know why you're investing. Everyone invests for different reasons, even if they share one overall goal—that of achieving financial security for themselves and their loved ones. Common investment goals include providing an emergency fund for unforeseen contingencies, meeting major expenses—a first house, college education, a daughter's wedding—and, most important, funding a comfortable retirement while accumulating an estate to pass on to future generations.

If you are already retired, you must ensure that your portfolio will provide you with the income necessary to meet ever-increasing living expenses. Without establishing objectives that account for your current financial situation as well as your longer-term financial needs, you'll have difficulty achieving your ultimate goal of financial security. Therefore, you need to know exactly what you want to accomplish with your investments in order to construct a suitable all-weather portfolio.

Once you have a clear idea of your investment goals, you should proceed with the following steps.

Step 1: Evaluate Your Current Portfolio Holdings

Reviewing and evaluating your current investments is one of the most important components of portfolio planning. Often, you'll find you have not paid sufficient attention to your investments, both from the standpoint of asset allocation and from the standpoint of selecting appropriate individual investments. You should also be sure to consider *all* investments over which you have control, either as to individual security selection and/or asset allocation. Most of us tend to review our investment accounts separately when they should be evaluated in their totality. Don't forget to include your retirement accounts in your evaluation—IRAs, 401(k) plans, and variable annuities. If you are involved in a company pension plan where you have a say as to how your portion of the plan is allocated between stocks and interest-earning investments—teachers and other employees of educational institutions that participate in TIAA/CREF, for example—be sure to throw them into your asset allocation pot, too. (The worksheet at the end of this chapter can help you summarize your investments.)

Step 2: Determine an Appropriate Allocation of Investment Assets

After evaluating your investment objectives and needs, and determining the asset allocation of your current investment holdings, you can begin to consider long-term asset allocation parameters. Allocating your investments prudently is as important to your investment success as is selecting good individual securities.

Step 3: Devise a Portfolio Redeployment Program

More often than not, your comparison will reveal substantial differences between how your investments are currently allocated and how they ought to be allocated. Many people invest in extremes, often resulting in either too much or too little investment risk. Similar to the asset allocation decision itself, devising a portfolio redeployment strategy requires a good deal of planning and judgment. Generally, if you find the need to make a significant restructuring in your portfolio, shift your investments gradually. Don't make a rapid reallocation. (See page 460 for an illustration of a gradual redeployment.)

Smart Money Move

Don't evaluate your investments one account at a time. The only way to get a good overview is to review all accounts together, including both personal and retirement accounts.

Step 4: Regularly Monitor Your Portfolio Composition and Performance

Monitoring your investment portfolio is a dynamic process because investment conditions are always changing. You should therefore review your portfolio composition and performance regularly. The extent of your involvement may range from periodically reviewing your holdings to being actively involved in investment selection. Don't get into the habit of worrying about your investments on a daily or even weekly basis, however. It will only make you anxious and more likely to make inappropriate changes in your investments.

Step 5: Coordinate Your Portfolio with Other Financial-Planning Areas

Don't forget that your investment portfolio plan may affect other important areas of your personal financial planning, such as income taxes, preparing for retirement, and structuring your estate to minimize estate taxes.

Investor, Know Thyself

Before getting into the nitty-gritty of asset allocation and creating a portfolio that's right for you, you should spend some time reviewing your own situation—age, marital status, current income and income prospects, and life-style. You'll do a better job putting together your portfolio if you understand how these "personal factors" should affect your investment planning.

Age

Age is *always* an important investment consideration because it creates a natural time horizon for your investment program. The horizon, or limit, is not necessarily death but could be that time when the main stream of your income is likely to decline or cease. Retirement is clearly the time when income usually declines. You invest to make up for this shortfall. In general, the younger you are, the more risk you can afford to take because your longer investment horizon provides time to make up for investment losses. That doesn't mean that if you are older—even retired—you should invest very conservatively. Even people in their sixties and seventies need to invest for growth as well as income because they will still live long enough to be affected by inflation.

Marriage and Family

Your marital status or marriage plans must also be accounted for in your investment planning, including whether you and your spouse have or plan to have children. If children are in the picture, you will need to set aside even more of your income to meet child-rearing and education costs. Of course, those who have children have more difficulty saving than those who don't, but who said life is fair? A two-income family may be able to set aside a higher portion of income for investment, although they all too often succumb to a high-spending yuppie life-style—which, of course, they will live to regret later on.

When the high cost of raising children is behind you, you may well be in a position where your savings have been depleted (remember those tuition bills?) and need substantial rejuvenation. However, don't let the apparent need to quick-fix your retirement coffers drive you to risky investments. With enough planning, you will be able to develop an all-weather portfolio that fits your current financial reality to your retirement dreams.

Income

Your current and potential income influences how much you can invest and how much risk you can afford to take. For example, if your income allows you to invest $4,000 each year, or if your modest annual savings start to accumulate, then you probably can't invest in individual stocks and bonds, but you could consider stock and bond mutual funds. On the other hand, if you can invest considerable sums each year, individual securities together with mutual funds make good sense, as might taking somewhat more risk in your investing.

Life-styles of the Rich and Not-Yet-Rich

Your life-style, particularly your spending habits, may also influence how you structure your portfolio. People who are prone to incurring large, unanticipated expenses, for example, require a higher percentage of liquid investments, since the forced sale of illiquid investments, such as real estate, could result in severe losses.

Asset Allocation

Asset allocation involves deciding how much of the money you have available for investments should be placed in each of the major investment categories: stocks, interest-earning investments, and if you are so inclined, real estate. At another level, asset allocation involves divvying up your investments within each category. For example, the portion which you may want to invest in stocks would normally be subdivided between directly owned stocks and stock mutual funds. Further, within the stock mutual fund area you'll need to decide how much of your investments should be placed in higher-risk, aggressive stock funds, more conservative stock funds, and international stock funds.

Definition

Asset Allocation: The process of deciding upon the portion of your savings that are invested in stocks, interest-earning securities, and perhaps real estate.

Asset allocation can be a very challenging and complex task if you want to make it so. You can consider many disparate and potentially volatile factors in deciding how to invest your money, including stock market conditions, interest rates, economic prospects, tax regulations, and investment product availability, not to mention your own personal finances. Confronted with all that, it's no wonder that so many investors prefer to focus on individual investments— for example, a stock mutual fund, a municipal bond, or a small apartment building—rather than to step back and look at investments in their totality. Thus, many people pay insufficient attention to asset allocation.

There is a middle ground, however. The problem with paying too little attention to asset allocation is that you really don't have a long-term investment plan. Your investments are probably inappropriately allocated, and unfortunately, you don't find that out until it's almost too late. On the other extreme, those who become obsessed with market conditions and the opinions of so-called experts are likely to flip-flop their asset allocation all over the place, which has been shown from time immemorial to be a recipe for investment mediocrity.

I like to refer to the middle ground as a "permanent portfolio structure." In other words, once you have determined an appropriate asset allocation—one that includes generous proportions of stocks and bonds—then you can stick with it over the long run. There's really no need to vary your asset allocation dramatically from the parameters you establish. History has shown that investors who maintain a relatively stable mix of investments do very well over the long run. Those who don't do this either invest in extremes or change their allocations frequently and often precipitously. In essence, they overreact.

Permanent portfolio structure doesn't mean that you never change your asset allocation. But you never make a *rapid* change in it. If you have been investing 50 percent of your money in stocks, for example, and you are particularly bearish on stocks, you may want to lighten up on your stock exposure somewhat. But since no one knows for sure which direction the market is going in, I wouldn't recommend going below 40 percent in the stock and stock fund investment category.

One Exception

If you become a short-term investor, you may want to invest more conservatively than you otherwise would. If you are about to buy a home, for example, or your children are going to start college in a few years, you would probably want to reduce the amount of stock investments that are earmarked for those purposes significantly, if not totally. The reason for this is that you can't afford the risk of a sharp decline of stock prices because you'll need the money within a short period of time.

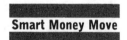

Smart Money Move

Asset allocation should be viewed as a relatively static apportionment of your investments, as opposed to one that involves frequent reallocation in response to market and economic conditions.

Four Steps to Investment Success

I 'll now explain the four-step asset allocation process. Later on, I'll illustrate it, so that you can understand how straightforward asset allocation can be.

Step 1

Determine the percentage of total available funds that should be invested in each of the three major investment categories (that is, stock investments, interest-earning investments, and real estate investments).

If you are not interested in real estate investments, the allocation will be between stock and interest-earning securities. Most of the asset-allocation illustrations that appear later in this chapter assume that you are not investing in real estate. There is certainly nothing wrong with avoiding real estate, particularly given the calamities that have befallen real estate investors in many areas of the country over the past few years.

Step 2

Evaluate which general kinds of investment vehicles within each category are suitable. This could be direct ownership of stocks, bonds, and real estate, or indirect ownership by means of mutual funds or real estate limited partnerships. Most often, the appropriate course is one of diversifying across investment vehicles. With respect to stock investments, for example, you may be best served by having some of your portfolio invested directly in specific company shares and some of it invested indirectly in stock mutual fund shares.

Step 3

Break down the general categories of investment into specific industry, market, or fund categories. Appropriate directly owned interest-earning investments might consist of short-term securities (like money-market accounts and Treasury bills) and long-term securities (like municipal bonds, government bonds, and corporate bonds). Assuming that you should also be invested in bond mutual funds, as is usually the case, you might want municipal bond funds, corporate bond funds, and convertible bond funds. The percentage or dollar amount of each investment in each specific category should also be decided.

Step 4

Select specific investments within each of the industry or fund categories delineated in the third step. Select a particular bond or stock issue or mutual fund, for example.

Asset Allocation Illustrated

I nvesting effectively is crucial to your ultimate financial well-being. The four-step process can help you develop your own plan to guide you both in deciding upon the types of investments to make and in reviewing your investments periodically. *Periodically* doesn't mean every day; otherwise, you'll become so concerned that you're likely to make investment changes too frequently. Rather, if you establish some sensible criteria now, you will be able to invest wisely and well without spending an inordinate amount of time worrying about your investments.

As the investment process is illustrated, I will periodically refer to the "Investment Allocation" figure that follows. It serves as the basis for your own investment decision-making.

INVESTMENT ALLOCATION

METHOD OF OWNERSHIP	INVESTMENT CATEGORY		
	STOCK	INTEREST-EARNING	REAL ESTATE
DIRECT OWNERSHIP			
INDIRECT OWNERSHIP (MUTUAL FUND/PARTNERSHIP)			

The following example shows how an appropriate investment "portfolio" can be put together.

Example

Rhea Bilitate, a therapist, has managed to set aside $25,000 over the past few years, which is now sitting in a money-market account. She has just read the above four steps to investment success and is ready to invest her money more sensibly.

Step 1

She decides that, while she may want to invest in real estate sometime in the future, she doesn't have enough money yet, and therefore she should restrict her investments to stocks and interest-earning securities. She decides that 60 percent of her $25,000, or $15,000, should be invested in stocks, and 40 percent, or $10,000, should be invested in interest-earning securities. (Note that most pension funds invest about 60 percent of their assets in stocks.)

STEP 1: DECIDING ON PROPORTION TO BE INVESTED IN EACH CATEGORY

METHOD OF OWNERSHIP	INVESTMENT CATEGORY		
	STOCK	INTEREST-EARNING	REAL ESTATE
DIRECT OWNERSHIP	60% ($15,000)	40% ($10,000)	0%
INDIRECT OWNERSHIP (MUTUAL FUND/PARTNERSHIP)			

Step 2

Because her portfolio isn't yet very large (although she fully expects it will be eventually), Rhea plans to invest most of her money in mutual funds. Nevertheless, she wants to become familiar with "direct" investing as well. So, she is going to invest $5,000 in stocks and $3,000 in directly owned interest-earning investments.

STEP 2: DECIDING HOW MUCH TO INVEST DIRECTLY AND INDIRECTLY

METHOD OF OWNERSHIP	INVESTMENT CATEGORY	
	STOCK	INTEREST-EARNING
DIRECT OWNERSHIP	$5,000	$3,000
INDIRECT OWNERSHIP (MUTUAL FUND/PARTNERSHIP)	$10,000	$7,000
GRAND TOTAL	$15,000	$10,000

Step 3

Rhea next needs to decide on the kinds of securities she will purchase within each of the four categories. After some deliberation, she decides upon the investments indicated in the figure for Step 3.

STEP 3: DECIDING ON APPROPRIATE KINDS OF INVESTMENTS

METHOD OF OWNERSHIP	INVESTMENT CATEGORY			
	STOCK		INTEREST-EARNING	
DIRECT OWNERSHIP	HIGH QUALITY GROWTH STOCK	$2,500		
	BLUE CHIP STOCK	2,500	CERTIFICATE OF DEPOSIT	$3,000
	TOTAL	$5,000	TOTAL	$3,000
INDIRECT OWNERSHIP (MUTUAL FUND/PARTNERSHIP)	MAXIMUM CAPITAL GAINS FUND	$3,000		
	GROWTH AND INCOME FUND	5,000	GOVERNMENT SECURITIES FUND	$4,000
	INTERNATIONAL STOCK FUND	2,000	CORPORATE BOND FUND	3,000
	TOTAL	$10,000	TOTAL	$7,000
	GRAND TOTAL	$15,000	GRAND TOTAL	$10,000

Step 4

Rhea now needs to select specific investments for each of the categories in which she has decided to invest. We will leave that up to her, although she, as well as you, might benefit from the investment suggestions contained in Chapters 55–62.

Issues in Asset Allocation

T he following guidelines will be helpful in determining the best way to allocate (or reallocate) your investments.

Avoid Extremes

All too often, investors invest in extremes. Even though you may think you have a well-balanced and well-diversified portfolio, you may be overlooking some kinds of investments that will help you achieve investment success. Therefore, before you do anything, you need to figure out how much of your total available investments (both now and in the future) should be invested in each of the three major investment categories: stock, interest-earning investments, and real estate. Some people may not be interested in real estate, in which case the allocation is between stock and interest-earning investments.

Younger People

Younger and middle-age people should weight their investments in favor of stocks and, if they are so inclined, real estate, because these investments have the best chance of beating inflation and producing good long-term returns. However, some of the portfolio should probably remain conservatively invested. A typical investment allocation for younger people is 40 percent stock, 30 percent interest-earning investments, and 30 percent real estate (excluding the family home). Most people prefer not to invest in real estate. They might choose an allocation of 60 percent stock and 40 percent interest-earning investments, or 50 percent–50 percent, which is perfectly okay and a lot easier to remember. Numerous studies of long-term stock and bond performance have indicated that a general portfolio mix of 50 to 60 percent stock and 40 percent to 50 percent interest-earning investments will provide very good long-term returns without taking too much risk.

Preretirees

Preretirees who are within about ten years of retirement should begin a gradual shift so that they increase the proportion of their money invested in more conservative securities. This tactic lessens the effects of being caught in a stock market downturn or real estate slump. Younger people have a longer "investment horizon" and can therefore weather the effects of a bear market better. If you, like most people, will need the portfolio to help meet your living expenses, an appropriate investment mix for imminent retirees might consist of 45 percent stocks and 55 percent interest-earning investments or, if you have real estate invest-ments, 30 percent stock, 20 percent real estate, and 50 percent interest-earning investments.

Retirees

Similarly, if you are retired, the amount of risk you can afford in your portfolio depends upon the extent to which you will have to rely on the funds to meet living expenses. Many retirees, of course, prefer investments that yield current income—either interest-earning securities or dividend-paying stocks. Since you also need capital appreciation to fund a (hopefully) long retirement, you should not abandon stocks entirely. Generally, unless you are very elderly, you should maintain about 40 percent of your portfolio in stocks and stock funds. Many retired people find that for the first time in their lives they have sufficient time to devote to stock market investing, and many do quite well at it.

Real Estate

Consider real estate on its economic merits, not its tax merits. For people who can afford it, real estate could be a component of a well-balanced portfolio because its long-term perfor-mance has been quite strong. For tips on buying real estate, see Chapter 60.

All-Weather Portfolios for the Rich and Not-Yet-Rich

We've said a lot about structuring an investment portfolio and selecting appropri-ate investments. Now we can look at how this might be done in real life. Incidentally, the same principles apply to both small and large portfolios. So the following illustrations will take you from a $1,000 portfolio to a $500,000 portfolio. All of the illustrations except for the $500,000 portfolio assume that the investor wants to main-tain an allocation of 50 percent stock investments and 50 percent interest-earning invest-ments—which, by the way, isn't a bad split for most of us.

The $1,000 Portfolio—Just the Beginning

What, a $1,000 investment portfolio? Why not? Unless you're some kind of heir, everyone starts at zero (or less). There's no reason why you shouldn't begin to develop good habits by investing your $1,000 much as a pension manager handles a multibillion-dollar portfolio. The rules are the same.

You can start out by putting $500 into a growth and income stock mutual fund and $500 into a government securities fund. Incidentally, there are many good mutual funds that have investment minimums of $500 or less. Alternatively, you could invest the $1,000 in a "balanced" mutual fund, which consists of both stock and interest-earning securities. The $1,000 portfolio is presented below.

SAMPLE $1,000 PORTFOLIO

METHOD OF OWNERSHIP	INVESTMENT CATEGORY	
	STOCK	INTEREST–EARNING
DIRECT OWNERSHIP		
INDIRECT OWNERSHIP (MUTUAL FUND)	GROWTH AND INCOME FUND $500	GOVERNMENT SECURITIES FUND $500

The $10,000 Portfolio—Passing Through

When you have $10,000 to invest, you can begin to expand your horizons somewhat, although you will still probably want to restrict your holdings to mutual funds and perhaps a CD. You aren't quite at a level where you can start to make direct investments. But don't fret—there are a lot of good mutual funds that will help you meet your investment objectives.

As the following table shows, you can divide your portfolio among several mutual funds. These funds will provide diversification as well as professional management of your hard-earned savings.

SAMPLE $10,000 PORTFOLIO

METHOD OF OWNERSHIP	INVESTMENT CATEGORY	
	STOCK	INTEREST–EARNING
DIRECT OWNERSHIP		
INDIRECT OWNERSHIP (MUTUAL FUND)	AGGRESSIVE GROWTH FUND $2,000 GROWTH AND INCOME FUND 3,000 TOTAL $5,000	GOVERNMENT SECURITIES FUND $3,000 CORPORATE BOND FUND 2,000 TOTAL $5,000

The $100,000 Portfolio—Getting There

Once your portfolio exceeds $20,000 or so, you can begin to make directly owned investments in stock and interest-earning securities if you want to. The illustration shows how a $100,000 portfolio might be structured so that $25,000 is invested in each of the four "boxes," thereby maintaining a 50 percent–50 percent split between total stock investments and total interest-earning investments. The directly owned stocks "box" includes $5,000 in each of five high-quality stocks. Most of the dividend-paying companies in which you would want to invest have dividend reinvestment programs. Be sure to participate in them so that your dividend checks can be used to purchase more stock.

The larger portfolio allows you to invest in a wider range of securities. Note that the stock mutual funds component now includes investments in an international fund and a small company fund.

Determining an appropriate split between directly owned and indirectly owned investments depends primarily on your experience with investing and the amount of time you can devote to monitoring your investments. In general, the less experience you have and/or the less time you have, the higher the proportion that should be invested indirectly in mutual funds. For a small annual fee, you pay experienced mutual fund managers to devote all or most of their time to managing your money.

SAMPLE $100,000 PORTFOLIO

METHOD OF OWNERSHIP	INVESTMENT CATEGORY			
	STOCK		INTEREST-EARNING	
DIRECT OWNERSHIP	$5,000 IN EACH OF FIVE HIGH-QUALITY BLUE CHIP STOCKS AND GROWTH STOCKS		CD	$5,000
			MUNICIPAL BONDS	10,000
			CORPORATE BONDS	10,000
	TOTAL	$25,000	TOTAL	$25,000
INDIRECT OWNERSHIP (MUTUAL FUND/PARTNERSHIP)	AGGRESSIVE GROWTH FUND	$5,000		
	GROWTH AND INCOME FUND	10,000	GOVERNMENT SECURITIES FUND	$10,000
	INTERNATIONAL FUND	5,000	MUNICIPAL BOND FUND	10,000
	SMALL COMPANY FUND	5,000	CORPORATE BOND FUND	5,000
	TOTAL	$25,000	TOTAL	$25,000

The $500,000 Portfolio—Wow!

In addition to making more of the same investments you made for your first $100,000, when (note that I don't say "if," because I have a lot of confidence in you) your portfolio exceeds

$100,000, you can begin to consider a number of additional investments, including: more speculative stocks and stock mutual funds, individual purchases of government securities and mortgage-backed securities, income-producing real estate, undeveloped land, and real estate limited partnerships. Tax-deferred annuities (discussed in Chapter 76) may also play a role in a larger portfolio. The illustration shows a well-balanced $500,000 portfolio, which includes some real estate investments.

SAMPLE $500,000 PORTFOLIO

METHOD OF OWNERSHIP	INVESTMENT CATEGORY				
	STOCK		INTEREST–EARNING		REAL ESTATE
DIRECT OWNERSHIP	$10,000 IN EACH OF TEN COMMON STOCK INVESTMENTS		CDS MUNICIPAL BONDS TREASURY NOTES CORPORATE BONDS	$25,000 25,000 25,000 25,000	
	TOTAL	$100,000	TOTAL	$100,000	
INDIRECT OWNERSHIP (MUTUAL FUND/ PARTNERSHIP)	AGGRESSIVE GROWTH FUNDS GROWTH AND INCOME FUNDS INTERNATIONAL FUNDS SMALL COMPANY FUNDS	$20,000 30,000 25,000 25,000	GOVERNMENT SECURITIES FUNDS $25,000 MUNICIPAL BOND FUNDS 25,000 CORPORATE BOND FUNDS 25,000 DEFERRED ANNUITY 25,000		TWO TO FOUR REAL ESTATE LIMITED PARTNERSHIPS*
	TOTAL	$100,000	TOTAL	$100,000	TOTAL $100,000

* Alternatively, investment in directly owned real estate could be made

Gradual Redeployment

O ne stone remains unturned in the all-important asset allocation process, and it is a crucial one. Many investors, once they get serious about allocating their investments appropriately, find that they have to make a major reallocation of their investments. If you have been investing in conservative money-market accounts, for example, and are now (hopefully) convinced that you need to invest in stocks and bonds, the crucial issue is, *how fast should you do it?* Or, if you have recently received a cash wind-

Smart Money Move

Never make a rapid change in the way you allocate your investments. Redeploy *gradually*.

fall—say, an inheritance—how fast should you invest it?

Unfortunately, if you give this money to a broker or an investment adviser, they're more likely than not to invest it all tomorrow. The risk, of course, is that you make a major investment in stocks just before the market declines or a major investment in bonds just before interest rates shoot up. The more uncertain market conditions are, the more difficult it is to decide on when to invest in the market.

All too often, investors become so wary of a possible loss amidst uncertain market conditions that they end up investing very conservatively—too conservatively. One way to reduce the risk of ill-timed investing is to devise a plan of *gradual redeployment* of your money, rather than taking the chance of investing a significant portion of your money at a stock market high and/or an interest-rate low.

Gradual deployment of your money is, in essence, a variation of dollar-cost averaging that is widely and successfully used for investing in individual stocks or mutual funds. The following table shows how you might devise an investment timetable over the next two years. This allows for a gradual investment of the available money rather than an immediate commitment. (For the sake of illustration, assume that you eventually want an allocation of 50 percent stocks and 50 percent interest-earning securities. Also assume that you would like your distribution to be fully invested within two years.) As the timetable indicates, while 15% and 25% of the available money is immediately invested in stocks and bonds, respectively, a large portion of the money initially sits on the sidelines in low-yielding cash-equivalent investments (see page 471) like money-market funds, short-term CDs, and Treasury bills. Alternatively, if you are willing to accept some interest-rate risk during the course of your investment program, you could use short-term bonds or short-term bond funds in lieu of cash-equivalents, which will probably enable you to get a somewhat better yield.

Within the first twelve months of the deployment program, your stock exposure is increased from 15 percent to 30 percent and fixed-income exposure from 25 percent to 35 percent. The third column shows a fully invested allocation that would be achieved within a two-year period of time.

Gradual redeployment of investments makes a lot of sense, particularly when you think stock prices are high and/or interest rates are low. Certainly, opportunities may be missed by following such a timetable, but on the other hand, costly mistakes may also be avoided.

INVESTMENT REDEPLOYMENT TIMETABLE

INVESTMENT CATEGORY	NOW	PERCENT OF TOTAL WINDFALL WITHIN NEXT 12 MONTHS	FROM 12 TO 24 MONTHS
STOCKS	15%	30%	50%
BONDS	25%	35%	40%
CASH—EQUIVALENTS	60%	35%	10%
TOTAL	100%	100%	100%

ALL-WEATHER PORTFOLIO CHECKLIST

☐ Find out how your investments are allocated now and devise a plan to allocate them more appropriately, if necessary.

☐ Even if you now have a small amount of money to invest, you should allocate and diversify your investments to reduce risk and achieve long-term investment success.

☐ If you have to make a major shift in the investments you now have or if you receive a cash windfall, redeploy these investments gradually to reduce the risk of investing a lot of money in stocks at a market high or investing a lot of money in bonds just before interest rates rise.

PERSONAL INVESTMENT SUMMARY WORKSHEET

Date at which market values are indicated: _____

DESCRIPTION	NUMBER OF SHARES OR FACE VALUE	DATE ACQUIRED	ORIGINAL COST	CURRENT MARKET VALUE	ESTIMATED ANNUAL INTEREST OR DIVIDEND

1. Cash-equivalent investments

Money-market funds and accounts

_____ _____ _____ $ _____ $ _____ $ _____

Savings accounts

»

DESCRIPTION	NUMBER OF SHARES OR FACE VALUE	DATE ACQUIRED	ORIGINAL COST	CURRENT MARKET VALUE	ESTIMATED ANNUAL INTEREST OR DIVIDEND
CDs					
_____	_____	_____	$ _____	$ _____	$ _____
_____	_____	_____	_____	_____	_____
_____	_____	_____	_____	_____	_____
_____	_____	_____	_____	_____	_____
_____	_____	_____	_____	_____	_____
Other cash-equivalent investments					
_____	_____	_____	_____	_____	_____
_____	_____	_____	_____	_____	_____
Total cash-equivalent investments			$ _____	$ _____	$ _____

2. Bond investments

U.S. government securities

_____	_____	_____	$ _____	$ _____	$ _____
_____	_____	_____	_____	_____	_____
_____	_____	_____	_____	_____	_____

U.S. government securities funds

_____	_____	_____	_____	_____	_____
_____	_____	_____	_____	_____	_____
_____	_____	_____	_____	_____	_____

Mortgage-backed securities

_____	_____	_____	_____	_____	_____
_____	_____	_____	_____	_____	_____
_____	_____	_____	_____	_____	_____

Mortgage-backed securities funds

_____	_____	_____	_____	_____	_____
_____	_____	_____	_____	_____	_____
_____	_____	_____	_____	_____	_____
_____	_____	_____	_____	_____	_____

»

DESCRIPTION	NUMBER OF SHARES OR FACE VALUE	DATE ACQUIRED	ORIGINAL COST	CURRENT MARKET VALUE	ESTIMATED ANNUAL INTEREST OR DIVIDEND

Corporate bonds

$ ———— $ ———— $ ————

Corporate bond funds

Municipal bonds

Municipal bond funds

Other fixed-income investments

Total bond investments $ ———— $ ———— $ ————

3. Stock investments

Common stock in publicly traded companies

$ ———— $ ———— $ ————

Stock mutual funds

»

DESCRIPTION	NUMBER OF SHARES OR FACE VALUE	DATE ACQUIRED	ORIGINAL COST	CURRENT MARKET VALUE	ESTIMATED ANNUAL INTEREST OR DIVIDEND
_____	_____	_____	$ _____	$ _____	$ _____
_____	_____	_____	_____	_____	_____

Precious metals and precious metal funds

| _____ | _____ | _____ | _____ | _____ | _____ |
| _____ | _____ | _____ | _____ | _____ | _____ |

Other equity investments

| _____ | _____ | _____ | _____ | _____ | _____ |
| _____ | _____ | _____ | _____ | _____ | _____ |

| Total stock investments | | | $ _____ | $ _____ | $ _____ |

4. Real estate investments

Undeveloped land

_____	_____	_____	$ _____	$ _____	$ _____
_____	_____	_____	_____	_____	_____
_____	_____	_____	_____	_____	_____

Directly owned, income-producing real estate

| _____ | _____ | _____ | _____ | _____ | _____ |
| _____ | _____ | _____ | _____ | _____ | _____ |

Real estate limited partnerships

_____	_____	_____	_____	_____	_____
_____	_____	_____	_____	_____	_____
_____	_____	_____	_____	_____	_____

| Total real estate investments | | | $ _____ | $ _____ | $ _____ |

5. Interest in privately held businesses

_____	_____	_____	$ _____	$ _____	$ _____
_____	_____	_____	_____	_____	_____
_____	_____	_____	_____	_____	_____

| Total interests in privately held businesses | | | $ _____ | $ _____ | $ _____ |
| **Grand total investments** | | | $ _____ | $ _____ | $ _____ |

How to Purchase Investments

hat used to be the Main Street form of investing—individuals buying their own stocks and bonds through a broker—is turning into a side road. At the same time, mutual funds are fast becoming the most popular avenue for approaching the market. The reason? The markets have become increasingly costly and complex for the individual investor to enter. With so many investment vehicles from which to choose, so many firms at your service—not to mention scores of discount stockbrokers and thousands of low- and no-commission mutual funds—and an ever-changing market, the process of purchasing investments often lives up to its reputation of being a financial jungle.

There are many ways to get through the jungle relatively unscathed by exorbitant brokers' fees, costly account service fees, and other costs that can give your finances jungle fever. This chapter guides you through the maze of "investment services" to the most cost-effective methods for purchasing investments—whether it's a municipal bond mutual fund or a round lot of stock in the New York Stock Exchange.

Opening a Brokerage Account

he mechanics of purchasing investments are less complicated than most people think. In fact, purchasing investments is, in many instances, only a matter of picking up a phone and placing your order.

Purchasing stocks requires that you set up a brokerage account. Again, the task is less arduous than you might think. In most instances, opening up a brokerage account is easier than opening up a checking account at your local bank. (Many full-service banks offer their clients the option of buying Treasury bills, bonds, and even stocks and mutual funds for a modest fee.) However, just because the mechanics of opening up a brokerage account are easy, that doesn't mean the task of selecting a suitable firm to meet investment needs is so.

The first thing you need to do is to think through your decision to open up such an account. Whether you are planning to be an active, semiactive, or hands-off investor will directly affect the type of account you should select. Second, you need to outline your investment plan and detail how you will go about putting your plan into action. Will you be making regular payments into your account or will you be adding more money sporadically? How will your funds be allocated, when will they be disbursed, and at whose command? With these general decisions made, you can begin to examine what kind of brokerage account fits your unique situation.

Warning: Blindly following brokers can be hazardous to your financial health. Many brokers (or "account executives") are unqualified to do anything more than sell you a product, be it a stock, a bond, or a limited partnership. When considering what account is best for you, be sure you know all the options as well as the cost of each. Also, ask your friends what types of accounts they have, and which types (and people) they are pleased and displeased with.

Where to Purchase Your Investments

Fees

Once you've decided that you want to open a brokerage account, you need to select a brokerage firm or mutual fund company that provides the account you need for the price you want. No matter what the outcome of your search, and no matter how you combine and use the various available services, always keep an eagle eye on what you're paying. More than a few apparently attractive trades have turned out to be mistakes because of unanticipated transaction fees. An important purchasing maxim: Know the fees you will be charged for each and every service that your brokerage or mutual fund company charges—and periodically check up on those fees, comparing them with other firms' fees to make sure you are paying a reasonable amount.

Full-Service Brokers

A full-service broker provides his or her clients with research and recommendations. Full-service brokers have research departments with analysts at the ready to support any recommendation or deliver an advisory answer to your question. If you're new to the market—haven't a clue about the most basic investment techniques and maneuvers—then you might decide to go to a full-service broker. But always *keep in mind* that since full-service brokers are paid on commission, they may be motivated to transact more business in your account than you need.

Discount Brokers

With a discount broker, you call all the investment shots. You are responsible for initiating the buy-and-sell orders. You pay a steeply discounted commission since there's no individual broker involved. The result is a more cost-effective way to invest, compared with the cost of doing business with a full-service broker. No wonder discount brokerage firms have been growing by leaps and bounds.

With more than a little (but less than a lot of) legwork, you can buy your own stocks and bonds with a minimum of "expert" advice and service. Here's a list of the ten largest discount brokerages, together with their toll-free numbers:

- **Brown & Co.**
  (800) 225-6707
  (617) 742-2600 (MA)

- **Fidelity Broker Services**
  (800) 544-7272

- **Jack White & Co.**
  (800) 223-3411
  (619) 587-2000 (CA)

- **Kennedy, Cabot & Co.**
  (800) 252-0090
  (800) 257-2045 (CA)

- **Muriel Siebert & Co.**
  (800) 872-0711
  (212) 644-2400 (NY)

- **Pacific Brokerage Services**
  (800) 421-8395
  (213) 939-1100 (CA)

- **Quick & Reilly**
  (800) 672-7220
  (800) 522-8712 (NY)

- **T. Rowe Price Discount Brokerage**
  (800) 638-5660
  (301) 547-2308 (MD)

- **Charles Schwab**
  (800) 435-4000
  (415) 627-7000 (CA)

- **StockCross**
  (800) 225-6196
  (800) 392-6104 (MA)

Many experienced and active investors find that they invest most effectively with both a full-service and a discount brokerage account. The discounter can be used when making transactions that the investor himself or herself initiates, and the full-service broker can be used to obtain research and recommendations and to buy investments based upon the firm's and broker's research and recommendations.

Types of Accounts

Brokerage firms offer a number of options when opening an account.

- **SINGLE ACCOUNT.** The account is registered in your name and your name only.

- **JOINT ACCOUNT.** For most couples, this may be the preferred choice. It allows either partner to authorize purchases and sales.

- **CASH ACCOUNT.** A cash account is a small investor's best choice. A cash account simply means that all your transactions must be done on a cash basis. In this age of too much debt, paying cash is a sensible way to build your investment portfolio.

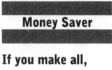
Money Saver

If you make all, most, or some of your investment decisions, save money by making your investments through a discount broker.

- **MARGIN ACCOUNT.** In contrast to a cash account, this account enables an investor to buy "on margin." Buying on margin is like taking out a loan to place a bet; in this case you take a loan—usually no more than 50 percent of your brokerage account balance—to purchase stocks or bonds. It's a risky way to invest unless you're an experienced investor, and you're charged interest (prime rate plus one to three percent) for the privilege of assuming such risk.

- **DISCRETIONARY ACCOUNT.** Another account that's worth avoiding. A discretionary account allows your broker to invest your money at his or her discretion without getting your authority to do so. No, no, no, no, no, no, no, no.

Other Great Ways to Purchase Investments

Stock-Purchase Plans

You may have the opportunity to participate in a stock purchase plan at your place of employment. Stock purchase plans offer employees convenience and, often, discounts in the purchase price of their company's stock. They provide employees a stake in the present and future of the company—a novel approach to pride and profitability.

But there's a rub. All too often, employees' savings have been wiped out. The cause? The company in which they owned stock fell on hard times, and the stock plummeted.

Nevertheless, the majority of larger corporations offer such plans, as do an already sizable and increasing number of smaller publicly traded companies. It's a route to stock ownership well worth considering—if it's available and if you're confident of your company's future success. But don't put too many eggs in one basket. If more than 20 percent of your investments are tied up in the stock of a single company, that's too much.

Smart Money Move

Take advantage of stock purchase plans if you can, but don't tie up more than 20 percent of your investments in the stock of a single company.

Dividend Reinvestment Plans

If you have already purchased stock in a company, and if you expect the company's stock to do well, then dividend reinvestment is one of the smartest ways to purchase new shares in the company. Why? Because you can instruct the corporation to buy new shares for you either through the automatic reinvestment of your dividends or by making an optional additional payment. What's more, they'll allow you to purchase and sell these shares at either no-commission or at a sharply reduced commission. Some companies even offer these shares to you at a slight discount. (For more information on dividend reinvestment plans, see page 446.)

Investment Clubs

An investment club is a group of investment-minded people who pool their resources to invest on a regular basis, and who meet regularly to review and revise their investments and investment strategies. There are thousands of investment clubs across the country. They offer both tangible and intangible advantages to their members. Among the tangible advantages are the ability to lower purchase and sales costs, and obtain greater diversification by pooling your money with other members of the investment club. The intangible benefits include the ability to share investment ideas and research with others as well as peer support to maintain a steady course during tough markets.

Mutual Fund Accounts

For the most part, buying shares in a mutual fund is as easy as picking up your phone and dialing the mutual fund company's toll-free number to request that an application be mailed to you. Many larger mutual fund companies also have investor service centers in large cities where you can open up your account. Like full-service and discount brokerage accounts, mutual fund accounts have a variety of bells and whistles including check-writing privileges, automatic investment programs, and sweep accounts that make sure that all of your money is working for you rather than sitting idle in a noninterest-bearing account.

The Best of Both Worlds

If you make all or most of your investment decisions yourself and you like to invest both in directly owned stocks and bonds as well as in mutual funds, you can get the best of both worlds by opening up a discount brokerage account that also has a mutual fund buying service. Schwab and Fidelity are the pioneers. They allow you to combine your direct investments and your mutual fund investments in one account. Each offers a wide range of no-load mutual funds that can be purchased through their mutual fund buying service. They assess a small charge for buying the fund, but this is a small price to pay for the wonderful convenience that these accounts offer.

The Rap on Wrap Fees

"Wrap fees" are the current rage among the brokerage fraternity. For an annual fee of about three percent (less if you have a lot of money to invest), the broker will select investment managers to manage your money and will include all brokerage commissions in the fee. Sound like a good deal? For some investors, perhaps, but 3

Smart Money Moves

Never give a broker the authority to invest your money at his or her discretion—not even if it's your son or daughter.

Combine the advantages of discount brokerage and no-load fund investing by opening up an account at a discount broker that also has a mutual fund-buying service.

percent taken out every year is mighty steep for what you get. (Ask your broker to break down who gets what with respect to the annual fee. You'll be surprised to learn that the most important players in this arrangement—the money managers—get only a very small portion [less than 20 percent] of the total fee.)

HOW TO PURCHASE INVESTMENTS CHECKLIST

☐

Learn about the many ways you can purchase investments. Compare the costs to make sure you don't pay for more services than you need.

☐

Take advantage of low-cost ways to purchase investments, like discount brokers, no-load mutual funds, and dividend reinvestment plans.

FOR FURTHER INFORMATION

The following two publications discuss the consumer-related aspects of investing:

Consumer's Financial Guide (free)

What Every Investor Should Know (free)

Branch of Consumer Affairs

Securities and Exchange Commission

450 Fifth Street N.W., Washington DC 20549

(202) 272-7440

56

Interest-Earning Investments

I nterest-earning investments belong in every investment portfolio. But what kinds are appropriate for you? After all, there are dozens of different kinds of interest-earning investments that range from the ultrasafe Treasury bill all the way down to the ultrarisky junk bond. In between these extremes lurk a variety of very interesting kinds of interest-earning investments. Although interest-earning investments are often viewed as the conservative counterparts of stock investments, the fact is that many do bear risk, so you must understand the risk in order to be comfortable with these investments. While it is true that common stocks have long been viewed as one of the better hedges against inflation, interest-earning investments also have a place in the portfolio of investors who are seeking attractive, inflation-beating rates of return with moderate risk.

Interest-earning investments have changed dramatically over the past decade. While the attention of many investors was riveted to the stock market during the latter half of the 1980s, bonds and other interest-earning investments were undergoing revolutionary changes that made them more complex, more volatile, and at the same time, more attractive as investment alternatives.

What Is an Interest-Earning Investment?

A ll interest-earning investments share the following characteristics. They pay interest at specified intervals, and they pay you back the face value of your investment either on demand or when the security matures, depending upon the type of security you're investing in.

Interest-earning investments can be broken down into two categories: cash-equivalent investments and fixed-income investments.

Cash-Equivalent Investments

Cash-equivalents are short-term interest-earning securities that can be readily converted into cash with little or no change in principal value. In other words, you get your original investment back—no more and no less—when you sell, plus you receive interest along the way. Cash-equivalent investments include money-market accounts (sold by banks), money-market funds (sold by mutual fund companies), and savings accounts. Other types of cash-equivalents include Treasury bills and short-term CDs. The interest paid on cash-equivalent investments fluctuates when overall interest rates change. Hence, if interest rates decline as they did in the early 1990s, investors who have a lot of money in cash equivalents will suffer because the interest paid on those investments will decline.

Cash-equivalent investments offer stability of principal and fluctuating yields. (In contrast, fixed-income investments, which are discussed next, offer stable yields but fluctuating principal.) Because the interest paid on cash-equivalents is always quite low in comparison with inflation, they are best viewed as a temporary parking place for your money while you are awaiting a more attractive investment opportunity. Many people also invest a small portion of their money (5 to 10 percent) in cash-equivalents as "safe money" that can be accessed quickly in an unexpected family emergency.

Fixed-Income Investments

"Fixed-income" means that the interest rate on the investment remains the same, or is fixed, regardless of what happens. But the value of the investment itself will change with prevailing interest rates. The easiest way to remember what happens to the principal value of your fixed-income investment is that it will move in the opposite direction of a change in interest rates. Therefore, if interest rates rise, the value of your fixed-income investment will decline and vice versa. Fixed-income investments have a maturity date, which is the date the owner of the investment is paid back the maturity value of the investment. When overall interest rates are declining, owning fixed-income investments provides two sorts of benefits to investors. First, they give you the opportunity to "lock in" an attractive interest rate; second, they may rise in value—creating a capital gain.

Some of the many available fixed-income investments include Treasury notes and bonds, mortgage-backed securities (like "Ginnie Maes"), municipal bonds, and corporate bonds.

Buying and Managing Interest-Earning Investments

You can buy cash-equivalent or fixed-income investments directly by buying individual securities through banks or brokers. Or you can buy them indirectly through a mutual fund where, in essence, you buy a portion of a diversified portfolio of interest-earning securities. You need to evaluate how interest-earning investments fit into your overall investment portfolio (including your retirement account investments), then decide the kinds of interest-earning securities that are most suitable for you. While interest-earning investments belong in every portfolio, the proportion of these investments in your total portfolio, as well as the type of investment vehicles, will depend on your unique financial situation.

Interest-earning investing will almost certainly continue to be a complex, yet potentially rewarding investment arena. The popularity of the many interest-earning investment vehicles that have come on the scene in the last decade will probably spur the development of still more products. Please note that new does not necessarily mean "improved." In fact, any new investment should be looked at with a healthy dose of skepticism.

A Quick Investment Primer

The best time to purchase fixed-income securities (or fixed-income mutual funds) is when you think interest rates are high and are unlikely to rise further. Since the rates of return on cash-equivalents fluctuate with changes of overall interest rates, you're better off in cash equivalents if interest rates are likely to increase. Of course, no one knows for certain where interest rates are headed. That's why fixed-income mutual funds are particularly appropriate for investors who don't want to make interest-rate "bets" with their hard-earned money. Indeed, fixed-income mutual funds should generally be a significant component of the interest-earning side of your investments.

Of course, fixed-income mutual funds can, and do, periodically decline in value when interest rates rise. But fund managers are generally much better able to protect a portfolio from the effects of changing interest rates than are individual investors.

Investments in unfamiliar fixed-income securities, such as foreign bonds, should definitely be made through a mutual fund with proven expertise in these areas.

Interest rates can fluctuate several percentage points within the course of a year, so price volatility is a factor that must be taken into account in planning and selecting interest-earning investments. Volatile interest rates, combined with the proliferation of many different kinds of interest-earning securities, have discouraged many investors from taking the plunge into these investments. Instead, they are content with short-term securities such as money-market funds. Yet with a little effort, you can increase your investment returns by taking advantage of the many attractive interest-earning investment vehicles that are available to individual investors.

A Brief Encyclopedia of
Interest-Earning Investments

A wide variety of taxable, tax-exempt, and tax-deferred interest-earning investments are described below. Don't be dismayed because you think that you have to have a king's ransom to afford to invest in some of these. Most can be purchased through a mutual fund with as little as $1,000—even less in some instances.

Directly Owned Investments
Directly owned investments are those individual securities like treasury bonds and CDs that you buy yourself.

Treasury securities

Treasury securities are the means by which the U.S. government borrows money. (As you know, Uncle Sam is pretty good at borrowing money.) Treasury bills, notes, and bonds are issued regularly by the Federal Reserve and are a popular investment, particularly for people who don't like risk and don't like paying state income taxes. *Treasury bills* are cash-equivalent debt instruments issued at a discount to the bearer and redeemed at face value on maturity. The difference between the discount and the face value represents the interest earned on the Treasury bill. See page 480 for more details.

Treasury notes and bonds are fixed-income obligations that have longer terms and pay interest semiannually at a fixed interest rate.

An interesting subspecies of U.S. Treasury securities is the so-called zero-coupon bond. These bonds pay no interest along the way. Instead, they are sold at a deep discount, which means that they are sold at a price that is much lower than the maturity value of the bond. While you don't get any interest along the way, your profit comes at the end in the form of a big increase in the amount you are paid at maturity compared with your original investment.

The main advantage in zero-coupon bonds is that you are guaranteed a set return insofar as the interest earned on these bonds is, in effect, reinvested at the original yield rate. Therefore, if interest rates decline you don't have to worry about reinvesting interest income at a lower rate. This automatic compounding also avoids your having to make decisions to invest the interest you would receive on a regular bond. Since there is no money to invest on your behalf along the way, many retail brokers hate to sell zeros.

The main drawback of these zeros is that even though you are not receiving interest along the way, for tax purposes the IRS assumes that you are, so you have to pay taxes on the "imputed" interest income. The upshot? These are good investments for tax-deferred retirement accounts such as IRAs and Keogh plans because you don't have to pay taxes on them before you retire, whether you receive the interest in cash or not.

Smart Money Move

Zero-coupon bonds make an excellent investment for your tax-deferred retirement accounts.

U.S. savings bonds

These are a popular way for savers to invest in government securities. Although they don't offer the highest rate of return, savings bonds are a sound way for savers to build up their savings. (As you will learn on page 481, they also offer some tax advantages.)

Mortgage-backed securities

These have peculiar-sounding names like Ginnie Mae, Fannie Mae, and Freddie Mac. These investments represent pools of mortgages. Their relatively high yields have been attracting a lot of investor interest, but the high investment minimums—typically $25,000—keep out the riff-raff. If your pockets aren't that deep, you can get a piece of the mortgage-backed security action through a Ginnie Mae mutual fund.

Collateralized mortgage obligations

If you dislike the unpredictable income streams that often accompany mortgage-backed securities, you might be attracted to collateralized mortgage obligations (CMOs). Technically, a CMO is a mortgage-backed security that represents a share in an organized pool of residential mortgages. Principal and interest payments are passed through to shareholders.

CMO pools are often divided into four share classes that correspond to the maturities of underlying mortgages, which may range from five to twenty years. Therefore, an investor can receive payouts in five, ten, fifteen, or twenty years. Other types of CMO pools place principal repayments in a redemption fund that randomly pays off CMO investors.

This scheme can deliver some very unpleasant surprises to investors who get their money back sooner than expected. (Note that like other mortgage-backed obligations, the pace of redemptions speeds up when interest rates drop and homeowners rush to refinance.)

A more recent type of CMO is the *companion CMO*, which is sold mainly to individual investors. These CMOs form part of a CMO issue consisting of both planned-amortization bonds (favored by large institutional investors because of their predictable cash flows) and companion CMOs. The fact that companion CMOs are not favored by large investors should tell you something.

When interest rates in general drop, companion CMOs are paid off first. If this sounds like a lousy deal, it's because it is. If interest rates rise, on the other hand, companion CMOs also suffer: Regular redemption payments are directed to institutional investors, who can then reinvest at higher interest rates. In return for the added prepayment and interest-rate risk that characterize companion CMOs, investors receive about one-quarter of one percent's worth of additional yield. It's not worth it. This is another example of the smaller investor getting the short end of the stick. Tell the CMO salesperson, "Thanks, but no thanks."

Smart Money Move

In spite of lofty promises, CMOs for smaller investors mainly offer the opportunity for some unpleasant surprises. Just say no.

Municipal bonds

These are used to finance long-term projects for cities, towns, villages, territories, and states. They don't appeal to people who enjoy paying federal income taxes, which means they're very popular. If you purchase bonds of issuing authorities in your own state (or bonds of Puerto Rico), you escape state income taxes and, perhaps, local income taxes. (Chapter 57 discusses tax-free investing in detail.)

Corporate bonds

Corporations issue a variety of debt securities, including secured and unsecured bonds, convertible bonds, and commercial paper. Many corporate interest-earning securities are no longer the safe haven for investors' money that they used to be. Many companies overloaded themselves with debt in the 1980s, and are consequently on shaky financial ground. Corporate debt securities must therefore be carefully chosen and closely monitored. Debt obligations of corporations vary significantly in quality, from triple-A rated all the way down to junk bonds. Purchasers of junk bonds (issuers prefer to call them "high yield" bonds) know well the perils of blindly chasing the highest-yielding corporate bond issues.

Convertible bonds

Convertible bonds are bonds that can be converted into stock at a predetermined price. They are more attractive to some investors than, say, regular bonds because they enable investors to gain from the appreciation of the issuing company's common stock. However, this conversion privilege usually means that the convertible bond yields one or more percent less than a "straight" bond. Corporations intend convertible bonds to be delayed sales of stock, and they can force you to convert into stock whenever the market value of such converted stock is equal to or greater than the call price of the bond.

The fact that convertible bonds may easily be called also needs to be considered if you are planning short- and long-term investment goals. Why? You could be forced either to redeem your bonds at a small premium and lose your former income or to buy shares of company stock. These complexities are beyond the abilities of the nonprofessional (in other words, you and me). So if you are attracted to convertibles (bonds, not cars), look for a mutual fund that invests in them. They're usually classified as "flexible income" funds.

Certificates of deposit

CDs are interest-bearing time deposits that are usually issued by banks. A CD is a loan of a set amount of money to a bank or other financial institution for a certain number of days at a predetermined interest rate. Their specified maturity typically ranges from thirty days to five or more years. Federally insured CDs are a major form of investment for many people. They shouldn't be, because better yields are usually available through other interest-earning investments.

Definition

Junk bond: A bond that carries a low rating (BB or lower) and is considered to have a high risk of default.

Indirectly Owned Investments

These are fixed-income mutual funds or money-market funds that in turn own interest-earning debt obligations of many issuers. Kinds of indirectly owned investments include the following:

Government securities funds

These funds invest in Treasury securities and/or mortgage-backed securities. The low investment minimums on these funds provide investors of all means with access to the government securities markets.

Municipal bond funds

Plenty of these funds are available, including single-state funds that provide double tax exemption to residents of a particular state. Like all mutual funds that invest in long-term debt obligations, muni funds can decline in value if prevailing interest rates rise. (See Chapter 57 for more on tax-free funds.)

Corporate bond funds

Corporate bond funds pay higher interest than municipal funds, but what matters is what you have left over after paying income taxes on the interest paid out by the corporate bond fund. Like municipal bond funds, each corporate bond fund states in its prospectus the quality of the bonds it will buy for its portfolio. Therefore, investors can select funds that invest in anywhere from the highest (triple-A) to the lowest (junk) quality corporate bonds.

Foreign bond funds

These invest in a variety of short-term and long-term foreign bond and money-market funds. Some invest only in money-market securities, others in corporate bonds, and still others in foreign government bonds. Since international investing is the wave of the future, you might take a look at foreign bond funds. But remember, they are a relatively new type of fund and, therefore, lack the kind of track record that instills confidence.

Money-market funds

These invest in short-term, usually very safe and stable securities, including commercial paper (short-term IOUs of large U.S. corporations), Treasury bills, and large bank CDs. Money funds are a very convenient place to stash your money and allow it to earn at least some interest while stashed. In other words, they beat stuffing your money in a mattress. While money-market funds are considered very safe, they are not federally insured. If you want the additional safety of federal deposit insurance, put your money in a *money-market deposit account* at a federally insured bank. But be aware that bank money-market deposit accounts usually pay an even lower rate of interest than the already paltry rates paid on money-market funds. Is the added safety worth the lower returns? I don't think so.

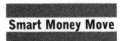

Smart Money Move

Don't invest too much of your money solely in CDs.

Interest-Earning Investing Know-how

Monitor Prevailing Interest Rates

It will serve you well if you develop rules of thumb about judging interest rates. For example, you may find that interest-earning securities are attractive when they beat inflation by a couple of percentage points after taxes are taken out. Many individual investors monitor the yield on long-term Treasury bonds (quoted in the financial pages of your daily newspaper) to get an idea of the current level of interest rates and interest-rate trends.

Keep Up to Date on Interest-Rate Changes

One key to investing successfully in interest-earning investments is to purchase longer-maturity securities when you think interest rates are high and likely to fall, in order to lock in high returns. Conversely, you should purchase shorter-maturity securities (or cash-equivalent investments) if you think prevailing interest rates are likely to rise.

Don't Speculate Heavily on Interest-Rate Changes

While your feelings about interest rates may influence the type of investments that you want to make, don't speculate heavily on your own (or anyone else's) opinion about future interest rates. Fixed-income security prices can, in fact, be more volatile than stock prices. So, for example, if you put a lot of money into long-term bonds and interest rates rise, you could lose a lot of principal.

Three Risks You Need to Know About

While some people think interest-earning securities have no risk, in fact they all have risk to some degree. Even Treasury bills have risk insofar as—in a period of low interest rates—your return is so low that you risk losing ground to inflation. The three major risks of interest-earning securities are these.

Smart Money Move

You could probably get a better return on a money-market fund than you could with a bank money-market deposit account.

1. Market risk

Also called "interest-rate risk," it is the risk that your investment's value will fluctuate with changes in interest rates. In general, if interest rates rise, the market value of a bond declines. Conversely, if interest rates decline, the market value of a bond increases. For example, if you purchased a bond that paid 7 percent and prevailing interest rates then fell to 5 percent, the value of your bond would have increased because it would be paying a higher rate of interest than a newly issued bond. Note that the amount that a bond's market value changes due to fluctuating interest rates depends upon its maturity. Longer-term securities' values tend to change more in reaction to changes in interest rates than do shorter-term securities.

2. Credit risk

This is the risk of default by the bond issuer. In other words, it's the risk that you won't get your money back or the issuer won't make an interest payment. This is why corporate and municipal bonds are risk-rated by rating agencies like Standard & Poor's Corporation and Moody's Investors Services (see below). Securities with a lower credit rating pay a higher rate of interest because investors generally demand more interest to compensate for the possibility that the issuer may default.

3. Call risk

This is the risk that a bond will be called (bought back prior to maturity by the issuer on demand). Not all tax-free bonds are callable, but those that are *may* be called after interest rates have declined. Calling a bond allows the issuer to reissue the bonds at a lower interest rate. Since bonds are usually called only after interest rates have declined, investors in bonds that are called will have to reinvest their money at lower interest rates.

Some bonds have "call protection," which is a guarantee that a security can't be bought back by the issuer or won't be called until a specific amount of time has elapsed. Be sure to ask about it. Treasury securities are almost without exception noncallable.

Risk Ratings

With so many different bond issues and so many issuers of fixed-income securities, it's difficult for individual investors to keep up to date on the relative risk of a particular issue. Fortunately, Moody's and Standard & Poor's bond-rating agencies provide ratings designed to help investors choose bonds that meet their own risk tolerance. Typically, the lower-rated bonds offer a higher yield but also more risk.

MOODY'S	STANDARD & POOR'S	MEANING OF RATING
Aaa	AAA	Best quality; issuer's ability to repay principal is extremely strong
Aa	AA	High quality; ability to repay is very strong
A	A	Upper-medium quality; ability to repay is strong; somewhat susceptible to adverse economic conditions
Baa	BBB	Medium quality; capacity to repay principal and interest can be weakened by adverse economic conditions. »

Smart Money Move

Purchase longer-maturity fixed-income securities when you think interest rates are high and are likely to fall. Purchase shorter-term securities (or cash-equivalents) if you think interest rates are likely to rise.

MOODY'S	STANDARD & POOR'S	MEANING OF RATING
Ba	BB	Speculative (spelled r-i-s-k); below investment grade; uncertain of financial future
B	B	Low grade; lacking the characteristics of a desirable investment
Caa	CCC	Very risky; issues may already be in default, or principal and interest may be in jeopardy
Ca	CC	Highly speculative; marked shortcomings, major risk
C	C	Lowest grade (not a passing mark!); outside of a miracle, no prospect of ever attaining any real investment standing
D	D	In default

Definition

Secondary market: Securities are bought and sold after their original issue on the secondary market. The initial sale of a new security (initial public offering) occurs in the primary market.

Smart Money Move

Save commissions by buying U.S. Treasury securities directly from the Federal Reserve Bank.

U.S. Treasury Securities

High interest from the federal government! Great tax breaks! No commission charges! No, this isn't a pitch for another "new and improved" investment product. But if the U.S. government ever decided to create a hard-sell ad for Treasury securities, it would probably read something like that. While other investments may earn better returns at times, Treasury securities consistently appear in a wide variety of investment portfolios.

U.S. Treasury issues—which, along with U.S. savings bonds, are the only types of securities that are direct obligations of Uncle Sam—have long been classic, bread-and-butter investments. Their appealing features include:

- **HIGH LIQUIDITY.** Individual investors must often pay higher fees when buying municipal and taxable corporate bonds because the market for small blocks of securities is limited. But the Treasury arena is so huge that an investor with $1,000 is on the same footing as someone with $100,000.

- **NONCALLABILITY.** Many investors who think they've locked in high yields for decades get a rude awakening when an issuer redeems (calls) its bonds before they reach maturity. This won't happen with Treasurys, though, since most of them cannot be called.

- **STATE TAX EXEMPTION.** Treasury securities are exempt from state and local income taxes. This is a big plus if you live in a state that levies high income taxes.

- **LOW OR NO SALES COMMISSIONS.** It costs nothing to purchase bonds through a local branch of the Federal Reserve Bank. You pay only a small sales charge when you buy them through a bank or broker, and you can purchase issues on the secondary market rather than waiting for federal auctions. Buying bonds from a bank or broker makes a great deal of sense if you are an active investor: it's a lot easier to trade bonds if they are held in a bank or brokerage account.

There are several species of Treasury issues from which to choose. Treasury bills come in minimum denominations of $10,000 and mature in one year or less. Treasury notes mature in one to ten years and have a minimum purchase requirement of $1,000 (except for two- and three-year notes, which have a $5,000 minimum investment requirement). Treasury bonds have maturities of more than ten years and up to thirty years and also have a $1,000 minimum purchase requirement. You can also invest in U.S. Treasury issues through a U.S. government securities mutual fund. Before investing, however, be sure to check on whether the interest paid by the Treasury mutual fund is exempt from state and local income taxes in your state.

U.S. Savings Bonds

Savings bonds occupy territory between cash-equivalents and fixed-income investments. Unlike the other long-term securities described in this chapter, U.S. savings bonds are not fixed-income investments. They pay a variable interest rate, the amount of which is recalculated every six months. This interest rate is set at 85 percent of the benchmark five-year Treasury yield, with a 6 percent floor that limits how far the bond's yield can sink downward. (For bonds purchased before November 1986, this floor is set

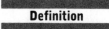

Definition

Secondary market: Securities are bought and sold after their original issue on the secondary market. The initial sale of a new security (initial public offering) occurs in the primary market.

Smart Money Move

Don't turn up your nose at the old-fashioned U.S. savings bond. State tax exemption, federal tax deferral, and not-too-shabby interest rates make for a respectable, if not spectacular, investment.

at 7.5 percent.) Finally, while investors are guaranteed their principal back when they redeem their bonds, they will incur stiff interest penalties by cashing in U.S. savings bonds before five years have elapsed.

Series EE Bonds

EE bonds sell for half their face or redemption value, which ranges from $50 to $10,000. A maximum of $30,000 face value ($15,000 cost) of Series EE bonds may be purchased per calendar year per person.

Tax-Deferral Features

U.S. savings bonds are not subject to state and local income taxes. Federal taxes on accrued interest is deferred until you redeem your bonds or until they reach maturity, whichever comes first. U.S. savings bonds have a variety of attractive features in addition to the Series EE tax deferral. An exchange provision allows Series EE bonds to be converted into Series HH bonds in increments of $500. Therefore, investors may purchase Series EE bonds, defer payment of taxes until maturity, then convert the EE bonds into HH bonds, thereby deferring payment of taxes once again. Tax must be paid on current income from the HH bonds, however.

> **EXAMPLE:** A maturing Series EE bond has a $10,000 value. If you cash in the bond, you have to pay federal tax on the accrued interest. Instead, you decide to use the deferral privilege. You exchange the bond for $10,000 in Series HH bonds, further deferring your tax liability, though you have to begin paying taxes on the 6 percent semiannual interest payments you receive from the Series HH bonds.

Series EE bonds have a thirty-year maturity and Series HH bonds have a twenty-year maturity. Series EE bonds might be a particularly attractive investment if you expect interest rates to rise. The adjustable-rate feature of the savings bond would allow you to enjoy the increased return occasioned by the rise. In addition, you may defer payment of federal income tax until the bonds are cashed in. Because savings bonds are exempt from state and local tax, they are particularly attractive for residents of highly taxed states and cities.

Smart Money Move

Buy U.S. savings bonds at the end of the month and redeem them at the beginning of the month.

Bonds of both series are subject to federal and state inheritance, estate, and gift taxes. If, upon the death of an owner, there is a surviving co-owner or beneficiary named on the bonds, the bonds do not form part of a decedent's estate for probate purposes. Although they are subject to applicable estate or inheritance taxes, if any, U.S. savings bonds become the sole and absolute property of the beneficiary.

The College Break

Interest on bonds purchased after December 31, 1991, may be free of taxes if they are used to pay for college tuition and educational fees for a dependent child, spouse, or yourself. However, the tax break is phased out gradually for families with adjusted gross incomes over a set amount when the bonds are redeemed. These income levels are adjusted for inflation, but parents earning over the maximum adjusted gross income when the bonds are redeemed will be ineligible for this favorable tax treatment. Parents must purchase the bonds themselves and hold the securities in one or both of their names in order for them to qualify for this tax break for a child. Don't put the bonds in your child's name if you expect to qualify for this break.

Transaction Tips

Keep copies of the issue dates and serial numbers in a safe place separate from your bonds. This will make it easier to replace them if they are lost or stolen. Make large purchases in small denominations so you have the option of gradually redeeming a large purchase at your local bank. It is possible to redeem part of a Series EE bond with a denomination of $100 or more, but the transaction will have to be handled through your local branch of the Federal Reserve Bank.

Since bonds are credited with interest for the entire month in which they are bought, it is best to purchase them at the end of the month. Before redeeming a bond, you should find out when the interest is credited. Older savings bonds are credited only once every six months, and if you cash in a bond a day early, you will lose six months' interest. Newer bonds are credited with interest monthly. It will be to your advantage, therefore, to sell the bonds early in the month, because you'll receive interest for the entire month. Sorry, Uncle Sam!

Even though you may purchase your bonds at a bank, you should direct important questions elsewhere, since banking personnel are often not well versed in the particulars of U.S. savings bonds. It is safer to get your information from the savings bond division of your local branch of the Federal Reserve Bank. They can send you helpful publications. You can also call the Savings Bond Information Office (304) 420-6112 to obtain information about investing in savings bonds.

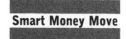

Smart Money Move

Buy longer-term CDs to protect yourself against falling interest rates and at the same time to take advantage of rising interest rates.

Certificates of Deposit

C Ds are popular among individual savers, perhaps because of their convenience, safety, and seemingly diverse range. (They're available in a range of maturities: one, two, three, six, and twelve months; two years, two and one-half years, five years, and ten years.) But CDs tend to provide less than meets the eye, especially once the double whammy of taxes and inflation have been taken into account.

Liquidity and federal insurance on deposits up to $100,000 (in a qualifying bank) are two reasons for the attraction of CDs. But it is their interest rates—which more often than not do not keep pace with other investment options—that receive the most attention. The problem arises when rates begin to fall and people who counted on CDs to provide them with a safe, convenient, and uncomplicated source of income begin to see their returns diminish—sometimes dramatically. Ugh!

Short-Term or Long-Term?

While most investors prefer shorter-term CDs, they may in fact be better off opting for long-term CDs, even if they risk incurring a penalty for early withdrawal. Why? Like any other fixed-income investment, the main risk that long-term CDs present is that if interest rates rise, you're stuck with a lower-yielding investment. But the interest penalty levied on the early withdrawal of a long-term CD is usually far less than the drop in value other fixed-income investments of similar maturity experience when interest rates rise. As interest rates rise, simply cash in the old CD, pay the interest rate penalty, and take out a new higher-interest CD. That way, you can take advantage of rates on the rise while defending yourself against falling rates that leave short-term CD investors in a lurch.

CASE STUDY: SUFFERING FROM DECLINING INTEREST RATES

"The truth is, I didn't used to have to think about what to invest in, but I can't sit and watch my interest income being hurt by falling interest rates. This disappearing interest act might make for a good magic show, but it won't be too long before I'm retired and will need this money to live on." That's how John Curwen, a fifty-seven-year-old super-market manager, sums up his financial situation.

"The problem is that I don't know how to approach the stock market. After all, you don't have to look as far back as 1929 to figure out that the stock market can be a roller-coaster ride that will make your heart jump. It dropped over 500 points in a single day in 1987!

"During the past I was content with the steadiness that came from investing in money-market accounts, CDs, and T bills. But interest rates have proven themselves to be volatile, and I've reached the point where I can't afford to let my hard-earned savings lose ground, particularly when you figure in taxes and inflation.

"What I want to know is whether I can find an investment that will be safe, consistent, convenient, *and* provide a higher yield than my CD investments."

Like millions of CD investors, John Curwen is concerned about the effect declining interest rates can have on his financial well-being. Fortunately, he is still working and has

»

a steady paycheck to meet his daily living expenses. But many retirees who have put a lot of money into short-term investments like money-market accounts, CDs, and Treasury bills can experience difficulty making ends meet because of a sharply lower interest-rate environment. Whatever your financial situation, one thing is clear: If you have put most of your savings in "safe" short-term interest-earning investments, you haven't made the best investment decision.

Over the long run, bond and stock investments have provided investors with consistently better returns than short-term interest-earning securities, in the form of interest and dividend income and growth in the value of the investment. While the short-term volatility Curwen described can be frightening to the novice, the fact remains that, over the long term, stacks provide the best returns around.

According to data compiled by Ibbotson Associates, over the ten-year period from 1982 to 1991, common stocks, as measured by Standard and Poor's 500 Index, provided a compound annual return of 17.6 percent. Over the same period, long-term government bonds provided a compound annual return of 15.6 percent, while short-term interest-earning securities—as measured by U.S. Treasury bills—provided a compound annual return of 7.7 percent.

Interest-Earning Investment Strategies

Make Interest-Earning Investments One Part of Your Well-Balanced Portfolio

Some people invest too much money in fixed-income investments or cash-equivalent investments because they are afraid of stocks. Others think stocks are the ultimate investment and have too little money in interest-earning securities. What everyone needs is balance. A well-balanced portfolio consists of approximately equal portions of stocks, interest-earning investments, and, if you are so inclined, income-producing real estate.

Ladder Maturities

Smart investors do what is known as "laddering" or "staggering" the maturities of their interest-earning investments. Rather than investing in a single issue or in several issues with roughly the same maturity, you should opt for a variety of maturities—some short term (less than three years), some intermediate term (three to ten years), and some long term (ten to thirty years). That way, if there is a significant change in interest rates, you will have avoided placing a heavy, and perhaps incorrect, bet on a single maturity. Simply stated, laddering maturities reduces the risk in your interest-earning

Smart Money Move

Reduce risk by purchasing fixed-income securities and bond mutual funds of varying maturities.

security portfolio. Don't forget to time some of the maturities to coincide with times when you may need the money—for instance, to meet college tuition bills or to cover livimg expenses during your first few years of retirement.

If you invest in interest-earning mutual funds, you can also follow a similar laddering strategy by spreading your money among money-market and short-term bond funds, intermediate-term bond funds, and long-term bond funds. There are literally hundreds of good mutual funds from which to choose.

Compare Interest Rates

Interest rates vary among various types of interest-earning securities, both within the same investment category and between alternative categories. Chances are that the CD rate paid on CDs at your local bank, for example, is not as good as it might be if you shopped around a little. Another example: Over the past several years, interest rates on tax-exempt bonds have been very attractive compared with the after-tax returns on Treasury securities and corporate bonds. Yet another example: Rates on medium-grade bonds are sometimes much higher than on high-grade bonds, even though the risk of default on medium-grade bonds is not much higher than with blue-chip bonds—that is, high-quality issues of financially strong companies or municipalities.

What's the lesson here? It pays to shop around for the best yields on your interest-earning investments, just as it pays to shop around for the umpteen million other financial products and services that you need to achieve your financial dreams.

Don't Chase Yield

While "shopping" for yield is a virtue, "chasing" yield is a sin. An interest-earning investment that pays 14 percent interest when prevailing rates are 8 percent is trying to tell you something. This is a junk bond or a close relative. Yet many investors erroneously think that the higher the yield, the more attractive the investment. This is not so. As many junk bond junkies found out to their dismay, some of these bonds go down the tubes. While it may be appropriate to allocate a very small proportion of your portfolio to a more speculative investment, be sure not to bet the ranch on it. One undeniable fact: The higher the yield, the higher the risk.

Emphasize Quality

Although there is no agreement on the outlook for interest rates, you should buy primarily high-quality interest-earning investments, such as Treasury securities, certificates of deposit from federally insured banks, and high-grade or medium-grade corporate and municipal bonds. If you invest in interest-earning mutual funds, opt for funds that emphasize high-quality securities.

Diversify

Unless you have only a very small amount of money to invest, don't concentrate your interest-earning investments in a single or very few securities. Select several different issues and several different categories of investments or mutual funds. (Important matters of diversification are discussed in Chapter 54.)

Emphasize Shorter Maturities

Even though longer-maturity interest-earning investments usually have slightly higher yields than shorter-maturity investments, many experts contend that there is usually not enough of a difference to justify the greater risks in concentrating on long-maturity bonds. Remember, the longer the maturity, the more the value of the bond will fluctuate in reaction to changes in interest rates.

Review Your Current Interest-Earning Investments

Because of the investment risks associated with our topsy-turvy economy, you need to review your interest-earning securities at least semiannually. The reason? You need to assure that the financial stability of the company or municipality that issued the securities has not deteriorated since you bought them. Does that sound time consuming? You bet it is. That's another reason why bond mutual funds make so much sense. You should also double-check that all of your bank deposits are federally insured in view of the problems in the banking industry. (This issue would have been much less of a concern a few years ago.)

Consider the Tax Effects

You may be able to increase your investment returns by carefully comparing the tax effects of alternative interest-earning investments. Some are fully taxable; Treasury securities are federally taxable but exempt from state taxes, and municipal obligations are usually exempt from federal and, perhaps, state taxes. It is important to keep in mind that the most heavily taxed (and usually higher yielding) securities should be placed in your tax-deferred retirement accounts. On the other hand, tax-favored investments like municipal bonds should be placed in your personal investment account.

High-quality municipal bonds are worth examining because their return may well be higher than what you'd receive from a taxable interest-earning security after taxes are taken out. (See discussion on tax-free securities in Chapter 57.)

INTEREST-EARNING INVESTMENTS CHECKLIST

■□■

If you have limited your interest-earning investing to one or two types of securities, learn about the broad range of products that are on the market.

Don't put much money in low-yielding cash-equivalent securities.

Avoid overexposure to interest-rate risk by purchasing interest-earning securities of varying maturities.

Compare yields before purchasing an interest-earning security—you will probably be well rewarded.

Avoid "chasing" yield. Securities that offer high yields also offer high risks.

Tax-Free Investing

You don't have to be rich to benefit from tax-free investing. Many investors can benefit from investing in municipal securities, although they may not realize it. Here's a quick rule of thumb: Consider investing in tax-free securities if your taxable income is expected to place you in the 28 percent federal tax bracket or higher. While the tax brackets are adjusted for inflation each year, you are probably in that bracket if your taxable income is around $25,000 if you file a single return or around $40,000 if you file a joint return. *Note:* Tax-free investments should not be placed in investment accounts that are already tax-advantaged, like IRAs.

Municipal Securities

Often referred to as "munis," municipal securities are debt obligations or IOUs issued by state and local governments and governmental agencies such as a highway department, airport authority, school district, even a sewer commission.

Tax Benefits of Municipal Investments

With few exceptions, the interest earned on municipal investments is exempt from federal income taxes, and in many instances from state and local taxes, too. Taxes take a heavy toll on your investments—federal income taxes alone can take almost one-third of your investment income. High state and local taxes rub salt in the tax wound. Here are some tax-free investing facts.

- **INTEREST FROM MUNICIPALS** is usually exempt from federal income taxes. Some securities that finance private ventures are taxable to all investors, and others may be taxable if you are subject to the alternative minimum tax (AMT).

- **THE INTEREST ON MOST MUNICIPALS** is exempt from state and local, as well as federal income taxes, if you are a resident of the state that issues the bonds. For example, if you reside in California, interest on municipal securities issued by the state of California or by California municipalities would be exempt from both federal and state income taxes. These are known as "double tax-free" bonds.

- **INTEREST ON MUNICIPAL SECURITIES** issued by U.S. territories (the Territory of Guam and the Commonwealth of Puerto Rico, for example) is generally exempt from both federal and state income taxes.

Types of Municipal Bonds

I f you buy individual municipal bond issues, you have a variety of choices.

General obligation bonds

Backed by the full faith, credit, and usually taxing power of the governmental authority that issues them, general obligation bond issues or (GOs) are repaid out of a government's general revenue, mainly taxes.

Revenue bonds

These are issued to finance public works projects that generate revenue from public use, such as a toll bridge, highway, tunnel, hospital, stadium, or water system. The bond interest and principal are repaid out of the revenue that the project generates.

Industrial development bonds

These bonds are issued by a state or municipal agency as a means of financing, or helping to finance, a private corporation's construction or equipment costs. Industrial development bonds are backed by the credit of the private corporation and may, under some circumstances, be subject to federal income tax.

Zero-coupon bonds

Municipal securities may be issued as "zero-coupon" bonds. So-called "zero munis" provide no interest to the bondholder until they mature—at which time all the accumulated interest is paid at once.

Insured bonds

Some municipal securities' principal and interest payments are insured against default by private insurers such as the American Municipal Bond Corporation (AMBAC) or the Municipal Bond Insurance Association (MBIA). The cost of this insurance is usually passed on to the bondholders, somewhat lowering the bond's yield. While municipal bond insurance may add an additional level of comfort, many experts predict that if an economic situation occurred where there were massive defaults on municipal obligations (although this is very unlikely), municipal bond insurers might not be able to make good on all their obligations.

Municipal notes

These are short-term obligations secured by specific sources of future revenues like taxes or the proceeds from a bond issue. Municipal notes usually have maturities of less than one year.

Types of Municipal Funds

Mutual funds provide investors with a variety of alternative ways to earn tax-free income.

Nationally diversified tax-free funds

Many tax-free funds hold securities issued by states and municipalities throughout the country. Income from such funds is usually exempt from federal income taxes, and a portion may be exempt from state and local taxes.

Single state or "state tax-free" funds

These funds invest in the securities of a single state so that investors who are residents of that state can save on both federal, state, and, if applicable, local taxes.

High-yield municipal funds

High-yield tax-free funds usually invest a substantial portion of their money in medium- and lower-rated tax-free securities. These funds may be appropriate for investors who are seeking a higher return and who are willing to take more risk to do so. They are suitable if you can afford a little more risk in exchange for a (hopefully) higher return.

Tax-free money-market funds

If you don't want to risk fluctuations in principal value, you can invest in tax-free money market funds. These operate similarly to the garden-variety money-market fund, except that your income is free of federal taxes. Of course, the return on a tax-free money-market fund is quite low.

A word to the wise: Periodically compare the returns on the taxable money-market funds (after-tax basis) with the return on tax-free money-market funds. Depending on market conditions, you may be better off putting your money-market dollars in one or the other. You might as well put your money into the type of fund that gives you the best return after taxes have been factored in.

The Tax Advantage

You don't need a Ph.D. in math to compare tax-free investments with taxable investments.

Calculating the Tax Advantage

Interest paid on municipals may *seem* lower than that of other types of taxable interest-earning securities like Treasury bonds and corporate bonds. But the yields on tax-free municipals and taxable securities can be compared only *after* you have taken into account the municipal's tax-free advantage. It's not hard to do, and you may be handsomely rewarded for your efforts.

To compare a taxable investment with a tax-free investment, first estimate what income tax bracket you're going to be in. Although income tax brackets are adjusted each year to account for inflation, the following table will help you make a rough approximation of your income tax bracket. (Be sure to check your exact tax bracket before making a tax-free investment.)

APPROXIMATE YOUR TAX BRACKET

INCOME TAX BRACKET	TAXABLE INCOME BASED ON FILING STATUS		
	SINGLE	JOINT	HEAD OF HOUSEHOLD
28%	OVER $22,000	OVER $37,000	OVER $30,000
31%	OVER $54,000	OVER $90,000	OVER $77,000

Next, use the following worksheet to determine how much a given taxable security would have to yield in order to equal a particular tax-free investment's interest income.

YOUR TAXABLE EQUIVALENT FIELD

	YOUR CALCULATION	EXAMPLE
(1) TAX-FREE YIELD	....	6.5%
(2) YOUR FEDERAL INCOME TAX BRACKET CONVERTED TO A DECIMAL	....	.31
	1.00	1.00
	- .	- .31
(3) SUBTRACT LINE 2 FROM 1.00	.	.69
(4) TAXABLE EQUIVALENT YIELD (LINE 1 DIVIDED BY LINE 3)	. = %	$\frac{6.5}{.69} = 9.42\%$

The formula for taxable equivalent yield enables you to compare a tax-free investment to a taxable investment.

$$\text{Taxable Equivalent Yield} = \frac{\text{Interest rate on a tax-free security}}{(1 - \text{your federal income tax bracket})}$$

Example

Gary and Sarah Williams are in the 28 percent federal income tax bracket. They're considering purchasing either a tax-free investment paying six percent interest or a Treasury bond paying 7.5 percent. In order to accurately compare the yields, they must first compute the taxable equivalent yield on the municipal bond. This can be done in the following way:

First, they need to convert their income tax bracket to its decimal equivalent: 28 percent becomes .28.

Second, they need to apply the above formula:

$$\text{Taxable Equivalent Yield} = \frac{6\%}{(1 - .28)} = \frac{6\%}{.72} = 8.33\%$$

For the Williamses, the taxable equivalent yield of the tax-free investment turns out to be 8.33 percent, compared with 7.5 percent for the Treasury bond. The tax-free investment has a lower interest rate but it provides more interest income than a taxable security.

Use the "Comparison of Taxable and Tax-Exempt Yields" table below to make a quick comparison between a taxable investment and one that is exempt from federal taxes. Use the table to find the approximate taxable equivalent yields for your tax bracket of a particular tax-exempt yield.

COMPARISON OF TAXABLE AND TAX-EXEMPT YIELDS

YOUR TAX BRACKET	28%	31%
TAX–EXEMPT YIELDS (%)	APPROXIMATE TAXABLE EQUIVALENT YIELDS	
3.00%	4.17%	4.34%
4.00	5.56	5.80
5.00	6.94	7.25
6.00	8.33	8.70
7.00	9.72	10.14
8.00	11.11	11.59

Double Tax-Free Securities

I f you hold municipal securities of issuers located within your own state, you get a double benefit: The interest on these bonds or notes is free of both federal and state taxes.

To compare a taxable investment to an investment whose income is free of both federal and state taxes, multiply the interest that you could receive on a double tax-free investment by the multiplier in the following table. Then use the "Your Double Tax-Free Yield" worksheet to calculate your yield.

MULTIPLIER BASED ON YOUR FEDERAL INCOME TAX BRACKET*

TAX RATE ON INTEREST INCOME FOR YOUR STATE	INCOME TAX BRACKET	
	28% BRACKET	31% BRACKET
2%	1.42	1.48
3	1.43	1.49
4	1.45	1.51
5	1.46	1.53
6	1.48	1.54
7	1.49	1.56
8	1.51	1.58
9	1.53	1.59
10	1.54	1.61
11	1.56	1.68
12	1.58	1.70
20% OF FEDERAL TAX LIABILITY	1.47	1.61
25% OF FEDERAL TAX LIABILITY	1.49	1.63

* The multipliers apply only to interest, not total return (interest plus capital gains).

YOUR DOUBLE TAX-FREE YIELD

	YOUR CALCULATION	EXAMPLE
(1) YOUR FEDERAL INCOME TAX BRACKET	.............%	31%
(2) YOUR STATE INCOME TAX RATE ON INTEREST INCOME	.............%	6%
(3) DOUBLE TAX EXEMPT EQUIVALENT MULTIPLIER FROM TABLE (BASED UPON YOUR FEDERAL INCOME TAX BRACKET AND STATE INCOME TAX RATE)	.............%	1.54%
(4) DOUBLE TAX EXEMPT YIELD	.............%	5.3%
(5) MULTIPLY BY THE MULTIPLIER FROM #3, ABOVE	....	1.54
(5) EQUALS THE EQUIVALENT YIELD ON A TAXABLE INVESTMENT	.............%	8.16%

Example

A 7 percent federal and state tax-free yield would be the equivalent of a 10.2 percent fully taxable yield for an investor in the 28 percent federal income tax bracket whose state tax rate on interest income is 5 percent (7% X 1.46 = 10.2%).

Purchasing Municipal Securities

Buying Your Own

Some people prefer to buy municipal bonds on their own. Like any other directly owned investment, there may be an advantage to a reliable and predictable stream of interest income, as well as the psychological advantage of controlling your own investment portfolio. But there are important facts to keep in mind if you are considering buying individual municipal bonds.

- THE MINIMUM PURCHASE PRICE for a single bond is usually $5,000.

- YOU WILL PROBABLY NEED $50,000 or more to acquire a diversified municipal portfolio.

The municpal bond market is the least organized of all major securities markets. Therefore, when buying or selling your own munis, it is very difficult to insure that you get a good price. Prices on the same municipal issue vary considerably, and it is unlikely that an individual investor will be able to secure a particularly attractive price. Also keep in mind:

- MUNICIPAL BOND PRICES are not listed in the newspaper.

- YOU WILL NEED TO MONITOR the municipal securities that you own because interest rate conditions change and the financial strength of municipal issuers can deteriorate. This is particularly important in the current environment when so many states and municipalities are having fiscal problems.

Unit Investment Trusts

Municipal bonds can also be purchased through a unit investment trust (UIT). These trusts hold a variety of municipal bonds, which are usually held until maturity or until they are called. Thus, unit investment trusts are unmanaged portfolios of munis. The advantage is that for a small investment, you receive a piece of a diversified portfolio of municipal securities as well as regular tax-free income.

But there are disadvantages to UITs as well. First, you pay a commission to invest (which can be avoided if you purchase a no-load muni fund instead). Because the portfolio is not actively managed, a UIT always risks the possibility that deteriorating bonds will not be sold on a timely basis. Also, if you want to sell your unit trust before maturity, you may get considerably less for it than you think, particularly if interest rates have climbed.

Be particularly careful if you are buying a "used" UIT—in other words, one that has already been issued. It is very difficult to evaluate whether you are getting a good deal with these. Chances are quite good that you're not, so steer clear of them. Your best bet is to only buy UITs at the initial public offering with the intention of holding them until maturity. Alternatively, and preferably, consider an actively managed muni bond fund.

Tax-Free Mutual Funds

Like UITs, tax-free mutual funds do not require a large initial investment. They have the added advantage of being able to reinvest your income and capital gains into the fund, as well as the ability to add to your fund investments regularly. In addition, tax-free funds provide continuous professional management. You can check the market price of your fund investments daily in the financial pages of the newspaper. Finally, you can select tax-free funds based upon varying maturities of the securities held in the fund: money-market, short, intermediate, and long-term funds. Many investors find that a combination of tax-free funds suits them best.

TAX-FREE INVESTING CHECKLIST

☐

Before making an interest-earning investment, compare the returns of municipal securities with those of corporate and Treasury securities to determine which offers the best after-tax returns.

☐

If you live in a state with a high state income tax, save on both federal and state income taxes by investing in tax-free securities of issuers in your state and/or single-state municipal bond mutual funds.

☐

Be sure to comparison-shop before investing in individual municipal bonds because the market for muni bonds is so unorganized. You will probably be better off investing in municipal bond mutual funds instead.

Stock Investments

I s there still a place for the individual investor in today's stock market? Absolutely! In fact, if you are not investing in today's stock market, you risk falling short of realizing your financial goals. And according to the National Association of Investors Corporation, over 51 million individual investors invest in the New York Stock Exchange alone.

But the market itself is no children's playground. While the individual investor is still a major participant, institutional investors play an active and, at times, disruptive role in the markets with their program trading and all-too-frequent brushes with scandal. This chapter will provide you with some guidance on understanding stock investing and how to do it wisely. One of the biggest mistakes an investor can make is to jump into the market, buying stock indiscriminately, with little or no regard to a stock's suitability for his or her particular portfolio. While getting into the stock market—by purchasing shares either directly or indirectly, through a stock mutual fund—is the right move for you, doing it suddenly, without planning, may imperil your finances in short order.

You may be one of the millions of people who feel that the roller-coaster ride of stock investing is just too risky. Yes, it is a roller-coaster ride, but *not* investing in stocks may be even riskier. Why? Because stocks have consistently proven to be the best inflation-beating investment around. According to statistics compiled by Ibbotson Associates of Chicago, a one-dollar investment made at the end of 1925 would have grown to the following by the end of 1991:

GROWTH OF ONE DOLLAR FROM 1925 TO 1991	
TREASURY BILLS	$11
LONG–TERM GOVERNMENT BONDS	$22
COMMON STOCKS	$675

In this day and age, if you don't beat inflation, you really don't stand a chance of making any headway in your financial life. So if you haven't invested in stocks, my advice to you is first, to learn about them, and then begin to invest in stocks *gradually*. There's no real rush, as long as you begin to add stocks to your investments. Incidentally, you may have nothing but disdain for stocks, but if you participate in a pension plan, you can bet that more than half of your pension plan's assets are invested in stocks.

Investing in some time to learn about common stocks, prior to investing in them, will help you avoid costly mistakes. This chapter explains the various types of stock investments, ways to invest in stocks, and when to buy and sell them.

Some stock markets are safer than others. In general, it's best to invest at home rather than abroad. Investing in foreign markets will increase the diversity of your overall investments—always a good idea—but unless you are investing through an American mutual fund company that specializes in international or global investing, chances are you won't have access to the information about the country's economic condition that you need. It is probably best to consider purchasing stocks traded on the major U.S. markets: New York Stock Exchange (NYSE), National Association of Securities Dealers Automated Quotation (NASDAQ), and the American Stock Exchange (AMEX).

Ways to Own Common Stocks

T here are two ways to own common stocks: directly and indirectly.

Direct Ownership

Direct ownership of a stock means that you (or your broker) hold the certificate of the stock of the company that you've purchased. (In the future, it may mean that you "hold" a serial number that designates the number of shares you purchased, since stock certificates are simply too inconvenient in this electronic age.)

Indirect Ownership

Indirect ownership of stocks is made possible by mutual funds, where as an investor, you own shares of a stock mutual fund. This fund, in turn, owns shares of the stock of many corporations. Stock mutual funds offer a lot advantages over stocks, particularly if you are a new investor or you don't yet have enough money to purchase several individual stocks. (For more information on stock mutual funds, see pages 516-17.)

One of the big advantages of owning shares directly relates to taxes. As long as you hold on to a stock, you don't have to pay taxes when it appreciates in value. You pay taxes only when you sell the stock at a profit. Since the stock mutual fund manager is constantly buying and selling stocks in the mutual fund (that's what he or she is supposed to do), you can't control the timing of the capital-gains taxes passed on to you by the fund.

So which is better, stocks or stock mutual funds? Since there are advantages and drawbacks to both, the answer may be a little of each, if you can afford it.

Types of Common Stocks

A *common stock* is a security that represents an ownership interest in a corporation. Investors in common stocks may benefit in two ways. First, the company may pay dividends to its shareholders. Second, investors may benefit through capital appreciation—an increase of the share price of stock. Not all common stocks are the same, however. Some pay dividends, and some don't. Some have relatively stable prices, while others are more volatile. Most common stocks are classified into one of several categories.

Income Stocks

Income stocks are usually bought for current income, as they have a higher-than-average dividend yield. Companies whose stocks fall into this category are typically in fairly stable industries (for example, telecommunications and utilities), have strong finances, and pay out a substantial portion of their earnings in dividends. Income stocks are popular with retirees and others who depend on stability and regular dividend income.

Growth Stocks

Investors buy growth stocks for capital appreciation. Because most growth companies have to finance their growth and are involved in research, most or all of their earnings are reinvested in the company for future expansion. Thus, while growth stocks have the prospect of increased market value, they pay little, if any, dividends. The prices of growth stocks usually rise in value more than do those of other stocks, but they also decline in price more significantly.

Blue-Chip Stocks

Blue-chip stocks are considered the highest quality of all common stocks because they are dominant companies that have the ability to pay steady dividends in both good and bad years. All of the thirty Dow Jones industrials, including General Electric and Coca-Cola, are blue-chip stocks. These companies hold dominant positions in industries that generally are not as vulnerable to cyclical market swings as other industries.

Cyclical Stocks

Cyclical stocks are issued by companies whose earnings tend to fluctuate sharply with their business cycles. When business conditions are good, a cyclical company's profitability is high and the price of its common stock rises. But when conditions deteriorate, the company's sales and profits fall sharply. For example, the housing and steel industries suffer when interest rates are high because high interest rates hurt their customers. Thus, the correct timing of transactions is crucial to a successful investment in cyclical stocks.

Speculative Stocks

In a sense, all common stocks are speculative stocks, since they offer a variable rather than a fixed return. But some stocks are more speculative than others. A speculative stock typically has a high stock price in relation to the company's earnings, extensive share price fluctuations, and a higher risk of loss of all or most of the investment. "Hot" new issues, high-flying glamour stocks, and penny mining stocks are speculative stocks.

You should avoid them unless you can easily afford the loss; they usually are traded successfully only by expert investors. The best way for the average investor to play speculative stocks is to buy shares of a mutual fund that specializes in them.

To decide upon which common stocks to emphasize, you need to step back for a moment and assess your own financial needs and investment objectives. Your age might also influence your investment selection. For example, although growth stocks are relatively risky, they are attractive investments if you are relatively young and are looking for long-term capital appreciation in your portfolio. On the other hand, income stocks tend to be less volatile. Such stocks may be useful if you are seeking an investment that can provide an income supplement in addition to the opportunity for some capital appreciation.

What Are the Risks?

The essential rewards of owning stocks—dividends and capital appreciation—are, of course, accompanied by risks. Risks of owning a common stock include the risk that the stock's price will decline and the risk that dividend payments will be reduced or eliminated. Stock prices can fall rapidly, particularly if there is a sudden and severe impairment in a company's well-being. You can reduce this risk if you diversify your holdings across several companies (always a good idea) and if you limit your stockholdings to larger, well-established corporations.

If a company's ability to generate profits is impaired, chances are its share price will fall. Changes in competition, demand for products, costs, or management all can affect a company and, hence, its stock. The best way to insulate or to protect yourself against such unfavorable changes is to keep up to date on both the overall economy and industry-specific factors that affect the company in which you've invested. This is a big task and all the more reason why you may want to emphasize well-established, dominant companies in your stock portfolio or make sure you have a financial adviser (stockbroker or investment manager) who will keep abreast of the company's profitability in relation to economic developments.

Price Fluctuations

Stock price fluctuations can simply happen. When they do, the pundits offer a range of "explanations." For example, even if a corporation's financial outlook does not change, the price of its stock can, and often does, fluctuate widely. Some causes: intermittent transactions by buyers and sellers of the stock, and investors' periodic preferences for different types of investments.

Moreover, the price of a stock you own may fluctuate simply because the stock market in general is moving upward or downward. As the saying goes, "A rising tide floats all ships."

While you can't ignore price fluctuations in stocks that you own, you shouldn't become obsessed with them, either. The only certainty in stock market investing is that prices will fluctuate. But you have to remind yourself that, to the extent that price fluctuations are caused by market forces in general (rather than company-specific forces), over the long run your willingness to accept the risks associated with stock investing will be rewarded with good, inflation-beating returns.

Suggestions for Investing in Common Stock

Never Buy Stocks Indiscriminately

Many investors buy stocks haphazardly simply because they have money to spend. This is a bad practice; investments should be made when you have a good reason to buy a particular stock.

Select a Promising Industry

At any given time, most industries in the economy are either on the upswing or on the downswing with respect to earnings potential. When choosing a stock to buy, start by selecting a promising industry. (You should always have a good reason for selecting an industry.) Then, look for a company within that industry whose future looks promising. The *Value Line Investment Survey* ranks industries as well as stocks each week.

Diversify

Try to own stocks in several different industries. The danger of having too many eggs in one basket can't be stressed too much. On the other hand, overdiversification with a small amount of money is unwise. You can keep track of five stocks more easily than twenty-five stocks. Incidentally, studies have shown that investors can achieve excellent diversification with as few as ten or twelve stocks.

Buy Low and Sell High

Condition yourself to buy stock when a company's share price is down and to sell it when the price is up. Stocks of good companies are more likely to gain when prices are low. Major selling opportunities come when the stock is hot (everybody wants to own it) and prices are high. This is the famous "buy low, sell high" rule.

Definition

Value Line Investment Survey provides rankings, descriptions, and evaluations of more than fifteen hundred stocks. It is available in many libraries.

Stay Abreast of Market Trends

It is always important when considering a stock to look at the general trend in the market. A stock that has already risen in value might be a good candidate for continued gains if the market is still rising. Conversely, a stock that does not respond to a general market rise may turn out to be a poor investment.

Use Stop-Loss Orders to Protect Against Loss

Remember, potential losses can be effectively limited by using stop-loss orders (they're not available on over-the-counter stocks), which "fence in" gains by restricting the effects of a price downturn on your stocks.

Stop-loss orders can also be used to force you to sell. For example, if you buy a stock at $12 per share and it rises to $18 per share (lucky you!), you might put a stop-loss order in at $15 per share to lock in a gain. The risk of this strategy is that you might get left behind at $15 per share if the stock dips to this level temporarily and then continues rising. But this may be less risky than a loss due to a plummeting stock price.

Maintain Long Holding Periods

The buy-and-hold strategy of investing usually works for high-quality stocks because the general market gains ground over time, and thus the value of most holdings increases. Only more experienced investors are consistently successful with a "trading" strategy—one that involves frequent buying and selling. Studies have shown that over most holding periods of ten years or longer, buy-and-hold investors have enjoyed returns well in excess of inflation. Active traders generally have not fared as well.

Buy Good Performers

Try to buy value. Companies with strong finances and solid earnings growth are consistently better long-run performers.

Use the "Low P/E and High Dividend" Strategy

Many successful long-term investors use the investment strategy of purchasing common stocks of companies with relatively low price-to-earnings (P/E) ratios and relatively high dividend yields. For example, using a "7 and 7" strategy, you can buy stock in companies with a P/E ratio of less than 7 and a dividend yield of greater than 7. The logic behind this is that the stock price is depressed (a low P/E ratio), and hence the stock is being purchased when no one else wants it. This is in itself a good strategy so long as the company has no major long-term problems.

The dividend yield of such stocks is already attractive, and what you're doing is betting that when the P/E ratio returns to normal (perhaps 12), the company will increase its dividend to maintain an attractive yield.

Participate in Dividend Reinvestment Plans

If you own stock in one of the over 1,000 corporations that offer dividend reinvestment plans, participating in the plan is a smart way to add to your holding. Why? First, the company will either waive or sharply reduce any commissions incurred when reinvesting your dividends or when making any optional additional purchases of stock that you can make simply by sending a check. Second, many companies also offer to sell you these additional shares at a slight discount. All in all, dividend reinvestment is a very convenient way to build up your stock investments. Only your broker won't agree.

The benefits go beyond building your portfolio at a minimum cost. Reinvestment is also a way for investors to force themselves to save. Of course, if you are investing for income, dividend reinvesting may not be for you, since you'll stop receiving the dividend checks. One other drawback: You have to pay income taxes on the reinvested dividends as if you had received and cashed them in yourself. And the discounted difference between the price at which you bought the shares and their market price is taxable to you.

Buy Stocks in Companies with Strong Dividend Payment Records

If you think the market is heading for troubled water, consider buying stocks in companies that have a consistent history of paying generous dividends. In a bear market, these companies have tended to decline less in price than companies that pay no dividend at all or that pay dividends erratically, since investors are confident that the dividends will keep coming through thick and thin. As always, check on the current financial position of any company before investing in it.

Evaluating Your Stock Investments

Knowing which stocks in your portfolio to sell, and when to sell them, is at least as important as knowing when to buy a stock. One general rule of thumb is that any stock that you now hold that you don't currently consider to be an attractive "buy" candidate should be considered a candidate for sale.

Warning Signs

There are several red flags that should alert you to the potential need to sell stock.

- **IF** a company's growth rate or earnings trend peaks and then falls, selling should be considered.

- **IF** a company cuts its dividend or ceases to pay a dividend, it is usually a sign that the company is in trouble. You should sell the stock.

- **MARKET EXPERTS** even go so far as to say that if a dividend remains steady, or if its rises are behind those of the market in general, it may be time to sell.

- **PRICE TARGETS** are another means of hedging against drops in the market. Shares generally hover in a range from which they depart only under extreme circumstances. If a share goes below its trading range, it probably should be sold.

- **WHEN** a stock reaches an apparent upper limit, it may also be time to sell. Realizing present profits may be better than waiting for an additional gain, which may not materialize.

General Market Guidelines

You may want to use some general guidelines for predicting market declines, although, of course, the market can never truly be predicted. The following indicators may signal that the market is headed for a drop. Most of the information to which they refer is easily obtainable in the financial press.

- **INTEREST RATES.** Rising rates can divert money from stocks to competing investments, depressing stock prices.

- **ECONOMIC CONDITIONS.** Historically, recessions have often been preceded by stock market declines. Therefore, early indications of an economic slump may be reason to lessen market exposure. On the other hand, stock prices have often rebounded before the end of a recession, which argues against selling stocks during a recession.

- **DIVERGENCE.** Conditions that cause one broad market index to rise while another declines often signal the end of a rally.

- **PRICE INFLATION.** Soaring price to earnings ratios and depressed dividend yields are often signs that market prices are unsustainable.

Guidelines for Selling

Although there are no foolproof methods for selling (or buying) stocks, the following suggestions and guidelines should be considered.

Haste makes waste

Don't make any investment with the intention of selling it within the next few years. One of the reasons you buy high-quality stocks, interest-earning investments, and mutual funds is to avoid having to worry all the time about whether or not you should sell them.

Two-year rule

If the performance of an investment over two consecutive years is "disappointing," sell it. Define "disappointing" as a stock that does not keep up with the Standard and Poor's 500 stock average over two consecutive years or a mutual fund that lags the annual average performance of its category for two consecutive years. This rule of thumb may mean that you hold on to a poor investment longer than you should, but that mistake is often better than selling too often. Selling too often does not work.

Timing

You should also evaluate the timing of a sale of stock in light of the taxes that will be paid on the capital gain. For example, there still may be situations in which it is beneficial for you to defer capital gains from one year to another. Put options may be useful toward this end (see page 510).

Tax Advantages

Securities that appreciate in value can be considered as tax-advantaged investments, because taxes on the gains are deferred until the securities are sold. For example, a 31 percent tax bracket investor who puts $25,000 into a 10 percent bond pays federal taxes each year plus any state taxes on the interest earned. Conversely, a $25,000 stock investment that increases 10 percent in market value incurs no tax liability. The 10 percent increase in market value of the stock is far from certain, but in the long run, stock investments tend to enjoy returns above the yields on interest-earning securities.

Even when the stock is sold and taxes are incurred, the income from capital gains on the sale may be taxed at a lower rate than you would pay on interest income.

Preferred Stocks

P referred stocks share features of both bonds and common stocks. A preferred stock is like a bond in that it pays a fixed dividend; it is similar to a common stock in that you cannot receive the dividend unless it is earned and declared by the corporation. Also, the preferred stock can increase (or decrease) in market value.

Type of Ownership

Like common stocks, the majority of preferred stock issues trade on the stock exchanges. But while preferred stock does represent a portion of ownership in a corporation, you, as an owner, normally do not have voting powers, as you do if you are a holder of common stock. Moreover, there's a major disadvantage of preferred stock: Its dividends do not rise, as common dividends often do.

Should a company be liquidated, the preferred shareholders receive priority over the common shareholders in the distribution of assets. Also, preferred stock is usually less volatile than common stock, so preferred stocks offer more stability to your stock portfolio.

Convertible Preferreds

About one-third of all preferred shares are convertible, at the option of the individual shareholders, into the company's common stock. If you're a holder of a convertible preferred share, you can benefit from this feature when the price of the common stock rises above a point where conversion into common stock is financially advantageous. Let's say you buy a thousand shares of a convertible preferred stock (that are convertible into a thousand shares of common stock) for $50 per preferred share. The price of the common stock rises from $45 to $52 per share. You can exercise the conversion option and make $2 per preferred share converted, an aggregate gain of $2,000. (Of course, you must weigh the income advantages of the preferred stock against the capital-gains advantage of the conversion.) The conversion option permits you to participate more fully in a company's success if it prospers, but allows you to retain your preferred position if it does not.

Foreign Stocks

There is always a bull market somewhere in the world, and it often isn't in the good old U.S.A. In fact, foreign stock markets have pretty consistently outperformed the U.S. stock market. As the global economy expands, the importance of foreign stocks will increase. What this all means is that you should be putting a portion of your investment money into foreign stocks. Otherwise, you will be missing out on some excellent investment opportunities.

Foreign stocks, quite simply, are shares of companies that are incorporated in a foreign country and are listed on an overseas stock exchange. Germany, Great Britain, and Japan have very large and well-established stock markets. Smaller markets operate in Australia, Hong Kong, Singapore, and Taiwan. There are many other, smaller and riskier markets as well.

Understand Foreign Currency Risks

How well you do when you invest in foreign stocks depends on two factors. First, the prices of the shares you own may rise or fall. Everyone understands that. Second, the value of the U.S. dollar will fluctuate against the foreign currency that you use to buy the stock. If the value of the U.S. dollar declines against a foreign currency, this means that the foreign currency is worth more compared with the U.S. dollar. This doesn't sound so good, but it is advantageous if you own a foreign stock in that currency, because when you sell the stock, a stronger foreign currency will translate into more U.S. dollars for you. Hence, you stand to gain on the foreign currency side of international investing if the dollar weakens.

On the other hand, if the dollar strengthens against a foreign currency, your foreign-currency-denominated investment will result in your getting fewer dollars from your investment, if and when you sell and convert the proceeds into U.S. dollars.

Foreign Taxing Matters

Capital gains are not taxed by most foreign governments, although you must include such gains on your U.S. income tax returns. The same U.S. capital-gains rate applies to both U.S. and overseas investments. Dividends are another matter. Most foreign governments tax income from dividends on stocks owned by nonresidents. But you are usually allowed to take a tax credit on your U.S. return for dividends that are taxed by a foreign country.

How to Invest Abroad

There are several ways to invest in overseas stocks, ranging from the inconvenient and impractical to the easy and straightforward. At one extreme, you can use a brokerage firm with foreign expertise. Many U.S. firms have departments that research and trade in foreign stocks. If you have got a ton of money, you may be able to afford this expensive and inconvenient route, which often requires that you keep the stock certificates in the foreign country. What a mess!

For most investors, the two sensible ways to invest in overseas stocks are by purchasing either American depository receipts or international mutual funds.

American depository receipts (ADR)

ADRs are negotiable receipts representing ownership of shares of a foreign corporation that is traded in the American securities market. ADRs allow you to buy, sell, or hold foreign stocks without actually taking possession of them. ADRs are traded and transferred in the same way that U.S. stocks are. Hundreds of larger foreign companies can be purchased with ADRs on the New York Stock Exchange, the American Stock Exchange, and the over-the-counter market. Examples of leading ADRs include British Airways, British Petroleum, Honda, NEC, and Unilever.

International mutual funds

There are three main categories of international mutual funds. Mutual funds that invest all over the world (including the United States) are called *global funds.* Those that invest only in non-U.S. companies are called *international funds.* Mutual funds that concentrate their investments in a specific country or geographic region are called *single country funds* or *regional funds.*

International mutual funds are clearly the easiest way to play this important market segment. They are also the best way, because with a broad-based international fund, you are assured of obtaining adequate diversification, not only within a single country but across several countries. Avoid the single country or regional funds. They are too much of a gamble and many investors who have chased after a "hot foreign market" have ended up with a lot less money. It's far better to let a good international mutual fund manager decide how much or how little a fund's money should be placed in a particular foreign market. (For more information about mutual fund investing in general, see Chapter 59.)

Initial Public Offerings

Initial public offerings (IPOs) carry both greater risks and greater possible rewards. As the name implies, IPOs are new issues of the stocks of companies that previously were privately held. Issuing stock gives the company a valuable new source of capital as well as a listing on a stock exchange.

There are two major reasons to purchase new issues: a speculative motive with a short-range time frame, and a growth motive with a long-range perspective based on the company's predicted performance.

Short-Term Speculation

If you want to speculate, the most important criterion for IPO investing success is timing. IPOs are very volatile—much more so than established common stocks. One rule of thumb: Stock prices may bear little relation to the company's actual performance. Regardless of a new company's eventual success or failure, you may reap short-term profits from an IPO because the high level of interest may generate substantial price action. New issues typically follow a cyclical pattern, with prices increasing in proportion to the public interest and perhaps falling rapidly thereafter. Of course, there are no guarantees. Many IPOs have dropped immediately and precipitously the moment they "go public."

Long-Term Investment

The long-term performance of many IPOs can be very positive. As with any other stock held for long-term investment, several questions about the company's financial health must be considered:

- IS the company operating in a growing industry? Does it hold a significant market share or are its products proprietary?

- IS the new company likely to be successful in the industry?

- IS the company an established organization with a proven record of profitability, or is it just starting up?

- DOES the company plan to use its capital in fiscally sound ways?

- IS the company being underwritten by reputable investment banking firms with successful track records?

Examine Company Data

Whether you are interested in an IPO as a short-term speculation or a long-term investment, by all means take the time to review the company's financial data, including the information that is contained in the prospectus.

The company's financial record is probably the most important part of the prospectus.

Declining earnings, past losses or low or non-existent revenues may be warnings of things to come. Companies with high debt levels should also generally be avoided.

The prospectus may contain valuable nonfinancial information as well. For example, legal actions taken against a company may have troubling implications. The prospectus should also specify why the company is issuing stock. For example, if a portion of the proceeds go to corporate officers, they are, in effect, reducing their own holdings. So much for their confidence in the company's future. The prospectus will also reveal how long the current management has been in place, as well as the background and prior experience of key managers.

I recommend that you do your own investigation into an IPO because most investors become so smitten with an "opportunity" preferred by their brokers to get in on the ground floor that they have no idea what they're getting into. Many IPOs are nothing but smoke and mirrors—yet investors flock to them like ducks to a June bug.

Of course, some IPOs turn out to be marvelous investments. A few of them may become another Xerox. But unless you're a major client of your broker, chances are that when you receive the call inviting you to get in on this once-in-a-lifetime opportunity, this particular IPO is not going to be one of the future great companies.

Options

I nvesting in options is highly speculative. If you don't think so, invest a small amount of money in an option—but make sure it is money you can afford to lose, because you're going to lose it. Buying a stock option is a bet on the magnitude and direction of a change in a security's price, and you probably do not have the information needed to predict the price of a security in the short term.

Options written on individual issues of stock are the most familiar type but they are not the only ones available. Options are also traded on various stock indexes, such as the NYSE Composite Index, Standard & Poor's 100 stock and 500 stock indexes, the AMEX Index, and many others. Options are also available on foreign currencies, certain debt instruments such as U.S. Treasury securities, and futures contracts. Hardly a week goes by without an introduction of some new-fangled type of option. Unfortunately, many otherwise intelligent people succumb to the temptation of playing these options.

How Options Work

There are many permutations and combinations of options. Basically, you can buy or sell two kinds: calls and puts. Buying a *call option* gives you the right—but not the obligation—to purchase one hundred shares of a particular widely held, actively traded common stock at a specific price at any time during the life of the option. Buying a *put option* gives you the right—but not the obligation—to sell one hundred shares of a particular stock at a specified price at any time before a specified time. Options are not written on all issues of common stock, only on the most popular ones.

Every option has an *exercise price*, or *strike price*. This is the price at which you may exercise the right you obtained when you bought the option. Every option also has an expiration date, which is the last day on which the buyer is entitled to exercise the option to buy or sell the stock (usually the third Friday of a specified month).

The Role of Options in a Portfolio

Although not all option trading is suitable for all investment goals, option trading can fulfill several types of investment goals in different ways.

Call options

Call options can be used to lock in the price of a stock you want to buy, provide diversity, and, of course, offer opportunities for speculation. If you wish to lock in the price of a stock that you want to purchase at some time in the future—say, when a bond matures—you may buy a call in the expectation that the stock will rise signficantly between now and the time you will be able to buy the stock.

Call options can also help diversify a portfolio. You may consider purchasing a call option on two or more different securities that you expect to rise in value in order to achieve a greater degree of diversification than would be possible if all of your available capital were invested in a single stock.

Since the majority of option *buyers* end up losing money, it stands to reason that the majority of option *writers* (those who are willing to sell the options to the buyers) stand to make money. You may want to consider writing covered options against stock that you now own. Some investors find this to be an attractive, low-risk way to increase their investment income. A word to the wise, however: writing options against stock you don't own (in other words writing uncovered ["naked"] options) is one of the riskiest investment ventures in the history of mankind.

Warning: 70 to 80 percent of all call options on individual stocks expire worthless, resulting in a net loss to the call option's buyer—and a net gain to that option's seller. This means that buyers of call options realize a gain only 20 to 30 percent of the time.

If you are a long-term speculative investor, call options are for the most part not suitable for you. You generally look for industries and companies that are likely candidates for substantial long-term growth. Because listed options are available only on stocks that are among the most widely held and actively traded, many small companies or new issues of stock that might be suitable for speculation do not appear on options listings. Furthermore, options are generally available for only nine months, although some longer-term options have been introduced.

Put options

Put options enable you to take advantage of falling stock prices. The purchase of put options can take the place of selling stock short, especially if you do not want to risk the stock's rising in value. Short-selling is a risky technique where you profit if a stock declines in value. If you sell a stock short, and it subsequently rises in price, your risk of loss is—theoretically, at least—unlimited. On the other hand, the most you can lose with a put option is the amount you paid for it. A major advantage of puts over selling short is that the risks are known and limited.

Tax Considerations

Option trading entails special tax considerations, some of which can be quite beneficial, especially in deferring capital gains.

The buyer of a call option, on exercise of the option, is considered for tax purposes to have purchased stock for a total cost that is equal to the exercise price plus the premium paid for the option (plus any commissions or other costs). Thus, the stock's basis is increased.

The writer of a call option that is exercised is considered to have sold the stock for a total value that is equal to the exercise price plus the premium received for the option (less any commissions or other costs). The period between the initial sale of the option and its exercise is irrelevant for tax purposes; all profits and losses are attributed to the holding of the security itself, which begins on the exercise date for the option buyer and ends on that date for the option seller.

The exercise of put options is treated similarly; for example, a shareholder who exercises a put option may deduct its cost from the gain on the sale of the stock when calculating taxable net capital gain.

If an option is allowed to lapse, you can deduct its cost as a capital loss.

STOCK INVESTMENT CHECKLIST

■□■

You should invest in stocks because they are essential to achieving long-term investment success.

■□■

Understand the general risks of stock investing and the specific risks associated with particular categories of stocks and stock mutual funds. That way, you'll be able to select appropriate stock investments.

■□■

Take advantage of dividend reinvestment plans to build up your stock portfolio.

■□■

Establish your own criteria for deciding when to sell a stock, and stick with it.

■□■

Diversify your stock portfolio, and take advantage of investment opportunities abroad by investing in international or global mutual funds and ADRs.

■□■

Avoid high-risk stocks or stock-related investments unless you fully understand the risks. Such investments include initial public offerings and stock options.

Mutual Funds

Mutual funds are the investment of choice in the 1990s and beyond. They have experienced explosive growth in recent years and are an excellent financial choice for investors who have either a little or a lot of money to invest. Mutual funds offer diversification and professional management to small- and medium-size portfolios that might not be able to afford them otherwise. For fat cats, mutual funds alleviate the burden of evaluating and selecting individual securities. Perhaps the best evidence of the legitimacy of mutual funds as an excellent investment choice is that the huge financial institutions—including pension funds—are entrusting more and more of their own investments to mutual funds.

Basically, a mutual fund is a pool of investors' money that is used to purchase a professionally managed, diversified portfolio of stocks, bonds, money-market instruments, or other securities. Pooling the money gives each investor the benefit of a greater portfolio than his or her funds alone could purchase. Each share in a mutual fund represents a small slice of the total fund portfolio.

The first open-end mutual fund, the Massachusetts Investors Trust, was started in 1924. Industry growth remained relatively sluggish until the postwar stock market boom of the 1950s and 1960s. Then in the late 1960s and early 1970s, a succession of bear markets caused a decline in their popularity. Sales picked up again in the late 1970s and have flourished in recent years with a bullish stock market and the introduction of a variety of bond and money-market funds.

A Competitive Industry

Mutual funds are playing an increasingly important role in individual and institutional investment management, and as mutual funds begin to demonstrate consistency of performance, more investors will see the benefits of this investment method. The mutual fund industry is very competitive, which provides both opportunities and problems for you. To capture investment dollars, mutual funds will offer even more attractive and convenient features, as well as a broader range of funds, particularly in the arena of international stock or bond funds. The almost-daily introduction of new funds will make fund selection that much more challenging. But, as I will show you in this chapter, selecting and monitoring a good mutual fund is a lot easier than selecting and monitoring a handful of individual stocks and bonds.

Every investor needs to consider investment alternatives that will perform well in bad times as well as good. Over the past decade, the *average* stock mutual funds' annual rate of return was almost 12 percent. In fact, many top-performing funds rewarded their investors with substantially greater results. No doubt, that's part of the reason why mutual funds grew from just over $100 billion in assets in 1980 to over $1 trillion in assets by 1991, and why there were more than 3,400 mutual funds from which to choose in 1992, compared with less than 500 in 1980.

Since mutual funds vary in size, objective, and the type of investments they hold, you need to know how and why they differ. The following sections will help you understand the many choices you have. While the range of choices may at first appear intimidating, you actually benefit insofar as there is a fund—or more likely, several different funds—that meet your exact investment requirements. First, let's distinguish among the major fund categories.

Mutual funds should play a major role in your investment program.

Mutual Fund Categories

Stock Funds

A stock (or equity) mutual fund invests its money in stocks of individual companies, large and small, new and old, here and abroad. There are many different types of stock funds, characterized both by the kind of companies in which the fund invests, and by the fund's particular objective. The portion of your portfolio that focuses on long-term growth should include stock funds.

Bond Funds

A bond mutual fund invests its money in bonds of companies or governments that are as varied as those in which the stock funds invest. Bond funds tend to be the more conservative growth- and income-producing portion of an investor's portfolio—although bond fund share prices can and do fluctuate in value. Some bond funds even deliver tax-free income to their investors.

Money-Market Funds

The most conservative and usually least lucrative type of mutual fund is a money-market fund. The net asset value of a money-market share doesn't change—only the interest rate fluctuates. The function of money-market funds—which tend to bring higher returns than a bank's money-market deposit account or savings account—is measured more in terms of their liquidity (easy access to your cash) and stability of principal (least risky).

Advantages and Drawbacks

F or most investors, the advantages of mutual funds far outweigh the disadvantages. On the positive side:

- **OWNING** mutual funds is a low-cost way to diversify your portfolio, thereby reducing investment risk.

- **MOST MUTUAL FUNDS** have low minimum investment requirements. Some funds have *no* minimum investment requirements. Moreover, you can add to your fund investments regularly and easily.

- **BOOKKEEPING TASKS,** such as depositing dividend and interest checks and keeping track of securities transactions, are avoided.

- **YOU HAVE** access to a number of convenient services, such as an option to automatically reinvest dividends and capital gains and make automatic investments at regular intervals. These features are useful for individuals who can benefit from a systematic, forced savings plan (which includes almost everybody). Fund families also often allow you to switch from one type of fund to another with a minimum of paperwork.

- **READILY AVAILABLE** current and past performance records are listed in newspapers, magazines, and other publications.

- **MUTUAL FUNDS** are able to reduce brokerage transaction costs because of the large amount of money they invest.

- **YOUR FUND INVESTMENTS** are selected and managed by experienced professionals who are responsible for monitoring them continuously.

The drawbacks are:

- **LIKE** the securities in which they invest, a stock or bond fund's asset value fluctuates with changing market conditions. (Of course, you face the same risk if you buy individual stocks and bonds.)

- **THE COMMISSION** and fee structures of mutual funds are confusing and often not well disclosed. The funds range from no-load funds, which carry no sales commission and are sold directly to the public, to low-load funds, which have a commission of one to three percent, to load funds, which charge a commission of up to 8.5 percent. Some funds assess a charge if you redeem your fund shares within a specified period of time. To make matters worse, some funds also charge a "sales distribution fee" each year you hold the fund. (You should always find out about a fund's fees before you invest in it.)

- **MUTUAL FUND INVESTORS** cannot control the timing of capital gains since it is the fund manager who makes the decisions about selling fund holdings. In contrast, if you held shares of individual stocks, you could control the timing of capital-gains recognition by simply selling or deferring the sale of a particular stock.

- **BOND FUND INVESTORS** are subject to interest-rate risk. This means that if interest rates rise, the value of your bond fund holdings will drop. (Happily, the opposite can happen as well.) If you held individual bond issues, you would not be subject to interest rate risk as long as you held the bonds until they matured.

Mutual Fund Smorgasbord

Within each of the three categories of mutual funds—stock funds, bond funds, and money-market funds—you have a variety of different types of funds from which to choose. In addition, several specialized funds have been introduced that allow investors to focus on narrow market segments or on particular investment techniques. These are all discussed below.

Stock Funds

Maximum capital-gains funds (also called aggressive growth funds)

These attempt to achieve very high returns by investing in more speculative stocks, maximizing capital-gains income while generating little or no income from dividends. For the manager of these funds, the potential for rapid growth is the primary criterion for investment. Of course, the potential for greater rewards means that these funds are quite risky; they tend to do very well in bull markets and very poorly in bear markets. *Small company growth funds* (also called *emerging growth funds*) are a type of maximum capital-gain fund specializing in stocks of promising small companies.

Long-term-growth funds

These seek capital gains from companies that have the potential for steady growth in earnings. These funds' growth is more stable, less volatile, and more consistent than maximum capital-gains funds. Growth funds aim to achieve a rate of growth that beats inflation without taking the risks necessary to achieve occasional spectacular success.

Growth and income funds

These seek a more balanced stock portfolio that will achieve capital appreciation as well as current income from dividends. These funds are less risky than growth funds, because the dividend may offset at least some of the periodic losses in stock prices. In times of high market volatility—in either an up or a down direction—growth and income funds are slower to respond.

Equity-income funds

These generally invest about half their portfolio in dividend-paying stocks and the rest in convertible securities and bonds. Equity-income funds may have capital growth as a secondary objective to providing current income.

International stock funds

These have been attracting investors' attention because foreign stock markets have pretty consistently outperformed the U.S. stock market. Moreover, there are many excellent companies that trade only on foreign stock exchanges. Therefore, international funds provide additional diversification to a portfolio. Most international funds invest throughout the world. Some invest only in one country or region. *Global stock funds*, however, differ only in that they also invest in U.S. securities.

Bond Funds

For many years, especially during the period of high inflation in the 1970s, bond funds performed poorly. But in the last decade they have performed very well, and they are very attractive to millions of mutual fund investors. Except for funds that invest solely in government bonds, all bond funds have some degree of risk of default; but the real risks of holding bonds or bond funds is that high inflation will outpace the returns and/or rising interest rates will reduce the principal value of the investment. You should also note that within each bond fund category, there are usually several funds that specialize in investments of either short-term duration, intermediate-term duration, or long-term duration.

Corporate bond funds

As the name suggests, these buy and trade bonds of corporations. There are two categories of corporate bond mutual funds: Investment-grade corporate bond funds, which are comprised of high-quality and/or medium-quality corporate bonds and seek high income with limited risk, and high-yield bond funds, which are described below.

Government bond funds

Backed by the full faith and credit of the U.S. government, these offer total protection from bond default, although the value of government bonds will fluctuate with interest rates like all bonds and bond funds. Most government bond funds hold U.S. Treasury securities. One variety of government bond fund, *government mortgage funds*, holds mortgage-backed securities such as those issued by the Government National Mortgage Association (GNMA).

Holders of GNMA funds receive both interest and a partial return of principal, which may be reinvested.

Municipal bond funds

Introduced in 1976, these provide investors with a means for tax-free income. Since municipal fund prices do not appear in the daily papers and are inconvenient for the individual investor to manage, muni bond funds are a useful way to invest in municipal bonds while avoiding these problems. Interest earned from bonds not issued in the investor's own state is fully taxable in his or her own state, so in order to produce maximum tax-free income, *single state funds* have been developed that hold municipal bonds from only one state. A New York resident investor owning the New York muni fund, for example, will avoid state as well as federal taxes on the fund's interest income.

Convertible bond funds

Convertible securities are bonds or preferred stock that can be exchanged for a fixed number of shares in the common stock of the issuing company. The conversion feature is intended to induce investors to accept a lower interest rate in the hopes that the accompanying stock will rise in value and bring up the convertible's value. When stocks rise, convertibles will rise as well—albeit at a slower rate—while when stocks fall, convertibles tend to fall less because of the benefit of their fixed interest yield. Convertible bond funds thus combine features of both stocks and bonds.

International bond funds

Yields on foreign bonds are often higher than those on U.S. bonds. These funds' returns also depend in part on the relative strength of the American dollar. An international bond fund typically invests primarily in high-quality foreign government or corporate bonds, and may enter into currency hedges. These funds can provide an investor with an additional degree of diversification.

High-yield bond funds

Also called junk bond funds, these specialize in low-quality, high-yield bonds that may offer substantial profits but that also carry higher risk. High-yield funds invest either in corporate bonds or municipal bonds. They can be very volatile, and investors in corporate high-yield bond funds have periodically been surprised to find their principal declining, sometimes significantly.

Money–Market Funds

First created in 1972, these have become the most widely held mutual fund category, holding a variety of short-term interest-earning securities. Their three main objectives are preservation of capital, liquidity, and as high an income as can be achieved without sacrificing the first two objectives. Money-market funds offer excellent liquidity—an investor need only write a check to transfer money. These funds are commonly used as a place to hold funds temporarily until new stock or bond investment opportunities arise. *U.S. government money-market funds* and *tax-exempt money-market funds* invest in short-term instruments of the U.S. government and states/municipalities, respectively. Like municipal bond funds, there are also some *single-state tax-exempt money funds.*

Specialized Funds

Specialized funds offer mutual fund investors even more choice. But be careful—the narrower the focus of a fund, the more risk it presents to the investor.

Balanced funds

These maintain a "balanced" combination of common stocks, bonds, and perhaps preferred stocks. Balanced funds may have income, growth, or growth-income as an objective. They provide diversification between stocks and bonds in the same fund with a low minimum investment and are thus a good investment for someone with a small amount to invest.

One of the advantages of balanced funds and a major reason they have done so well as long-term investments is the forced discipline that they impose on the fund manager. As stock prices rise, the fund manager is forced to sell stocks to bring the portfolio back into balance. Conversely, if stock prices decline, the fund manager will be purchasing stock to bring the fund back into balance. Thus, the manager is forced to "buy low" and "sell high." Would that all of us could enforce that discipline upon our investments! Balanced funds are the one fund to own if you own only one fund. (They're a great IRA investment, too.)

Specialized industry funds

Also known as sector funds, these invest only in the stocks of a single industry, such as biotechnology, waste management, utilities, or energy. Sector funds, unlike well-diversified funds, zero in on a particular area of the stock market that may or may not have attractive prospects. The lack of diversity across industries means that sector funds can rapidly switch from excellent to abysmal performance. Sector funds behave more like individual stocks than diversified funds, and selection of a sector fund cannot be made by using the same criteria (such as past track record and management skill) that usually guide the purchase of funds.

Don't be surprised if you see sector funds dominating the list of high-performing mutual funds over the past quarter or year. But before rushing to make an investment, realize that you'll probably find this fund ranked among the worst performers a year later.

Asset allocation funds

These provide extremely broad diversification. They generally invest in up to five or six different markets, so that any one market's losses may be offset by another's gain. Variable funds, commonly referred to as *market timing funds*, may shift allocation according to large economic trends and are thus more flexible. Many investors are attracted to the ability of market timing funds to get in and out of the market. But these funds haven't performed very well and are unlikely to perform well simply because no one has yet been able to accurately time when you should be in or out of the stock and bond markets.

Precious metal funds

Often called gold funds, these usually invest in stocks of gold-mining firms and other companies engaged in the business of precious metals. Some funds may actually purchase and store the metal itself. These funds tend to move in synchronization with precious metal prices. Historically, precious metal funds have been considered an inflation hedge, but lackluster performance in recent years has brought this into question.

Option funds

Stock options are so complex an investment that a well-managed fund is a very effective way of entering the options market. Most option funds are conservative and income oriented. In a long-term bull market, option funds tend to perform poorly; they are at their best in a flat market.

Index funds

These replicate the performance of all of the stocks in an index—the Standard & Poor's 500, for example. These "unmanaged" funds have always attracted the attention of institutional investors who have had a very difficult time beating the market. By simply duplicating a broad section of the market, an institution can save a lot of money on management, research, and trading fees. You can do the same through an index fund.

Socially responsible funds

Several funds limit their investments to companies they consider to be socially responsible. For example, some funds do not invest in companies that manufacture defense-related products or tobacco products. Other funds are committed exclusively to companies that make a contribution to world peace.

Open-End versus Closed-End Funds

 Mutual funds can also be divided into the way they are organized and how their shares are priced.

Open-End Funds

Open-end funds can issue unlimited numbers of shares so that any investor who wants to purchase shares in it can do so. (A few open-end funds have closed their doors to new investors, generally because the fund has enjoyed a spectacular performance record and therefore risks attracting more money than the manager feels he or she can effectively manage.) The disbursement of the new money into a fund is left to the discretion of the fund manager(s). He or she may invest it immediately or may hold it in reserve for future purchases.

There are many investment advantages to open-end mutual funds, but there is one particular advantage that open-end funds offer a new investor: small minimum-initial-investment requirements. Many large fund families require initial minimal investments in the $2,000 to $3,000 range, but you can begin to invest in many open-end funds with as little as $100. Some funds have no minimum. This makes them an attractive place for first-time investors, young investors just starting out, and even as gifts for children. (Starting your children off on the road to investing doesn't have to cost you an arm and a leg. For more ideas about introducing your child to investing, see Chapter 20.)

The value of open-end fund shares is based on the daily market value of the investments held by the fund. If the investments in the fund rise in value, the net asset value (NAV) of the fund's shares rises, too. The NAV of a fund is the price of one share in the fund based on the total value of the fund's investments divided by the number of the fund's outstanding shares. It is calculated at the end of every trading day and is listed the following day in the financial section of most city newspapers. That doesn't mean you should look at the price of your mutual fund NAV every day in the newspaper. It will do nothing but create anxiety if you do so.

An open-end fund will also provide its investors with dividends and interest earned on the securities in which it invests. The shareholder can choose to receive those profits or to automatically reinvest them (a wise move). Similarly, most mutual funds generate realized capital gains for their shareholders which you can choose to receive in cash (a check, really) or to reinvest (also a wise move).

Closed-End Funds

Also known as "publicly traded funds," a closed-end fund has a fixed capital structure—just like that of an ordinary corporation—and a fixed, limited number of shares outstanding. A set number of shares are issued, then publicly traded among investors on one of the stock exchanges. Many closed-end funds are managed by the most successful and best-known money managers in the business. This factor increases their attractiveness to would-be investors hoping to capitalize on the manager's expertise and record of success.

Closed-end funds have a net asset value, just as open funds do, but there's a twist: If the demand for the closed-end fund's shares is great, the price of the shares may trade above, or at a *premium* to, the NAV. Likewise, if demand for the shares declines, the shares may trade at a *discount.* If you buy a closed-end fund's shares at a discount, and they later trade at a NAV premium, you will realize a gain, all other things being equal.

In some instances, closed-end shares can be bought at a substantial discount from their net asset value per share. For example, a closed-end mutual fund might have a NAV of $15 per share but might be selling at a 15 percent discount, or at $12.75 per share. Therefore, for every share the investor purchases, he or she buys $15 worth of investment assets for $12.75. The discounts, however, can widen. There is no obvious reason for closed-end funds to trade at a discount or premium from net asset values, so playing the closed-end market in anticipation of a narrowing discount or increasing premium is speculative at best.

Warning: New issue closed-end funds are often heavily promoted, but because of the high likelihood that the closed-end fund will trade at a discount immediately after issue, you should avoid them.

Commissions and Fees

I t's very important to understand and consider all commissions, annual expenses, and management fees *before* you invest in a fund. While such expenses and fees won't knock all the potential profit out of your investment, they can certainly cramp your investment's performance. How much? Say you invest $1,000 in a fund that charges a 6 percent load (commission) and turns in a 10 percent performance for the year. You still earn the 10 percent—but not on $1,000. Rather, you earn 10 percent on $940. That may not sound like a lot, but since you start out with less money working for you at the outset with a load fund, the ultimate return will be less, all other things being equal. But don't make a common mistake of thinking that no-load funds mean no management fees whatsoever. Every fund charges management fees and expenses. (Some may temporarily waive these charges as an inducement to new investors.) Nevertheless, some funds' fees and expenses are far more reasonable than others. You'll need to shop around—for the best fund with reasonable annual fees and expenses.

Smart Money Move

Never buy shares in a newly issued closed-end fund. New closed-end funds almost always decline in value after they begin trading on the secondary market.

Load Funds

A load is an up-front sales commission charged and deducted from your initial investment amount. Load charges range as high as 8.5 percent, but most are in the 4 to 6 percent range. Is the load justified? If you really need someone to advise you on selecting a mutual fund, that person deserves to be compensated. On the other hand, you wouldn't be reading this book if you weren't interested in taking charge of your own financial life. By doing a little of your own research, you can avoid paying a load, and you'll have more money going to work for you from day one. Don't believe the common sales pitches that load funds outperform no-load funds or that load funds have lower annual expenses than no-load funds. With a little bit of effort, you can find a no-load fund that is every bit as good as any load fund.

Low-Load Funds

Another subspecies of mutual fund is the *low-load* fund. These funds typically charge a fee of between 1 and 3 percent. While this assessment isn't too onerous, it's up to you whether it's worth paying to get into the fund.

No-Load Funds

No-load fund investing is a great way to invest. No-load funds charge no initial sales commission fee, so not only are you taking advantage of one of the most successful, simple, and strategic investment vehicles—mutual funds—but you are doing it at a minimum cost to yourself. (See the listing of major no-load mutual fund companies at the end of this chapter.)

Other Fees and Expenses

Back-End Loads

More commonly known as "redemption fees" (although there's little that is redeeming about them), they are taken from the net asset value of your shares when you sell them. The immediate result is that your profit is diminished, or your loss is increased. Sour grapes!

Deferred Loads (Contingent Deferred Sales Charges)

Some funds impose a deferred load that kicks in if you redeem your shares before a specified time, often five years. In such instances, your initial investment amount is docked a percentage amount, and this percentage usually declines the longer you hold the fund. Even though deferred loads may seem disagreeable, in principle they make some sense. How so? They are meant to discourage investors from jumping into and out of the fund.

Reinvestment Loads

If you have chosen to have your dividends reinvested—usually a very wise choice—be aware of the fact that a few fund companies will charge you for the privilege. The way it's done is to charge a load on your reinvested dividends, interest, and capital gains. Again, check the prospectus of each fund carefully so that you can cull such a ridiculous charge (and the fund that charges it) from your list of funds in which to invest.

Waived Fees

A section on fees may not be the best place to mention this, but I couldn't resist. Some funds actually temporarily waive all fees! These funds are worth tracking down and researching to see if they otherwise suit your investment needs. The price is right, and all other things being equal, it will increase your return. Take advantage of their generosity!

12b-1 Fees

Some funds deduct the costs associated with advertising and marketing themselves directly from the fund's overall assets rather than from management fees. The charge associated with such deductions is called a 12b-1, and it typically amounts to one-quarter to one-half of one percent, but can range as high as 1.25 percent. Some funds even feed a portion of the fee to the broker who sold you the fund. Avoid funds with 12b-1 fees greater than .25 percent.

Expense Ratio

Located in every fund's prospectus, the expense ratio is a critical management-cost indicator for would-be fund investors. It is the cost of running a fund expressed as a percentage of the fund's assets. Mutual fund expenses include all annual costs of running the fund including the 12b-1 fee, if any, but excluding brokerage commissions for buying and selling the fund's securities.

Expense ratios vary from fund to fund—often widely. So it behooves you to check out a fund's expense ratio. Bond funds are cheaper to run than stock funds. A bond fund should generally have an expense ratio of less than 1 percent, while any stock fund with an expense ratio of more than 1.25 percent is on the high side. Excluded from these general rules of thumb are specialized funds, particularly international funds, which may have considerably higher expense ratios because of the specialized nature of their investment activities. While the most important criterion in selecting a mutual fund is past performance, don't ignore expense ratios. Look around. You'll find many good-performing funds with low expense ratios—the best of all worlds.

The Prospectus

How can you tell one mutual fund from another? Each fund has a specific objective that dictates what the fund invests in and how it will be managed. You find out about such details by reading the fund's *prospectus*.

What You Should Look For in a Prospectus

- HOW the fund has performed in the past

- HOW the fund is managed

- WHAT the fund's objectives are

- WHAT the minimum investment amount is

- WHAT FEES, if any, are associated with purchasing and operating the fund

- HOW you can purchase and redeem shares.

Why a Fund's Objective Is So Important

A fund's objective is its investment credo. It states the kinds of investments that the fund will make, as well as the investment strategies that the fund manager uses. Since funds vary considerably in the amount of risk they assume to achieve their objectives, you need to know what each fund's objective is so that you can find a fund that matches the amount of risk you can live with.

How to Purchase Mutual Fund Shares Yourself

The mechanics of purchasing shares in most mutual funds couldn't be easier, even if you're doing it yourself by buying a no-load fund. All you need to do is dial the investment company's twenty-four-hour toll-free number and request the prospectuses for the funds in which you're interested. If you don't know what funds they offer, or if you don't know which fund group—stock, bond, money-market, tax-free—to choose from, ask the investor representative to send you a range of fund prospectuses that fall within your investment purview.

In a matter of days, you'll have a host of material to read and act upon. Many of the fund companies also have helpful brochures that explain about mutual fund investing in general and individual fund selection. They also may have brochures that will show you how you can use mutual funds to meet specific financial goals, such as providing a college education for your children or retirement. Make sure to ask about them when you phone a fund company or speak with your broker.

Investor Service Centers

Many larger no-load mutual fund companies have investor service centers in major cities. These are hosted by genial account representatives who are well versed in the art of opening accounts quickly and efficiently.

Automatic Investing

You can set up an automatic mutual fund investment account for most funds. It's as simple as requesting, receiving, and filling out an application form in which you authorize the fund to withdraw a specified amount from your checking or savings account on a periodic basis—usually monthly. In some instances, automatic investing can also be done as a direct deposit from your paycheck.

The Kind of Service You Deserve

In addition to offering automatic reinvestment of dividends and capital gains, fund companies offer a variety of services including transfers between funds, regular withdrawal plans, check-writing, and IRA and Keogh accounts.

Selecting a Fund Portfolio That's Right for You

The task of assembling a portfolio of mutual funds may seem daunting at first, given the wide variety of funds that are available. But you will find that with a little effort, you can construct a very suitable group of funds that will help you achieve your financial objectives. Funds have a wide variety of investment objectives, such as maximum capital gains, growth and income, or income. Many investors are well served by investing a part of their money in several funds in different categories. There are four levels of analysis that are necessary before actually selecting individual funds.

1. Determine Your Investment Objectives

Before you can start to acquire appropriate investments, you need to clearly specify your investment objectives. How much risk can you afford to take? What major future financial hurdles, such as college-education costs, will you need to overcome, and when? What are your future income prospects? By realistically assessing your current situation and future needs, you can begin to identify what you want to accomplish with your investments. From there, you can begin to identify the kinds of mutual funds that will help you meet your investment objectives.

2. Determine an Appropriate Portfolio Allocation

The portfolio allocation process involves assigning appropriate percentages of your total investment portfolio (no matter how small or large it may be) to stock, bond, and cash-equivalent investment alternatives. Virtually everyone should have stock investments, and many experts suggest that stocks constitute 50 to 60 percent of a portfolio for younger people and 40 to 50 percent of a portfolio for older people, including recent retirees.

3. Identify Appropriate Categories of Mutual Funds

After you have decided on your portfolio allocation, the specific categories of investments within the stock portion and interest-earning portion must be determined. You need to consider several things, including your investment objectives, current financial status, the current investment climate, and your familiarity with the various fund categories. The following table, "Sample Mutual Fund Portfolio Allocation," is an illustration of a typical allocation, based upon a 50-50 split between stock funds and interest-earning funds.

SAMPLE MUTUAL FUND PORTFOLIO ALLOCATION

INVESTMENT CATEGORY	PERCENTAGE OF TOTAL PORTFOLIO
Stock funds:	
MAXIMUM CAPITAL GAIN	10 %
GROWTH AND INCOME	20
INDEX	10
INTERNATIONAL	10
SUBTOTAL: STOCK FUNDS	50
Interest-earning funds:	
CORPORATE BOND	10
GOVERNMENT BOND	15
MUNICIPAL BOND	15
MONEY MARKET	10
SUBTOTAL: INTEREST-EARNING FUNDS	50
TOTAL FUND PORTFOLIO:	100 %

Note that the stock fund portion of the portfolio includes aggressive funds but is heavily weighted in favor of more conservative funds. International stock funds are also included. The interest-earning side of the portfolio is broadly diversified among a variety of interest-earning investment categories. Mutual funds are an excellent way for you to assemble an appropriate portfolio even though you don't yet have a lot of money.

Well diversified, this portfolio could be assembled with less than $20,000.

4. Select Good Funds in Each Category

Selecting a good mutual fund is not a difficult task because there are so many good funds within each category. If you rely on someone else to recommend a fund for you, be sure to ask them why they're high on the fund. Especially if you're paying them for their advice.

If you want to select your own fund, the best thing to do is to go over to the library and check one of the mutual fund monitoring services such as Wiesenberger/CDA or Morningstar. Also, the major financial newspapers, including *The Wall Street Journal* and *Barron's* and the financial magazines, including *Money, Kiplinger's Personal Finance, Forbes*, and *Business Week*, provide periodic coverage of mutual fund performance.

What should you be looking for? Long-term performance is the single most important criterion. Ideally, the fund should have been in existence at least five, and better, ten years. That way, the organizations and periodicals that rate performance can evaluate the fund in both up and down markets. A fund that consistently ranks above average *within its category* is probably a good choice so long as the fund itself invests in securities that you are comfortable with. Ideally, it will rank above average over the past one, three, five, and ten years.

Evaluating Your Fund Portfolio

Once you have put together a mutual fund portfolio, you will need to evaluate it periodically in terms of both the allocation of the total portfolio and individual fund performance.

With respect to the portfolio as a whole, you will need to refigure how the total fund assets are allocated. Is the allocation in line with your parameters? If not, perhaps some reallocation is necessary. In other words, if stock prices have risen sharply, the proportion of stocks in relation to your total portfolio is probably higher than you had originally determined was appropriate. If so, you should sell some of your stock funds and buy additional interest-earning funds. Note that you would do the opposite if stock prices fell. As you may surmise, this disciplined approach to fund evaluation forces you to sell stock funds when prices are high and buy stock funds when prices have dropped. This is exactly what most investors should be doing, but few have the discipline, and most do the opposite. How often should you reallocate? Certainly no more than once per quarter and probably less frequently, unless there has been a precipitous change in stock or bond prices.

Beyond having to sell certain funds as part of a portfolio reallocation, you also need to periodically make an objective evaluation of each individual fund in your portfolio. If you selected good funds in the first place, you are probably better off holding on to them even if they disappoint you for a few months or quarters. But if a fund that you own consistently turns in results that are below average for its fund category, you should consider replacing it with a better performing fund. I follow this rule of thumb: I won't sell a fund unless it performs below its category average for two consecutive years. This doesn't happen very often, however. Most important, don't fret over short-term fluctuations in either market conditions or in the performance of individual funds in your investment "stable."

FOR FURTHER INFORMATION

Major no-load mutual fund companies

This list provides the names, addresses, and telephone numbers of investment companies offering no-load mutual funds. Some of the companies listed also offer load funds. No-load funds do not charge sales commissions and can be purchased directly through the offering company without going through a broker. Call or write the specific company for information on their funds. Products and services vary from company to company.

»

Benham Management Corporation
1665 Charleston Road
Mountain View, CA 94043
(800) 321-8321

Boston Company Advisors Group
One Boston Place
Boston, MA 02108
(800) 225-5267

Columbia Funds Management
Company
1301 S.W. Fifth
P.O. Box 1350
Portland, OR 97207
(800) 547-1707

Dimensional Fund Advisors
1299 Ocean Avenue, Suite 650
Santa Monica, CA 90401
(213) 395-8005

Dreyfus Corporation
144 Glenn Curtis Boulevard
Uniondale, NY 11556
(800) 242-8671

Evergreen Asset Management
Corporation
2500 Westchester Avenue
Purchase, NY 10577
(800) 235-0064

Federated Research Corporation
Federated Investors Tower
Pittsburgh, PA 15222-3779
(800) 245-2423

Fidelity Management & Research
Corporation
82 Devonshire Street
Boston, MA 02109
(800) 522-7297

Founders Asset Management
Founders Financial Center
2930 East Third Avenue
Denver, CO 80206
(800) 525-2440

Harris Associates L.P.
(Acorn Fund)
2 North LaSalle Street, Suite 500
Chicago, IL 60602-3790
(800) 922-6769

Heine Securities Corporation
(The Mutual Series Funds)
51 John F. Kennedy Parkway
Short Hills, NJ 07078
(800) 448-3863

INVESCO Fund Group
(Financial Funds)
P.O. Box 2040
Denver, CO 80201
(800) 525-8085

Investors Research Corporation
(Twentieth Century Funds)
4500 Main Street
P.O. Box 418210
Kansas City, MO 64141-9210
(800) 345-2021

Janus Capital
100 Fillmore Street, Suite 300
Denver, CO 80206
(800) 525-3713

Jones & Babson, Inc.
Three Crown Center
2440 Pershing Road
Kansas City, MO 64108
(800) 422-2766

»

Neuberger & Berman Management
605 Third Avenue, 2nd Floor
New York, NY 10158
(800) 877-9700

Nicholas Company
700 Water Street, Suite 1010
Milwaukee, WI 53202
(414) 272-6133

Price (T. Rowe) Associates
100 East Pratt Street
Baltimore, MD 21202
(800) 638-5660

Reich & Tang L.P.
100 Park Avenue
New York, NY 10017
(800) 221-3079

SAFECO Mutual Funds
P.O. Box 34890
Seattle, WA 98124-1890
(800) 426-6730

The Scudder Funds
P.O. Box 2291
Boston, MA 02107-2291
(800) 225-2470

SEI Financial Management
Corporation
53 State Street

Boston, MA 02109
(800) 345-1151

SteinRoe & Farnham
P.O. Box 1143
Chicago, IL 60690
(800) 338-2550

Strong/Corneliuson Capital
Management
100 Heritage Reserve
P.O. Box 2936
Menomonee Falls, WI 53201
(800) 368-3863

USAA Investment Management
Company
USAA Building
San Antonio, TX 78288
(800) 531-8181

Value Line
711 Third Avenue
New York, NY 10017
(800) 223-0818

Vanguard Group
Vanguard Financial Center
P.O. Box 2600
Valley Forge, PA 19482
(800) 662-7447

MUTUAL FUND CHECKLIST

Mutual funds should play an important role in your investment program. Make maximum use of them by understanding the wide range of products and services that are available.

■□■

Help your mutual fund investments grow by reinvesting dividends and capital gains.

■□■

Explore the widely varying commissions and fees associated with buying and owning mutual funds so that you can minimize them.

■□■

Look for mutual funds that have demonstrated consistently superior long-term performance. Avoid purchasing a fund that has recently shown spectacular performance.

■□■

Avoid selling an otherwise good fund on the basis of poor short-term performance.

60

Real Estate Investments

Traditionally, real estate has been one of the best ways for people of average means to build their wealth. But as many real estate investors have recently learned, it is also possible to lose a great deal of money in the real estate market. Like all good investments, real estate carries a degree of risk. If you own real estate, you may either be troubled by the deteriorating real estate markets or be delighted by stable or rising prices. Much depends on where your property is located. If you are a potential real estate buyer—tempted by the "bargains" flooding the market in some locales—remember that, as with any investment, you must educate yourself thoroughly before making a decision to buy an investment property.

This chapter examines the real estate investment options available to you and explains the principles of investing in income-producing real estate. (If you are interested in buying a home, see Chapter 12.)

There are many kinds of properties that fall under the investment real estate umbrella, but each fits into one of two broad categories: residential and commercial. The following sections describe the various types of properties in these two categories.

Residential Rental Property

As an investment, residential rental property ideally produces a steady and predictable cash flow, which minimizes costs while the property (hopefully) increases in value. A residential rental property can be anything from a single-family or two-family house to a large multiunit apartment building. Location, condition, available utilities, and occupancy rate will all affect the property's value, as can local population movement and zoning changes.

As you probably know, the most important consideration in any real estate parcel is location. This truism is particularly crucial to residential real estate investing. While a few savvy real estate investors have been able to benefit by taking early stakes in "turnaround neighborhoods," that sort of gambling is best left to the professional.

Single-Family Homes

If you have a relatively limited amount of money to invest in real estate, a single-family house is one way for you to learn the ropes of real estate investing. These units require a smaller amount of capital upfront than do multifamily apartments—usually 20 to 30 percent of the total cost. Mortgage financing is generally available on satisfactory terms, and you may realize certain tax benefits from operating the property (see below).

The potential for capital appreciation with single-family units varies. Such residences have provided attractive returns over the long term—ten years or longer. Many short-term speculators in single-family homes in hot real estate markets have been badly burned, however.

The main problem with buying single-family residences for rental purposes is that it is difficult to locate properties that are priced low enough that the rental income is sufficient to cover mortgage and operating expenses. You'll soon tire of pumping money into a property that is not self-supporting. And if you invest in such a property, you are in essence placing a heavy bet that the property will appreciate smartly and soon. Remember, housing prices do not rise forever.

Vacation Homes

Second homes or vacation homes are a popular form of real estate ownership because they can serve as both investment property and a place to get away from the normal living routine. Second home ownership provides many of the tax advantages of primary home ownership, and it also offers economic advantages through its rent-producing potential.

Unfortunately, the tax benefits of vacation homes are generally very limited. In essence, if the home is often used for personal purposes, its tax deductibility is severely restricted. If a vacation home is rented for fewer than fifteen days a year, the resulting income need not be reported to the IRS. If the residence is used solely as a rental property, however, all income must be reported. In this event, the IRS allows the investor to deduct that proportion of expenses corresponding to the number of days the house was used as an income producing investment.

Smart Money Move

Don't invest in residential rental properties unless you can find a property that will generate enough rent to be self-supporting.

In addition to maintenance and depreciation deductions, real estate taxes and mortgage interest allocatable to rental use are subtracted from rental income. More than likely, taking all these deductions will create a taxable loss that is not allowed if the property is personally used for more than fourteen days or 10 percent of the total period when the property was rented, whichever is greater. If you rent the home for fifteen days or more, and the days of your personal use are fewer than the days fixed by the fourteen-day/10 percent rule, you are not considered to have made any personal use of the residence. Therefore, losses may be deductible if you meet certain tax regulations pertaining to your income level and the extent to which you were involved in the management of the property.

Many people consider vacation homes to be investments because they have the potential to produce rental income. Unfortunately, in more than a few cases, the investment value of vacation home ownership turns out to be an illusion, because rental income is insufficient to cover ownership expenses. If you take at face value the broker's or owner's projection of rental income, you are going to be disappointed. The safest way to evaluate a vacation home is to assume that it will generate no income. In other words, buy it purely for pleasure. If you are then able to realize some income on rentals, it will be an added bonus to the pleasure of owning a "house in the country."

Time-Sharing Ownership

Time-sharing—or interval—ownership offers the exclusive right to occupy a unit in a resort development for a specified period of time each year and represents a variation of vacation home investment.

There are two types of time-sharing ownership: simple fee and right-to-use. *Simple-fee* owners purchase a slice of the property and receive title by means of a deed. The property is legally theirs; simple-fee owners have the rights of homeowners. They can obtain insurance on the time-share property, sell or lease it, or have it transferred by will. In short, simple-fee ownership offers many of the advantages of regular home ownership.

Right-to-use owners have a membership that assures them the right to use a specific unit for a specific period of time over a certain number of years. At the end of that time, possession of the property reverts to the "real" owner, usually the contractor, developer, or manager. Time-sharers under this arrangement are usually prohibited from transactions that simple-fee ownership allows.

There are a few factors that you should consider before entering into a time-sharing contract. Time shares must be marketed very heavily, since developers may need to find upward of fifty owners per unit. Aggressive marketing has led to limits on information disclosure, questionable selling practices, and unlicensed vendors. Many time-sharing ventures have earned bad reputations as a result of their marketing strategies. While some projects are very straightforward, and a good number of owners are pleased with their time-sharing investments, the majority are of dubious value. There is almost no secondary market for time-share properties, a fact that severely limits their utility from an investment standpoint. Never look at a time-share as an investment in anything but your pleasure.

Condominiums

Condominiums are apartment units contained within larger multi-unit buildings. Each unit is individually owned and controlled. Owners are free to mortgage their property as they wish, since all financing is done on an individual basis.

Condominium living has become more popular in recent years as detached housing has become more expensive. While condominium units are generally cheaper than equivalent single-family homes,

Smart Money Move

Be realistic in estimating rental income before purchasing a vacation home.

condominium ownership provides the same sort of tax advantages as does home ownership. Amenities and common areas like foyers, yards, and parking lots are generally owned by condominium owners' associations, which usually hire a building or site manager to maintain the common areas. Each unit is individually financed, so that if one owner defaults on his or her mortgage, the other residents need only assume the defaulting owner's share of operating expenses. Many first-time real estate investors purchase condominiums for rental purposes. Unfortunately, many have ended up paying too much for the property in relation to the rental that it generates. As with all real estate investments, if you are contemplating a condominium purchase for investment purposes, make sure the rental income is sufficient to support your ownership costs.

Cooperatives

A cooperative—as opposed to a condominium—usually takes out a blanket mortgage on an entire building, so that if an owner defaults, the remaining tenants must assume the extra share of carrying costs. My reservations about condominium investing, noted above, apply to cooperatives as well. Nevertheless, condominiums or cooperatives may be viable investments in areas where rents can be increased significantly over time. In recent years, however, many areas of the country have been overbuilt with condos and co-ops, causing price declines in both rentals and property values.

Multifamily Units and Apartments

There are greater opportunities for tax advantage and positive cash flow with multifamily apartments than with single-family structures. Included in this category are small two-, three-, and four-family homes that are often owner-occupied. In fact, if you want to purchase your own home and get into the rental real estate game, you can do both at the same time by buying a duplex or a triple-decker and living in one of the units.

Multifamily dwellings require a greater initial investment, but the cost per dwelling unit is lower. Multifamily units are relatively easy to finance for investors with sufficient resources to make the down payment, as lenders see the potential rental income as protection on their loans.

Smart Money Move

Don't fall for the time-share hard sell. Time shares don't have any investment value.

A major problem with large apartment units in some communities is the presence of rent control restrictions (either present or potential). Other drawbacks include the possibility of overbuilding in a community and the difficulty of selling the property quickly in the event the owner needs the money.

As with any other real estate, the property's location can make or break the investment—a prospective buyer should avoid areas of depreciating property values. Proximity to main avenues of transportation and to shopping, recreation, schools, and work is particularly important to the apartment dweller. If the physical condition of the property has been neglected, the costs of repair could boost expenses dramatically. Unexpected expenses such as reroofing or replacing the electrical or heating systems may arise, so an investor who purchases an apartment building is well advised to have sufficient reserves to meet such contingencies.

Commercial Property

O ffice buildings, shopping centers, other retail property, and industrial real estate all offer investors with substantial resources an opportunity for significant gain, albeit at a significant risk. As the size of the property increases, however, buying and managing become more complicated, so you should already be experienced in real estate investing and be especially well informed about the specifics of the purchase. With the exception of very small, well-located, and fully occupied properties, commercial real estate is best left to the experts.

You may, however, want to consider making a commercial property investment via either a real estate limited partnership or a real estate investment trust. These "indirect" investment methods are discussed later on in this chapter, but the main areas of commercial real estate investment are briefly described below. If you are contemplating indirect investment in commercial properties, you should become familiar with the various categories of commercial property.

Office Buildings

Office buildings for investment may range from suburban office parks to central business district buildings. As with all real estate, location plays a critical role. With respect to office buildings in particular, occupancy rates are more unpredictable, and even a moderate number of vacancies can be disastrous to an office building.

Shopping Centers

Shopping centers fall into five main categories: regional or super-regional, community, neighborhood, discount, and specialty. Many of the smaller shopping-center types are losing customers to super-regional, "mega" shopping centers. Shopping centers can offer substantial returns, but like office buildings, this type of property has not fared well in weak economies. Also, older shopping centers are losing out to newly constructed shopping centers.

Industrial Real Estate

Industrial property includes warehouses, wholesale and assembly sites, and manufacturing plants. While industrial property may be

Smart Money Move

Become a home-owner and a landlord at the same time by purchasing a small apartment building and living in one of the units. This is a great way to get started as a real estate investor.

unfamiliar to the average investor, it can be an attractive investment. Industrial property ranges from industrial parks to miniwarehouse complexes. (Many of the latter are sold as limited partnerships.) One great benefit to industrial real estate investments is that maintenance is usually minimal and tenant turnover is often lower than it is in office buildings.

Undeveloped Land

While undeveloped land might seem to be an ideal investment for a first-time real estate investor, it's been left for last here because it is often the least appropriate investment. Why? Raw land purchases often end up being raw deals. Successful investors in undeveloped land need deep pockets—and more. Since undeveloped land doesn't generate any income, your money will be tied up for a long time. It's difficult to finance undeveloped land for more than a few years. In addition, successful land investors understand the current value and can anticipate the potential value for development of a given area. Investors should also be familiar with how regulatory and zoning issues affect, or may affect, a particular parcel of land. The importance of the regulatory environment can't be overemphasized. Legislation like the Federal Wetlands Act and several state-level laws, as well as environmental protection regulations, have made otherwise valuable land nearly worthless.

Another cautionary note: Large parcels of land that sell for peanuts usually spell trouble, not bargain. The price is cheap for a number of good reasons—lousy location, difficult access, bad drainage. So if the land you want to purchase has more moose per square mile than people, don't expect to make any money on it. Land in particularly desirable areas, on the other hand, is always expensive to purchase but may, with some luck and a lot of skill, appreciate considerably in value.

Evaluating Potential Real Estate Investments

Smart Money Move

Don't buy inexpensive undeveloped land. You won't live long enough to see it become valuable.

Suppose you come across a building that really appeals to you. It is in good condition, has some architectural character, and seems to be located in an up-and-coming neighborhood. While all these factors may make you want to buy the property, they are meaningless until you know what it costs to operate the building and how much income it generates. Once you have these figures in hand—and have a good idea of the property's selling price—you can then determine whether buying it makes any sense. The following yardsticks and formulas for evaluating real estate investments will help you make just that decision.

Rent Multiplier

The simplest way to evaluate a property is to compare the price you'd have to pay for it with its current gross annual rental. Any property selling for much more than seven or eight times the gross annual rental is likely to yield a negative cash flow—in other words, your rental income won't be sufficient to cover your mortgage and operating expenses, let alone make a profit. To determine the rent multiplier, which compares the total selling price with the current gross annual rental, use the following formula:

$$\text{Rent multiplier} \quad = \quad \frac{\textbf{Selling price}}{\textbf{Gross annual rental}}$$

For example, a duplex selling for $180,000 generates $15,000 in annual rent. The rent multiplier is calculated as follows:

$$\text{Rent multiplier} \quad = \quad \frac{\textbf{Selling price}}{\textbf{Gross annual rental}} \quad = \quad \frac{\$180,000}{\$15,000} \quad = \quad 12$$

In other words, the property is selling for twelve times the annual rental. As we noted earlier, any property that is selling for much more than seven times the gross annual rental is probably not going to be a particularly good investment. Also remember that if you put a sizable cash down payment into the property to assure a positive cash flow, you're only fooling yourself because there's an opportunity cost associated with tying up a lot of cash that could otherwise be earning interest. You might be interested in knowing that professional real estate investors generally will not pay more than five to six times the gross annual rental.

Similarly, if a real estate limited partnership pays more than seven times the gross annual rental to buy a property, the partnership is probably paying too much, unless it can reasonably expect a dramatic increase in the value of the property (for example, immediate condo conversion). Of course, the salespeople always expect great things out of the deal, although a less optimistic prognosis would often be more accurate.

The Capitalization Rate

Calculating the capitalization rate—or "cap rate," as veteran real estate investors call it—is a more detailed method of evaluating a property. The cap rate is determined as follows:

$$\text{Capitalization rate} \quad = \quad \frac{\textbf{Net operating income}}{\textbf{Total amount invested}}$$

For example, a limited partnership investment in an apartment building requiring a total investment of $3,500,000 has an estimated net operating income of $300,000. The cap rate is $300,000 divided by $3,500,000, or 8.6 percent. A cap rate of 8 percent or higher is considered desirable.

Whether you are investing in real estate directly or through a limited partnership, make sure the amounts that go into the cap rate formula are realistic. The sum used for the "total amount invested" should include both the down payment and the borrowed money necessary to buy the property, while the "net operating income" is the total rental income (allowing for vacancies) less all the expenses except mortgage interest and principal.

Beware of a favorite trick called "bumping to market," which is used by real estate agents and general partners in order to make a deal look more attractive. "Bumping to market" is raising rent projections from what they actually are to what they "ought to be" according to a so-called market level. Don't believe these pie-in-the-sky projections.

Four Ways to Invest in Real Estate

Real estate investing can play an important role in a well-balanced investment portfolio for those investors who have the resources and time to research, and, if necessary, manage real estate investments. Nevertheless, many people choose not to invest in real estate, and for good reasons—volatile prices and illiquidity chief among them. But if you are interested in real estate investing, there are three main ways to go about it.

1. Own It Yourself

Purchasing real estate yourself provides the greatest returns—and the greatest risks. A lot of wealthy people in this country have achieved their wealth through real estate investing. But it takes a lot of hard work, and you have to have the right disposition to be a landlord.

The best way to start out is to buy a small property, probably an apartment, to test the waters. You will find out in relatively short order whether you are cut out to be a landlord. If you get hooked, chances are that ten years from now you'll own ten buildings, and you'll be on your way to real estate riches. Along the way, however, don't overextend yourself. Remember, too much debt can be disastrous when the inevitable downturn occurs—vacancies rise and real estate prices drop. Finally, if you are on your way to becoming a real estate investor, don't waste your money on those ridiculous "no money down" real estate courses. If you're going to get into and thrive in the real estate investment business, you're going to need to use and always have available some of your own money.

Smart Money Move

Calculate the rent multiplier and the capitalization rate before investing in any income-producing real estate—either on your own or through a limited partnership.

2. Real Estate Limited Partnerships

Real estate limited partnerships are a way to pool money from a group of people to invest in larger properties.

Advantages

Advantages of investing in real estate limited partnerships include:

- **EASE OF BUYING IN.** While direct ownership requires a system of transfer, an investor in a limited partnership needs only to complete some documentation and send a check to the general partner. The partnership's prospectus gives you access to information necessary to make a reasonably quick decision.

- **FIXED CASH REQUIREMENTS.** After you make the initial payment, you will not usually be responsible for financing any further cost overruns.

- **NO MANAGEMENT RESPONSIBILITY.** This is often a blessing, particularly to older investors. The general partner is responsible for finding tenants, maintenance, bookkeeping, tax reporting, and all other management duties.

- **LIMITED LEGAL LIABILITY.** As a limited partner, your maximum legal liability is limited to the total amount you have invested in the partnership, so your other assets are not at risk.

- **SMALLER INITIAL INVESTMENT.** In most deals you need to invest as little as $5,000 (less if you invest through an IRA or other retirement plan) to receive the benefits of a large real estate project.

- **LOWER OVERALL RISK.** Diversification and professional management can make limited partnership investments less risky than direct ownership.

Disadvantages

Naturally, there are also disadvantages to investing in real estate limited partnerships. These include:

- **LESS CONTROL.** A limited partner has no say in the management of the property, nor can he or she dictate when or to whom the property is sold.

- **LOWER OVERALL RETURN.** This is due to fees and commissions paid to set up the partnership, to operate the property, and upon liquidation of the partnership.

- **LIMITED TAX-SAVING OPPORTUNITIES.** Under current tax rules, tax shelter opportunities for limited partnerships have been either severely restricted or eliminated outright.

- **ILLIQUIDITY.** Because there is little demand for existing limited partnership investment units, if they can be sold at all, they will likely sell for far less than the original investment. This could be a major drawback for anyone who may need to sell the investment on short notice to provide income or who wants to remove illiquid investments from their estate.

Best course of action

Avoid making any new partnership investments until the national real estate market turns around, and never make any if there is the slightest chance that you'll need the money in the foreseeable future. Remember that the people who sell you these partnerships may tell you that the market has already turned around, that the partnership will be liquidated in just a few years, and that you'll be able to sell your interest readily on the secondary market if you need to. That's all bull. Don't let any of these assertions influence your decision to purchase a limited partnership interest.

Real Estate Investment Trusts

A real estate investment trust (REIT) is a corporation that invests in real estate or mortgages. REIT shares trade on the stock exchange so, for no more than the cost of buying some shares of stock, you can participate in the real estate market without the hassle of management and without the problem of liquidity or deceptive sales tactics.

Therefore, the least expensive and most liquid way to invest in real estate is through purchasing shares in a REIT. Capital gains realized through the trust go directly to the shareholders, the diversified portfolio minimizes risks, and the ability to trade provides greater liquidity than other real estate investments.

REITs, like mutual funds, bring the advantages of centralized, professional management to individual investors. They are subject to strict regulations and thus tend to be well managed.

Before you conclude that REITs are the best thing since sliced bread, you need to know that REIT share prices suffer in bad real estate markets just as much as limited partnerships or directly owned investments. Many REITs invest in major commercial properties, and overbuilt real estate markets have adversely affected leasing environments. The specter of the Resolution Trust Corporation's vast holdings of real estate flooding an already depressed market could cast a pall over the REIT industry and hold down share prices.

Nonetheless, if you want to play the real estate market, the REIT route may still be best. It certainly is cheapest, and you can sell your investment and receive cash in a matter of days. What's more, REITs have traditionally provided a rich dividend yield. Real estate investments are renowned for their extreme boom/bust cycles, and it's at the perceived bottom of a cycle that experienced real estate professionals jump in and reap extraordinary returns. The REIT vehicle was legislated into existence specifically to enable the smaller investor to participate in such gains. If you want to take the plunge, look for REITs that specialize in apartments or cater to the elderly. They should hold up relatively well during the 1990s.

3. Real Estate "Rich" Companies

There is one final way by which you can invest in real estate. Consider purchasing stock in companies with substantial real estate holdings. Investment professionals often point to large paper companies, and some retailers that own a lot of their outlets, as attractive real estate "rich" companies. By investing in these companies, you can possibly gain some of the benefits of owning real estate while skipping the hassles of direct real estate ownership and the risks of limited partnerships.

Real Estate Investment Strategies

Real estate is a tricky investment to gauge. In a strong economy, identical houses, built by the same company but set in different states, can vary in price and value by $100,000 or more. In a weak economy, even properties in the best locations can suffer dramatic losses in value. It has always been the case, as with stock and bond investing, that many experienced investors have lost substantial amounts of money due to changing market conditions that left them buying too high or selling too low. While the real estate investment professional may be able to identify and take advantage of attractive investments, the part-time real estate investor is ill-advised to make investments in a depressed real estate market.

While investors may have an opportunity to purchase properties at attractive prices in a depressed market, the problem is that markets get depressed because of overbuilding and vacancy problems. If the property can not be fully rented, it doesn't matter how cheaply the property was purchased—it is headed for trouble.

What to Avoid

The following is a list of real estate investments to avoid:

- MOST REAL ESTATE LIMITED PARTNERSHIPS
- NO-MONEY-DOWN REAL ESTATE COME-ONS
- CHEAP LAND DEALS
- FOREIGN LAND OR PROPERTY
- UNINSPECTED PROPERTY.

Finding the Right Investment

The following suggestions will help you make the right real estate investments and thereby avoid making costly mistakes.

Buy what you know

Consider purchasing parcels that are close to your home. Since real estate is so closely tied to local economies, your best chances for investment success are tied to your knowledge of the locale in which you invest. Those who are familiar with the real estate market in their local community enjoy a significant advantage over those who try to purchase real estate in an unfamiliar locale.

Distressed properties may cause distress

There are always distressed properties available, and some regions of the country have more than their fair share. You may be attracted to the appealing notion of obtaining a property at a foreclosure auction or through the Resolution Trust Corporation (RTC), which is charged with disposing of the foreclosed properties of defunct savings and loans.

Both methods of acquiring property are fraught with peril. Extensive investigation of each property is required before bidding commences, but most auctions disallow the time it takes to do a thorough job, selling the property "as is," without contingencies for inspection and without warranty. Moreover, foreclosed properties sold at auction are often in very poor condition. There also may be liens on the property or clouds in the title. You'll need an attorney to scrutinize it. Finally, dealing with the RTC can be a time-consuming bureaucratic nightmare. (A local real estate broker may be able to assist you—for a fee.)

Real estate limited partnerships offer little

Although the deals are structured much more sensibly than they were when they were packaged as tax shelters (prior to 1986), most deals rely on price appreciation—not something that can be guaranteed anymore. Maybe one deal in a hundred will be worthwhile.

Real estate investing can be profitable—in spite of all the negatives. Some investors—in both up and down markets—do well. Some professional investors emphasize that down markets present unprecedented opportunities for investing in real estate. Still, this is the kind of opportunity that only experienced real estate investors can exploit. More often, it is the new investor who is exploited.

When to Sell

Don't Sell in a Weak Market

If you own income-producing real estate, you may be confronted with an unusually competitive market for tenants at the same time that the real estate market is weak. You must plan for the possibility that you may have to go to unusual lengths to retain and/or attract tenants—lowering rents, providing more amenities, refurbishing dings and dents. Build up your cash reserves in anticipation of potentially more difficult times. You need to plan ahead to avoid being forced to sell your property in weak markets.

Real Estate Limited Partnerships

If you are a limited partnership owner and you want out, you will probably have to take your lumps. The secondary market for limited partnerships will pay top dollar only for successful partnership investments, which you wouldn't want to sell in the first place. In short, there isn't much you can do about a soured partnership. If you absolutely, positively need the money, you may be able to sell the partnership on the secondary market, but you'll take a beating. Ask the person who sold you the partnership (if he or she is still in the business) to recommend a reseller of your partnership.

REITs

Your decision to hold on to a REIT may depend on the kind of income you are receiving from it. Many may have attractive dividend yields but such yields are hardly guaranteed. The decision on holding or selling a REIT should hinge on whether the REIT is likely to perform well or not over the next year. It's not unlike the decision to sell or hold a stock.

Rule Numero Uno

W hatever way you want to play the real estate market, the single most important ingredient to success is *economic viability*. If the investment relies on tax gimmicks, like rehabilitation credits, it could be headed for trouble. If the deal relies on capital appreciation to make any money, it's a recipe for disappointment, if not disaster. If the deal relies on increasing anemic occupancy rates or raising rents, it's a pipe dream. The only worthwhile real estate investments are those that can not only survive on the basis of their own economic merits but thrive on them.

The really successful real estate investors share one characteristic in common—patience. If they can't get the right property at the right price, they'll be quite content to sit on the sidelines. They also have the staying power to be able to survive in slow real estate markets because their properties are more than self-sustaining. I have a friend who, starting from scratch, has made over $50 million in real estate. Yet for the past five years, he has owned no real estate (not even a home). He just hasn't been able to find the right property at the right price, so he's very happy to wait until the right opportunity comes around. In the meantime, he's driving his wife crazy in their apartment.

REAL ESTATE INVESTMENTS CHECKLIST

Own-it-yourself real estate is the best way to build up your wealth, but it is also the riskiest. Be particularly wary of the following common first-time real estate investments: time shares, vacation homes, condominiums, and single-family homes purchased for rental. Rental incomes from these properties are very unlikely to cover their carrying costs.

When evaluating a particular property or a limited partnership investment, apply some simple evaluation techniques like the rent multiplier and the capitalization rate.

███

Don't invest in undeveloped land unless you have both the experience and the financial resources to buy prime properties.

███

Evaluate any potential real estate limited partnership investments thoroughly and with a healthy dose of skepticism.

FOR FURTHER INFORMATION

National Association of Real Estate Investment Trusts
1129 Twentieth St. NW,
Suite 705,
Washington, DC 20036
(202) 785-8717

For a list of repossessed properties in your area, call the Resolution Trust Corporation at (800)782-3006 (there is a $5.00 fee)

For other RTC publications, call (800)431-0600

For a list of foreclosed properties offered by the Federal National Mortgage Association (Fannie Mae), call (800)553-4636

To find a qualified real estate appraiser, check your local Yellow Pages or contact the Appraisal Institute at (312)335-4100.

Request the *Directory of Members*.

The following two publications provide helpful information for the potential real estate investor:

The Basics of Interest Rates (free)
The Federal Reserve Bank
of New York
Attention: Public Information
13th Floor
33 Liberty Street
New York NY 10045
(212) 720-6130

Buying Lots from Developers (free)
Department of Housing and Urban Development (HUD)
Program Information
451 Seventh Street S.W.
Washington DC 20410
(202) 708-1420

Other Investments

M ost, if not all, of your personal investment program can be handled quite effectively with stocks, interest-earning securities, and real estate. There are, however, certain other kinds of investments that may be of interest to you. They include:

- STOCK PURCHASE WARRANTS

- COMMODITY FUTURES

- STOCK INDEX FUTURES

- PRECIOUS METALS

- COLLECTIBLES

Most of these are of dubious value to your wealth-building program, in spite of what some commissioned salespeople may tell you. In fact, many of these have been used to dupe people into putting their money into "can't lose" investments that—you guessed it—lost a lot of money. So caution is called for. Even under circumstances where these investments are used for legitimate purposes, they are riskier than "old-fashioned" investments like stocks and bonds.

Stock Purchase Warrants

S tock purchase warrants guarantee you the right to buy a fixed number of shares of a company's stock at a fixed price for a fixed time period. Unlike options, warrants are issued by the corporation itself (usually with new issues, bonds, or preferred stock) and are traded on the stock exchanges. On the expiration date of such rights, the warrants lose all trading value. The value of warrants—defined as the difference between the market price and the price at which the warrant guarantees you can buy the stock—is intrinsically more volatile than that of the underlying stocks.

Therefore, as with options, you can get more bang for your buck by buying warrants than by buying shares of common stock. The problem, of course, is that in exchange for the slight possibility of making a lot of money, you risk losing most or all of your investment. Warrants are speculative investments. You should buy warrants only on companies whose stock you would like to own anyway and whose stock price you think stands a good chance of rising rapidly before the expiration date of the warrant.

Commodity Futures

Commodity futures are traded in order to speculate on price changes in basic commodities such as cocoa, copper, corn, eggs, frozen concentrated orange juice, lumber, oats, platinum, pork bellies, potatoes, silver, soybeans, and wheat. If you have devoted your life to a certain commodity and you are an expert in commodities, commodity futures may play a role in your investment program. Otherwise, don't waste your time and money.

Commodity Markets

The Chicago Board of Trade was established in 1848 and remains one of the most active futures exchanges in the nation. Today there are many other organized commodity futures exchanges, including:

- CHICAGO MERCANTILE EXCHANGE

- COMMODITY EXCHANGE (NEW YORK)

- MINNEAPOLIS GRAIN EXCHANGE

- INTERNATIONAL MONEY MARKET (CHICAGO)

- INDEX AND OPTIONS MARKET (CHICAGO)

- KANSAS CITY BOARD OF TRADE

- MIDAMERICA COMMODITY EXCHANGE (CHICAGO)

- NEW YORK COFFEE, SUGAR AND COCOA

- NEW YORK COTTON EXCHANGE

- NEW YORK FUTURES EXCHANGE

- NEW YORK MERCANTILE EXCHANGE

Smart Money Move

You almost certainly have no business playing with commodity futures. So don't do it.

Sources of Information

Investment advisory services and newsletters report on developments in futures markets and predict price changes. Brokerage and commodity firms, which handle buy and sell orders, also can give recommendations. Brokers can trade for you in a discretionary account, in which the broker makes buy and sell decisions. This can be dangerous to your financial health, of course. You can also contract with a managed commodity service, which pools investors' money in a fashion similar to a mutual fund.

How to Lose

Profits are won (but usually lost) by buying and selling futures contracts in a particular commodity. *Futures contracts* are agreements to buy or sell a commodity at a stated price on a specified date. Although a contract calls for the actual delivery of a commodity (visions of truckloads of pork bellies being dumped on your front yard come to mind), this is rarely done. Rather, speculators in commodity futures close out their positions before the contracts mature.

Nonprofessionals should stick to the most liquid markets if they play this market at all. Be aware of the risky nature of futures trading, which is much like that of options trading. Although there can be very large and quick profits in commodity futures, speculators lose most of the time, so you should invest only if you can easily afford to lose your investment.

Buying on Margin

When you are buying on margin (with borrowed money, in other words), your account is screened daily to see whether the money in it meets the minimum requirement for that day (as prices change). If it does not, you are required to pay the difference; if you do not, the broker must liquidate that portion of your futures investment necessary to meet the margin requirements. If the broker closes out your position and your account balance does not reach zero, as may easily happen, you are indebted to the broker for the losses. This open-ended risk allows you to lose much more than your original investment; some investment firms set minimum standards of annual income and net worth before opening a commodity trading account for you. But why go through that just for the privilege of losing your shirt?

Stock Index Futures

Stock index futures are hybrid instruments that share characteristics of both the stock market and the commodities market. Like commodity futures contracts, stock index futures are a legal commitment between two investors in which the buyer agrees to buy a certain amount and quality of a product at a prearranged price and within a specified time period. In the case of stock index futures, however, the product is not a commodity like soybeans or corn, but a stock market index.

Consult Your Psychic

Stock index futures are for those of you who think you can call the direction of the market but not of individual stocks. (If you are convinced that you can predict the direction of the market, please give me a call. It's not that I want you to tell me where the stock market is headed. Rather, I want to recommend an institution where you can take a long rest.) These investments are considered very risky, and a thorough working knowledge of the stock market is necessary to survive in an arena dominated by professional traders, institutional investors, and other financial experts.

Stock index futures do allow you to play the full stock market with relatively small amounts of money. This large leverage is considered one of their main advantages. Investing in actual stocks requires putting up at least 50 percent of the value of the stock in a margin account, whereas futures trading allows the investor to play the market for as little as 10 percent of the contract's value. A subsequent 10 percent rise in the underlying index produces a 100 percent increase in the investment, but investors all too often incorrectly predict price movements and thus incur substantial if not total losses. This is a game for the pros. Stay away!

Precious Metals

P recious metals—gold, silver, platinum, and others—are tangible investments whose values used to rise during times of economic or political unrest and inflation. They haven't "behaved" that way in the past few years, however.

Profits in precious metal investments are usually made only during times of economic turbulence. Otherwise, precious metals should constitute at most only a small portion of your investment portfolio. There are better and more secure returns elsewhere. While investment experts used to suggest that precious metals might make up about ten percent of your investments, many are now suggesting that, after years of lackluster performance, you eliminate all precious metals investments.

How to Invest

If you are going to invest in precious metals, the most common ways to do so include:

Smart Money Move

Gold lost its luster as an inflation hedge and a hedge against world crisis. Don't invest in it unless you're going to wear it.

Gold bullion

Gold bullion can be bought in bars or ingots and held in depositories in the United States or in other banking centers. Owners are charged for storage and insurance costs. If you choose to buy and store bullion—please, please, please, be sure you do it *only* through well-known dealers who will store the metal at a major bank. In other words, don't buy gold over the telephone from a guy named Bill who promises to store it in his cousin Henry's bank.

Gold bullion coins

Gold bullion coins are attractive to investors who prefer a smaller investment than bars or ingots. They are sold through international dealers, banks, and brokerage houses at a small premium above the value of the gold contents. They are also sold by some of the biggest crooks this world has ever seen. Know thy seller.

Silver can be purchased and stored in a similar fashion to gold. Unless you purchase a large amount of silver, typically at least 10,000 ounces, however, you will usually pay a premium over the market price.

Precious metals mutual funds

The best way to invest in precious metals is to purchase a precious metals mutual fund. Most invest solely or predominantly in gold either through purchase of shares of gold-mining companies or by purchasing the bullion itself. In addition to offering you a chance for capital gains if the price of gold rises, these funds also usually pay small dividends. Precious metals funds are certainly a lot less hassle than buying and storing bullion or coins.

Collectibles

Collectibles run the gamut from old masters paintings to baseball cards. Most collectibles are simple objects that were once used for everyday use that have since increased in value due to interest in the cultures or the eras that produced these objects.

Collectibles include antique furniture, porcelain pieces, paintings, Art Nouveau and Art Deco objects, folk art and Americana, coins held primarily for their numismatic value, books, autographs, stamps, rugs, sculptures, toys, games, comic books, baseball cards, and other reminders of past eras. Because of the sheer range and number of collectibles, an investment-grade object is defined stringently:

- **IT SHOULD** be relatively scarce.

- **IT SHOULD** be historically significant compared with other collectibles of the same type.

- **IT SHOULD** be historically significant within the larger context of the culture that produced it.

- **IT SHOULD** be in excellent condition.

If you look carefully at the above list, you should conclude that "investment-grade" collectibles cost a bundle of money. As investment items, collectibles are at a disadvantage because of the care that must be given to preserve their value and because of widespread fraud and price manipulation.

There are numerous pitfalls in investing in collectibles. The market for collectibles is poorly organized. Prices and grading of items

Smart Money Move

Unless you are a professional collector, don't rely on the value of your collectibles to meet future financial needs. Enjoy them instead.

are rarely standardized, and there is no reliable and easy method to assess a collectible's value. Many items simply have no resale market. Recent years have witnessed numerous fads that initially drove prices up but failed to sustain them and ended in a rapid price decline.

Most experts agree that investing for profit in collectibles usually requires considerable start-up capital, perhaps in the six- or seven-figure range. Moreover, considerable expertise, is necessary. Either you possess the expertise or you must have enough money to consult experts.

If you have some collectibles, great. They are wonderful to look at, walk on, or sit on. But don't expect to retire on your collectibles.

OTHER INVESTMENTS CHECKLIST

◼️◻️

Don't risk any more money than you can easily afford to lose on such high-risk investments as commodity futures, stock index futures, and stock purchase warrants.

◼️◻️

Do business only with established, well-known firms if you are investing in commodity futures or precious metals.

◼️◻️

Don't consider money spent on collectibles an investment unless you have a lot of experience and can afford expensive pieces.

FOR FURTHER INFORMATION

For information on puts and calls:
Chicago Board Options Exchange
Literature Area
400 LaSalle
Chicago IL 60605
(800) 678-4667

The following publication explains the basics of gold investing:

"Your Introduction to Investing in Gold"
($5.00)
The Gold Institute
1112 16th Street N.W.

Washington DC 20036
(202) 835-0185

The following organizations provide a number of pamphlets on futures trading:
Chicago Board of Trade
Attention: Educational and Marketing
Publications
141 West Jackson Boulevard
Chicago IL 60604-2994
(312) 435-3500

Chicago Mercantile Exchange
Office Services

»

30 South Wacker Drive
Chicago IL 60606
(312) 930-8210

For information on investing in stamps, send a stamped, self-addressed envelope to:

American Stamp Dealers Association
3 School Street
Glen Cove NY 11542
(516) 759-7000

62

Coping with Market Uncertainty

T he investment markets—they're a-changin'. In the old days (prior to the mid-1980s) they used to be reasonably predictable. No longer. Whatever investments you are into—stocks, bonds, real estate, or plain vanilla savings accounts, you're headed for a new era of investment volatility and market uncertainty in the 1990s. If market conditions ever make you unsure of how to proceed, if recent movements in security or real estate prices have you downright scared, then take two aspirin (or have a martini) and review this chapter. It will help you keep a cool head amidst chaos.

Guidelines

M any investors overreact to unexpected market fluctuations. The really jittery types dump all their stock and bond investments and retreat to the safety of low-yield, short-term investments like money-market accounts. The following guidelines will help you invest successfully in the face of market uncertainty.

Do Nothing

Most investors react too suddenly to adverse market conditions, and they almost always do the wrong thing. Selling when one should be holding, if not buying, is an almost surefire way to lose money. In fact, doing nothing may be the best way to react during a crisis. In general, you should never "sell into market weakness." Wait until things settle down. Also, be very wary of the immediate opinions of experts amidst and right after the crisis. Ask yourself: "If they're such experts, why didn't they predict this mess in the first place?"

SO MUCH FOR EXPERT OPINION

It's risky to follow the advice of a single expert. But following the advice whenever there is a consensus among experts is downright dangerous. In early January 1991, on the eve of Operation Desert Storm against Iraq, a clear consensus emerged that once the war commenced, stock prices would take a steep tumble, interest rates would skyrocket, and fuel prices would go through the roof. Woe betide any investor who took action in accordance with this consensus! What actually happened was the opposite. Stock prices rose,

»

and interest rates and oil prices declined. Perhaps the best thing to do when there is a consensus among the experts is to do the opposite of what they suggest.

Diversify

Once again, it pays to follow this most basic and time-honored investment truism. All too many people have too much of their money invested in the stock of one or a very few companies, in money markets, or in real estate. This can be a recipe for disaster if the particular investment sector on which you are concentrating falters badly. The better diversified you are, the better position you will be in to emerge from the scary market relatively unscathed.

Take a Long-Term Perspective

The 500-point, single-day drop in the Dow Jones Industrial Average on October 19, 1987, did not provoke another Great Depression. Indeed, the total decline during the October 1987 market erased only one year's gain in the Dow. (The Dow actually ended 1987 with an overall gain, not a loss.) Flat (if not down) twelve-month stock markets aren't that uncommon, yet few people remembered this fact during the 1987 postcrash hysteria. Investing for the long term—a principle equal in importance to diversifying—will usually reward you with greater returns on your investments and with better nights' sleep.

Buy Quality

True, the market is driven by rumors and unfounded fears. True, short-term changes in stock and bond prices often have little to do with companies' underlying value or financial health. But shares of quality, dividend-paying companies with no or low debt and with bonds of financially sound issuers are favored during volatile markets. Higher-quality securities will have more staying power if market conditions do continue to deteriorate.

One way to fine-tune your investments without falling into the trap of making a major shift in your investment allocations is to prune out lower-quality securities (or mutual funds that invest in such companies or bonds) and replace them with higher-quality securities or funds.

Ladder the Maturities of Your Fixed-Income Investments

Smart Money Move

When in doubt, don't follow the advice of the experts.

If your interest-earning investments mature simultaneously, you may find yourself rather abruptly burdened with a lot of cash. This situation can easily be avoided if you pick fixed-income investments with varying maturities. You will be better off in a period of skyrocketing interest rates if your fixed-incomes mature periodically. That way, you won't risk being stuck with a lot of money during a time when investment markets are either unattractive or particularly volatile.

Opt for Mutual Funds That Have Good Track Records in Down Markets

Stock mutual funds have typically performed abysmally during bear markets, but not all have done so. The value of most bond mutual funds declines when interest rates rise, but not all. Some funds have proven to be better suited at coping with adverse market conditions than their competitors. How do you identify these funds? In addition to reporting long-term performance, many mutual fund monitoring services report performance of these funds in both up and down markets. (Check the several sources and investment magazines listed in Chapter 59.) Again, you can identify some funds that have proven themselves to be particularly adept at coping with unfavorable market conditions.

Use Stop-Loss Orders on Stocks

A stop-loss order will help protect your stocks against sharp and/or rapid market drops. They are not foolproof, however. In a volatile market, for example, you may be sold out of a stock that subsequently rebounds in price.

Avoid Investing with Borrowed Money

The investors who are really hurt by sharp market downturns are those who invest "on margin"—they use borrowed money to invest. The only way for them to cover their margin calls is to sell some of their stock holdings at a most inopportune time. While the judicious use of margin investing can be an effective means of increasing the returns on a stock or bond portfolio, heavily margined investors expose themselves to considerable risk. If you are heavily margined and are concerned about market conditions, do the prudent thing and reduce your margin now.

When in Doubt, Seek Safe Havens

If you are totally daunted by market conditions, you may want to move *some* of your investment money into safe cash-equivalent investments like money-market funds, Treasury bills, and short-term certificates of deposit. While you may not be earning a particularly attractive return, at least you are protecting your assets. Note that the emphasis here is moving *some* of your money—in other words, lightening up on stocks or bonds. Avoid the temptation of making a major shift in your investments, because maintaining a steady course is the most important ingredient to long-term investment success—in both good and lousy markets.

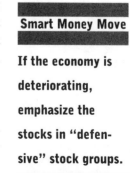

Smart Money Move

If the economy is deteriorating, emphasize the stocks in "defensive" stock groups.

Stay Alert

The best way to quell market jitters is to stay on top of your investments at all times. Knowing what you're invested in, and knowing why you invested in it in the first place, will make the decision to hold or sell rational more than emotional.

Defensive Investment Strategies

Y ou will hear a lot about "defensive investing" when stock market conditions are particularly worrisome. Defensive investing emphasizes avoiding serious mistakes or losses by concentrating on investments that are thought to be resistant to significant loss. When investment market conditions are unusually uncertain or adverse, many investors prefer defensive investments. In the stock arena, defensive investors opt for high-quality stocks in so-called "defensive" industries. This does not mean investing in weapons manufacturers. A defensive investment is one made primarily to protect yourself against declining stock prices.

Defensive stock groups listed below should, but won't necessarily, perform better than other groups during a rocky economy. (Note that these groups produce goods and services that we use under any economic conditions.)

- BEVERAGES
- COSMETICS
- DRUGS
- FOODS
- HEALTH CARE
- LIQUOR
- SUPERMARKETS
- TELEPHONES
- TOBACCO
- UTILITIES

Smart Money Move

If you're particularly concerned about the possibility of a drop in stock or bond prices, select mutual funds that have good track records in down markets.

A defensive fixed-income investment strategy involves the selection of high-quality fixed-income securities—typically Treasury issues, or municipal and corporate bonds that are highly rated by the rating agencies, namely Standard and Poor's and Moody's. Defensive investors also may prefer shorter-maturity fixed-income investments, which will fluctuate in value less than longer-maturity fixed-income investments in response to changes in prevailing interest rates. A final defensive investment strategy is to temporarily emphasize high-quality cash-equivalent investments for absolute protection of invested funds against loss. (See Chapter 56.)

Ten Stable Investments for the Downright Frightened

Do you want absolute or almost-absolute protection against loss of all or a portion of your investments? You can't go wrong with any of the following stable cash-equivalent investments. Another advantage: If inflation heats up, the interest rates on these securities will, sooner or later, increase as well. The drawback to these investments is that after you pay income taxes on the interest, you'll probably barely beat inflation. But if you are ever truly frightened, these may be a worthwhile tradeoff. So select any of these stable investments, and sleep tight. (Several of these investments are issued by banks, savings and loans, or credit unions. Be sure to buy only investments that are federally insured.)

1. **CERTIFICATES OF DEPOSIT**

2. **MONEY-MARKET DEPOSIT ACCOUNTS**

3. **MONEY-MARKET MUTUAL FUNDS**

4. **MUNICIPAL NOTES**

5. **SAVINGS ACCOUNTS**

6. **SINGLE-STATE, TAX-EXEMPT MONEY-MARKET MUTUAL FUNDS**

7. **TAX-EXEMPT MONEY-MARKET MUTUAL FUNDS**

8. **TREASURY BILLS**

9. **U.S. SAVINGS BONDS**

10. **U.S. TREASURY MONEY-MARKET MUTUAL FUNDS**

COPING WITH MARKET UNCERTAINTY CHECKLIST

No matter how volatile or uncertain market conditions may be, avoid the temptation to make any major shifts in your investments.

Any changes in your investment strategy amidst market uncertainty should be directed toward diversifying your investments, emphasizing high-quality securities, and reducing margin loans.

Part VIII

Income Tax Planning

63

Planning Ahead to Minimize Taxes

Taxes are the most universally disliked of all personal finance matters. Rich or poor, Democrat or Republican, northerner or southerner, easterner or westerner, Americans dislike taxes, and they dislike the system that has been established to collect them. Each American reasons that the only fair tax is one that he or she doesn't have to pay.

Nevertheless, good tax planning can save you money. If you think about it, finding sensible ways to save on taxes is the least painful way to cut your expenses. Every taxpayer can benefit from learning ways to cut their taxes. In fact, figuring out ways to save on taxes is as American as apple pie and baseball. Yet whether out of ignorance or fear, many people pay more taxes than they have to—even though the law has consistently upheld the American right to pay only the minimum legal tax. In the often-quoted words of Judge Learned Hand: "Over and over again courts have said that there is nothing sinister in so arranging one's affairs as to keep taxes as low as possible. Everybody does so, rich or poor; and all do right, for nobody owes any public duty to pay more tax than the law demands; taxes are enforced exactions, not voluntary contributions."

Don't overpay your taxes. Profit from spending some time learning about sensible tax-saving techniques.

Don't Go Overboard

On the other hand, many tax-saving strategies simply aren't worth the effort, and they may end up backfiring. The best example is giving money to your children to save taxes and pay for college (see page 165). Just because there are legal ways to reduce your tax bill doesn't mean that each and every option makes sense or will benefit you this year or in future years. Intelligent tax planning often means knowing when *not* to undertake tax-saving strategies as well as knowing which tax strategies to use. (How many billions of dollars were invested during the past decade in now-worthless real estate limited partnerships?) It is always important to remember that tax planning is an important part of personal financial planning—but *it is just one part.* Any investment or financial decision should include an evaluation of its tax ramifications, but none should be regarded solely or even primarily on that basis. There are many cases in which the option that results in a lower cut for Uncle Sam also results in a lower cut for you!

Don't allow your savings strategies to be guided by grandiose tax-saving schemes. These often lack economic substance (in spite of what the colorful brochures tell you). Many people also rely too heavily on their tax preparers. While they may provide you with sound advice, they are obviously not as familiar with your own situation as you are. In fact, effective tax planning often takes years to accomplish.

One final note: The tax "complification" act of 1986 reduced our tax rates so significantly that finding a "tax shelter" is no longer a significant issue. Things were a lot different when you were taxed at forty or fifty cents on the dollar—but no longer. The more you say, "What is the income tax impact of this transaction?" the more likely you are to become so tax driven that you jeopardize your financial status in exchange for very little tax savings.

FIFTY USEFUL IRS PUBLICATIONS (THEY'RE FREE, TOO!)

These publications, available free from the IRS, can be very helpful in understanding income tax matters that pertain to you. You can order any of these publications by calling (800) 829-3676.

PUBLICATION NUMBER	PUBLICATION TITLE
1	Your Rights As a Taxpayer
17	Your Federal Income Tax
54	Tax Guide for U.S. Citizens and Resident Aliens Abroad
225	Farmer's Tax Guide
334	Tax Guide for Small Businesses
448	Federal Estate and Gift Taxes
463	Travel, Entertainment, and Gift Expenses
501	Exemptions, Standard Deduction, and Filing Information
502	Medical and Dental Expenses
503	Child and Dependent Care Credit
504	Tax Information for Divorced or Separated Individuals
505	Tax Withholding and Estimated Tax
508	Educational Expenses
514	Foreign Tax Credit for Individuals
520	Scholarships and Fellowships
521	Moving Expenses
523	Tax Information on Selling Your Home
524	Credit for the Elderly or the Disabled
525	Taxable and Nontaxable Income
526	Charitable Contributions
527	Residential Rental Property
529	Miscellaneous Deductions

»

TAX-PLANNING CHECKLIST

☐

Familiarize yourself with the tax advantages available to you.

☐

If you have a sideline business, familiarize yourself with the tax advantages available to the self-employed.

■□■

Coordinate your income tax planning with other important personal financial-planning areas, including investments and retirement planning.

■□■

Carefully analyze any investment or transaction that is being recommended to you or that you intend to make primarily on the basis of tax saving. It probably isn't worth it.

■□■

Don't lose sight of the role of "old-fashioned" tax-advantaged investments like tax-exempt bonds and buying and holding stock and real estate.

■□■

Maintain complete and well-organized income tax records throughout the year. Your tax record-keeping should be coordinated with your personal record-keeping system.

■□■

Spend some time after tax season with your adviser, if applicable, or yourself, planning to minimize your income taxes over the next several years. Effective income tax planning is both a year-round process and a multiyear process.

Tax-Saving Strategies

Tax planning consists of much more than simply taking advantage of every possible deduction. Rather, tax planning consists of developing a coherent, long-term strategy to reduce taxes for years to come. Timing plays an important role in the well-designed tax plan—"when" can have as great an effect as "how much" on your tax bill, as far as both income and expenses are concerned. Because timing is so important, tax planning is a year-round process, not to be disposed of between Thanksgiving and Christmas. Good planning requires advance planning.

One of the best things about multiyear tax planning is that you eventually learn to avoid the mistakes you made in the past. It doesn't take a big-time commitment to become "tax aware." It just takes a commitment, and you're sure to benefit. Remember that "tax aware" doesn't mean "tax driven." The days of tax-motivated transactions have, mercifully, come to an end, and you are far better off by making investment decisions primarily on the basis of their economic merits. While you need to be aware of the tax implications of your day-to-day personal and business activities, they should no longer be motivated by their impact on your personal tax status.

The purpose of this chapter is to help you develop a coherent tax plan that will serve you well in the long run. (Chapter 65 deals more specifically with particular tax deductions and how to take advantage of them.)

Capital-Gains Taxes

If you are building up a solid investment portfolio—and you should be—dealing with the capital-gains tax effectively will be one of your best tax-saving strategies. According to the Internal Revenue Code, when an investment rises in value, taxes must be paid only when that property is sold—that is, when the capital gains are *realized*. As long as you hold on to your investments, you don't pay any capital-gains taxes on the increase in value these investments have (hopefully) enjoyed. Indeed, the portfolios of many wealthy families consist largely of either real estate or common stock that has been owned for a long time. These assets have significant unrealized capital gains, and the annual rent or dividend income the assets produce can easily be as much as 20 to 30 percent of their original cost basis.

Why are these returns so high? With real estate investments, for instance, rents have been increased over the years, while expenses—including mortgage payments—have stayed relatively low. In the case of stocks, investments have been made in good companies that have strong dividend-paying records. Over the years, dividends have increased to the point where the dividend itself represents 20 percent, 30 percent, or more of the investment's original cost. The key to this approach to wealth creation is avoidance of the capital-gains tax bite by "buying and holding." (Your broker won't want me to tell you this.)

STEELWORKER 1, UNCLE SAM 0

A good friend of mine who is a very successful stockbroker as well as radio talk-show host related the following true story to me: "A few years ago a recently retired steelworker came into my office to ask for some investment advice. He said that he was very embarrassed about his situation and had avoided speaking with an investment adviser about it for many years.

"About twenty-five years earlier he had inherited $40,000 worth of stock from his father. He told me that at that time he didn't know anything about investments, although he recognized the names of all the companies whose shares he had inherited. So he put the stock certificates in his safe-deposit box, where they sat for twenty-five years. He then went on to say that he had been receiving dividend income all along, and he noted that it had increased considerably over the years.

"I told him to retrieve the certificates from the safe-deposit box so we could figure out what they were worth. Well, as you might suspect, his stock was worth over $500,000. He hadn't paid one cent of income tax on the over $450,000 of appreciation in value because he had held on to the shares. His annual dividend income was almost $20,000, which is half of what the total stock investment itself was worth twenty-five years earlier!"

Tax–Exempt Investments

Tax-exempt investments are a smart investment, and you don't need a six-figure income to benefit from them. Over the past several years, the yield on many long-term tax-exempt bonds has not been much less than the yield offered by taxable long-term Treasury bonds. When you consider that you don't have to pay federal income tax on the interest, tax-exempt bonds begin to look like a pretty good addition to a diversified investment portfolio. For example, an investor in the 31 percent federal tax bracket would have to earn over 10 percent on a taxable bond to match a 7 percent tax-exempt yield after taxes have been factored in. Municipal bonds issued in your state (or municipal obligations of Puerto Rico) can provide exemption from both federal and state income taxes.

An alternative to buying individual municipal issues is to invest in municipal bond mutual funds and unit investment trusts that offer tax-free compounding, diversification, and professional securities selection for a low price (see page 518).

Tax-Deferred Investments

T ax deferral, most often in the form of retirement-oriented investment accounts, is a useful way to build your retirement funds. The money you contribute to tax-deferred investment plans accumulates with no tax liability until it is withdrawn. In addition, when you contribute to some of these plans, you can deduct the amount you contribute from your current earnings. Tax-deferred investing is discussed in Chapter 57. To sum up my feelings on tax-deferred investing, anyone with work income should establish an individual retirement account (IRA); anyone with any income from self-employment should contribute to a self-employed retirement account such as a Keogh or simplified employee pension (SEP) plan; and anyone whose employer offers a 401(k) plan or thrift plan should be sure to participate to the maximum.

Year-End Tax Planning

N o matter how much you concentrate on planning for the long haul, when the end of the year rolls around, you may want to take some strategic actions to minimize your tax bill. Remember, miscellaneous expenses are deductible only to the extent that they exceed two percent of your adjusted gross income, and medical expenses are similarly subject to a 7.5 percent floor. You may therefore need to accelerate the payment of these sorts of expenses in a given tax year if you are at or near these thresholds. Similarly, if your income is likely to put you into a higher tax bracket, you should try deferring some income to the next tax year if that will keep you in a lower bracket.

The following additional tips provide some other useful strategies for gaining some year-end tax savings.

- **IF YOU MAKE** estimated state income tax payments, rather than paying the last installment in January, you may want to pay it in late December so that it can be deducted this year. Make sure your tax savings will exceed the amount of interest lost by paying early, however.

- **THE END OF THE YEAR** is the season to give vent to your charitable impulses. Don't forget that donations of such items as old clothing, furniture, and books are deductible at fair market value. Keep track of any expenses you incur while driving your famous chocolate swirl pound cake to the church bake sale—your mileage is deductible at an IRS set rate per mile. Donations of appreciated stock are often even better than cash, since in addition to your income tax deduction, you can avoid paying tax on the capital gain.

- **TO AVOID A PENALTY,** make sure your withheld and estimated taxes will equal or exceed either last year's tax bill or 90 percent of what you'll owe for the current year. If you think you'll come up short, there may still be time to compensate by increasing the taxes withheld from your salary at the end of the year.

TEN EASY WAYS TO SAVE ON TAXES

1. **KEEP METICULOUS TAX RECORDS.** Unless you want to pay more taxes than you have to, improve your tax record-keeping system. Have a notebook handy to keep track of miscellaneous tax-deductible expenses.

2. **PREPARE YOUR OWN TAX RETURNS.** This is the best way to learn about tax-saving techniques. The IRS provides many free pamphlets (see pages 564-65) and there are many books on the market that can help you out. When you prepare your own return, show the IRS that you take your tax-preparation duties seriously. A typed return will send that message. Furthermore, typing your return will eliminate at least one reason for IRS agents to make inquiries about your return: illegibility!

3. **REQUEST IRS PUBLICATION 17.** Call or write the IRS to request a copy of IRS Publication 17, "Your Federal Income Tax." This is an excellent source of information on how best to prepare your tax return. You may well find Publication 17 informative and thorough enough to make purchasing other tax-preparation guides unnecessary.

4. **MAKE A CHARITABLE DONATION** of stock that has appreciated in value rather than giving cash. If you donate stock that has appreciated in value to charity, you get a deduction for the current market value of the stock—thereby avoiding any capital-gains tax. This is an attractive money-saving maneuver that is far better than donating an equivalent amount of cash.

5. **KEEP A RECORD** of all cash charitable contributions you make. If you are like most people, you make a "guesstimate" of your cash charitable contributions when tax time rolls around. Unfortunately, even if you have underestimated the amount of your contributions, the IRS is wary of unsubstantiated deductions. So keep a log or diary of your cash contributions. Or better yet, make all but your smallest donations by check.

6. **DONATE UNNEEDED CLOTHING** and other personal items to recognized charities. If you have usable clothing, furniture, or other personal property you don't need, donate it

»

to a recognized charity. You can take a tax deduction for the donated items' fair market value. Let Uncle Sam subsidize your generosity!

7. **FILE RETURNS SEPARATELY** (rather than jointly) if it will result in lower taxes. Sometimes married taxpayers end up paying less in taxes when they file separate returns than when they file a joint return.

8. **IF YOU'RE OWED A REFUND,** send in your tax return early. File early. Don't procrastinate. Send in your tax return ahead of time if you're going to get some money back. After all, the federal government isn't going to pay you interest on it.

9. **IF YOU OWE THE IRS MONEY,** don't send in your tax return early. As long as you have paid enough during the tax year to avoid a penalty, there's no reason to file your tax return early if you owe money to the IRS. This is one instance where procrastination allows you to keep your money working for you until the last minute.

10. **IF YOU OVERPAID TAXES** the previous year, amend your return and get a refund. But don't wait—there's a time limit.

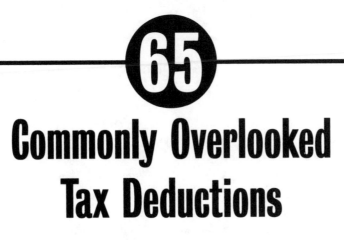

Commonly Overlooked Tax Deductions

D o you have a room at home that is used as an office? Do you find yourself picking up the tab when you are out on business trips? Have you been saddled with a lot of hospital bills and medical expenses this year? For child care? All these expenses are tax-deductible—albeit subject to an often-maddening variety of caveats, qualifications, and restrictions. This chapter shows you how to take advantage of these deductions, which are all too often misunderstood and underused, if not overlooked altogether. Some of the deductions discussed here may seem "old hat," but read on, and you will probably find some things that will take a bite out of your tax bill. It's worth your time. After all, finding a new tax deduction is like finding money; it doesn't require any sacrifice to obtain it.

Homeowner's Expenses

H ome ownership is an expensive proposition. So it's nice to know that at least some homeowner's expenses are tax-deductible. Everyone knows that mortgage interest and property taxes are deductible, but did you know that you can also deduct those annoying "points" you pay when you take out a mortgage or refinance? If you refinance, you can't deduct all the points in one year—they must be spread out over the term of the mortgage. Also, remember that if you refinance, any interest prepayment penalties are deductible.

Moving Expenses

If you're just moving across town to a bigger house, you probably won't qualify for a moving expense deduction. But if you are moving because you are changing jobs—or are being transferred to a new location by your employer—you are eligible. One caveat: The IRS requires that to qualify for the deduction, your new work location must be more than thirty-five miles from your old home. Generally, your move must take place within one year of your commencing work at your new place of employment.

You can also deduct up to 80 percent of the costs you incur house- or apartment-hunting, so long as your move has been prompted by career considerations. You can deduct as many as thirty days' worth of these expenses. During the move itself, the cost of food and lodging on the day before and the day of arrival can be deducted. Be sure to keep records of these expenses.

Business and Job-Related Expenses

The way job-related expenses are treated on your tax return depends on whether they are reimbursed by your employer. All reimbursed employee business expenses are deductible from your gross income. But since the reimbursed amount is part of your gross income, the deduction is essentially canceled out. Unreimbursed employee business expenses, on the other hand, including car expenses and travel, are claimed as "miscellaneous itemized deductions." Since miscellaneous itemized deductions must exceed two percent of your adjusted gross income (AGI) before the deduction is allowed, it is quite possible that none of your unreimbursed expenses will be of help in reducing your taxable income. But you never know until you add up all your miscellaneous itemized deductions. You may be in for a pleasant surprise if they exceed two percent of your AGI.

If you are claiming business expenses as an employee, you are required to file Form 2106, "Employee Business Expenses," with your tax return. Self-employed persons will generally record all business expenses on Schedule C of Form 1040.

Travel Expenses

Deductible travel expenses generally consist of transportation costs incurred while away from home on business. Your "tax home" is (a) your regular place of business; (b) the principal one if you have several places of business; or (c) your residence. If you are temporarily assigned to another locale as part of your job, you may generally deduct travel expenses while you are temporarily employed away from home.

Smart Money Move

Review a list of tax-deductible items to uncover tax-saving deductions of which you may not be aware. Many tax-preparation guides have these lists.

With respect to local transportation, you are entitled to deduct as a business expense local transportation costs incurred in traveling (a) from your principal place of business to another location where business-related activities occur and (b) between one place where business-related activities occur and another such place.

Most expenses associated with business travel away from home are deductible if they are reasonable. Deductible travel costs include the expense of attending business meetings and conventions in the United States, as long as the agenda is related to your occupation. Apportionment of expenses between personal and business-related activities may be necessary if the trip is part pleasure. If you take your spouse on a business trip, part of your total trip expenses will not be deductible. Generally, the nondeductible amount is the difference between the total expense and what it would have been if you had taken the trip by yourself.

Business expenses associated with foreign travel are also usually deductible, although transportation costs may have to be allocated when the trip involves some nonbusiness activities. If the foreign trip lasts less than one week or if the time spent on personal pursuits is less than 25 percent of the total time away from home, you do not have to divide your expenses between business and personal activities. The deductibility of business expenses associated with attending *foreign* conventions as well as meetings on cruise ships are subject to much stricter rules.

Automobile Expenses

If you use your automobile in connection with your business or occupation, you may be able to deduct part or all of your car expenses using either a standard mileage rate or the actual cost. The standard mileage rate is certainly more straightforward to use, and you can deduct parking fees and tolls incurred during business use on top of it. Nevertheless, the actual cost method will usually give you a greater tax deduction. You must keep thorough records of all car-related operations and costs to substantiate your deductions. If you employ the actual cost method and use your car partially for personal purposes and partially for business purposes, the interest on any car loans that is attributable to business use should be included in total car expenses for determining the deduction. The proportion of interest expense that is attributable to personal use is no longer deductible since it is considered personal interest.

Meals, Entertainment, and Gifts

It is often hard to determine whether the cost of a business meal, entertainment, or gift is tax-deductible. As a rule, you can deduct 80 percent of the cost of these items, although the burden is on you to prove that the meal, gift, or entertainment expense was truly business-related.

Club dues and fees are generally not deductible unless you use the club facility primarily (more than half the time) for business purposes. If you do deduct dues and fees, you must prorate your deduction based on the percentage of time you used the club for business engagements. For instance, if your monthly club dues were $200 and three-quarters of your visits to the club were for business purposes, you could deduct $150. You cannot deduct more than $25 per year per business-gift recipient.

Maintaining an Office at Home

If you use your home to conduct business, you may be able to deduct certain expenses pertaining to its use. To be eligible for the office-at-home deduction, you must use your home in at least one of the following ways: as the principal place of business, as a place to meet with patients, clients, or customers in the regular course of business, or in connection with a trade or business. The key sticking point: The part of the house that you use for business must be used exclusively and regularly for business purposes in order for your office-at-home to be deductible.

Record-Keeping for Business Expenses

Good record-keeping is necessary in order to maximize business-related deductions and substantiate them later. Perhaps the best way to do this is to keep a diary with you at all times in which you can note day-to-day business-related expenses, including travel itineraries and notations of business meetings and entertainment. That diary could save you several hundred dollars in taxes each year.

Medical Expenses

You can deduct out-of-pocket medical expenses that exceed 7.5 percent of your adjusted gross income (AGI). Medical expenses include dental and drug expenses. If there is any likelihood that your medical expenses will exceed the 7.5 percent of AGI threshold, you should tally them up in November or early December. If you're over the threshold, try to pay as many medical expenses as you can before the year ends so that you can take maximum advantage of the deduction. You may even be able to prepay some medical procedures that will be performed in the next year.

The following medical expense deductions are frequently overlooked.

- ALCOHOLISM AND DRUG ABUSE TREATMENT
- CHILDBIRTH PREPARATION CLASSES (FOR THE MOTHER, NOT FOR THE COACH)
- CONTACT LENSES
- CONTRACEPTIVES (IF BOUGHT WITH A PRESCRIPTION)
- HEALTH INSURANCE COSTS FOR SELF-EMPLOYED PERSONS
- LEAD PAINT REMOVAL
- TRAVEL EXPENSES INCURRED EN ROUTE TO MEDICAL TREATMENT
- MEDICAL EXAMINATION REQUIRED BY EMPLOYER
- MEDICALLY PRESCRIBED ITEMS
- ORTHOPEDIC SHOES
- PARKING FEES AND TOLLS
- PRESCRIBED DIET FOODS
- SPECIAL EQUIPMENT FOR THE DISABLED OR HANDICAPPED
- SPECIAL DIET FOODS

Smart Money Move

Keep a diary handy to record your deductible expenses.

- TRAVEL (SUBJECT TO LIMITATIONS)

COMMONLY OVERLOOKED TAX DEDUCTIONS

The following items *may* be tax deductible, although a lot of taxpayers don't realize it. Be careful, however, because many of these items are deductible only under certain circumstances—for example, only if they are associated with business activities. To find out more, check one of the many income-tax-preparation guides or the applicable IRS publications listed on pages 564-65.

- ACCOUNTING FEES for tax-preparation services and IRS audits

- APPRECIATION on property donated to a charity

- BUSINESS GIFTS of $25 or less per recipient

- CASUALTY LOSS

- CELLULAR TELEPHONES

- CLEANING and laundering services when traveling

- COMMISSION on sale of property

- DEPRECIATION of home computer

- DUES to labor union

- EMPLOYEE EDUCATIONAL EXPENSES

- EMPLOYEE MOVING EXPENSES, including those related to house-hunting, selling your old home or settling an unexpired lease, and travel

- EMPLOYMENT AGENCY FEES

- FEES for a safe-deposit box to hold investments

- FOREIGN TAXES PAID

- GAMBLING LOSSES to the extent of gambling gains

- IRA TRUSTEE'S ADMINISTRATIVE FEES billed separately

- OUT-OF-POCKET EXPENSES relating to charitable activities, including standard mileage deduction

- PASSPORT FEE for business trip

- PENALTY for early withdrawal on savings

»

- **POINTS ON HOME MORTGAGE** and certain refinancing

- **SELF-EMPLOYMENT TAX** up to 50 percent of amount paid

- **STATE PERSONAL PROPERTY TAXES ON CARS**

- **THEFT LOSSES**

- **TRADE OR BUSINESS TOOLS** with life of one year or less

- **UNIFORMS AND WORK CLOTHES** not suitable as ordinary wearing apparel

- **WORTHLESS STOCK OR SECURITIES**

66

Easing the Chore of Preparing Your Taxes

W hether you prepare your own tax returns or pay someone else to prepare them, the annual chore of income tax preparation is at best agonizing. The mechanics of tax-return preparation can be puzzling and difficult, and nobody is about to give the IRS a special award for its lucid and succinct use of the English language. To make matters worse, the tax rules are always changing. As the saying goes, the only two things in life that are certain are death and taxes. But at least death doesn't get worse every time Congress convenes.

For these reasons, many people opt to have their taxes prepared by a professional, whether it be a national chain like H&R Block or a CPA in private practice. It's a shame that millions of people have to pay someone else to perform duties required of them as citizens. A lot of people who pay someone to prepare their returns should probably be doing them themselves. The best way to learn tax-saving techniques is to prepare your own tax return. If you simply throw up your hands and give all your information to a tax preparer, you can rest assured that you are paying too much tax on top of having to pay someone to do your return. If your tax situation is not that complex and you have cultivated the habit of having someone else prepare your return, consider doing it yourself next time. Or perhaps you could strike a deal with your tax preparer, wherein you do the best you can in filling out your return. It would then be reviewed and corrected by the tax preparer for a lower fee than if the preparer were to start from scratch.

Even when you hire a tax preparer, however, you can't entirely escape the often mindnumbing tasks that accompany tax season. Nonetheless, tax time doesn't have to be a total nightmare, and if you approach it properly, it can be short if not sweet. It's all a matter of:

- GETTING ORGANIZED

- BECOMING TAX AWARE.

Preparing for April Starts in May

If you find yourself tearing your hair out with frustration and stress every tax season, making tax preparation a year-round task may not strike you as the perfect solution to your problem. But if you take the time to establish a good record-keeping system and properly file away your bills and statements, life will become a good deal more bearable when 1040 time rolls around.

Even if you have your taxes professionally prepared, being well organized will save you time and expense. The more time your tax preparer must puzzle over incomplete material, the more he or she will charge you. The more frequently your accountant has to call to ask you to dig up a particular bill, the more time you waste ransacking your house and getting into arguments with family members over lost documents.

Once your records are in order, you won't have to spend the second week in April trying to find last year's receipts. While periodically sorting through and organizing old records is hardly a pleasant task, the long-term payoff will be substantial. (For pointers on setting up a user-friendly record-keeping system, consult Chapter 4.)

Working with a Tax Preparer

Once you understand some general tax and investment rules, you need to figure out how to put them to work for you. The first question is: Do you need a tax preparer? Many of the best-prepared tax returns from the standpoint of accuracy and tax minimization are prepared by the individual taxpayer. Many people don't mind doing their own taxes because they have time to become informed about tax-saving matters. If your individual tax situation isn't too complicated, there's nothing wrong with doing your own taxes. It will also save you some money.

On the other hand, tax preparation and planning are intimidating, frustrating, and downright unpleasant for many working and retired people. The extensive tax reforms of the 1980s have managed to confuse just about everybody, and as soon as you begin to feel that you understand the current rules, the Congress is probably going to change them. A good tax adviser can be a life-saver. He or she will help you minimize your tax bill by keeping you informed on strategies you can use and by knowing how different expenses and income are treated. Also, a good tax adviser will help you stay up to date on tax-saving techniques and the latest changes in tax law.

Tax preparers come in all sizes, shapes—and competencies. They range from people operating from their kitchen table whose knowledge of income tax preparation ranges from quite competent to downright ignorant, to storefront tax-preparation chains, to CPAs and lawyers. Like any other service business, the quality of tax-preparation service varies greatly, and it pays to be a wise consumer. High-cost tax preparers don't necessarily do a better job than do less-expensive preparers.

You may need a highly qualified tax preparer—a CPA or lawyer—if your tax situation is unusually complicated. For example, if you are involved in buying and selling property, complex investment transactions or a lot of limited partnerships, you may need to go first class. Another advantage of going with a full-time tax professional is that he or she will be able to advise you on sensible long-term tax-planning strategies. But this talent doesn't come cheap, and most people don't need that kind of service, particularly if they are willing to spend a little time learning tax-saving strategies themselves.

The Burden Is on You

Whoever you choose, you still have to work with your tax adviser because only you are fully aware of your financial situation. You shouldn't expect your tax adviser to be a miracle worker who can make sense out of the unorganized mass of receipts and forms you give him or her around April 1. You should organize your records, keep them organized throughout the year, and always keep tax considerations in mind before making any financial transaction. Simplify your tax life and your tax adviser's job as much as you reasonably can. Consolidate investments, keep the best and most complete records you can, and avoid all sorts of supposed tax shelters. Keep a notebook handy to record miscellaneous deductible expenses, such as costs associated with medical care and volunteer activities. Remember, tax minimization and tax planning are year-round processes, so expect your adviser to advise you throughout the year, and listen to the advice. A good tax adviser will be available year-round not only to answer your questions but also to review the tax implications of contemplated investments and to suggest tax-saving strategies.

Don't just sign your completed tax form without checking it over first. No matter how competent your tax preparer is, mistakes can—and do—happen. At the very least, you should make sure that the numbers on the return match the numbers you supplied before affixing your John Hancock to your 1040. Should the IRS spot an error on your return, you will be the one to suffer the consequences, not the tax preparer. It also makes good sense to verify that your return will be completed on time. Like any business operation, tax preparers can be prone to clerical errors. To insure that the return is being completed on schedule, check in with the preparer every couple of weeks or so to see how matters are progressing. Your calls will be a subtle reminder that you are relying on him or her to get the job done.

Doing It Yourself

I f you are one of those fearless (and, in my opinion, smart) individuals who are committed to preparing their own taxes, you have a number of tools at your disposal, including tax-preparation guides, tax-preparation software, and free IRS tax-advisory services.

Tax-Preparation Guides

In the early months of each year, the tax-preparation guides—some of which are as large as big-city telephone directories—flood the bookstores. Most of these guides are excellent. I favor *J.K. Lasser's Your Income Tax*, the granddaddy of them all, and *The Ernst & Young Tax Guide*. But before taking my advice, take a good look at how each guide is put together before you buy it. You'll be living on very intimate terms with your guide, so it's important to be comfortable with the way that it is organized. Even if you don't prepare your own taxes, these guides can go a long way in helping you become "tax aware."

Tax-Preparation Software

If you own a personal computer or have access to one at work—and have a little skill at operating it—a good tax-preparation software could speed and simplify the chore of preparing your taxes. There are many different programs on the market, but all of them are capable of doing the job. The cost of these programs generally ranges from $50 to $100. You may also be able to buy a separate program to do your state taxes, although it may not justify the extra expense if your state taxes are fairly straightforward. Two of the best programs are Turbo Tax sold by ChipSoft ([619] 453-8722) and TaxCut 1040 sold by MECA Software ([800] 288-6322). The software may be purchased directly from the manufacturer or from a local software retailer. Income tax-preparation software has really caught on in recent years, and for good reason. It is a user-friendly way to do your taxes.

Obtaining Free Help with Your Return

You are doing your return yourself. You've bought a good tax-preparation handbook. But you're still experiencing difficulties with your return. You can get assistance from the IRS, should your tax preparation run into a snag. The IRS has established a whole network of telephone tax consultants and information audiotapes. District offices also offer walk-in assistance to taxpayers.

You can obtain a comprehensive catalogue of teletax numbers by ordering IRS Publication 1137, "Toll-Free and Tele-Tax Telephone Numbers." Publication 910, "Guide to Free Tax Services," details the kinds of walk-in service your local IRS Service Center can offer you.

Filing Your Return Electronically

The advent of electronic tax-return filing is profoundly changing the tax experience for many individual taxpayers. Now that the IRS has finally come "on-line," the bureaucratic behemoth is slowly becoming more service oriented. More and more people are taking advantage of this quick and convenient method of filing, no doubt largely because taxpayers who file electronically get their refund checks a lot faster than taxpayers who file the old-fashioned way. If getting your refund check a few weeks early sounds appealing, all you need to do is make a few telephone calls to local income tax preparers. Many of them are sure to be set up for electronic filing. If you use income tax-preparation software, you can also file your return automatically. One thing to remember, however: You'll have to pay for the privilege—around twenty dollars.

How to Avoid an Audit

Being audited is every taxpayer's worst nightmare, and every taxpayer would love to know how to make his or her return audit-proof. Unfortunately, there is no fool-proof method of avoiding an audit. A careful assessment of your deductions, how-ever, can significantly reduce the chance that you will be summoned by the Inquisition.

Any deduction for which you may not have adequate documentation is open to IRS scrutiny. The following deductions are difficult to prove if you have failed to maintain ade-quate records:

- **CASUALTY LOSS.** The IRS assumes that taxpayers will not have the receipts required by law to prove a casualty loss.

- **AUTO AND ENTERTAINMENT.** Again, because taxpayers usually do not keep sufficient records and receipts for unreim-bursed business expenses, auto and entertainment deductions are fertile fields for the auditor.

- **CASH CONTRIBUTIONS.** The amount of money deducted for cash contributions to eligible civic, religious, charita-ble, scientific, literary, and educational organizations is always open to readjustment by the tax auditor, since the amount is not itemized. Because this deduc-tion does not require receipts to substantiate it, tax-payers often guess at the exact amount. Anytime guess-work is involved, the IRS is within its rights to adjust the amount of the deduction during the audit if the auditor feels that the amount is too large.

- **CHILD CARE.** Because many people pay their child-care providers in cash, a large number of child-care deduc-tions cannot be substantiated. It is impossible to prove a deduction without receipts, so a large claim for child-care credits may invite an audit.

Returns claiming deductions that are commonly misunderstood, especially those involving depreciation, often bear fruit—for the IRS. The IRS has a vested interest in ensuring through audits that the technicalities governing these sophisticated deductions have not been overlooked and that the correct method of deduction has been chosen.

Definition

Casualty Loss: For income tax pur-poses, deductible losses arising from the destruction of property from an unidentifiable event that is sudden, unexpected, and unusual in nature. Examples of casual-ty losses: damages from floods, fires, tornadoes, hurri-canes, sonic booms, vandalism, storms, and automobile accidents.

Types of Audits

K nowing how the IRS's audit program works can help you lower your own chances of being audited.

Taxpayer Compliance Management Program (TCMP)

Undertaken every three years for individual returns, the TCMP is the foundation of the IRS's enforcement procedure. The program's objective is to develop profiles of "typical" returns for various levels of income in the United States. A representative sample of roughly fifty thousand returns is randomly drawn.

The good news about a TCMP audit is that because the selection is entirely random, there is not necessarily a discrepancy on the return. Thus, if you are chosen, you don't need to feel that the IRS suspects you of being a tax cheat. Indeed, one out of every fifteen taxpayers audited through the TCMP learn that they have overpaid their taxes and walk away from the process with a refund check in hand.

The bad news is that the TCMP audit is the IRS's most painstaking, thorough, and arduous examination. You will find the cost in time and aggravation substantial.

Every return submitted is scored by a computer program according to its resemblance to the typical return. The greater the deviation, the higher the score will be, and all returns whose scores exceed a certain level are earmarked for further scrutiny. Most of these will result in one of the three conventional civil audits: the mail, office, or field audit. A few returns are given a criminal audit.

Mail Audits

If your tax return includes fairly straightforward problems, it can be easily corrected by mail. If you make a mathematical error or deduct an unallowable item on your return, for example, the IRS will merely mail you a letter explaining the problem and giving the recalculated tax. You may need to complete additional forms or submit copies of receipts to provide the IRS with information concerning a particular item on the return; in many cases all communication is conducted by mail.

Office Audits

Returns with more complex problems are forwarded to IRS district offices. At this stage, an agent examines your return and organizes a portfolio of discrepancies concerning the items in question. You are then notified by mail of the problems and scheduled for an appointment at the district office. The notification letter also specifies what records and receipts should be brought to the meeting in order to substantiate the claims.

Field Audits

If your return has several complex problems, an IRS field agent will handle the case. The agent will examine your return, formulate a list of potential problems, notify you that you are being audited, and arrange a time to visit you at home or at work. This type of audit may take anywhere from one to several days to complete.

Criminal Audits

If you've been filing honest returns, you probably don't have to worry about being subject to a criminal audit, which the IRS initiates if it suspects criminal fraud. Severe penalties and even jail sentences can lie at the end of a criminal audit. If you are going to be the subject of a criminal audit, retain a lawyer to help you.

Being Audited—and Living to Tell the Tale

If the IRS informs you that you are subject to an office or field audit, avoid the temptation to jump out the nearest window. True, your luck is not the greatest—only slightly more than one out of every one hundred personal income tax returns is audited each year. On the other hand, many people who are audited by the IRS walk away owing no more or less than when they originally filed. The best defense against an audit is filing an honest tax return. Quite simply, an honest tax return is one in which you include all taxable income and don't lie about deductions.

The most important thing is not to lose your head. As soon as your office or field audit notice arrives in the mail, call the IRS office to which the notice refers you. Ask the agent how much time you will need to set aside to meet with your auditor. Should the agent tell you to set only a few hours aside, chances are that your interview will be short-lived. If the agent tells you that you need to set aside a whole week to discuss matters, pack your sleeping bag.

If someone else prepared your tax return, you may want to bring them along to the examination. Discuss this with the tax preparer. Obviously, having representation may lessen the aggravation, but it will increase the expense. If matters come down to some sort of settlement (in larger cases they do), your tax professional will handle negotiations over how much you will pay in additional taxes, penalties, and fines.

Be prepared to marshal as strong a documentary case as possible to support the deductions you made on your return. The more hard evidence you can bring forth to bolster your position, the more likely it is that you will emerge from the audit process relatively unscathed. Don't offer more information than is requested. *One caution:* While you must make a forceful argument as to the legitimacy of your returns, don't become belligerent or treat the agent rudely. The IRS is a huge machine, and once it gets you in its grip, it can be very hard to extricate yourself. The last thing you want is to have the agent who is auditing you take a personal dislike to you.

You have the right to appeal. Initially, you may appeal to the examiner's supervisor or request an informal conference. Beyond that you could go to Tax Court to state your case. The decision to appeal to the Tax Court should not be taken lightly, for fighting the IRS is an expensive and time-consuming uphill battle.

TAX-PREPARATION CHECKLIST

☐

Unless your tax situation is particularly complicated, you should prepare your own tax returns. The best way to learn about tax-saving techniques is to prepare your own returns.

☐

Organize your tax records throughout the year to avoid a last-minute marathon.

☐

Whether you prepare your own returns or not, purchase one of the many excellent tax-preparation guides to learn about how to reduce your taxes under the current rules.

☐

If you prepare your own returns, buy one of the many excellent tax-preparation software packages to ease the chore.

☐

Understand the "red flag" areas on your tax return to reduce the chances of an audit.

☐

Always maintain good tax records. The best defense against an audit is adequate documentation to prove your income and deductions.

Part IX

Retirement Planning

It's Never Too Early to Start Planning for Retirement

To a large extent, everything you do during your working years—from saving regularly to maintaining adequate insurance coverage—is directed toward your most important objective: to be able to retire comfortably. During the remainder of this decade and well into the new century, retirement planning is likely to become an even more important issue, as the postwar baby-boomers enter their fifties and begin to ponder their prospects of achieving and maintaining financial security in their "golden years."

Increasingly, both employers and the federal government are expecting individuals to fund a substantial portion of their retirement income from their own personal savings. On the employer's side, pension plans are already under pressure because of the increasing costs associated with funding those plans. Many companies, in fact, are replacing traditional pension plans, which provide a guaranteed income at retirement, with plans that base corporate contributions on annual profits. In addition, many pensions do not provide post-retirement cost-of-living increases; and those that do have generally not kept pace with inflation in recent years.

Let Uncle Sam Help

Many experts feel that Social Security benefits—once considered a legislative sacred cow—will eventually be subject to a means-based test. Should this occur, relatively affluent workers may find that their Social Security benefits are less than they had planned on.

On the other hand, the federal government has introduced a number of tax-advantaged retirement-savings programs to help boost the sagging personal savings rate. Employers, too, now offer tax-advantaged savings plans, like 401(k) plans, that often have incentives such as matching contributions. Financial institutions also feature numerous products and services to take advantage of the growing retirement market. So while it is becoming increasingly important to save for your own retirement, there is an attractive array of investment and savings alternatives to help you do so. It is largely up to you, however, to acquaint yourself with these various opportunities.

Benefit from Planning Early

Ideally, retirement planning should start when individuals are in their twenties or thirties. While it is difficult to predict retirement income and expenses, younger individuals can begin saving for retirement by taking advantage of an individual retirement account (IRA) or other tax-advantaged savings plans, determining an appropriate investment strategy, and making regular plan contributions.

Chances are that you haven't yet accumulated a substantial nest egg for retirement. If you are like most people, you have experienced more pressing and immediate concerns, such as buying a home and raising and educating children. Whatever your circumstances, however, you should regularly direct some attention to planning for your retirement.

Don't Put Off Until Tomorrow What You Should Do Today

Whether you are twenty-two or sixty-two or somewhere in between, you should be actively planning for your retirement. Retirement planning can appear so complex that many people don't know where to begin, so they put off doing it. This chapter is a retirement-planning primer that introduces you to the various matters that need attention when developing a reliable, solid retirement plan. The chapters that follow explain in more detail the important but by no means overwhelming matters that need your attention.

Along the way, of course, I will offer a lot of suggestions that will help you not only plan but, more importantly, achieve your retirement dreams. Don't despair over your retirement prospects. That will only cause you to further delay your planning.

Changes in the Retirement Landscape

Planning for retirement ain't what it used to be. You need to be aware of several changes in the retirement landscape, because they will affect your planning. It's sad to say, but these trends make it all the more important for you to take the action necessary to achieve a financially secure retirement as soon as possible.

Great Expectations

Most of us have very ambitious retirement expectations—we want to be able to maintain the same life-style when we retire as we have during our working years. This is quite a change from previous generations, who generally expected to have to cut back somewhat when they retired. There's nothing wrong with setting high retirement expectations—as long as you are willing to take the actions necessary to achieve them.

Early Retirement

Many people aspire to, or are forced to consider, early retirement. According to the Social Security Administration, half of Social Security-eligible workers begin collecting Social Security at age sixty-two, the earliest they can begin to collect benefits. (If early retirement is in your future, read Chapter 77.)

Life Expectancy

Longevity has increased dramatically since the beginning of this century. It used to be that workers who lived long enough to retire at age sixty-five lived only a few years longer. Now, a person who retires at sixty-five should plan on living another twenty-five years, and many will live well beyond ninety. You may work for thirty-five or forty years, during which time you will have to accumulate enough retirement funds to last twenty-five years or more.

Inflation

Inflation makes it tough to accumulate sufficient resources in advance of retirement and to maintain an adequate living standard throughout a long retirement. One of the biggest mistakes that people make in planning for their retirement is to ignore or underestimate the effects of inflation. Even though inflation is much lower now than it was during the double-digit days of 1979-81, it still takes its toll on your purchasing power.

Many experts now recommend that people who are making financial projections assume a future annual inflation rate of three to five percent. Some experts think that even higher inflation rates are in the offing. Incidentally, the average annual inflation rate during the 1980s, including the high rates of the early 1980s, was 4.7 percent. I recommend using a rate of 3.5 to 4.5 percent when making projections, which means that the cost of living will double every fifteen to twenty years.

Social Insecurity

Fiscal pressures on the government and employers are increasing the likelihood that to assure an adequate retirement income, we will have to rely less on Social Security and company pension plans and more on personal investments and savings. With respect to company pension plans, an unmistakable shift is taking place in moving the burden on funding retirement-income needs away from the employer to the employee.

The Five Basic Steps in Retirement Planning

There are five basic steps in the retirement-planning process. These steps are introduced below and discussed in more detail in the chapters that follow.

1. Decide how you want to live when you retire

Once you have an idea of how you want to live in retirement, you can estimate your expenses—first in current dollars, then in future, inflated dollars. In order to maintain the same standard of living in retirement that you enjoyed during your working years, you will probably spend approximately 75 percent of the amount you *spend* during your working years.

You must also consider the possibility of a forced early retirement. What chance is there that it could happen? You may need to plan for that contingency. Are you prepared to settle for a more modest retirement life-style? The last thing you want to happen is to be forced into an unplanned early retirement, only to find yourself pounding the pavement for a new job at sixty. (If this happens or is likely to happen, read Chapters 28 and 31.)

2. Estimate how much income you will need during retirement

If you are twenty years away from retirement, estimating your income requirements at retirement age may be of little concern to you now, but you should still pay attention to it. After all, you may well spend over one-third of your life retired! If, on the other hand, you are within ten years of retiring, you must begin to think in great detail about your retirement expenses and your sources of income. This is also the time to give some thought to the all-important decision about where you want to live.

3. Figure out how much you need to accumulate to fund your retirement

Once you have estimated how much you expect to spend when you retire, you need to forecast how much you will need to accumulate personally, in addition to estimated Social Security and your pension benefits, to provide for your needs for the rest of your life. (The so-called three legs of the retirement stool are your pension, Social Security, and your personal resources.) Don't forget to factor in inflation at around 4 percent per year for twenty-five to thirty years after you retire in order to calculate how much money your investments will have to generate in order to at least keep pace. Inflation takes such a heavy toll on retirees that most of them must continue saving well into their seventies in order to set aside enough money to meet ever-increasing living expenses in their eighties and nineties.

Smart Money Move

Go over the five steps to achieving a comfortable retirement at least once each year.

4. Take stock of your progress in meeting your retirement needs

Estimating how much you will need to accumulate by the time you reach retirement age can be startling. If you are still young, this amount may seem more like the gross national product of a small country, but it is attainable. *Caveat:* Don't include the value of your home in your retirement-related assets unless you plan to sell the house and become a renter when you retire.

5. Take action to close the gap between the resources you now have

and the resources you will need to retire

Figuring out how much you need to retire in comfort usually leads to the realization that you don't yet have enough money to meet these needs. If misery does love company, there is some solace in the fact that very few people achieve financial independence until they are very near retirement. But what is most important is to make sure you take action today to provide for your financial needs *throughout* your retirement.

FOR FURTHER INFORMATION

American Association of Retired Persons (AARP)
601 E Street N.W.
Washington DC 20049
(202) 434-2277

For an $8 annual membership fee, you will receive a subscription to *Modern Maturity* magazine, assorted AARP booklets, and be able to attend AARP-sponsored seminars.

RETIREMENT-PLANNING CHECKLIST

Don't delay planning carefully for your retirement. It's the end result of all you do during your working life, so it merits your careful attention.

Regularly—at least annually—go through the five steps to achieving a comfortable retirement to gauge your progress.

Don't get discouraged over your retirement prospects. Every worthwhile goal takes time to achieve, and the sooner you begin to take action, the better.

Determining Your Retirement Life-Style

I f you want to live a fast-lane retirement life-style—buying a shiny convertible sports car to match your balding pate—you'd better make sure you die before your biological speedometer hits seventy. Otherwise, you'll end up spending the rest of your retirement years in the breakdown lane. My advice for oldsters is the same as for youngsters: Living beneath your means is the only way to achieve financial security. So stop dreaming about sports cars, balmy beaches, and bronzed bods. Set your financial sights on having the retirement time of *your* life.

The amount of money you will need to finance a long and happy retirement obviously depends on how expensive your tastes are. Your choice of housing, including your choice of community or surroundings, is usually the single most important standard-of-living consideration. (Living in a log cabin in Manhattan, Montana, certainly imposes different financial and social obligations from inhabiting a penthouse in Manhattan, New York.) But there are many other factors to consider, such as when you are going to retire (early, on your sixty-fifth birthday, or later); what you're going to do with your time; how you're going to manage your retirement investments (before and during your retirement); insurance and health-care matters; and activities like traveling and financially helping out your children and grandchildren, which, of course, increases the cost of your retirement living. I've said it before and I'll say it again: Don't go overboard giving financial assistance to your children and grandchildren unless they genuinely need it. Also, try to devise a plan to spend all your money before you die. You deserve your money a lot more than your heirs do.

The Housing Dilemma

M ost retired people choose to live in the same home they occupied prior to their retirement, although from a purely financial standpoint this is often short-sighted. Others decide to live in another area or try a new life-style, such as living in a condominium, a smaller house, a retirement community, or a continuing-care community. Ideally, you should try out, or at least seriously evaluate, any such arrangement *before* retirement. During retirement, when funds are limited, it's far more difficult to go back to your former housing arrangements or locale once a change has been made.

Housing expenses can present a serious problem for many fixed-income retirees. Many who do not own their homes are confronted with rent or alternative housing costs that rise faster than inflation—but with an income that barely keeps up. Even if you bought your home in anticipation of being mortgage-free by retirement, property taxes—which reflect the value of the property rather than your income or ability to pay—may present a serious financial burden. Many people who would prefer to stay in their own homes wind up selling their homes to find a cheaper and more manageable housing arrangement. This is often a good idea, even if you can afford your old home.

Many people choose to move at retirement even though neither their health nor their financial circumstances compel them to do so. Some wish to adopt a new life-style by moving into a different type of housing. Others just want a change of scenery or climate, and still others decide to sell their home and buy a smaller one or rent in order to use the equity in their home for additional income. If you do plan to move at retirement, you will probably want to take advantage of the one-time exclusion from tax on the sale of a home for taxpayers over age fifty-five. (See Chapter 13.)

If you are contemplating a change of residence, you should thoroughly explore the types of housing available. Housing advertisements are often a good place to start to get an idea of what's available. By the time your search gets serious, you should have a fairly good idea of what you want, need, and can afford. You also need to know the area. The last thing you want is to move to a neighborhood that is in the throes of becoming unsafe. Ask the local police about the area. They'll give you a straight answer. Take a vacation or two to the various destinations that you think might make great retirement havens.

Money Saver

Save money by moving into less-expensive living quarters rather than staying in your old home, which is larger than you need and will probably become more difficult and expensive to maintain.

Any decision to buy a house depends on many variables. You should take enough time to choose carefully a home in which you intend to live for the next ten, twenty, or thirty years. Some common issues to consider:

- IS THE HOME convenient to transportation, shopping, and recreation?

- IS THE GENERAL NEIGHBORHOOD declining or improving?

- HOW EXPENSIVE are property taxes, and have they been rising at a rapid rate?

- ARE SENIORS offered any local tax breaks?

- DOES THE COMMUNITY offer programs to senior citizens that you may want to use?

- WHAT ARE the advantages and disadvantages of the particular type of housing? Old houses may be less energy efficient and may require ongoing maintenance. Newer houses may be more expensive and of inferior construction. Condos and co-ops may have less storage space, and some have inadequate soundproofing, allowing footsteps and voices to be heard from neighboring units.

- **DO YOU PLAN** to live in the home for the rest of your life or only for the next few years? If you anticipate spending only a few years in the neighborhood, you should try to pick a home that will be easy to resell.

Household Finance

Since most people's financial resources are not as abundant in retirement as they were during their working years, the financial and tax climate are primary considerations for people considering later-life moves. If you haven't started planning, but do intend to move— whether in two or in ten years' time—your contemplated destination's cost of living is an important consideration. Costs and standards of living vary considerably between urban and rural areas, among different regions within the United States, and among different countries of the world. Even within the United States, differences between state income and estate tax rates can make a dramatic difference on a retiree's standard of living and on the taxes assessed on his or her estate.

Retiring Abroad

More and more Americans are choosing to retire overseas to stretch their incomes or join their friends or family. Unless you live in certain prohibited countries (you probably wouldn't want to live in countries like Albania or Democratic Kampuchea anyway), your Social Security benefits will not be affected by where you choose to receive them. On the other hand, you will probably lose your Medicare coverage. Of course, many foreign countries have at least partially state-provided health-care systems, so you may not need to pay for it after all. But you'll need to be absolutely positive that you are covered for medical and health-care conditions. Quality of health care should also be an important consideration.

Your estate may be subject to foreign tax and legal requirements, and your heirs may have difficulty probating your will. Your income tax situation will also probably be complicated. Unless you renounce your American citizenship, you may continue to be subject to U.S. income tax, even if your income is earned elsewhere, although some tax breaks are available. You may also be subject to taxes in the foreign country, which may or may not be deductible in the United States, depending on tax treaties.

What Will You Do?

All our lives we long for free time, and then, when at last our wishes are answered, we mope around the house in a state of boredom. But a multitude of experiences await the adventurous retiree. Doing volunteer work or hobbies; joining gardening clubs, poker clubs, or fishing clubs; joining the alumni or fellowship committee of your alma mater or church; or taking up a new sport—these are all possibilities.

Some may cost more than others, however, and it's important to play within your limits. For example, buying a top-of-the-line golf set and paying dues for an exorbitant country club when you've never hit a golf ball before isn't very smart. Nor is volunteering to work in the Amazonian rain forest. (The price of the trip alone might mean you'd never be able to get back home—and then there's the question of medical attention.) A smarter move would be to work for the rain-forest cause here—where the money and political clout are—and then, if you're still interested in seeing the rain forest firsthand, join a travel group that specializes in educational vacations. Be ambitious when planning your retirement activities, but be realistic.

Helping Your Family

Many seniors hope to be able to help their children and grandchildren out with their finances. But be careful—don't let your generosity impair your retirement. If you are intent on doing certain things for your children or grandchildren—helping with college tuition, for example—you will need to factor in that expense when doing your retirement planning. It may turn out that it isn't feasible, that it is less feasible than you thought, or in the best possible circumstance, that you can afford to do so with no troubling effects on your overall financial condition.

Some people harbor visions of grandeur when it comes to giving money to their children. You've no doubt heard of retirees who annually give $10,000 to each child, child-in-law, and grandchild. This type of gifting can go a long way to reducing estate taxes since the money is removed from the giver's taxable estate. But you have to have a lot of money in the first place to be so munificent. Generally, you should not undertake a program of large annual gifts unless your estate exceeds $1 to $1.5 million. The reason? Many years of large annual gifts could erode your savings to a point where your security is actually impaired, particularly if either you or your spouse has to enter a nursing home.

Smart Money Move

Avoid giving large annual cash gifts to children and grand- children unless you're rolling in dough.

Plan Ahead

When it comes to your retirement, you are in the driver's seat. Whatever route you decide to take to get there—a prudent financial one or a spendthrifty one—will affect the outcome of your ultimate destination. With sensible financial planning, careful and regular investing, and moderate life-style, you'll most likely end up with a comfortable and secure retirement. If, however, you've been eating out five nights a week, spending money as soon as it comes in rather than saving and investing some of it, buying a new wardrobe every year, or buying enough shoes to make Imelda blush at the expense, then you're heading for a retirement that could be the least enjoyable time of your life. But the answer is simple. If you want to achieve a financially worry-free retirement, you can have it by working toward it. Hard work, careful planning, and curbing thy spending habits will truly make your retirement years your golden years. The choice is yours.

RETIREMENT LIFE-STYLE CHECKLIST

■□

Plan what you want to do when you retire well before you retire.

■□

Consider alternative housing arrangements and various locales before deciding on a change.

■□

Consider moving to a less expensive locale and/or into less expensive housing. It's an excellent way to keep retirement living expenses in check.

■□

Resist the temptation to make large cash gifts to children and grandchildren unless you can easily afford to do so.

Projecting Retirement Income and Expenses

T his chapter takes a hands-on approach to projecting your retirement income and expenses. The worksheets herein will help you prepare financially for retirement by finding out where you stand and what you need to do in order to meet your retirement objectives. The worksheets include:

- RETIREMENT–EXPENSE FORECASTER

- RETIREMENT–RESOURCES FORECASTER

- RETIREMENT–SAVINGS ESTIMATOR

- RETIREMENT–LIVING EXPENSE SUMMARY

Estimating retirement expenses and income need not be complicated, as the worksheets will show. By all means, complete these worksheets. They'll work whether you are forty years or four months from retirement. Don't chicken out. Gauging your financial progress toward retirement is arguably the most crucial thing you do in your personal financial planning. After all, everything you do during your working years is either directly or indirectly geared toward being able to afford a comfortable retirement. You must periodically review your progress, or lack of progress, toward preparing for retirement.

Estimating Your Retirement Expenses

W hen you retire, your cost of living usually falls. There are four reasons for this. First, upon reaching retirement, most people reduce the amount of money they save each year. Although many retirees think they no longer need to save anything for their later years, most need to continue saving some of their income so that more funds will be available later to meet increased living costs.

Second, work-related expenses are no longer a part of the family budget. This may not be a significant change for some, but for many others parking, business entertainment and travel, business clothing, meals away from home, transportation, and other job-related expenses can add up to a fairly large savings. In addition, unless you decide to work part time, Social Security taxes will no longer need to be paid.

Third, with respect to insurance, retirement often lessens or eliminates the need for various types of insurance, including disability and life insurance.

Fourth, many discounts are available to senior citizens, including public transportation and entertainment. Although these may seem like minor expenses, if used regularly, the discounts will lower your overall retirement living expenses.

Warning: Don't just assume that your living expenses will decline when you retire. They may not, particularly if you plan to travel and/or divide your time between two locales in summer and winter. Also, inflation will steadily increase your living expenses.

Estimating Your Living Expenses

One convenient way to prepare a rough estimate of retirement living expenses, particularly for those nearing retirement age, is to use the following formula:

> **Annual income (in current dollars) necessary to maintain living standard during retirement years = (Current gross annual income – amount of annual savings) x 75%**

For example, if your current income is $45,000 and you save $5,000, that means you spend, including taxes, $40,000. To calculate the annual income in current dollars necessary to maintain this living standard during retirement years, you would multiply the amount you spend, or $40,000, times .75. This equals $30,000 ($40,000 x .75).

The .75 multiplier is a general rule of thumb as to the amount of income necessary during retirement to maintain a preretirement standard of living. Of course, everyone's situation is different, so the appropriate factor for you may be above or below 75 percent.

To project your necessary retirement income when you reach retirement age, you must adjust the results of this calculation upward to account for inflation between the present and the date of your retirement.

Use these four worksheets to forecast the amount of retirement expenses and income you will require and to estimate the amount of savings you will have to accumulate to meet your retirement income needs.

RETIREMENT EXPENSE FORECASTER

This worksheet helps you approximate the amount of annual retirement income that will allow you to maintain your preretirement standard of living. First, the approximate income necessary to maintain your current living standard in current dollars is calculated. Then, by referring future value tables and using the assumed rate of inflation, you can project this amount to your estimated retirement date.

»

1.	CURRENT GROSS ANNUAL INCOME[1]	$ ....
2	LESS: AMOUNT OF ANNUAL SAVINGS[2]	(..............)
3.	SUBTOTAL (THE AMOUNT YOU SPEND CURRENTLY)	....
4.	MULTIPLY BY 75%[3]	x .75
5.	APPROXIMATE ANNUAL COST (IN CURRENT DOLLARS) OF MAINTAINING YOUR CURRENT STANDARD OF LIVING IF YOU WERE RETIRING THIS YEAR	$ ....
6.	MULTIPLY BY INFLATION FACTOR (REFER TO INFLATION FACTOR TABLE)[4]	x ....
7.	ESTIMATED ANNUAL LIVING EXPENSES AT RETIREMENT AGE (IN FUTURE DOLLARS)	$ ....

Notes:

(1)   Current gross annual income includes all income from all sources.

(2)   Annual savings includes—in addition to the usual sources of savings—reinvested dividends, capital gains, and any contributions to retirement plans that are taken from your annual income.

(3)   The general rule of thumb is that a retiree can maintain his/her preretirement standard of living by spending roughly 75 percent of his/her preretirement income. Of course, individual circumstances may dictate a higher or lower percentage. Ideally, you should prepare a retirement budget that details expected expenses. You may find a multiplier less than .75 in some circumstances (like low housing costs due to paid off mortgage) or, in other circumstances, a higher multiplier (due to, say, extensive travel plans). To make a more precise estimate of your expected retirement living expenses, prepare the Retirement Living Expense Summary on page 606.

(4)   In order to project retirement expenses to retirement age, current-dollar living expenses must be multiplied by a factor to account for inflationary increases. The inflation factor table can be used for that purpose. The assumed long-term inflation rate is 4.5 percent.

INFLATION FACTOR TABLE

NUMBER OF YEARS UNTIL RETIREMENT	FACTOR
5	1.2
10	1.6
15	1.9
20	2.4
25	3.0
30	3.7
35	4.7
40	5.8

RETIREMENT-RESOURCES FORECASTER

There are three legs to the retirement income stool: company pension plan benefits, Social Security benefits, and income from personal investments. This worksheet can be used to forecast pension and Social Security benefits at retirement age, then to approximate the total amount of personal savings and investments that will be needed by retirement age to cover any shortfall between Social Security/pension benefits and your total income needs.

	CURRENT DOLLARS	INFLATION FACTOR[1]	FUTURE (RETIREMENT AGE) DOLLARS
1. ESTIMATED ANNUAL LIVING EXPENSES AT RETIREMENT AGE (FROM LINE 7 ON PAGE 603)			$ ....
2. ANNUAL PENSION INCOME (PROJECTION AT RETIREMENT AGE AVAILABLE FROM EMPLOYER)[2]	$ x	.... =	$ ....
3. ANNUAL SOCIAL SECURITY BENEFITS (PROJECTION AT RETIREMENT AGE AVAILABLE FROM SOCIAL SECURITY ADMINISTRATION)[3]	$ x	.... =	$ ....
4. SUBTOTAL: PROJECTED PENSION AND SOCIAL SECURITY INCOME (ADD LINES 2 AND 3)			....
5. SHORTFALL (IF EXPENSES ARE GREATER THAN INCOME) THAT MUST BE FUNDED OUT OF PERSONAL SAVINGS/INVESTMENTS (SUBTRACT LINE 4 FROM LINE 1)			....
6. MULTIPLY BY 17[4]			x 17
7. AMOUNT OF SAVINGS/INVESTMENTS (IN FUTURE DOLLARS) THAT NEED TO BE ACCUMULATED BY RETIREMENT AGE TO FUND RETIREMENT[5]			$ ....

Notes:

(1)   Use Inflation Factor Table on page 603 for the appropriate factor.

(2)   Employers usually provide pension plan projections at retirement age, expressed in current dollars. If

»

(3) Social Security estimates are expressed in current dollars and therefore they should be adjusted for inflation, as on line 2.

(4) As a general rule of thumb, for every $1,000 of annual income you will need to fund at retirement age, you will need to have at least $17,000 in savings/investments in order to keep up with inflation. If you plan to retire before age sixty-two, use a factor of 20, rather than 17. If you want to be ultraconservative, use a factor of 25.

(5) You may be dismayed by the magnitude of this figure, which can easily exceed $1,000,000 for younger persons and people with minimal pension benefits. Nevertheless, good savings habits combined with the power of compounding can usually close the gap between current resources and eventual needs.

so, the amount should be multiplied by an inflation factor to approximate benefits in future dollars.

RETIREMENT-SAVINGS ESTIMATOR

This worksheet can be used to estimate the annual amount of savings that is required to accumulate the funds necessary to meet your retirement objectives. The amount arrived at on line 7 equals the required *first year* savings. The annual savings should be increased by 5 percent in each succeeding year until you retire. For example, if the Retirement-Savings Estimator shows that you need to save $4,000 over the next year, you will have to increase that amount by 5 percent to $4,200 in the following year, $4,410 two years thence, and so forth.

1. AMOUNT OF SAVINGS/INVESTMENTS (IN FUTURE DOLLARS) THAT NEED TO BE ACCUMULATED BY RETIREMENT AGE TO FUND RETIREMENT (FROM LINE 7, PAGE 604) $ ....

2. LESS: RESOURCES THAT ARE CURRENTLY AVAILABLE FOR RETIREMENT PURPOSES[1] $ ....

3. MULTIPLY BY APPRECIATION FACTOR (REFER TO ANNUAL APPRECIATION FACTOR TABLE)[2]   X ....

4. ESTIMATED FUTURE VALUE OF RETIREMENT RESOURCES THAT ARE CURRENTLY AVAILABLE (MULTIPLY LINE 2 BY LINE 3)   (...............)

5. RETIREMENT FUNDS NEEDED BY RETIREMENT AGE (SUBTRACT LINE 4 FROM LINE 1)   ....

6. MULTIPLY BY ANNUAL SAVINGS FACTOR (REFER TO ANNUAL SAVINGS FACTOR TABLE)[3]   X ....

7. EQUALS SAVINGS NEEDED OVER THE NEXT YEAR (MULTIPLY LINE 5 BY LINE 6)[4] $ ....

Notes:

(1) Resources that are currently available typically include the current value of all of your investment-related assets that are not expected to be used before retirement. Don't include the value of your home unless you expect to sell it to raise money for retirement. Don't include any vested pension benefits if you have already factored them in on line 2 of the Retirement-Resources Forecaster on page 604.

(2) The appreciation factor is used to estimate what your currently available retirement resources will be worth when you retire. The appreciation factor assumes a 7.5 *after-tax* rate of appreciation per year.

»

(3) The annual saving factors computes the amount you will need to save during the next year in order to begin accumulating the retirement fund needed by retirement age, as indicated on Line 5. The annual savings factor assumes a 7.5 percent *after-tax* rate of return.

(4) The annual savings needed to accumulate your retirement nest egg assumes that you will increase the amount of money you save by 5 percent each year until retirement.

ANNUAL APPRECIATION FACTOR TABLE

NUMBER OF YEARS UNTIL RETIREMENT	
5	1.4
10	2.1
15	3.0
20	4.2
25	6.1
30	8.8
35	12.6
40	18.0

ANNUAL SAVINGS FACTOR TABLE

NUMBER OF YEARS UNTIL RETIREMENT	
5	.1513
10	.0558
15	.0274
20	.0151
25	.0088
30	.0054
35	.0034
40	.0022

RETIREMENT-LIVING EXPENSE SUMMARY

This worksheet can be used to determine how your expenses will change when you retire and to estimate what your total retirement living expenses will be. The best way to estimate your expenses in retirement in the second column is to estimate those amounts in *current dollars*. This will give you an idea of the amount your retirement expenses will change compared with the expenses you now incur. If you want to estimate what your retirement expenses will be when you retire (in future dollars, in other words), multiply the total that you have calculated on this worksheet by the inflation factor from the table on page 603 for the approximate number of years until you expect to retire.

EXPENSES	CURRENT EXPENSE LEVEL (19___)	ESTIMATED EXPENSE LEVEL AT RETIREMENT YEAR:_____	COMMENTS ON EXPECTED CHANGE IN EXPENSE LEVEL DURING RETIREMENT YEARS
1. Fixed expenses			
Income taxes	$...............	$...............	....
Rent/mortgage	....	....	....
Home heating	....	....	....
Utilities	....	....	....
Water	....	....	....
Telephone	....	....	.... »

Loan payments	....	....	....
Property taxes	....	....	....
Auto insurance	....	....	....
Medical, dental insurance	....	....	....
Homeowner's/renter's insurance	....	....	....
Other insurance	....	....	....
Other	....	....	....
Subtotal	$	$..............	

2. Discretionary and semidiscretionary expenses

Food	$	$..............	....
Alcohol, tobacco	....	....	....
Household maintenance	....	....	....
Furnishings, equipment	....	....	....
Clothing	....	....	....
Transportation	....	....	....
Medicine, medical care	....	....	....
Personal care, grooming	....	....	....
Education	....	....	....
Recreation	....	....	....
Travel	....	....	....
Contributions, donations	....	....	....
Gifts	....	....	....
Laundry	....	....	....
Other	....	....	....
Subtotal	$	$..............	....
Total (Sections 1 + 2)	$	$..............	

Notes..

....

....

....

Social Security

T he Social Security system resembles most other government programs in that the rules are complex and subject to frequent modification. This chapter will help you understand the system so that you can factor in Social Security benefits as part of your retirement planning.

There's a myth about Social Security that must be dispelled at the outset. Contrary to what many people still think, the Social Security system was never intended to satisfy all your retirement income needs—despite the extraordinary amount that you and your employers have had to contribute to support the system. As your only retirement resource, Social Security would barely keep you above the poverty level. Social Security benefits will probably support you in a moderate life-style for about one week in each month. Assuming that you want to live the other three weeks of each month, you will need other income sources—pension plans or personal investments.

Nevertheless, as part of a comprehensive retirement portfolio, Social Security is a basic building block of guaranteed income. Social Security benefits have an important benefit that is lacking in most retirement annuities: They are indexed for inflation. Although they may lag behind the rate of inflation somewhat, the inflation adjustment is particularly crucial in light of the higher inflation confronting retirees now as compared with previous generations.

Will Social Security Be Around When You Retire?

Social Security is, without a doubt, the most maligned government program ever devised by mankind. Not only is it maligned, it's distrusted. Many people are convinced that Social Security won't be around when they get ready to retire, in spite of the tens (if not hundreds) of thousands of dollars they have personally sunk into the system.

Of course, Social Security *will* be around when they retire. But how beneficial it will be remains to be seen. For example, it may be tougher for high-income retirees to get much in the way of Social Security benefits if, in fact, a means-based test is applied. But for most of us, Social Security will be there, right as rain, providing a *small* portion of our total retirement income needs and more. More? The critics of the Social Security system often forget, or seem to forget, that there's a lot more to Social Security than making monthly payment to retirees. Social Security benefits are available to widows, children of deceased workers, the disabled, and others.

Who Is Covered and How the System Is Funded

Who Is Covered?

You are probably "covered"—Social Security tax is withheld from your earnings, in exchange for which you accumulate credit toward certain benefits. If you have worked for the federal government since before 1984, or if you work for some state and local agencies, certain non-profit groups, or the railroads, you are probably not covered. If you're uncertain, check with your employer.

What You Pay

During your working years, a tax—currently 7.65 percent—is withheld from all your earnings up to a maximum income wage base, and your employer pays a matching amount. (If you are self-employed, you are responsible for the entire 15.3 percent, half of which is tax-deductible.)

There is a maximum amount of work-related income beyond which Social Security taxes aren't withheld. This maximum is adjusted each year for inflation. If your income exceeds or reaches this maximum, you may be surprised to find out that the total amount that is contributed on your behalf to the Social Security system, including the employer's portion, is over $10,000 per year! If you are a higher-income self-employed person, you will have to pay the total amount yourself.

Smart Money Move

Be sure you understand the many benefits you may be eligible for from the Social Security system come retirement, disability, or, in the event of your death, the benefits for members of your family.

What You Get

Another common misperception about Social Security is that what you put in, you will eventually receive back. But what you pay today supports current retirees and other benefits receivers, as, in turn, your benefits will be paid (at least in part) by future workers. The vast majority (almost 95 percent) of all workers participate in the Social Security system, and one in six American citizens is currently drawing benefits.

Establishing Eligibility

If you reach age sixty-two *after* 1990, you will have to have participated in the Social Security system for at least 40 quarters—ten years—to be eligible for any benefits. There is some confusion as to what constitutes a quarter, but it's straightforward. You must earn at least fifty dollars in each fiscal quarter for that quarter to be counted in the SSA's record of earnings. However, if you earn the maximum Social Security income in any year, you will automatically get credit for four quarters, even if you earned less than fifty dollars in a given quarter. In other words, you can receive up to four credits per year, regardless of how your earnings are actually distributed throughout the period. The earnings quarters do not have to be consecutive.

If you leave the work force before you have enough credits to qualify for benefits, your credits will remain on your Social Security record. This way, if and when you return to work later on, you can add more credits so you can qualify. There are exceptions to the rule. For example, employees of nonprofit organizations who were fifty-five or older as of 1984, or anyone born before 1929, may qualify for benefits with fewer credits.

Applying for Social Security Benefits

Social Security benefits are not paid out automatically. *You* must initiate the monthly payment process yourself. You won't receive a penny, a plugged nickel, not one thin dime of what is rightly yours, until such time as you get your act together and initiate the process.

How to Apply

You must apply in person or by telephone, but all the follow-up can be done through the mail. Of course, no matter which initiation and follow-up options you use, you'll need to be certain to keep either photocopies of documents sent or accurate phone records—including the date, time, and individual you spoke with—so that, in the event of a foulup, you'll have covered your own assets.

When to File

Unless you are receiving disability benefits, you should file a claim with your local SSA office *at least three months before you would like your benefits to commence.* Three months might seem like enough lead time to respond to several thousand claims, let alone one. But, of course, that's precisely what is taking place.

Selecting When to Receive Your Benefits

You can elect to begin receiving benefits as early as age sixty-two, or you can postpone them until as late as age seventy. The later you receive your benefits, the higher your monthly benefit payment will be. Your actual date of retirement is irrelevant, although your earnings after you begin collecting Social Security may reduce your benefits.

Necessary Documents

You will need all of the following documents:

Smart Money Move

Have your Social Security check deposited automatically into your bank or credit union account.

- **YOUR SOCIAL SECURITY CARD** or a record of the number

- **PROOF OF DATE OF BIRTH** (driver's license, passport, birth certificate)

- **YOUR MOST RECENT** IRS W-2 form and tax returns (so that your latest earnings will be included in calculating your benefit amount)

- **VETERAN'S** discharge papers (if applicable)

- **DIVORCE DEGREE** (if applicable)

- **YOUR CHECKBOOK** or savings passbook (if you want your benefits deposited directly to your bank account—a very good idea).

You will need original documents or copies certified by each document's issuing office, but Social Security can, and upon request will, make photocopies and return the originals to you.

Don't delay your application because you don't have all the information. If you don't have a document you need, Social Security can help you get it. If you aren't sure whether you qualify for a particular benefit, go ahead and apply for it, and Social Security will evaluate your eligibility. There's no penalty for trying!

Your Benefit Amount

The amount of your benefit is based on your earnings averaged over most of your working career, using a formula that places the greatest emphasis on wages in your most recent years of work. Other important pieces to the benefits puzzle:

- **HIGHER LIFETIME** earnings result in higher benefits.

- **IF YOU HAVE** some years of no earnings or low earnings, your benefit amount may be lower than if you had worked steadily.

- **YOUR BENEFIT AMOUNT** is also determined by the age at which you start receiving benefits.

Smart Money Move

- **THE EARLIER** you start collecting retirement benefits, the smaller the size of your monthly payments for life.

Request a personal-ized benefit esti-mate from Social Security.

- **ONCE YOU START** receiving benefits, the amount will be adjusted subsequently to account for inflation.

OBTAIN AN ESTIMATE OF YOUR SOCIAL SECURITY BENEFITS

The Social Security Administration (SSA) will provide you with a personalized benefit estimate at your request. Call 1-800-772-1213, and ask for Form SSA-7004, *Personal Earnings and Benefits Statement.* If you are age 62 or older, the SSA should be able to provide you with an earnings estimate over the phone. (See the following table for an approximation of your retirement benefits.)

For the asking, they'll send you a simple form to complete and return. They'll mail back your complete earnings history along with estimates of your benefits for retirement at age sixty-two, at full retirement age (which will be somewhere between sixty-five and sixty-seven, depending on your age), and at age seventy.

You'll also receive estimates of disability and survivors benefits that might be payable in the event of your disability or death. Since Social Security will play a role in funding your retirement income needs, you should know what you can expect to receive. Of course, it doesn't make as much sense for a thirty-three-year-old as it does for a forty-three- and fifty-three-year-old. But being overinformed never hurt anyone (except maybe Benedict Arnold). As retirement nears, it's smart to request these statements every few years, in order to assure that your earnings are being credited properly.

APPROXIMATE MONTHLY BENEFITS IF YOU RETIRE AT FULL RETIREMENT IN 1992 AND HAD STEADY LIFETIME EARNINGS

YOUR AGE IN 1992	YOUR FAMILY	YOUR EARNINGS IN 1991				
		$20,000	$30,000	$40,000	$50,000	$55,000 OR MORE[1]
45	YOU	$878	$1,159	$1,302	$1,436	$1,491
	YOU AND YOUR SPOUSE[2]	1,317	1,738	1,953	2,154	2,236
55	YOU	796	1,052	1,150	1,231	1,258
	YOU AND YOUR SPOUSE[2]	1,194	1,578	1,725	1,846	1,887
65	YOU	748	977	1,038	1,081	1,088
	YOU AND YOUR SPOUSE[2]	1,122	1,465	1,557	1,621	1,632

1   Use this column if you earn more than the maximum Social Security earnings base.

2   Your spouse is assumed to be the same age as you. Your spouse may qualify for a higher retirement benefit based on his or her own work record.

Note: The accuracy of these estimates depends on the pattern of your actual past earnings and on your earnings in the future.

Early versus Late Retirement

Social Security currently considers sixty-five a normal retirement age, although this will slowly be moved back until it reaches sixty-seven in the year 2027. For every month you retire before you reach sixty-five, your benefits will be reduced by five-ninths of 1 percent—that's a whopping 20 percent reduction if you retire at 62! The following table shows the amount your benefits will be reduced if you begin collecting Social Security benefits before age sixty-five.

SOCIAL SECURITY BENEFIT REDUCTIONS FOR EARLY RETIREES

Multiply your estimated benefits at age 65 as provided by the Social Security Administration by the appropriate reduction factor.

MONTHS BEFORE AGE 65	REDUCTION FACTOR								
		6	.966	14	.922	22	.877	30	.833
		7	.961	15	.916	23	.872	31	.827
		8	.955	16	.911	24	.866	32	.822
1	.994	9	.950	17	.905	25	.861	33	.816
2	.988	10	.944	18	.900	26	.855	34	.811
3	.983	11	.938	19	.894	27	.850	35	.805
4	.977	12	.933	20	.888	28	.844	36	.800
5	.972	13	.927	21	.883	29	.838		

Retiree benefits cannot commence before age 62. Dependent spouses who retire early have a somewhat greater reduction factor; a dependent spouse who retires 36 months before age 65 has a reduction factor of .750 (versus .800 for the early retiree).

The Effects of Early Retirement on Your Benefits

Think more than twice about collecting Social Security benefits early. The Social Security system offers lower monthly retirement checks with early retirement. Since subsequent cost-of-living adjustments are all based on your initial benefit, your benefits will stay low and lag further and further behind what they could have been. Shall I rub some salt in the wound? If you die, the benefits to your spouse will also be lower.

Smart Money Move

Don't begin collecting Social Security benefits early if you expect to receive enough part-time work income to reduce your Social Security benefits.

The Effects of Later Retirement on Your Benefits

A later retirement *increases* your benefits by three percent each year your retirement is postponed until age seventy. This delayed retirement credit will gradually be increased from now to 2008 to a level of eight percent per year, which can dramatically increase benefits for late retirees.

After the year 2007, if you postpone retirement for five years beyond age sixty-six, which will then be the normal retirement age, your Social Security benefits *will increase by 40 percent.* Early retirees will still be able to collect benefits at age sixty-two, but the penalty will be greater since they will be collecting benefits for a longer period before reaching full retirement age.

The table below shows the amount of Social Security benefit increases for late retirees.

SOCIAL SECURITY BENEFIT INCREASES FOR LATE RETIREES

Increase your estimated benefits at age 65 as provided by the Social Security Administration by the appropriate percentage factor. For example, assuming that you become age 65 in 1993, and you expect to begin collecting Social Security at age 67, your initial Social Security benefits will be 8 percent higher (yearly percentage of 4 percent times 2 years) than they would have been had you begun collecting benefits at age 65.

YEAR AGE 65 ATTAINED	MONTHY PERCENTAGE (OF 1 PERCENT)	YEARLY PERCENTAGE				
1990-91	7/24%	3.5%	2000-2001	1/2	6	
1992-93	1/3	4	2002-2003	13/24	6.5	
1994-95	3/8	4.5	2004-2005	7/12	7	
1996-97	5/12	5	2006-2007	5/8	7.5	
1998-99	11/24	5.5	2008 OR LATER	2/3	8	

Important Questions and Concerns

Is it advantageous to begin collecting benefits prior to normal retirement age?

Some argue that it is, since the total amount of benefits received by someone collecting benefits beginning at age sixty-two, even though lower than the benefits received at age sixty-five, will still total more than the benefits received by an age-sixty-five retiree for twelve years or more. The reason for this is that if you begin collecting benefits at age sixty-two, you have already collected three years' worth of benefits by the time the age-sixty-five retiree begins receiving benefits. It takes about twelve years for the person collecting at age sixty-five to catch up! But don't forget that your monthly payments will be much lower if you begin collecting at age sixty-two, and with a long life expectancy, it's quite likely that you will be better off waiting until age sixty-five to begin collecting.

Will you need to begin collecting benefits earlier in order to meet expenses?

If you need to collect Social Security retirement benefits early in order to be able to afford to retire early, I have one thing to say to you—seriously reevaluate your decision to retire early. You simply may not be able to afford it over the long run, particularly as inflation begins to erode the purchasing power of your retirement income.

What if you are forced to retire early?

If poor health forces you to retire early, look into Social Security disability benefits (described later in this chapter). If you are eligible for these benefits, you will receive the same amount as you would for your full, unreduced retirement benefit instead of the diminished retirement benefit for collecting before full retirement age.

Effect of Extra Earnings on Benefits

The other side of the early-retirement coin is the effect of extra earnings on your benefits. The amount of unearned income you receive—such as dividends, interest, and pension benefits—does not affect the *amount* of your Social Security benefit, no matter how old you are. But your benefits may be taxed if your total income exceeds certain limits. Income is considered to be money earned from full- or part-time employment and can significantly *reduce* Social Security benefits for persons under seventy.

Benefits are reduced for people over age sixty-five whose job income is above the annual exempt amount, which is adjusted each year for inflation (it was $10,200 in 1992). Retirees aged sixty-two to sixty-five could earn up to $7,440 per year in 1992 without having their benefits reduced. (This amount is also adjusted for inflation each year.) If you are under sixty-five, earned income in excess of the annual exempt amount will reduce Social Security benefits at a rate of one dollar for each two dollars of earnings above the limit. If you are between age sixty-five and seventy, your benefits will be reduced at a rate of one dollar for each three dollars of earnings above the limit. However, benefits for persons over seventy are *not* reduced regardless of income. Starting in the year 2000, the age at which the one-dollar-per-two-dollars rate applies will increase as the retirement age increases.

When you file for retirement benefits and at the beginning of each subsequent year, Social Security will ask you to estimate your future income and will base your benefit amount on that estimate. You must report any changes as they occur. And above all else, don't try and pull a fast one. Social Security gets a copy of the W-2 your employer sends the IRS. If you don't file an earnings report and your earnings were over the limit, or if you don't file an adjustment report and your earnings exceeded your estimate, you will owe Social Security a penalty in addition to the amount you were overpaid.

Social Security Keeps Track of Your Earnings

In January, Social Security will send you an annual report (Form SSA-777) so you can compare your estimate with the amount you actually earned over the last year. If you have earned more than you expected, you will have been paid too much by Social Security. You can send Social Security a check for the amount you were overpaid (you can pay in installments), or you can have the amount deducted from your future benefits checks.

If you earned less money than you expected, your next few benefit checks will include adjustments for the amount you were underpaid in the prior year. My advice: It's usually wise to report any changes in your income as soon as they occur.

A special rule applies (only) in the year you retire. Under this rule, you can receive your monthly benefit for any month in which your wages do not exceed a specified monthly limit. This rule ensures that you will not be denied benefits in the months immediately following your retirement just because your income from the months you were still working already exceeded the annual income limit.

Taxation of Social Security Benefits

B oth the Social Security Administration and the Internal Revenue Service have numerous free brochures and pamphlets that explain tax matters pertaining to Social Security benefits and help you determine your income tax liability. You can call those toll-free numbers to request these documents:

- **SSA:** (800) 772-1213

- **IRS:** (800) 829-3676

And while you'll receive detailed reading material aplenty, the following tax considerations should be duly noted.

If you're a recipient whose adjusted gross income (AGI) exceeds a certain limit, you'll incur federal taxes on half the amount of your benefit. The income limit is determined on a different basis from the one used to determine your AGI for a regular tax return. Here's how to calculate it: To half of your Social Security benefits, add all income derived from wages, taxable pensions, interest, dividends, and all other taxable income plus tax-exempt interest. If the total does not exceed $25,000 for single filers or $32,000 for married couples filing jointly, you don't owe any tax. If your income exceeds the limits, you pay tax on 50 percent of the excess or 50 percent of your benefits, whichever is less.

If you're married, don't think about filing separately to lower your income. The maximum for married persons filing separately is zero, so you will have to pay tax on half of your benefits anyway. The only way to avoid or reduce this taxation of Social Security benefits is to reduce your adjusted gross income. Sorry!

Special Circumstance: Retiring Abroad

T he good news is that if you're a United States citizen, you can live or travel in most foreign countries without affecting your eligibility for Social Security benefits. That's fortunate, considering that more and more Americans are retiring abroad— where they can enjoy a lower cost of living while still receiving their "American" Social

Security and pension income. The bad news is that if you're eligible for Social Security but you are neither a U.S. resident nor a U.S. citizen, up to 15 percent of your benefits will probably be withheld for federal income tax.

Take note: If you *work* outside the United States, different rules apply in determining if you can get your benefit checks.

Benefits for Family Members

D id you know that if your spouse is not eligible to receive retirement benefits based on his or her own work record, he or she can still receive an amount equal to up to half of your benefit? That could mean that together you'll receive 150 percent of your individual benefit amount. What if your spouse is eligible either for spousal benefits or for benefits based on his or her own work record? Not to worry—your spouse will get the larger of the two.

No matter when you (that is, "the worker") decide to start collecting benefits, your spouse is entitled to his or her benefits from age sixty-two on. But your spouse's benefits will be reduced as a percentage of yours if he or she elects to receive them before age sixty-five. There's an exception: A spouse who is taking care of a child who is under sixteen or disabled gets full spousal benefits (50 percent of your benefit) regardless of age.

Other Eligible Members

Some other members of your family may be eligible to receive benefits when you retire.

- YOUR FORMER WIFE or husband of age 62 or older, if the marriage lasted at least ten years, if you have been divorced at least two years, and if the former spouse did not remarry prior to age sixty. (The amount a former spouse receives will not affect the amounts for which you and/or your current spouse are eligible.)

- DEPENDENT CHILDREN under age eighteen.

- DEPENDENT CHILDREN age eighteen to nineteen, if they attend elementary school or high school.

- CHILDREN of any age who were disabled before age twenty-two.

- DEPENDENT GRANDCHILDREN (subject to various conditions)

Family Maximum Benefit

There's always a limit to how good things can get. Your family's total benefits cannot exceed the Family Maximum Benefit, which is based on your earnings record and full retirement benefit. (Your divorced spouse's benefits do not count toward your family maximum amount.)

Survivors' Benefits

Many people associate Social Security with retirement alone. But it can also provide benefits to people who are much younger than retirement age. Social Security provides benefits to both disabled workers and survivors of deceased workers—regardless of age—as long as the specified work credit hours have been fulfilled.

The Social Security Administration estimates that 98 percent of American children are eligible to receive some level of benefits should one or both working parents die.

For your survivors to be eligible for this benefit, however, you must have satisfied the same "work credit" requirements (indexed by age) that govern all Social Security benefits. As long as you have earned 1.5 work credits over the past three years, your children will still be covered by Social Security. (In 1992, one work credit was equal to $570 in earnings.)

If you were to die while covered by Social Security, your spouse would be eligible for full benefits at sixty-five or reduced benefits at sixty; disabled widows/widowers can get benefits at fifty to sixty. If your spouse is left to care for children who are under age sixteen or disabled, he or she is eligible for benefits regardless of age. Furthermore, your unmarried children under age eighteen (or nineteen, if they are full-time elementary- or secondary-school students) would be eligible for benefits. Finally, grandchildren (under limited circumstances) and dependent parents sixty-two or older are also eligible for survivor's benefits.

At the time of your death, either your spouse or your children would receive a $255 one-time death benefit.

Applying for Benefits

How survivors sign up for benefits depends on whether they were receiving Social Security benefits at the time of the worker's death. If the survivors weren't getting Social Security benefits at the time of the death, they must file for benefits at the nearest Social Security office. Information and documents needed to file an application include:

- THE SURVIVING SPOUSE'S Social Security number and birth certificate

- CHILDREN'S Social Security numbers and birth certificates

- THE DECEASED SPOUSE'S W-2 forms or federal self-employment tax returns for the most recent year and death certificate

- MARRIAGE CERTIFICATE or divorce papers, if the application is being made as a divorced spouse

- CHECKBOOK or savings passbook, if direct deposit of Social Security payments is desired.

If the surviving spouse has already been receiving benefits on the spouse's record, however, they will automatically be changed to survivor's benefits. (If the Social Security Administration requires more information, they will contact the surviving spouse.) If the surviving spouse has already been receiving benefits on his or her own record, he or she will need to fill out a survivor's benefits application.

Level of Benefits

The level of survivor's benefits that the surviving spouse and children will receive ultimately depends on how much the deceased paid into the system. A widow or widower sixty-five or older can expect to get 100 percent of the deceased's benefits. A widow or widower aged sixty to sixty-four can expect to get between 71 and 94 percent. A widow of any age with a child under sixteen can expect 75 percent, and children can expect 75 percent. There is a cap to how much in total benefits a single family can receive: It ranges from 150 to 180 percent of the deceased's benefit rate, depending on family circumstances. To receive an estimate of your survivor's benefits, call the SSA at (800) 772-1213.

The following table approximates monthly benefits for the family of a worker who died in 1992. Benefit amounts change each year to account for inflation.

APPROXIMATE MONTHLY SURVIVOR'S BENEFITS IF THE WORKER DIES IN 1992 AND HAD STEADY EARNINGS

WORKER'S AGE	YOUR FAMILY	DECEASED WORKER'S EARNINGS IN 1991				
		$20,000	$30,000	$40,000	$50,000	$55,000 OR MORE[1]
35	SPOUSE AND 1 CHILD[2]	$1,112	$1,476	$1,658	$1,840	$1,878
	SPOUSE AND 2 CHILDREN[3]	1,375	1,722	1,934	2,146	2,190
	1 CHILD ONLY	556	738	829	920	939
	SPOUSE AT AGE 60[4]	530	703	790	877	895
45	SPOUSE AND 1 CHILD[2]	1,110	1,474	1,636	1,752	1,770
	SPOUSE AND 2 CHILDREN[3]	1,373	1,721	1,910	2,044	2,064
	1 CHILD ONLY	555	737	818	876	885
	SPOUSE AT AGE 60[4]	529	703	780	835	843
55	SPOUSE AND 1 CHILD[2]	1,108	1,462	1,566	1,640	1,652
	SPOUSE AND 2 CHILDREN[3]	1,372	1,705	1,828	1,914	1,927
	1 CHILD ONLY	554	731	783	820	826
	SPOUSE AT AGE 60[4]	528	696	747	782	787

(1) Use this column if the worker earned more than the maximum Social Security earnings base.

(2) Amounts shown also equal the benefits paid to two children, if no parent survives or surviving parent has substantial earnings.

(3) Equals the maximum family benefit.

(4) Amounts payable in 1992. Spouses turning 60 in the future would receive higher benefits.

Note: The accuracy of these estimates depends on the pattern of the worker's actual past earnings.

Disability Benefits

T he whole question of the danger of disability and the effect it can have on your financial well-being is thoroughly discussed in Chapter 42. While you will most likely need to have an employee-provided disability insurance policy and/or purchase a private disability insurance policy to truly protect your family and yourself, the Social Security system does provide limited disability coverage.

Who Is Covered

You can get Social Security disability benefits at any age, although after age sixty-five they automatically become retirement benefits (the amount remains the same). Certain family members of a disabled worker may also qualify for benefits on his or her record, including:

- **UNMARRIED CHILDREN** (in some cases grandchildren may qualify) under age eighteen. The cap is age nineteen for children who are full-time elementary- or secondary-school students. Disabled children whose disability predates their twenty-second birthday are not subject to the age cap.

- **SPOUSE** over age sixty-two.

- **SPOUSE** of any age if he or she is caring for a child of the disabled person, if the child is under sixteen or is disabled and also receiving disability payments.

Applying for Benefits

You should apply for benefits as soon as you become disabled, but be forewarned: Even if your claim is approved, benefits will not begin until the sixth full month of disability. The waiting period begins with the first full month after the onset of disability.

Qualifying Requirements

When you apply for disability benefits, the Social Security Administration puts your application through a rigorous screening process to determine whether you meet the agency's definition of disability. The following five questions are generally asked by the SSA to determine your status. As you will see, the requirements are stringent—much more so than the requirements for employer-provided or private disability insurance.

1. Are you working?

If you are working and are earning more than $500 a month, the SSA generally won't consider you disabled.

2. Is your condition "severe"?

Your impairments must interfere with basic work-related activities for your claim to be considered further.

3. Is your condition found in the list of disabling impairments?

The SSA maintains a list of impairments for each of the major body systems that are so severe that they automatically mean an applicant is disabled. If your condition is not on this list, the SSA must determine whether it is of a severity equal to those on the list. If it is, the claim is approved. If it is not, the next question is asked.

4. Can you do the work you did previously?

If your condition is severe but not as severe as those on the SSA master list mentioned above, the administrators must determine whether the condition interferes with your ability to do the work you have been doing for the past fifteen years. If it does not, the claim will be denied. If it does, the claim merits further consideration.

5. Can you do any other type of work?

If you cannot do the kind of work you did over the last fifteen years, the SSA looks to see if you can do any other type of work. Your age, education, past work experience, and transferable skills are reviewed in light of the job demands of occupations, as determined by the Department of Labor. Basically, if the SSA deems you unfit for any occupation, your claim will be approved. Otherwise, it will be denied.

Necessary Documents

The Social Security disability benefits claims process is quite drawn out—it typically takes sixty to ninety days from start to finish. Determining the answers to the five questions above is a slow process. When you go to your local SSA office to file your claim, life will be somewhat easier if you bring along the following items:

- THE SOCIAL SECURITY number and proof of age for each person applying for payments. This includes your spouse and children, if they are applying for payments.

- NAMES, addresses, and phone numbers of doctors, hospitals, clinics, and institutions that treated you, and the dates of treatment.

- A SUMMARY of where you worked in the past fifteen years and the kind of work you did.

- A COPY of your W-2 Form (Wage and Tax Statement), or if you are self-employed, your federal tax return for the past year.

- DATES of any prior marriages, if your spouse is applying.

Work Credit Hours

The number of work credit hours needed to receive disability benefits depends on your age when you become disabled.

- **BEFORE** age twenty-four—you need six credits in the three-year period ending when your disability starts.

- **AGE** twenty-four to thirty-one—you need credit for having worked half the time between twenty-one and the time you become disabled.

- **AGE** thirty-one or older—you need the same number of work credits as you would need for retirement, as shown in the following table.

BORN AFTER 1929, BECOME DISABLED AT AGE	BORN BEFORE 1930, BECOME DISABLED BEFORE 62	WORK CREDITS YOU NEED
31 THROUGH 42		20
44		22
46		24
48		26
50		28
52		30
53		31
54		32
55		33
56		34
57	1986	35
58	1987	36
59	1988	37
60	1989	38
62 OR OLDER	1991 OR LATER	40

Level of Benefits

The amount of your monthly disability benefit is based on your lifetime average earnings covered by Social Security. In 1992, the average monthly benefit for a disabled worker was $608, and the average payment for a disabled worker with a family was $1,045. Payments continue until age sixty-five, at which time retirement benefits begin.

The following table approximates monthly benefits for a worker who became disabled in 1992. Benefit amounts are adjusted for inflation.

APPROXIMATE MONTHLY BENEFITS IF YOU BECOME DISABLED IN 1992 AND HAD STEADY EARNINGS

YOUR AGE	YOUR FAMILY	$20,000	$30,000	YOUR EARNINGS IN 1991 $40,000	$50,000	$55,000 OR MORE[1]
25	YOU	$745	$987	$1,109	$1,231	$1,266
	YOU, YOUR SPOUSE, AND CHILD[2]	1,118	1,480	1,664	1,847	1,899
35	YOU	740	984	1,105	1,221	1,240
	YOU, YOUR SPOUSE, AND CHILD[2]	1,111	1,476	1,657	1,831	1,860
45	YOU	739	983	1,086	1,159	1,170
	YOU, YOUR SPOUSE, AND CHILD[2]	1,109	1,475	1,629	1,738	1,755
55	YOU	739	974	1,044	1,094	1,101
	YOU, YOUR SPOUSE, AND CHILD[2]	1,109	1,462	1,567	1,641	1,652
64	YOU	746	975	1,034	1,076	1,082
	YOU, YOUR SPOUSE, AND CHILD[2]	1,119	1,463	1,551	1,614	1,623

(1)   Use this column if you earn more than the maximum Social Security earnings base.

(2)   Equals the maximum family benefit.

Note: The accuracy of these estimates depends on the pattern of your actual past earnings.

Returning to the Workplace

As you have read, Social Security disability benefits are quite limited. Most people receiving benefits, in fact, would like to return to employment as soon as possible. Should you be receiving benefits and decide to make a go of it in the working world, you won't necessarily lose your "disabled" classification and the checks that accompany it.

The SSA allows disability benefit recipients to take advantage of a so-called "trial work period," which is nine months long. During the trial work period, you may work without jeopardizing your benefits. You need not work the nine months consecutively; you must use up your nine months within a five-year time span for your work to be considered a trial work period at all.

A trial work month is one in which you earn more than $200 of income. After you have worked for nine trial work months, your period is over, and your earnings will be evaluated to see whether they qualify as "substantial." If your trial work period earnings average over $500 per month, your benefits will stop after a three-month grace period has elapsed. Otherwise, benefits will continue unabated.

Your Right to Appeal

A final item that concerns many people is a failure of Social Security's records of your earnings to match your W-2 Forms—in other words, a mistake! You can ask them to revise their records, and if you disagree with a decision made on your claim, you may ask the Social Security Administration to reconsider it. If you are still not satisfied, you have the right to representation by an attorney or anyone else you choose. You also have the right to appeal decisions made by the SSA concerning your benefits. Two fact sheets, "The Appeals Process" and "Social Security and Your Right to Representation," are available from your local SSA office or by calling (800) 772-1213.

SOCIAL SECURITY CHECKLIST

■■

Estimate how much Social Security benefits you will receive by requesting a personalized benefit estimate from the SSA.

■■

Apply for Social Security benefits at least three months before you would like them to commence.

■■

Apply for Medicare benefits within three months of your sixty-fifth birthday, since delays can be costly.

■■

Plan ahead to minimize the effects of a reduction in Social Security benefits for recipients who continue working and taxation of Social Security benefits for retirees whose income exceeds certain thresholds.

■■

If you are ever eligible for Social Security disability or survivor's benefits, you must apply for these benefits to receive them. Understand your rights.

71

Company Pension Plans

The burden of accumulating sufficient retirement funds is shifting from your employer to you. (That's why companies love to sponsor 401[k] plans—you foot most of the bill!) Nevertheless, if you are fortunate enough to work for a business or institution that has its own pension plan, and you stay there for a long time, and the company stays financially fit for the duration, you may retire with a pension that goes a long way toward covering your retirement needs.

The important thing to do now, however, is to find out through the projections provided by your employer just how "generous" the plan truly is. Granted, you may also be permitted to make additional "after-tax" contributions to the plan—to increase your future benefits. But you shouldn't be hasty about it. For one thing, that money might earn a better return elsewhere. For another, you need to be careful about putting too many eggs in one basket.

Variations of the traditional company pension plan are employee thrift and savings plans and 401(k) plans. These plans usually require you to make your own contributions, which are either wholly or partially matched by your employer's contributions. That's good news. Even though there may be no immediate tax benefits (there are with 401[k] plans), you are at least getting something for nothing—your employer's contribution—and you will benefit from tax deferral. Therefore, you *should* participate.

The extent to which a pension plan can contribute to meeting your retirement income needs can vary from zero (more than half of the nation's private-sector employees are not covered by pension plans) to a considerable amount.

Types of Pension Plans

Although each company's pension plan is somewhat different, all plans share certain features. Most pension plans are formal plans. They have defined rights, benefits, and eligibility standards, and they use predetermined formulas to calculate your benefits. The reason for all this formality is self-interest. Federal regulations, largely promulgated by ERISA (the Employee Retirement Income Security Act), require company pension plans to conform to certain rules in order for your employer's contributions to the plan to be tax-deductible.

There are two basic types of pension plans: defined benefit and

Smart Money Move

If you have a choice, opt to work for companies that have generous employer-paid pension plans.

627

defined contribution plans.

In a *defined benefit plan*, the benefits you receive on retirement are determined in advance, although contributions made to the retirement fund are not. Defined benefit plans concentrate on benefits to be received by you (the retiree), so that you can budget your income accordingly—and expect a specific amount of benefits no matter how well or badly the pension investments perform. From both sides of the equation—your employer's and your own—defined benefit plans create a certain amount of risk. How so? Your employer is responsible for delivering the goods—your specified pension benefits—upon your retirement. It's conceivable that employers who suffer severe financial difficulties may not be able to provide all of the projected benefits to you.

A *defined contribution plan* is somewhat less secure—for you. With this plan, your employer makes a certain contribution to the pension fund each and every year. When you retire, you receive a monthly amount based on whatever happens to be in the fund at the time. If this sounds like pot-luck, you pass the hearing test. This plan is usually advantageous if you have a long working life and if your employer contributes enough to build up a substantial retirement fund. A defined contribution plan, although not ensuring that there will be enough income upon retirement to support a desired standard of living, also does not limit how much will be set aside in the plan for your retirement.

Vesting

Vesting is the rate at which your pension contributions permanently accrue to your account. In order to understand how vesting works and when it occurs, you should read the provisions of your employer's pension documents very carefully, which must be made available to all employees. Current vesting schedules for most plans require five-year "cliff" vesting (100 percent vesting upon completion of five years of service) or an alternative, seven-year, graduated vesting schedule (20 percent after three years of service and 20 percent for each year thereafter).

Should you terminate your employment with a company and receive vested benefits, the benefits must be put into a rollover IRA within sixty days. If they are not, they will be regarded as taxable income for that year, and they will usually be subject to a 10 percent penalty tax for distributions received before age fifty-nine and a half. Therefore, if you ever leave a company in which you have vested pension benefits, roll the benefits over into an individual retirement account (IRA) within the sixty-day limit after the employer pays you your vested portion. Otherwise you can kiss a substantial portion of it good-bye since taxes will take a heavy toll.

Smart Money Move

If you're contemplating a job change, check to see where you stand on vesting. You may benefit from delaying the change until you become further vested.

You may also have the option of keeping your vested pension benefits in the company until you reach retirement age, at which time you can draw a small pension. The decision as to letting the money sit or rolling it over into an IRA is up to you. If you are confident that you can manage your own resources, the IRA alternative is probably better. If not, keep the money in the company pension plan.

Whatever you do, don't withdraw the money for your own use. Younger people in particular are inclined to view what may be a relatively small amount of money as unimportant for their retirement. The result is that they end up doing something stupid with money that should remain earmarked for their retirement, like buying a new car. Not only are they heavily taxed and penalized for their profligacy, they sacrifice some resources that may be important to their retirement well-being.

The decision to roll or not to roll over your company pension benefits is a little less clear if you are laid off. If you think you might be out of work for a long time, you may need to use these retirement benefits to meet living expenses. Do that only as an absolute last resort.

Don't Be a Job Hopper

Chronic job hoppers, even if they dutifully roll over whatever pension benefits they receive, usually end up with far less pension income than those who are less peripatetic because most large-institution pension plans are skewed heavily in favor of those employees who have many years of service.

Vesting is also affected by a break in the employee's service in which he or she leaves the company for an extended period of time because of illness, an accident, or personal reasons. Although ERISA strictly regulates this aspect of pension plans, you can lose all the benefits you have accrued to a certain point if you are unable to work for a long time. For this reason, it's very important to understand your employer's policy on breaks in service.

Plan Benefits

Your pension plan may allow for a combination of benefits. Although most people think the only benefit that they will receive from their plan is a retirement income, there are other benefits that you should know about. Depending upon your company's plan, you may have the option of taking either a lump-sum payout at retirement age or an annuity. (If you do have this choice, see page 631.)

In general, ERISA requires retirees who have been married at least one year before retirement and who will be receiving benefits in the form of an annuity to designate at least one-half of the benefits as a survivor annuity payable to their spouse. The level of benefits is lower, of course, when survivor benefits are included. ERISA

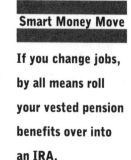

Smart Money Move

If you change jobs, by all means roll your vested pension benefits over into an IRA.

does permit you to reject the provision for a joint-and-survivor annuity, but it must be done in writing, accompanied by your spouse's signature, which must be witnessed by a notary. (More on this below.)

If you die shortly after retiring—perish the thought—certain allowances are customarily made for your spouse and dependents so that they don't have to endure financial hardship. Contributory plans refund the balance of all funds you contributed to the plan while working, minus the money paid out by the plan to you before you died. Because ERISA requires that married employees be covered under a joint-and-survivor annuity pension, benefits after your death are paid to your spouse or other beneficiary (unless you waived the joint-and-survivor annuity option).

If you die before retiring—it happens—ERISA requires that provisions be made for your surviving spouse if you were married for at least twelve months prior to your death. The plan must include an option that will pay your spouse not less than one-half of your retirement income. This is an optional benefit, available to you only after you have become eligible for early retirement or are within ten years of normal retirement age.

Early retirement because of permanent disability could impose a severe financial hardship on your family and dependents. Therefore, recognizing your need for protection, some pension plans provide for disability by allowing for the distribution of a reduced income previously slated for your retirement. Other plans have a disability plan that's separate from the retirement plan, and some pension plans also have provisions for accumulating funds for medical benefits.

Don't Waive the Joint-and-Survivor Annuity Option

Be aware and wary of a retirement-funding technique that has been vigorously promoted by the insurance industry: opting for a straight life annuity and, surprise, buying a life insurance policy to provide for your spouse. As you probably know, straight life annuities provide payments only during your life—they do not continue payments to your spouse upon your death. (A joint-and-survivor annuity does provide payments to your surviving spouse.) What's the attraction of a straight life annuity? Higher monthly payments. (Less money is being set aside to cover your spouse.)

Smart Money Move

Don't fall for the "use life insurance in lieu of a joint-and-survivor annuity pension" sales pitch without a very careful and objective analysis.

Theoretically, part of those larger pension payments could be used to buy an insurance policy on your life, in order to provide insurance proceeds for your spouse in lieu of a continuing annuity. This is what the insurance industry is touting. But there are problems. Can you afford sufficient life insurance coverage? Can you keep up the payments? What happens if the insurance company gets into financial trouble? Additionally, your surviving spouse must be capable of managing the proceeds effectively in order to ensure a continuing income. This may be particularly difficult if your surviving spouse is unacquainted with managing money, elderly, or in poor health. Thus, any strategy that uses insurance in lieu of a joint-and-survivor annuity must be evaluated over and over again. It may sound like a good idea, but often it isn't.

Taxation of Lump-Sum Benefits

First too little, then too much. If you receive your pension benefits in a lump sum, you have a few choices as to how these benefits will be taxed. And though your choices may be few, the consequences of your decision can multiply or divide your benefits. Choosing what's best for you depends, naturally enough, upon your particular situation. In fact, making an exception to my own rule about your being your own best financial adviser, I think you really should speak with an accountant or financial planner who has the know-how (and a computer program to go with it) to help you figure out which way to go.

You may want to take special *five-year or ten-year averaging* treatment on the proceeds in lieu of an IRA rollover. In using the five-year or ten-year averaging method, the calculation assumes that the distribution was received by five individuals (ten for ten-year averaging) in the current year and that each of these individuals had no other income. As a result, most of the income is taxed at the lowest rates on the single-taxpayer tax-rate schedule. The tax for each of these fictional individuals is then added up and becomes your tax on the pension distribution. Five- or ten-year averaging can be used *only* if you were born before 1936.

This may sound like the instructions for getting Rubik's cube right, but it's not as difficult as it seems. Special averaging is not allowed once you've put the money in an IRA, and it's generally permitted only once. Before making an IRA rollover, you should determine what the tax is under the five-year averaging method (or ten-year averaging method under the old tax rates, for some people) and compare it with an estimate of tax payable on a later distribution of the rolled-over IRA account.

You'll also want to evaluate the desirability of making this one-time election on these benefits or, if you're entitled to any future distributions, waiting until a future distribution, for which forward averaging might provide even greater benefits.

Which is better—forward averaging or an IRA rollover? It all depends. That's why you need a professional to look the situation over. Usually, but not always, the chips will fall in favor of the IRA rollover.

Choosing Between a Lump Sum and an Annuity

While some pension plans require participants to take an annuity

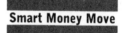

Smart Money Move

If you take a lump-sum pension distribution, ask a professional to evaluate whether you should take special forward averaging treatment or roll the benefits over into an IRA.

when they retire, your plan may allow you the option of taking a *lump-sum payout*. There may be some advantage to taking a lump sum, but this option must be considered carefully.

If the monthly payments provided by an annuity are not adjusted for inflation (and most are not), and if you are confident that you can invest the lump-sum amount more profitably, then the lump-sum option may be a good choice (if it's available). Why? Because you'll probably be able to generate more income than the annuity and at the same time do a better job at quieting inflation's toll.

But there may be a serious drawback to taking a lump sum. If you or your spouse should incur substantial uninsured medical expenses (like a long-term nursing home stay), or if you should otherwise be subject to the claims of creditors or to the mismanagement of money that may occur in old age, your lump-sum retirement fund may be jeopardized. In the worst-case scenario, it could seriously erode or altogether wipe out your pension resources. This eventuality must be weighed against the fact that money that is in an annuity is usually protected from these adverse occurrences.

What is the solution? A partial lump-sum settlement and a partial annuity may be a desirable compromise. Or if an annuity is your best option, don't necessarily take the first one that's offered to you. Why? Payout rates on so-called immediate-pay annuities vary widely (see page 671). Shop around for a financially hale company that offers the most attractive terms.

If you take a lump sum, you have some homework to do as well. You may be able to take advantage of forward averaging to reduce the tax impact of the distribution, or if you can afford it, you can further postpone taxes on your plan's distribution by rolling it over into an IRA. This way, you won't pay tax until you begin withdrawing money from the IRA. (For more on IRAs, see Chapter 75.)

Smart Money Move

Choosing between a lump sum and an annuity is never easy since both have their disadvantages. Consider taking part lump sum and part annuity with your pension distribution.

Excess Distributions

The infamous 1986 tax "Complification" act imposes a 15 percent excise tax on so-called "excess distributions" from company retirement plans, IRAs, and most other retirement plans. Like most of the provisions of the act, the rules are very complicated. Suffice it to say that if you are fortunate enough to expect an annual income from your retirement plan(s) in excess of $150,000 and/or you expect to take a lump-sum distribution in excess of $750,000, you should speak with an income tax professional about your potential exposure to this onerous tax. The threshold amounts will eventually be indexed for inflation, so if you are many years from retirement, you may escape its clutches. It all depends upon how much you will have accumulated. If you are likely to find yourself subject to this excise tax, you should speak with a tax accountant about certain strategies that you might take to minimize its effects. For example, you may not want to make additional IRA contributions if they are going to be later subject to an excise tax. Advance planning may be helpful.

FOR FURTHER INFORMATION

The following publications will help you better understand how your company pension plan works:

What You Should Know About the Pension Law ($.50)

Consumer Information Center
Attention: R. Woods
Pueblo CO 81009
(719) 948-3334

A Guide to Understanding Your Pension Plan: A Pension Handbook ($3.00)

AARP
Worker Equity
601 E Street NW
Washington, DC 20049
(202) 434-2060

COMPANY PENSION PLANS CHECKLIST

If you work for a company that has an employer-paid pension plan, learn about its features and your expected benefits under the plan.

Pay careful attention to the vesting requirements if you are contemplating a job change.

If you are married and are going to take an annuity, waiving the joint-and-survivor annuity option is usually inappropriate.

If you have the option of choosing between a lump sum and an annuity, weigh carefully the advantages and disadvantages of each.

If you are going to take a lump-sum distribution, evaluate carefully whether you should use special forward averaging treatment or IRA rollover treatment of the distribution.

If you are likely to be subject to the 15 percent excess distributions tax, plan ahead to minimize its effects.

401(k) Plans

I f you haven't heard of 401(k) plans—also called salary reduction plans—don't be embarrassed. Not everyone has had *your* opportunity to vacation on Mars. If you truly haven't heard, 401(k)s are among the most attractive tax-advantaged retirement investment vehicles your money can buy. Sound too good to be true? In this case it isn't.

When you participate in a 401(k), your employer diverts a fixed portion of your pretax salary into a company-sponsored investment plan. There are two immediate advantages to this: Your overall taxable income amount is reduced, and you've started investing in your own future. While 401(k) plans have long been available to employees of large corporations, they are now becoming available in an increasing number of smaller companies. Many employers are even matching part of each employee's contribution to 401(k)s!

If you are lucky enough to work for an employer who has established a matching program, don't pass up the golden opportunity to participate. In fact, employer matching or not, I urge you to participate in your company's 401(k) plan if it's offered. Amazingly, of the millions of workers who are eligible to participate in 401(k)s, over 40 percent are out to lunch when it comes to investing in them. Maybe retiring in good wealth means nothing to them.

401(k) plans are easy to join and convenient to use. Direct withdrawal from your paycheck makes it more likely that you will invest—rather than spend—the money you need to be salting away for retirement. This chapter describes in detail how 401(k) plans work, and how you can best put one to work for you.

Build up a large retirement nest egg by participating in your company's 401(k) plan.

How 401(k)s Work

When it comes to 401(k) plans, you can tell your company where to go. When you agree to participate in your company's plan, you instruct your employer to deduct a percentage of your income and put it into a retirement account. Typically, you can elect to have anywhere from two percent to ten percent of your total compensation put into a 401(k).

Read my lips: "*tax-advantaged.*" Perhaps the most immediate attraction of a 401(k) plan is that it saves federal income taxes. It does this in two ways. First, earnings placed into a 401(k) are deducted from your gross pay, so that the more you put into your plan, the less there is for the feds to tax you on. Because money in a 401(k) plan is deferred compensation—as distinct from a deductible IRA contribution—the 401(k) money doesn't appear on your W-2 Form and thereby escapes both federal income tax and Social Security taxes (unless your gross income after the 401[k] contribution exceeds the maximum income for which Social Security is withheld). Also, depending upon where you reside, your 401(k) contribution may escape state and local income taxes.

Unfortunately for some, the IRS *has* put a cap on the amount of money you can divert into your 401(k): As of 1992, the maximum salary reduction was $8,728. (This maximum amount is increased annually for inflation.)

The second tax benefit is that the money invested in the plan can grow tax-free until you are ready to begin making withdrawals. Dividends, interest, and capital gains won't be taxed as long as they are reinvested into the plan.

Choosing an Appropriate 401(k) Investment Program

For better or for worse, you must decide how you want your 401(k) funds invested. Of course, where you invest the money depends upon what options your company offers. Four common options that most plans provide are stock funds, bond funds, money-market funds, and guaranteed investment contracts (GICs). Many also offer the option of purchasing shares of the company's stock.

Here are some suggestions about investing your 401(k) money so that you can take maximum advantage of the alternatives that are available to you.

Don't go overboard on GICs

GICs are fixed-income investments sold by insurance companies. When you buy a GIC, the insurance company promises to pay a specified interest rate over a specified period of time. GICs have been a very popular 401(k) investment option—it is estimated that six out of every ten dollars invested in 401(k) plans are invested in GICs.

While GIC rates may seem very attractive, over the long run you will probably do better with bond funds and stock funds. Don't place more than 20 percent of your 401(k) money in GICs. Also, don't believe for one minute that *guaranteed* means "absolutely, positively guaranteed." Remember, GICs are insurance company products, and insurance companies have not been immune from suffering financial problems.

Invest your 401(k) plan funds much as you would invest any other long-term investment money

Chapter 54 provides guidance on allocating your investments for long-term growth so that you can achieve financial security.

Avoid the option of adding shares of your own company's stock in your 401(k)

You need diversification in this important retirement-earmarked money, and *as optimistic as you might be about your company's financial future and fortunes, you never know what's going to happen to its stock price.* A lot of 401(k) plan participants have seen years of savings wiped out because they put too much money in their own company's stock. When the bottom fell out of the company's stock price, the 401(k) plummeted, too.

Advice for Preretirees

I f you are within several years of retirement and your employer has a company pension plan, you may want to consider dropping out of the 401(k) plan. Why? Many company pension benefits are based on the level of compensation that employees earned during the last three to five years of employment. If this is the case, you may want to receive your full compensation during those crucial years rather than continue participation in the 401(k) plan and consequently lower your company benefits. You should check with the people in your company responsible for employee benefits to determine whether this course is desirable for you. Your company's plan may base your pension plan benefits on income before deferral, in which case it would be okay to continue participating in the 401(k).

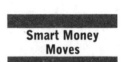

Smart Money Moves

Don't invest any of your 401(k) plan money in the stock of the company you work for.

Don't invest more than 20% of your 401(k) money in guaranteed investment contracts. You will do better with stock funds and bond funds.

CASE STUDY

Jack Wilkes is forty-six and makes $32,000 per year. He's been putting away a little bit regularly in his 401(k) plan for the past seven years. Counting his employer's contributions, Jack has accumulated about $22,000 in 401(k) retirement savings. Jack's problem is that he doesn't know how best to invest these savings. Thus far, his money has been going into a guaranteed investment contract. Jack's money has been put into a GIC because he's been too busy to do the research necessary to determine what sort of investment would best suit his needs. He feels that he doesn't know enough about investments and doesn't have the time necessary to keep track of the market. Also, Jack is fairly conservative about money, and since his 401(k) is his main retirement-savings fund, he doesn't want to risk losing it. Another concern: He's probably going to have to help support his wife's mother in a few years.

Where should Jack be investing his 401(k) funds?

First things first

There is a problem with putting all or most of your 401(k) eggs in a single investment "basket"—no matter how safe, sound, and "guaranteed" the investment seems. By investing all his funds in GICs alone, Jack is settling for lower overall performance in return for what he perceives as a high degree of security. But by settling for lower returns, he is running the risk that his savings will barely keep pace with inflation, let alone achieve capital growth. Stocks and bonds have generally provided better returns than GICs over the long run.

Smart Money Move

No later than 5 years before you plan to retire, check with your employer about the effect, if any, of your 401(k) plan participation on your pension benefits.

Diversify—the golden rule

Jack should first find out what other investment options his 401(k) plan offers. He should spend some time studying the brochures and other material that describe the various investment options—it will be time well spent. Since this money is earmarked for retirement purposes and Jack has a long time to let his investments grow until he retires, he should consider diversifying his investments along the following lines: 55 percent stock funds, 30 percent bond funds, and 15 percent in the GIC.

Jack has been laboring under the delusion that he can remove all degree of risk if he invests only in ultraconservative securities. But the risk of taking no risk is that, over the long run, Jack's GIC may badly underperform a well-balanced portfolio of stocks and bonds.

Preretirement needs

Jack is also concerned about the need to meet the costs of elder-

»

care and college. Since his 401(k) investments are earmarked for retirement and can be withdrawn only in the event of financial hardship, he should plan to provide for these expenses outside the 401(k) plan. Funds invested outside the 401(k), particularly those that will pay for his son's college education, should be invested much like 401(k) plan investments. Funds that may be needed to care for Jack's mother-in-law should be invested a bit more conservatively (in other words, in a higher proportion of bonds and guaranteed income securities like CDs and a lower proportion of stocks), since he will need them in a few years. Generally speaking, the shorter your investment horizon, the more conservatively you should invest your money.

Checking up

Jack can keep track of how his investments are doing by reviewing his 401(k) plan statements and, for the mutual funds or stocks that he owns through his plan, by checking the prices in the financial section of the newspaper if they are published.

A simple strategy

Finally, Jack will need to know whether and when to readjust his 401(k) portfolio allocations. If Jack buys reasonably good investments—and buys them in the correct proportions—chances are that he won't have to readjust his portfolio too often. A simple strategy for him would be to review his portfolio every ten to twelve months in order to determine what percentage he should have in stocks and what percentage he should have in interest-earning securities.

A typical portfolio

The Asset Allocation Models table shows how a typical 401(k) portfolio might be arranged at different stages of an individual's work life.

401(K) ALLOCATION MODELS

	25 TO 40 YEARS OLD	40 TO 55 YEARS OLD	55 THROUGH RETIREMENT
GICS	10%	15%	20%
STOCK FUNDS	60%	55%	50%
BOND FUNDS	30%	30%	30%

Managing Your Investments

Some employers grant their employees a degree of latitude in managing their own 401(k) investments. Depending upon your employer, you may be able to choose from among only a limited number of mutual funds, or you may be able to invest your funds in a wide (and sometimes wild) variety of investment vehicles.

You have the right to switch the instruments in which your 401(k) is invested up to a minimum of four times per year. Of course, you can switch only into those accounts that are preset by your employer. The rules regarding shifting are specific to your company's policy. Contact your employee-benefits department to find out what they are.

When is the best time to shift? That's a tricky one to answer. For the most part, you should not be shifting your investment at every possible time. Instead, you should develop a general awareness of the economy and how it affects your investment's performance. (Chapter 32 should be of help in this regard.) If the performance of a particular investment is steadily deteriorating over several quarters—in other words, if your investment's performance stinks compared to the rosy performances of similar kinds of investments—then it's probably a good idea to consider alternative investments.

Getting Access to Your 401(k) Savings

Early Withdrawal

Rumor has it that the regulations governing early withdrawals from 401(k) plans are more lenient than those for IRAs. If you turned on your radio and it said the Martians had landed and were making war with the world, would you believe that, too? Don't be fooled. There's a 10 percent penalty tax for early withdrawal, not too mention that making an early withdrawal from your 401(k) is usually more difficult than doing so from your IRA.

Here's what you can believe: Your 401(k) plan contributions may not be distributed to you earlier than when you reach age fifty-nine and a half unless:

Smart Money Move

Take advantage of favorable borrowing terms by borrowing from your 401(k) plan—but only for good purposes.

- YOU RETIRE

- YOU DIE

- YOU BECOME DISABLED

- YOU LEAVE OR LOSE YOUR JOB

- YOUR PLAN IS TERMINATED, AND NO SUCCESSOR PLAN IS ESTABLISHED

- YOU DEMONSTRATE EXTREME (AND I MEAN EXTREME) NEED

As a last resort, it is possible to withdraw funds early from your

401(k). But you must first demonstrate both an immediate and substantial financial need as well as an inability to meet that need with any other resources. Purchasing your principal residence, meeting deductible medical expenses that exceed 7.5 percent of your adjusted gross income, and paying postsecondary tuition are demonstrations of substantial financial need, as is need related to the imminent foreclosure of your principal residence.

To the extent that a distribution is not necessary, or to the extent that it exceeds the amount needed, it will be (or should be) denied.

Taking Out a Loan

Loans from 401(k) funds are permitted for up to half the account balance up to $50,000, though loans of less than $10,000 may exceed one-half the balance. Such loans must be for a stated interest rate and have a predetermined repayment schedule. Except for home loans, the maximum loan period is five years. For one thing, interest on such loans is not tax-deductible. For another, the interest rate on such loans is seldom fixed. Instead, it is geared to the prime rate or other applicable federal rate or, in some instances, to some other index.

If you don't repay the loan within the specified time period, then the (outstanding) balance is taxable and subject to the 10 percent penalty (if you are under age 59 1/2).

Rolling Funds Over into an IRA

Taking a loan from your *retirement* fund may sound to you like one of the worst ideas that you can think of (good for you!). But one of the worst, and most repeated, ideas is *spending* the whole kit and kaboodle. How can this happen? Simple. If you decide to leave your job—for any reason—you can take your whole 401(k) sum with you, the idea being that you reinvest it in another tax-advantaged retirement plan. What happens? You know how tempting a new car, a trip to Europe, or a mini-vacation in Bermuda can be—especially to someone in the younger set, for whom retirement is something that only grandparents do. The result is that money earmarked for retirement is spent for current living needs rather than rolled over. Not only is the retirement money being spent, it is being taxed. Stupid, stupid, stupid!

One way to avoid paying the penalty tax—and to avoid spending your retirement resources prematurely—is to roll over your 401(k) money into an IRA within sixty days. You can do so as long as you roll over at least 50 percent of your balance. (That still means you'll be taxed on any amount you didn't roll over.) You'll be thankful you did.

Other strategies besides rolling over a lump-sum distribution can still offer you some tax advantage as long as you are over fifty-nine and a half. If you need the money today, for example, and you were born before 1936—that's the law laid down by the IRS—you can use a strategy called *five-year averaging*. Five-year averaging provides favorable tax treatment of your distribution (see page 631). You can also use a ten-year averaging technique that is similar to five-year averaging. Either way saves you taxes and allows you to get access to your funds.

That said and done, I strongly urge you to leave well enough alone. Your retirement money should be used for one thing only—your retirement. But don't just take my word for it, listen to the most convincing retirement experts I know—people just like you.

CASE STUDY I

Elizabeth Manter, a twenty-seven-year-old accountant at a large multinational corporation, recently joined her company's 401(k) plan. As she sees it, "I may be thirty or forty years away from retirement, but I'm beginning to realize how important it is to start setting some money aside for retirement. What motivates me? My parents are getting ready to retire, and I can see that it's not going to be easy for them. I don't want to have to worry like they do about whether or not I'll be able to afford to retire. Also, I saw someone working in a fast-food restaurant last week who must have been over seventy. That's not for me!"

Younger people are beginning to realize the importance of saving for retirement even though retirement is a long way off. The sooner you start saving, the more you'll be able to take advantage of the dramatic effects of compounding. 401(k) plans are an ideal way to begin a retirement savings program. Employee contributions to the plan are not taxed, your money grows free of taxes until you begin making withdrawals, and your investments are professionally managed. If Elizabeth puts $2,500 per year into her 401(k) plan, and it grows at an average rate of 8 percent she will have almost $600,000 in her plan by the time she's sixty-five!

CASE STUDY II

Stan and Millie Zaborowski are concerned about what Stan calls "life's two great expenses"—college education for the kids and retirement. "I don't consider a house to be a big expense anymore. Millie and I paid less for our house than we are going to pay in college tuition for just one of the three kids." Stan and Millie are both forty-seven, and they have a combined income of just over $50,000.

"The way I look at it, Stan and I have to save for the kids' tuition bills *and* at the same time put money away for retirement. I don't want to be like other couples we know who have spent everything they had on college-education costs. Once their children have graduated, these parents are almost starting from scratch again, and retirement isn't that many years off."

Middle-age parents often feel like they're "stuck in the middle." Tuition bills have to be met, and retirement is no longer decades off. It used to be that most people were empty-nesters by the time they were in their mid- or late forties. They still had a lot of

»

time to save for retirement. But the combination of starting families later in life and the desire on the part of many people to retire early means that the time between the kids leaving the nest and the parents' retirement is shortened considerably. To make matters worse, cutbacks in federal and state tuition-aid programs mean that only the neediest families will qualify for much college financial aid. While they may feel that they are needy, Stan and Millie will be considered middle-class homeowners who, at best, will qualify for very little college financial aid for their three children.

As Millie mentions, parents should not become so preoccupied with meeting college education costs that they lose sight of the need to provide for their own retirement. Millie and Stan are fortunate in that both of their employers offer a 401(k) plan, and they are determined to continue making regular contributions to them. "There may come a time, when we have two kids in college at once, when we may have to reduce our 401(k) plan contributions somewhat. But we want to stay active in the plans, since Millie and I both feel that these plans will be crucial to our being able to retire comfortably. And that's every bit as important a goal for us as is being able to provide the kids with a college education."

CASE STUDY III

Claudia and Phil Gabler are looking forward to retiring in five years. Claudia is fifty-eight and Phil is sixty, and they have a combined income of $67,000. While they have managed to set aside quite a bit of money over the years, they are still concerned about whether their savings, company pension plan, and Social Security will be enough to allow them to retire comfortably. They want to travel some when they're retired and would like to spend the winters in a warmer clime. Phil wonders about the 401(k) plan that his company recently introduced. "I don't know if I should be participating in the company 401(k) plan since we're so close to retiring," he says. "I think these plans are designed primarily for younger workers. If you contribute to them for twenty or thirty years, the money will really add up. But we're only a few years from retirement, so it won't amount to a whole lot. Also, Claudia and I already do an IRA every year."

It's never too late to participate in retirement-savings plans. Since you can defer taxes on the income from a retirement-savings plan—interest, dividends, and capital gains— you're better off putting money that is earmarked for retirement into these plans, even if for only a few years. Phil apparently thinks the tax benefits of a 401(k) end at retirement. In fact, the Gablers can let their 401(k) plan money continue to grow tax-free many years after they retire.

The added advantage of participating in a 401(k) plan, even if only for a few years, is that the money you put into the plan each year is not taxed. Because of their income

»

level and active participation in a company pension plan, Claudia and Phil cannot deduct their IRA contributions. Therefore participating in the 401(k) plan is more advantageous for them than contributing to an IRA.

401(K) PLAN CHECKLIST

☐ Participate to the maximum in your company's 401(k) plan. If you can't afford to participate to the maximum, make at least some regular contribution and strive to increase it to the maximum as soon as you can.

☐ Invest your 401(k) plan assets just as you would any other long-term investment portfolio. Maximize stock and bond funds and minimize money-market funds, guaranteed investment contracts, and stock in your own company.

☐ Take advantage of favorable loan terms by borrowing from your 401(k) plan—but borrow only for worthwhile purposes. Inability to repay could result in tax penalties as well as jeopardize important retirement investments.

73

403(b) Plans for Employees of Nonprofit Organizations

I f you work for an educational institution or other nonprofit organization, you may be eligible to participate in a 403(b) plan. In many ways, a 403(b) plan is the non-profit sector's answer to the 401(k) plan. 403(b)s—also known as *tax-sheltered annuities*—are a special type of salary-reduction retirement-savings plan. These plans are available only to employees of educational institutions and other speci-fied nonprofits.

While most workers in the nonprofit sector do not enjoy high incomes, many do partici-pate in generous pension plans. Nonprofit organizations often provide pension plans that are far more generous than those found in the private sector. Even if you are covered by one of these pension plans, however, it probably won't provide you with enough income to guarantee that your retirement will be truly comfortable. Do you think your pension alone will do the job? Put your convictions to the test and calculate your projected retirement income and expenses, using the worksheets provided in Chapter 69. You will probably find that you need to set aside some of your own money for retirement purposes. If you work in the nonprofit sector, 403(b) plans are the way to go.

Using 403(b)s, educators and administrators, janitors and coaches, clerks and therapists can all accumulate tax-sheltered retirement savings with relative ease. Most institutions offering 403(b)s make available to their employees several plans from which to choose. To find out what your organization offers, simply contact your personnel office and request the appropriate literature. Don't neglect to read the information you receive very carefully. As you have already read, 403(b)s have features in common with 401(k) plans. Just as with 401(k)s, there is no excuse not to participate.

If you work for a nonprofit organization, build up needed tax-sheltered retirement savings by participating in your organization's 403(b) plan.

Opening Your 403(b)

I f you want to participate in a 403(b), you must agree to have your employer deduct a special portion of your current salary. The employer then takes the deducted portion of your salary and transfers it into a 403(b) account. You generally have several options as to how you can invest your 403(b) funds. Since your paycheck will be reduced by the amount of money that your employer takes out of it, your tax bill will decrease. Meanwhile, the funds invested in your 403(b) will generate dividends, interest, and capital gains totally free of taxes until you begin making withdrawals during retirement.

Contribution Agreement

Before you can participate in a 403(b) plan, you have to sign a contribution agreement that tells your employer how much of your salary to withhold. You can initiate your 403(b) plan at any time during the year. However, once you have chosen a date and signed the agreement with your employer, you can't alter the agreement—except to terminate the remaining payments due for that year.

Investing Your 403(b) Funds

O nce you've signed your 403(b) contribution agreement, the next step is to decide how to invest the funds you'll be salting away into the plan. Employers who offer 403(b) plans generally provide participants with several investment alternatives from which to choose.

As with any other long-term investment, you ought to invest your 403(b) savings for growth along the lines described in Chapter 54.

Smart Money Move

Shop carefully for the best tax-sheltered annuity in terms of investment selection, reasonable restrictions, commissions, and fees.

TEACHERS INSURANCE AND ANNUITY ASSOCIATION/COLLEGE RETIREMENT EQUITIES FUND (TIAA/CREF) SYSTEM

TIAA/CREF is a nonprofit corporation organized to provide a "universal" retirement plan for teachers who are not eligible for state pension funds and who—in the course of their lives—may teach at several institutions. Employees of a number of other qualifying nonprofit organizations can also participate in TIAA/CREF-sponsored plans.

The TIAA/CREF system of retirement plans consists of two basic funds. The TIAA fund is invested primarily in fixed-income securities (bonds and mortgages). The CREF fund is invested in the stock market. There is also a money-market fund. TIAA/CREF offers three different annuity products: retirement

»

annuities (RAs), group retirement annuities (GRAs), and supplemental retirement annuities (SRAs).

Because the type of plan in which you participate (as well as the investment alternatives you choose within that plan) has a major effect on how much income you'll receive during retirement, you should take an active role in running your 403(b) portfolio. Not only do you need to select appropriate investments from among those offered to you, you must monitor their performance.

As with IRAs and 401(k)s, you need to scrutinize each of the types of investments your 403(b) plan offers. Annuities are a product rife with restrictions, commissions, fees, and penalties, and it pays to shop around. Don't select a plan that has a lot of restrictions, penalties, and fees if more flexible and lower-fee plans are available. Tax-sheltered annuities are heavily marketed, so you are likely to be on the receiving end of a lot of sales pitches. Remember, it's your hard-earned money. Just because the sales person is nice to you and seems very interested in your well-being doesn't mean that his or her tax-sheltered annuity is the best one for your money.

Other Considerations

Contribution Limitations

When you set up a 403(b), your employer automatically diverts a portion of each paycheck into the plan. But you can also make *voluntary* additional plan payments—up to certain limits. There are three limitations that affect your plan: elective deferral limitation, annual limitation, and overall limitation.

Elective Deferral Limitation

Ordinarily, your annual voluntary contributions to your 403(b) cannot exceed $9,500. If you are already making contributions to a SEP or 401(k), you may find that the amount of voluntary 403(b) contributions that you can make is lower than the usual maximum. In general, the more you contribute to a SEP or 401(k) plan, the less you will be allowed to voluntarily contribute to your 403(b) plan.

If you have been working for your current employer for more than fifteen years, *and* your previous contributions to tax-sheltered annuities with your current employer have not exceeded $5,000 per year, you can make annual contributions of $12,500. You can make these larger $12,500 contributions for only 5 years, however; after that, you must comply with the standard $9,500 ceiling.

Annual Limitation

However you cut it, the sum of your total annual voluntary contributions cannot exceed 25 percent of your reduced salary—the salary remaining after the contribution amount has been deducted from it—in any given year. While 25 percent would be nice to set aside, most of us can't afford that amount. Try 10 to 15 percent or whatever you can afford. The important thing is to participate.

Overall Limitation

The law limits the total amount you can invest in a 403(b) based on a variety of factors, including your employment history and your use of other retirement plans. Check with your employee-benefits administrator to see how the overall limitation rules may affect your participation in a 403(b) plan.

Borrowing from Your 403(b)

Subject to specific amounts (maximum $50,000) and duration limitations (no longer than five years), some annuity plans provide their participants the option to borrow their 403(b) plan investments prior to reaching fifty-nine and a half without incurring the 10 percent penalty tax. While you generally must pay back a 403(b) loan within five years, you can take longer to repay it if you use the proceeds toward the purchase of your home. The interest paid to yourself on these loans is not tax-deductible.

Any borrowing from a 403(b) plan—or from any retirement plan, for that matter—should be done only as a last resort. After all, you're tapping into valuable tax-advantaged retirement money. When you raid your retirement funds, the opportunity cost is great—the money you've taken out could have been generating tax-free compounded investment returns for you.

Rolling Over into an IRA

403(b) plans allow you to roll your savings over into an IRA using a lump-sum payment option. When you are setting up your 403(b), avoid purchasing a tax-sheltered annuity that lacks a lump-sum payment option if others are available to you that do permit lump-sum payouts. It's nice to have the rollover option available, even if you never actually use it.

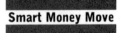

Smart Money Move

Let your 403(b) plan continue to grow tax-deferred by rolling it over into an IRA.

Unless you really need access to your 403(b) plan savings when or shortly after you retire, it usually pays to roll the funds over. By rolling your lump-sum distribution into an IRA, your money can continue to grow tax-deferred.

Taxes are levied only when withdrawal commences. Moreover, unlike an annuity—where you select a plan and are relatively bound and tied to it—an IRA offers you considerable flexibility and control both in terms of what you invest in and in terms of how your accumulated funds are redistributed to you. The rollover option would usually be taken upon leaving your employer or after you reach age fifty-nine and a half. Otherwise, if you withdraw 403(b) funds prior to that time, you will be socked with a 10 percent penalty tax. The 10 percent early-withdrawal penalty may also be waived if the funds are withdrawn under certain circumstances. Check with your employee-benefits administrator.

Mandatory Distribution Rule

Benefits accruing from 1987 or later are subject to a mandatory distribution rule that takes effect when you reach seventy and a half. The rules that govern 403(b) mandatory distribution are, with a few exceptions, the same as those that govern IRA mandatory distributions (see page 665).

403(B) PLAN CHECKLIST

■□■

If you work for a nonprofit organization, you should participate in its 403(b) plan, if available, to build up essential retirement savings.

■□■

Choose a tax-sheltered annuity plan that offers an attractive array of investment options and that imposes reasonable restrictions and fees.

■□■

Manage your 403(b) plan investments carefully, just as you would any other investment account. Invest for growth, and avoid overemphasis on low-yielding options like money-market funds and guaranteed investment contracts.

■□■

Avoid the temptation of borrowing from your 403(b) plan, unless the purpose of such borrowing is very worthwhile—for example, to purchase a home.

Retirement Plans for the Self-Employed

T he number of people who are self-employed, full and part time, is steadily increasing. It seems that being your own boss, and even bossing other people, has a mythic appeal: sleeping late, working the hours you want to work, taking extended vacations, never missing a weekend or holiday. Of course, the reality is that if you're self-employed, you're probably working twice as hard, with no time to take a vacation, let alone take a solitary Sunday off. In the hurly-burly world of self-employment, it's easy to see why so many self-employeds are completely focused on the present—getting the job done and surviving the slings and arrows of business as usual.

But there's a danger that transcends the present, immediate demands of everyday work. That danger is forgetting that, no matter how distant it seems, there will come a time when you retire. And like everything else about self-employment, making a successful go of your retirement is completely in your hands.

If you are a self-employed professional or if you own your own business, you will need to make a decision now or in the near future about how to establish a retirement plan through your business, for yourself, and if you're not flying solo, for those whom you employ. The benefits are obvious. Contributions to a self-employed retirement plan are tax-deductible, and retirement plan investments are tax-deferred until they are withdrawn during your retirement.

If you have no employees, you should almost without exception establish and fund a retirement plan. It's not as tough to do as many seem to think. Generally, you should be setting aside on a regular basis money that is earmarked for retirement. There's no better way to do so than through a tax-deductible, tax-deferrable retirement plan.

If you have employees (other than family members), you have to weigh the benefits to yourself (as well as to your employees) of establishing a retirement plan, even a modest one, against a company's ability to afford the plan. This is a decision you will need to make, although if you cannot yet afford to provide a retirement plan, you may be able to afford one in the future.

ARE YOU A MOONLIGHTER?

If you earn income from moonlighting, you can establish your own self-employment retirement plan, even if you are participating in a company pension plan. If you have any income from self-employment, seriously consider one of these retirement plans. Just like a full-time small business owner, you get the same double tax benefit—tax-deductibility of the money going in, and tax-deferral along the way.

Who Qualifies for Self-Employed Retirement Plans?

If you are self-employed either full or part time, you are eligible to set up your own retirement plan. Even if you are employed by another organization that has a pension plan, you can most likely establish a self-employed plan, too. The general rule of thumb: If you have any income from self-employment, you can establish a self-employed retirement plan. My advice is, do it now. Even if you stop working for yourself, you can continue letting your self-employed retirement plan investments grow, although you won't be able to make additional contributions to the plan.

Two plans are worthy of your serious consideration (if you are serious about being able to retire comfortably): a Keogh plan and a simplified employee pension, or SEP, plan.

Take note. Like all other retirement plans, the money you invest in a tax-advantaged or tax-deferred retirement account is out of reach—or within reach only with steep early-withdrawal penalties—until you reach age fifty-nine and a half. Don't put money into a self-employed retirement plan that you will need to access before you reach that age. College-tuition funds and family emergency funds, for example, should not be invested in retirement plans.

Smart Money Move

Let the financial institution of your choosing do all the detailed work regarding setting up your Keogh plan. They'll be delighted to help you.

Some critics argue that the benefits of tax-deductibility and tax-deferral are not sufficient to offset the disadvantages of tying money up for such a long period of time. My feeling is that having easy access to your money is of secondary importance to investing regularly in your own retirement. After all, wouldn't you rather have your money "tied up" now so that, when it comes time to retire, you will have enough money to retire and cut loose on?

If you are a small business owner or self-employed professional or if you have income from a sideline business, take advantage of the powerful tax incentives offered by retirement plans for the self-employed.

Keogh Plans

K eogh plans have been around for some time now. Originally introduced in 1964 by the congressman after whom they are named, their purpose is to provide self-employed individuals the opportunity to establish a private pension fund for their own retirement. This private pension fund is modeled after the large-company pension plans and can be set up by *unincorporated* self-employed persons and their employees. Even if you participate in a pension plan at your place of employment, you may also set up a Keogh plan if you earn income from another line of work.

Keogh plans are subject to a lot of complex and confusing rules. But many financial institutions have established "prototype plans" that make the process of establishing and contributing to a Keogh as easy as pie. Banks, brokerage firms, mutual fund companies, and other financial institutions can help you set one up, explaining the details to you. Some important details about Keogh plans follow that you should know before you seek out help.

What Is a Keogh Plan?

A Keogh plan is a formal arrangement in which the owner or owners of an unincorporated business (a sole proprietorship or a partnership) establish a program to provide tax-deferred retirement benefits to the owners or partners and their eligible employees, if any. Keogh plans permit small business owners to set aside a considerable amount of money each year. As with a large company retirement plan, all contributions to the account are tax-deductible, and all interest accumulates tax free until withdrawn.

Keogh plan characteristics

Keoghs are generally set up as *defined-contribution* plans (see page 628). They can be structured to allow you to contribute, and deduct, up to 25 percent of your net income from self-employment (actually, 20 percent of your income before you make the contribution) or $30,000, whichever is less. You can tailor the plan to suit your own needs and resources.

Smart Money Move

If you have employees, you *must* extend this benefit to them and make contributions at the same percentage-of-income level that you do for yourself. If you have employees, you should weigh the costs of making contributions on their behalf against the benefits you will receive from your own retirement funding. It may simply be too costly. On the other hand, you might find that it is in your best interest to establish such a plan. If you can't afford to set up a retirement plan that provides for both you and your employees, remember that you somehow need to build up a retirement nest egg outside the business. Start with an IRA.

High income professionals should look into the rapid tax-sheltered retirement plan buildup power of defined-benefit Keogh plans.

There are two types of Keogh plans: *money-purchase* and *profit-sharing* plans. Both of them are defined-contribution plans. With a money-purchase plan, your contribution amount is a fixed percentage of the participant's income—no matter how little or how much you make, you're obligated to provide the set percentage. A profit-sharing plan is far more flexible. You can contribute as much (up to the maximum, which will be roughly 15 percent of your earned income) or as little as you want. In fat years you can contribute to the max. In lean years you can cut way back, or even contribute nothing at all. (If you're the owner of the business, there is usually no difference between the two plans, but if you have employees, there is.)

Defined-benefit advantages

A *defined-benefit* Keogh plan may be the best way to accumulate a substantial retirement nest egg (see page 628)—if you fit this description: You are a high-income professional, are over fifty, and have no other employees. The reason? A defined-benefit plan can be structured to allow very high annual tax-deductible contributions, well in excess of the $30,000 cap on defined-contribution Keoghs.

Important deadline

No matter which Keogh plan you choose, you must establish it by December 31 of the tax year when you want to begin taking the deduction, even though you can delay making the contribution until your tax return is filed (including extensions) in the succeeding year. (If you missed the deadline but it is not yet April 15, you can set up a SEP, described below.)

Keogh Accounts and IRAs

If you have a Keogh plan, and you are contributing the maximum deductible amount you can under the rules, but you want to contribute more to a retirement-earmarked account, you could open up or add to an existing IRA. (See Chapter 75 for the scoop on IRAs.) You can also make voluntary contributions to your existing Keogh of up to 10 percent of your earned income on top of what is normally contributed. While these contributions are not tax-deductible, the earnings are tax-deferred.

Smart Money Move

Maximize your self-employed retirement plan contributions by setting up a Keogh plan by the end of your business's tax year.

Contribution and Deduction Limitations

Because of the way Keogh plan legislation has been written, there can be a lot of confusion concerning the maximum amounts that may be contributed and claimed as a deduction on your tax return each year. The amount contributed and the amount deducted are not always equal to each other, although in no case may the deduction exceed the contribution.

The amount of the contribution you may claim as a deduction depends on which type of Keogh plan you're using. If you are using a money-purchase Keogh plan, your deduction is limited to a maximum of 25 percent of your compensation as long as it doesn't exceed $30,000. If you are using a profit-sharing plan, your deduction is limited to the lesser of 15 percent of compensation or $30,000. These percentages are based on net income after Keogh deductions are accounted for, which can make the computations complicated. For money-purchase plans, actual deduction percentages are figured by dividing 25 percent by 125 percent (total income plus the Keogh deduction divided by the maximum percentage) to arrive at 20 percent for money-purchase plans. For profit-sharing plans, the deduction percentage is derived by dividing 15 percent by 115 percent to arrive at 13.0435 percent.

The two plans can be, and frequently are, used in combination: This allows for the maximum percentage deduction permitted by the law. How so? With a combined money-purchase and profit-sharing plan, you can contribute 10 percent to money-purchase and 15 percent to profit-sharing.

Borrowing against Your Plan

As soon as one finishes talking about how to set up a retirement plan, the question of how to get the money out—in case of an emergency, or just because—arises. Under certain conditions, employees of a business who are *not* owners of the business may borrow against their Keogh plans. Loans to owner-employees (individuals who own more than 10 percent of the business) are prohibited and subject to the following penalties: a 5 percent penalty assessed in the year the prohibited loan is made, and another 5 percent assessed with each following year until the loan is repaid with interest. A 100 percent penalty is imposed if the loan is not repaid. (That's right—100 percent!)

Individuals who qualify as *employees*—in other words, they own 10 percent or less of the business—may borrow up to $10,000 or 50 percent of the vested Keogh plan benefits (with a ceiling of $50,000), whichever is greater. These loans must be repaid over a five-year period, except for residential loans, which may be repaid over a longer period. Fail to do so, and you will be taxed on the outstanding balance and, if you're under fifty-nine and a half, pay a 10 percent penalty tax to boot.

Annual Information Returns

If your Keogh plan covers only yourself, or you and your spouse, and if the assets you have in your Keogh plan at the end of the plan year exceed $100,000, you must file IRS Form 5500 EZ by the end of the seventh month following the end of the plan's fiscal year (or July 31 if your plan year is the calendar year). You do not have to file an information return if the plan assets are $100,000 or less. If you're uncertain about the rules on annual information returns, by all means check with an accountant.

Smart Money Move

Continue to make contributions to your Keogh or SEP plan. You can do this even after reaching age seventy and a half as long as you still have self-employment income.

Simplified Employee Pension Plans (SEPs)

S implified employee pension plans (SEPs) are simple to set up, simple to maintain, and simply wonderful retirement savings vehicles for self-employed people. Instead of maintaining a separate pension plan (required with a Keogh), SEP contributions are deposited directly into your (and if applicable, to your employees') IRA account(s).

A SEP plan offers small businesses, closely held or otherwise, the opportunity to establish either an employer- or employee-funded pension plan for stockholders and eligible employees. An employer establishing a SEP does not necessarily have to be an incorporated firm.

With respect to an employer-funded SEP, employees establish IRA accounts into which their employers make contributions. If you do not have an IRA, your employer must establish one in which to deposit your contributions. The employer then makes contributions established by a specified limit into the IRA accounts. Once a SEP is established, your employer must contribute to the accounts of each employee over age twenty-one who has performed services in at least three of the five preceding calendar years.

The SEP has tax advantages similar to those of regular qualified retirement plans. Employer contributions to SEPs are tax-deductible up to a designated limit. The deductible employer contribution is the lesser of $30,000 or 15 percent of your compensation, although your employer may set up a percentage of less than 15 percent. The same percentage must apply to all employees. Contributions made within three and a half months after the close of a calendar year are treated as if they were made on the last day of the calendar year. Employer contributions are not subject to FICA or Federal Unemployment Tax Act (FUTA) tax withholdings, although state income tax usually has to be paid on the contribution.

Smart Money Move

Small business owners, set up a retirement plan for your employees at small cost by establishing a salary-reduction SEP.

Important Deadline

You may establish a SEP after the end of the tax year in which you want to begin taking the deduction, as long as it is set up and funded before April 15.

Therefore, if you are self-employed, and you miss the December 31 deadline for establishing a Keogh plan, it's still possible to set up a SEP as late as April 15 of the following year. It will be tax deductible for the previous tax year, and the deductible SEP contributions can be made at any time until the April 15 deadline.

Generally, the amount you may contribute is 15 percent of your gross self-employment income, up to $30,000 per annum. You can also kick in an IRA contribution on top of the SEP contribution.

Withdrawals from a SEP are taxed as ordinary income, unless

they occur before age fifty-nine and a half, death, or disability, in which cases they are subject to a 10 percent penalty. Forward averaging is not available for a lump-sum distribution from a SEP. In order to start a SEP, an employer must file IRS Form 5305-SEP.

As with Keogh plans, you have to offer a SEP plan to your employees if you have employees. Moreover, as with a Keogh, "chronic" workers can still contribute to a SEP plan after age seventy and a half.

Salary-Reduction SEPs

A salary reduction SEP is available to certain small businesses. As with a 401(k) plan, employees elect to have their contributions deducted from their pay (rather than their making the SEP payments in addition to their salary). You may establish a salary-reduction SEP if you or your employer have twenty-five or fewer employees at any time during the preceding year and at least 50 percent of them agree to participate in the salary-reduction SEP.

Employee-funded SEPs contain a salary-reduction provision allowing employees to reduce their salaries and to have the reduction amount (called elective contributions) deposited in the plan. But there are limitations on the total amount of annual elective contributions an employee can make under all salary-reduction plans. This limitation is increased annually by an inflation factor (see page 603).

I told you at the beginning of this chapter that the rules governing Keoghs and SEPs are complex. But don't let the complexity of the rules that govern them dissuade you from actively participating in them. Remember that participation is the easy part of these excellent retirement savings vehicles.

Smart Money Moves

If you miss the December 31 deadline for setting up a Keogh plan, you have until April 15 to establish a SEP.

Consider a SEP an easier alternative to a Keogh plan. While the percentage of your self-employment income that can be set aside is lower, SEPs have the advantage of being easier to set up and maintain.

FOR FURTHER INFORMATION

Retirement Plans for the Self-Employed, IRS Publication 560 (free)
(800) 829-3676

SELF-EMPLOYED RETIREMENT CHECKLIST

Take advantage of the many tax benefits available to the self-employed who set up their own retirement plans.

■

If you have income from a sideline business or moonlighting, you should set up your own self-employed retirement plan.

■

Avoid the expense and aggravation of setting up a Keogh plan, either by using the prototype plans that many financial institutions offer, or by setting up a SEP plan.

■

If you have employees, consider a salary-reduction SEP so that you have a low-cost way to enable your employees and yourself to fund their own retirement plans.

Individual Retirement Accounts (IRAs)

When it comes to retirement-oriented investments, most people think of one tax-advantaged investment—the individual retirement account (IRA). IRAs are the best-known form of tax-advantaged investment accounts. In fact, more than eight million Americans have at least one IRA account, representing almost $500 billion in retirement-earmarked investments.

In spite of this large number, the reality is that many more workers could and should be contributing to an IRA. Moreover, many of those who are participating aren't investing their IRA money as well as they should. What follows should help novice and experienced IRA investors alike make the most of their IRA investments.

Build up valuable and needed retirement investments by making an annual IRA contribution.

Don't be intimidated by the many rules associated with IRA investments. They're not all that complicated. There are three major areas with which you need to become familiar: opening the account, managing the funds you invest in the account, and planning withdrawals from your account when you retire. Read on, and in a few minutes you'll be an IRA expert.

Opening an IRA Account

The mechanics of opening an IRA are as easy as calling or visiting your local bank, brokerage house, mutual fund company, or insurance company, and asking for an IRA application form. The whole process can be done over the telephone, so you might as well save time and do it that way. You can also make IRA investments over the telephone. But first, simply call and request an application. (The one exception to calling: If you're making a last-minute IRA contribution, just before April 15, don't rely on the mail. Open the IRA account in person.) There's a good reason why it's so easy to open an IRA account. The financial institutions love these accounts, since once it is opened, chances are that the investor will stick with that institution for many years to come.

Which Institution?

While opening an IRA account is easy no matter which institution you choose, the choice of the right financial institution is not as straightforward. Nevertheless, it is critical. The reason is that the place where you open your IRA account will affect the range of investment options available to you, which in turn may affect the long-term performance of your IRA funds.

If you're going to make your own investment decisions, you should probably opt for a discount brokerage account or no-load mutual fund family. Generally, brokerage firms and mutual fund companies offer a wider array of investment options than do banks and insurance companies, but banks and insurers are rapidly expanding their investment options.

Types of IRA Contributions

There are two types of IRA contributions—tax-deductible and nondeductible.

Tax-deductible IRAs

If you are not an active participant in a qualified retirement plan, you may make tax-deductible IRA contributions regardless of your income. The money you invest in your IRA account must come from earned income, however. Generally, when high-income earners and/or their spouses are already *active participants* in qualified retirement plans, they cannot deduct IRA contributions on their joint income tax return. You are considered an active participant in a defined-benefit plan if you are included under the eligibility requirements of your employer's defined-benefit plan for any part of the year ending within your tax year. You are also deemed an active participant in a profit-sharing or stock-bonus plan if a contribution is added or a forfeiture is allocated to your account during your tax year.

Smart Money Move

Open an IRA account at a financial institution that offers a variety of investment products—ideally a discount broker or no-load mutual fund company.

An exception to the active-participant rule allows some low- and middle-income people to make contributions to IRAs even if they or their spouses are active participants in a qualified plan. Single people with AGIs of $25,000 or less, for instance, can take full advantage of the IRA deduction. Married individuals filing a joint return who have an AGI of less than $40,000, and married individuals filing separate returns if a spouse has an AGI of less than $10,000, may also be able to deduct IRA contributions.

For a married person filing a separate return for any taxable year, the IRA deduction will be either reduced or eliminated if his or her spouse is an active participant in an employer-maintained retirement plan. This rule does not apply to married people who file separately and who live apart from their spouses during the entire tax year.

Partial deductibility is afforded to single people who make slightly more than the above cutoff amounts. Single people who are active participants and whose AGI is between $25,000 and $35,000 qualify for partial deduction. For active-participant married individuals who file joint returns, the applicable AGI is between $40,000 and $50,000 for partial deductibility. This rule also holds true for married individuals filing separate returns if one spouse has an AGI below $10,000. To calculate how much you can deduct, use the following rule: For every five dollars that your AGI increases above the applicable cutoff amount, your maximum IRA deduction is reduced by one dollar. This is equivalent to a 20 percent reduction.

For example: William Congreve is an active participant in his employer's retirement plan. He files a joint return with his wife, who is employed but does not participate in a retirement plan. Their total AGI is $44,000. Because their total AGI is over the $40,000 ceiling for a fully deductible IRA but is below the $50,000 ceiling, Congreve must reduce his maximum deduction of $2,000 ($4,000, if both he and his wife contribute to IRAs) by the proportional amount their combined AGI exceeds $40,000. The maximum deduction must be reduced by $800 ($4,000 x 20 percent). Thus, Congreve's maximum deductible contribution to his IRA is $1,200 ($2,400 if both he and his wife contribute). The fact that Congreve's wife is not an active participant in a qualified plan does not allow the couple a larger IRA deduction.

A taxpayer whose AGI is within the range qualifying for partial deductibility can make a $200 deductible contribution regardless of the 20 percent phaseout rule discussed above. For example, if the phaseout calculation indicates that you can make a $60 deductible contribution, you can raise this amount to $200. Also, a taxpayer who is entitled to a partially deductible IRA can make an additional nondeductible contribution up to the $2,000 limit.

Nondeductible IRAs

If you are an active participant in a qualified plan and therefore may not be eligible to make even partially deductible IRA contributions, you may be able to make designated nondeductible contributions (DNCs). Tax on the earnings of these DNCs is deferred until withdrawn. Your DNC cannot exceed the lesser of $2,000 ($2,250, in the case of a spousal IRA) or 100 percent of your total compensation that exceeds the amount you can take as a deductible IRA contribution. Thus, a single taxpayer whose earned income is at least $2,000 and who is permitted a $900 deductible IRA contribution may contribute an additional $1,100 in nondeductible contributions. IRS Form 8606 is required of taxpayers who make nondeductible IRA contributions.

Contribution Limitations

The $250 spousal IRA contribution is permitted even when your

Smart Money Move

Don't let inability to qualify for a deductible IRA discourage you from making a nonde-ductible contribution. You'll still enjoy tax-deferred buildup.

spouse receives some income over the year. Generally, if one spouse has compensation of less than $250 for the year, a spousal IRA is more advantageous than a regular IRA.

The deduction phaseout rules that may have reduced or even eliminated your own IRA deduction also apply to a spousal IRA. If you have a spousal IRA, are covered by an employer retirement plan, and your income is within the applicable phaseout range (see page 660), you can take only a reduced spousal IRA deduction.

A divorced person may contribute up to $2,000 of alimony or other compensation to continue to build up an IRA established by an ex-spouse. Alimony is now considered earned income.

Once you reach age seventy and a half, you cannot continue to contribute to your IRA, although if you have a younger spouse, you can make contributions to his or her account.

The deadline for opening or contributing to an IRA is April 15 (tax day) for the previous year's IRA. If you send your tax return to the IRS early, however, the contribution does not have to be made before the return is sent. On the other hand, an extension for filing a tax return no longer allows an extension to contribute to an IRA beyond April 15. Contributions do not need to be made every year, and the annual contribution does not need to be made all at once.

Although the IRA contribution can be deferred until April 15 of the following year, investors realize a substantial increase in the return on their IRA if their deposit is made at the beginning of the tax year. This allows the contribution to accumulate tax-free for as much as 15.5 months extra. With annual contributions of $2,000 and a 10 percent rate of return, in twenty years an account would be worth $16,000 more if the contributions were made in early January rather than 15.5 months later. In addition, by making the IRA payment early in the year, interest or dividend income that would otherwise be taxed in that year will be tax-sheltered.

It may be advantageous, however, for you to wait until after the end of the year if during the year you are unsure whether IRA contributions will be deductible, or if your financial situation precludes your making the contribution earlier.

Acceptable IRA Investments

Smart Money Move

Don't delay. Make your IRA annual contribution as early in the year as possible.

When you open an IRA account, you direct where your money will be invested. Your options can be one or more of the following: certificates of deposit, U.S. government securities, money-market funds, mutual funds, stocks and corporate bonds, zero-coupon securities, unit investment trusts, limited partnerships, options (for self-directed IRAs only), and U.S. gold and silver coins.

How to Manage Your IRA Funds

Y ou should manage your IRA account(s) with as much diligence as you do your other investments. Some people think that because their IRA money is earmarked for retirement, it should be invested very conservatively. Hence, a lot of IRA money languishes in money-market accounts, CDs, and low-yield securities. Rather, this money should be invested in securities that offer the opportunity for capital growth as well as current income. (See Chapter 54 for guidance on investing for long-term growth.)

Once you have selected your IRA investments, don't forget about them. You may need to shift your IRA investments periodically in response to changes in interest rates or stock market conditions. An 8 percent CD, for example, might be an appropriate place to put a portion of your IRA funds. But if CD rates drop considerably, when the 8 percent CD matures, you should probably look for alternative investments (a stock or bond mutual fund, for example) rather than taking the easy way out and rolling the money over into a new, lower-yield CD.

IRA investments to avoid include gold and silver coins. You may get taken, and even if you don't get taken, they won't appreciate very well. Municipal securities should also be avoided—it makes no sense to put tax-free money into an already tax-free account. Avoid real estate limited partnerships as well—they've proven themselves to be a pretty awful investment, and it's unlikely that they will improve for many years to come.

If You Have a Lump Sum to Roll Over

Deciding how to invest a lump-sum distribution, particularly one that will be used to provide retirement income, is never easy. Unless you think stocks are unusually cheap or interest rates are exceedingly attractive, you should probably devise a plan to gradually invest your lump-sum distribution rather than investing it in stocks and bonds all at once. (To get an idea of how you can do this, see page 459.)

The Mechanics of Shifting IRA Investments

This section explains the often-confusing mechanics of shifting IRA investments *between* accounts. There are two ways in which funds can be shifted: direct transfer (the most common), and rollover.

Direct transfer

When you want to transfer funds directly into a new account, you sign a form provided by the new custodian. The new custodian sends this form to the old custodian, who then transfers the IRA account assets. Don't expect the transfer to take place overnight. There is often some delay in transferring the investments. Sometimes the old custodian delays the transfer, being reluctant to let go of the account. Or you may encounter the ever-present red tape of administrative inertia. Don't hesitate to voice your displeasure regularly to both custodians if the delay is causing you fits. Transfers within a single custodian—a mutual fund family or brokerage account, for example—avoids this problem. That's a good reason to establish an IRA account at a financial institution that offers a wide range of investment alternatives. You may make as many direct transfers as you want.

Rollover

A lot of people are confused about IRA rollovers. The source of this confusion is that there are really two distinct kinds of rollovers. You may make a tax-free rollover of funds *from an employer or self-employed pension plan to an IRA*, or you may make a tax-free rollover of funds *from one IRA to another.*

In the first circumstance, the rollover is used to add pension funds to an IRA. Virtually everyone who receives vested pension benefits prior to age fifty-nine and a half should either roll them over into an IRA or, possibly, into another pension plan. (Many people over that age will also benefit from doing this kind of IRA rollover.) You must make the rollover into the IRA within sixty days of the time you receive the pension plan money. Otherwise, it will be taxed, which could be a major financial disaster. Whatever you do, memorize the sixty-day deadline. Better yet, write it on the back of your hand in indelible ink, and even then, don't wait until the last minute to make the rollover.

In the second circumstance you personally transfer your IRA funds, by withdrawing all or part of the investments from one custodian and reinvesting them with another. This differs from the direct transfer described above in that you temporarily receive the IRA funds involved in the rollover. Under a direct transfer, you don't get your hands on the funds, since it is a transfer between custodians.

There are a couple of reasons why you may want to use a personal IRA rollover. First, by taking charge of the transfer between custodians, you may reduce the likelihood of a delay in making the transfer. The disadvantage is the risk of penalty if the IRA money is not rolled over within sixty days.

The former custodian must be specifically notified of your intention to rollover the funds. Otherwise it must withhold the 10 percent penalty when the funds are withdrawn. Remember also that you are entitled to only one personal rollover in a twelve-month period, whereas direct transfers may be made as often as desired.

Smart Money Move

If you're temporarily short of cash to make an IRA contribution, borrow from your existing IRA fund to pay for your new IRA fund.

Personal loan from your IRA

Another use of a personal IRA rollover would be to make personal use of your IRA funds for up to sixty days while rolling over your account(s). But this once-a-year "opportunity" can easily be abused. For example, you may succumb to temptation and spend the money and thereby not have the money on hand to complete the rollover within sixty days. If this happens, you'll pay taxes and penalties on the money withdrawn. On the other hand, a possible beneficial use of a personal transfer, if you are short of cash, would be to use the money to fund a new IRA before the April 15 deadline, using old IRA money. Of course, you'll have to come up with new money within sixty days to refund your old IRA.

Transfers to a spouse resulting from divorce or death

If you receive your former spouse's IRA, the transfer is generally not taxable to either spouse so long as it is the divorce decree or, if you are legally separated, a decree of separate maintenance. IRA rollovers are also permissible if you receive a share of your spouse's or former spouse's benefits from an employer pension plan.

If you inherit your spouse's IRA upon death, you may elect to treat it as your own IRA. You will then be subject to all the provisions and regulations pertaining to IRA owners. If you inherit an IRA from someone who is not your spouse, the rules get more complicated. You may not treat it as your own IRA account, and the way you receive funds from the account depends upon the provisions of the IRA plan you inherited. Plans usually give you the option of receiving funds over your life expectancy and/or over the five-year period following the IRA owner's death.

Withdrawal

Many people are so intent upon managing their IRA accounts—or on avoiding anything to do with managing them—that they neglect to plan for the actual withdrawal of their funds. But if you understand the rules and plan ahead, you stand to maximize the tax-advantaged returns from your IRA investments. You will have that much more money available at a time when many retirees need it most—late in life. Before we get into the details, remember one general rule regarding IRA withdrawals: The longer you can postpone withdrawing IRA funds, the better.

When You May Begin to Withdraw

You *may* begin withdrawing from your IRA at age fifty-nine and a half, or earlier if you become permanently disabled. Any other withdrawals before that age are subject to a 10 percent penalty in addition to the proceeds being taxed as regular income. (If part of a premature distribution is tax-free because it is an allocation of nondeductible contributions [you've already paid tax on it], the 10 percent penalty applies only to the taxable portion of the distribution.) The exceptions are that the 10 percent penalty does not apply to distributions payable to a beneficiary upon the death of an IRA owner or payable to his or her estate. Also, if the before-age-fifty-nine and a half distribution is part of an annuity over your life expectancy or the joint life expectancy of yourself and the beneficiary, the distribution is not taxed. The rules are complicated, so you need expert assistance if you're going to buy a lifetime annuity with your IRA before age fifty-nine and a half.

Unfortunately, many people who have diligently saved and accumulated an IRA succumb to temptation when they reach the magic fifty-nine and a half or shortly thereafter. I've often seen people who are still working tap into their IRA accounts to buy cars, take vacations, and the like. They will live to regret their shortsighted decisions.

When You Must Begin to Withdraw

You *must* begin IRA withdrawals by the April 1 following the year you turn seventy and a half. (Failure to do so can cost you a whopping penalty from the IRS—fifty percent of the difference between the amount you should have received and the amount you did receive.) Minimum withdrawals must be made each year, taking into account your life expectancy or, if you've designated a beneficiary, your joint life expectancies.

The rules regarding minimum withdrawals are awful, period. But you can manage them if you buy a good tax preparation guide or request IRS Publication 590, "Individual Retirement Arrangements (IRAs)." If you can afford to postpone drawing on your IRA account until age seventy and a half, and you can afford to follow the minimum withdrawal schedule, the computational nonsense and complexities you have to go through each year are well worth the effort, because the money remaining in your IRA account continues to grow tax-free.

Computing Minimum Withdrawals

To compute the minimum withdrawals that are required for IRA owners over age seventy and a half, follow these steps.

1. **DETERMINE** the account balances in all of your IRAs as of the previous December 31.

2. **FIND OUT** your life expectancy or the joint life expectancy of you and your beneficiary. The IRS provides life expectancy tables that give the fraction used to compute the minimum amount that must be withdrawn from an IRA.

3. **CALCULATE** the minimum amount you must withdraw. This is done by dividing the amount of money in your IRA accounts (Step 1) by the life expectancy factor (Step 2). A single woman, age seventy, with a fifteen-year life expectancy, for example, would take out one-fifteenth of her IRA savings upon reaching age seventy and a half. The next year she would take out one-fourteenth of the remainder, and so on.

Smart Money Move

Delay withdrawing your IRA money as long as possible to maximize the tax-deferral advantage.

One of the advantages of following the minimum withdrawal schedule is that the funds left in the IRA continue to accumulate tax-free. The following table shows how much this can actually increase the funds that you will receive during your retirement. The table calculates total withdrawals of $67,314 over nineteen years. (The table does not assume that the withdrawals begin at age fifty-nine and a half, but it does assume that the withdrawals will commence by the time you reach seventy and a half.) If you took this IRA in a lump sum, you would receive $25,000 in the first year. If, instead, the money is withdrawn in installments and the withdrawal schedule is refigured each year by a changing life expectancy, the accumulation is greater. (See below.) For the highest accumulation, it is best to take out the smallest amount possible while allowing for your financial needs. The table assumes 10 percent interest on an account with minimum withdrawals.

ADVANTAGES OF FOLLOWING THE MINIMUM WITHDRAWAL SCHEDULE

YEAR	BEGINNING YEAR BALANCE	FRACTION	MINIMUM WITHDRAWAL AMOUNT
1	$25,000	1/19	$1,315
2	26,052	1/18	1,447
3	27,065	1/17	1,592
4	28,021	1/16	1,751
5	28,896	1/15	1,926
10	31,025	1/10	3,102
15	24,983	1/5	4,996
19	7,315	REMAINDER	7,315

If your IRAs are spread among more than one account, the minimum withdrawal schedule will be the same for each, but you may decide from which accounts the withdrawals will be taken.

An Even Better Deal

It is now possible to lower withdrawals by refiguring life expectancy every year. Because the age to which the retiree is expected to live increases each year, refiguring makes the fraction smaller. This recalculation will deplete the funds more slowly and allow you to continue to let your IRA investments grow tax free. Another possibility is to stretch the withdrawals jointly over the combined life expectancies of the IRA owner and spouse or other beneficiary.

Warning: If the minimum withdrawal schedule is not followed, the IRS is allowed to take 50 percent from every dollar in the IRA that falls behind the schedule. (This penalty is rarely waived.) Also, note that the table is only a minimum schedule and that after age fifty-nine and a half, your withdrawals can be as large as you desire. If in any year a withdrawal is larger than the minimum, your remaining minimum withdrawals will be reduced.

Lump-Sum Withdrawal

Some people may prefer taking the whole IRA in one lump sum. One reason to do this is that it eliminates any risk of the 50 percent penalty for falling behind the minimum withdrawal schedule. But the money withdrawn will be taxed and what's left should be reinvested in non-IRA accounts, which will be subject to tax on capital gains, dividends, and interest (except municipal bond interest).

IRA Annuities

As a retiree, you may use your IRA to purchase an annuity. Buying an annuity that begins regular payments by age seventy and a half satisfies the IRS's minimum withdrawal rules. It can be purchased for your life expectancy or jointly for the combined life expectancies of you and your spouse or other beneficiary. One advantage of this option is that it guarantees you payments for your lifetime or, in the case of a joint annuity, for the lifetime of both you and your beneficiary. There may also be a provision in the annuity that provides for payments to heirs. Experienced investors can generally do better than annuities, while inexperienced investors and those who have little else to rely on for retirement other than IRA funds should consider the safety of an annuity.

Designating Beneficiaries

Designating beneficiaries is an important matter that is often not given sufficient attention. The rules and choices governing the receipt of IRA funds by the beneficiary in the case of the IRA owner's death are important, as they can significantly affect the beneficiary's tax liability.

When you open your IRA account, you designate a beneficiary—your spouse, estate, another person, or a group of people. Unlike you, however, your beneficiary has fewer options for withdrawing the funds. An individual other than your spouse who inherits an IRA may not treat it as one established on his or her behalf. The result: The IRA distribution to the nonspouse will have to be paid out in accordance with the plan provisions. But if your designated beneficiary is your spouse, he or she can take over the IRA as the equivalent of an IRA rollover. In this case, the same rules apply as to a regular IRA; that is, your spouse cannot withdraw funds without penalty until age fifty-nine and a half and can delay withdrawals until turning age seventy and a half. Finally, the unlimited spousal estate tax deduction means that any bequests to a spouse are not subject to federal estate tax. (They may be subject to state death taxes.)

FOR FURTHER INFORMATION

Individual Retirement Arrangements (IRAs), IRS Publication 590 (free)
(800) 829-3676

INDIVIDUAL RETIREMENT ACCOUNT CHECKLIST

■□■

Everyone with earned income should get into the habit of contributing to an IRA. If you can't afford the full amount, you should contribute at least something.

■□■

Open an IRA account at a financial institution that provides a variety of investment alternatives.

■□■

Make your IRA contribution as early in the year as possible to maximize tax-deferred buildup of the investments.

■□■

Withdraw your IRA money as late as can be afforded. However, minimum withdrawal schedules must be strictly adhered to after age seventy and a half to avoid penalty.

Annuities

nnuities often play a role in accumulating retirement savings or in providing a steady source of income for retirees. Like any other insurance product, annuities create a lot of confusion. Much of the confusion is due to there being two distinct kinds of annuities—*deferred annuities*, which are essentially retirement-savings plans, and *immediate-pay annuities*, which are used by retirees as a source of regular income.

While annuities can be an important part of building a secure retirement, purchasing them should be approached with careful consideration. The reason for this is that annuities usually entail a permanent commitment on the part of the investor, so it's important to be absolutely sure that an annuity suits your financial needs and objectives before you sign on the dotted line.

One important rule of thumb: Whatever kind of annuity you are purchasing, chances are that you will be able to find a better one than the one that someone is trying to sell you. In other words, you can do nothing but benefit from shopping around for the best annuity product.

Annuities are less attractive than a well-managed, self-directed retirement plan. Many annuities are laden with an array of fees and commissions that reduce the purchasing power of your investment dollars. Nevertheless, an annuity may be an alternative worth considering. Tax-deferred annuities, for example, offer the opportunity to build up retirement savings tax-deferred. They operate much like a nondeductible IRA, except that there's no limit on the amount you may place in a tax-deferred annuity. Similarly, an immediate-pay (or "lifetime") annuity may be a good choice for an individual who wants an assured income for the rest of his or her life and, if desired, his or her spouse's life. Provided the company selling the annuity is sound, immediate-pay annuities guarantee a secure and steady source of income, which may be a blessing to a retiree who lacks the wherewithal or the knowledge to manage retirement investments on his or her own.

Deferred and Immediate-Pay Annuities

asically, an annuity is an investment contract between you and an insurance company (no matter who's selling it to you). You purchase an annuity by paying a lump sum of money (minimum purchases range from $2,000 to $10,000) to a life insurance company in order to receive either a deferred annuity or an immediate-pay annuity. As

I mentioned, there is a considerable difference between the two.

Deferred Annuity

A deferred annuity is typically used to accumulate retirement savings. You purchase it and let your investment capital grow, tax-deferred.

Make no mistake about it: Deferred annuities are not really annuities. They are tax-deferred savings plans. In fact, only select deferred annuities allow you the option of taking a lump-sum settlement when you retire rather than forcing you to "annuitize." Tax-deferred does not mean tax-free. You eventually pay taxes when the money is withdrawn for retirement purposes, either in a lump sum or in an annuity. Moreover, you receive no tax deduction on the amount of money you initially invest to establish your annuity.

Deferred annuities may be purchased in one of two ways. Single-premium annuities are purchased with a lump sum, and flexible-payment annuities may be purchased with installment payments over a period of years.

Immediate-Pay Annuity

An immediate-pay annuity is used to provide retirement income. It starts with your investment of a lump sum of money and begins generating periodic, usually monthly, income payments as soon as it is purchased. An immediate-pay annuity may be appropriate for a new retiree who has just received a lump-sum pension distribution.

Immediate-pay annuities are often used by those who want a guaranteed, periodic income for the rest of their lives, and, if desired, the life of the spouse. Several important decisions must be made before committing to an annuity because this is, indeed, a commitment for life. These issues concern how you want the benefits distributed, and finding the best annuity from a highly rated company. (These important matters are discussed on pages 675-77.)

Fixed and Variable Annuities

Smart Money Move

Evaluate all your retirement investment options carefully before purchasing an annuity.

To make matters more confusing, both immediate-pay and deferred annuities may be purchased as either fixed or variable investment instruments. As their respective labels imply, a *fixed annuity* provides a fixed rate of return based upon the amount invested and—with respect to an immediate annuity—your age, as filtered through the insurance company's actuarial tables. A *variable annuity*, on the other hand, provides a variable rate of return based upon the performance of the investment instruments (usually mutual funds) in which you select to place your money.

The fixed-rate annuity seems like the more secure and reliable investment, until you factor in inflation. But a variable-rate annuity, while it may keep pace with or even outdistance inflation, is subject to stock and bond market volatility. Thus, a fixed-rate annuity may provide you with a reliable and predictable accumulation or monthly benefit, but its purchasing power may diminish, while a variable-rate's accumulation or installments will vary—sometimes higher, sometimes lower—depending on the stock and bond markets.

Fixed Annuities

Fixed annuities guarantee you a specified interest rate for a specified period of time. Be sure you understand what happens after the high "come-on" rate period expires. After the specified period, your interest rate will change in accordance with prevailing rates. This may sound like a positive way for your annuity to remain competitive with other interest-earning investment options, but it is really the way the insurance companies hedge against declining interest rates.

Some do's for the fixed annuity buyer

- **LOOK FOR** companies that are well established in the annuity business and that are rated highly by insurance rating bureaus like Best's.

- **MAKE SURE** your contract has a competitive interest-rate floor—a limit to how low your interest rate can go.

- **SEE IF** you can find annuities that provide you with an exit clause. Typically, such companies allow you thirty to sixty days to find another, better annuity (at no surrender charge) if you have become dissatisfied with their performance or "renewal" rate during a predetermined time of usually no more than five years.

Some don'ts for the fixed annuity buyer

- **IF A COMPANY'S** fixed interest rate is sky high compared with others, *don't* buy its product. It's just a come-on.

- **DON'T GET ENSNARED** by a company that charges exorbitant early-withdrawal fees. There are plenty of other companies in this very competitive business that don't.

- **DON'T GET FOOLED** by a company offering "low" exit rates. Paying its exit rate (typically 1.5 to 2 percent) will almost certainly be in your worst interest.

- **DON'T BUY** from a company that rewards those who stay

Smart Money Move

Don't be duped by a high annuity "fixed" interest rate.

with it and penalizes those who don't. If it can't earn your staying power, then you shouldn't have to pay more for its poor performance.

- **DON'T BUY** CD annuities. They're not federally insured (the way CDs are), and even though they have no maturity date, you will most likely run up against tax penalties if you withdraw the money before you reach fifty-nine and a half.

Variable Annuities

Variable annuities are meant to protect your money from the effects of inflation. The buildup in your deferred annuity's savings is based not on a fixed interest rate but on the performance of a pool of mutual funds that you select. The purpose here is to provide you with the opportunity for a return that is in excess of the return you could get out of a fixed contract. The risk, of course, is that the mutual funds may lose value.

Fees must also be taken into consideration when purchasing variable annuities. A sales commission may be deducted from each contribution to the annuity, as well as fees for the insurance company and the investment managers. If you are considering a variable annuity, look for one that has both good performance in its underlying mutual funds and low fees. A few of the no-load mutual fund companies have started their own variable annuity products, and their fees are generally lower than the fees associated with stockbroker or insurance agent–sold deferred variable annuities.

Since nothing in personal financial planning is either/or, you may want to divide your deferred or immediate-pay annuity purchases between fixed and variable annuities. The net result will be the holding of "balanced" annuities.

Smart Money Move

Consider a variable annuity for retirement savings, but only after you have taken out an IRA and have participated to the maximum in your company-sponsored retirement-savings plans.

Consequences of Early Withdrawal

Don't even think about early withdrawal. While you may bail out of a deferred annuity contract, it probably won't make your wallet happy if you do so. Therefore, don't invest in a deferred annuity unless you are certain that you will not need to tap into the money before age fifty-nine and a half.

Unfortunately, even if the company that holds your annuity contract is financially troubled, you probably can't pull your money out without incurring withdrawal fees and perhaps tax penalties.

Income taxes and penalties may also be levied if you take money out of your annuity, unless you roll it over into another annuity. The more you take out, the more you will owe to the IRS.

Your friendly insurance company will turn downright nasty—fee-wise—should you decide to quit your annuity contract. The penalty is usually graduated—for example, a six percent early-withdrawal fee if you quit the contract in its second year, declining each year thereafter. This can mean that the later in the contract you quit it, the better. But some companies aren't nearly as lenient and will assess a penalty fee throughout the life of the contract.

Exceptions to the Rules

While having a change of mind can be costly, you shouldn't be penalized for withdrawing your money under the following circumstances:

- THE POLICYHOLDER has reached age fifty-nine and a half or has become disabled.

- THE DISTRIBUTION is a payment under an annuity for life or at least sixty months.

- THE PAYMENT is to a beneficiary (or estate) after the policyholder's death.

Important note: While concern over an insurance company's health is certainly not to be taken lightly, if you are investing in a variable annuity, you need not be as concerned about the insurance company that sponsors the annuity program. The reason for this is that variable annuity investments are maintained in mutual funds that are kept separate from the insurance company's assets. These are called "separate accounts." Since they are legally separate from the insurance company, they are generally not affected by a deterioration in the financial health of the sponsoring insurance company.

Immediate-Pay Annuities: Further Issues

Distribution of Benefits

Immediate-pay annuities also vary according to their benefit distribution.

Straight-life annuities

Straight-life annuities make payments to the annuitant until death do you part. A straight-life annuity is a win-or-lose deal. You can win by living longer than the insurance company figures you will live, or you can lose by dying earlier than the company estimates. (Heirs get nothing under these arrangements.) Remember that insurance companies want to make a profit and have a great deal of experience in working with mortality tables. There is a better-than-even chance of losing at least part of the money that you invested in the annuity.

Joint-and-survivor annuities

Joint-and-survivor annuities deal with the risk of loss by guaranteeing that neither you (the annuitant) nor your spouse will outlive the income. Payments will continue to your spouse even after you die, should you die first, although the survivor will be paid smaller install-ments than both received previously. Also, because the annuity is intended for a longer period of time, the regular payment to both spouses will be smaller than with a straight-life annuity.

In the vast majority of situations, couples are well advised to take joint-and-survivor annuities to protect the surviving spouse. Don't let an insurance agent talk you into waiving a joint-and-survivor annuity in your pension plan by buying an insurance policy. While this may work in some instances, be sure to understand the pitfalls before making such a significant and irreversible commitment. (See page 630.)

Life annuities with certain installments

Life annuities with certain installments provide a way of overcoming the risks of straight-life annuities. They resemble straight-life annuities in that they guarantee regular payments until death. In addition, a certain number of payments are guaranteed: If death occurs before a specified number of years have elapsed, the balance of the guaranteed payments will be paid to your survivors.

Most commonly, the guaranteed payments are for a period of ten years, which is usually shorter than life expectancy at retirement. Thus, premature death results in a smaller monetary loss for the family with this type of annuity than for one with a straight-life annuity. But the periodic annuity payment is less as well.

Refund annuities

Refund annuities alleviate some of the risk inherent in straight-life annuities by guaranteeing that the retiree or his survivors will receive back part or all of the money that was originally paid into the purchase. Therefore, if the retiree dies prematurely, a "refund" will be paid to his or her beneficiaries. This refund can be paid either in one lump sum (a cash-refund annuity) or in regular installments (an installment-refund annuity).

Note: It is important not to misunderstand the meaning of the term *refund.* It does not mean that the money originally paid can be returned at any time—only upon the annuitant's death. There is still a risk of loss in this annuity, as money is tied up in the annuity and may not be used for personal investing to create more income. Both refund annuities and life annuities with certain installments offer lower annuity payments than straight-life annuities do.

Family annuities

Family annuities (also called private annuities) present another way of dealing with the potential for loss of money due to premature death. Family annuities are purchased from a family member rather than an insurance company. To do this, transfer a portion of your property, such as a family business or real estate, to one of your children or other relatives in exchange for their paying a certain monthly installment until the annuitant's death. This eliminates the involvement of an insurance company. Family annuities have complex income and estate tax implications, so consult a tax professional.

Shopping for an Immediate-Pay Annuity

As with any other financial product, it pays to shop around for an annuity. Don't accept the first one that is offered you. Even if your company pension plan offers you an annuity, see if you can do better elsewhere if you have that option. You may be pleasantly surprised to find the often-significant differences in benefit-payment amounts among several companies. One source of information that may be helpful is the semiannual *Best's Retirement Income Guide*, which provides comparative information on company annuity plans. Check your local library.

Better alternatives?

Always approach the purchase of annuities cautiously—not because they are inappropriate retirement investments but rather because there are preferable investments. You could gain many of the same advantages of annuities, for example, and fewer of their disadvantages, by purchasing U.S. savings bonds.

The main concerns

Annuities have a relatively low yield. The fixed payments to annuitants may erode with inflation. You are likely to encounter high fees, commissions, and penalties. And there's a possible loss of a substantial part of an estate as a result of your premature death. Despite these drawbacks, an annuity may be a good choice if you are not or do not plan to remain an active manager of your investments. Similarly, an annuity may be a good choice for a retiree and his dependents who are neither financially secure upon retirement nor capable of managing and conserving money. The annuity ensures them an income, which, in these circumstances, may be important.

ANNUITY-PLANNING CHECKLIST

Remember that even though annuities have many advantages for your retirement-planning program—and many professionals advise investing in them—they do pose risks.

Check with your state insurance officials on what protection, if any, that state offers. Protection of annuities varies from state to state. Some, like New York, strictly regulate companies offering annuities and maintain a guaranty fund to cover a default. Others, including many large states, have no guaranty fund and do not have the staff to police the insurance companies under their jurisdiction.

Because annuities are not federally insured, you should invest in two or more smaller fixed annuity policies with different companies rather than one large one. With this kind of diversification, the risk of a major loss is significantly reduced.

■□

As with any other purchase, check the financial strength of the company offering a fixed annuity or the mutual fund track record of the company offering a variable annuity.

■□

Factor into your retirement income-and-expense forecast the fact that fixed annuities do not rise with inflation. Inflation can therefore seriously erode the annuity's purchasing power.

■□

Check the fees, commissions, and penalties associated with the annuity before you invest in it. They have been a major drawback, although charges have begun to drop to more reasonable levels.

Early Retirement

Ahhh, early retirement! How many times each day do we dream about being able to bid the workaday world adieu. Turning the dream of early retirement into a reality is a huge financial challenge. Unfortunately, many people who are retiring early now will eventually realize that they could not afford to do so. The truth is that most people cannot afford to retire early—even if they think they can, and even with a generous company-sponsored incentive plan.

Many employees who leave their jobs under company-sponsored early-retirement plans often discover—too late—that they won't have enough income to support themselves. Many end up having to reenter the work force late in life—not a pleasant thing to *have* to do!

If you would like to retire early, you need to take a hard look at how you will be able to meet your living expenses—not just the year you retire but ten, twenty, thirty, or more years thereafter. If you have been or expect to be offered an early-retirement "package," some down-to-earth advice for evaluating such offers appears later in this chapter.

Disadvantages of Early Retirement

Inflation's Toll

If you aspire to take early retirement, inflation is even more of an issue in determining whether your pension and savings are sufficient to support you than it would be if you retired at sixty-five. Why? Since you will be spending more years in retirement, you will therefore be more heavily affected by inflation. The table on the following page gives you an idea of how much more inflation affects early retirees. It shows how much living expenses will increase between retirement and the time you reach age eighty. As the table shows, people who retire at normal retirement age experience an 80 percent increase in living expenses by the time they reach age eighty. Those who retire at sixty experience a 120 percent increase, and those who retire at age fifty-five will experience a 170 percent increase in the cost of living by the time they reach eighty. Many

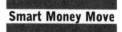

Smart Money Move

Inflation takes a particularly heavy toll on early retirees. Always factor in the effects of inflation in projecting your retirement income and expenses.

early retirees (and for that matter, age-sixty-five retirees) who neglect to account for inflation in their retirement planning are headed for an unpleasant surprise.

EFFECTS OF INFLATION ON EARLY RETIREES

RETIREMENT AGE	HOW MUCH LIVING EXPENSES WILL INCREASE BY AGE 80*
65	80%
60	120%
55	170%

* Assuming a 4 percent annual inflation rate.

Taxes

Many people mistakenly assume that their tax burden will lighten significantly at retirement. You will avoid some taxes, but on the other hand, taxes could go up again and cost you more than they do now. One thing you can be sure of: Income tax rates will never be lower than they are now.

Life-Style

Unless you are willing to curtail your life-style considerably, you should figure on spending about 75 percent of the amount you spend during your working years. Many retirees spend more than 75 percent.

Health Insurance

One commonly overlooked expense is health insurance. Unless you're taking an early-retirement package that extends your company health insurance coverage until age sixty-five, you'll need to factor in high health insurance premiums for an individually purchased policy until you become eligible for Medicare at age sixty-five. Most early-retirement incentive plans extend your company health insurance coverage after you leave work. If yours doesn't, you'll have to pay high premiums for an individually purchased policy until you become eligible for Medicare at sixty-five.

Smart Money Move

Be realistic in assessing your part-time employment prospects after you take early retirement.

Part-Time Work

Many early retirees count on working part time to supplement their retirement income. Part-time employment answers the two most frequent complaints of early retirees: too much time and too little money. But don't count on this option. Good part-time jobs that are financially and emotionally rewarding may not be as plentiful as you think. Good part-time jobs may be even harder to find than good full-time jobs. Don't simply assume you'll be able to get a part- or full-time job.

Planning for part-time employment should take into account not only the additional income it produces, but the additional costs it may incur, such as higher income taxes and reduced Social Security benefits.

Social Security

Your Social Security benefits will be reduced if you opt to collect before age sixty-five. You can receive reduced benefits upon your sixty-second birthday. Not only are the monthly checks lower, but the future cost-of-living increases are also proportionately lower because they are calculated from a lower initial benefit amount. As a result, benefits for early retirees will lag further and further behind inflation. (See page 614 for information on Social Security benefits for early retirees.)

It still may be appropriate for you to begin drawing Social Security benefits at age sixty-two. But one rule of thumb I use in advising people who are considering early retirement is that if your projections show that you will *have* to begin drawing Social Security benefits at age sixty-two to help meet living expenses, you probably can't afford to retire early.

Personal Retirement Plans

Any funds that you have set aside to supplement your retirement pension through individual retirement accounts (IRAs), Keogh or simplified employee pension (SEP) plans, 401(k) plans, or deferred annuities may be affected by your early-retirement decision. Not only will you have contributed to the plans for fewer years when you retire, you probably also will begin withdrawing from the plans sooner than you would have otherwise.

Penalties

You generally cannot withdraw funds from personal retirement savings plans before age fifty-nine and a half without incurring a steep penalty.

Fewer available funds

Even if you can afford to delay payments and avoid the penalties, there will be less money available to withdraw than if you had contributed for a few more years.

Smart Money Move

If your early retirement projections indicate that you will have to begin collecting Social Security benefits before age 65 in order to meet living expenses, you probably can't afford to retire early.

Need for personal investments

As a consequence of these reductions, personal savings and investments are even more crucial to early retirees than to workers who wait longer to retire.

401(k) plan penalties

Distributions from a 401(k) or other company-sponsored tax-deferred savings plan may be subject to a 10 percent penalty if you elect to take them before age fifty-nine and a half. Your best bet is to roll any such distributions over into an IRA within sixty days of receiving the funds and let these funds continue to grow free of taxes until you begin withdrawing. Live off your severance and personal savings.

Company Pension Plans

Normally, company pension plans penalize early retirees, and the penalty is often severe. While most early-retirement incentive plans waive this penalty, believe me, you're going to end up with considerably less than if you had remained with the company until normal retirement age—often less than half as much.

Warning Signs

If a large portion of your retirement income is going to be fixed—a retirement annuity, for example—and you will not be able to save a portion of it each year to help pay for ever-increasing future living costs, you may not be able to afford an early retirement. In other words, you should plan to save some of your retirement income each year.

Another warning sign: If you are likely to have to rely heavily on income from your personal retirement savings plans (IRAs, 401(k)s, 403(b)s, etc.) to meet living expenses before age sixty-five, you may not be able to afford an early retirement.

The Brighter Side

Early retirement is a very attractive prospect for many people. If you've been looking forward to an early-retirement that might be augmented by an early-retirement incentive plan, the above caveats may seem discouraging. It is possible to retire early and retire well, but you need to be very certain of your long-term financial security. If you have accumulated sufficient personal resources, your projections may indeed show that you can afford to retire early.

I cannot overemphasize the importance of making thorough projections. It may be well worth the expense to hire an accountant or financial planner to help you make your early-retirement income and expense projections. All I ask is that you be very careful and realistic in projecting your income and expenses until age ninety. If the numbers work and if you want to take early retirement, by all means do so. I envy you.

Keys to Successful Early-Retirement Planning

I f there's one common characteristic of people who can afford to retire early, it is sacrifice. This is how they do it.

They Plan Early

You can't decide when you're fifty that you want to retire at fifty-five. It doesn't take years of planning—it takes decades. Many successful early retirees begin planning for their dream in their twenties and thirties. They set their sights on early retirement and take action to achieve it. They work for companies with generous pension plans and avoid hopping jobs so that they can accrue substantial pension benefits. Some couples make the decision not to have children so they won't incur the expenses of raising them. Many live in low-cost cities and towns.

They Sacrifice During Their Working Years

Where most people have trouble saving 10 percent of their salary, successful early retirees realize that they need to save 20 or 30 percent of their income during their working years. They are experts at living well below their means. They often live in inexpensive housing, and they become experts at keeping their living expenses low. Those that own homes get out from under their mortgage as soon as they can, certainly no later than when they plan to retire.

They Sacrifice After Their Working Years

Even though they have spent many years living modestly, successful early retirees cut back even further when they retire. They realize how much money they will have to continue saving in order to make ends meet thirty or forty years hence. They relocate to low-cost areas of the country. Some even move out of the United States and settle in countries whose living costs are much lower than in the United States.

Early-Retirement Incentive Plans

Smart Money Move

If you *really* want to retire early, begin taking action to do so in your twenties or thirties.

E arly-retirement incentive programs, also called window incentives, are now the most popular means companies use to achieve a reduction in the work force. And for companies in the midst of mergers, takeovers, or downsizing, they have been one way to reduce layoffs.

When times get worse, companies downsize. Early-retirement plans are usually the way they try to do so in as humane a manner as possible. The advantages and disadvantages of the plans are very clear-cut and quantifiable for employers.

Early-retirement incentive plans may sound particularly appealing to you if times are tough and you feel there are no guarantees that you'll be able to keep your job if you don't accept the offer. The plans are fairly compelling, but on the other hand, many of them offer a lot less than meets the eye. Making matters worse, chances are that if you're confronted with an early-retirement incentive plan, you'll have only a month or so to evaluate the offer. That is very little time to weigh all the financial repercussions of the decision.

Often, company-sponsored early-retirement incentive plans are made to look particularly appealing. For instance, the company's benefits officer may show you how much more you'll receive with the plan than if you were to quit your job now without it. But unless you were considering retiring anyway, this isn't really a useful comparison. A better comparison would be between the package that is being offered and what you could expect if you stayed in your job as long as you originally intended. You would be sacrificing something; if you weren't, how would your company be saving money?

Even a beefed-up early-retirement pension is likely to be considerably smaller than the pension you could expect if you continued to work. That's because your pension is probably based on the average of what you earned in the last few years you worked. Even if the early-retirement incentive plan adds bonus years of employment and bonus years of age to your pension formula, it won't be able to make up the difference between your average salary for the last five years and your presumably higher average salary for your last five years if you were to continue working.

Smart Money Move

Assess realistically the financial implications of an early-retirement incentive plan. While you may have no alternative but to accept it, you need to realistically assess where you will stand financially should you accept the offer.

If the extra years of leisure are worth the reduced benefits to you, then the crucial issue for you is not how the early-retirement package compares with the normal retirement options but whether the package is sufficient to meet your retirement-income needs. To answer that you will have to project your retirement income and expenses.

Before you sit down to compare the psychological ramifications of working and early retiring (by drawing up a list of the pros and cons), or before trying to project your retired versus working income and expenses for the next thirty years, you need to figure out a way to assess your situation realistically. If you're worried about your job future at the company, the early-retirement plan may well be your most palatable option. If future layoffs appear likely, you may have little choice but to participate in an early-retirement program.

Assessing the Plan

The most important thing is for you to be realistic.

Do you know what sort of deal you have been offered?

Do you have it in writing and have you read and understood the fine print? Do you *have* to take the deal offered you? (If you can't answer this question, then you probably need to go back and reread the material that you have been given.) What is the likelihood of continued employment if you decline the current offer?

Have you noticed anything that indicates how badly the company is doing?

You have at least one thing working in your favor—you're on the inside. If things are really bad, the incentive plan might be only the beginning of a reduction in the work force in which you will be laid off anyway, have your pay frozen or cut, or be transferred to a less desirable job.

Have there already been layoffs at the company, and if so, how were they implemented?

Some companies that have not been able to reduce their payroll sufficiently through relatively humane early-retirement options resort to layoffs.

Is the early-retirement offer itself limited to one plant or one department?

If so, it probably signals significant change for those who remain. If, on the other hand, the company is offering the option across the board—say, to all employees over age fifty-five with over ten years of experience—your job may not be subject to future eliminations. *In general, the narrower the cut, the worse it bodes for those who refuse it.* If you have no choice but to take the early-retirement offer, you must plan for the future. If you have some choice, you still need to plan for the future, and your plans may influence whether or not you will take the offer.

Assuming you do have a choice and that you still enjoy working, you've got a lot of factors to weigh before making your decision. While it's true that many early-retirement incentive programs look appealing at first glance—incentives may include additional or enhanced pension benefits, retiree health insurance, and lump-sum cash benefits—you should keep in mind that the high cost of living and the erosion of purchasing power due to inflation may make such benefits much less attractive in only a few years. The following checklist will help you evaluate an early-retirement offer.

CHECKLIST FOR EVALUATING AN EARLY-RETIREMENT INCENTIVE PLAN

Determine how much choice you really have. What will happen to your company in the future? What will happen to your job? If the likely alternative is being fired, take the offer while you have the chance.

■

If you have a choice, compare the package to the retirement benefits you would receive if you continued to work—not to those you would receive if you retired immediately without the package.

■

Examine how you feel about your job, and consider how you would like to spend the next thirty or forty years of your life. Would you enjoy the leisure of leaving your job, or would you feel bored and restless?

■

Project your retirement income and expenses until age ninety. The retirement benefits that look so generous now look a lot different when you see how thirty or more years of inflation can erode your purchasing power.

■

Determine how your other resources would be affected by an early retirement.

■

Ascertain how long your severance pay and personal resources alone would be able to support you so that you can avoid steep penalties on early-retirement fund withdrawals and let your personal retirement accounts accumulate tax-free.

■

Examine prospects for continuing employment realistically. If your company offers postemployment job counseling, take advantage of it.

EARLY-RETIREMENT CHECKLIST

■

If you want to retire early, you will need to spend years planning and sacrificing to get into a position where you can do so.

■

Whether you are offered an early-retirement incentive plan package or not, you must be realistic in projecting your income and expenses. Take inflation into account, and assess your job prospects should you need to continue working.

■

If you genuinely want to retire early, expect to curtail your life-style during your retirement years. For many, the prospect of more years in retirement is worth lowering their standard of living somewhat.

Countdown to a Successful Retirement

After reading the previous chapters, you may think that you won't be able to retire until you're one hundred. But remember, virtually everything you do to preserve and improve your financial well-being during your working years is helping you prepare for retirement. Many people get a late start on saving for retirement, yet they manage quite well. All the financial hurdles you have or will have to overcome—like paying off your own education loans, buying a home, and educating your children—have been preparing you for the sacrifices that may be necessary to fund a comfortable retirement. You've succeeded in the past, and you will succeed in your retirement planning. The Retirement Planning Timetable and the Retirement Action Plan will help guide you.

Successful retirement planning begins when you begin your career and continues for the rest of your life. Take action throughout your working years to assure that you will be able to retire when you want to and how you want to.

Retirement–Planning Timetable

It's never too early to plan for retirement. To prepare for a financially comfortable retirement, you need to take action throughout your working years. These important steps to take at various ages will help you on your way to retirement.

During All Working Years

1. **MAKE** sure you always have adequate and continuous insurance coverage.

2. **GET** into the habit of living beneath your means and avoiding too much debt.

3. **PARTICIPATE** in any employer-sponsored retirement-savings plans, such as 401(k) plans and 403(b) plans.

4. **CONSIDER** the ramifications of any contemplated job change on future pension benefits. Job hopping can curtail pension benefits severely.

5.   **ROLL OVER** any vested pension benefits you receive as a result of a job change into an IRA or other tax-deferred retirement plan.

Before Age 40

1.   **CONTRIBUTE** regularly to an IRA or other retirement-earmarked savings fund.

2.   **PURCHASE** a home so that by the time you retire your housing costs will be under control.

3.   **DISCUSS** the fine points of the company pension plan with your company's benefits officer.

Age 40 to 49

1.   **PERIODICALLY CHECK** with Social Security by requesting and filing Form SSA-7004 (see page 613). You will receive a "Personal Earnings and Benefit Statement" to verify that your wages are being properly credited to your account and to help prepare retirement-income projections.

2.   **ANALYZE** your personal investments and your retirement-savings plans, and work out a plan for funding an adequate retirement income.

3.   **ACTIVELY MANAGE** your IRA and other retirement funds, with appropriate emphasis on stock and bond investments.

4.   **MAKE** a will, and review it every three years or when moving to another state. Also, prepare a durable power of attorney (or living trust) and a living will. Discuss other estate-planning techniques with an experienced estate-planning attorney.

Age 50 to 59

1.   **REQUEST** your Social Security "Personal Earnings and Benefit Statement" periodically.

2.   **REVIEW** your status with your company's pension plan regularly.

3.   **REVISE** your retirement income and expense projections, taking inflation into consideration.

4.   **REVIEW** the beneficiary and policy ownership designations on life insurance policies.

5.   **MONITOR** your personal and retirement-plan investments regularly. While you may want to reduce the risk in your investments somewhat as you approach retirement age, you still need to invest for the long term, so stocks and bonds should still play an important role in your investments.

6. **CONSIDER** devising a plan to pay your mortgage off by the time you retire.

7. **JOIN** the American Association of Retired Persons to take advantage of the many sources of information and help that they offer. (The address is: AARP, 601 E Street N.W., Washington DC 20049, (202) 434-2277.)

8. **IF YOU** are contemplating an early retirement, discuss the advantages and disadvantages with your employer's personnel officer and the local Social Security office. Evaluate thoroughly and realistically whether you can afford early retirement before doing so.

Age 60 to 64

1. **COLLECT** the documents necessary to process Social Security benefits:

   - **BOTH** spouses' Social Security cards

   - **PROOF** of both spouses' ages

   - **MARRIAGE CERTIFICATE**

   - **COPY** of latest income tax withholding statement (Form W-2)

2. **DON'T TAKE** any major actions, such as selling the house, before weighing carefully the financial and personal ramifications.

3. **DETERMINE** what your health insurance needs will be in retirement, and decide how these insurance needs will be met.

4. **IF YOU** have the option of taking a lump sum, annuity, or combination pension settlement, plan how to take the settlement. Don't forget to consider the income tax implications of each of the pension settlement options available to you.

5. **DETERMINE** the status and duration of ongoing financial commitments such as mortgages and loans.

6. **PREPARE** detailed cash-flow projections from the estimated year of retirement until at least age ninety, taking inflation and income taxes into consideration.

7. **PRACTICE** living for a month under your planned retirement income.

8. **CONSIDER** different retirement locations. If a location other than your present home is chosen, try living there for a while before making the move.

Right Before Retirement

1. **ESTABLISH** what your retirement income will be, and estimate as closely as possible what your retirement costs of living will be.

2. **CALCULATE** how much you will need to continue saving during your retirement years. (Most retirees must continue saving until at least age seventy-five.) Prepare a plan for investing these savings.

3. **HAVE** your employer's personnel officer determine exactly what your pension benefits will be, what company or bank will send the pension, and when the first check (or lump-sum distribution) will arrive; what can be done about accumulated vacation time; whether there are any special annuity benefits; and whether supplemental medical or hospital insurance is available.

4. **DISCUSS** with your spouse and family members your wishes concerning health-care needs in retirement, including contingency plans in the event of a prolonged illness, incapacity, or death of a spouse.

5. **DETERMINE** which sources of income you will access to meet living expenses during the first ten years of your retirement. You will generally be better off deferring the receipt of tax-deferred investment income such as IRAs for as long as possible.

6. **REGISTER** with the Social Security Administration for Social Security and Medicare benefits at least three months before retirement.

7. **INQUIRE** about possible entitlement to partial pensions from past jobs.

RETIREMENT ACTION PLAN

Begin by preparing projections of your retirement income and expenses. If you are within ten years of retirement, prepare these projections annually.

You cannot rely on pension and Social Security benefits alone to provide for an adequate retirement. Therefore, get into the habit of setting aside some money each year that is earmarked solely for retirement. An IRA (whether it is deductible or not) is an effective means of starting to get into this habit.

If you change jobs, roll any vested pension benefits over into an IRA immediately—no matter how small the amount may be and no matter how badly you want to use the money to buy something.

»

■ If you are self-employed, set up a retirement plan that is appropriate to your circumstances and needs.

■ If you have any net income from moonlighting (even if you are covered by a pension plan where you work), set up a simplified employee pension (SEP) plan or a Keogh plan to contribute tax-deductible money for retirement.

■ Try to be mortgage-free by retirement age. If you are a renter or will still have a large mortgage when you retire, remember that you will need a considerably larger nest egg to cover your housing costs.

■ Review your retirement-plan investments periodically. Be sure to consider them in conjunction with your entire investment portfolio—personal investments as well as retirement-plan investments.

79

Wanderlust for the Senior Set

Wanderlust for the senior set—you bet! (But you don't have to bet your bottom dollar.) Traveling is a significant life-style and financial factor for many retirees. There is an amazing array of interesting travel possibilities—often at substantial discounts of 50 percent or more—that are yours for the asking. Not surprisingly, well-informed retirees are having the traveling times of their lives.

But many aren't aware of the numerous travel discounts that are available to them. Knowing what options are available to you will allow you to take advantage of them. That's what this chapter is about. One of the best ways to begin is to read up on *how* to travel before you begin to read about where you want to go. Check out Joan Heilman's *Unbelievably Good Deals & Great Adventures That You Absolutely Can't Get Unless You're Over 50*, published by Contemporary Books; and *Get Up and Go: A Guide for the Mature Traveller*, available from P.O. Box 50820, Department 6, Reno NV 89513-9905, which is very informative, too. There are even newsletters aimed at retirees, such as *The Mature Traveller*, from P.O. Box 50820, Department 6, Reno NV 89513.

Deciding How to Go

If you are planning a trip, think about how you want to go. A prearranged tour? The cost is attractive. Solo? Too lonely and expensive for most. With a companion? You'd better pick the right one.

Many retirees enjoy the advantages that group tours offer, while others find the idea unthinkable. (For the latter, the idea of being herded from place to place with an imagined mangle of polyester tourists is as pleasurable as eating hot jalapeños for breakfast.) And while many find being left to their own devices in a foreign city frightening, many others find it exhilarating. Of course, you may prefer a compromise: traveling with a group to major destinations—countries or cities—while planning your own itinerary once you arrive.

Group Benefits

There is safety *and* savings in numbers. And don't underestimate the value of the peace of mind that comes with traveling via a prepackaged group tour, where professional guides handle the headaches of getting you and your luggage there and back. If you deal with a reputable, established tour company, you should be able to pack your worries away. AARP has its own travel services. (For land and air travel, call [800] 927-0111, and for cruises call [800] 745-4567.) Grand Circle Travel is a private firm that has specialized in senior tours for many years ([800] 221-2610).

Membership Has Its Privileges

Even if you don't like to travel in a group, just being a member of one has its privileges. For example, AARP offers its members a host of discounts on everything from cars to cruises. The National Alliance of Senior Citizens provides members with car and lodging discounts, and the National Council of Senior Citizens gives its members discount travel services.

Goodbye, Columbus

If you prefer to plan your own trip, you probably have a particular destination in mind. If, however, you know that you want to travel but haven't already chosen some specific destinations, consult the travel pages of your Sunday newspaper. *The New York Times* is a most helpful resource. It contains practical information about the mechanics of getting you from one place to another, lists of hotels, inns, bed and breakfasts, and the likes. It also advertises hotel, resort, and airline ticket deals. In addition, it includes features focusing on the art, literature, cuisine, and music of various countries and cities. Inspire yourself.

Knowledge Is Its Own Reward

Good planning, naturally enough, follows from being well informed. Did you know that most major airlines offer a variety of discount arrangements for retirees? But don't let planning be an obstacle to enjoyment. Be flexible. A great deal of the pleasure in traveling is the unforeseen opportunities for adventure that simply present themselves.

Arm Yourself with Information

There are many sources for planning your trip—home and away. Your local library should have any number of informative travel guides, and a variety of informational booklets and pamphlets published by the federal government are helpful. (See the list at the end of this chapter.) And don't overlook your travel agency. A good travel agent should be able to help you plan an affordable and interesting trip whichever way you decide to go.

Money Saver

Stretch your travel dollars by learning as much as you can about money-saving ways to travel.

Transportation

While planes, trains, and automobiles are the preferred means of transportation, you might consider something more unusual, leisurely, or adventurous.

Cruising

If you like the idea of traveling but hate checking in and out of hotels, consider taking a cruise. You can look forward to visiting a number of ports of call without having to heft a suitcase once. But don't hesitate to contact several cruise lines—Discovery, Holland, Premier, Princess, and Sitmar, to name a few—to inquire about senior discounts or other discount programs.

Take a freighter

If you have the time—thirty to one hundred and eighty days—a freighter can take you to the *most* exotic ports of call for half the cost of a cruise ship. The food and accommodations on many freighters rival those of any ship at sea, and the experience is truly once in a lifetime.

Travel to Learn

A number of programs, many of them conducted by major universities, give you the chance to tour a country or region accompanied by a scholar specializing in its art, culture, and/or history. Because many retirees are enjoying longer and longer retirements, many have chosen to continue their education in their later years. Contact your college or university's alumni office—many institutions sponsor tours of this type with faculty members.

Another possibility is Elderhostel, which sponsors programs located on university campuses; rather than going on a tour, participants travel to a campus and are housed in dormitories. In the mornings participants take classes; on afternoons and weekends, they can take part in organized trips or travel individually. Elderhostel's address is 75 Federal Street, Boston, MA 02110-1941, (617) 426-8056.

Traveling with Grandchildren

Taking trips with your grandchildren can be the most rewarding way of developing a friendship with the younger members of your family, and often it can be done at very little added cost to you. Many airlines, hotels, motels, train, and bus lines offer 50 to 100 percent discounts for your younger traveling companions. You will have to plan your trip carefully, so that everyone, both young and old, enjoys themselves and doesn't become bored or irritable. (Avoid long hours visiting art museums.) Do consult with your travel companions (as well as their parents) about itineraries. You might be in for something of a surprise. Children often choose points of interest that will appeal to you, too, while other sites, described by adult travel guide writers as "perfect for children" hold all the interests of a deflated balloon.

Keep Your Financial Wits about You

After you pack your bags, remember not to throw financial caution overboard. Travel often transforms an average savings-oriented couple into big spenders. Ordinarily thrifty seniors all too often patronize the best restaurants and shops, spend inordinate sums of money on symphony, theater and opera seats, and take enough cab rides to make even a New Yorker's head spin. As if that weren't enough, they buy the most expensive exotica for their grandchildren. What's a two-year-old going to do with that silk sarong? Use it for a bib?

How can you protect your savings from such temporary insanity? You could stay home. Instead, why not double-check the following money-saving travel tips? Whether traveling near or far, they'll show you how to go and get back without saying "bon voyage" to your savings.

TEN GREAT WAYS TO CUT YOUR TRAVEL COSTS

1. **MAKE SURE** you are adequately insured if you are traveling abroad. Most of us know whether we're adequately insured for trips within the United States. But few of us check to see if our coverage, particularly medical insurance, reaches overseas. Most standard health insurance policies are effective there, but Medicare provides almost no coverage outside the United States. If you are insured under Medicare or your policy doesn't provide the overseas coverage you need, ask your travel agent about obtaining supplementary insurance for your trip.

2. **ALWAYS GET** a second or third opinion before buying an airline ticket. Trusting a travel agent to sell you the lowest-priced ticket is like trusting a car salesman to make you a deal. Call several different agencies, and while you're at it, call the airline directly. You'll probably be amazed at the range in quotes you receive.

Smart Money Move

Always carry your prescription medications in your travel bag. Let lost luggage ruin your trip, not your health.

3. **MAKE** all airline reservations well in advance—or at the last minute. This may sound contradictory, but it isn't. There are two tried and true ways to save money on airline tickets. One is to purchase them well in advance of your departure date (three or more weeks in advance). The other is to fly standby or buy discounted travel tickets from air charter companies or cruise lines. (Many travel agents now specialize in deeply discounted travel arrangements.)

4. **GIVE UP** your seat if your flight is overbooked. For a small inconvenience you'll be amply rewarded. A free round-trip ticket to anywhere the airline flies is the usual bounty. »

5. **JOIN** frequent flyer programs. You have nothing to lose and a lot to gain (in terms of saving) by taking advantage of frequent flyer programs if you travel more than sporadically. Don't be put off by the paperwork—you'll be paid (in terms of tickets later received) about $100 per minute to fill out the application.

6. **TRAVEL** with cheap luggage. Unless you want to impress a baggage handler with your good taste, buy Naugahyde, not leather. Not only will your grandchildren think you are hip to animal rights, you will probably save enough money to spend an extra two or three days at your destination.

7. **INQUIRE** about discounts when making hotel or motel reservations. If you don't ask, no one is likely to tell you. But the truth is that discounts are almost always available for the asking—especially if you're traveling in the off-season.

8. **FIND** inexpensive places to eat. Two things to avoid like the plague, because they'll cause a plague on your pocketbook: eating in the hotel (room service is even costlier) and eating at a touristy restaurant. Find out where the locals eat. Just ask. The locals like to show off their knowledge. Another tip: Don't even open the door to your hotel room's minibar!

9. **RENT** a condo or vacation cottage rather than a room at a hotel. If you are traveling to a place that offers this choice, try it. You will have to shop around, and by all means haggle to make the price right, but it's worth it. Chances are you'll save money and have more room to relax in.

10. **NEVER EVER BUY** a trinket from a hotel or airport gift shop. You would impress your friends and relatives far more by burning a hundred-dollar bill than by spending it on a bronzed replica of the Eiffel Tower (made in Korea).

Useful Government Publications on International Travel

The U.S. government provides some excellent publications that will help you plan your international travel.

- *Health Information for International Travel* is a comprehensive listing of immunization requirements of foreign governments. In addition, it gives the U.S. Public Health Service's recommendations on immunizations and other health precautions for the international traveler. Copies are available for $6.00 from the Superintendent of Documents, U.S. Government Printing

Office, Washington DC 20402-9325; tel. (202) 783-3238.

- *Know Before You Go: Customs Hints for Returning U.S. Residents* gives detailed information on U.S. customs regulations, including duty rates. This pamphlet is available from any local customs office or by writing to the Department of the Treasury, U.S. Customs Service, P.O. Box 7407, Washington DC 20044; tel. (202) 927-6724.

- *Traveler's Tips on Bringing Food, Plant and Animal Products into the United States* explains what you can and can't bring home from your travels. This pamphlet may be obtained free of charge from the U.S. Department of Agriculture, Document Management Branch, Room #G110, 6505 Belcrest Road, Hyattsville, MD 20782; tel. (301) 436-8633.

- *Your Trip Abroad* provides basic travel information—tips on passports, visas, immunizations, and more. It will help you prepare for your trip and make it as trouble-free as possible. This publication may be ordered for $1.25 from the Superintendent of Documents, U.S. Government Printing Office, Washington DC 20402-9325; tel. (202) 783-3238.

- *A Safe Trip Abroad* gives travel security advice for any traveler, but particularly for those who plan trips to areas of high crime or terrorism. This publication may be ordered for $1.25 from the Superintendent of Documents, U.S. Government Printing Office, Washington DC 20402-9325; tel. (202) 783-3238.

- *Foreign Entry Requirements* lists visa and other entry requirements of foreign countries and tells how to apply for visas and tourist cards. This pamphlet may be purchased for fifty cents from the Consumer Information Center, Department 454Y, Pueblo CO 81009; tel. (719) 948-3334.

- *Key Officers of Foreign Service Posts* gives addresses, telephone, Telex, and fax numbers for all U.S. embassies and consulates abroad. A yearly subscription to this publication may be obtained for $5.00 from the Superintendent of Documents, U.S. Government Printing Office, Washington DC 20402-9371; tel. (202) 783-3238.

- *Background Notes* are brief, factual pamphlets on each of 170 countries in the world. They give current information on each country's people, culture, geography, history, government, economy, and political conditions. They also include a factual profile, travel notes, a country map, and a suggested reading list. These pamphlets may be purchased for $1.00 each from the Superintendent of Documents, U.S. Government Printing Office, Washington DC 20402; tel. (202) 783-3238.

Bon voyage!

SENIOR TRAVEL CHECKLIST

■□■

Plan any travel arrangements well ahead of time so that you can take the trip that you want at the price you want.

■□■

Avoid the inevitable temptation to overspend when traveling. The more you save on this trip, the sooner you can take another one.

■□■

Take advantage of the many excellent publications for travelers that are available from the U.S. Government as well as your bookstore.

Part X

Estate Planning

80

Estate Planning for the Here and Now As Well As the Hereafter

I n the pecking order of interesting personal-financial planning matters, estate planning undoubtedly ranks at the bottom. No one likes to contemplate his or her own mortality, but that's exactly what estate planning requires. The majority of adults do not even have the most basic estate-planning documents, and those who do often neglect to revise their estate plans to reflect changes in their personal circumstances or new laws and regulations.

Of course it's unpleasant to think about death, but knowing that your affairs are in order and that your heirs will be provided for is a real comfort. Chances are, your personal records will also be better organized once you get your estate in order. Whatever your situation—whether your estate is worth $2,500 or $2,500,000—the following chapters will help you focus on the all-too-easy-to-put-off topic of estate planning. As unappetizing as putting your estate in order may be, you'll feel better once it's done.

The Basics and Beyond

Every adult needs a will, and most people also need a durable power of attorney, living will, and letter of instructions. If you don't have these basic documents, you will probably cause both yourself and your loved ones a lot of grief not only after your death but during your lifetime if you become incapacitated or terminally ill. Beyond these basics, there are several more sophisticated estate-planning techniques of which you should be aware—and you don't have to be a millionaire to take advantage of them.

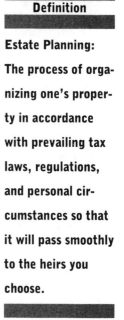

Definition

Estate Planning: The process of organizing one's property in accordance with prevailing tax laws, regulations, and personal circumstances so that it will pass smoothly to the heirs you choose.

Fundamentals of Estate Planning

E very stage of your estate planning should be concerned with minimizing inconvenience and legal problems and saving taxes. But the most important goal of estate planning is retaining control over *your* assets, both during your lifetime and even after death. Through careful planning, you can control the distribution of your estate free of interference from the government and the court system. Hence, every estate plan should include a will that specifies exactly how the estate is to be divided. By taking the time to draw up a will, you are assured that your estate will be settled in the way you want. Without a will, the probate courts will distribute the estate and more than likely will follow a set of prescribed formulas and procedures. The result is not only higher-than-necessary legal fees but a badly distributed estate as well. If you die without a will when your children are quite young, for example, do you know that in most states your children will inherit half of your estate? If you had a will, you would almost certainly have bequeathed all of your estate to your spouse.

The way you own property may also be important in estate planning. The type of ownership—whether sole tenancy, joint tenancy, or in trust—affects the rights and limitations of ownership. Shifting funds into trusts, either during one's lifetime or after death, is one way to transfer funds to your heirs in accordance with your wishes, but this strategy may be too inflexible to take into account any future changes in family circumstances.

Of course, a will is only the first step in a sound estate plan. The main drawback of a simple will is that it cannot fulfill the second objective of estate planning, which, for people who have large estates, is tax savings. To save as much in estate taxes as possible and hence to increase the value of the estate you can pass on to your heirs, an estate plan should balance the many options available. And while you probably understand the need to have certain basic estate-planning documents, including a will, you may not be familiar with the range of estate-planning stategies and techniques that can help you in the here and now as well as benefit your heirs in the hereafter.

Estate-Planning Objectives

T he following objectives should be kept in mind when devising your estate plan.

Minimize the problems and expenses of probate, and avoid potential family conflicts

The more tangled an estate plan you weave, the greater the expense—and the greater the possibility of family conflict—you bequeath. Detail your intentions about your estate so that confusion over your intentions doesn't lead to your inheritors squabbling over and squandering your estate.

Provide your surviving spouse with as much responsibility and flexibility in estate management as desired, consistent with potential tax savings

If he or she is up to the challenge, you should give your spouse or partner the necessary understanding and power to steer your estate during its most crucial passage through tax-infested waters. But when you sit down to chart this out, don't forget about testamentary trusts. (See page 739.) Such trusts, while removing your spouse from direct control of certain aspects of your estate, could in fact end up being in the best interest of your beneficiaries.

Provide for the conservation of your estate and its effective management following your death or the death of your spouse

If you have a spouse, children, and/or grandchildren, don't leave home without making sure your estate plans are in order. Your estate plan should include contingency plans to provide for your survivors in the event of your death.

Minimize death taxes as well as income taxes after death

If your estate is large enough to incur state death taxes and federal estate taxes, there may be actions you can take now to minimize them. The sooner you undertake estate-tax-saving strategies, the better.

Avoid leaving your children "too much too soon"

Many people become so concerned about providing generously for their children that they overlook matters that should influence how their estate should be distributed. Don't make this mistake. For example, consider the varying degrees of need that each child has, and don't turn a blind eye to tell-tale signs of financially inept children.

Provide for adequate liquidity to cover taxes and other expenses at death without the necessity of forced sale of assets

Given the variety of investments that can be easily "cashed in," it is surprising how many people forget to factor them into their estate planning. Lack of adequate liquidity at the time of your death could burden your heirs with the stressful task of forced sale of your estate assets in order to provide immediate capital. At-death and after-death expenses are numerous and must be accounted for:

- EXPENSES OF FINAL ILLNESS AND FUNERAL EXPENSES

- FEDERAL ESTATE TAXES AND STATE DEATH TAXES

- FEDERAL AND STATE INCOME TAXES

- PROBATE AND ADMINISTRATION EXPENSES

- PAYMENT OF MATURING DEBTS

- MAINTENANCE AND WELFARE OF THE FAMILY

- **PAYMENT OF SPECIFIC CASH BEQUESTS**

- **FUNDS TO CONTINUE RUNNING A FAMILY BUSINESS**

These needs must be estimated so you can devise an estate plan that will provide your survivors with ready access to sufficient resources to meet these needs.

Provide for estate management in the event of serious disability of you or your spouse

Plan for the event of serious disability—it's not uncommon these days. Provide for someone to look after your finances in the event you are unable to do so.

Assemble copies of all important documents affecting your estate plan in a documents portfolio. Make certain all appropriate family members know where to find them

A thorough letter of instructions accompanied by supporting documentation will go a long way toward easing the burden on your survivors of settling your estate. Also, make it a point to review and update your document portfolio at least annually.

Inform all family members about your overall estate plan

Make a point of periodically discussing the specifics of your estate plan with your spouse and children or other family members.

Getting Started

I n order to save time and fees, you should gather together all the necessary information before sitting down with an estate planning attorney. In addition, you should discuss estate-planning objectives with your spouse and adult children beforehand so that any personal family disagreements can be settled and decisions made without the estate planner being paid to act as a referee.

Money Saver

Organize your records (and thoughts) before going to see your estate-planning attorney.

Necessary Information

The following information should be gathered:

- **YOUR FULL NAME,** including any nicknames or other names used in the titles to any of the estate property.

- **THE FULL NAMES** of your spouse, children, grandchildren, and any other parties that you would like to include in the estate-planning documents.

- **YOUR DATE OF BIRTH,** address, state of legal residence, and pertinent medical history; the same applies for your spouse, children, grandchildren and any other beneficiaries.

- **A SUMMARY** of investments, pension plans, Social Security status, and any other benefits that are producing or will produce income for you.

- **FUNDS** that you are receiving or will receive as the beneficiary of a trust.

- **YOUR RESPONSIBILITIES** as a guardian or trustee for another party, if any.

- **GIFTS** made to children or others and any taxes paid on these gifts.

- **NAMES** and addresses of persons you appoint as guardians of minor children and details of specific requests to these guardians, if any.

- **NAMES** and addresses of persons who will be named as executors, health-care proxies, trustees, and any other fiduciaries.

- **IN ADDITION,** copies of pertinent documents, such as deeds, income tax returns, insurance policies, and certificates should be made available to the person who will prepare your will and other estate-planning documents.

Once this information has been gathered, you and your estate planner should prepare an estimate of your estate's value. Your estate's value is the total value of all your property, less any debts you have as well as funeral costs, executor compensation, and a few other items. You need to have a good idea of your estate's value so that the appropriate estate planning tools and strategies can be utilized.

ESTATE SIZE ESTIMATION WORKSHEET

Your estate planning will be easier—and ultimately more successful—if you have an accurate idea of the overall value of your estate before you begin thinking about how you would like to dispose of it. This worksheet will help you determine how much your estate will be worth after settlement costs.

Gross estate

CHECKING AND SAVINGS ACCOUNTS	$...............................
MUTUAL FUND INVESTMENTS	....
STOCK INVESTMENTS	....
INTEREST–EARNING INVESTMENTS	....
REAL–ESTATE INVESTMENTS	....
LIFE INSURANCE PROCEEDS	.... »

Smart Money Move

Estimate the size of your estate in order to determine the best estate-planning strategies.

ESTATE SIZE ESTIMATION WORKSHEET < CONT'D >

PERSONAL PROPERTY AND OTHER ASSETS ....

TOTAL VALUE OF GROSS ESTATE $....................................

Liabilities

UNPAID MORTGAGE BALANCE(S) ....

MISCELLANEOUS DEBTS AND LIENS ....

SETTLEMENT COSTS (executor's commissions, attorney's fees, etc.
These costs usually amount to 5 to 10% of an estate's
gross value.) ....

FUNERAL EXPENSES ....

TOTAL LIABILITIES ....

ESTIMATED TAXABLE ESTATE VALUE $....................................

By subtracting the total liabilities from your gross estate, you will know the net pretax value of your estate. Now you can begin deciding how to structure your estate plan and, if necessary, to undertake strategies to minimize your estate tax liability.

Guidelines for an Appropriate Strategy

Of course, the value of your estate will change over the years. That's why your estate plan needs to be reviewed periodically. The following guidelines may be helpful in deciding on an appropriate estate-planning strategy:

- FOR ESTATES BELOW THE $600,000 FEDERAL ESTATE TAX EXEMPTION LIMIT: Federal and state death tax savings are of little concern here since estates under $600,000 are not subject to federal estate taxes, although in some states, the state death tax burden might need to be considered. A proper combination of joint ownership of property between you and your spouse along with a will and, perhaps, a living trust should provide for an uncomplicated settlement of the estate. Trusts incorporated in your will can be used if there are minor children, other dependents, or unusual circumstances.

- FOR ESTATES JUST ABOVE THE AMOUNT OF THE FEDERAL ESTATE TAX EXEMPTION: The use of annual gifts should bring the estate value closer to, if not below, the $600,000 exemption limit. Such planning, along with joint ownership of property between you and your spouse, plus a will, should reduce taxes and simplify probate proceedings. If you have an estate of this size, however, be cautioned against giving away so much money that you jeopardize your future financial well-being. Your estate planning attorney might recommend the use of a so-called "bypass" trust (see page 742) as an estate-tax-saving strategy.

- **FOR ESTATES VALUED WELL ABOVE THE $600,000 EXEMPTION LIMIT:** A variety of methods may be used to achieve estate-planning objectives (like a bypass trust). For the largest estates, plans can be complicated and should be drafted by an experienced estate-planning attorney.

Making Important Estate-Planning Decisions

Property Ownership Designations

Joint ownership of property is common, particularly among married couples, and it can be advantageous from an estate-planning standpoint if the estate is fairly small. But jointly held property is not desirable in many instances; in fact, it is possible that the property may be subject to estate taxation twice in the case of property held jointly with someone other than a spouse. (See page 722 for more information to help you make the correct property ownership designations.)

Selection of an Executor

A close relative is a natural choice for an executor, and while it usually works out well, sometimes it does not. The reasons a relative may not be an appropriate executor include inexperience (particularly with complicated estates), lack of time to devote to any details of proper estate administration, or inability to get along with other relatives (see page 722).

Multistate Property Ownership

More and more people divide their time between two states and/or own property in more than one state. Those in this situation need to be particularly careful about establishing primary residence in one state—ideally the one with the more advantageous (to you) state death tax rules. Even when your state of residence is well established, there may still be problems if you own property in more than one state: each state may attempt to collect death taxes on your property. Sometimes a living trust can alleviate these problems, but you will need legal advice.

Spousal Transfers

The unlimited marital deduction allows one spouse to pass his or her entire estate to the other, completely free of federal estate taxes. The regulations regarding marital deductions in individual states vary. But giving all of your estate to your spouse may not always be the best method of transferring property between spouses (see page 730).

711

Lifetime Gifts

The *annual gift tax exclusion* allows you to give up to $10,000 per year to any number of people ($20,000 per year to married couples), as well as direct payments of tuition to educational institutions and for medical expenses. While gifts to children and grandchildren are a convenient way for affluent families to reduce the size of their taxable estate during their lifetimes, you should be cautioned against being so generous that you end up jeopardizing your own financial well-being. Be particularly wary of giving money to children with the expectation that they will pay it back.

Finally, avoid giving money to relatives so that you can qualify for Medicaid in the event you must enter a nursing home. This practice is riddled with problems, not the least of which is that you may not get your money back if and when you later need it.

Disposition of a Family Business

If you own a closely held business, you face particularly thorny estate-planning issues. Careful planning is necessary to assure that your business can continue operating successfully should you die.

If and when you get ready to sell your business, whether to family members or outsiders, other estate-planning matters may need to be considered, particularly if you intend to keep the business in the family (see page 714).

Charitable Gifts

Charitable gifts made during your lifetime provide a dual tax advantage. First, you get a charitable deduction on your tax bill. Second, when you make such a gift, its value (plus any future appreciation) is removed from your estate, which will eventually save estate taxes. There are certain limitations on charitable deductions with which you should become familiar if you intend to make substantial charitable gifts.

When you make a charitable bequest in your will, your taxable estate is reduced by the amount of the gift. There are no limitations. Charitable giving can also be carried out through a so-called *charitable remainder* arrangement. Charitable remainder trusts (described on page 743) allow you to have your cake and eat it, too. In return for a donation of property or cash, you are entitled to a partial tax deduction for the amount of your donation, plus, of course, you remove this property from your taxable estate. There is more: In return for your donation the charity provides you with a lifetime annuity income.

Trusts

Whether they are established during your lifetime (living trusts) or take effect upon your death (testamentary trusts), trusts can provide a great deal of flexibility in how your estate is handled and distributed. For example, some people are uncomfortable with the thought that their spouses and children will receive inheritances with no strings attached. But a simple will (and most wills are simple wills) does just that. Some trusts have the added advantage of saving taxes and/or protecting your estate from creditors. (Chapter 82 explains many trust arrangements.)

A DOZEN WAYS TO REDUCE YOUR ESTATE TAXES

Most people think that they don't have enough money to be concerned about estate taxes—but many of them are wrong. Even though you may not have much in the way of assets now, you may in the future. Therefore, it behooves you to at least consider techniques that you can employ to reduce your estate taxes. While most planning strategies end up saving money only after your demise, some may actually provide tax savings during your lifetime.

1. **IF** you have a large estate and can afford it, take advantage of the annual gift exclusion to transfer assets to children and grandchildren. You can reduce the size of your taxable estate by giving as much as $10,000 away per donee. In other words, you and your spouse could give as much as $20,000 per year to each of your children and grandchildren, and anyone else, for that matter. Of course, they will love to receive the money.

2. **A "BYPASS TRUST"** can increase the amount of money your heirs will inherit. The estate tax savings of a bypass trust can be dramatic, although you won't live to see them. If you are married and your estate is likely to exceed $600,000 in value, you should consult your attorney about establishing a trust under the terms of your will. On the death of your spouse, your heirs will save as much as $235,000 in estate taxes by having the language necessary to establish this straightforward trust established in both your and your spouse's wills. (See page 740.)

3. **CONSULT** with an attorney about taking advantage of the $600,000 unified credit during your lifetime. Affluent individuals are often advised to make transfers of up to $600,000 to their heirs during their lifetime, rather than deferring the credit until the estate is eventually settled. Incidentally, the $600,000 unified credit is the maximum amount of your estate that you can pass on free of federal estate taxes, either during your lifetime or after your death. This is *in addition to* the $10,000 annual gift exclusion.

4. **TRANSFERRING ASSETS** to irrevocable trusts during your life can reduce estate taxes. Irrevocable trusts have a variety of advantages, including their ability to reduce the taxes that would eventually be levied on your estate. But as the name suggests, these transfers can't be undone, so they require a great deal of thought on your part.

»

5. **CONSIDER** putting your life insurance policy into a life insurance trust. Taking this action could result in dramatic estate tax savings for your heirs. When you simply name beneficiaries to your life insurance policy, the policy's proceeds will be included in your estate for tax purposes. If you think that your—or your spouse's—estate will be sufficiently large to be subject to estate taxes, consider transferring your life insurance policy into a life insurance trust.

6. **TRANSFER** an unneeded life insurance policy to a charity. If you own a life insurance policy that your heirs don't need, consider naming a charity as its beneficiary. That way, your estate won't have to pay taxes on the death benefits. You'll get a charitable deduction for the donation and possibly other benefits as well.

7. **CHECK** with your lawyer to see if there is any action you should take to minimize state death taxes. Just as there are ways to reduce, if not eliminate, federal estate taxes, state death tax-saving opportunities may be available in your own state. Ask your estate-planning attorney to review your situation and suggest any actions that should be taken to minimize these taxes.

8. **MOVE** to a state that has lower death taxes. The death tax that a state can assess varies dramatically from state to state. You can save your heirs a considerable amount of money by moving to a state that levies low death taxes.

9. **DON'T DESIGNATE YOURSELF** as custodian for a child's investment account. It may be customary and convenient to name yourself as custodian when you give money to your kids. But this could backfire since the IRS will still include those assets in your taxable estate if you die before your child reaches age eighteen or twenty-one, depending on state law.

10. **PAY** college tuition for grandchildren directly to the college. In estate-planning parlance, there is an unlimited gift tax exclusion for qualifying payments of tuition. In plain English this means that, in addition to the $10,000 annual gift exclusion, you are permitted to make tuition payments on behalf of grandchildren (or anyone else for that matter) without running afoul of the gift and estate tax rules. Be sure to make these payments directly to the educational institution so that there is no question about how the money is used.

11. **INVESTIGATE** ways to transfer your family business to younger family members in order to reduce your estate tax liability. While Congress has tightened the rules on passing family businesses on to children, there are still opportunities to make a transfer while minimizing estate taxes. What is required? A lot of planning, in consultation with an expert in these matters.

»

12.   **DON'T DELAY** if you are planning to utilize sophisticated estate-planning techniques. Of course it's unpleasant dealing with estate-planning matters because they remind us of our own mortality. But there is reason not to tarry, beyond the obvious one that we never know when the grim reaper will come calling. Congress has been threatening over the past few years to curtail many of the estate-tax-saving benefits available to people with large estates. Someday Congress will make good on this threat, although it is very unlikely that the more restrictive rules will apply to those estate plans and trusts that have already been implemented. So don't waste time.

FOR FURTHER INFORMATION

The following IRS publications address key areas of estate taxes:

*   *Federal Estate and Gift Taxes,* Publication 448

*   *Tax Information for Survivors,* Publication 559

All are free. Call the Internal Revenue Service at (800) 829-3676.

ESTATE PLANNING ACTION PLAN

This Estate Planning Action Plan will help you get your estate in order. If you are uncertain whether some of the items apply to your situation, review the next three chapters, where important estate-planning matters are discussed in further detail.

		CURRENT STATUS	
		NEEDS ACTION	OKAY, OR NOT APPLICABLE
1.	**DETERMINE** your wishes for the ultimate disposition of your estate.	[ ]	[ ]
2.	**HAVE** an attorney prepare an up-to-date will that is consistent with your personal wishes and circumstances.	[ ]	[ ]
3.	**NAME** an appropriate executor. (Your spouse or children may not be the best choice.)	[ ]	[ ]

»

	CURRENT STATUS	
	NEEDS ACTION	OKAY, OR NOT APPLICABLE
4. PREPARE and keep up to date a letter of instructions.	[ ]	[ ]
5. ESTABLISH a durable power of attorney or living trust that protects you in the event of incapacity.	[ ]	[ ]
6. DESIGNATE competent guardians for your children and, if applicable, disabled adults.	[ ]	[ ]
7. PREPARE a living will and health care proxy.	[ ]	[ ]
8. MARRIED PEOPLE often assume that one spouse—typically, the husband—will predecease the other spouse. Evaluate the personal and estate-planning effects if the assumed order of death does not occur.	[ ]	[ ]
9. DECIDE if your estate plan should include provisions for any heir or dependent who may have special needs.	[ ]	[ ]
10. ESTIMATE the amount of state and federal taxes your estate will have to pay.	[ ]	[ ]
11. DETERMINE if your estate has enough readily accessible money to meet the immediate cash needs of your survivors.	[ ]	[ ]
12. MAKE SURE that the title in which you hold property (single ownership, joint partnership, etc.) is appropriate from an estate planning standpoint.	[ ]	[ ]
13. MAKE SURE any gifts to relatives and/or charitable contributions are compatible with your financial condition and overall estate planning.	[ ]	[ ]
14. IF you own property in more than one state, take appropriate actions to minimize probate problems upon your demise.	[ ]	[ ]
15. IF you have your own business, provisions for		

»

		CURRENT STATUS	
		NEEDS ACTION	OKAY, OR NOT APPLICABLE
	its disposition in the event of your death should be made.	[ ]	[ ]
16.	**CONSIDER** the use of revocable and irrevocable trusts as part of the estate-planning process.	[ ]	[ ]
17.	**INFORM** your family and other beneficiaries of your estate plans.	[ ]	[ ]
18.	**INFORM** your family of any employee benefits that will be paid or available upon death.	[ ]	[ ]
19.	**MAKE** your funeral wishes known to your family.	[ ]	[ ]
20.	**IF** you have elderly parents, inquire periodically as to the status of their personal finances and estate plans.	[ ]	[ ]
21.	**BE SURE** that the attorney who handles your estate planning is up to the task. If your estate is quite large or complex, you should retain a highly qualified and experienced estate-planning attorney.	[ ]	[ ]

81

Basic Estate-Planning Documents

S ome things you can't live without. This chapter, and the two that follow, concern matters in your financial life that you can't (or shouldn't) die without. Chief among them is a will, but there are others, including a durable power of attorney or living trust, a living will, and a letter of instructions. Many of us fail to complete even the most basic estate-planning documents, or we neglect to revise our estate plan to reflect changes in personal circumstances or new laws and regulations. While it's unpleasant to contemplate the possibility of our own demise, it is far more satisfying to know that our affairs have been put in order. Beyond these basics, there are several more sophisticated estate-planning techniques of which you should be aware—and you don't have to be a Rockefeller to take advantage of them. These are discussed in Chapter 82.

Your estate may well be worth more than you realize. Even if you have prepared an estate plan in the past, your estate—or your attitude toward it—may have changed since you last reviewed matters. Have you had any children or grandchildren since you last revised your will? Have any of your intended heirs died, married, divorced, or become disabled since your will was prepared? These events may require a revision of your estate-planning documents. It's certainly worth the time and possible expense to update an out-of-date estate plan. You'll sleep more soundly, and your heirs will be grateful.

What Is Congress Up To?

Another matter of importance: Congress is beginning to pay more attention to the estate and gift tax as a means of raising additional revenue. This doesn't bode well for even moderately affluent families. According to many experts, this tightening of estate and gift tax laws will probably not affect existing estate plans. The looming possibility of estate tax reform *makes it all the more important* to attend to estate-planning matters sooner rather than later.

Estate planning need not be complicated to be effective. A simple estate plan can save legal fees, prevent unnecessary delays, and ensure that your estate will be distributed according to your wishes. It may also have some positive effects while you are still alive. If you are single, you should certainly plan your estate, because state laws governing intestacy (dying without a will) may not distribute the estate the same way you would have. You may want to leave at least a portion of your estate to a friend or to charity, for example, but if you die without a will, the court will generally require that the estate be distributed to your blood relatives—and the relatives who end up with your estate may not be the ones of your choosing.

A Stripped-Down Estate Plan

A minimum estate plan usually consists of four documents:

- A VALID AND UP-TO-DATE WILL

- A DURABLE POWER OF ATTORNEY OR LIVING TRUST

- A LIVING WILL

- A LETTER OF INSTRUCTIONS

Each of these documents is discussed in detail below.

Prepare and keep up-to-date basic estate planning documents (unless you dislike your heirs).

Valid and Up-to-Date Will

Everyone knows the importance of preparing and maintaining a will, yet many people have never written one. Your will should specify exactly how your estate is to be divided, including, if appropriate, a list that indicates which heirs are to receive which specific items of personal property. More on this below.

Although your will should be drawn up by a lawyer, you (and when possible, your heirs) should be familiar with its general form and contents. The following items should be included:

- YOUR FULL NAME

- A STATEMENT that the document is a will

- THE DATE

- A STATEMENT revoking all previous wills

- SPECIFIC BEQUESTS and provisions for the death of the named beneficiaries. (A specific bequest is for the transfer of a particular piece of property to a named beneficiary.)

- GENERAL BEQUESTS (which do not specify from which part of the estate the property is to be taken), with provisions for the death of the named beneficiaries

- INSTRUCTIONS for dividing the residuary (that is, the total amount of the estate remaining after these specific and general bequests have been made).

- PROVISIONS for trusts, if any, including the names of selected trustees and successor trustees

- **STATEMENTS** of who should be presumed to have died first (either husband or wife), should both die in a common accident. (This allows both wills to be processed without complications.)

- **NAMES** of guardians and alternative guardians for minor children, if necessary, or for a handicapped dependent under your care

- **NAMES** of the executor and substitute executor

- **YOUR SIGNATURE.** Your will should be signed in the presence of witnesses. In general, it is preferable to have disinterested witnesses at the signing of the will. In some states, the validity of the will may be questioned or denied if the signing is witnessed by individuals who have an immediate financial interest in your will.

- **ANY MAJOR CHANGES** in the form of codicils (a will amendment). Codicils must be witnessed and signed, just like the original will.

Important Considerations in Drafting a Will

A will is an essential estate-planning document—don't leave home without it! A common misconception is that a will limits your flexibility. This is by no means the case, as a will can always be changed to reflect changes in your circumstances or desires. In fact, changing the will to reflect such changes is an important part of estate planning. Getting married or divorced, starting a family, losing loved ones, and becoming disabled all are changes that more likely than not will require revisions in your will. Indeed, in many states, marriage, divorce, or a new baby invalidates any existing will. You can either write a new will that declares any previous wills to be invalid or append a codicil to an existing will. Moving to a new state may invalidate a will drawn up under the laws of your previous state. Codicils are subject to the same legal stipulations as are wills. Earlier wills should be saved for reference: If a current will is declared invalid, the latest dated, legally valid will is considered as your legal will.

Smart Money Move

If there's a change in your family circumstances or if you move to a new state, ask your attorney if your will needs to be changed.

Before your death, your will is a private document, the contents of which need not be known to anyone other than you and your attorney. The two signing witnesses must see you—the testator—sign the document, and they must know that you intend the document to be your will, but they do not need to know its contents. In some states, the witnesses do not even have to see you sign as long as you acknowledge to them that the signature is yours.

Upon your death, however, the will becomes a publicly accessible legal document that is under the jurisdiction of the probate court system. I recommend that, despite the privacy afforded by a will, its contents be discussed with your intended heirs. Doing so not only gives you the opportunity to explain or clarify certain will provisions to those directly involved, it improves the chances that your will's provisions will be carried out as indicated, without doubts or animosity.

Deciding who gets what

The first step in drawing up your will is to decide which of your assets should go to which inheritor. All valuable possessions should be clearly identified in the will, along with your designated inheritors. It is also advisable to include the manner in which your less valuable personal possessions are to be distributed. Alternatively, a list indicating specifically how personal possessions are to be distributed could be included in your letter of instructions. (A letter of instructions, however, does not have the legal standing of a will.) Very elderly individuals who have not yet divided up their personal possessions might be advised to place color stickers in an inconspicuous place on individual possessions, each color indicating a specific heir. The explanation of which color belongs to which heir can be included in the letter of instructions.

Disposing of certain possessions before death may also be advisable for older people who may no longer need certain items. They will save themselves (and their heirs) a great deal of trouble by giving away, donating, or selling unneeded possessions before they die.

Designating Your Executor(s)

When your will is created, you will have to appoint an executor (also referred to as a personal representative) to ensure that the settlement of your estate is properly administered upon your death. Otherwise, the courts will appoint one.

What does an executor do?

An executor ensures that your will is probated and that the wishes stipulated in your will are properly carried out. The executor assembles and arranges for the appraisal of your assets, liquidates assets as required, and distributes the estate according to the will. He or she also files income tax, estate tax, and inheritance tax returns and pays the debts and taxes for the estate. All these matters need to be settled in accordance with legal and tax requirements. Failure to do so may result in penalties.

Smart Money Move

Avoid family squabbles by stipulating in your will who gets which specific personal possessions.

An executor should have financial knowledge, be a reliable record-keeper, and be sensitive to the needs of your beneficiaries. He or she should also be trustworthy, have high ethical standards, and have sufficient time to perform all the duties of an executor—which can be time-consuming. Family members may not be up to the task. If you want to appoint a family member as an executor but don't want to burden them with all the details, mention in your will that you expect them to hire necessary professionals (lawyers, accountants, and the like) to assist in settling your estate. For a large estate, you could consider appointing a bank trust department, estate-planning attorney, or other professional to serve as the executor. Assigning a professional to this position removes the burden from your family and lowers the possibility that any conflicts of interest might arise. On the other hand, professionals may be rather impersonal for a family that has suffered a traumatic loss. A solution could be to appoint co-executors (for example, a bank trust department and a family member) and thus get both the financial expertise and the personal touch.

Where should you store your will?

There should be only one original copy of a will at any given time, although it is advisable to make photocopies for your files and for family members. Deciding where to keep the original copy of the will is a vexing problem. Options including a home safe, a business safe, a bank safe-deposit box, your lawyer's office, a trust company if one has been named as an executor, or the clerk of your local probate court, who will hold it for safekeeping in a sealed envelope.

Where you should ideally store your will really depends on state and local probate law. Many such statutes automatically seal the safe-deposit box upon death, making the will inaccessible pending a court order. Wherever you decide to store your will, always make certain that the location of your original will is known by family members or close friends.

Review your will regularly

Things change. Family circumstances change, and your financial status changes as well. People move to different states. Federal and state tax laws change. Therefore, you must periodically review and revise your will to ensure that its contents conform to current laws and regulations and that it reflects your current status and desires.

Joint wills are a bad idea

Some related parties, particularly married couples, prepare a joint will, under the terms of which they leave everything to each other or to specified beneficiaries if they die together. Joint wills can create problems and unexpected litigation. Questions naturally arise as to whether one of you can change the terms of the will without the consent of the other. Separation and divorce can cause additional problems. Some joint wills obligate the survivor to make bequests to specific persons. This may, under some state laws, not qualify for the marital deduction and could therefore be subject to tax. Joint wills are a bad idea—everyone should have his or her own individual will.

Smart Money Move

If you choose a family member as executor, make sure he or she is up to the task. If necessary, empower your executor to hire the necessary professionals to settle your estate.

If You Die Without a Will

The legal term for dying without a valid will is dying *intestate.* If you die intestate, your heirs will be faced with estate planning's worst-case scenario. If you simply "haven't gotten around to" drafting a will, consider this: If you die without one, the state will have complete power to determine the disposition of your estate.

State intestacy laws

When you die intestate, the state courts will step into the fray. Each state has its own laws governing intestacy. In most states, however, the first action the court will take is to appoint an *administrator* for your estate. Your spouse will probably be saddled with that thankless task, or the court may appoint one of your children or grandchildren. Essentially, the court will go through the line of succession until it reaches the first qualified individual able to administer your estate. In cases where no survivors are available or able to serve as administrator, the court appoints a public administrator.

State law often hobbles the ability of the administrator to act effectively. For instance, should real estate need to be sold to pay your estate's bills, a court order may first be necessary if minors have any claim to the property. (Under most state laws, real estate passes intact to your survivors. Any decision about disposing of real estate must thus be unanimous.) Obtaining a court order can be costly, as can having to post a bond, which your estate's administrators must also do.

In addition, your administrator will have no say over how the property is distributed to heirs. Instead, a group of statutes known as the *laws of descent and distribution* mandate to whom the estate will go once all liabilities have been satisfied. Typically, the law would divide your property between your spouse and children—approximately half to the spouse and half to the children. The exact proportion involved would depend on the particularities of a given state's intestacy code. There are a thousand permutations of the law designed to meet every possible combination of survivors. The law is rigid in its prescriptions, however, and more than a few intestate estates have been gerrymandered under laws that reflected very little of the survivors' actual needs. Indeed, the laws of descent and distribution almost never reflect the decedent's wishes, particularly where a spouse and children are involved. Enough said.

Durable Power of Attorney, or Living Trust

If you ever become incapacitated (through accident, illness, or just plain aging) and are unable to handle your own affairs, a court order may revoke your right to manage your own money and appoint a guardian or conservator. It is possible that the court will not appoint the guardian that you would have chosen. Even if the court ultimately does approve your choice of guardian, the approval process will be subject to unnecessary red tape and confusion. The simplest way to protect yourself—and to ensure that your property will continue to be managed as you see fit—is to appoint a guardian for yourself through a durable power of attorney.

Preparing a durable power of attorney ensures that if you ever become unable to manage your own financial and personal affairs, someone that you trust will act on your behalf. A power of attorney may be special—applying to only certain situations—or general, giving the attorney-in-fact virtually limitless control over your affairs. General powers of attorney may be dangerous, are subject to abuse, and are usually unnecessary.

If you use special powers of attorney, you can give different people responsibility for different jobs. For example, you may want one person to make decisions regarding your health care and housing but another to manage your finances. A power of attorney may also be either indefinite (durable) or last for a specific length of time. No matter how it is assigned, it may be canceled at any time, and it terminates immediately upon your death.

Living Trusts

An alternative to a durable power of attorney is a living trust. Living trusts can provide a variety of estate-planning advantages, such as avoiding probate and keeping your financial matters private. Living trusts allow you to specify who you want to take over your financial affairs if you become incapacitated. Living trusts may be preferred by residents of states where the probate process is particularly burdensome.

A *funded living trust*—not to be confused with a living will—is used to hold your property, naming yourself as the principal beneficiary. Regardless of your age or mental condition, the trustee is legally bound to act in your best interests according to the trust's instructions.

A variation of the funded living trust is the *standby trust,* which can be established under a revocable agreement stating that assets can be transferred into the trust only if you become unable to manage your own finances. As long as the trust remains unfunded, there may not be any administration fees.

Living trusts have become a hot product of late, and many attorneys and financial institutions have been aggressively promoting them. Many people have been led to believe that living trusts are the answer to every problem of their estate planning. This is not necessarily the case. While many people can benefit from living trust arrangements, for others, establishing a living trust is a waste of time and money. How do you determine if a living trust makes sense for you?

Don't rely on an attorney who advertises or gives seminars on living trusts—it's obvious what these people will tell you. Instead, speak with an attorney who is experienced in estate planning but who doesn't ballyhoo the supposed virtues of living trusts. In other words, consult with an attorney who can give you an objective evaluation of whether a living trust is right for you. (For more on living trusts, see page 741.)

Living Will

A dvances in medical technology mean, plain and simple, that people's lives can be sustained even when they are terminally ill. A living will is a document, signed by you and witnessed, that tells your health-care provider that you do not want life-prolonging medical procedures when recovery from the condition is impossible and there is no chance of your regaining a meaningful life. Living will laws vary from state to state in specific details, but each permits an individual to direct his or her own terminal care and protects the attending physician from liability.

Specific information on living wills can be found by consulting with an attorney or by contacting Choice in Dying. (The address and telephone number for this organization, which publishes several informative booklets, appears at the end of this chapter.)

The legal and religious aspects of living wills are controversial. Nevertheless, a living will in the hands of family, physician, clergy, or attorney may persuade the court to allow the individual his or her right to die. Everyone should consider preparing a living will. It is advisable for anyone who spends significant time (such as winters or summers) in a state away from his or her home state to execute the correct statutory living will documents for *that* state as well as his or her home state. Choice in Dying provides living will forms that are recognized by the individual states.

Numerous right-to-die court decisions have emphasized the necessity of having "clear and convincing" evidence of a patient's wishes before a person can exercise his or her right to die. If you write a living will, explicitly state your wishes to ensure that your intent will later be judged sufficiently clear that it can be honored. To further clarify this intent, attach a *medical directive* to the living will specifying treatments in different scenarios. In addition, compose a personal statement explaining the rationale and feelings behind these choices.

You should consider redating and resigning your living will periodically before witnesses and a notary. Not only will a recent reaffirmation carry extra weight with doctors, hospitals, and judges, it will force you to reconsider your position as circumstances change.

Smart Money Move

Living trusts are greatly oversold. Make sure you will truly benefit from a living trust before going to the expense.

Health-care proxy

In conjunction with a living will, your attorney may also recommend (and many states require) a health-care proxy. This document designates the person whom you want to make health-care decisions on your behalf in the event you become incapacitated. Generally, a health-care proxy and a living will each carries out a distinct function. A living will provides guidance to health-care personnel and family members as to your wishes regarding life-sustaining treatment, while a health-care proxy names the person who is responsible for making health-care decisions on your behalf.

Remember, your living will must be written and executed while you are competent and of sound mind. Choose two adult witnesses who are not related to you, are not entitled to any part of your estate, and are not your doctor, and have the document notarized.

Letter of Instructions

A letter of instructions is not as important as a will, durable power of attorney, or living will, but many people—myself included—think it's the one thing you can do that will most ease the way for your survivors during a difficult time. You'll certainly be doing your heirs and survivors a big favor by preparing one. A letter of instructions is an informal document (you don't need a lawyer to prepare one) that gives your survivors information concerning important financial and personal matters. Although it does not carry the legal weight of a will, the letter of instructions is very important because in it you can clarify any further requests to be carried out upon your death and provide essential financial information, thus relieving the surviving family members of needless worry and speculation.

The most common areas covered in letters of instructions are as follows:

- **INSTRUCTIONS** on whom to contact and what to do immediately after your death

- **FUNERAL INSTRUCTIONS**

- **DIRECTIONS** for handling other important financial matters that need immediate attention

- **AN INVENTORY** and explanation of investments, insurance policies, and other important personal financial matters

- **PERSONAL WISHES.** Although this letter is not a binding legal document, this may be the place to express your wishes about the education of your children, how you would like your heirs to spend their inheritances, or anything else.

A detailed Letter of Instructions Checklist appears at the end of this chapter. Obviously, your survivors will benefit if you prepare a letter of instructions, but so will you. A well-prepared letter of instructions is a great way to organize your records. Be sure to keep it up to date, since the information it contains is likely to change. Finally, make sure your family members know where the letter is! (Perhaps you should tape it to the door of your refrigerator.)

Smart Money Move

Living will laws are changing. Make sure your living will meets current state regulations.

Special Estate-Planning Considerations

Guardianship for Children

Guardianship generally refers to responsibility for a minor child's (or disabled adult's) care and upbringing if the parents die early. Although most parents would rather not think of someone else raising their children, it is important to consider the possibility of your death before the children are able to care for themselves. Lawyers are increasingly urging their clients who have children to make detailed guardianship arrangements and to make them earlier in life.

These lawyers and estate planners are entirely correct. Deciding who should take care of your minor children can be a very difficult process. Today, however, a failure to make such decisions can lead to greater custodial and financial problems than families have encountered in the past. With the increasing number of less traditional family situations, such as divorced parents and step-parents, the possible complications are obvious.

Alarming statistic

Estate planners estimate that 80 to 90 percent of parents with young children have no formal instructions specifying who will care for the children in the event of their death—never mind who will manage the children's finances. As a result, such decisions fall to overloaded state courts, where battles over custody and money can leave orphans in limbo for months or longer.

The trend toward more complex guardianship arrangements is occurring for good reason. Divorce and remarriage are commonplace among parents, and if one parent dies, the determination of who gets custody of the children may not be clear-cut. It's no longer automatic that the parents' first choice will be the court's first choice.

Under most state laws, the natural parent has paramount right to custody of the children. But in a dispute, the judge will make the decision based on factors such as the length of the marriage, how involved the biological parents were in the children's lives, and the wishes of the children. If the step-parent has adopted the children or has made them inheritors, the case to retain them is much stronger. This is where the wishes of the deceased natural parent can play a crucial role in the decision-making process.

On the other hand, courts tend to work very slowly when there is no written instruction available from the deceased parent. Another problem that arises when instructions for guardianship are absent is that economics tends to play a larger role than many parents would like. Simply put, it's not always the relative with the most affection for the child who receives custody, but the relative with the most money.

Consider dividing guardianship duties

Your attorney may advise you to divide guardianship duties so that the responsibility for taking care of the children's health and well-being is given to a personal guardian, and the responsibility for taking care of their financial affairs is given to a property guardian. There are several reasons for separating guardianship responsibilities between a personal guardian and a property guardian. The most important reason is that the particular relative or friend whom you trust completely with your child's upbringing may not have the expertise to deal with money that will be left to the child. Indeed, if no written instruction from you is available, the court itself may well appoint both a personal guardian and a property guardian.

But there is another side to the question of division of responsibilities. The separate trustee of the child's assets may be unaware of—and even at odds with—your and your guardian's financial priorities. Of course, this is more likely to be the case when the court appoints property guardians without the benefit of a written instruction from you. In many states, the guardian must hire a lawyer and petition the court annually to be reimbursed for even the most routine childrearing expenses.

Since the main goal of appointing a property guardian is to protect an estate until a child reaches the age of majority, courts are often reluctant to allow any expenses that will decrease the principal. In one case, the guardians of a twelve-year-old disabled child received only $5,200 per year for her care, even though the assets available to her totaled six figures. Don't allow this to happen. Include clauses in your will or trust that empower your guardians to spend the money in your estate that is necessary to raise the children as you would want them to be raised.

A thoughtful provision

If your estate is likely to be considerably greater than the resources of the guardian, it is conceivable that your children will grow up in a household where there is some resentment of their inheritance. If this is a possibility, you may want to consider empowering the property guardian to provide additional resources to the personal guardian's family to minimize the potential for resentment. For example, some parents provide for the payment of college tuition out of their estate for the guardian's children as well as for their own.

Finally, regardless of how the guardianship arrangement is made, it is vital that you discuss your wishes with the potential guardians prior to putting them in the will or trust. If the children are old enough, they should be included in the discussion, too. Parents are too often embarrassed to do this or afraid to start a fight within the family. Don't you be. Realize that it is of the utmost importance to inform guardians. Otherwise, upon the event of your death, serious problems could arise when your designated guardians suddenly realize they are responsible for the lives of *your* children.

Property Ownership

Because estate planning deals with the eventual transfer of property to others, the way in which you own your property is critical. The following section looks at how you can designate property ownership in the best manner to meet the needs of your heirs and to minimize estate taxes.

Transferring property to your heirs

A well-designed estate plan allows your estate to transfer property to your designated beneficiaries with a minimum of fuss and a maximum of tax savings. Assets that you completely or partially control are usually included in the estate, and shifting the title to these assets to your spouse or heirs (either in total or as co-owners) almost always reduces the estate tax burden and ensures a speedier transfer of assets. But this course has an overwhelming disadvantage: Such transfers of title usually must be *irrevocable*. Also, you could have to pay gift taxes if you transfer ownership of a lot of assets to anyone but your spouse.

Defining ownership of property also defines each owner's or co-owner's rights to and limitations regarding that property. Generally, each form of ownership tends to maximize one advantage (such as control), at the expense of another (such as reduced tax liability).

The following list summarizes the important considerations that you should keep in mind when deciding on a particular form of property ownership:

- **SOLE OWNERSHIP.** Sole ownership is outright ownership. Sole owners can sell the property, use it as collateral, or give it away. They can pass it on to heirs in any way they wish.

- **JOINT OWNERSHIP.** Joint ownership means that two or more persons have ownership rights in property. There are two kinds of joint ownership:

- **JOINT TENANCY WITH RIGHT OF SURVIVORSHIP** can exist between anyone, not just husband and wife. The main feature of joint tenancy with right of survivorship is that if one of the joint owners dies, interest in the property automatically passes to the other joint owner or owners.

- **TENANCY BY THE ENTIRETY** is similar to joint tenancy with right of survivorship, but there are some important differences. First, tenancy by the entirety can exist only between spouses. Also, in many states, survivorship rights cannot be terminated without the consent of all joint owners.

The advantages of joint ownership are that it is convenient and often works well for small estates since it avoids probate and thus provides the surviving family member with immediate access to the decedent's property. Joint ownership of property may also protect the property from being lost to a lawsuit during the owners' lifetimes (see below).

For estates that will be subject to estate taxes, however, joint ownership may have adverse estate tax consequences (see page 742). Also, anyone transferring property from sole ownership to joint ownership usually loses full control of property during his or her lifetime and relinquishes the power to unilaterally decide who will inherit it. Joint ownership arrangements are difficult to unwind—both legal and tax problems may arise. Finally, a joint tenancy between nonspouses may incur income and estate taxes.

- **TENANCY IN COMMON.** Tenancy in common differs from the other kinds of joint ownership primarily in that tenants in common do not have the right of survivorship. Instead, a tenant-in-common's interest in a property passes at death to his or her beneficiaries. Also, while joint tenants and tenants by the entirety always have equal interests, tenants in common can have unequal interests. For example, one tenant in common could have a 65 percent interest while the other has a 35 percent interest.

- **COMMUNITY PROPERTY.** Under community property laws, each spouse is co-owner of any property that is acquired by either spouse during the marriage if a joint effort was made in acquiring the property. Upon death, each spouse can dispose of only his or her half of the community property by will. The states of Arizona, California, Idaho, Louisiana, Nevada, New Mexico, Texas, and Washington all treat spousal property in this manner. Similar legislation is in effect in Wisconsin. Community property laws in each state are not uniform, so if you are a resident of a community property state, be sure to learn about the regulations.

Insulation from lawsuits

If you are unable at any time to pay financial debts, the properties that you own individually are subject to creditors' claims. If you are on the receiving end of a negligence, malpractice, or other lawsuit against you personally, your assets may also be seized by a court order. If, however, the property is held in joint ownership or is owned by some form of irrevocable trust, it may be partially or completely immune from these claims simply because of a foresighted joint ownership status.

There must be a legitimate reason to transfer ownership from one form to another besides avoiding personal financial obligations. In other words, the deliberate transfer of assets into another form of ownership merely to avoid paying your debts is considered fraudulent and may be overturned by the court. To protect assets from litigation, obtain sufficient umbrella and, if applicable, professional liability insurance coverage. In many circumstances, joint, trust, and community ownership ensures the safety of your property for your spouse and heirs. But remember that this assurance must be weighed against the partial or total loss of control and convenience that accompanies joint ownership arrangements.

LETTER OF INSTRUCTIONS CHECKLIST

It's really up to you what you want to put in your letter of instructions. Since a letter of instructions is not a legal document like a will, you have a lot more leeway in both its language and contents. Your letter is a good place to put personal wishes and final comments, but your heirs will be very grateful if you include some more useful information. This checklist suggests what to put in your letter of instructions. Even if you're not planning to die in the near future (for heaven's sake, I hope not!), preparing a letter of instructions is a good way to start getting your records in order. Your heirs will also be very grateful.

FIRST THINGS TO DO

- **ACQUAINTANCES** and organizations to be called, including Social Security, the bank, your employer

- **ARRANGEMENTS** to be made with funeral home

- **LAWYER'S** name and telephone

- **NEWSPAPERS** to receive obituary information

- **LOCATION** of insurance policies

CEMETERY AND FUNERAL

- **DETAILS** of your wishes, and any arrangements you have made

FACTS FOR FUNERAL DIRECTOR

- **VITAL STATISTICS,** including your full name, residence, marital status, spouse's name, date of birth, birthplace, father and mother's names and birthplaces, length of residence in state and in the United States, military records/history, Social Security number, occupation, and life insurance information

INFORMATION FOR DEATH CERTIFICATE AND FILING FOR BENEFITS

- **CITIZENSHIP**, race, marital status, name of next of kin (other than spouse), relationship, address, and birthplace

EXPECTED DEATH BENEFITS

- **INFORMATION** about any potential death benefits from your employer (including life insurance, profit sharing, pension plan, or accident insurance), life insurance companies, Social Security, Veterans Administration, or any other source

SPECIAL WISHES

- **ANYTHING** you want your survivors to know

PERSONAL EFFECTS

- **A LIST** of who is to receive certain personal effects

PERSONAL PAPERS

- **LOCATIONS** of important personal documents, including your will, birth and baptismal certificates, communion and confirmation certificates, diplomas, marriage certificate, military records, naturalization papers, and any other documents (like adoption and divorce papers)

SAFE-DEPOSIT BOX

- **LOCATION** and number of box and key and an inventory of contents

POST OFFICE BOX

- **LOCATION** and number of box and key (or combination)

INCOME TAX RETURNS

- **LOCATION** of all previous returns

- **LOCATION** of your estimated tax file

- **TAX** preparer's name

LOANS OUTSTANDING

- **INFORMATION** on loans other than mortgages, including bank name and address, name on loan, account number, monthly payment, location of papers and payment book, collateral, and information on any credit life insurance policies on the loan

DEBTS OWED TO THE ESTATE

- **DEBTOR,** description, terms, balance, location of documents, and comments on loan status/discharge

SOCIAL SECURITY

- **FULL NAME,** Social Security number, and location of Social Security card

LIFE INSURANCE

- **POLICY NUMBERS** and amounts, location of policy, whose life is insured, insurer's name and address, kind of policy, beneficiaries, issue and maturity date, payment options, and any special facts

VETERANS ADMINISTRATION

- **IF YOU** are a veteran, information on collecting benefits from local Veterans Administration office

OTHER INSURANCE

- **IF ANY** other insurance benefits or policies are in force, including accident, homeowner's/renter's, automobile, disability, medical, personal or professional liability, give insurer's name and address, policy number, beneficiary, coverage, location of policy, term, how acquired (if through employer or other group), and agent

INVESTMENTS

- **STOCKS:** company, name on certificates, number of shares, certificate numbers, purchase price and date, and location of certificates

- **BONDS/NOTES/BILLS:** issuer, issued to, face amount, bond number, purchase price and date, maturity date, and location of certificates

- **MUTUAL FUNDS:** company, name on account, number of shares or units, and location of statements and certificates

- **OTHER INVESTMENTS:** for each investment, list amount invested, to whom issued, maturity date, issuer, other applicable data, and location of certificates and other vital papers

HOUSEHOLD CONTENTS

- **LIST** of contents, with name of owners, form of ownership, and location of documents, inventory, and appraisals

AUTOMOBILES

- **FOR EACH CAR:** year, make, model, color, identification number, title in name(s) of, and location of title and registration

IMPORTANT WARRANTIES, AND RECEIPTS

- **LOCATION** and description

DOCTORS' NAMES, ADDRESSES, AND TELEPHONES

- **INCLUDING** dentist, children's pediatrician, and children's dentist

CHECKING ACCOUNTS

- **NAME** of bank, name on each account, account number, and location of pass–book (or receipt) for all accounts

CREDIT CARDS

- **FOR EACH CARD:** company (including telephone and address), name on card, number, and location of card

HOUSE, CONDO, OR CO-OP

- **HOME:** in whose name, address, legal description, other descriptions needed, lawyer at closing, and locations of statement of closing, title insurance policy, deed, and land survey

- **MORTGAGE:** held by, amount of original mortgage, date taken out, amount owed now, method of payment, and location of payment book, if any (or payment statements)

- **LIFE INSURANCE ON MORTGAGE:** policy number, location of policy, and annual amount

- **PROPERTY TAXES:** amount and location of receipts

- **COST OF HOUSE:** initial buying price, purchase closing fee, other buying costs (real estate agent, legal, taxes), and home improvements

- **IMPROVEMENTS:** what each consisted of, cost, date, and location of bills

- **FOR RENTERS:** lease location and expiration date

FUNERAL PREFERENCES

- **SPECIFY** *whether or not* you would like to have any of the following done: donate organs, autopsy if requested, simple arrangements, embalming, public viewing, least expensive burial or cremation container, or immediate disposition. Remains should be: donated (details of arrangements made), cremated (and the ashes: scattered, buried at), disposed of as follows (details), or buried (at)

- **SPECIFY** which of the following services should be performed: memorial (after disposition), funeral (before disposition), or graveside to be held at: church, mortuary, or other

- **SPECIFY** where memorial gifts should be given or whether to omit flowers

- **IF PREARRANGEMENTS** have been made with a mortuary, give details

SIGNATURE AND DATE

FOR FURTHER INFORMATION

For information on living wills and the rights of the terminally ill, contact:

Choice in Dying
200 Varick Street, 10th Floor
New York, NY 10014
(212) 366-5540

BASIC ESTATE PLANNING DOCUMENTS CHECKLIST

☐

If you haven't already done so, prepare a will, a durable power of attorney, and a living will.

☐

Exercise particular care in choosing and informing guardians for your minor children or disabled dependents.

☐

Make sure that the title in which you hold property is appropriate for achieving your estate-planning objectives.

☐

Make sure your estate planning documents are up-to-date. Changes in family relationships or circumstances, relocation, or changes in laws and regulations may require that your estate plans be reviewed and, if necessary, revised.

Trusts and Other Estate-Planning Strategies

M any people can benefit from establishing trusts, although they may not know it. Trusts are often incorrectly viewed as inflexible arrangements reserved only for the wealthy. In fact, trusts can provide advantages both to you during your lifetime and to your heirs after your death. When you set up a trust, you (as the grantor) transfer assets to a separate legal entity that holds your assets and disburses them as you see fit.

Because you determine who will serve as trustee—whether it be yourself, one or more individuals of your choice, or a financial institution—certain trusts let you continue to maintain control over your assets even after you have transferred them to the trust.

Used effectively, trusts can accomplish many important estate-planning goals. They can ensure the sound management of your assets after your death; they can protect your property from creditors; they can minimize or reduce probate while guaranteeing that your estate passes to your heirs exactly as you wish; and finally, they can reduce estate taxes.

There are many different types of trusts that are designed to accomplish a variety of lifetime and after-death objectives. This chapter examines a variety of commonly used trusts and how they function—protecting your estate, reducing your estate taxes, or reaping the benefits of being charitable—as well as which type of trust may be appropriate for your particular needs.

Choosing Trustees

B ecause your trustee is considered your personal representative, designating the trustee may well be the most important decision you make in drawing up your trust. You can name any person or institution—including yourself, a member of your immediate family, or the beneficiary(ies)—as the trustee. Although a relative is a good choice in some circumstances, it is not if the main objective of the trust is to reduce taxes.

Definition

Trust: The transfer of property by the trust creator (the settlor, grantor, or trustor) to a trustee for the purpose of holding such property in a prescribed manner for the benefit of another (the beneficiary).

In general, the IRS frowns on naming the grantor or the beneficiary as the trustee if the main reason for drawing up the trust is to reduce income and estate taxes. From a tax perspective, appointing an independent party as a trustee—an unrelated business partner or a bank or trust corporation—is your best alternative. With such a third party, however, the factor of disinterest must be added to your concerns. A third party will never be as familiar with your family's needs as a relative will be.

Furthermore, many bank and trust institutions prefer to deal only with trust funds of more than $100,000. A common compromise: Appoint your spouse or other close relative as a co-trustee along with an independent third party. From a tax-planning standpoint, as long as the spouse can be outvoted by the other trustee(s), the trust is considered sufficiently independent not to be included in the grantor's income and estate tax return.

This arrangement is an especially popular alternative when the trustee is empowered to "sprinkle" income among the beneficiaries. The spouse's or other family member's concern and knowledge about the beneficiaries' welfare can then be combined with the management expertise of the bank or other financial institution without forfeiting the tax advantage you worked so hard to provide.

When choosing a bank, trust company or other financial institution as a trustee, you should first examine the institution's trust department. How long has the trust department been in existence? How qualified are its personnel? What has been the past performance of the trust portfolios? Are the fees for administration and services competitive?

Irrevocable and Revocable Trusts

An irrevocable trust transfers the trust assets outside your ownership, and the assets are immune from lawsuits and creditors' claims against you. Revocable trusts do not have these advantages, although they have other benefits. Trusts are not subject to the same stringent rules regarding wills and are thus less likely to be successfully contested after your death.

Irrevocable Trusts

Smart Money Move

Consider using trusts to accomplish your estate-planning objectives.

In general, an irrevocable trust is advisable when your primary concern is to reduce your estate tax liability. But transferring assets into an irrevocable trust is a big step that should not be taken lightly. Why? Irrevocable trusts significantly restrain your powers and freedom of action and therefore are considered primarily in the context of estate taxes. An irrevocable trust is a completed gift at the time of the property's transfer into the trust, and gift taxes may therefore be assessed at the time of the transfer. You retain no reversionary interest and little power to control the trust. The best property to place in an irrevocable trust is property that is likely to appreciate in value, since any future appreciation in value will not be subject to either gift or estate taxes. This is one of the major advantages of irrevocable trusts. A less drastic but nevertheless effective way to accomplish a reduction in estate taxes is to make use of the $10,000 annual gift exclusion (or $20,000 with your spouse's consent). (See page 712.)

Revocable Trusts

A revocable trust, on the other hand, offers no tax advantages and therefore should be considered for reasons other than reducing the estate tax bite. There are a variety of possible benefits to establishing a revocable trust. For one, assets placed in a revocable trust will not be subject to the delays and inconvenience caused by probate. This assures the payment to beneficiaries of proceeds from life insurance, pension, and profit-sharing plans, and other benefit plans without going through probate. A revocable trust also reduces vulnerability to postdeath contest among the heirs and reduces access of creditors and claimants to the decedent's estate. The decedent's financial affairs remain private, as the trust plan is not subject to public inspection.

Competent management by professional trustees, if desired, assures that the grantor's wishes will be adhered to. At times, grantors have created a revocable trust as a "test run" for creating an irrevocable trust, to measure both the competence of the chosen trustees and the viability of the trust.

Testamentary Trusts

A testamentary trust is a trust created according to your will. Creating a trust this way has some advantages over leaving property outright. First, it allows you, rather than your inheritors, to control the disposition of your estate. (Otherwise, your inheritors would be able to have complete control over how they dispose of their share of your estate.) Second, a testamentary trust may save on estate taxes that would have to be paid on the demise of your inheritor. For example, a married couple's use of a testamentary trust can result in significant estate tax savings upon the death of the second spouse (see page 742).

Third, a testamentary trust may provide for professional management of your estate after your death, and it can eliminate or reduce the need to sell stock and property for distribution of the estate among your heirs.

The major drawbacks of testamentary trusts (as opposed to living trusts) are their inclusion in the taxable estate. Because a testamentary trust can be created only by a will and all wills are subject to probate, a testamentary trust can be created only after the probate process. Sometimes an improperly drawn will that has been thrown out of court blocks the creation of a testamentary trust altogether.

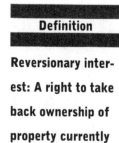

Definition

Reversionary interest: A right to take back ownership of property currently held in a trust.

The property in the trust also is considered as part of your estate and thus is subject, after your death, to estate taxation. (An irrevocable living trust, on the other hand, would not be included in your taxable estate.)

A SIMPLE WILL CAN BE AN EXPENSIVE ($235,000) MISTAKE

The garden-variety will for married people, which in essence says "all to my spouse," could end up costing your children or other heirs a lot of money. Assume the husband has an estate of $1,200,000 (which, by the way, is by no means an unusually large estate for older persons), and he dies leaving all of it to his wife. No federal estate taxes are owed because the transfer qualifies for the unlimited marital deduction.

But what if the wife dies right after the husband? She's got at least $1,200,000 to bequeath, but she has only the $600,000 tax-free exemption available to reduce estate taxes. Her taxable estate, therefore, is $600,000 (the $1,200,000 gross estate minus the $600,000 exemption). The federal estate tax on this $600,000 is a whopping $235,000, which could have been avoided altogether with some modest estate planning.

The husband should have limited the wife's taxable estate to the amount covered by her $600,000 exemption by not willing everything he owned to her. He could have done this by allowing her the full use of all of the property to meet her needs, while placing a part of his estate in a trust for her that would not be subject to estate tax at her death.

Of course, the wife might have died first, but the estate could have been structured to avoid some or all estate taxes no matter who died first. In the above example, the husband could have, during his lifetime, given his wife $600,000 (there are no gift taxes on transfers to a spouse), and she could have left that sum to him in her will to use if he survived her.

Incidentally, these arrangements go under a variety of monikers, including "bypass trusts," "marital-deduction trusts," "A-B trusts," "unified credit trusts," "power-of-appointment trusts," and "qualified terminable interest property (QTIP) trusts." If you're married, if your estate is likely to be over the $600,000 threshold, and if you don't have one of these trusts in your will, check with an experienced estate-planning attorney. You won't be around to enjoy the estate tax savings, but your heirs will certainly appreciate your foresight.

Trusts That Can Protect Family Members

Minor's Testamentary Trust

This trust is created in a will for the purpose of protecting the children's inheritance. The trustee of this trust handles its assets for the children's benefit. This prevents poor management of their inheritance by an incompetent guardian. Also, a minor's testamentary trust can establish limits and control your heirs' access to their inheritance until they reach the age at which you feel they are mature enough to handle the entire sum wisely.

Testamentary Discretionary Spendthrift Trust

This trust is also created in a will. It provides security for a disabled beneficiary. It supplements government assistance by allowing for the trustee to distribute income from the fund to the disabled beneficiary. If he or she is unable to handle the money, it is given to the guardian to spend in the best interest of the beneficiary.

Irrevocable 2503(c) Trust

Although the law limits the tax benefits of putting money in your minor child's name, there are still reasons to open an irrevocable 2503(c) trust. When you establish this trust, you are giving up control of the trust property and the power to change the trust agreement. Thus, the trust's assets are no longer a part of your taxable estate. With an irrevocable 2503(c) trust, you may restrict the beneficiary from obtaining the trust's income and principal until he or she reaches the age of twenty-one or even older if the beneficiary fails to claim the assets within thirty to ninety days of turning twenty-one. There may also be some income tax reduction possibilities with a 2503(c) trust.

Irrevocable Crummey Trust

This trust has essentially the same income and estate tax benefits as the irrevocable 2503(c) trust. But one major difference is that the Crummey trust does not have to terminate when your child turns twenty-one. The beneficiary of a Crummey trust can withdraw up to $10,000 a year—the value of the annual gift exclusion. If the beneficiary waives the right of withdrawal (this is what the parents hope will be done), the money in the trust will accumulate. Establishing either a Crummey or a 2503(c) trust is an expensive proposition, so a considerable amount of money must be placed in the trust in order to make it cost-effective.

Living Trust

A living trust is a trust into which you transfer your assets while you're alive. A living trust's immediate advantage is that it can circumvent probate. This may be particularly advantageous if you live in a state that has particularly onerous probate laws. If all your assets are held in a living trust, there is nothing to transfer through the will. The trust is not obligated (in most states) to pay any remaining debts, and it ensures continuous management of the assets, uninterrupted by your death. If at any point you become disabled or otherwise unable to make an important decision concerning the assets, your co-trustee can take responsibility. (If you do not want to manage all your assets during the remainder of your life, you can appoint a co-trustee.)

A living trust, compared with a simple will, provides more assurance that your desires will be carried out. A trust document can specify exact conditions about the distribution of your assets (such as at what age a child will receive an inheritance) and can allow the trustee the discretion to withhold or distribute extra assets if it is prudent or necessary.

A living trust can also serve as a receptacle for estate assets and death benefits from your employee-benefit plans and life insurance. Also, it can unify in one location all your assets and thus avoid administration of the estate in different places. Compared with a testamentary trust, this trust is protected from public inspection and may be less vulnerable to attack on grounds of fraud, incapacity, or duress.

Moreover, if your living trust is revocable, it permits you to alter it as necessary or desired. But while an irrevocable living trust is not included in your estate for estate tax purposes, a revocable trust provides you with no tax savings (although if you die without revoking the trust, it automatically becomes irrevocable).

Living trusts aren't for everyone, and they're vastly oversold, but they still merit your consideration.

Trusts That Can Reduce Estate Taxes

E ven married couples whose estates are less that $1 million can take advantage of certain trust arrangements that can end up saving the next generation well over $100,000 in federal estate taxes.

Bypass

Bypas (or "unified credit") trusts can be set up to hold that portion of the estate that is exempt from taxes upon the death of the first spouse by reason of the $600,000 unified credit. The bypass trust is designed to exempt the assets placed in it from estate taxation upon the death of the second spouse. This estate tax savings strategy can be accomplished with a general power of appointment trust or a qualified terminable interest property (QTIP) trust. Both are discussed below.

General Power of Appointment Trust

The most distinctive characteristic of a general power of appointment trust is that it gives the surviving spouse the power to name (usually in a will) the ultimate beneficiary of the trust's assets. If the surviving spouse fails to name a beneficiary of the assets, they will go to the beneficiary named by the spouse who died first. Two other essentials for setting up a general power of appointment trust are that it must give the surviving spouse a lifetime right to the income earned on the trust property, and it must give the trustee or surviving spouse the power to withdraw and use the trust principal for certain purposes.

Qualified Terminable Interest Property (QTIP) Trust

This trust can be used to insure that you, rather than your surviving spouse, choose who is to ultimately inherit your estate. People who are concerned that their spouse may remarry and that the "new spouse" will end up with most or part of the estate will find QTIP trusts appealing. Like a general power of appointment trust, the lifetime right for the surviving spouse to receive income will qualify for the marital deduction, so the ultimate estate tax savings features remain. In essence, a spouse can get income from the trust over his or her lifetime, but upon death, the principal in the trust passes on to whomever you choose—usually your children.

In addition to the estate tax saving aspects of marital trusts, both the general power of appointment trust and the QTIP trust allow you to be sure that your spouse is adequately provided for without somehow squandering estate assets during the spouse's lifetime. This may be particularly useful if your spouse is not very experienced in managing money.

Irrevocable Life Insurance Trust

In order to avoid incurring estate taxes on life insurance proceeds, you can place your policies in an irrevocable life insurance trust. By doing this, you prevent your heirs from having to raise money to pay taxes on the money they received from your life insurance. On the other hand, when you set up a life insurance trust, you must give up all ownership rights. This includes the ability to borrow against the policies and to change the beneficiaries. Also, if you die within three years of setting up the trust, your insurance will be included in your taxable estate anyway.

Charitable Remainder Trust

If you are charitably inclined, charitable trusts offer a variety of advantages both during your lifetime and when your estate is eventually settled. When you set up a charitable remainder trust, you place the property you want to donate into an irrevocable trust. The income from this trust is distributed to anyone you choose—usually yourself and your spouse, but sometimes children are included. Depending upon what you want, this income is usually distributed to you or your beneficiaries for life. Once the last income recipient dies, the property in the trust is given to a charity.

A number of benefits are provided by charitable remainder trusts. First, you receive a partial income tax deduction for your donation based on the value of the property that the charity will ultimately receive. This property is also removed from your estate so that estate taxes will not be paid on it upon your death. Finally, of course, you receive a lifetime income in return for your donation. Not a bad deal. While charitable remainder trusts usually require a contribution of at least $50,000, many charitable organizations have programs that provide similar advantages for persons who prefer to donate less money—as little as $5,000. These programs are called *pooled income funds* and *charitable gift annuities.*

Charitable Lead Trust

In many respects a charitable lead trust operates in the opposite way from a charitable remainder trust. The income provided by property that is placed into a charitable lead trust is given to a qualified charity (rather than the donor). But a charitable lead trust also includes the provision that upon the death of the donor, the property is to be given to specified noncharitable beneficiaries—typically, family members. From the time the trust begins operation, the value of the property in the trust is no longer included in your taxable estate, but there is no immediate tax deduction granted to you upon opening the trust. Therefore, a charitable lead trust can provide significant estate tax savings while keeping the property "in the family." The price you pay, of course, is that you give up the income generated by the property for the rest of your life.

TRUST AND OTHER ESTATE-PLANNING STRATEGIES CHECKLIST

■□■

You should consider establishing trusts either during your lifetime or upon your death to accomplish important estate-planning objectives.

■□■

Use an experienced estate-planning attorney to advise you as to what trusts or other estate-planning strategies may be appropriate for you.

■□■

Don't automatically assume that you should have a living trust just because a lot of attorneys are pushing them. Seek objective advice before going to the expense of setting up a living trust.

■□■

If you are charitably inclined, charitable remainder trusts, charitable lead trusts, pooled income funds, and charitable gift annuities offer a variety of tax and other advantages.

Funeral Planning

You can ease a good deal of the trauma and confusion—not to mention the expense—of planning your funeral by making your wishes known in advance. This chapter focuses on keeping funeral costs under control—either yours or a loved one's.

The Importance of Making Your Wishes Known

If you haven't already done so, talk to your parents about what their funeral plans are—or talk to your adult children about your own. It's not an easy subject to discuss, but it is a matter of great importance. The reason: Funerals have become increasingly *and* needlessly expensive. By communicating openly with your family members about your and their plans, you will avoid the risk of making a loved one's death become the death of your finances.

Memorial Societies

Local memorial societies can be very helpful to funeral planning. A one-time membership fee is nominal and often transferable if you move to another city. These societies may be able to obtain lower prices on funeral expenses for members.

Memorial societies can also recommend funeral homes and ceremony directors. You can skip the memorial society if you want, although it may take extra initiative and effort since the arrangements will then have to be made directly with a funeral director.

Choosing a Funeral Home

If you decide that you wish to have a funeral home handle your arrangements, then finding an appropriate funeral home will be the most important step in your funeral preplanning.

A member of the clergy can often recommend a funeral home. The place that will take care of all the details concerning disposal of the deceased's body, especially in the case of an earth burial, should meet with your personal and financial approval. You will generally be better off using a home that charges separately for each item.

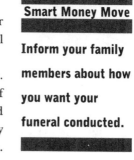

Smart Money Move

Inform your family members about how you want your funeral conducted.

Avoid funeral homes that tout "package deals"—the prices of these deals may well include a good deal of padding. At the very least, you could end up paying for frills that you don't need and don't want.

When paying for a funeral in advance, make sure that the funds can be withdrawn or refunded if you or your family change your mind about what sort of arrangements you want.

Above all, don't be afraid to bargain. Remember that funeral directors aren't immune to seeking financial gain from your misfortune. While most won't try too hard to convince the bereaved to order the most expensive funeral possible, many won't exhaust themselves pitching the most economical ones either. It is far less likely that they will use this tactic on a living, preplanning, and hopefully prepaying consumer. They would rather service your less-than-grandiose funeral needs than lose your business to a more sensible competitor.

FUNERAL PLANNING AND THE LETTER OF INSTRUCTIONS

A letter of instructions is a supplement to a formal will (see page 727). It helps ensure that your survivors know exactly how to proceed at the time of your death. A letter of instructions should include the following information pertaining to your funeral:

- PREVIOUSLY arranged or preferred funeral arrangements.

- NOTIFICATION and pertinent information if you are an organ or body donor. (Include the location of your uniform donor card.)

- NAMES and addresses of the memorial society, funeral home, and/or crematory with which you contracted.

- TYPE OF CEREMONY and details of service.

- CASKET AND GRAVE-MARKER preferences.

- PREFERRED death notice

Disposing of the Remains

E verybody should spend some time thinking about what they want to happen to their body after they die. Planning one's own funeral is certainly the most emotionally difficult aspect of financial planning, but your heirs will be better off if you make the hard decisions yourself. Over the centuries, mankind has devised countless ways to dispose of the dead; the methods common to late twentieth-century America are discussed below.

Naturally your religious beliefs and/or secular attitudes about death will influence the route you decide to take. At the very least, however, the following information will allow you to compare the available alternatives on a practical level.

Donation to a Medical School

If you are of a practical and unsentimental turn of mind, donating your body to a medical institution is the most cost-effective way to dispose of your body. Many people who choose to donate their bodies to science also have humanitarian matters on their mind—they know that their actions will support medical research while saving their heirs money.

Check with the school or institution of your choice about its detailed requirements. Different medical institutions have different requirements and guidelines for accepting the remains. Some bodies may be unsuitable. Make sure that the institution will accept your body and pay for its transportation. Also, be sure to have a backup plan for unexpected events, such as death occurring at a place too far away to transport your body to the medical school.

Organ Donations

An alternative to donating the entire body is to donate only specific organs for transplant. The designated organs must be removed immediately after death in order for them to have any value. The rest of your body will be released in time for the funeral. If you are interested in donating organs, ask your doctor for information on making the appropriate arrangements.

Cremation

Next to donating your body to a medical school, cremation is the best choice from a purely financial standpoint: It is cheap and straightforward. A simple, low-cost fiberboard container is all that is needed to contain the body. The Federal Trade Commission has explicitly prohibited crematoria from requiring the use of a casket or the embalming of the body. If the body is delivered directly to the crematorium, even the presence of a funeral director is unnecessary, further reducing the cost.

After cremation, there are a number of economical ways to handle your remains. Most families scatter or bury the ashes in a place familiar to the deceased, although local laws may prohibit or restrict this. As an alternative, the urn can be placed in a niche at a special mausoleum called a columbarium, or in a cemetery's mortuary chapel.

Earth Burial

Earth burial is the most expensive and complicated way to dispose of your body. If you want to have an earth burial, it can take place either immediately after the death, or after a funeral home viewing and/or church (or graveside) service have taken place. In any case, the largest expense involved in an earth burial is the cost of the coffin. Because so many expensive coffins are on the market, you should choose one yourself in advance and make sure that your letter of instructions makes your choice clear. That way, if you want a simple coffin, your heirs won't be overcharged by overzealous coffin salespeople. If you're not pre-pared to select your own coffin now (and you can't be faulted for that), at least inform your family members that you'll be perfectly happy to be ensconced in an average coffin rather than a mahogany and teak one. Also, suggest that you'll be perfectly comfortable without an innerspring mattress in the coffin.

A funeral home might also try to sell burial vaults to enclose the casket, asserting that the cemetery requires it. Even if the cemetery does require a grave lining (to prevent cave-ins), a simple metal or concrete liner is more than sufficient and is at most half the cost of a vault.

As far as embalming is concerned, it is unnecessary if burial occurs soon after death. Embalming is only required when there will be a delay in burial or when the body is to be shipped a great distance.

Choosing a Cemetery

I f you've made up your mind to have your body interred, you have to think about where you want to be buried. Consider a place where family and friends won't be too inconvenienced. Then, consider the costs—they vary widely. Municipal cemeteries are usually less expensive than private ones. Urban areas are generally more expensive than rural locations. Above-ground mausoleums tend to be costlier than earth burial. Different areas within the same cemetery may cost more or less depending on the specific location. (If the less expensive lot lacks a view of a bubbling fountain or a sunrise view would you real-ly mind?)

Buying a Cemetery Plot

Consider buying the plot in advance. You may save some money for yourself and your heirs by locking into today's price for tomorrow's plot. It's a good anti-inflation investment. (Plot prices have risen dramatically in the past, far outstripping inflation rates.) On the other hand, if you end up moving to a new place far away from the purchased plot, prepurchasing a lot may complicate rather than simplify your plans. Exchange plans are available but often have many restrictions. If you don't have an exchange plan you have to arrange for a private sale. (The salesperson for the cemetery may be able to help you sell it—for a commission.)

Final Rites

A fter deciding on the disposition of the body, the second most important considera-tion is the funeral service. A great deal of money can either be spent or saved, depending on how well one plans. It is important to remember that the purpose of the service is to assuage the survivors' emotional needs. For example, a family may feel that the deceased deserves a big sendoff. But they're the ones who may live to regret the expense of the bowers of roses, the fleet of limousines and the solid bronze casket.

Funeral Service

The most expensive type of ceremony is the funeral service. By definition, a funeral service is one held in presence of the body. If there is a time lapse before the burial, the body will have to be embalmed, and for an open coffin ceremony, cosmetic work is required. Also, if there is a viewing, rental charges may be imposed. A funeral parlor is usually rented for the ceremony, but the funeral director may transport the body to another meeting place, or church. These details add up. Remember, a memorial society can be of great help. If you're not getting assistance from a memorial society, choose a trusted friend or relative to help you make your preferred arrangements.

Memorial Service

The second type of ceremony is a memorial service. It differs from a funeral service in that it typically takes place after the body has been cremated or interred. The focus of a memorial service therefore tends to be on the life of the persona grata rather than on the corpus delicti. Also, because there are no calendar constraints on the disposal of the body, a memorial service offers greater flexibility in location and time. It can be performed at virtually any place that is desired and does not require the assistance of a funeral home. A memorial service can be far less expensive than a funeral service, as all the items required by a funeral service (cosmetic work, elaborate coffin, funeral parlor, and so on) are unnecessary. In general, memorial services tend to be less elaborate and more thoughtful than funeral services. A common feature is to suggest that friends make a donation to some specified charitable organization. They will be thankful because such donations are thoughtful—and tax-deductible.

Financing the Funeral

When it's time to pay the piper, how will you (or your survivors) do it? Death and the procedures that accompany it are so expensive that some families have to go into debt in order to finance the funeral of a loved one. What could be more stressful? Making your family aware of all the anticipated and contracted funeral expenses—including any possible special sources of funds you've set aside to cover them—can make the funeral ordeal less stressful.

There are three main ways of meeting the expenses associated with a death. One is for the funds to come from the family coffers. If so, be sure there are enough readily available resources around to pay these costs. A second way is through a particular investment account. A regularly renewed certificate of deposit (CD) is a good vehicle for this purpose, especially since the penalty for early withdrawal does not apply if the owner dies. Finally, the cost of burial can be included in the estimate of final expenses in determining your life insurance needs.

Other Sources of Funeral Funds

Along with your self-created means of building funds to cope with the financial strain of your funeral, you may also be able to find some outside sources that can help reduce the burden. Double-check the following sources:

- **CHECK** your life insurance policy to see if it provides for burial and cremation costs. If you have burial insurance, be sure your family knows about it.

- **NOTIFY** your family in advance about any job-related death benefits. For example, they may be eligible for assistance through your worker's compensation plan. In any event, ask them to notify the employee benefits office at your work place, as there may be some benefit connected with the pension or the company's life insurance program.

Sources of Death Benefits

I f you're a fully insured worker under Social Security or have credit for a year and a half out of the three years before death, there is a $255 lump-sum death benefit. However, as with other Social Security benefits, a survivor has to apply to the Social Security Administration to receive the benefit. Your surviving spouse and children may also be eligible for survivor benefits (see page 619).

Veterans

Certain honorably discharged wartime or peacetime veterans can qualify for a $300 allowance for funeral expenses. If death is caused by service-related factors, this allowance may go up to $1,500. In addition, veterans, their wives, and minor children can obtain free burial in a national cemetery where space is available.

Simple headstones are available at no cost to veterans, and spouses and minor children may receive markers free of cost if buried in a national cemetery. If the body required shipment *and* (a) the veteran died of a service-related cause in or in transit to a VA hospital or (b) had any service-related disability, then the VA will pay for it. Also, all eligible veterans are entitled to the draping of an American flag over the casket. You can get further information at a VA office or veterans' service organization. Call (800) 827-1000 for further information.

Other Sources

Among the other sources of available benefits are liability insurance, state employee survivor benefits, trade unions, fraternal organizations, and specific occupation benefits—for example, benefits available to the survivors of railroad workers. The relevant information about your or a loved one's association with such unions and organizations is yours for the asking.

EIGHT WAYS TO PUT A LID ON YOUR "FINAL EXPENSES"

1. **MAKE YOUR FUNERAL WISHES KNOWN.** Tell your relatives exactly how you want your funeral handled. Better yet, include these details as part of your will. By making your wishes clear, you will save your survivors the pain of agonizing over these details at such a distressing time.

2. **ASK FOR A MODEST FUNERAL.** One of the best ways to encourage your family not to go broke with a lavish funeral is to describe in writing the kind of modest funeral or memorial service you want. The more detailed the instructions, the more likely they will conform to your wishes.

3. **PAY FOR YOUR FUNERAL TODAY.** Perhaps the best way to ensure that your funeral costs are kept under control is to prepay your funeral. Most funeral homes offer prepayment plans.

4. **BUY A FAMILY BURIAL PLOT.** You have heard of economies of scale. You can take advantage of this basic rule of economics by purchasing one large burial plot instead of several individual ones. That way you can divide up the plot's cost among of all its future residents.

5. **SHARE A BURIAL PLOT.** Check to see if you can be buried on top of another family member—two for the price of one.

6. **ASK FOR A MODEST TOMBSTONE.** However you plan for your funeral, don't forget to ask for a modest tombstone or marker. I think you will agree that there is no need to adorn your final resting place with a twenty-foot-tall Carrara marble obelisk or a poured-concrete replica of the Pietà. Come to think of it, who could rest with all that weight pressing down on them anyway?

7. **DONATE YOUR REMAINS TO SCIENCE.** You can help advance scientific knowledge while reducing what are euphemistically called "final disposition costs" if you donate your remains to a medical school.

8. **ASK TO BE CREMATED.** While you won't enjoy any benefits from this expense-saving tactic, your heirs will.

Coping with a Sudden Death

sudden death can wreak emotional havoc on surviving family members and friends. For the partner closest to the deceased, to whom most of the decisions regarding disposition and funeral services are left, the situation can be overwhelming.

For this reason it is imperative that, in the event that no preplanning was done, no one person be allowed to decide on the issues of disposition and interment—especially a spouse or child. If you or someone you know is in this situation, then consider this advice:

- **CALL** your closest and most trusted friend. You will need to rely on their help and judgment in the days to come.

- **DON'T GO** directly from the hospital to a funeral home. You will only risk agreeing on a too-elaborate funeral that will end up costing you time, emotion, and money.

- **CALL** your immediate family members and ask them to convene as soon as possible and confer with you as a whole.

- **CONTACT** the deceased's attorney for legal guidance concerning the immediate matter of the will as it relates to funeral arrangements, about which you may not have been informed.

- **DON'T COMMIT** to any funeral-related costs until you have discussed the items with your friend, family and/or lawyer. It is an exhausting and unpleasant task but one that must be done. Never go it alone.

- **DON'T TAKE** any calls from strangers who claim to have known the deceased or want to help you with your future finances.

FOR FURTHER INFORMATION

Continental Association of Funeral and Memorial Societies, Inc.
6900 Lost Lake Road
Egg Harbor, WI 54209-9231
(800) 458-5563

FUNERAL-PLANNING CHECKLIST

☐ Make your funeral wishes known to your family members.

☐ If they haven't already, ask your parents to make their funeral plans known.

☐ Consider the many and varied ways to keep funeral costs in check.

Part XI

You Can Achieve
Financial Security

A Strategy to Get Rich Sensibly

There are four ways to get rich:

1. INHERIT A LOT OF MONEY

2. MARRY SOMEONE WHO HAS A LOT OF MONEY

3. WIN THE LOTTERY

4. DO IT YOURSELF

There is certainly nothing wrong with inheriting or marrying a lot of money. Winning the lottery is fine, too, but far too many people are spending themselves into the poorhouse buying lottery tickets. A dollar or two a week is cheap fun. But if you spend more than that, take heed: You won't win the lottery, so you're wasting hard-earned money that should be put to sensible use.

If your only opportunity to get rich is by doing it yourself, take heart. This is the American dream. This is what people envy. Those who have become wealthy by having the good fortune of being born into it or marrying it are forever tainted. We may envy them, but we also think that they don't deserve their good fortune. (If it's any consolation to you, those with inherited wealth or those who "marry well" harbor their own doubts of self-worth.) As for lottery winners, forget it. Everyone in the world knows that they don't deserve their wealth. The quickest way to lose your friends is to win the lottery. But don't think you can replace them with rich friends. Rich people pooh-pooh lottery winners.

What's a Do-It-Yourselfer to Do?

Many people waste a lot of time thinking about how nice it would be to be rich, but they don't take any action to get rich. Others think it is impossible to get rich, so they do nothing about it. If you want to become wealthy, you first need to set realistic objectives. The sooner you conclude that you're not going to accumulate the amount of wealth that the more visible rich folks among us have (or appear to have), the easier it will be to set a reasonable target. Anyway, do you really want to be superrich? Let me name a few of the more conspicuous superrich among us: Ivan Boesky, Leona Helmsley, Charles Keating, Imelda Marcos, Michael Milken, and Donald Trump. Just because you're rich doesn't mean you're forever happy.

What constitutes "rich"? If you have enough money set aside to support yourself comfortably (maybe with a few extras thrown in, like travel) for the rest of your life, taking inflation into consideration, as far as I'm concerned, you're rich enough. Maybe you want to set your sights a little higher, but don't go overboard. If you do, you'll spend the rest of your life being frustrated because you'll never meet your goal. By the way, don't burden yourself by thinking that you need to pass some of your riches on to your children. After all, you wouldn't want to taint them with their ill-gotten inheritance, would you? It's better to spend it all before you die.

The Strategy

I f you are ready to get down to the business of getting rich sensibly, you may be surprised to learn that there's no magic to it—no schemes, no can't-lose ways to double your money every year, no secrets to be revealed. Instead, what's required is some *sacrifice*, some *common sense*, and some *consistency*. Here is the five-point strategy.

1. **BE REALISTIC.** The first step to getting rich sensibly is to be realistic in your definition of *rich*. If you think you need $100 million to be rich, forget it. Be reasonable, so that you'll have a target that you can reach.

2. **SAVE REGULARLY.** Saving should become habitual. You don't necessarily have to save a lot right away in order to get rich. But if you develop the saving habit, you'll probably be able to increase your rate of savings over the years. A steadily increasing rate of savings, combined with the compounding of money already set aside, might not have Robin Leach of *Lifestyles of the Rich and Famous* knocking at your door, but you'll be a VIP whenever you visit your banker. The table on page 757 shows how dramatically saving a hundred dollars per month will grow over the years.

3. **INVEST YOUR SAVINGS SENSIBLY.** While both are essential, there's a big difference between saving and investing. You'll never get rich sticking your money in a savings account or money-market account. Instead, you should invest your savings in a variety of stock and interest-earning investments that, over time, have proven to provide attractive rates of return.

4. **PROTECT WHAT YOU'VE ACCUMULATED.** There's nothing more discouraging than being well on your way to financial independence, only to suffer an uninsured loss that requires you to tap into your funds prematurely. Gaps in insurance coverage can literally wipe out years of savings. Always carry comprehensive insurance coverage.

5. **STEER CLEAR OF SETBACKS.** Don't let a financial setback jeopardize your accumulated wealth. Improper borrowing, for example, can jeopardize your stash. Divorce can also seriously interrupt a wealth accumulation program. While some financial setbacks may be unavoidable, you should do whatever is within your power to mini-

mize the possibility that they may occur.

It doesn't take much luck to get rich, as long as you're willing to sacrifice a little and spend a little time working on your wealth accumulation program. As with most important things in our lives, the choice is yours. There are many people out there whose financial circumstances are almost identical to yours. Some of them will never accomplish anything in their financial lives, while others will undoubtedly get rich—slowly and sensibly.

GROWTH OF A $100 MONTHLY DEPOSIT

INTEREST RATE	5 YEARS	10 YEARS	15 YEARS	20 YEARS	25 YEARS	30 YEARS	35 YEARS	40 YEARS
5%	$6,829	$15,593	$26,840	$41,275	$59,799	$83,573	$114,083	$153,238
5 1/2	6,920	16,024	28,002	43,762	64,498	91,780	127,675	174,902
6	7,012	16,470	29,227	46,435	69,646	100,954	143,183	200,145
6 1/2	7,106	16,932	30,519	49,308	75,289	111,217	160,898	229,599
7	7,201	17,409	31,881	52,397	81,480	122,709	181,156	264,012
7 1/2	7,298	17,904	33,318	55,719	88,274	135,587	204,345	304,272
8	7,397	18,417	34,835	59,295	95,737	150,030	230,918	351,428
8 1/2	7,497	18,947	36,435	63,144	103,937	166,240	261,395	406,726
9	7,599	19,497	38,124	67,290	112,953	184,447	296,385	471,643
9 1/2	7,703	20,066	39,908	71,756	122,872	204,913	336,590	547,933
10	7,808	20,655	41,792	76,570	133,789	227,933	382,828	637,678

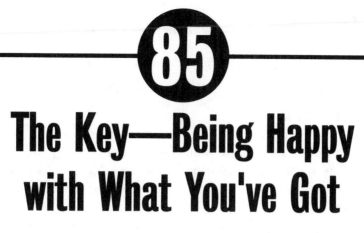

The Key—Being Happy with What You've Got

y now, you've realized that this book is a far cry from those get-rich-quick compendiums hawked by various financial rainmakers. It won't have you leaping over your financial worries in a single bound. It doesn't promise instant gratification and Hawaiian vacations with your favorite football team's cheerleaders. It is a sensible approach to the long-term growth of your money so that you will be able to meet life's financial hurdles one at a time—and reach the retirement finish line in good financial condition.

There's Nothing Wrong with Being Happy with What You've Got

There is far too much preoccupation with money these days—and not enough with personal financial planning. Most people waste precious time thinking they would be on Easy Street if they only earned $10,000 more than they do currently. But $10,000, after taxes and inflation are factored in, wouldn't pay off more than one credit card balance for many people. Instead of obsessing over more money, people should be thinking of ways to do better with what they have.

We all want financial security, of course. Believe it or not, some people spend all they earn during their working years thinking that they'll be able to live off Social Security when they're retired. But Social Security will support most people only about one week of each month. Assuming you'd like to provide for the other three weeks as well, you must accumulate a sizable investment portfolio by the time you retire. In order to create an investment portfolio, you have to save regularly. In order to save regularly, you have to spend less than you earn. In order to spend less than you earn, you'll have to learn to *be happy with what you've got.*

No matter how obvious that sounds, many of us have difficulty practicing it. But the best way to spend less than you earn is to be happy with what you've got. A lot of people don't like to hear this. They want a fancier car or an imported kitchen or an exotic vacation or a larger house. After all, the advertisers tell us that we have to have these things to be happy, and by golly, our neighbors have some of these things, and they sure seem happy. What a crock of—beans that is. The neighbors, even the ones who do make $10,000 more per year than you do, probably feel the same way about you that you feel about them. But if you can be happy with what you've got, you'll find it a lot easier to save the money to make the investments that will allow you to achieve financial security. It's as simple as that.

You *Can* Get There from Here

How many times have you told yourself that you don't make enough money to invest, let alone save one thin dime? Chances are, within twenty-four hours of convincing yourself that what you say is true, you'll have spent twenty-five dollars or so on "things" you don't need. Perhaps you'll write out a check to the cable TV for all sorts of movie channels, then go out and rent a couple of videos. Sure—using that money to add to a mutual fund investment account isn't as much fun now. But it may allow you to have a little fun when retirement time rolls around. Is seeing *Rambo 3* for the fifth time really a wise choice when, at age seventy, you're flipping burgers in a fast-food joint just to make ends meet? I don't think so. The fact of the matter is that a little sacrifice can go a long way to achieving financial security—and a little overspending can go a long way in preventing you from achieving this goal.

Every chapter in this book offers you ways through the morass of planning for a successful financial future, but taking action is up to you. I can spur you on with tales of the consequences of bad saving habits, and I can encourage you with examples of the rewards that await those who save and invest regularly. But if you can't see the value of being happy with what you've got, then there's little that I—or anyone—can truly do for you.

Rather than spending money in pursuit of happiness, take pleasure in the security it can bring. No one needs a new car every two years. No one needs a speedboat that can outrace a jet airplane. No one needs to live in the Taj Mahal of their neighborhood. In fact, when you get down to it, living sensibly, beneath your means, *means* that you will always be able to invest some of your current earnings in your future, rather than in someone else's—for example, the guy who would love to sell you that speedboat.

What a Difference in Attitude

Evaluating where you stand financially and beginning to plan for the future is a lifelong process. So are saving and investing. In the end, you not only reap the reward of financial security by planning and taking appropriate action, you benefit along the way. For example, consider those who have to face financial uncertainty—a recession, a layoff, disability—when they're heavily in debt. At best they face a lot of sleepless nights. Contrast that feeling with the feeling of those who can confront financial uncertainty with money in the bank—or better yet, in an investment account. There's quite a difference in attitude between the two scenarios. Depending on your own circumstances, you should begin to build your savings, or regularly add to your savings, so that you will be able to look forward to a more secure financial future.

86

Looking into the Next Century—How Trends Will Affect You

The question of what the future holds perplexes even our most distinguished economic forecasters and pundits. Much depends upon how—and whether—we can solve the problems that currently bedevil our nation: an enormous deficit, a crumbling infrastructure, a dysfunctional educational system, an endangered environment, and a health-care system that everyone—liberal, moderate, and conservative alike—wants to see overhauled.

Meanwhile, the country continues to muddle along, neither entirely solving nor completely ignoring these problems. I do have some ideas where current trends will probably take us. As you go about running your financial affairs, keep an eye on them. They may have a major effect on your financial well-being.

A Graying Country

Perhaps the most salient demographic feature of the beginning of the new century will be the continued graying of America. As the leading edge of the baby-boom generation enters retirement, the already-high demand for services and products directed toward senior citizens will significantly increase.

Another result of the aging of the American population will be an enormous transfer of wealth from today's seniors to their children and grandchildren. By the year 2010, several trillion dollars will be inherited. This great wealth transference means that many individuals will have to make major modifications in their financial plans.

Estate Taxes

Federal estate taxes are a fertile area for revenue enhancement, and one that is not likely to be unpopular to the majority of Americans—until they realize that they themselves might actually leave (or inherit) an estate that is large enough to be taxed. Some states may also consider increasing death taxes in their attempts to bridge chronic budget deficits.

Retirement Planning

Almost every working person in the United States is either preparing to retire or has parents who are preparing to retire. Working people of all ages will become more concerned about their prospects for achieving a comfortable retirement. The financial services industry will become more responsive to the financial planning needs of the vast numbers of retired people.

Changing Responsibilities for Meeting Retirement Needs

There is a clear trend toward requiring employees to take more responsibility for setting aside and managing their own retirement-earmarked investments. The burden of funding retirement-income needs will continue to shift from employer to employee. Moreover, affluent clients will have to plan for an even smaller share of Social Security benefits, which will eventually be subject to a means-based test. The combination of lower employer-provided pension benefits and lower Social Security benefits means that workers will have to shoulder more of the burden of providing for a comfortable retirement.

The combination of longer life expectancies and delayed childbearing will create enormous financial burdens on an increasing number of so-called "sandwich generation" families. These families must simultaneously provide for both aging parents and dependent children.

Banking in the 1990s

As banks emerge from the current industry shakeout, you are likely to see a smaller number of very large, nationally and regionally oriented institutions dominating the industry. Fears left over from the debacle of the late 1980s will cause many lenders to continue to be stringent in their lending policies. On the other hand, banks are aggressively moving into new areas of service, and you are likely to see banks evolving into "one-stop" financial service centers. The debate over how much banking laws should be relaxed to allow banks to develop along these lines will persist.

Insurance

As the population ages and as many individuals and families join the ranks of the affluent, insurance needs will change, though this will not necessarily be readily apparent. The insurance marketplace will grow increasingly competitive, and companies will have to offer new and innovative products designed specifically for an aging and affluent population.

The financial problems experienced by many insurance companies in the early 1990s will result in a greater concern on the part of policyholders over their insurer's financial stability—particularly for life insurance companies.

The Investing Landscape

The growth of the no-load mutual fund industry has already shown that investors from all walks of life have become better informed about investing. The ease with which mutual funds can be purchased—combined with other attractive aspects of mutual fund investing—will bring former noninvestors into the marketplace. During the 1990s and into the next century, then, stock mutual funds will enjoy high asset growth as individual investors better understand the advantages of stock investing in general and of stock mutual fund investing in particular.

The Global Economy

Many experts predict that the volatility in world stock, fixed-income, and real estate markets that was so prevalent in the late 1980s will become the norm of the future. Your investment program should protect against the effects of uncertain markets through greater diversification and more attention to asset allocation. Investors will have to learn to cope with sporadic market volatility.

The rapid development of many foreign economies means that American investors should no longer restrict themselves to U.S. securities. Therefore, foreign investments will become an important component of well-diversified investment portfolios.

Investor Benefits

Investors will benefit from two different trends in the investment arena. First, the continual introduction of new investment products will make it easier for informed individual investors to choose appropriate investments. The flip side of all this innovation is that it will confuse and tempt uninformed investors.

The second competitive trend involves the area of investor services. Intense competition for investor dollars will force full-service financial institutions to reduce commissions and sales fees. Investors will increasingly prefer no- and low-load products and discounted brokerage fees. In addition, financial institutions will constantly be introducing new and more convenient services to attract and retain business.

Interest-Earning Investments

Increasingly volatile interest rates will complicate interest-earning investment decisions. Individual investors will continue to benefit from the intense competition among financial institutions that offer interest-earning investments. This competition will reward investors who comparison-shop for the most attractive interest-earning investments.

Real Estate Investments

The real estate industry will probably not recover from the excesses of the 1980s until the new century. Real estate investors will have to exercise considerably more caution in selecting investments, particularly in areas suffering from overbuilding and high vacancy rates.

The beleaguered real estate limited partnership industry will continue to cause headaches for investors. New real estate partnership projects will likely be and should be met with investor skepticism.

Long-Term Planning

The financial excesses of the 1980s are being followed by serious concern about long-term financial security. This concern, combined with the aging of the American population, will translate into a higher savings rate. The new century will see a higher proportion of people who are not only concerned about achieving financial security, but who are also willing to take the action or actions necessary to achieve it.

It's Up to You

There are so many important matters to attend to in your personal finances that at times it may seem overwhelming. You can't do everything, of course, and you can't do all that you need to do at once. Nevertheless, there are always some things that you can do to improve your financial well-being— one step at a time. Good personal financial planning doesn't have to be a time-consuming, daily process. But it won't happen automatically either.

Here are several basic guidelines that will help you focus on important financial planning and money management matters. I can't promise you financial nirvana, but if you adhere to these ten financial planning guidelines, you will be able to enjoy some peace of mind, knowing you are well on your way to financial security.

1. Be happy with what you've got

Putting on the ritz is the quickest way to the poorhouse that I can think of. People who overextend themselves usually do so in an attempt to maintain a life-style beyond their means. The only way to accumulate wealth is to live *beneath* your means, and the only way to live comfortably beneath your means is to be happy with what you've already got.

2. Stop believing that because your income and assets may be limited, you can't do any financial planning

Many people go through life with the mistaken assumption that they don't earn enough to be able to do financial planning. Not only is this a mistaken assumption, it's a perilous one. Basic financial-planning matters such as insurance, saving, building up investments, planning for retirement, and preparing estate-planning documents apply to everyone. If you still don't believe me, look around. You'll find your friends, peers, and others in circumstances similar to yours who are doing very well with their personal financial planning.

3. Close all gaps in your insurance coverage

A single gap in your insurance coverage could easily wipe out years of savings and investments, or worse. Everyone needs comprehensive and continuous insurance coverage. You need to be particularly careful to assure that you have adequate insurance coverage in those areas that are not provided by your employer.

4. Save at least 10 percent of your income (hopefully more)

It is inexcusable not to save at least 10 percent of your *gross* income (not net), no matter what your circumstances. If you say you can't do it, you haven't looked hard enough at how you spend your money. Unless you inherit it or marry it, you will never accumulate enough money to achieve retirement security without saving regularly.

5. Maintain a balanced investment portfolio that is appropriate to your own financial situation

Most people invest in extremes, either taking too much risk or too little risk. The best portfolio structure is one that includes stock investments, interest-earning investments, and perhaps real estate investments. Your chosen asset allocation—even if your investment portfolio is very small—should be considered a long-term allocation, one that is not altered materially in response to current market conditions or, worse, to the opinions of some "expert."

6. Develop a reasonable investment strategy and stick with it

You don't have to be an investment expert to invest well. Fill your balanced investment portfolio with sensible (some might say dull) investments that you wouldn't mind holding for the rest of your life. Don't overlook the many advantages offered by mutual funds. Above all, be consistent in carrying out your investment strategy.

7. Save taxes by becoming more "tax aware"

Most people pay too much income tax. One of the easiest ways to save money is to pay only the minimum amount of taxes that you are legally obliged to pay. This doesn't mean that you need to make complicated (and often money-losing) investments in tax shelters. Instead, become more aware of the many opportunities there are for people of average means to reduce their taxes. On the other hand, don't let income tax saving considerations outweigh more important financial-planning matters. Rather than asking, "Is this going to save me taxes?" you should ask, "Is this a worthwhile cost or investment?"

8. Take maximum advantage of retirement plans

Recognize that it will cost a fortune to retire comfortably, so begin preparing now. Much of what you do in your year-to-year financial planning is directly or indirectly geared toward assuring you a comfortable retirement. Yet many people still fall short. No matter how young or old you are, don't delay projecting your retirement needs and planning to meet them. Take advantage of the many tax-advantaged retirement savings plans available.

9. Prepare and keep up-to-date necessary estate-planning documents

If you are one of the many who don't yet have a will, durable power of attorney, and a living will, by all means ask an attorney to prepare them. Believe it or not, you will feel better for having done so. Higher income and/or net worth people may benefit from more elaborate estate planning techniques.

10. Take control of your personal finances

Don't rely too much on others to tell you what is good for your own situation. You know best. You may be very busy with your job and family, but you still need to devote some time to managing your money and other important financial planning matters. It doesn't take a lot of time and it's time well spent.

FINANCIAL PLANNING "THINGS TO DO" LIST

Before you put this book away, please write down three things that you need to do now to help improve your personal finances. They don't need to be the most crucial; instead, they should be matters that you can accomplish with relative ease, like arranging with your bank to have some money automatically and regularly withdrawn from your checking account and placed in a savings or investment account. After you have accomplished these three tasks, you'll be encouraged to do more, and you'll be well on your way to a successful financial life.

1. ....
....
....
....
....

2. ....
....
....
....
....

3. ....
....
....
....
....

Remember, good financial planning begins with good common sense. Financial security may still be a long way off, but as you begin to take control of your financial future, you'll find that many rewards accompany the sacrifices along the way. Don't get discouraged, and always remember that you are your own best financial planner. Good luck!

Index

O

P

Q

R

S